Assessment Strategies for Monitoring Student Learning

JAMES S. CANGELOSI
Utah State University

LONGMAN

An imprint of Addison Wesley Longman, Inc.

New York • Reading, Massachusetts • Menlo Park, California • Harlow, England
Don Mills, Ontario • Sydney • Mexico City • Madrid • Amsterdam

Editor-in-Chief: Priscilla McGeehon
Acquisitions Editor: Arthur Pomponio
Supplements Editor: Joy Hilgandorf
Full Service Production Manager: Eric Jorgensen
Project Coordination and Text Design/Electronic Page Makeup: Electronic Publishing Services Inc., NYC
Cover Designer/Manager: Nancy Danahy
Cover Illustration/Photo: Dan Sorenson/Photospin, Inc.
Photographers: Donna Korchner and Ted Hansen
Senior Print Buyer: Hugh Crawford
Printer and Binder: The Maple Vail Book Manufacturing Group, Inc.
Cover Printer: Coral Graphic Services

Library of Congress Cataloging-in-Publication Data

Cangelosi, James S.
    Assessment strategies for monitoring student learning / James S. Cangelosi.—1st ed.
    p. cm.
    Includes bibliographical references (p.) and indexes.
    ISBN 0-321-02332-3 (hard)
    1. Educational tests and measurements—United States
    2. Examinations—United States.   I. Title.
    LB3051.C342   1999
    371.26'4—DC21

                                     99-10749
                                       CIP

Please visit our website at http://www.awlonline.com

ISBN 0-321- 02332-3

12345678910—MA—02010099

BRIEF CONTENTS

Contents   v

Introduction   xvii

1 Difficult Decisions You Face as a Teacher   1

2 Making Formative Judgments as You Teach   42

3 Communicating Your Summative Evaluations of Student Learning   121

4 The Art of Making Informed Decisions About Student Learning   176

5 Pinpointing What Students Are to Learn   210

6 Systematically Developing Measurements   255

7 Monitoring Students' Progress as They Construct Concepts and Discover Relationships   292

8 Monitoring Students' Development of Knowledge and Process Skills   367

9 Monitoring Students' Development of Comprehension and Communication Skills   408

10 Monitoring Students' Progress with Problem Solving   433

11 Monitoring Students' Progress with Creative Thinking   450

12 Monitoring Students' Attitudes   463

13 Monitoring Students' Development of Psychomotor Skills   484

14 Interpreting Systemwide and Standardized Test Results   509

15 Examining the Relevance of Measurements   576

16 Examining the Reliability of Measurements   594

17 Examining the Effectiveness of Mini-Experiments   638

Glossary   G1

References   R1

Name Index   I1

Subject Index   I3

CONTENTS

Introduction   xvii

CHAPTER 1   Difficult Decisions You Face as a Teacher   1

Goal of Chapter 1   1

Teaching Cycles   2

Decisions in Every Teaching Cycle   7

How You Make Decisions   8

Measurements and Decision-Making   10

What Are Tonja and Reggie Learning?   10

Empirical Observations, Measurement Results, and Decisions   30

Measurements for Monitoring Students' Learning   31

Why "Monitoring"?   31

Unplanned Measurements   31

Planned Measurements   33

Sequences of Mini-Experiments   33

A Mini-Experiment   34

Prompt for Students   35

Observer's Rubric   35

Measurement Error   37

Synthesis Activities for Chapter 1   39

Transitional Activity from Chapter 1 to Chapter 2   41

CHAPTER 2   Making Formative Judgments as You Teach   42

Goal of Chapter 2   42

Summative Evaluations and Formative Judgments   43

Formative Judgments for Designing Curricula   44

Curricula   44

Planning and Organizing for the School Year   44

Designing Teaching Units   51
   Teaching Unit Sequences   51
   A Goal and Objectives for Each Teaching Unit   51

Formative Judgments for Designing Lessons   57

Formative Judgments for Setting the Tone for the School Year   61

Formative Judgments During Learning Activities   70

Formative Judgments for Managing Student Behaviors   86

Students' Use of Formative Feedback to Monitor Their Own Learning   91
   Self-Monitoring   91
   Sharing Measurement Results with Students   91
   Prompting Students to Use Feedback as They Learn   108

Portfolios as a Formative Feedback Mechanism   111

A Classroom Environment Conducive to Formative Feedback   115
   Focusing on What Students Do, Not On Who They Are   115
   Focusing on Formative Judgments   116

Synthesis Activities for Chapter 2   118

Transitional Activity from Chapter 2 to Chapter 3   120

CHAPTER 3   Communicating Your Summative Evaluations of Student Learning   121

Goal of Chapter 3   121

Evaluate Students' Learning, Not Students   122

Who Should Know What About a Student's Achievement?   122
   Violations of Professional Trust   122
   Privileged Information   124

Periodic Reports   125
   Clearly Defined Purpose   125
   Grading Scales   134
   Norm-Referenced Evaluations or Criterion-Referenced Evaluations?   136
   Grades and Cooperative Learning   137
   Grades and Class Participation   138
   Grades and Homework   141
   A Recommendation   143
   Report Formats   145

Student-Parent-Teacher Conferences   145

Portfolios for Communicating Summative Evaluations of Student Achievement   148
   The Complexity of Student Learning   148
   Individualized Student Portfolios   152

Assigning Grades to Measurement Scores   154
   Scoring and Grading   154
   Criterion-Referenced Grading   154
      The Traditional Percentage Method   154

Checking-Off Objectives   157

Norm-Referenced Grading   163
Classical Curve Grading   163
The Visual Inspection Method   163

Compromise Grading   164
A Conflict Between the Theoretical and the Practical   164
A Resolution   165
Point and Counterpoint   165

Assigning Grades for a School Term   166
Condensing Information   166
Weighting Goals and Weighting Measurement Results   167
Deriving One Grade from a Set of Grades   171

Developing a System That Works for You and Your Students   173

Synthesis Activities for Chapter 3   173

Transitional Activity from Chapter 3 to Chapter 4   175

CHAPTER 4   The Art of Making Informed Decisions About Student Learning   176

Goal of Chapter 4   176

Informed by What?   177
Valid Measurement Results   177
Usable Measurements   180

Measurement Validity   181

Measurement Relevance   181
Subject-Content Relevance   181
Learning-Level Relevance   182

Measurement Reliability   183
Internal Consistency   183
Observer Consistency   186
Intra-Observer Consistency   186
Inter-Observer Consistency   189

Designing and Selecting Valid Measurements   189
Designing Measurements   189
Designing Relevant Measurements   189
Designing Measurements That Produce Internally Consistent Results   190
Designing Measurements with Observer Consistency   193
Selecting Measurements   199
Using Unplanned Measurements   201

The Need for Pinpointing What Students Are to Learn   203

Synthesis Activities for Chapter 4   203

Transitional Activity from Chapter 4 to Chapter 5   207

CHAPTER 5   Pinpointing What Students Are to Learn   210

Goal of Chapter 5   210

Meaningful Learning   211

Rationale for the Advanced Organizer for Specifying Subject-Content and Learning Level   217

  Needed Abilities, Attitudes, and Skills   217

  Simplifying Objectives by Operationally Defining Words   217

  No Need for Behavioral Objectives   217

  A Suggestion for Writing Objectives   219

Subject-Content Specified by an Objective   219

  Specifics   219

  Concepts   222

  Relationships   226

  Discoverable Relationships   226

  Relationships of Convention   228

  Processes   230

  Other Ways of Classifying Subject-Content   230

The Learning Level Specified by an Objective   230

  The Need to Classify Learning Levels   230

  Learning Domains   230

Cognitive Objectives   231

  Memory-Level and Reasoning-Level Cognition   231

  Memory-Level Cognitive Objectives   231

  Simple Knowledge   231

  Process Knowledge   236

  Reasoning-Level Cognitive Objectives   236

  Construct a Concept   236

  Discover a Relationship   237

  Comprehension and Communication Skills   237

  Application   238

  Creative Thinking   240

Affective Objectives   242

  Appreciation   242

  Willingness to Try   243

Psychomotor Objectives   243

  Physical Fitness   243

  Psychomotor-Skill   244

Defining the Goal with a Set of Weighted Objectives   248

Synthesis Activities for Chapter 5   250

Transitional Activity from Chapter 5 to Chapter 6   254

CHAPTER 6   Systematically Developing Measurements   255

Goal of Chapter 6   255

Why Not Follow Common Practice?   255

A Systematic Program   257

A Computerized Folder of Mini-Experiment Files   257

  Organizing and Setting Up the Folder   257

Mini-Experiment Formats   259

Difficulty Levels   259

Cross-Referencing the Mini-Experiments   268

Creating a Computerized Folder   268

Modifying Mini-Experiments and Expanding the Files   273

Developing the Measurement Blueprint   275

An Example of a Measurement Blueprint   275

Administration Time and Dates   275

Accommodation for Students with Special Needs   278

Distribution of Points and Weights of Objectives   280

Final Elements of the Blueprint   281

Synthesizing the Measurement   282

Administering the Measurement   283

Student Cheating   284

Nine Incidents   284

Prevalence and Causes of Cheating   286

Strategies for Preventing and Dealing with Cheating   287

Incorporating Individualized Student Portfolios in Your System   289

Synthesis Activities for Chapter 6   290

Transitional Activity from Chapter 6 to Chapter 7   291

CHAPTER 7   Monitoring Students' Progress as They Construct Concepts and Discover Relationships   292

Goal of Chapter 7   292

How Students Construct Concepts   293

Concept Attributes   293

Example Noise   293

Inductive Reasoning   297

Sorting and Categorizing   297

Reflecting and Explaining   298

Generalizing and Articulating   298

Verifying and Refining   299

Indicators of Progress as Students Engage in Construct-a-Concept Lessons   299

Indicators of Students' Achievement of Construct-a-Concept Objectives   325

Mini-Experiments Relevant to Construct-a-Concept Objectives   325

Performance-Observation Mini-Experiments Relevant to Construct-a-Concept Objectives   328

Essay Mini-Experiments Relevant to Construct-a-Concept Objectives   328

Essays Prompting Students to Reflect on Concept Construction   328

Time for Essays   331

Flexibility of Expression but Taxing Writing Skills   333

Overcoming Common Weaknesses of the Essay Format   334

Oral-Discourse Mini-Experiments Relevant to Construct-a-Concept Objectives   336

Multiple-Choice Mini-Experiments Relevant to Construct-a-Concept
Objectives   336

   Prompting Students to Select the Example from the Alternatives   336
   The Role of Example Noise   339
   Parallel Alternatives   339
   Number of Alternatives, Guessing, and Number of Prompts   341

Interview Mini-Experiments Relevant to Construct-a-Concept
Objectives   344

Product-Examination Mini-Experiments Relevant to Construct-a-Concept
Objectives   345

How Students Discover Relationships   345

Discovering Relationships for Oneself   345
Experimenting   347
Reflecting and Explaining   348
Hypothesizing and Articulating   348
Verifying and Refining   348

Indicators of Progress as Students Engage in Discover-a-Relationship Lessons   348

Indicators of Students' Achievement of Discover-a-Relationship Objectives   352

Mini-Experiments Relevant to Discover-a-Relationship Objectives   352
A Variety of Formats for Mini-Experiments Relevant to Discover-a-Relationship
Objectives   360
Short-Response Mini-Experiments Relevant to Discover-a-Relationship
Objectives   360

Synthesis Activities for Chapter 7   362

Transitional Activity from Chapter 7 to Chapter 8   366

**CHAPTER 8   Monitoring Students' Development of Knowledge and Process
Skills   367**

Goal of Chapter 8   367

How Students Acquire and Remember Information   368

Information to Be Remembered   368
Retention of Information   368
Facilitating Reception and Retention of Information Through Direct
Instruction   369
Exposure   369
Mnemonics   372
Reinforcement   373
Overlearning   374

Indicators of Progress as Students Engage in Simple-Knowledge Lessons   374

Indicators of Students' Achievement of Simple-Knowledge Objectives   376

Mini-Experiment Relevant to Simple Knowledge Objectives   376
   Stimulus-Response   376
   Avoiding Responses Beyond Simple Knowledge   378
Short-Response Mini-Experiments Relevant to Simple-Knowledge
Objectives   379

Multiple-Choice Mini-Experiments Relevant to Simple-Knowledge
Objectives   380
    Controlling for Difficulty   380
    Correct Responses for the Wrong Reasons   382
    Incorrect Responses for the Wrong Reasons   383
    Placement of Correct Responses   384
    Matching Multiple-Choice Format   384
    An Ill-Advised Variation of the Multiple-Choice Format   388

How Students Develop Process-Knowledge Skills   388
Acquiring and Polishing Process-Knowledge Skills   388
Delineating the Steps in the Process   391
General Overview of the Process   393
Step-by-Step Explanation   394
Trial Execution of the Process, Error-Pattern Analysis, and Correction   395
Overlearning the Process   395

Indicators of Progress as Students Engage in Process-Knowledge Lessons   395

Indicators of Students' Achievement of Process-Knowledge Objectives   397
Mini-Experiments Relevant to Process-Knowledge Objectives   397
Display-Process Mini-Experiments Relevant to Process-Knowledge
Objectives   398
Performance-Observation Mini-Experiments Relevant to Process-Knowledge
Objectives   400
Multiple-Choice Mini-Experiments Relevant to Process-Knowledge
Objectives   405

Synthesis Activities for Chapter 8   406

Transitional Activity from Chapter 8 to Chapter 9   407

CHAPTER 9 Monitoring Students' Development of Comprehension and
Communication Skills   408

Goal of Chapter 9   408

**How Studentsz Learn to Interpret, Extract Meaning from, and Communicate
Messages   408**
Messages for Students to Comprehend and Communicate   408
Lessons for Comprehension and Communication of Messages   409
    Literal and Interpretive Understanding   409
    Learning Activities for Literal Understanding   416
    Learning Activities for Interpretive Understanding   422
Lessons for Comprehension and Fluency with Modes of Communication   423

**Indicators of Progress as Students Engage in Comprehension-and-Communication-
Skills Lessons   423**

**Indicators of Students' Achievement of Comprehension-and-Communication-
Skills Objectives   428**
Modes of Communication for Prompts and Responses   428
Insightful Responses   430

Synthesis Activities for Chapter 9   431

Transitional Activity from Chapter 9 to Chapter 10   431

CHAPTER 10   Monitoring Students' Progress with Problem Solving   **433**

Goal of Chapter 10   433

How Students Learn to Solve Problems   433

Application-Level Learning   433

Deductive Reasoning   433

Problem Confrontation   434

Analysis and Rule Articulation   436

Subsequent Problem Confrontation and Analysis   438

Extension Into Subsequent Lessons   438

Indicators of Progress as Students Engage in Application Lessons   438

Indicators of Students' Achievement of Application Objectives   440

Deciding How to Solve Problems   440

Avoiding "Give-Away" Words   440

Mixing Subject-Content   445

Synthesis Activities for Chapter 10   447

Transitional Activity from Chapter 10 to Chapter 11   449

CHAPTER 11   Monitoring Students' Progress with Creative Thinking   **450**

Goal of Chapter 11   450

Some Thoughts on Creativity   450

Divergent Reasoning   450

Preserving Creativity   451

Fostering Creativity   452

Metaphors and Analogies to Stimulate Students to Think Creatively   452

Synectics   452

Direct Analogies   452

Personal Analogies   453

Compressed Conflicts   453

Indicators of Progress as Students Engage in Synectics Activities   453

Indicators of Students' Achievement of Creative-Thinking Objectives   455

Synthesis Activities for Chapter 11   457

Transitional Activity from Chapter 11 to Chapter 12   462

CHAPTER 12   Monitoring Students' Attitudes   **463**

Goal of Chapter 12   463

The Role of Affective Objectives   463

**How Students Develop Attitudes Conducive to Learning
and Cooperation   465**

Connecting Content to Existing Values   465

Freedom to Experiment, Question, Hypothesize, and Make Errors   468

Reinforcement   469

Indicators of Progress as Students Engage in Affective Lessons   469

Indicators of Students' Achievement of Appreciation Objectives   471

Is Appreciation Measurable?   471

Presenting Choices   473

Indicators of Students' Achievement of Willingness-to-Try Objectives   477

Observing Behaviors   477

Inferring Behaviors   479

Self-Reports   479

Synthesis Activities for Chapter 12   483

Transitional Activity from Chapter 12 to Chapter 13   483

CHAPTER 13 Monitoring Students' Development of Psychomotor Skills   **484**

Goal of Chapter 13   484

Prerequisites for Development of Psychomotor Skills   484

Physical Fitness   484

Cardiovascular Endurance   485

Body Composition   486

Flexibility   486

Muscular Strength and Endurance   486

Agility   486

Static and Dynamic Balance   489

Coordination   489

Power   489

Speed   489

Reaction Time   489

Measurement Instruments and Procedures Relevant to Physical Fitness   490

How Students Develop Psychomotor Skills   491

Integration with Process-Knowledge Lessons   491

Analysis of Initial Trials   494

Step-by-Step Trials with Coaching   501

Practice with Coaching   504

Extended Practice for Overlearning   505

Indicators of Progress as Students Develop Psychomotor Skills   505

Indicators of Students' Achievement of Psychomotor-Skill Objectives   505

Synthesis Activities for Chapter 13   507

Transitional Activity from Chapter 13 to Chapter 14   508

CHAPTER 14 Interpreting Systemwide and Standardized Test Results   **509**

Goal of Chapter 14   509

Systemwide Tests   510

School District Testing Programs   510

Statewide and District-wide Core Curriculum Tests   519

Political Accountability and High-Stakes Testing   519

Standardized Tests   526

Test Item   526

Achievement Test   526

Aptitude Test   526
Norm Group   526
Test Norms   528
Raw Score   528
Derived Score   531
Student's Grade Level   531
Test Level   531
Test Form   531
Edition of a Test   532
Test Manuals   532
Concurrent Validity   532
Predictive Validity   533

Establishing a Norm-Referenced Point of Comparison   535
How Large Is 27?   535
Central Tendency   537
Measures of Central Tendency   538
Median   538
Arithmetic Mean (μ)   539
Mode   539

Frequency Distribution   541
Establishing a Norm-Referenced Unit for Comparison   543
Variability   543
Measures of Variability   546
Range   546
Mean Deviation (MD)   546
Variance (σ^2)   548
Standard Deviation (σ)   549

z-Scores   549
Distribution of Norm-Group Scores   550
Grade-Level Norms ($\mu_{g.m}$, $\sigma_{g.m}$)   550
Normal Distributions   550
Commonly Used Derived Scores   553
Standard Scores   553
Percentiles   553
Normal Curve Equivalents (NCEs)   557
Scaled Scores   560
Grade Equivalent Scores   560
Stanines   563

Interpreting Standardized Test Scores for Students and Their Parents   564
Uses and Abuses of Standardized Tests   570
Synthesis Activities for Chapter 14   571
Transitional Activity from Chapter 14 to Chapter 15   575

CHAPTER 15   Examining the Relevance of Measurements   576
Goal of Chapter 15   576

Measurement Validation Studies   576

The Case for Relevance of a Measurement You Designed   577

Assessing the Relevance of an Existing Measurement Instrument   579

A Systematic Analysis   579

Item-by-Item Examination   582

Content and Learning-Level Relevance   582

Think-Aloud Trials   584

Expert Judgments   586

Comparing Actual to Targeted Weights   586

Assessing to What a Measurement Is Relevant   587

Other Models for Examining Relevance   587

Synthesis Activities for Chapter 15   592

Transitional Activity from Chapter 15 to Chapter 16   593

CHAPTER 16   Examining the Reliability of Measurements   594

Goal of Chapter 16   594

The Mini-Experiments' Outcomes Matrix   595

Classical Test-Reliability Theory   599

Measures of Consistency   601

$(+, +)$ and $(-, -)$ Versus $(+, -)$ and $(-, +)$ 601

Scatterplots   602

Correlation Coefficients   603

Evolution of Reliability Coefficients   608

Test-Retest Method   608

Equivalent Form Method   609

Split-Halves Method   610

Odd-Even Method   611

Adjusted Odd-Even Method   611

Kuder-Richardson Methods   613

Discovery and Invention   613

Coefficient α *614*

Kuder-Richardson 20   615

Kuder-Richardson 21   619

Interpreting Reliability Coefficients   620

Reliability Coefficients You Compute   620

Reliability Coefficients Reported by Commercial Test Publishers   621

Standard Error of Measurement (SEM)   622

Derivation of SEM   622

Pieces in the Puzzle   622

Test-Retest Reliability Model   622

A Normal Distribution of Reliability Error   623

The Ratio Reliability Model and Theoretical True Scores   624

Solving for the Standard Deviation Due to Reliability Error   624

Using SEM to Interpret Scores   625

Assessing Reliability When Kuder-Richardson Methods Are Inappropriate   627

Measurements Used for Criterion-Referenced Evaluations   627
The Problem   627
Variation from the Criterion   627
Either Meets or Fails to Meet the Criterion   628
Homogeneous True Scores   630
Measurements with Many Weighted-Scored Items   631
Measurements Administered to Only a Few Students   632

Assessing Observer Consistency   632

Synthesis Activities for Chapter 16   635

Transitional Activity from Chapter 16 to Chapter 17   637

CHAPTER 17   Examining the Effectiveness of Mini-Experiments   638

Goal of Chapter 17   638

The Effectiveness of Mini-Experiments   638

The Concept of Effectiveness   638
Why Assess Effectiveness   641

Developing a Process for Assessing Effectiveness   641

Classical Item Analysis   644

Identifying Groups of Varying Achievement Levels   644
Index of Discrimination (D_j) 647
Selecting N_H and N_L 649
D_j as a Measure of Effectiveness   649
Interpreting D_j 650
Index of Difficulty (P_j) 650

A Refinement of Classical Item Analysis   650

Dependence of D_j on P_j 650
Index of Item Efficiency (E_j) 654
Interpreting Item Analysis Data   654

Assessing Effectiveness of Mini-Experiments When Classical Item Analysis Is Inappropriate   655

When the Measurement Lacks Validity   655
When the Number of Mini-Experiments Is Small   655
When the Number of Students Is Small   656

Using Item Analysis Data   656

Synthesis Activities for Chapter 17   659

Transitional Activity from Theory to Practice   662

Glossary   G1

References   R1

Name Index   I1

Subject Index   I3

INTRODUCTION

An analysis of the work of professional teachers reveals an overwhelming complex of decisions that are continually being made:

"Did Austin hear what I just said?" "What example should I use to help Randy construct the concept of surface area?" "Is Luanda ready to discover the dependence of plant life on light?" "Is Maxine approaching her frustration level with this problem?" "Should I pick up the pace or slow down this lesson?" "How did my new strategy for introducing the difference between nouns and pronouns work?" "Does Vincent have the psychomotor skills to write legibly?" "What grade should I assign for Miguel's achievements during this unit on creative writing?" "How will this assignment affect their attitudes about homework?" "Is my strategy for teaching Kara to pay attention to her classmates' answers to questions beginning to work?" "Rosalie's father wants a progress report. What should I tell him?" "Are these students actually learning how to apply Newton's laws of motion or are they just remembering them?" "How should I respond to Haeja's question about the importance of nutrition? If I probe with a question of my own, will it stimulate her to form her own hypothesis or will it just frustrate her?"

Although not always aware of the process by which they make decisions, teachers' answers to such questions are influenced by empirical observations they make. For example, Haeja's teacher decides to probe with a question of her own rather than answering Haeja's question directly because the teacher (a) notices that other students appear wide-eyed and attentive to the question, (b) calls to mind several students' comments during prior lessons (e.g., "I like it when we figure things out for ourselves"), (c) recalls Haeja's high score on a previous test that emphasized students' examining their own hypotheses, and (d) notes that eight of the 15 minutes allocated for the learning activity are still available for addressing Haeja's question. Because the success teachers experience is so dependent on the accuracy of the decisions they make, *Assessment Strategies for Monitoring Student Learning* is designed to lead you and other preservice and inservice teachers to develop the art of making complex instructional decisions.

Fortunately, principles from psychometric theory and the field of educational measurement and evaluation provide a scientific basis for suggested instructional practices leading to improved decision-making, especially when one considers the empirical observations that influence teachers' decisions as measurements. Unfortunately, such principles are too often only associated with traditional, formal achievement and aptitude tests (e.g., tests consisting of multiple-choice or essay items). The so-called "alternative" or "authentic" test-reform movement is a reaction against traditional school tests that emphasize low-level memory skills while ignoring more meaningful forms of learning (e.g., concept construction, discovery of relationships, or applications to real-life situations). This reform movement calls attention to methods of assessing learning that are not solely dependent on traditional tests. Teachers need to practice these alternative methods. However, in some circles within the teacher-education community, this test-reform movement is being played out so that sound fundamental measurement and evaluation principles are abandoned as traditional testing practices are rejected. Consider, for example, the following case.

CASE 1

Mr. Delgado's experiences as a middle-school science teacher have taught him that traditional tests are inadequate indicators of what students learn. Thus, he enthusiastically follows recommendations from such professional references as *National Science Education Standards* (National Research Council, 1996) by applying alternative assessment strategies. His students, for example, maintain individualized portfolios as a record of their progress in the courses he teaches. As one means of getting students to demonstrate what they have achieved during a physical science unit on heat, he directs students to produce an exhibit illustrating how the concepts of heat conduction, convection, and radiation can be applied to address real-life problems.

Several days later, he is examining the colorful, eye-catching poster Eva produced in response to this task. Mr. Delgado thinks to himself, "Fantastic! She must have spent hours locating and cutting out these pictures showing how heat is transmitted by conduction, convection, and radiation." He tells Eva, "Your work merits an A+. This poster shows a great deal of effort. And, wow! What art work! I suggest you include this in your portfolio. It really demonstrates your work ethic and talent for illustrating science."

How well does Eva's poster reflect what she learned about applying the concepts of conduction, convection, and radiation to address real-life problems? According to Mr. Delgado's thoughts and comments, the poster demonstrates artistic talent, a conscientious effort, and that she can illustrate the process for transmitting heat. But it's not very evident how well she can apply that knowledge to address real-life problems—the learning objective he seemed to be targeting. Contrast Case 1 to Case 2.

CASE 2

Ms. Bohrer, like Mr. Delgado, is a middle-school science teacher who applies alternative assessment strategies as recommended by various professional references. She begins designing mini-experiments for detecting how well her students are learning to apply the concepts of heat conduction, convection, and radiation to address real-life problems. She thinks to herself, "Okay, the content of the objective I want to measure involves three modes of heat transmission: conduction, convection, and radiation. It's at the application learning level, so I should present them with some sort of problem situation and see if they can decide how, if at all, their understanding of those three modes can help them solve the problem." After going through a list of possible problems, she decides to go with the problem of designing outdoor shelters for dogs so that the dogs are protected from extreme temperatures. For her initial attempt at a prompt for students, she writes, "Apply your knowledge of heat conduction, convection, and radiation to design an outdoor shelter for a dog that will help keep the dog cool on hot summer days." Then she thinks, "Oh, no! Since this is an application objective, I need to see if they come up with the idea of using conduction, convection, and radiation on their own. So I shouldn't tell them to 'apply their knowledge of conduction, convection, and radiation,' but just direct them to design the shelter so that it helps keep the dog cool." After thinking of examples of how conduction, convection, and radiation can be applied to both deflect heat from the shelter and transmit it to the shelter, Ms. Bohrer produces the following mini-experiment:

Prompt for students

The students are shown a picture of a dog in a large fenced-in yard on a hot day. Ms. Bohrer directs them to design a shelter for the dog in the picture. Ms. Bohrer explains that they can choose any materials and can plan the shelter for any reasonable size for the yard. However, they have no artificial power source (e.g., electricity for air conditioning), nor can the shelter be supplied with ice or any kind of cooling substance (although the dog is supplied with regular meals and fresh drinking water). The purpose of the shelter is to help keep the dog cool on hot sunny summer days. Each student's design is to be explained and illustrated with a diagram on a poster to be considered for the student's portfolio.

Similarly, the students are shown a picture of another dog in a fenced-in yard on a cold wintry day. She directs them to design a shelter for the second dog, who must stay in the yard on cold wintry days. Ms. Bohrer explains that the rules are the same; again there is no artificial power source to supply heat. Also, they cannot build fire just as they couldn't bring in ice for the first dog. Each student's design is to be explained and illustrated with a diagram on a poster to be considered for the student's portfolio.

Ms. Bohrer' Scoring Rubric as She Examines Each Pair of Posters

For each of the following criteria, score +2 if the criterion is clearly met, +1 if it is unclear as to whether or not the criterion is met, and +0 if the criterion is clearly not met:

____ The shelter is likely to produce an overall cooler environment for the dog than outside the shelter.
____ At least one aspect of the design uses heat radiation in a way that will cool the dog.
____ No aspect of the design will use heat radiation in a way to warm the dog.
____ At least one aspect of the design uses heat convection in a way that will cool the dog.
____ No aspect of the design will use heat convection in a way to warm the dog.
____ At least one aspect of the design uses heat conduction in a way that will cool the dog.
____ No aspect of the design will use heat conduction in a way to warm the dog.

Ms. Bohrer's comments about the design relative to how the design applies the concepts of heat radiation, convection, and conduction:

_____

_____

Ms. Bohrer examines the design for the second dog using the same rating scale for each of the following criteria:

____ The shelter is likely to produce an overall warmer environment for the dog than outside the shelter.
____ At least one aspect of the design uses heat radiation in a way that will warm the dog.
____ No aspect of the design will use heat radiation in a way to cool the dog.
____ At least one aspect of the design uses heat convection in a way that will warm the dog.
____ No aspect of the design will use heat convection in a way to cool the dog.
____ At least one aspect of the design uses heat conduction in a way that will warm the dog.
____ No aspect of the design will use heat conduction in a way to cool the dog.

Ms. Bohrer's comments about the design relative to how the design applies the concepts of heat radiation, convection, and conduction:

_____

_____

Ms. Bohrer's mini-experiment will not be a perfect indicator of how well her students apply their conceptions of conduction, convection, and radiation to real-life problem situations. The prompt and rubric she designed should only be one part of a measurement used to monitor students' progress toward the goal of her physical science unit on heat. Results of that measurement will be influenced by measurement error. However, unlike Mr. Delgado, Ms. Bohrer at least applies a fundamental psychometric principle by designing the experiment so that it focuses not only on the content of her objective (i.e., heat conduction, convection, and radiation), but also on the objective's learning level (i.e., application or problem solving).

Impetus for integrating authentic assessment strategies into instructional practices is provided by numerous curriculum-reform project reports (see, e.g., *Assessment Standards for School Mathematics* (National Council of Teachers of Mathematics, 1995), *National Science Education Standards* (National Research Council, 1996), *Standards for the English Language Arts* (National Council of Teachers of English & International Reading Association, 1996), and *National standards for history grades K–4: Expanding Children's World in Time and Space* (National Center for History in Schools (1997)). Such reports suggest that teachers should collect evidence of student learning not only after learning activities but also as part of learning activities. For such non-traditional monitoring of students' learning to help teachers make accurate instructional decisions, it needs to be based on sound measurement principles.

You hardly learn to systematically apply fundamental measurement principles to all aspects of instructional decision-making by simply reading a traditional textbook. Thus, *Assessment Strategies for Monitoring Student Learning* not only presents information and explanations, but it also engages you in hands-on, thought-provoking activities that enable you to tailor a monitoring system to meet your own needs and the needs of your students. The following features are included:

- A goal is stated and defined by a set of objectives for each chapter.
- Principles, suggestions, and techniques are brought to life via 210 cases drawn from actual experiences from primary, elementary, middle, and secondary school classrooms involving a wide range of subject-matter specialties (e.g., foreign language, health and physical education, language arts, mathematics, science, and social studies). The cases are presented not only to demonstrate principles and suggestions; they are developed and sequenced to lead you to construct concepts, discover relationships, and formulate your own strategies. Besides being used to teach the contents of the sections where they appear, many of the cases are also used to set the stage for subsequent learning.
- Along with the many cases, the text includes an unusually high number of illustrations, 328, because of the following reasons:
  - Concepts are constructed, relationships are discovered, and ideas are stimulated by exposure to examples and interactions with concrete models. Examples and models require illustrations.

- You need to integrate the principles, strategies, and processes you learn from your work with this book into complex classroom environments. Designing curricula, preparing lessons, managing behaviors, interacting with students, obtaining formative feedback, regulating instruction, and making summative evaluations are inextricably interrelated. Thus, topics are not presented in isolation, but rather continually interwoven. The pedagogy of the book is such that you are frequently prompted to connect work from prior chapters to what you are working on at the moment. This requires routine trips back to previously read sections. This referring back to prior work is facilitated by having much of the material in clearly numbered illustrations and cases.
- Throughout the book you are prompted to engage in problem-solving, cooperative-learning, and self-assessment activities designed to promote productive thinking and to lead you to monitor your own learning.
- Near the end of each chapter is a sequence of synthesis activities designed to help you (a) further interrelate principles, strategies, and techniques and apply them to your own teaching specialty, (b) reinforce and extend what was learned, and (c) assess what you gained from the chapter so that you can identify areas of proficiency and topics to be reviewed. By engaging in these synthesis activities for Chapters 1–13, you gradually build your own computerized files of measurement instruments and procedures that should be relevant to your particular teaching specialty.
- At the end of each of the first 16 chapters, a transitional activity is included to help you (a) connect the content of one chapter to that of the next and (b) set the stage for the subsequent chapter. The transitional activity at the end of Chapter 17 is intended to prompt you to reflect on your work with the entire book.
- "Measurement and Analysis Tool," the accompanying compact disk (CD-ROM), provides the software to enable you to easily set up a computerized file system for facilitating the measurement development strategies you develop as you work with Chapters 1–13. Furthermore the CD-ROM provides user-friendly routines for applying the statistical models for interpreting measurement results and conducting measurement validation studies that you learn as you work with Chapters 14–17.
- For convenient reference, a glossary of technical terms introduced in the book follows the last chapter.

Seventeen chapters are included:

Chapter 1, "Difficult Decisions You Face as a Teacher," leads you to analyze your own instructional activities, focusing on the many complex decisions you must make within every teaching cycle. Examinations of decision-making in classrooms illustrate that the accuracy of those decisions depends on empirical observations (i.e., measurements), measurement error, and judgment. The need for systematic, accurate decision-making is established. You become cognizant that, as a teacher, you continually make unplanned measurements—measurements that influence your instructional activities, especially how you interact with students. You also construct the concept of planned mini-experiments, with each mini-experiment composed of a prompt for students and an observer's rubric.

Chapter 2, "Making Formative Judgments as You Teach," reinforces the idea that monitoring student learning (involving measurement, concern for measurement error, and judgment) is an integral part of teaching. Cases are used extensively to illustrate how to use formative feedback for designing curricula, setting the tone for the school year, designing teaching units, designing lessons, leading students to monitor their own learning, regulating learning activities, and managing student behaviors. The use of individualized student portfolios as a formative feedback mechanism is emphasized and illustrated.

Chapter 3, "Communicating Your Summative Evaluations of Student Learning," begins with cases and explanations leading you to recognize the importance of communicating summative evaluations of student achievement in a highly professional manner—a manner that helps build students' trust, confidence, and cooperation. A variety of traditional and nontraditional reporting methods are illustrated and explained. The use of individualized student portfolios as a tool for building and maintaining a record of student learning is emphasized and illustrated. Conventional techniques for converting measurement results to grades are illustrated, as is a novel technique.

Chapter 4, "The Art of Making Informed Decisions About Student Learning," takes fundamental psychometric principles, ordinarily applied only to traditional tests, and extends their applications to all types of measurements used in monitoring student learning. Thus, the quality of even authentic, performance, and alternative measurements is considered in terms of relevance, reliability, and usability. Qualitative strategies for examining measurement error are introduced and illustrated. You are led to view student achievement as a variable and discover the need for defining learning outcomes so that learning can be monitored.

Chapter 5, "Pinpointing What Students Are to Learn," reminds you that a teaching cycle (e.g., an instructional unit) targets a goal defined by a set of objectives. You engage in activities by which you specify what you want students to learn within your own teaching specialty. The chapter introduces a classification scheme for categorizing subject-matter content (i.e., specifics, concepts, relationships, processes) and learning levels (i.e., construct a concept, discover a relationship, simple knowledge, process knowledge, comprehension and communication skills, application, creative thinking, appreciation, willingness to try, physical fitness, and psychomotor skill). This scheme accommodates the integration of constructivist and behaviorist instructional strategies.

Chapter 6, "Systematically Developing Measurements," introduces, explains, and illustrates a systematic process for developing valid and usable measurements. You integrate a practical measurement-management system into your own instructional practices. The system includes the use of computerized files of mini-experiments and individualized student portfolios.

Chapter 7, "Monitoring Students' Progress as They Construct Concepts and Discover Relationships," begins with a treatise on how students construct concepts and on the design of lessons that lead students to construct concepts for themselves. Strategies and techniques for gauging students' progress during those lessons are explained and demonstrated. The problem of how to design mini-experiments relevant to achievement of construct-a-concept objectives is then addressed with explanations, illustrations, exercises, and demonstrations with a variety of measurement formats (e.g., performance observation, essay, oral discourse, multiple choice, interview, and product examination). The second half of the chapter focuses on students' discovering relationships in the same way that the first half focused on students constructing concepts.

Chapter 8, "Monitoring Students' Development of Knowledge and Process Skills," is organized similarly to Chapter 7; however, Chapter 8 focuses on students' acquiring and remembering information and on students' developing process-knowledge skills.

Chapter 9, "Monitoring Students' Development of Comprehension and Communication Skills," is organized similarly to Chapter 7; however, Chapter 9 focuses on students' developing comprehension and communication skills.

Chapter 10, "Monitoring Students' Progress with Problem Solving," is organized similarly to Chapter 7; however, Chapter 10 focuses on students' addressing problems and applying prior learning to new situations.

Chapter 11, "Monitoring Students' Progress with Creative Thinking," is organized similarly to Chapter 7; however, Chapter 11 focuses on students being stimulated to think divergently and their achievement of creative-thinking objectives.

Chapter 12, "Monitoring Students' Attitudes," is organized similarly to Chapter 7; however, Chapter 12 focuses on monitoring students' attitudes and their progress toward appreciation and willingness-to-try objectives.

Chapter 13, "Monitoring Students' Development of Psychomotor Skills," is organized similarly to Chapter 7; however, Chapter 13 focuses on students' achievement of psychomotor objectives.

Chapter 14, "Interpreting Systemwide and Standardized Test Results," explains and illustrates how tests are standardized, as well as common uses and misuses of systemwide and standardized tests in schools. Statistical models for establishing norms and estimating measurement error are developed and applied to the interpretation of standardized test results. Exercises lead you to practice and develop your skills communicating standardized test scores to students and their parents. Strategies for combating common abuses of standardized tests are illustrated.

Chapter 15, "Examining the Relevance of Measurements," leads you to develop strategies and techniques for assessing the relevance of your own measurements and the relevance of commercially developed tests.

Chapter 16, "Examining the Reliability of Measurements," leads you to develop strategies and techniques (both qualitative and quantitative) for assessing reliability and estimating error ranges of measurements you use with your students.

Chapter 17, "Examining the Effectiveness of Mini-Experiments," builds upon item-efficiency models to develop useful strategies and techniques (both qualitative and quantitative) for assessing the effectiveness of individual mini-experiments used to monitor student learning. Exercises lead you to apply the techniques for the purpose of improving your measurement-design talents.

Assessment Strategies for Monitoring Student Learning is designed to be used in teacher-education programs at colleges and universities in the following manner:

- Chapters 1–12 and 14 serve as the textbook for measurement and evaluation courses for preservice teachers that carry 3 semester or 5 quarter credits. Chapter 13 will also be important for primary-grade teachers, music teachers, art teachers, health and physical education teachers, and special education teachers, but not necessarily important for secondary-level mathematics, science, social studies, and other teachers who only teach to cognitive and affective objectives.
- All 17 chapters serve as the textbook for graduate-level measurement and evaluation courses for inservice teachers that carry 3 semester or 5 quarter credits.
- Chapters 1–12 (and 13 for primary-grade, music, art, health and physical education, and special education teachers) serve as the textbook for measurement and evaluation courses for preservice teachers that carry 2 semester or 3 quarter credits.
- Chapters 1–12 (and 13 for primary-grade, music, art, and health and physical education teachers) serve as the textbook for a component of teaching methods courses for preservice teachers that carry at least 4 semester or 5 quarter credits. This use would be for teacher-education programs that do not require a separate measurement and evaluation course.

As an aid to professors who incorporate this book into their courses, an instructor's manual/test-bank is available from Addison-Wesley Longman. The manual includes (a) suggestions for taking advantage of the book's features in a variety of course structures, (b) a detailed sample syllabus, (c) plans for 30 class meetings as well as corresponding homework assignments, and (d) five unit tests with each test accompanied by a scorer's form with detailed rubrics.

ACKNOWLEDGMENTS

I am indebted to the hundreds of teachers and students who stimulated the ideas for the decision-making strategies embodied in this book and especially to the teachers who field-tested those strategies in their classrooms. Joe Koebbe's creative talents are responsible for the development of "Measurement and Analysis Tool," the accompanying CD-ROM disk, that makes it practical for busy classroom teachers to implement techniques explained in Chapters 6, 14, 16, and 17. I am grateful for Art Pomponio's willingness to embrace an innovative project. *Assessment Strategies for Monitoring Student Learning* is a highly-complex learning tool. Without the extraordinary work of its production editor, Lake Lloyd, as well as Eileen Smith's copyediting it would not be a reality. The following scholars provided expert reviews of the manuscript: Mary Bicouvaris of Christopher Newport University, Susan Brookhart of Duquesne University, Charles Eiszler of Central Michigan University, R. L. Erion of South Dakota State University, Steve Hoover of St. Cloud State University, Charles Isler of Central Michigan University, Craig Mertler of Bowling Green State University, Kouider Mokhrari of Oklahoma State University, Peggy Perkins of the University of Nevada at Las Vegas, Michael Trevisan of Washington State University, and Ann Weber of Illinois State University.

Difficult Decisions You Face as a Teacher

◈══ GOAL OF CHAPTER 1

Chapter 1 is designed to lead you to analyze your own instructional activities focusing on the many complex decisions you make within every teaching cycle and to examine how measurements and judgments influence those decisions. More specifically, the objectives are as follows:

A. From examining your own instructional activities as well as descriptions of activities of other teachers, you will identify various teaching cycles imbedded in those activities (construct a concept)[1] 20%[2].

B. You will want to develop a systematic method of making instructional decisions (appreciation)[1] 10%[2].

C. You will distinguish between examples of measurements and examples of decisions (construct a concept)[1] 20%[2].

D. From examining the process by which you make instructional decisions, as well as descriptions of the process by which other teachers make decisions, you will discover the dependence of the effectiveness of decisions on measurements, measurement error, and interpretation of measurement results (discover a relationship)[1] 30%[2].

E. You will incorporate the following technical terms and phrases in your working professional vocabulary: "teaching cycle," "empirical observation," "measurement," "planned measurement," "unplanned measurement," "measurement results," "measurement error," "monitoring students' learning," "mini-experiment," "prompt for students," and "observer's rubric." (comprehension and communication skills)[1] 20%[2].

---

[1]Indicates the learning level of the objective as defined in Chapter 5 of this text. (It is not necessary for you to be concerned with this scheme for categorizing learning levels until you've reached Chapter 5.)
[2]Indicates the relative importance assigned to the objective as explained in Chapter 5 of this text. (It is not necessary for you to be concerned with this weighting method until you've reached Chapter 5.)

TEACHING CYCLES

Classroom teaching is not brain surgery; teaching is far more complex. Brain surgery involves (1) studying a patient's symptoms and determining the need for surgery, (2) specifying what the surgery is to accomplish, (3) planning for the surgical procedure, (4) conducting the surgery (with assistance) and monitoring the patient's progress, and (5) evaluating the outcomes of the operation. The work of classroom teachers is conducted in cycles that parallel the stages of brain surgery. However, unlike the brain surgeon, the teacher does not have the luxury of working with only one client (i.e., student or patient) at a time. Typically, a teacher deals with about 30 students at a time. Whereas the brain surgeon only engages in one surgery at a time, focusing on one aspect of the patient (e.g., removing an intraaxial neoplasmic tumor from the occipital lobe) while others (e.g., an anesthesiologist) monitor variables (e.g., the patient's respiratory rate), the teacher (usually working alone) is expected to concurrently engage in numerous teaching cycles with about 30 students while monitoring a myriad of variables (e.g., self-image, aptitude, motivation, achievement, attention level, interest in the lesson's content, progress toward long-range goals, success with moment-to-moment objectives, and on/off-task behavior).

Teaching is an extremely complex art; consider, for example, Case 1.1.

CASE 1.1

While designing one of the mathematics units for his class of 26 second-graders, Mr. Chacone thinks to himself, "For mathematics to be meaningful and useful to my students, they need to connect some key mathematical ideas to their own everyday lives. Let's see. This unit involves some fundamental geometry. Circle is one of the key concepts with which this unit should deal. I don't want them just to remember that a circle is something that's round. They need to construct the concept of circle for themselves—internalizing the attributes of a circle and understanding how round is different from straight. Okay, if I think of some point as the center of my circle and some distance from that point as my radius, then my circle is made up of all the points in a plane that are that same distance from the center point. At this time in their school lives, they don't need a formal definition of circle with technical words like "radius," "equidistant," and "plane" until they've conceptualized circles." (See Illustration 1.1.)

Mr. Chacone decides to include the following among the objectives for the unit he is planning:

Students construct the concept of circle.

He then designs the lesson for the objective. It's now several days later; Mr. Chacone is with his students outside in the schoolyard, engaging them in the lesson he designed. He places a soccer ball on the ground and marks a straight line about 15 meters from the ball. He directs the students to stand side-by-side on the line as shown in Illustration 1.2 and explains the rules of a game they are about to play.

In the game, Mr. Chacone calls out two students' names in rapid succession. Upon hearing their names, those students race from their places on the line and, without contacting one another, try to kick the ball before the other. After each race, the ball is replaced and another pair of names is called. As Rosita waits for her name to be called following the second race, she shoves her way from an outside position on the line to one closer to the middle of the line. Mr. Chacone thinks, "It's good that Rosita has figured out that she gains an advantage by being nearer the middle of the line—that's going to help her discover the attributes of a circle. But she also needs to comply with my directions and behave politely or else someone could get hurt. To get her to learn to follow the rules and cooperate, I'll intervene by applying the principle of negative reinforcement" (Cangelosi, 1997, pp. 49–50, 362). He calmly signals Rosita to come stand by him. After the third race, he tells her, "Rosita, you may rejoin the game as soon as you make up your mind to keep your place in line and respect your classmates' rights." Rosita: "But it's not fair; Jamie

Given a distance *r*, a circle with radius *r* is the set of all the points in a plane that are *r* from its center. Thus, the following figure is a circle with radius approximately equal to 2.1 inches. Its center, C, and the broken line segments indicating the length of the radius are not part of the circle.

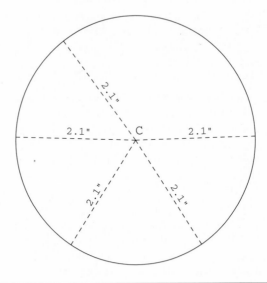

ILLUSTRATION 1.1

The Concept of Circle Mr. Chacone Wants His Second-Graders to Construct for Themselves

ILLUSTRATION 1.2

Early in Mr. Chacone's Mathematics Lesson

is closer to the ball than me!" Mr. Chacone: "Yes, I know. You may rejoin the game as soon as you make up your mind to keep your place in line and respect your classmates' rights." After the fourth race, Rosita jogs over to her original place on the line. Through the next two races, Mr. Chacone observes her waiting to hear her name in compliance with the rules. To positively reinforce this on-task behavior, Mr. Chacone calls out her name along with a student's who is located even farther from the ball than Rosita.

Although students aren't shoving one another or getting out of line, they are squeezing closer to the middle of the line in anticipation of their names being called. As the races continue, they grumble about the game not being fair. Mr. Chacone calls a halt to the proceedings and engages them in a discussion to explain why they think the game isn't fair. They agree that everyone should be "just as close to the ball." Mr. Chacone directs them to change the rules so they are fair to everyone, but he insists that they don't shorten the distance between the starting line and the ball because everyone needs the exercise. The students discuss the problem and decide that everyone would have the same distance to run if they lined up around the ball. They arrange themselves as shown in Illustration 1.3 and continue the game under the revised rules.

The following day, Mr. Chacone continues the lesson in the classroom, with the students describing and illustrating why and how they revised the game. Aware students knew the word "circle" prior to the lesson, he writes it on the board and has students list those things that make circles special. The list includes "circles are round and smooth," "circles are around something, always the same amount away," "circles are flat, unless you stand them up, which is when they're skinny," "circles have a huge hole in the middle," "a circle is like the outside of a hole which has been dug real even," and "circles don't have any wiggles in them." Such comments help Mr. Chacone to judge that most students are achieving the objective of the lesson.

A classroom (whether in the schoolyard or inside the building) is a complex social environment in a constant state of flux with multiple events and agendas interacting concurrently. To examine the art of teaching in this complex environment, it is helpful to focus on teaching cycles. A *teaching cycle* is any sequence of events in which a teacher (1) recognizes a need one or more students have, (2) decides to address that need by determining an objective or a set of learning objectives, (3) decides how to lead students to achieve the objective(s), (4) implements the plan, and (5) determines how well students achieved the objective(s).

ILLUSTRATION 1.3

Later in Mr. Chacone's Mathematics Lesson

At any point during a school day, a teacher is orchestrating many interrelated teaching cycles. In Case 1.1, Mr. Chacone executed one teaching cycle by designing and conducting the lesson on circles:

1. He recognized a student need when he decided, "For mathematics to be meaningful and useful to my students, they need to connect some key mathematical ideas to their own everyday lives. They need to construct the concept of circle for themselves—internalizing the attributes of a circle and understanding how round is different from straight."
2. He determined an objective that addressed the need by deciding to lead students to construct the concept of circle.
3. He decided how to lead students to achieve the objective by designing the lesson involving the racing game with the soccer ball.
4. He implemented the plan by engaging the students in the lesson that included the racing game with the soccer ball.
5. After observing students' activities and listening to their comments near the end of the lesson, he determined how well students achieved the objective by judging that most were in the process of learning.

Case 1.1 also relates another teaching cycle involving Mr. Chacone teaching Rosita to supplant an off-task behavior with an on-task behavior:

1. He recognized a student need when he decided Rosita needed to comply with his directions and behave politely.
2. He determined an objective that addressed the need when he decided to lead Rosita to follow the rules and cooperate.
3. He decided how to lead a student to achieve the objective by planning to use the principle of negative reinforcement.
4. He implemented the plan by signaling Rosita to stand by him and interacting with her as described in Case 1.1.
5. He determined how well Rosita achieved the objective after observing her waiting at her place in compliance with the rules.

Note that Mr. Chacone's judgment that Rosita achieved the classroom management objective influenced him to initiate another teaching cycle, one with the objective of positively reinforcing Rosita's on-task behavior. Of course, Mr. Chacone was also in the process of orchestrating another teaching cycle by designing and implementing the teaching unit of which the lesson on circles was a part.

Identify the two teaching cycles Ms. Anderson completes in Case 1.2; for each, note what she does in the stages listed in Illustration 1.4.

CASE 1.2

Ms. Anderson, an English teacher at Carver Middle School, believes her students need to improve their abilities to communicate in writing. In her judgment, they should become aware of the different ways readers interpret what they write and be able to edit their own writing to convey their messages as unambiguously as possible. Thus, for one of her classes of 32 students, Ms. Anderson designs a creative writing unit with the following learning goal:

Students will be aware of the different ways their writing can be interpreted and will edit what they write in light of that awareness.

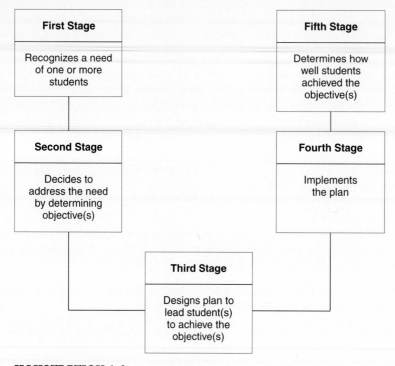

ILLUSTRATION 1.4

Five Stages of a Teaching Cycle

For the unit, she plans, prepares, and implements a number of learning activities over a 10-day period. For example, one day she divides the 32 students into five cooperative-learning groups of six or seven each. Within each group, one student reads a paragraph he or she wrote for homework. The other students then discuss the meaning of the paragraph as if the writer were not present. The writer, who is not allowed to enter into the discussion, listens and takes notes on how classmates interpreted the paragraph. The writer is to later modify the paragraph in light of the discussion. This activity is to continue until all students have had a chance to read their paragraphs and hear them discussed. However, as Ms. Anderson is moving toward the group that includes Howard, Chen, Austin, Cecilia, Angel, and Tomasina, she overhears the following exchange:

Howard:	"I don't want to read mine; it's horrible!"
Tomasina:	"Oh, go ahead; it's your turn. We'll be kind to you."
Howard:	"Naw, you guys will just make fun of me!"
Austin:	"We'll make fun of you whether you read it or not—so read it."

Turning to Ms. Anderson, Tomasina says, "Howard doesn't want to read his. Does he have to?" The following thoughts flash through Ms. Anderson's mind: "Howard needs to understand that no one is supposed to judge him by his paragraph—in fact, they're supposed to interpret his paragraph, not critique it. But I've already told them that, and another lecture from me on focusing on the paragraph's meaning rather than the person isn't going to help here. I could get by this uncomfortable moment and just tell the group that Howard doesn't have to read his now. On the other hand, he really needs to get through this and learn to get feedback on his writing. But if I push him to read it and he's embarrassed by what they say, his attitude might be further damaged. Too bad Chen is in the group; she's more likely to say something Howard would personalize than the rest. Austin and Tomasina tried to encourage him, but neither echoed my directions to separate the writing from the person. Maybe, I'll take some pressure off of him by reading it for him. Then I'll make a comment that'll get the discussion going in the right direction. I can't spend too much time with this group and still be supervising the rest." Turning to Howard, she says, "May I read your paragraph?" Grinning, he says, "I guess so."

After reading the paragraph in a serious, businesslike fashion, Ms. Anderson comments, "The paragraph got me to think about how the weather affects my behavior. I never thought about it before I read this, but the day's weather is one of the first things I think about when I get up in the morning. Did you think about that when you heard the paragraph, Angel? Keep the discussion going." As Angel responds, Ms. Anderson continues to listen and observe Howard's body language as she positions herself to supervise all of the groups' activities. Later, when the bell ending the period rings, she pulls Howard aside and asks, "Did hearing the guys discuss your paragraph help you decide how to edit your paragraph?" Howard: "Yeah, but I don't think they liked it." Ms. Anderson is unsure about the success of her strategy.

Near the end of the 10-day unit, Ms. Anderson uses a posttest to help her evaluate just how aware of readers' interpretations her students have become and how effectively the students learned to edit what they wrote.

Make sure you've analyzed Case 1.2, identifying the two teaching cycles before comparing your analysis to mine in the next two paragraphs.

The idea of Ms. Anderson's unit grew out of her belief that the students needed to improve their writing and editing abilities. Deciding to do something about that need, she entered the second stage of a teaching cycle by determining the goal for the unit (i.e., Students will be aware of the different ways their writing can be interpreted and will edit what they write in light of that awareness). In the third stage, she designed lessons to help students accomplish the goal (e.g., the lesson that included the cooperative group activities described in Case 1.2). The fourth stage, of course, was the actual implementation of the lesson plans (e.g., conducting the cooperative group activities). Her posttest results provided one of the data sources she used in the fifth stage to decide how well students achieved the unit goal.

Case 1.2 relates another teaching cycle triggered by Ms. Anderson overhearing the conversation from Howard's group. She decides that Howard needs to understand that no one is supposed to judge him by his paragraph. She also decides that he and the group need to get on with their activities without extending the delay caused by Howard's reluctance to share his paragraph. In stage two, Ms. Anderson decides to take a chance and try to get Howard to engage in the activity and progress toward the objective. In stage three, she decides to read his paragraph herself and set the tone for a productive discussion, which she does in stage four. Stage five left her undecided as to how well her plan actually worked.

DECISIONS IN EVERY TEACHING CYCLE

Studying teaching cycles dramatizes the huge role decision-making plays in your teaching—decisions with far-reaching impacts on your students and on your success as a teacher. Four of the five stages of a teaching cycle are a matter of making decisions. The first stage requires you to determine student needs, in the second you decide on objectives, in the third you decide how to accomplish objectives, and in the fifth you decide how well those objectives were accomplished. But it's during the fourth stage, in which you are orchestrating learning activities, that you are continually making one decision after another—decisions about classroom management, what to do next, how to handle a problem, whether to move on to the next phase of the lesson or continue in the present one, whether you should revisit a prior phase of the lesson, how to respond to a student's request, and on and on. Students' learning (whether it be learning about academic content, how to be cooperative, a skill, or to willingly engage in an activity) is in a constant state of flux that you need to continually monitor. One way or another, instructional decisions are about students' learning. Decisions, of course, are more likely to be effective if they are made systematically rather than haphazardly. Let's begin developing systematic methods for making instructional decisions by examining the process by which the teachers in Cases 1.1 and 1.2 made their decisions.

HOW YOU MAKE DECISIONS

The following were among the decisions made by the teachers in Cases 1.1 and 1.2; for each, identify possible factors that might have influenced that decision:

1. Mr. Chacone decides that Rosita needs to comply with his directions and behave politely.
2. Mr. Chacone decides to apply the principle of negative reinforcement for the purpose of getting Rosita to follow the rules and cooperate.
3. Shortly after he applies the principle of negative reinforcement, he judges that Rosita is complying with the rules and is on-task.
4. Near the end of the lesson on circles, Mr. Chacone judges that most students are successfully constructing the concept of circle.
5. Ms. Anderson decides that Howard needs to learn that he is not to be judged by his paragraph and that his classmates are supposed to interpret, not critique, his paragraph.
6. After implementing her plan with Howard, Ms. Anderson is unsure of how well Howard has learned that he is not to be judged by his paragraph and that his classmates are supposed to interpret, not critique, his paragraph.
7. Near the end of the unit, Ms. Anderson judges how well students edit their own writing.

If you can conveniently do so, compare the factors you identified with those of a colleague; discuss the bases for your responses. In Case 1.3, two preservice teachers, Kisha and Elwin, discuss their responses.

CASE 1.3

Kisha:	"We don't know Chacone's history with Rosita—her prior classroom behaviors and so forth—so there's no way we can know all the factors that influenced his decision about Rosita's need to comply with his directions and behave politely. But at least we know from Case 1.1 that he saw her shove her way toward the middle of the line. Obviously, that's what triggered his thoughts about needing to do something to teach her to be more cooperative."
Elwin:	"That's what I listed as the factor—that he saw her shoving other students. But what influenced him to decide to apply the principle of negative reinforcement? There's nothing in the case suggesting anything."
Kisha:	"I agree; we aren't given anything to go on at all. So I just used my imagination and thought about what he might have called to mind to make him think of negative reinforcement."
Elwin:	"Oh yeah! Like past experiences with similar situations."
Kisha:	"Right. And recalling what he had previously learned about when to use negative reinforcement. In this situation, it seemed appropriate since Rosita wanted to play the game."
Elwin:	"What would make him think she wanted to participate in the game? She wasn't cooperating."
Kisha:	"But he saw her trying to move to a more advantageous position in line. Don't you think that observation tended to make him think she really wanted to participate. By"

excluding her from the game while giving her the choice of returning by displaying appropriate behavior, he applied the principle of negative reinforcement."

Elwin: "So a factor influencing his decision was his noting that the circumstances of the moment were similar to circumstances for which he knew negative reinforcement could be applied. Okay, the next one is obvious. He decided that Rosita complied with the rules and was on-task because he saw her maintaining her original place in line and waiting her turn."

Kisha: "Okay, that brings us to the fourth one: Mr. Chacone judges that most students are successfully constructing the concept of circle."

Elwin: "For that one he was influenced by observing the students' list of things that make circles special."

Kisha: "I agree. There were probably other factors not given in the case—like particular things he saw and heard them say while they were changing the rules of the game and while they were describing why and how they revised the game."

Elwin: "The fifth one is from Case 1.2: Ms. Anderson decides that Howard needs to learn that he is not to be judged by his paragraph and that his classmates are supposed to interpret, not critique, his paragraph."

Kisha: "Again, I'm sure there were more factors influencing that decision than we were given in the case, but we do know that Anderson overheard that exchange with Howard, Tomasina, and Austin. That was the trigger for the decision."

Elwin: "Along with Tomasina's question for Ms. Anderson. Now, about the sixth one: Anderson is unsure of how well Howard has learned that he is not to be judged by his paragraph and that his classmates are supposed to interpret, not critique, his paragraph."

Kisha: "If she's unsure, did she really make a decision?"

Elwin: "I would say so, because how well Howard learned the lesson is a matter of degree. A teacher can never decide for sure just how well a student has learned something. One doesn't either absolutely learn or not learn—we learn in degrees. Anderson made a decision that the evidence of Howard's degree of understanding of the purpose of his peers discussing his paragraph was not sufficiently positive or negative for her to be sure one way or another."

Kisha: "That evidence being what?"

Elwin: "First of all, she watched Howard's behavior—the case mentions body language—during and after she read his paragraph to the group. At least we aren't told that he continued to protest or interrupted the ensuing discussion. I interpreted that as positive or, at best, as not a negative indicator of his understanding. But then his response to her after class—when he said, 'Yeah, but I don't think they liked it'—seemed to be a negative indicator to me because he was still thinking about them judging rather than interpreting the paragraph."

Kisha: "Okay, I follow what you're saying. Now for the last one in which she judges how well students edit their own writing. The case doesn't tell us what her judgment or evaluation was—how well she thought they achieved the lesson's objective."

Elwin: "I guess that would differ from student to student."

Kisha: "Sure. She has to evaluate the achievement of each student, and then she also thinks about what the class as a whole learned. The case tells us that she gave a posttest. I would guess that students' scores from that posttest were the factors influencing her judgment of how well they learned."

Note that the teachers in Cases 1.1. and 1.2, like you and all other teachers, don't make decisions in a vacuum. Your decisions are influenced by your empirical observations (i.e., what you see, hear, taste, smell, or feel) and by prior knowledge you call to mind. Decision-making is a two-step process: (1) Information is gathered through your empirical senses or recalled from prior experiences, and (2) you make a judgment.

MEASUREMENTS AND DECISION-MAKING

WHAT ARE TONJA AND REGGIE LEARNING?

You are the teacher in Case 1.4.

CASE 1.4

You are planning the first meeting with your third-period U.S. history class at Greystone High School. Among your objectives for the history lesson you'll initiate that day is the following:

Students discover that we base our beliefs about the past on observations of today's phenomena and events, examinations of artifacts and documents, and interviews with people.

Because this is the first day, you also want your students to begin learning the importance of arriving to class on time and completing homework assignments by their due dates. Thus, you decide to get the initial class meeting off to a purposeful start and assign homework for which students will be positively reinforced for completing.

You begin the first third-period class meeting by directing students to complete the questionnaire shown in Illustration 1.5. As the students respond to the questionnaire, you take care of administrative chores (e.g., distributing textbooks and checking the roll) and observe students as they work. You note, for example, that instead of answering the second question after writing down her name, Tonja looks around the room as shown in Illustration 1.6. Aloud, she asks students around her, "Why do we have to do this? I thought this was supposed to be history!" You walk over to her and in a hushed voice you say, "Tonja, I need for you to answer these questions as soon as possible; I will use your answers to plan tomorrow's class." Frowning, she begins writing as she says, "Okay, but I don't see what this has to do with history!"

After collecting the questionnaires, you engage the class in a discussion about their responses, discuss expectations and requirements for the history course, give each student a copy of a two-page essay by historian Mariya Jefferson, and give the following homework assignment:

Carefully read Mariya Jefferson's essay, "Looking at the Past with Today's Eyes." Note her descriptions of how she studies current events, artifacts, and documents, and how she talks to people in order to learn things about the past. This assignment is due for tomorrow's class.

That evening, in preparation for the second class meeting, you read students' responses to the questionnaire. Illustrations 1.7 and 1.8 display Tonja's and Reggie's responses.

As soon as the third period begins on the second day, you administer the test shown in Illustration 1.9. Tonja spends most of the 15 minutes you allot for the test as shown in Illustration 1.10. Reggie arrives to class 13 minutes late. As you hand him the test paper, he says, "I had to go to my locker to put my orchestra stuff away." He takes a seat and begins writing, but then you call for the papers to be turned in. Reggie complains, "I didn't have time to get started!" Seeming to ignore his complaint, you begin playing off students' responses to the test to engage them in a discussion about how all of us use our experiences with today's world to make inferences about what occurred in the past. During the lively discussion, Reggie says,

Third-Period History 😊 Meeting #1

1. What is your name? _____

2. Think of something that happened before you were born that you
   think almost everyone in this room also knows about. In two
   sentences, tell what happened.

   _____

   _____

   _____

   _____

3. What makes you think what you just wrote actually happened?

   _____

   _____

   _____

   _____

4. Think of something that happened before you were born that you
   think no one else in this room (other than yourself) also knows
   about. In one or two sentences tell what happened.

   _____

   _____

   _____

   _____

5. What makes you think what you just wrote actually happened?

   _____

   _____

   _____

   _____

ILLUSTRATION 1.5

Questionnaire Your History Students Complete During the First Class Meeting

(Continued)

ILLUSTRATION 1.5 (Continued)

6. Explain one way in which you influenced history.

   _____

   _____

   _____

   _____

7. Suppose that you are walking down a path through a
   forest. Just around a
   curve, you look to your
   left and observe the scene
   pictured to the right:

   Describe exactly what you see. _____

   _____

   _____

   _____

   _____

   Now, explain what you would infer happened at this site at
   some time in the past before you arrived.

   _____

   _____

   _____

   _____

ILLUSTRATION 1.6

You Observe Tonja as the Class Begins Responding to the Questionnaire

"That Mariya woman said that she read old diaries and stuff to learn about things before she was born. That's kind of like when I look at the old pictures my mom has hanging on the wall—pictures of her great grandma and stuff. Then I know how they used to dress and look and stuff. Of course real historians, like the one that wrote that paper we read, are more careful and scientific than we are when we just look at pictures or something." At one point in the discussion, you ask Tonja if she has anything she'd like to add. She responds, "No, I didn't know we were going to have a test. I didn't get to do the homework." You say, "I understand. Now let's go back to Reggie's point paralleling the work of professional historians to what we do all the time when we look into the past."

Near the end of the period, you give a homework assignment that is due on the third day. Tonja asks, "Will we have another test tomorrow like we did today?" You answer, "Yes, we will."

That night, as you prepare for the next day, you score the test papers using, for each student, the scoring form and criteria displayed by Illustration 1.11. Tonja's paper with her responses and that of another student, Salina, are displayed by Illustrations 1.12 and 1.13. Most students' scores (e.g., Salina's, as indicated by Illustration 1.14) are very high, but Tonja's score is only 10 out of 40, as indicated by Illustration 1.15. You don't record a score for Reggie since he simply wrote across his paper, "Not enough time to do this, but I could if I did."

On the third day, you again give a short quiz at the very beginning of the period; the students' success with the test is at least partially dependent on their having completed the homework assignment. Both Reggie and Tonja are on time with their homework. Out of a possible 30 points, Tonja's test score is 23 and Reggie's is 30. As with the first test, you designed this second test to be relevant to students' progress toward the following objective:

Students discover that we base our beliefs about the past on observations of today's phenomena and events, examinations of artifacts and documents, and interviews with people.

Third-Period History 😊 Meeting #1

1. What is your name? _Tonja Adams_

2. Think of something that happened before you were born that you
   think almost everyone in this room also knows about. In two sentences, tell what happened.

   (My mother was born)

   George Washington was

   the first president

   Move to 4

3. What makes you think what you just wrote actually happened?

   (Because she had to be born for me to be born.)

   I just did. Everyone knows.

4. Think of something that happened before you were born that you
   think no one else in this room (other than yourself) also knows
   about. In one or two sentences tell what happened.

   Move to 5

5. What makes you think what you just wrote actually happened?

ILLUSTRATION 1.7

Questionnaire Tonja Returned to You

(Continued)

ILLUSTRATION 1.7 (Continued)

6. Explain one way in which you influenced history.

   History is in old books that were written before I was born.

   So I couldn't influence history.

7. Suppose that you are walking
   down a path through a forest.
   Just around a curve, you look
   to your left and observe the
   scene pictured to the right:

   Describe exactly what you
   see.

   I see a place where people were camping.

   There was a fire.

   Now, explain what you would infer happened at this site at
   some time in the past before you arrived.

   The people put out the fire.

Third-Period History 😊 Meeting #1

1. What is your name? _Reggie King_

2. Think of something that happened before you were born that you think almost everyone in this room also knows about. In two sentences, tell what happened.

   There was a large music festival called Woodstock that took place in the 60's. Lots of popular bands played and people tore down the fences to get in

3. What makes you think what you just wrote actually happened?

   I've heard about it from others. There are documentary programs on TV about it. Recently, big music producers have tried to copy the idea of Woodstock.

4. Think of something that happened before you were born that you think no one else in this room (other than yourself) also knows about. In one or two sentences tell what happened.

   The boarded-up building across the street from where I live was built in 1912. It used to be a fish market where people could buy fish to eat.

5. What makes you think what you just wrote actually happened?

   On the top of the building is carved "Erected in 1912" and below is Seafood Emporium. I asked my mom what that meant and she said her Dad said it was a fish market that closed a really long time ago.

ILLUSTRATION 1.8

Questionnaire Reggie Returned to You

(Continued)

ILLUSTRATION 1.8 (Continued)

6. Explain one way in which you influenced history.

   I taught my friend Drew to play drums and now he wants to become a percussionist. Another was is because I was born, I changed the data in the census and census data will always be part of recorded history.

7. Suppose that you are walking down a path through a forest. Just around a curve, you look to your left and observe the scene pictured to the right:

   Describe exactly what you see.

   I see a pile of ashes that looks like it's from an old camp fire. I see rocks in a circle around it and an old log on the ground. There are trees growing in the back.

   Now, explain what you would infer happened at this site at some time in the past before you arrived.

   Somebody lit a fire and probably sat on the log and either cooked some thing or just ~~sat~~ sat around and stared at the fire.

```
            Opportunity to Demonstrate Your Understanding of How
                         We Discover History

                              Meeting #2

1. What is your name? _____

2. Yesterday, when you answered the questionnaire at the beginning
   of class, you thought of two things that happened before you
   were born.  For homework, you read historian Mariya Jefferson's
   explanations of how she learns about the past.

     A. What is one inference about the past that Jefferson
        related in her essay?

        _____

        _____


     B. Describe a process she used to obtain information from
        which she made the inference you listed for "A" above.

        _____

        _____

        _____

        _____


     C. What is one inference about the past that you have made?
        (It could be one of the ones you listed on the question-
        naire yesterday, but it doesn't have to be.)

        _____

        _____


     D. Describe a process you used to obtain information from
        which you made the inference you listed for "C" above.

        _____

        _____

        _____

        _____
```

ILLUSTRATION 1.9

Document for the Test You Administered on the Second Day

(Continued)

ILLUSTRATION 1.9 (Continued)

E. Explain how the process you described in "D" above was
    SIMILAR to the process you described in "B" above.

    _____

    _____

    _____

    _____

    _____

    _____

F. Explain how the process you described in "D" above was
    DIFFERENT from the process you described in "B" above.

    _____

    _____

    _____

    _____

    _____

    _____

As the teacher in Case 1.4, you are faced with some decisions about what Tonja and Reggie are learning. Address the following questions:

1. How did Tonja's progress toward the following objective evolve during Case 1.4?

> Students discover that we base our beliefs about the past on observations of today's phenomena and events, examinations of artifacts and documents, and interviews with people.

In your answer, describe how her understanding of how we and historians learn about the past changed from the beginning to the end of Case 1.4.

2. What factors influenced your answer to the above Question 1? In other words, identify the empirical observations and recollections of information you made that influenced your decision about Tonja's progress with the objective.

ILLUSTRATION 1.10

You Observe Tonja Taking the Test

3. How did Reggie's progress toward the objective listed for Question 1 evolve during Case 1.4?
4. What factors influenced your answer to the above Question 3?
5. How did Tonja's attitude about and willingness to do homework evolve during Case 1.4?
6. What factors influenced your answer to the above Question 5?
7. How did Reggie's attitude about punctuality and his willingness to arrive to class on time evolve during Case 1.4?
8. What factors influenced your answer to the above Question 7?

In a discussion, compare your responses to those of a colleague.

Now eavesdrop on the discussion Kisha and Elwin have in Case 1.5 as they discuss their responses to the exercise.

CASE 1.5

Kisha: "What did you put for the first question? Describe Tonja's progress toward the history objective."

Elwin: "I got the impression that Tonja arrived on the first day of class with a narrower perception of history than she had by the third day. Initially, she made no connections between our beliefs about the past and any process we use today to obtain information."

```
            Scoring Form for _____
                                    (name)
                      on Meeting #2's Opportunity

Note: For each criterion listed for Items 2A-2F, points are awarded
as follows:

     +2 if the criterion is clearly met
     +1 if it is unclear as to whether or not the criterion is met
     +0 if the criterion is clearly not met

Each encircled numeral (either 0, 1, or 2) indicates the number of
points your response received for the given criterion.

2-A:
   Identifies something that Jefferson
    related in her essay   ----------------------------- 0   1   2
   The thing identified is an inference
    about the past   ------------------------------------ 0   1   2
   Includes nothing erroneous or extraneous ------------ 0   1   2
                                                         (06)_____


2-B:
   Describes something that Jefferson did according
    to the essay   ------------------------------------- 0   1   2
   What is described is a process by which Jefferson
    collected information   --------------------------- 0   1   2
   The process described was used by Jefferson in
    making the inference listed for "2-A" -------------- 0   1   2
   Includes nothing erroneous or extraneous ----------- 0   1   2
                                                         (08)_____


2-C:
   Identifies an inference about the past
    she/he could have reasonably made ----------------- 0   1   2
   Includes nothing erroneous or extraneous ----------- 0   1   2
                                                         (04)_____


2-D:
   Describes an information-gathering process
    she/he could reasonably have done ----------------- 0   1   2
   What is described is a process by which the
    inference listed in "2-C" could be made ----------- 0   1   2
   Includes nothing erroneous or extraneous ----------- 0   1   2
                                                         (06)_____
```

ILLUSTRATION 1.11

Scoring Form You Used for Each Student's Test Responses

(Continued)

ILLUSTRATION 1.11 (Continued)

```
2-E:
  Is an explanation relating what she/he wrote for
   "2-D" to what she wrote for "2-B" ------------------  0   1   2
  Identifies similarities in the two processes --------  0   1   2
  Draws relevant parallels between the informal
   process and the process used by historians  --------  0   1   2
  Includes nothing erroneous or extraneous ------------  0   1   2
                                                      (08)_____

2-F:
  Is an explanation relating what she/he wrote for
   "2-D" to what she wrote for "2-B" ------------------  0   1   2
  Identifies differences in the two processes  --------  0   1   2
  Draws relevant parallels between the informal
   process and the process used by historians  --------  0   1   2
  Includes nothing erroneous or extraneous ------------  0   1   2
                                                      (08)_____


  Score for this opportunity: (40) _____
```

Kisha:	"Why do you say that?"
Elwin:	"Well, that gets me into the second question about factors that influenced me. But that's okay. On the first day she seemed really perplexed by the questionnaire asking her to think of something that happened before she was born. She seemed to think that history only resides in textbooks and didn't have much to do with what we do every day."
Kisha:	"Oh, because she said, 'I don't see what this has to do with history.'"
Elwin:	"And look at her answers on the opening-day questionnaire, like, 'History is in old books that were written before I was born.' Compare that to Reggie's answers; he jumped right in making connections between information gathering and inferring things about the past. In contrast to Salina's, Tonja's responses on the first test suggest she doesn't even know what an inference is."
Kisha:	"Maybe so, but she couldn't have done well on the first test because she hadn't done the homework assignment."
Elwin:	"But the homework assignment was designed to help her achieve the objectives; by not doing it, she prevented herself from progressing toward the objective."
Kisha:	"So why do you think her perceptions of history broadened between the second and third day?"
Elwin:	"At least she did her homework for the third day, and she did better on the second test than she did on the first. But let's stay focused on the first question; I'd like to hear how you answered the first question."
Kisha:	"I said I didn't have enough information to make a decision about how well she discovered that we base our beliefs about the past on observations of today's

Opportunity to Demonstrate Your Understanding of How
We Discover History
☻
Meeting #2

1. What is your name? _Tonja Adams_

2. Yesterday, when you answered the questionnaire at the beginning
of class, you thought of two things that happened before you
were born. For homework, you read historian Mariya Jefferson's
explanations of how she learns about the past.

   A. What is one inference about the past that Jefferson
related in her essay?

     _____

     _____

   B. Describe a process she used to obtain information from
which she made the inference you listed for "A" above.

     She found out things

     _____

     _____

     _____

   C. What is one inference about the past that you have made?
(It could be one of the ones you listed on the questionnaire yesterday, but it doesn't have to be.)

     George Washington was president. But I didn't do an inference. I

     already knew it.

   D. Describe a process you used to obtain information from
which you made the inference you listed for "C" above.

     I already knew it.

     _____

     _____

     _____

ILLUSTRATION 1.12

Tonja's Responses on the Test Paper

(Continued)

ILLUSTRATION 1.12 *(Continued)*

E. Explain how the process you described in "D" above was
   SIMILAR to the process you described in "B" above.

   What people said.

   _____

   _____

   _____

   _____

F. Explain how the process you described in "D" above was
   DIFFERENT from the process you described in "B" above.

   She wrote about history.

   _____

   _____

   _____

   _____

phenomena and so forth. Like you, I think she made some progress, but I can't be sure. She didn't seem to connect our knowledge of history with what we know about today's world. The factors I listed for the second question are (1) her comments about the questionnaire not having anything to do with history, (2) her answer about history being in old books, (3) and her answer on the first test that 'George Washington was president. But I didn't do an inference. I already knew it.' I didn't put much stock in the tests because the first one didn't really measure her achievement of the objective as much as it measured whether or not she did the homework. As far as the second test, Case 1.4 didn't display it, so we don't know what it really measured."

Elwin: "That's true, but since I was the teacher in Case 1.4, I assumed that I designed the test like the first one so that it would be a good indicator of how well students achieved the objective—at least for students who had done their homework."

Opportunity to Demonstrate Your Understanding of How
We Discover History

☻

Meeting #2

1. What is your name? ___Salina Mutombo___

2. Yesterday, when you answered the questionnaire at the beginning
   of class, you thought of two things that happened before you
   were born. For homework, you read historian Mariya Jefferson's
   explanations of how she learns about the past.

   A. What is one inference about the past that Jefferson
      related in her essay?

      Before 1910, bears roamed in the woods that surround Greystone Park.

      _____

   B. Describe a process she used to obtain information from
      which she made the inference you listed for "A" above.

      She studied pictures taken of some old cabins and they showed beask bearskins hanging
                              found
      up on the walls. Also she ⊗⊗ old newspapers that told about men going out to shoot

      bears. She interviewed people who told her that their grandfathers told them about going

      hunting where Greystone Park...

   C. What is one inference about the past that you have made?
      (It could be one of the ones you listed on the question-
      naire yesterday, but it doesn't have to be).

      The girls that went to school here before I was born weren't allowed to wear pants.

      They had to wear skirts or dresses.

   D. Describe a process you used to obtain information from
      which you made the inference you listed for "C" above.

      My Dad told me one day when he saw how I was dressed for school.
                saw
      Later, I ~~was~~ an old yearbook in the school office and all the girls wore

      skirts or dresses.

      _____

ILLUSTRATION 1.13

Salina's Responses on the Test Paper

(Continued)

ILLUSTRATION 1.13 *(Continued)*

E. Explain how the process you described in "D" above was
SIMILAR to the process you described in "B" above.

Mariya Jefferson looked at pictures like I did, and, like me, she listened to stories

people told. We both found out about the past by looking around us right now.

F. Explain how the process you described in "D" above was
DIFFERENT from the process you described in "B" above.

She did that triangulation stuff and checked out her sources. I just took ~~this~~ mine on

faith, believed what people said. Dr. Jefferson looked up records and documents and

interviewed people for the purpose of finding out about the past. My Dad just happened

to ~~find out~~ tell me about how they used to dress and I just happened to see the

yearbook. I didn't start out trying to find out about history.

Kisha: "Okay, so you have more confidence in your test-design talents than I have in mine. For the third question about Reggie's progress with the objective, I said that, compared to Tonja, he showed up the first day with a better understanding of the connection between our beliefs about the past and the observations we make today. But I really couldn't gauge if that understanding improved during the first three days of class. The factors I listed for the fourth question are his responses on the questionnaire about Woodstock, the Seafood Emporium, teaching Drew to play the drums, and the census data. Then, of course, he scored 30 out of 30 on the second test, but again I don't know what that test really measured. I wish he had shown up on time on the second day so I'd have another data point with which to work."

Elwin: "We have Salina's responses to that test, but we're not even asked to judge her achievement."

Scoring Form for *Salina Mutombo*
                    (name)
      on Meeting #2's Opportunity

Note: For each criterion listed for Items 2A-2F, points are awarded
as follows:

    +2 if the criterion is clearly met
    +1 if it is unclear as to whether or not the criterion is met
    +0 if the criterion is clearly not met

Each encircled numeral (either 0, 1, or 2) indicates the number of
points your response received for the given criterion.

2-A:
   Identifies something that Jefferson
    related in her essay   ------------------------------ 0 1 (2)
   The thing identified is an inference
    about the past   ----------------------------------- 0 1 (2)
   Includes nothing erroneous or extraneous ------------ 0 1 (2)
                                                          (06)   6

2-B:
   Describes something that Jefferson did according
    to the essay   -------------------------------------- 0 1 (2)
   What is described is a process by which Jefferson
    collected information ---------------------------- 0 1 (2)
   The process described was used by Jefferson in
    making the inference listed for "2-A" -------------- 0 1 (2)
   Includes nothing erroneous or extraneous ------------ 0 1 (2)
                                                          (08)   8

2-C:
   Identifies an inference about the past
    she/he could have reasonably made ------------------ 0 1 (2)
   Includes nothing erroneous or extraneous ------------ 0 1 (2)
                                                          (04)   4

2-D:
   Describes an information-gathering process
    she/he could reasonably have done ------------------ 0 1 (2)
   What is described is a process by which the
    inference listed in "2-C" could be made ------------ 0 1 (2)
   Includes nothing erroneous or extraneous ------------ 0 1 (2)
                                                          (06)   6

ILLUSTRATION 1.14

Scoring Form You Completed for Salina's Test Responses

(Continued)

ILLUSTRATION 1.14 (Continued)

```
2-E:
   Is an explanation relating what she/he wrote for
    "2-D" to what she wrote for "2-B" ------------------ 0  1 (2)
   Identifies similarities in the two processes -------- 0  1  2
   Draws relevant parallels between the informal
    process and the process used by historians -------- 0  1 (2)
   Includes nothing erroneous or extraneous ----------- 0  1 (2)
                                                   (08) ___8__

2-F:
   Is an explanation relating what she/he wrote for
    "2-D" to what she wrote for "2-B" ------------------ 0  1 (2)
   Identifies differences in the two processes -------- 0  1 (2)
   Draws relevant parallels between the informal
    process and the process used by historians -------- 0  1 (2)
   Includes nothing erroneous or extraneous ----------- 0  1 (2)
                                                   (08) ___8__

   Score for this opportunity: (40) ____40____
```

Kisha: "I think that was included in the case to give us a point of comparison to interpret Tonja's responses. Why don't you tell me how you answered questions 5 and 6? I think Case 1.4 gives more to go on to judge their changes in attitude about doing homework and showing up on time than it does about their achievement of the history objective."

Elwin: "I think Tonja's willingness to do homework improved between the second and third day. Why? My indicators are (1) she didn't have her homework for the second day, (2) I looked at her in Illustration 1.10 and she appeared frustrated and unhappy taking the test on the second day, (3) when I tried to involve her in the class discussion on the second day, she said 'I didn't know we were going to have a test; I didn't get to do the homework,' (4) she asked me right after I gave the second homework assignment if we would have another test the next day, (5) she has her homework for the third day, and (5) her score for the test after she did her homework was higher than it was for the test when she hadn't done the homework."

Kisha: "That's close to what I put; however, I'm not as certain of my conclusions as you are of yours. I'd rather withhold judgment about Tonja learning to do homework until I make more observations over a longer period of time. Will she continue to show up with her homework? How did you answer questions 7 and 8?"

Elwin: "Maybe I jump to conclusions faster than you, but I thought Reggie really learned his lesson about being to class on time. He was late the second day and complained that he didn't have time to take the test. He engaged in the discussion on the second day as if he would have done well on the test had he been there to take it. Most importantly, he was in class on time for the third meeting and scored 30 out of 30 on the test."

Scoring Form for _Tonja Adams_
(name)
on Meeting #2's Opportunity

Note: For each criterion listed for Items 2A-2F, points are awarded
as follows:

+2 if the criterion is clearly met
+1 if it is unclear as to whether or not the criterion is met
+0 if the criterion is clearly not met

Each encircled numeral (either 0, 1, or 2) indicates the number of
points your response received for the given criterion.

2-A:
Identifies something that Jefferson
related in her essay ------------------------------ ⓪ 1 2
The thing identified is an inference
about the past ----------------------------------- ⓪ 1 2
Includes nothing erroneous or extraneous ------------ 0 1 ②
(06) _2_

2-B:
Describes something that Jefferson did according
to the essay ------------------------------------- 0 ① 2
What is described is a process by which Jefferson
collected information ---------------------------- ⓪ 1 2
The process described was used by Jefferson in
making the inference listed for "2-A" -------------- ⓪ 1 2
Includes nothing erroneous or extraneous ------------ 0 1 ②
(08) _3_

2-C:
Identifies an inference about the past
she/he could have reasonably made ------------------ 0 1 ②
Includes nothing erroneous or extraneous ------------ ⓪ 1 2
(04) _2_

2-D:
Describes an information-gathering process
she/he could reasonably have done ------------------ ⓪ 1 2
What is described is a process by which the
inference listed in "2-C" could be made ----------- ⓪ 1 2
Includes nothing erroneous or extraneous ------------ 0 ① 2
(06) _1_

ILLUSTRATION 1.15

Scoring Form You Completed for Tonja's Test Responses

(Continued)

ILLUSTRATION 1.15 (Continued)

```
2-E:
   Is an explanation relating what she/he wrote for
     "2-D" to what she wrote for "2-B"  ------------------ ⓪ 1   2
   Identifies similarities in the two processes  -------- ⓪ 1   2
   Draws relevant parallels between the informal
     process and the process used by historians  -------- ⓪ 1   2
   Includes nothing erroneous or extraneous  -----------  0   1  ②
                                                         (08) __2__

2-F:
   Is an explanation relating what she/he wrote for
     "2-D" to what she wrote for "2-B"  ------------------ ⓪ 1   2
   Identifies differences in the two processes  -------- ⓪ 1   2
   Draws relevant parallels between the informal
     process and the process used by historians  -------- ⓪ 1   2
   Includes nothing erroneous or extraneous  ----------- ⓪ 1   2
                                                         (08) __0__

   Score for this opportunity: (40) _____ 10
```

EMPIRICAL OBSERVATIONS, MEASUREMENTS, MEASUREMENT RESULTS, AND DECISIONS

As human beings, we detect stimuli from our surroundings through our five empirical senses. Our experiences hearing, seeing, smelling, touching, and tasting along with our memories by which we recall prior experiences are the sources of the factors that influence the decisions we make. In Case 1.4, for example, your decisions about how well Tonja and Reggie were achieving the history objective and how well they were learning the importance of doing homework and arriving to class on time were influenced by what you heard them say, saw them do, and saw on their questionnaire and test papers. You were also influenced by your memory of prior experiences making empirical observations. For example, you may have decided that Tonja appeared frustrated while taking the test because she displayed body language and facial expressions that were reminiscent of behaviors you had seen others display when they were frustrated.

When you make an empirical observation (i.e., hear, see, smell, taste, or touch something), you collect information that can be stored in your memory or recorded in some manner. For example, you remember from Case 1.4 that you saw Tonja frown and heard her say, "Okay, but I don't see what this has to do with history." As her teacher, you read her responses on the first test, used Illustration 1.15's scoring form to record your analysis of those responses, and kept a record of her score of 10 (e.g., on a computer file). Your knowledge of this information influenced your decisions about her progress.

A *measurement* is defined as the process by which (1) information is collected through empirical observations and (2) that information is remembered or recorded. The memory or record of the information is called the *measurement result*.

Each decision you make depends on the combination of measurement results you choose to use and on how you decide to interpret those results.

MEASUREMENTS FOR MONITORING STUDENTS' LEARNING

WHY "MONITORING"?

The term "monitoring" is used herein because, as a teacher, you need to stay apprised of what your students are learning and doing as you conduct lessons. Monitoring students' learning requires you to make continual decisions, and thus, ongoing measurements.

UNPLANNED MEASUREMENTS

Most of the measurements influencing your decisions are unplanned; that is, you collect information that you did not set out to collect. In Case 1.4, for example, you made a measurement by overhearing Tonja ask students around her, "Why do we have to do this? I thought this was supposed to be history!" But you didn't plan that measurement ahead of time; you didn't direct the students to respond to the questionnaire to stimulate Tonja's comment. However, hearing that comment influenced your perception of Tonja's attitude about following directions and her perception of history. It appears from his comments in Case 1.5, that when Elwin put himself in the role of the teacher in Case 1.4, Tonja's comments influenced him to decide that she arrived on the first day of class with a relatively narrow perception of history. You made another unplanned measurement by hearing Reggie tell you as he arrived late for class, "I had to go to my locker to put my orchestra stuff away." Doesn't the fact that Reggie said this lead you to believe that Reggie has an interest in music? Consequently, you might decide to use a music-related example when explaining some aspect of history to Reggie.

Although you don't control this continual flow of information from unplanned measurements as you do from the less frequent measurements you plan ahead of time, it's important for you to control which results from unplanned measurements you let influence your instructional decisions. Put yourself in the role of the teacher in Case 1.6.

CASE 1.6

You are an English teacher at Sumac Creek Middle School conducting your first class meeting of the school year. You would like to engage the class in a discussion about different types of literature they encounter every day. According to your lesson plan, you should initiate the discussion by asking one of the students to tell the class about a selection he or she recently read. You believe the discussion would get off to a more efficient start if the initial selection that's discussed is of a more complex variety (e.g., a short story, novel, or think-piece from a magazine) rather than a simpler one (e.g., a commercial catalog or book of pictures). You are not yet acquainted with any of the students in the class. You look at the class and see the students sitting at their desks with the name tags you gave them at the beginning of the meeting. Illustration 1.16 depicts your view.

On whom should you call? Choose a student to call on—one who is likely to cooperatively talk about the type of reading selection you would prefer discussed at this point in the lesson. Of course, you do not have enough measurement results to make an informed decision, but for purposes of this exercise, make a decision based on the insufficient information you have at your disposal.

Fourth Row:

SAM　LAWRENCE　CATHERINE　LAMOS　SARAH

Third Row:

LESTON　SAMUEL　HARMONY　ALENA　BARTON

Second Row:

ISMAIEL　BOBBY　AMOS　SANDRA　HAE-SING

First Row:

ISLEY　LEE　MALEANA　ANITA　ERNESTO

ILLUSTRATION 1.16

Decide on Whom You Will Ask to Talk About a Recent Reading Experience

We cannot know which choice of students would prove effective in moving the ensuing class discussion in a productive direction. The following is a list of responses different teachers made to this exercise; each includes a rationale for the selection:

- "It's not very fair to ask me to make a decision based on a snapshot of the class. The dynamic classroom environment would give me much more information on which to base my decision. So, I'm just going to make a random choice. . . . I'll call on Samuel."
- "I first thought of asking Hae-Sing because she appears to be Asian-American and Asian-American families have the reputation of encouraging their children to read and succeed academically. Also at this age, girls tend to read more than boys. Thus, she might be more likely to have done some serious reading before the start of the school year. And then I realized that I was stereotyping my students by their appearances. Then I feared that by calling on Hae-Sing, I might be accidentally sending the message to my class that I expect more from females who appear to be Asian-American than I do from others. More importantly, the behavior of an individual should not be predicted on the basis of aggregate characteristics of the culture to which that individual belongs. To do so would be prejudicial. So I decided to ask Anita because she was looking right at me."
- "I have no basis for judging who among my students recently read a serious selection. So, I based the decision on my desire to get Ernesto to pay attention. I'll ask Ernesto."
- "At first, I thought I should pick someone who is making eye contact with me. I want this discussion to start off right; students who are looking at me, like Lawrence or Harmony, are more likely to respond in an on-task way than those who are not. But then I remembered that in some cultures, a person shows respect by casting their eyes down, so I decided to ask Bobby."
- "Sam's appearance and the fact that he's looking away and seated in the far corner of the room leave me with the impression that he is on the fringe of this group. I want to send a message on the first day of class that I expect all my students to participate. I'll call on Sam."
- "The student on the far left of the second row seems to be fidgeting, but he's looking at me. I get the impression, he'd like me to call on him. I want to call on him. But to tell you the truth—this is embarrassing—I don't know how to pronounce his name. If I pronounce it incorrectly, he might be insulted or others might laugh at me. I'm going to ask Lee."

Obviously, we cannot know the best choice for the situation, but it is important for you to be aware of the information that influences your instructional decisions and be able to satisfy yourself that decisions are based on tenable rationale that is consistent with sound pedagogical principles.

PLANNED MEASUREMENTS
Sequences of Mini-Experiments

Not only do you need to control which results from unplanned measurements influence your decisions, but you also need to be able to design and use planned measurements that produce relevant, accurate information. In Case 1.4, your use of the test on the second day is an example of a planned measurement. You developed, administered, and scored the test for the purpose of collecting information relevant to your students' progress toward a history-related learning objective. You may also have used the test to teach students the importance of doing homework and attending class on time. That's the nature of the complex art of teaching; you conduct activities for multiple purposes. But because one of the purposes of the test was to collect information that would influence a decision you needed to make, the test is an example of a planned measurement.

Not all planned measurements are formal tests such as the one you administered on the second day. In Case 1.4, you intentionally set up and controlled a situation in which your students would display their willingness to do homework. By assigning the homework without telling them whether or not the next day's test would depend on having completed the assignment, you set up an experiment in which you could observe behavior indicative of who in your class already understood the value of doing homework. It was an experiment because you set up a trial and observed the outcome. Think of your planned measurements as *sequences of mini-experiments*. Re-examine Illustrations 1.9 and 1.11. Note the components of the test document with which you confronted your students. 2-A, for example, prompts students with a question, "What is one inference about the past that Jefferson related in her essay?" A two-line blank provides for their written response. You then read each student's written response and record your observations using the scale labeled "2-A" in Illustration 1.11. Each component of the test (i.e., 2-A, 2-B, 2-C, 2-D, and 2-F) is a little experiment you conduct for the purpose of compiling information to help you make a decision.

A Mini-Experiment

Put yourself in the place of the teacher in Case 1.7.

CASE 1.7

You are a first-grade teacher in the midst of a mathematics unit on addition of one-digit whole numbers. You have already conducted lessons for the following two objectives:

A. Given two one-digit whole numbers, a and b such that $a + b = c$, students demonstrate why $a + b = c$ (e.g., explain why $3 + 5 = 8$ or $9 + 2 = 11$).

B. Given any two one-digit whole numbers, students recall the sum of those two numbers.

You want to develop a measurement that will provide you with information to help you decide how well students are progressing toward Objectives A and B.

Design two mini-experiments to be included on the measurement you want to develop for Case 1.7. The first should provide you with information relevant to how well students have achieved Objective A; the second should do the same for Objective B. Exchange and discuss the mini-experiments you design with a colleague.

In Case 1.8, Kisha and Elwin discuss their responses to the exercise.

CASE 1.8

Elwin:	"Designing a mini-experiment for Objective B was easy. I'd just ask individual students a question like, "What is 4 plus 8?" If the student says "12," I record that as a positive indicator of learning; if the student says something else, I record a negative indicator of learning. But a mini-experiment for Objective A is more difficult to come by. I guess I'd just ask them to explain why 5 plus 8 is 13 and listen to what they say."
Kisha:	"But what would you look for in their explanation?"
Elwin:	"Just if they said it right or not. What did you put?"
Kisha:	"I struggled with Objective A too. To come up with a mini-experiment for Objective A, I had to examine my own understanding of why the sum of two whole numbers is

whatever it is. After a lot of thought, I came up with the idea of why 5 plus 3 is 8. It's because if you take 5 things, like 5 red apples, and put them together with 3 other things that weren't part of the original set of 5—like 3 other apples—let's make the three additional apples yellow to keep it all straight—then altogether you have 8 apples. To demonstrate that, I would give students a pile of manipulatives of some kind—apples, blocks, whatever. I'd start with more than we need for the demonstration to see if she or he would count out the right numbers in each set. I'd direct the student by saying, 'Use these things to show me why 5 plus 3 is 8.' Then I'd watch to see if the student first counted out either 5 or 3 things and put them aside and then counted out the other number 3 or 5 so that the set of 5 things and the set of 3 things had no element in common. And then see if the student would join the two sets and show me that the joined sets had 8 things by counting the total."

Elwin: "Did you write all this down?"

Kisha: "Yes, here it is."

Kisha shows Elwin Illustration 1.17.

Prompt for Students

Note that each mini-experiment begins with a prompt for students. The prompt for students sets up the situation in which students are stimulated to behave in a manner that is indicative of what you want to measure. The prompts for students for the two mini-experiments displayed by Illustration 1.17 are labeled. In the less formal mini-experiment in Case 1.4 in which you measured students' willingness to do homework, you prompted students by assigning the homework, thus setting up a situation in which they had a choice of either completing or not completing the assignment in time for the next day's meeting. What is the prompt for students for mini-experiment 2-D of the test shown in Illustration 1.9? It is the directions that appear on the test document:

D.   Describe a process you used to obtain information from which you made
     the inference you listed for "C" above.

_____

_____

_____

_____

Observer's Rubric

Besides a prompt for students, each mini-experiment also includes an observer's rubric. A mini-experiment's *observer's rubric* is the set of rules, key, or procedures you follow whenever you record your analysis of a student's response to the prompt. Kisha labeled the observer's rubrics for the two mini-experiments in Illustration 1.17 as "Scoring Form" because when she designed them she had not yet been introduced to the term "observer's rubric." She must have noted the term "scoring form" in Illustration 1.11. The scoring form in Illustration 1.11 lists the observer's

Kisha's Mini-Experiment for Objective B from Case 1.7:

Prompt for Students:

Oral directions given by me with written response by students:

Directions: Write the number in the box that makes the statement true:

5 + 3 = ☐

Scoring Form:

Score +1 for "8," otherwise score +0.

Kisha's Mini-Experiment for Objective B from Case 1.7:

Prompt for Students:

I interview each student one-on-one:

Student meets me at one of the work tables in the back of the classroom. I show her/him a set of at least 20 manipulatives (e.g., beads, cards, coins, or plastic cubes). Then I direct her/him to use the things to show me why 5 plus 3 is 8.

If she/he hesitates or asks me for help, I only clarify directions without actually helping her/him perform the task.

Scoring Form:

Note: For each criterion listed, points are awarded as follows:

+2 if the criterion is clearly met
+1 if it is unclear as to whether or not the criterion is met
+0 if the criterion is clearly not met

Each encircled numeral (either 0, 1, or 2) indicates the number of points the response received for the given criterion.

The student counts out 5 objects from the
set and separates them from the rest ----------- 0 1 2
The student counts out 3 objects from the
set and separates them from the rest ----------- 0 1 2
The subsets of 5 and 3 objects
have no object in common ---------------------- 0 1 2

ILLUSTRATION 1.17

Two Mini-Experiments Kisha Designed

(Continued)

ILLUSTRATION 1.17 (Continued)

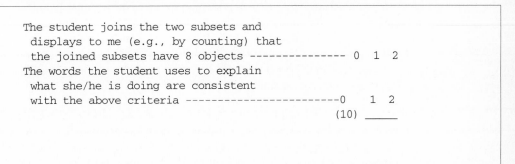

```
The student joins the two subsets and
  displays to me (e.g., by counting) that
  the joined subsets have 8 objects --------------- 0  1  2
The words the student uses to explain
  what she/he is doing are consistent
  with the above criteria -----------------------0    1  2
                                             (10) _____
```

rubrics for the individual mini-experiments that make up the test. What is the observer's rubric for mini-experiment 2-D of the test shown in Illustration 1.9? It is the directions labeled "2-D" in Illustration 1.11:

<u>2-D</u>:
Describes an information-gathering process she/he could
  reasonably have done. 0   1   2
What is described is a process from which the inference
  listed in "2-C" could be based 0   1   2
Includes nothing erroneous or extraneous 0   1   2

                                                            (06) ____

What is the observer's rubric for the mini-experiment you conducted in Case 1.4 in attempting to measure students' willingness to do homework? The answer is not explicitly given in Case 1.4. Had the homework assignment required students to produce a document (e.g., written answers to questions about Mariya Jefferson's essay), then the observer's rubric could simply involve you checking either "Yes" or "No" for each student, depending on whether or not the student shows up to class with the completed document. However, the homework assignment you gave in Case 1.4 was for students to read the essay; no concrete evidence that the essay was read is required. One possible observer's rubric for the mini-experiment might have been the following:

> Students' scores for mini-experiments 2-A and 2-B of the test (see Illustrations 1.9 and 1.11) are indicative of whether or not they read Jefferson's essay. Thus, note the score out of the possible total of 14 as an indicator of whether or not they completed the homework assignment prior to the beginning of the second class meeting.

By following observer's rubrics for a measurement's mini-experiments and compiling the outcomes or scores from each mini-experiment, you produce the measurement results. The measurement results of a formal test, such as the one from Case 1.4 and shown by Illustrations 1.9 and 1.11, are often expressed in the form of test scores (e.g., Tonja's score of 10, as reflected by Illustration 1.15).

MEASUREMENT ERROR

Your decisions are influenced by measurement results. But what influences measurement results? Call to mind some of the measurement results you obtained in Case 1.4. The scores obtained from the second day's test are examples of measurement results. Those scores were supposed to reflect students' progress relative to the stated history objective. Thus, if the scores are at least somewhat accurate, they are influenced by how well students are progressing with the objective. Salina's score of 40 is 30 points greater than Tonja's 10, supposedly indicating that Salina achieved the objective to a greater degree than Tonja. However, wouldn't you suspect that factors other than students' actual progress toward the objective also influenced those scores? Here are some possibilities:

- Maybe the puzzled and distressed look Tonja displayed in Illustration 1.10 as she took the test wasn't really caused by her being perplexed with questions about history. Maybe she did do her homework and progressed toward the objective but was so distressed over something in her personal life (e.g., she just had a fight with her boyfriend right before third period) that she didn't think straight while taking the test.
- Possibly Salina hadn't achieved the objective as well as her score of 40 suggests. Maybe, without really understanding the difference between information-gathering processes and making inferences, she just remembered facts from the essay and fortuitously happened to list the inferences for mini-experiment 2-A and examples of Jefferson's reported activities for 2-B.
- Students' scores on the test might be more indicative of their reading comprehension skills and how well they express themselves in writing than how well they achieved the history objective.
- While applying the observer's rubrics and filling out the scoring form, you may have read ideas into students' responses that they didn't intend to express. For example, in scoring 2-F, you might have assumed a student was drawing a relevant parallel that she or he wasn't. Another student may have expressed a relevant parallel in a way that you didn't detect as you hurriedly worked your way through the papers.
- Maybe some of the mini-experiments on your test don't really focus in on the more important aspects of the history objective.

If such factors did make a difference in the test scores, then they are sources of *measurement error*. Thus, the test scores in Case 1.4 were a function of two variables: (1) how well students were achieving the history objective, and (2) measurement error.

The results from unplanned measurements are also influenced by measurement error. In Case 1.4, for example, as Tonja began the opening-day questionnaire, you heard her say, "I don't see what this has to with history." Elwin indicated in Case 1.5 that when he put himself in the role of Tonja's teacher, hearing that comment influenced him to decide that Tonja arrived on the first day of class with a relatively narrow perception of history. If your opinion about Tonja's perception of history was also influenced by results from that unplanned measurement, then consider some possible sources of measurement error:

- Maybe Tonja made that comment not so much because of her perception of history, but because she was trying to draw attention to herself or conducting her own experiment—seeing how you, as her new teacher, would respond to a comment challenging the purpose of the questionnaire.
- Possibly, the comment was her way of expressing surprise at the unusual way you began the first day of class. She might have been expecting you to begin the first meeting as do many high school teachers—taking time with administrative chores and explaining what the course is all about.

In general, anything influencing measurement results that is not part of the question you're using the results to answer contributes to *measurement error*. In other words, the results of a measurement are dependent on both (1) the correct answer to the question which the measurement is being used to decide, and (2) measurement error. Thus, your decisions should not only be based on measurement results; they should also be made in light of the measurement error that influenced those results. Chapters 4–17 of this book are designed to help you (1) design measurements that produce results that are influenced more by truth than by measurement error, and (2) assess measurement error so that you account for measurement error when interpreting measurement results.

SYNTHESIS ACTIVITIES FOR CHAPTER 1

The synthesis activities for each chapter are intended to (1) help you bring together the chapter's content, (2) reinforce and extend what you learned, and (3) assess what you gained from the chapter so that you can identify your areas of proficiency and the topics you need to review. Another purpose is to encourage you to articulate your thoughts about principles, strategies, and methods for monitoring students' learning in both writing and discussion. Understanding is enhanced through such activities (Santa & Havens, 1991).

Here are the synthesis activities for Chapter 1:

  1. Examine Case 1.9 and then respond to the prompts listed A–N that follow:

CASE 1.9

Ms. Hall is a middle school health teacher. While supervising students on the school campus, she overhears one sixth-grader tell another, "I need some crack. My last hit finished me." Ms. Hall is aware of the alarming rate of drug use among pre-teens and teenagers. Consequently, she decides that her sixth-grade students should become more aware of the physiological and psychological effects of drug abuse.

She organizes and conducts a three-week unit (which includes videotape programs, a guest lecture, and small-group discussion sessions) that she hopes will increase students' understanding of the effects of drug abuse. During the presentation by the guest lecturer, Ms. Hall notices that Kevin and Gabrielle are especially attentive, but Emalee appears to be sleeping. She believes Emalee needs to hear the lecture, but rather than disturb the presentation, she leaves her alone. However, after Sally makes a loud wisecrack during the lecture, Ms. Hall passes a note to her directing her to say nothing until the speaker has concluded his remarks. Ms. Hall decides that the note worked because Sally remains quiet for the rest of the lecture.

Near the end of the unit, Ms. Hall administers a 60-point test that produces scores she uses to help her judge students' understanding of the effects of drug abuse. Ms. Hall is confident that most of the 16 students with scores greater than 45 got a lot out of the unit. She also believes that most of the 9 students with scores less than 25 have very little understanding of the effects of drug abuse. She's unsure of what the remaining 12 students learned from the unit.

Prompts:

  A. In Case 1.9, Ms. Hall completed two teaching cycles. In one cycle she developed and implemented a teaching unit for an academic goal relative to the effects of drug abuse. In the other cycle she dealt with a classroom management problem. Refer to Illustration 1.4 and list what she did in each of the five stages for the cycle involving the teaching unit for the academic goal.
  B. Ms. Hall's decision to develop the unit was based on her belief that some of her sixth-graders needed to be more aware of the physiological and psychological effects of drug abuse. Identify one measurement result that influenced Ms. Hall's belief that her students had this need.
  C. Did the measurement result you identified in your response to "B" above come from a planned or unplanned measurement? Explain your answer.

   D. Speculate on possible sources of measurement error that may have influenced the measurement result you identified in your response to "B" above.

   E. Near the end of the unit, Ms. Hall made a decision about how well students understand the effects of drug abuse. Identify one measurement result that influenced that decision.

   F. Did the measurement result you identified in your response to "E" above come from a planned or unplanned measurement? Explain your answer.

   G. Speculate on possible sources of measurement error that may have influenced the measurement result you identified in your response to "E" above.

   H. List what Ms. Hall did in each of the five stages for the cycle involving the classroom management problem.

   I. Ms. Hall decided that some of her students were not paying attention to the guest speaker. Identify two measurement results that influenced this decision.

   J. Did the measurement results you identified in your response to "I" above come from planned or unplanned measurements? Explain your answer.

   K. Speculate on possible sources of measurement error that may have influenced the measurement results you identified in your response to "I" above.

   L. Near the end of the teaching cycle for the classroom management problem, Ms. Hall decided her strategy for teaching Sally to stay on task succeeded. Identify one measurement result that influenced that decision.

   M. Did the measurement result you identified in your response to "L" above come from a planned or unplanned measurement? Explain your answer.

   N. Speculate on possible sources of measurement error that may have influenced the measurement result you identified in your response to "L" above.

2. Compare your responses to Synthesis Activity 1 with those of a colleague; discuss similarities and differences.

3. For each of the following multiple-choice prompts, select the one best response that either answers the question or completes the statement:

   A. In Case 1.1, Mr. Chacone decides that Rosita needs to learn to comply with his directions. That decision was influenced by his memory of Rosita shoving her way toward the middle of the line. That information he remembered is an example of a(n) _____.
   a) unplanned measurement result
   b) planned measurement results
   c) unplanned measurement
   d) planned measurement
   e) measurement error
   f) mini-experiment

   B. In Case 1.1, Mr. Chacone writes the word "circle" on the board and directs students to list those things that make circles special. That action _____.
   a) is an unplanned measurement
   b) is an example of measurement error
   c) produced an observer's rubric for a mini-experiment
   d) produced a prompt for a mini-experiment
   e) is an example of a measurement result

   C. In Case 1.1, Mr. Chacone judges that most students are constructing the concept of circle. That action _____.
   a) is an unplanned measurement
   b) is a planned measurement
   c) is an example of a measurement result
   d) falls within the second stage of a teaching cycle
   e) falls within the fifth stage of a teaching cycle

D. In Case 1.1, when Mr. Chacone decided to apply the principle of negative reinforcement, he was operating within the _____ stage of a teaching cycle.
   a) first
   b) second
   c) third
   d) fourth
   e) fifth

E. In Case 1.2, when Ms. Anderson overheard Howard say, "I don't want to read mine; it's horrible!" she was _____.
   a) making an empirical observation
   b) making a planned measurement
   c) making a decision
   d) producing an observer's rubric as part of a mini-experiment
   e) producing a prompt-for-students as part of a mini-experiment

F. In Case 1.2, when Ms. Anderson overheard Howard say, "I don't want to read mine; it's horrible!" she was _____.
   a) operating within the fifth state of a teaching cycle
   b) deciding that Howard had a need
   c) collecting information
   d) presenting Howard with a prompt as part of a mini-experiment

4. Compare and discuss your responses to the multiple-choice prompts from Synthesis Activity 3 with a colleague. Also, check your choices against the following key: A-a, B-d, C-e, D-c, E-a, and F-c.

5. With two or three colleagues, review Cases 1.1 and 1.2. For each case, identify two measurements the teacher made. For each measurement, discuss possible sources of error that might alter the measurement results.

TRANSITIONAL ACTIVITY FROM CHAPTER 1 TO CHAPTER 2

The transitional activity from one chapter to the next is designed to set the stage for your work in the subsequent chapter. In discussion with two or more of your colleagues address the following questions:

1. What are some effective ways for us to monitor our students' learning so that we have feedback that will help us plan instruction?

2. What are some effective ways for us to monitor what our students are learning and doing so that we have feedback to guide us as we conduct lessons?

3. What are some effective ways for us to monitor what our students are doing and learning that will help us keep students on task and engaged in learning activities?

4. How can we lead our students to monitor their own learning and use feedback to guide their own learning activities?

5. How, if at all, should we incorporate individualized student portfolios in our teaching?

Making Formative Judgments as You Teach

⟸ GOAL OF CHAPTER 2

Chapter 2 is designed to lead you to develop strategies for making formative judgments to guide your teaching and your students' learning. More specifically, the objectives are as follows:

A. From examining your own instructional activities as well as descriptions of activities of other teachers, you will distinguish between examples of formative judgments and examples of summative evaluations (construct a concept)[1] 10%[2].

B. You will develop strategies and techniques for making formative judgments that will guide the way you design curricula, teaching units, and lessons (application)[1] 20%[2].

C. You will develop strategies and techniques for making formative judgments as you conduct lessons for your students (application)[1] 20%[2].

D. You will develop strategies and techniques for making formative judgments to help you gain and maintain students' cooperation in a classroom environment that is conducive to learning (application)[1] 20%[2].

E. You will develop strategies and techniques for leading your students to monitor their own learning and make formative judgments to guide their own learning activities (application)[1] 20%[2].

F. You will distinguish between examples of expressions that communicate value judgments of students themselves and expressions that describe students' behaviors or accomplishments (construct a concept)[1] 05%[2].

G. You will incorporate the following technical phrases in your working professional vocabulary: "formative judgment," "summative evaluation," and "individualized student portfolio" (comprehension and communication skills)[1] 05%[2].

---

[1]Indicates the learning level of the objective as defined in Chapter 5 of this text. (It is not necessary for you to be concerned with this scheme for categorizing learning levels until you've reached Chapter 5.)
[2]Indicates the relative importance assigned to the objective as explained in Chapter 5 of this text. (It is not necessary for you to be concerned with this scheme weighting method until you've reached Chapter 5.)

SUMMATIVE EVALUATIONS AND FORMATIVE JUDGMENTS

Case 2.1 is a continuation of Case 1.4; once again, you are the teacher.

CASE 2.1

For the first week and a half of the third-period U.S. history class, you conducted a unit for the purpose of leading your students to understand methods for doing historical research and to apply some of those methods in their attempts to find out about the past. Throughout the one-and-a-half weeks, you operated numerous teaching cycles. One cycle you initiated in Case 1.4 involved Reggie and other students learning the importance of getting to class on time. As part of the fifth phase of this teaching cycle, each school day after the second class meeting, you observed Reggie arrive on time carrying his music bag. Recalling that he told you when he arrived late on the second day, "I had to go to my locker to put my orchestra stuff away," you decide that he now thinks arriving on time is important enough for him to quit stopping by his locker between second and third periods. You judge your strategy a success and close that teaching cycle.

Another teaching cycle you're about to close is the first teaching unit on methods for doing historical research. The purpose of the second unit is for the students to increase their understanding of some Native American cultures prior to 1500. You decide to make the transition between Units 1 and 2 by engaging students in activities in which they apply historical-research methods they acquired in Unit 1 to begin examining Native American cultures prior to 1500. The lesson you design requires students to work in six cooperative groups, each to conduct research on an aspect of the cultures. Trying to decide on which cultural aspects the groups should focus, you think to yourself, "On the opening-day questionnaire (Illustration 1.8), Reggie wrote that he impacted history by teaching Drew how to play the drums. He's in the school orchestra. Apparently, music is a major interest for him, as it is for quite a few others in this class. I'll assign one group the task of finding out about the music of some of the Native American cultures of the time; Reggie will be a member of that group. Now, for another group. Clothing or dress would interest some. On the first quiz, for example, Salina wrote about how girls at Greystone High used to dress (Illustration 1.13). I'll put her in a group assigned to study clothes. Sports and games of the different Native American cultures will be interesting to some. Tonja told me she's on the volleyball and soccer teams; I'll assign her to be the chairperson of a group that will focus on sports and games.

Within the fifth stage of one of the teaching cycles from Cases 1.4 and 2.1, you decided that Reggie learned the importance of coming to class on time. A decision that is made for the purpose of judging the success of a teaching cycle is known as a *summative evaluation*. Thus, you made a summative evaluation by judging your strategy with Reggie to be a success. Whenever you assign a grade to a student's achievement of some learning goal (e.g., at the end of a unit based on the results of a unit test), you are making a summative evaluation. The grade depends on your judgment of how well the student achieved the goal.

In Case 2.1, you were designing a transition lesson between Units 1 and 2. You made some decisions about students' interests and needs that influenced the lesson's design. Such decisions made for the purpose of guiding how you teach are not summative evaluations, but rather *formative judgments*. A decision that affects how you teach is known as a *formative judgment*. In Case 2.1, what measurement results influenced your formative judgment that the cooperative groups will be organized so that Reggie's group is to focus on music, Salina's on clothes, and Tonja's on sports? Those results included (1) Reggie wrote that he impacted history by teaching Drew how to play the drums, (2) Reggie is in the school orchestra, (3) Salina wrote about how women at Greystone High used to dress, and (4) Tonja told you she's on the volleyball and soccer teams.

The focus of this chapter is using formative judgments; Chapter 3 emphasizes the use of summative evaluations.

FORMATIVE JUDGMENTS FOR DESIGNING CURRICULA

CURRICULA

Your responsibilities as a teacher begin well before the opening day of the school year. You establish the direction for *curricula* your students will experience. Curricula exist on at least two levels:

- A *school curriculum* is a system of planned experiences (e.g., coursework, school-sponsored social functions, and contacts with school-supported services, such as the library) designed to educate students.
- A *course or classroom curriculum* is a sequence of *teaching units* designed to provide students with experiences that help them achieve specified learning goals.

A *teaching unit* includes four components:

1. A learning goal defined by a set of specific objectives
2. A planned sequence of lessons, each designed to lead students to achieve one of the specific objectives
3. Mechanisms for monitoring student progress and using formative feedback to guide lessons
4. Summative evaluations of student achievement of the learning goal

As their teacher, you exert far greater control over curricula your students experience than anyone or anything else. State-level, district-level, and school-level curriculum guidelines are articulated in documents housed in the files of virtually every school. These guidelines, as well as professional curriculum standards (e.g., *Curriculum and Evaluation Standards for School Mathematics* [National Council of Teachers of Mathematics, 1989] and *National Science Education Standards* [National Research Council, 1996]), establish parameters for you to follow. However, how you decide to interpret and implement these guidelines influences your students' curricula more than the guidelines themselves.

PLANNING AND ORGANIZING FOR THE SCHOOL YEAR

You begin designing curricula prior to the start of the school year. Even before meeting your students for the first time, you make formative decisions about their needs so that you can establish the initial goals for the year or course and tentatively set subsequent goals. Long-range planning and organizing require you to anticipate what you and your students will be doing throughout the year or course. Consider the many formative decisions Ms. Kimura makes in Case 2.2.

CASE 2.2

In three weeks, Amy Kimura will begin her fourth year as a first-grade teacher at Stewart Avenue Elementary School. Surrounded by curriculum materials including unit plans from last year, textbooks adopted for this year, curriculum guidelines, the daily time schedule outline shown in Illustration 2.1, and

8:30 A.M.	
8:45 A.M.	
9:00 A.M.	
9:15 A.M.	
9:30 A.M.	
9:45 A.M.	
10:00 A.M.	
10:15 A.M.	
10:30 A.M.	
10:45 A.M.	
11:00 A.M.	
11:15 A.M.	
11:30 A.M.	
11:45 A.M.	
12:00 P.M.	
12:15 P.M.	
12:30 P.M.	Lunch and Recess
12:45 P.M.	Lunch and Recess
1:00 P.M.	Lunch and Recess
1:15 P.M.	
1:30 P.M.	
1:45 P.M.	
2:00 P.M.	
2:15 P.M.	
2:30 P.M.	
2:45 P.M.	

ILLUSTRATION 2.1

The Daily Time Frame Within Which Ms. Kimura Has to Work

the school district calendar which provides for 180 instructional days including three days in the fall and three days in the spring for standardized testing, Ms. Kimura sits in front of her computer, reflecting on last year's experiences. She resolves to do a better job of integrating curricula from the various course content areas for which she is responsible (i.e., art and music, health and physical education, mathematics, reading, science, social studies, and writing and speaking). She ponders the problem of how to develop this integrated classroom curriculum while also maintaining enough separation among the courses to address curriculum guideline goals and use the adopted textbooks and programs.

Seeking information that will help her address the problem, she uses her computer to visit several web sites where teachers share ideas with one another. Also, she reads articles about integrating curricula for primary-grade students in professional journals including *Reading Horizons*, *School Arts*, *Science and Children*, *Social Studies and the Young Learner*, and *Teaching Children Mathematics*. Later she confers with two other primary-grade teachers to discuss alternatives. Assimilating the information from these measurements, she analyzes various time/course/unit configurations and decides to design her classroom curriculum around periodic themes. She thinks, "Every course will focus on a common theme for a week or two at a time. I'll formulate a sequence of topics that would interest the students. The classroom displays and just about everything else will have something to do with that topic for the week or two. Maybe more time should be spent on some themes than others. No, I think the period should be the same for all; then the children can anticipate starting and stopping points. That'll lend an air of organization. Whatever the time period is, this will provide opportunities to integrate across courses without locking me into having to integrate when it isn't practical to do so. This is a great compromise between what I think I should do and the administrator's concern for sticking to the adopted programs. But this is going to take some fancy coordination among the themes and the course units. First, I should make a tentative list of themes, but as I do it, I should keep the textbook chapters and curricula guideline chapters in mind. The mathematics, art, music, and language arts units can be related to almost any theme, but the science and social studies contents are organized around their own themes. Oh! Also, the reading program is organized into units, each focusing on a story that dictates a theme. This is going to be more complicated than I first thought!"

Ideas for themes are stimulated by her review of the textbook chapter titles, topics from curriculum guides and adopted instructional programs as well as her recall of experiences with prior classes, and examples from web sites and journal articles. She considers a myriad of complex factors that influence her choice of themes and how they should be sequenced. For example, she knows her students represent a wide variety of backgrounds, subcultures, and home environments. She must be careful to select topics that will be of interest to virtually everyone but that will offend hardly anyone. Themes should celebrate the diversity among her students while serving to bring them together around common interests. It will be easier to make these decisions after she's spent time interacting with the students. But at this point in time, she doesn't yet enjoy that luxury. She anticipates modifying her plans, and thus curricula, as she obtains formative feedback throughout the school year. After two more days of thought, she develops the theme sequence displayed by Illustration 2.2.

Since she'll be working with first-graders, Ms. Kimura decides to use the first two weeks as an orientation to the school and the classroom, establishing standards for conduct, routine procedures, and a safe, nurturing classroom community conducive to the business of learning. She plans to immediately involve students in every course during this orientation period. As she was deciding on Illustration 2.2's theme sequence, she was also developing ideas for the courses and titles for the units. After further conferences with colleagues, visits to web sites, reviews of journal articles, and recall of experiences with prior classes, she decides on some tentative grouping and scheduling patterns. Illustration 2.3 displays the course unit sequence she develops over the next three days. For each unit, she writes a goal. However, she only defines the goals for the first

Week	Theme	Week	Theme
1-2	Our School: Stewart Avenue	19-20	Games
3-4	Where We Live	21-22	Things That Grow
5-6	Friends and Pets	23-24	Birth and Death
7-8	Toys	25-26	Peace
9-10	Wild Animals	27-28	Television
11-12	Our Environment	29-30	Eating & Exercising
13-14	Taking Care of Ourselves	31-32	Technology
15-16	Government	33-34	Looking Back
17-18	Exotic Neighbors	35-36	Looking Forward

ILLUSTRATION 2.2

Ms. Kimura's Tentative Two-Week Themes to Help Her Integrate Her First-Grade Courses

unit of each course at this time. Determination of specific objectives for subsequent goals will depend on formative judgments about student needs that she'll make during the school year. Thus, in light of information yielded by her monitoring of student learning, she plans to decide on specific objectives for each unit about a week before the unit is scheduled to begin.

At any one point in time throughout the year, all seven unit sequences listed in Illustration 2.3 will be focusing on the theme of the time. At the beginning of the fifth week, for example, the focus of all units Ms. Kimura is conducting at the time will shift to friends and pets.

Depending on her usual sources of conferences with colleagues, professional web sites and journals, and recall of prior knowledge and experiences, she considers the relative advantages and disadvantages of various time schedules. She decides to begin with a stable, daily schedule at least for the first quarter of the school year; it's displayed by Illustration 2.4. She included daily community meetings to take care of administrative matters and provide time for discussions on how the class is governed; to raise, air, and deal with common-concern problems; to hear suggestions and ideas that don't specifically pertain to course content; and to deal with general procedural matters. She believes this will help students accept their share of the responsibility for the well-being of the classroom community.

In devising the schedule, she thinks about how she wants to structure lessons so that intense activities are followed by more relaxed ones, physical inactivity is followed by physical activity, quiet times alternate with noisy ones, and low-appeal activities are followed by high-appeal ones. She believes time should be organized so that the first-graders aren't expected to remain engaged in any one activity for an extended period of time and that their anticipation of an appealing activity helps motivate them to cooperatively complete a less appealing one.

In Case 2.2, Ms. Kimura made decisions about students whom she has yet to meet. Unable, at the time, to involve students themselves in mini-experiments for acquiring information to guide her formative judgments about curricula, she depended on her (1) recollection of prior knowledge and experiences with other students, (2) examinations of curriculum guides, textbooks, and instructional materials from adopted programs, (3) conferences with colleagues, (4) visits to professional web sites, and (5) professional journal readings. Besides the sources

Art & Music

1. The Art in Our School	11. Musical Stories
2. The Music in Our School	12. Picture Stories
3. The Art in Our Homes	13. Musical Games
4. The Music in Our Homes	14. Art Games
5. Making Toys	15. Musical Instruments
6. Lines That Tell Stories	16. Choral Singing
7. Cutting and Pasting	17. An Orchestra
8. Mixing and Using Colors	18. Happy and Sad Art & Music
9. Music and Art in Nature	19. Our Art & Music Show
10. Drawing People	

Mathematics

1. Problem Solving	12. More about Geometry
2. Measuring by Counting	13. Adding Whole Numbers II
3. Comparisons: $\neq$, $\approx$, $>$, $<$, $=$	14. Subtracting Whole Numbers II
4. Picturing Relationships I	
5. Counting and Naming Numbers	15. Numbers between 0 and 1
6. Multiples	16. Even More Geometry
7. Addition with Whole Numbers	17. Picturing Relationships II
8. Subtraction with Whole Numbers	18. Geometric Measurements
9. Place Value in Addition	19. Looking Back
10. Place Value in Subtraction	20. Looking Ahead
11. Adding Whole Numbers I	

Physical Education

1. Playing at Our School	10. Fitness Games
2. Playing for Health at Home	11. Growing Up Healthy
3. Eating for Health	12. Things to Avoid
4. Sports Toys	13. Team Sports III
5. Outdoor Recreation	14. Watching Sports on TV
6. Team Sports I	15. Exercising by Ourselves
7. How Our Bodies Work I	16. Individual Sports
8. Team Sports II	17. Our Own Olympics I
9. How Our Bodies Work II	18. Our Own Olympics II

Reading

1. Reading about School	16. "Kareem" and "Beautiful Music"
2. "Get Ready, Get Set, Go!"	
3. "Sunny Days" and "I Wonder"	17. "The Gingerbread Woman"
4. "A Place to Live"	18. "The Little Turtle"
5. "The Secret Hiding Place"	19. "Saying No"
6. "I Met a Man"	20. "What Animals Need"
7. "Teeth, Teeth, Teeth"	21. "I Can Decide for Myself"
8. "Heather's Feathers"	22. "Sebastian and the Bee"
9. "I Make Myself Happy"	23. "Deer Friends"

ILLUSTRATION 2.3

Titles of Teaching Units Ms. Kimura Plans for Her First-Grade Courses

(Continued)

ILLUSTRATION 2.3 (Continued)

10. "Breakfast Time"
11. "My Space"
12. "Germs"
13. "I Wonder Where the Clouds Go" and "I See the Wind"
14. "Gilbert and the Wind" and "City Lights"
15. "Rainbow Days"

24. "Dear Friends"
25. "The New Baby Pig"
26. "The Yellow Kite" and "The Lost Ship"
27. "The Seasons"
28. "An Old Friend"
29. "Pigeons" and "Gilbert"
30. Looking Back and Looking Forward

Science

1. The Ecology of Our School
2. The Ecology of Our Homes
3. Plants
4. How Animals Move
5. How Animals Eat
6. Body Coverings
7. Care of Plants and Animals
8. Comparing Matter
9. Measuring Matter
10. Moving Things
11. Producing Sound
12. Producing Motion
13. Using Machines

14. Rocks
15. Soil
16. Seasons and Weather
17. Seasons and Living Things
18. Our Sun
19. Stars
20. Seeing and Hearing
21. Smelling and Tasting
22. Touching
23. Emotions
24. Inventions
25. Looking Back
26. Looking Forward

Social Studies

1. Our School Community
2. Families
3. Friends
4. Our Neighborhood
5. Our City
6. Government
7. Communities: Birth, Growth, & Death
8. Making Maps
9. Using Maps

10. Our State and Country
11. Other Countries
12. Peace in the World
13. Navigation
14. Communications
15. World Technology
16. Individual Sports
17. Looking Back
18. Looking Forward

Writing and Speaking

1. Listening and Speaking
2. Speaking and Writing
3. Grammar: Sentences
4. Writing: Sentences
5. Grammar: Nouns
6. Writing: A Group Story

7. Grammar: Verbs
8. Writing: A Thank You Note
9. Grammar: Adjectives
10. Writing to Describe
11. More About Sentences
12. Writing: A Book Report

```
1. Plant Cells and Organisms      8. Electricity
2. Animal Cells and Organisms     9. Geology
3. Reproduction                  10. Meteorology
4. Structure of Matter           11. Human Anatomy
5. Laws of Motion                12. Human Physiology
6. Energy                        13. Preventing Diseases
7. Sound and Light               14. Treating Diseases
```

ILLUSTRATION 2.4

Ms. Kimura's Schedule for Her First-Grade Class

of information Ms. Kimura used in Case 2.1, you might also consider using *students' academic records* and, if available, *individualized student portfolios* from prior years as you develop curricula prior to the beginning of the school year.

Students' academic records typically housed in either the school counselors' offices or the principal's office may be of some value. Each student's cumulative folder typically provides personal background data (e.g., number of siblings, birth place, and with whom she or he is living), some account of the student's school history (e.g., co-curricula activities, prior report cards, attendance data, and anecdotal accounts of incidents involving the student), and standardized test scores. Be extremely cautious when you use students' records. They contain confidential information to which only school professionals (e.g., you or your principal) should have access for professional purposes (e.g., designing curricula). Be careful not to allow accounts of students' past performances and behaviors to prejudice how you monitor their learning as you work with them. Keep in mind, that children and adolescents display dramatic changes in performance and behavior from one year to the next. Expect some to respond to you much differently than they did to some of their other teachers. Furthermore, students' records do not present a complete or necessarily accurate picture of students' school history. Anecdotal accounts are sometimes haphazardly placed in files. Standardized test scores are not nearly as meaningful as most people think. (Proper interpretation of standardized test scores is the focus of Chapter 14 of this book.)

An *individualized student portfolio* is a collection of products, artifacts, and demonstrations of the student's schoolwork assembled for the purpose of providing a representative sample of the student's achievement. If your students' prior teachers had them develop individualized portfolios, you may be able to access at least some of those portfolios before the start of the school year. At some schools, students' portfolios are retained at the end of one school year and returned to students for further development during the subsequent year. A properly developed portfolio provides a rich source of information on what a student has learned. Incorporating individualized student portfolios in your teaching is addressed in a subsequent section of this chapter as well as in Chapters 3 and 6.

Until students are present so that you can begin monitoring their learning, you must depend on sources such as (1) recollection of prior knowledge and experiences with other students, (2) examinations of curriculum guides, textbooks, and instructional materials from adopted programs, (3) conferences with colleagues, (4) visits to professional web sites, (5) professional journal readings, (7) students' records, and (8) if available from prior years, individualized student portfolios.

DESIGNING TEACHING UNITS

Teaching-Unit Sequences

If you organize each course you teach into teaching units, as do most teachers, then you need to go through the same type of decision-making process Ms. Kimura went through in Case 2.2 when she developed Illustration 2.3. Other examples of teaching-unit sequences that four other teachers (Mr. Santiago, Mr. Eicho, Ms. Begin, and Ms. Fisher) developed for their courses are displayed by Illustrations 2.5, 2.6, 2.7, and 2.8.

A Goal and Objectives for Each Teaching Unit

Designing a teaching unit requires you to set a goal by expressing the overall purpose of the unit (i.e., what students will learn if the teaching unit is successful). By broadly identifying what students will learn, the learning goal provides direction for designing the unit. However, teaching is a complicated art. Leading students from where they are at the beginning of the unit to where you've decided they need to be at the end of the unit involves a complex of different learning stages requiring varied teaching strategies. For students to achieve the learning goal, they must acquire a number of specific competencies and/or attitudes. Thus, to guide the design of the unit's lessons, you should define the goal by a set of *specific objectives*, each indicating the specific competency or attitude that is a necessary, but insufficient, component of learning-goal achievement. Each time students accomplish an objective, they take a step toward achieving the unit's learning goal.

Note Unit 17 listed in Illustration 2.8; in Case 2.3, Ms. Fisher defines the goal for that unit with a set of objectives.

CASE 2.3

It is early March; Ms. Fisher's first-period U.S. History class is in the final stages of Unit 15, "A Cold Peace." She already planned Unit 16, "The Politics of Conflict and Hope," which she anticipates the class will complete within nine calendar days. Sitting in front of her computer with reference materials and notes, she begins designing Unit 17, "The Civil Rights Movement." She reads Unit 17's goal from the course outline she developed in August:

> "Students will trace the struggle for human equality in the United States from efforts to end racial segregation and disfranchisement in the 1950s, through the challenges of the black power advocates of the late 1960s, and to issues faced by minorities in the country today. They will also understand factors influencing the outcome of the struggle and their influence on current events."

She recalls that when she organized the course back in August, she decided to devote an entire unit to the civil rights movement although the topic corresponds to only one 21-page chapter in the textbook; the chapter title is "The Civil Rights Movement from 1945 to 1970." She reviews the chapter and its annotations for teachers, reflects on the students' progress to date, estimates the time the class can afford to spend on Unit 17, and thinks about which of her strategies seemed to succeed in previous units and which seemed to fail. She then makes a decision about the historical content of the unit by extending the era covered by the unit beyond that covered by the textbook. She plans to have students review content from previous chapters that will help them understand the roots of segregation and also deal with current issues that are affected by the historical events from the era studied.

Keeping in mind some fundamental learning theory based in cognitive science, she thinks, "To define this goal with objectives—first of all, I want my students to discover for themselves how segregation both de jure as well as de facto impacts the lives of all people—not only those who are the

1. Plant Cells and Organisms	8. Electricity
2. Animal Cells and Organisms	9. Geology
3. Reproduction	10. Meteorology
4. Structure of Matter	11. Human Anatomy
5. Laws of Motion	12. Human Physiology
6. Energy	13. Preventing Diseases
7. Sound and Light	14. Treating Diseases

ILLUSTRATION 2.5

Titles of Teaching Units Mr. Santiago Listed for His Middle School General Science Course

1. Saying What You Mean	8. Conversing
2. Listening to What Is Said	9. Making Speeches
3. Understanding What People Mean	10. Writing Stories and Skits
4. Getting People to Understand	11. Producing Skits
5. Writing So People Understand	12. Poetry
6. Persuading People	13. Creative Communications
7. Writing for Fun	

ILLUSTRATION 2.6

Titles of Teaching Units Mr. Eicho Listed for His Second-Grade Language Usage and Communications Course

1. Algebra and Its Language	10. Extending Functions
2. Numbers and Arithmetic Operations	11. Systems of Open Sentences
3. Operations on Rational Numbers	12. Extending Powers and Radicals
4. Algebraic Inequalities	13. Extending Quadratics
5. Powers	14. Operations with Rational Polynomials
6. Polynomials	15. Extending Work with Rational Polynomials
7. Factoring and Polynomials	16. Specific Functions with Natural Numbers
8. Quadratic Equations	17. Extending What You've Learned
9. Algebraic Functions	

ILLUSTRATION 2.7

Titles of Teaching Units Ms. Begin Listed for Her Algebra I Course

1. Looking Ahead in Light of Past Lessons; Historical Methods
2. The First Americans, Exploration, and Colonization
3. A New Nation
4. The U.S. Constitution and the New Republic
5. Expansion
6. The Civil War and Reconstruction Eras
7. Emergence of Industrial America, New Frontiers
8. Urban Society and Gilded-Age Politics
9. Protests and the Progressive Movement
10. Expansionism
11. World War I
12. The Roaring Twenties
13. The Great Depression and the New Deal
14. A Search for Peace and World War II
15. A Cold Peace
16. The Politics of Conflict and Hope
17. The Civil Rights Movement
18. The Vietnam War
19. Dirty Politics
20. Toward a Global (and Cleaner) Society
21. The New Nationalism
22. Extending What You've Learned Into a New Century

ILLUSTRATION 2.8

Titles of Teaching Units Ms. Fisher Listed for Her High-School U.S. History Course

targets of discrimination, but also members of the so-called 'privileged' group. Hopefully, they'll see that everyone loses in such a society. But I'm not going to include any affective objectives here. One or two reasoning-level objectives are needed to get them to discover some relationships. If those discoveries happen to influence attitudes for the better, so be it, but I'm only going to commit myself to making summative evaluations of cognitive outcomes at the end of the unit. Of course, I'll be making formative judgments about both cognitive and affective learning throughout the unit.

"They'll need to construct some concepts like de jure segregation and de facto segregation and comprehend readings that use vocabulary with some nuances that they don't yet understand, so I'll write an objective targeting some key words. Then they should be able to recount events to tell the story of the movement past to present; that'll involve comprehension of some historical accounts, recall of some processes, and discovery of some relationships. This unit is going to have some complex objectives."

After an hour of thinking, rethinking, writing, and rewriting, Ms. Fisher formulates Objectives A through H as listed in Illustration 2.9.

Illustrations 2.10, 2.11, and 2.12 list the goals and objectives Mr. Santiago, Mr. Eicho, and Ms. Begin each determined for one of the units from Illustration 2.5, 2.6, and 2.7 respectively. When you study Chapter 5, you will learn a method for formulating objectives that facilitates monitoring students' progress with those objectives.

Goal:

Students will trace the struggle for human equality in the United States from efforts to end racial segregation and disfranchisement in the 1950s, through the challenges of black power advocates in the late 1960s, to issues faced by minorities in the country today. They will understand factors influencing the outcome of that struggle and their influence on current events.

Objectives:

A. Students explain how segregation of black people from white people whether *de jure* segregation in the South or *de facto* segregation virtually everywhere in the U.S. affected the lives of all citizens both collectively and individually (discover a relationship)[1].

B. Students differentiate between examples and nonexamples of *de jure* segregation as well as between examples and nonexamples of *de facto* segregation (construct a concept)[1].

C. Students will translate the meaning of the following terms or expressions in the context of communications relative to the civil rights movement: "*de jure* segregation," "*de facto* segregation," "integration," "desegregation," "states' rights," "black urbanization," "equality of opportunity," "black separatism," "black power," "role models," "white backlash," "affirmative action," "reverse discrimination," "political power," "economic power" (comprehension and communication skills)[1].

D. Students describe a chronology of the civil rights movement from approximately 1863 to the present (in greater detail after 1950 than prior to 1950) (process knowledge)[1].

E. Students describe the following factors in the civil rights movement as presented in the textbook and in *Historical Accounts from Diverse Perspectives* and explain the significance of each: *Emancipation Proclamation*, *Thirteenth Amendment to the Constitution*, *Civil Rights Act of 1866*, *Fourteenth Amendment to the Constitution*, *Fifteenth Amendment to the Constitution*, *Plessy v. Ferguson*, National Association for the Advancement of Colored People (NACCP), Jim Crow laws, Truman's executive order of 1948, *Brown v. Board of Education of Topeka*, Southern Manifesto, lynching of Emmett Till, Montgomery bus boycott, White Citizens Council, confrontation in Little Rock, *Civil Rights Act of 1957*, Gandhi's policies of

ILLUSTRATION 2.9

Goal and Objectives Ms. Fisher Decided on for Unit 17

(Continued)

ILLUSTRATION 2.9 (Continued)

nonviolent resistance, lunch counter sit-ins, protest marches, sleep-ins, boycotts, kneel-ins, wade-ins, Ku Klux Klan (KKK), Southern Christian Leadership Conference (SCLC), Student Non-violent Coordinating Committee (SNCC), freedom riders, Inter-state Commerce Commission laws, Supreme Court decisions, black urbanization, religion, Constitutional rights, mass media, African independence movements, violence and arrests in the South, the march on Washington, *Civil Rights Act of 1964*, Freedom Summer Project, Mississippi Freedom Democratic Party (MFDP), *Voting Rights Act of 1965*, urban violence in the West and North, Black Muslims, black power movement, Black Panther Party, Black Panthers, the Kerner Commission, *Civil Rights Act of 1968*, white backlash, assassination of Martin Luther King, Jr., American Civil Liberties Union (ACLU), elections of black politicians, extension of strategies used in the struggle against racial prejudice into other movements (e.g., women's rights, environmental protection, consumer action, gay rights activists, etc.) (comprehension and communication skills)[1].

F. Students identify the following personalities and their roles in the civil rights movement: Charles Houston, Harry Truman, Thurgood Marshall, Martin Luther King, Jr., Earl Warren, Rosa Parks, Orville Faubus, Dwight Eisenhower, James Lawson, Medgar Evers, James Meredith, Ross Barnett, John Kennedy, George Wallace, Eugene Connor, Lyndon Johnson, Malcom X, Elijah Muhammad, Robert Kennedy, Douglas Wilder, Jesse Jackson (simple knowledge)[1].

G. Students explain how various stages of the civil rights movement from the early 1950s to today affected or affect the lives of all U.S. citizens both collectively and individually (discover a relationship)[1].

H. Given a real-life problem or current event, students address that problem or interpret that event in light of the lessons of the civil rights movement (application)[1].

[1] Indicates the learning level of the objective as defined in Chapter 5 of this text. (It is not necessary for you to be concerned with this scheme for categorizing learning levels until you've reached Chapter 5.)

Goal:

    Student will explain the effects of Newton's three laws of motion, gravity, and friction on speed and acceleration and apply their understanding of these effects in real-world situations

Objectives:

A. Students discriminate between speed and acceleration (construct a concept)[1].

B. Students state definitions for "speed," "acceleration," "force," "mass," and "distance" (simple knowledge)[1].

C. Students measure the speed of moving objects (process knowledge)[1].

D. From either observations of a moving object or utilizing sufficient data, students determine whether the object is or isn't accelerating (process knowledge)[1].

E. Students explain Newton's First Law of Motion (discover a relationship)[1].

F. Students state Newton's First Law of Motion (simple knowledge)[1].

G. Students explain the effects of friction and gravity on the speed of a moving body (discover a relationship)[1].

H. Students explain Newton's Second Law of Motion (discover a relationship)[1].

I. Students state Newton's Second Law of Motion (simple knowledge)[1].

J. Students explain Newton's Third Law of Motion (discover a relationship)[1].

K. Students state Newton's Third Law of Motion (simple knowledge)[1].

L. Given a real-life problem, students determine whether or not any combination of Newton's first three laws of motion apply to the solution of that problem and if so formulate a solution to the problem using that combination (application)[1].

[1] Indicates the learning level of the objective as defined in Chapter 5 of this text. (It is not necessary for you to be concerned with this scheme for categorizing learning levels until you've reached Chapter 5.)

ILLUSTRATION 2.10

Goal and Objectives Mr. Santiago Decided on for Unit 5 from Illustration 2.5

Goal:

Students will empathize with readers of their writing and focus on getting a specified message across as well as improving their writing mechanics (e.g., handwriting, spelling, and sentence structure)

Objectives:

A. Students approach a writing task via the following procedure:

1) Describe the targeted readers
2) Summarize the principal message to be communicated
3) Outline a plan for writing
4) Write the piece
5) Read the piece
6) Edit the piece
7) Rewrite

(process knowledge)[1].

B. Students accept constructive criticism about their own writing (willingness to try)[1].

C. Students write with a specified purpose in mind (application)[1].

D. Students utilize writing mechanics appropriate to the writing task (application)[1].

[1] Indicates the learning level of the objective as defined in Chapter 5 of this text. (It is not necessary for you to be concerned with this scheme for categorizing learning levels until you've reached Chapter 5.)

ILLUSTRATION 2.11

Goal and Objectives Mr. Eicho Decided on for Unit 5 from Illustration 2.6

FORMATIVE JUDGMENTS FOR DESIGNING LESSONS

In Case 2.3, Ms. Fisher's formative judgments about Unit 17's objectives were influenced by her knowledge of some fundamental learning theory based on cognitive science. For example, research literature (e.g., Cangelosi, 1996, pp. 49–174; Davis, Maher, & Noddings, 1990; Greene & Ackerman, 1995; Schuell, 1990; Steffe & Gale, 1995; Tobin, Tippins, & Gallard, 1994) strongly supports the following principles:

Teaching units should be designed so that students are led through inquiry instruction to construct a concept for themselves before they're engaged in a direct instructional lesson to learn a conventional name for that concept (e.g., in Case 1.1, Mr. Chacone used inquiry instruction to lead students to discover the concept of circle before he used the word "circle" and associated it with its meaning). Similarly, a relationship should be discovered before a statement of that relationship is articulated and committed to memory (e.g., in Case 2.3, Ms. Fisher decides that

Goal:

Students will understand why certain factoring algorithms work and how to use them in problem solving

A. Students explain how factoring polynomials can facilitate problem solving (discover a relationship)[1].

B. Students translate the meaning of the following terms in the context of communications relative to algebraic polynomial expressions: "factor," "prime factorization," "greatest common factor," "difference of squares," "perfect square trinomial," and "prime polynomial" (comprehension and communication skills)[1].

C. Students explain why the distributive property of multiplication over addition can be used to express a polynomial in factored form (discover a relationship)[1].

D. Students factor polynomials expressible in the form $ax + ay$ (process knowledge)[1].

E. Students explain why polynomials expressible in the form $a^2 - b^2$ can be expressed in factored form as $(a + b)(a - b)$ (discover a relationship)[1].

F. Students factor polynomials expressible in the form $a^2 - b^2$ (process knowledge)[1].

G. Students explain why polynomials expressible in the form $a^2 + 2ab + b^2$ can be expressed in factored form as $(a + b)^2$ (discover a relationship)[1].

H. Students factor polynomials expressible in the form $a^2 + 2ab + b^2$ (process knowledge)[1].

I. Students explain why some polynomials expressible in the form $ax^2 + bx + c$ (where x is a real variable and a, b, and c are rational constants) can be expressed in factored form as $(dx + e)(fx + g)$ (where d, e, f, and g are rational constants) and others cannot (discover a relationship)[1].

J. Given a polynomial expressible in the form $ax^2 + bx + c$ (where x is a real variable and a, b, and c are rational constants), students determine if it can be expressed in factored form as $(dx + e)(fx + g)$ (where d, e, f, and g are rational constants) and, if so, do so (process knowledge)[1].

ILLUSTRATION 2.12

Goal and Objectives Ms. Begin Decided on for Unit 7 from Illustration 2.7

(Continued)

ILLUSTRATION 2.12 (Continued)

> K. Students write and use computer programs to execute the algo-
>   rithms alluded to in the above listed objectives (process
>   knowledge)[1].
>
> L. Given a real-life problem, students explain how, if at all,
>   factoring polynomials can be utilized in solving that problem
>   (application)[1].
>
> [1] Indicates the learning level of the objective as defined in Chapter 5 of this text.
> (It is not necessary for you to be concerned with this scheme for categorizing learn-
> ing levels until you've reached Chapter 5.)

her students should discover for themselves how segregation impacts people before delving into accounts of the effects of segregation). Relationships underlying step-by-step procedures should be understood via inquiry instruction before direct instruction is used to help students become skillful with that procedure (e.g., you may choose to use inquiry instruction to teach for Objective A from Case 1.7 before you use direct instruction to teach for Objective B). Furthermore, fundamental principles for teaching reading comprehension and other language arts skills should be applied to teach students to comprehend conventions (e.g., vocabulary) and to communicate. Finally, inquiry instructional strategies should be applied for lessons to develop students' abilities to apply content in real-world situations and to develop their creativity with the content.

Ms. Fisher has these principles firmly implanted in mind during Case 2.4 as she continues to design Unit 17.

CASE 2.4

As she develops general guidelines for Unit 17's lessons, Ms. Fisher thinks, "The way I've organized these objectives, packing content into Objectives C through G, these objectives should be taught in pieces after students have achieved Objectives A and B. Then Objective H is the climax. Okay, I've got to get a grip on the whole picture."

She sketches Illustration 2.13, breaking Objectives C through G's content into five time periods, and continues thinking: "So first we go through a discovery lesson getting them to experience the consequences of a segregated society—that's going to take some creative planning on my part—doing it effectively while avoiding repercussions is going to be tricky. Then there's a construct-a-concept lesson for Objective B. What about the next five objectives? I'll deal with the background review content for those five objectives to set the stage for the central part of the unit. Then we address Objectives C through G again but for the period from 1945 to 1960, then again for 1960 to 1975, then for 1975 through 1999, and then we deal with Objectives C through G relative to current times. Finally, we get to the application lesson for Objective H.

"The lessons are pretty much going to follow some things I've done with previous units, except for Objective A—I'm going to have to take special care designing its lesson. There are some video programs and reading selections about what it was like to be black in various parts of the country during the 1950s. But most of my students have already been exposed to programs like those. They also need to learn what it was like to be white during that period. I'd like for them to experience some of the gut-level emotions that go along with arbitrarily-sanctioned unfairness—unfairness that's born out of tradition. I'd better check out some of my standard resources for ideas."

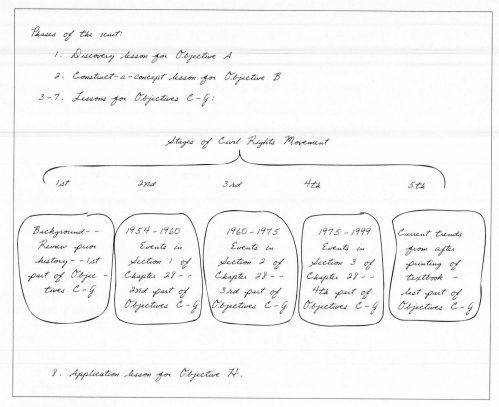

Phases of the unit:

1. Discovery lesson for Objective A

2. Construct-a-concept lesson for Objective B

3-7. Lessons for Objectives C-G:

Stages of Civil Rights Movement

| 1st | 2nd | 3rd | 4th | 5th |

Background -- Review prior history -- 1st part of Objectives C-G

1954-1960 Events in Section 1 of Chapter 28 -- 2nd part of Objectives C-G

1960-1975 Events in Section 2 of Chapter 28 -- 3rd part of Objectives C-G

1975-1999 Events in Section 3 of Chapter 28 -- 4th part of Objectives C-G

Current trends from after printing of textbook - last part of Objectives C-G

8. Application lesson for Objective H.

ILLUSTRATION 2.13

A Sketch Ms. Fisher Made While Planning Unit 17

Stimulated by a conference with a colleague, a review of her file of journal articles and instructional materials from inservice workshops and a university teaching methods course, and visits to several web sites for history teachers, she thinks, "One possibility would be to simulate a segregated community with my Afro-American students role playing the dominating group and my Euro-American students experiencing the discrimination. But I don't want to emphasize those distinctions in the classroom; some of my Afro-Americans come from more so-called 'privileged' homes than some of my Euro-Americans. Then where do I put my Native American, Latino, and Asian-American students in this scheme? I also don't want to send the message that racial segregation is a problem of only one race—this lesson should not dichotomize the students according to their actual ethnic differences. I need to think of another way of imposing a segregated society—something arbitrary, and untenable—some way that group membership is clearly visible like black and white, but I won't use black and white!

"There was that one journal article describing an activity where a teacher had students wear different types of hats. But hats can be a source of disruptions; I need something that they wear but doesn't fly off like hats. I've also got to be careful that I don't end up creating a gang-like atmosphere. We've already had too much trouble with gang activity in the neighborhood without me instigating some insignia or article of clothing for them to rally around! Whatever we try, whatever group designation I come up with has to be confined strictly to the time they're in first-period history class. It can't spill out of my classroom or else I'm asking for trouble. It would be nice if they were segregated for only one class meeting so animosities aren't carried outside of class where I'm not around to supervise. Maybe the possible repercussions aren't worth attempting something like this. The standard 'what it's like to be black' videotape programs and essays would surely be a safer route."Armbands! Colored armbands would work. I pass them out at the beginning of class—immediate segregation; I collect them after class—boom, end of segregation! I've got to pick some innocuous colors. Yellow, black, brown, white, red, pink all have some racial associations—blue is probably okay and then some other color that's clearly different but not all that different. I want them to ask themselves, 'What's the difference? Why is this happening to us?' Green, I'll use green. Now how should I split the class, 50–50 or what? I'm in charge of the class, so I should be a member of the 'privileged' group. I'll make the assignment of the armbands seem random, but I'll make sure that certain students are placed apart to avoid personality conflicts. There are a few who might be tough to manage in the discriminated-against group and a few who would be tough to manage it they thought they could exert power over others.

"Now, what can I do to set up a situation that'll get them to experience a segregated society within a class period? It would be more effective if I could pull it off before they read any of the textbook sections on the civil rights movement—before they recognize what the unit is all about. Maybe I could sneak this into the end of Unit 16, while they're still thinking about the politics of conflict and hope. It'd make a nice transition. I could do something on the Unit 16 posttest—distribute the armbands and administer the test under conditions that favored the 'blues' and discriminated against the 'greens.' The trouble with that is it would contaminate the validity of the test. But then I could always retest after they discovered what I was doing. But I don't have the luxury of the extra days that would take. I've got it! We'll try this on the day we go over Unit 16's posttest results—the day after the test, but before they know we're actually in Unit 17! Oh, that's beautiful! They show up curious about how they did, anxious to go over the test. They're more likely to tolerate my shenanigans when they're looking forward to something like going over the test results."

Excited by her own ideas, Ms. Fisher works out the general plan for Objective A as described for the first phase in Illustration 2.14. She spent an extraordinary amount of time planning the lesson for Objective A and described it in greater detail in Illustration 2.14's unit plan because she hadn't before tried a lesson similar to this one. The lessons for the other objectives resemble numerous other ones she's conducted in the past. Thus, as indicated by Illustration 2.14, she doesn't describe them in much detail. Details for all lessons will be worked out in her daily plans.

The account of Case 2.4 you just read does not explicitly delineate the many measurements Ms. Fisher used to influence her formative judgments for designing lessons. You can, however, implicitly identify them. For example, for information she depended on her recall of principles from cognitive science, interviews with colleagues, journal readings, web site visits, review of prior lessons plans, and recall of experiences with her students. Those unplanned and planned measurements you make while in the presence of students are, of course, critical.

FORMATIVE JUDGMENTS FOR SETTING THE TONE FOR THE SCHOOL YEAR

The beginning of a school year or new course is filled with uncertainties. Because students are uncertain about you, they will be watching your reactions, judging your attitudes, predicting what the relationships among you and the students will be, assessing their individual places in the social order of the classroom community, and determining how they will conduct themselves. It's a time for establishing expectations for the year or course. It's also your initial opportunity to empirically observe their behaviors, thus collecting critical information for formative judgments. In Cases 1.4 and 2.1, for example, you used Illustration 1.5's

Course: U.S. History

Unit #: 17th out of 22

Title: The Civil Rights Movement

Goal and Objectives (see Illustration 2.9)

Textbook Page References: 708-729, R-19, R-26, R-28 (Unless otherwise indicated, page numbers referred to in the overall lesson plan are from the course textbook.)

Overall Plan for Lessons:

The lessons are to be conducted in eight phases:

1. A lesson for Objective A is to begin the last day of Unit 16, the day in which I return and review the test for Unit 16 that the class will have taken the previous day. Without announcing the purpose of the exercise, 14 of the 27, as well as I, wear blue armbands in the classroom during history period. The other 13 students wear green armbands. The classroom is re-arranged so that the "greens" are physically segregated from the "blue" students (but not from me who is a blue). During the period, I will review the test results with the blues first, responding to their questions while the greens work on some menial task (e.g., sharpening pencils for the blues) while waiting for the test review session with the blues to end. The blues are then assigned some thoughtful task (e.g., completing a form critiquing the test -- possibly using the pencils that the greens just sharpened) while I spend the remaining time going over the greens' test results with them. The armbands are turned in at the end of the day's session without further explanation from me.

   The following day, the armbands are redistributed and the class is again segregated during a brief session in which I engage the blues in a critique session about the test using the questionnaires to which they responded the previous day. In the meantime, the greens are involved in another menial task. I'll halt the session before it "goes too far," collect the armbands, desegregate the groups, and engage the class in a questioning/discussion session relative to their feelings during the simulated segregation.

   The lesson may extend into a third day depending on the direc-tion of the discussion. Possibly, students may be assigned to write an essay expressing their feelings and then sharing them

ILLUSTRATION 2.14

Ms. Fisher's Plan for Unit 17

(Continued)

ILLUSTRATION 2.14 (Continued)

in either large or cooperative group sessions in which they develop hypotheses about the effects of living in a segregated, racially discriminatory society.

2. For the construct-a-concept lesson for Objective B, I'll engage them in four types of activities: (1) A sort-and-categorize exercise in which they'll discriminate among examples of *de jure* segregation, examples of *de facto* segregation, and nonexamples of segregation, (2) a question-discussion session leading them to reflect on and explain their categories from the prior activity, (3) a question-discussion session in which they develop definitions of the two types of segregation, and (4) a cooperative-group session in which they verify and refine their definitions.

3. Lessons for objectives C, D, E, F, and G are conducted relative to events prior to 1945 that established the roots and set the stage for the civil rights movement. The lessons will be integrated with direct instructional strategies for objectives D and F as well as the literal comprehension aspects of objectives C and E. Inquiry instruction will be applied for Objective G as well as for interpretive comprehension aspects of objectives C and E. Primary emphasis in this phase of the unit will be on relating experiences from phase 1's lessons to relevant content from previous units (e.g., slavery, Emancipation Proclamation, Thirteenth Amendment, etc.). Readings and videotape programs will be used. 1.25 class periods are anticipated for Phase 3.

4. This phase will also pertain to objectives C, D, E, F, and G except that the content will focus on pertinent events described in Section 1 "Origins of the Civil Rights Movement" (pp. 709-715) of Chapter 28 covering roughly the period between 1945 to 1960. Methods will be similar to that for Phase 3. 1.75 class periods are anticipated for Phase 4.

5. This phase will also pertain to objectives C, D E, F, and G except that the content will focus on pertinent events described in Section 2 "Freedom Now" (pp. 715-720) of Chapter 28 covering roughly the period between 1960 to 1975. Methods will be similar to that for Phase 3. 1.5 class periods are anticipated for Phase 5.

6. This phase will also pertain to objectives C, D, E, F, and G except that the content will focus on pertinent events described in Section 3 "High Hopes and Tragic Setbacks"

(Continued)

ILLUSTRATION 2.14 (Continued)

(pp. 721-727) of Chapter 28 covering roughly the period between 1975 to 1999. Methods will be similar to that for Phase 3. Two class periods are anticipated for Phase 6.

7. This phase will also pertain to objectives C, D, E, F, and G except that the content will focus on pertinent events since 1999 and current events and issues. Methods will be similar to that for Phase 3. 1.5 class periods are anticipated for Phase 7.

8. In this phase, an application lesson will be used to achieve Objective H. The selection of example and non-example problems raised during this will depend on formative judgments of students' interests in various issues raised during previous phases. Two class periods are anticipated for Phase 8.

<u>Formative Feedback and Summative Evaluation</u>:

Besides formative feedback throughout, brief tests following homework and individual work assignments will be routine. A day long unit test will be given at the end of the unit and the results will be reviewed with the class the following day.

<u>Extraordinary Learning Materials and Equipment Needed</u>:

1. 13 green and 15 blue armbands

2. Five videotape programs: "Unrecognized Achievement," "Who Looks Like Me?" "I Have a Dream," "Passive Resistance," "Different Perspectives on Affirmative Action"

3. The booklet *Historical Accounts from Diverse Perspectives* as well as magazine articles and newspaper clippings from my "Civil Rights" file

questionnaire to begin establishing expectations as well as to set up opportunities for you to observe behaviors indicative of their perceptions of history, willingness to follow directions, and reading and writing skills.

In Cases 2.5, 2.6, and 2.7, teachers take advantage of their initial interactions with students to make planned measurements that provide useful information for formative judgments.

CASE 2.5

Ms. Elabiad met most of her 23 first-graders and their parents individually during a two-day orientation session before the start of the school year. The following are among the objectives she targets as she plans the first class meeting:

A. Students feel comfortable and safe in the classroom working with one another and me and begin developing a sense of community.

B. Students begin developing the impression that schoolwork relates to their individual interests, that they are expected to make judgments, and those judgments are valued by me and their classmates.

C. Students discover that they are expected to perform challenging tasks in this class—tasks in which they can succeed.

Ms. Elabiad also wants to engage all students in the same activity so that she can observe how individuals follow directions and identify individuals who need closer supervision than others. The activity should provide opportunities for her to obtain indicators of individuals' interests, preferences, communication skills, and willingness to attempt tasks. She locates Illustration 2.15's tasksheet in a professional reference book and adapts it for one of the first-day's activities. Among other things, she plans to use students' responses from the tasksheets in subsequent lessons to help students understand academic content. For example, Ms. Elabiad intends to conduct a lesson on the concept of community during the second week. One of the activities she plans for that lesson is for students to compare their drawings from the tasksheets to demonstrate how different people in a community view things differently.

On opening day, she gives each student a copy of the tasksheet with the stickers. Step-by-step, she walks the class through the tasksheet as she observes their behaviors. At the end of the school day, she examines the responses to each mini-experiment task from the tasksheets. For example, she notes that on David's sheet a smiling-face sticker is on the picture of the boy who appears to have just fallen from his bike and hurt his arm. This raises a question in her mind about whether David interpreted the picture differently than she intended, misinterpreted the directions, found the incident depicted by the picture to be funny, or what. Consequently, to gain more insights into David's thinking, she decides to take David aside the next day and ask him to explain why he put the smiling face on that picture.

CASE 2.6

It is the opening day of a new term at Lincoln Middle School. The bell ending the second period rings, and the bell indicating the beginning of third period will ring in five minutes. Mr. Asgill-Jones, in preparation for the arrival of his third-period earth science class, turns on a video player showing a tape on a prominently displayed monitor with the audio volume control turned up rather loudly. As required by school policy, Mr. Asgill-Jones stations himself just outside the classroom door between second and third period. As students enter the room, they hear Mr. Asgill-Jones's voice coming from the video monitor: "Please have a seat at the desk displaying a card with your name. If no desk has a card with your name, please sit at one of the desks with a blank card. There you will find a marking pen for you to print and display your first name. Once seated at your desk, please take out one sheet of paper and a pen or pencil. You will need them when the third period begins. I would appreciate you clearing your desk top of everything except your name card, pencil or pen, and paper. This message will be repeated until the beginning of third period. After the bell, the directions for today's first lesson will appear on the screen." The message, which is printed on the screen while it can be heard in Mr. Asgill-Jones's voice, is repeated continually until five seconds after the third-period bell. Mr. Asgill-Jones has moved into the room. He moves among the students, gently tapping one inattentive student on the shoulder and pointing toward the monitor. Several times he gestures to the monitor in response to students trying to talk to him.

The message on the video changes. Mr. Asgill-Jones's image appears on the screen with this message: "I am about to perform an experiment. It will take six and a half minutes. During that time, carefully watch what happens. When the experiment is completed, you will be asked to *describe* in writing just what you *observed*. Remember those two words, 'describe' and 'observe.' They will be very important during this course in earth science."

As the experiment appears on the screen, Mr. Asgill-Jones watches the students (see Illustration 2.16). After the videotape is over, the students are directed to spend seven minutes writing a paragraph describing what they saw. Mr. Asgill-Jones circulates around the room reading over students' shoulders as they

These 25 stickers are in an envelope attached to Olga's taksheet:

Olga Bailey

1.

2.

3.

ILLUSTRATION 2.15

Taksheet with Which Ms. Elabiad Engaged Her Students on the First Day of School

Adapted from pp. 99–100 of *Classroom Management Strategies: Gaining and Maintaining Students Cooperation* (3d ed.)(Cangelosi, 1997) with permission from Addison-Wesley/Longman.

(Continued)

ILLUSTRATION 2.15 (Continued)

1.

Oral directions to be explained by the teacher to the students - - one item at a time using an illustrative tasksheet:

1. Pinned to the sheet is an envelope with three kinds of stickers. Take out the stickers and find the one with your name. · · · Now put the others back in the envelope. · · · Thank you. Now stick your name in this first box. · · ·

2. Now, draw a picture of your teacher - - that's me, Ms. Elabiad - - right here in this big box. · · · Thank you. I like looking at these pictures of myself.

3. Now, picture in your head what the outside of our school building looks like. · · · Now draw the outside of our school building in this big box. · · · Thank you. I like looking at the different ways you pictured our school.

4. Now turn to the last page and look at all the pictures. · · · Take the rest of the stickers out of your envelope. · · · Put a smiling face sticker on each picture that shows something you like to do. Put a frowning face sticker on each picture showing something you <u>don't</u> like to do. When you're finished, put the leftover stickers back in the envelope and raise your hand so I can bring you something.

write. At the end of the seven minutes, he calls on several students to read their paragraphs. Other students are then brought into a discussion session in which a distinction is made between describing observations and making judgments.

Mr. Asgill-Jones judges the learning activity a success because all students seemed to realize that they had made and described observations. He then outlines the course, making frequent references to observing and recording experiments, such as the one everyone had just commonly shared.

Information Mr. Asgill-Jones gained that first day influences formative judgments he makes for weeks. For example, prior to the opening of school, when Mr. Asgill-Jones first planned the first two units, he intended to get students to discover scientific relationships without much concern with how clearly they communicate their discoveries. However, while reading what they wrote during that initial activity, he noted that nearly half the students strung together a few expressions that did not really constitute a paragraph. Thus, he decides to refocus those first two units so that more emphasis is placed on how they communicate science.

CASE 2.7

Ms. Adreas' fifth-period physical education course at Westdale Junior High is organized so that, for the first half of the year, different units focus on different team sports. But rather than begin the school year with Unit 1 on a single sport such as flag football or basketball, she decides to spend the first week observing students trying to play various team sports as she makes planned measurements for formative judgments about their physical conditioning and readiness for different sports, skill-levels with various sports, their attitudes about sports, how well they cooperate with teammates, how well they follow directions, and which sports they prefer. For example, on the second day of the first week, she engages the students in volleyball games as she observes a sample of students using Illustration 2.17's form for each student in the sample.

At the end of the week, she analyzes the measurement results as recorded on the forms to help her plan the units. She makes formative judgments to address questions such as the following: Which sports should I include in the course? How long should I spend on each unit (i.e., sport)? For each unit, how much time should I spend on conditioning before I actively involve them in playing the sport? For each unit, how much time should I spend teaching them specific skills before involving them in games? For each unit, what levels of instruction should I include (e.g., beginner, intermediate, and/or advanced) and how should I group students according to levels?

ILLUSTRATION 2.16

Mr. Asgill-Jones Observing His Earth Science Students Respond to Tasks on the First Day of Class

```
                        Volleyball Rating Scale

Student's name _____    Date _____

Performance level relative to grade level:
   +5 for exceptionally high, +4 for clearly above average, +3 for
   near average, +2 for clearly below average, +1 for exceptionally
   low, ? for no judgment due to lack of opportunities

Performance areas:

   I.   Team play
           A. Decision-making      5   4   3   2   1   ?
           B. Positioning          5   4   3   2   1   ?
           C. Hustle               5   4   3   2   1   ? Average _____
  II.   Defense
           A. Digging/saving       5   4   3   2   1   ?
           B. Blocking             5   4   3   2   1   ?
           C. Decision-making      5   4   3   2   1   ? Average _____
 III.   Passing
           A. Positioning          5   4   3   2   1   ?
           B. Footwork             5   4   3   2   1   ?
           C. Handwork             5   4   3   2   1   ?
           D. Accuracy             5   4   3   2   1   ?
           E. Decision-making      5   4   3   2   1   ? Average _____
  IV.   Setting
           A. Positioning          5   4   3   2   1   ?
           B. Footwork             5   4   3   2   1   ?
           C. Handwork             5   4   3   2   1   ?
           D. Accuracy             5   4   3   2   1   ?
           E. Decision-making      5   4   3   2   1   ? Average _____
   V.   Hitting
           A. Angles               5   4   3   2   1   ?
           B. Speed/pace           5   4   3   2   1   ?
           C. Accuracy             5   4   3   2   1   ?
           D. Decision-making      5   4   3   2   1   ? Average _____
  VI.   Serving
           A. Toss                 5   4   3   2   1   ?
           B. Hand & Footwork      5   4   3   2   1   ?
           C. Variety              5   4   3   2   1   ?
           D. Placement            5   4   3   2   1   ?
           E. Speed/pace           5   4   3   2   1   ?
           F. Accuracy             5   4   3   2   1   ? Average _____
```

ILLUSTRATION 2.17

Rating Form Ms. Adreas Uses During Observations of Her Students Playing Volleyball

Before continuing with this chapter, imagine yourself planning the first meeting with one of your own classes. Design an activity that will help you set the tone for the year or course and that provides you opportunities to collect information that will influence formative judgments you must make. Consider developing a questionnaire or tasksheet for the activity. Exchange and discuss your plans with colleagues.

In Case 2.8, Elwin and Kisha discuss Kisha's opening day plans.

CASE 2.8

Kisha:	"One of my two teaching specialties is mathematics, so I made plans for the opening session of a high-school geometry course. I took an idea from Case 1.4 and developed a questionnaire for my students to work on while I observed them and took care of some first-day administrative chores. Here's the questionnaire."

Kisha shows Elwin Illustration 2.18.

Elwin:	"This looks more appropriate for an art or perception course than for geometry."
Kisha:	"Think about the tasks I'm asking them to do. When they try to describe the differences and similarities in the two trees, people, or whatever, they'll be looking at geometric characteristics like height, shape, surface area, and relative position. That's what geometry is all about."
Elwin:	"Now that you say that, I'm seeing triangles, rectangles, angles, and arcs where I didn't notice them before. So I'll bet you you'll throw their own descriptions back to them as you introduce various topics."
Kisha:	"Right! And look what I added at the bottom. Mini-experiment task 6 will give me a lot of information about their interests and concerns that I can use to build examples and problems in my lessons that'll interest them."
Elwin:	"And it'll give you a head start on knowing them."

FORMATIVE JUDGMENTS DURING LEARNING ACTIVITIES

Traditionally, teachers think of themselves as making summative evaluations of what students learned during the fifth stage of teaching cycles. During the fourth stage, they think of themselves as too busy conducting learning activities to be able to actively monitor students' learning. However, it is precisely during the fourth stage, while you're actively engaging students in learning, that the richest opportunity for collecting information for formative judgments about students' learning occurs. That is why much of this book addresses the question of how to design and use planned measurements as students learn. Chapters 7–13 focus on strategies for designing mini-experiments for such *planned* measurements. The purpose of this section is for you to heighten your awareness of the formative judgments you make as you teach and to develop some strategies for designing learning activities so that you are in a position to collect useful information from *unplanned* measurements.

Compare Case 2.9 to Case 2.10.

CASE 2.9

Ms. Snyder has designed an integrated mathematics and science lesson for the purpose of leading her fifth-grade students to achieve the following objective:

Students discover that the speed of a moving object can be measured by dividing the distance the object traveled by the time it took the object to travel the distance.

1. What is your name?_____

2. Carefully look at the photograph of the two trees. Write a
   description of how one tree looks different from the other.

   _____
   _____
   _____
   _____

   Write a *description* of how the two trees look the same.

   _____
   _____
   _____
   _____

3. Carefully look at the photograph of the two people. Write a
   description of how one of the people looks different from the
   other.

   _____
   _____
   _____
   _____

   Write a *description* of how the two people look the same.

   _____
   _____
   _____
   _____

ILLUSTRATION 2.18

Questionnaire Kisha Developed for the First Day of Her Geometry Course
Adapted from Cangelosi, 1996, pp. 352–353.

(Continued)

ILLUSTRATION 2.18 (Continued)

4. Carefully look at the photograph of the two balls. Write a *description* of how one ball looks different from the other.

_____

_____

_____

_____

Write a *description* of how the two balls look the same.

_____

_____

_____

_____

5. Carefully look at the photograph of the two kites. Write a *description* of how one of the kites looks different from the other.

_____

_____

_____

_____

Write a *description* of how the two kites look the same.

_____

_____

_____

_____

6. Make a list of 10 important questions about which you're going to have to make a decision during the next 9 months.

ILLUSTRATION 2.18 (Continued)

a. _____

b. _____

c. _____

d. _____

e. _____

f. _____

g. _____

h. _____

i. _____

j. _____

The lesson plan calls for Ms. Snyder to use an overhead transparency to display a path with equally spaced grid lines and to move a tiny image of a car at a slow steady speed along the path, as depicted by Illustration 2.19. She will have a student use a stopwatch to time how long it takes the image to cross a number of grid lines. Then she'll repeat the demonstration several times, but with each trial she either moves the image at a different steady speed or varies the number of grid lines the image crosses. All along, she plans to raise questions and provide explanations that will lead students to discover the relationship specified by the objective. By recording the number of lines crossed (i.e., the distance) and the time it took for each trial on the board, she hopes to get students to make comparisons demonstrating that the faster the image moves, the greater the ratio of distance to time.

Ms. Snyder is now standing in front of the class conducting the planned demonstration on the overhead projector. "Now count how many lines the car crosses this time," she directs the class as Yoshi operates the stopwatch. "There, 8 lines that time. What was the time, Yoshi?" she asks. Yoshi: "A little over 12 seconds." Ms. Snyder: "So that time the car took about 12 seconds to cross 8 lines. How does that compare to the last trip when it took about 17 seconds to cross 8 lines?" Manny quickly answers loudly, "This time the car went faster." "I agree with Manny. The car went faster this time because it took less time to cross the same number of lines," Ms. Snyder says as she turns to add the results of this latest trial to the data already on the board. Based on Manny's response, she thinks that he answered "faster" because he recognized that the car crossed just as many lines in less time. However, while she is writing on the board and starting the next trial, she doesn't hear the following exchange between Manny and Frank, who is sitting next to him off to one side of the room:

Frank: "How did you know the answer?"

Manny: "Couldn't you see her move her hand faster that time. I didn't count no lines. I don't know what she's talking about."

Occupied at her place in the front of the room, Ms. Snyder also did not notice Rosalina in the back of the room starting to raise her hand just as Manny blurted out his answer. If Rosalina had had the opportunity to respond, she would have said, "The time before, the car took 17 seconds to go 8

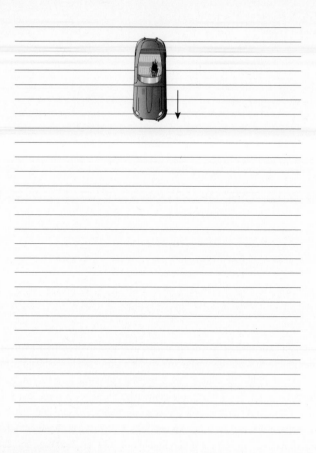

ILLUSTRATION 2.19

Ms. Snyder Uses an Overhead Transparency to Demonstrate
Speed of a Moving Object

lines. That's about 2 seconds for one line. But this time, the car took only 12 seconds to go 8 lines; that's like 1 ½ seconds for one line."

Consequently, Ms. Snyder makes an erroneous formative judgment about Manny's progress and misses an opportunity to make a measurement relevant to Rosalina's progress. More importantly, the whole class would have profited from a discussion stimulated by Rosalina's thoughts had she shared them.

After completing all the trials using the overhead, Ms. Snyder sums up what has been said: "So you see, we find out the distance by counting the number of lines crossed and the time with our watch. Then the rate of speed is the distance, or number of lines crossed, divided by the time. When the car crossed 15 lines in 5 seconds, its speed was 3 lines per second. What would its speed be if it took 10 seconds to go 15 lines?" Mindy: "1.5 lines per second." Ms. Snyder: "Does everyone understand how Mindy found the speed?" Some students nod positively; others stare straight ahead or look down. "Good!" Ms. Snyder responds. "Any questions? Yes, Parker." Parker: "I see how Mindy got 1.5, but I don't know why." Ms. Snyder: "Because the rate of speed is the distance, or number of lines crossed, divided by the time. Do you understand, now?" Parker: "Uhh,—okay, yeah."

Throughout the activity, Ms. Snyder was so busy from her place by the overhead projector and the board that she missed a myriad of indicators of who was on task, who was off task, who had insightful comments to make, who was following the discussion, and who got lost in the process. See Illustration 2.20.

CASE 2.10

Mr. Heaps devises a lesson plan for his fifth-grade students that targets the same objective that Ms. Snyder targeted in Case 2.9. His approach is similar to the one Ms. Snyder employed in Case 2.9. However, instead of standing in the front of the classroom by the overhead projector and board, Mr. Heaps conducts the lesson while circulating about the room, spending more time in the back of the room than the front. One student, Jorge, stands in front, operating the overhead projector with the gridded pathway and image of a car, as directed by Mr. Heaps. Another student, Nakisha, records data from the trials on the board while Jason operates the stopwatch, as Yoshi did in Case 2.9.

Because he is not busy manually carrying out the trials in front of the room and recording the results, Mr. Heaps is free to move among the students, as shown by Illustration 2.21. He gives step-by-step directions to Jorge on how to perform each trial. Everyone in the classroom also hears the directions, thus making it easier for them to understand the procedure. Furthermore, he has the students at their places respond to the prompts on the tasksheet shown by Illustration 2.22.

At one point in the activity, Mr. Heaps directs Jorge: "For this third trial, start the car at the second line on the path and move it at steady pace for 10 seconds. Wait until Jason gives you the signal to start. The rest of us will count how many lines the car crosses." As the trial is performed, Mr. Heaps observes who is following the procedure; then he directs the class to fill in the data for the third trial on the tasksheets. He quickly surveys a sample of the students' responses, noting that most wrote down "18" and "10 seconds," as did Nakisha on the board, but that Brett wrote nothing for Trial #3, and Mitsuko wrote "10" for the number of lines crossed and "18" for the time. Quickly and discreetly, he puts his finger on the blanks on Brett's tasksheet and then points to the data on the board. Quietly, he sends Mitsuko

ILLUSTRATION 2.20

Ms. Snyder Misses Some Important Opportunities for Unplanned Measurements

ILLUSTRATION 2.21

Mr. Heaps Conducts the Activity So That He Is Free to Make Empirical Observations for Formative Judgments

a hand signal indicating that she should transpose the two numbers. He notes that they both comply with his directions—directions that hardly anyone else in the class noticed.

As students work on the tasksheet after the fourth trial, Mr. Heaps walks around the room, sampling their responses and watching them use their calculators in response to the last four-part prompt of the tasksheet. Illustration 2.23 contains three of the completed tasksheets he read.

At this stage of the lesson, he only expects a few students to have discovered that speed can be measured by dividing the number of lines crossed by the number of seconds. He sees that Woofa has used her calculator to compute the actual number of lines per second, as indicated by the numbers at the bottom of her tasksheet. But he also interprets her explanations of why the speed was fastest in the third trial and her choice of trials 1 and 2 for the slowest as indicative of a misconception. Apparently, she only considered number of lines crossed without factoring in how much time it took to cross those lines. But yet, she computed the correct rates.

From Julie's explanations of her choices for fastest and slowest trials, Mr. Heaps judges that she's developed very sophisticated insights about the targeted relationship. However, he's confused by the numbers written at the bottom of her sheet. Instead of the expected higher numbers for higher speeds, she has lower numbers for higher speeds.

Saul's responses suggest to Mr. Heaps that Saul reasoned that the greater the number of seconds, the faster the speed. Since he judges Saul's progress with the lesson's objective to be behind the progress of the vast majority of the class, he decides to not discuss Saul's responses at the moment, but rather to work with Saul individually at a more convenient time.

He begins a class discussion by having Julie read her explanations for her choices of Trial #3 as the fastest and Trail #1 as the slowest. A comparison of Julie's responses to those of some other students leads

Trial #1:

      Number of lines crossed _____

      Time in motion _____

Trial #2:

      Number of lines crossed _____

      Time in motion _____

Trial #3:

      Number of lines crossed _____

      Time in motion _____

Trial #4:

      Number of lines crossed _____

      Time in motion _____

During which of the four trials did the car travel fastest? _____

      Why do you think your answer is correct? _____

      _____

      _____

      _____

During which of the four trials did the car travel slowest? _____

      Why do you think your answer is correct? _____

      _____

      _____

      _____

Write a number that indicates the speed of the car during:

      Trial #1 _____   Trial #2 _____

      Trial #3 _____   Trial #4 _____

ILLUSTRATION 2.22

Tasksheet Mr. Heaps' Students Use as They Follow the Demonstration Jorge Conducts from the Front of the Room

<u>Woofa's</u>

Trial #1:

       Number of lines crossed _____8_____

       Time in motion _____15.4 sec._____

Trial #2:

       Number of lines crossed _____8_____

       Time in motion _____7 1/2 sec._____

Trial #3:

       Number of lines crossed _____18_____

       Time in motion _____10.0 sec._____

Trial #4:

       Number of lines crossed _____15_____

       Time in motion _____9.0 sec._____

During which of the four trials did the car travel fastest? __#3____

       Why do you think your answer is correct? _____because it_____

crossed the most lines _____

_____

_____

During which of the four trials did the car travel slowest? _#1 and 2_

       Why do you think your answer is correct? _#1 and 2 because_____

_____

_____

Write a number that indicates the speed of the car during:

       Trial #1 _.52____   Trial #2 _1.1___

       Trial #3 _1.8___   Trial #4 _1.7___

ILLUSTRATION 2.23

Woofa's, Julie's, and Saul's Tasksheets

(Continued)

ILLUSTRATION 2.23 *(Continued)*

<u>Julie's</u>

Trial #1:

      Number of lines crossed ____8____

      Time in motion __15.4 seconds__

Trial #2:

      Number of lines crossed ____8____

      Time in motion ___7.5 seconds___

Trial #3:

      Number of lines crossed ____18____

      Time in motion ____10 seconds____

Trial #4:

      Number of lines crossed ____15____

      Time in motion ___9 seconds___

During which of the four trials did the car travel fastest? __3__

      Why do you think your answer is correct? _Because it took_
only about half a second to cross a line. The others took longer for a line. #4
took just a little longer #2 took about 1 second and #2 #1 took about 2
seconds

During which of the four trials did the car travel slowest? _#1_

      Why do you think your answer is correct? _Because of what_
I said above

Write a number that indicates the speed of the car during:

    Trial #1 _1.92_   Trial #2 _.93_

    Trial #3 _.55_   Trial #4 _.6_

ILLUSTRATION 2.23 (Continued)

<u>Saul's</u>

Trial #1:

      Number of lines crossed _____8_____

      Time in motion _____15.4 seconds_____

Trial #2:

      Number of lines crossed _____8_____

      Time in motion _____7.5 seconds_____

Trial #3:

      Number of lines crossed _____18_____

      Time in motion _____10 seconds_____

Trial #4:

      Number of lines crossed _____15_____

      Time in motion _____9 seconds_____

During which of the four trials did the car travel fastest? __1__

      Why do you think your answer is correct? __15.4 is the__

      most times _____

      _____

      _____

During which of the four trials did the car travel slowest? __9__

      Why do you think your answer is correct? __9 seconds is__

      the shortest _____

      _____

      _____

Write a number that indicates the speed of the car during:

      Trial #1 __?__   Trial #2 __~~~~__

      Trial #3 __?__   Trial #4 __~~~~__

the class to agree that speed is a function of distance and time. Then Mr. Heaps asks Julie to explain what he considers mysterious numbers at the bottom of her sheet. She says, "My numbers tell us the average number of seconds the car took to cross one line." Now Mr. Heaps realizes that her computations are perfectly consistent with her explanations. Each of the numbers is a ratio of time to distance, rather than the ratio of distance to time as he had anticipated.

A very productive discussion ensues, with most students recognizing that Julie's method and the more conventional method provide equally accurate measures of speed. Rather than raise general, vague questions such as, "Does everybody understand?" Mr. Heaps directs pointed queries at specific students to gauge their progress. For example, he asks, "Since Woofa's numbers are different from Julie's, how could they both be equally good indicators of how fast the cars were going?"

Consider the following ideas for designing lessons so that, as you teach, you collect useful information for making formative judgments:

- You are in a far better position to detect what your students are doing and thinking when you are circulating among them than when you are confined to a single area of the classroom (e.g., at the board, by the overhead projector, or behind a lab table). Organize your lessons so that you can conduct learning activities while remaining free to move about the classroom. In Case 2.10, Mr. Heaps put students on the "stage" in front of the room while he directed the activities as he moved about the room in close proximity with the learners. Students can operate projectors, display illustrations, and perform experiments and demonstrations as you direct them from any point in the room. It isn't necessary for students to be watching you to learn from you.
- Take advantage of technology to free you from having to stand in front of the classroom while making presentations. Electronic image writers, remote-controlled video players, and notebook computers with presentation software (e.g., *PowerPoint*) are examples of devices for controlling visual and audio presentations while moving about the classroom.
- Arrange your classroom so that you can easily move between any two points and can get near a student who needs to be observed closely without disturbing other students. Compare the four different classroom arrangements depicted by Illustration 2.24. Discuss with a colleague the relative advantages and disadvantages of each with respect to facilitating your being able to easily move between any two points.
- While conducting learning activities, continually survey the entire room, making eye contact with one student and then another. Students are likely to give you nonverbal feedback on what they are thinking when they see you acknowledging them by looking at them.
- Asking students, "Do you understand?" is unlikely to produce responses that are indicative of what students understand or misunderstand. Rather than raising such vague questions as Ms. Snyder did in Case 2.9, conduct an impromptu mini-experiment, as Mr. Heaps did in Case 2.10, by asking a very pointed question (e.g., "Why do you think Woofa decided to divide the two numbers instead of multiplying them?") or directing students to perform a specific task (e.g., "Show me how you got the .53 you wrote on the tasksheet").
- Continually employ prompts for students to respond to during presentations and other teacher-centered learning activities. If you're giving a lecture or presenting a demonstration, pepper it with questions for students to answer to obtain feedback on their engagement and comprehension. By reading over students' shoulders as they wrote on the tasksheet shown in Illustration 2.22, Mr. Heaps collected information that helped him decide how to proceed with the lesson.

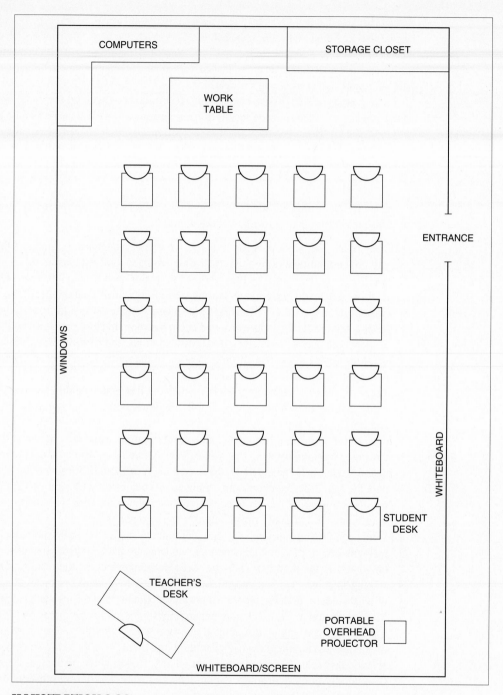

ILLUSTRATION 2.24

Which of the Four Classrooms Are Arranged So That You Can Easily Move Between Any Two Points?

Copied with permission from Cangelosi (1997), pp. 227–235.

(Continued)

ILLUSTRATION 2.24 (Continued)

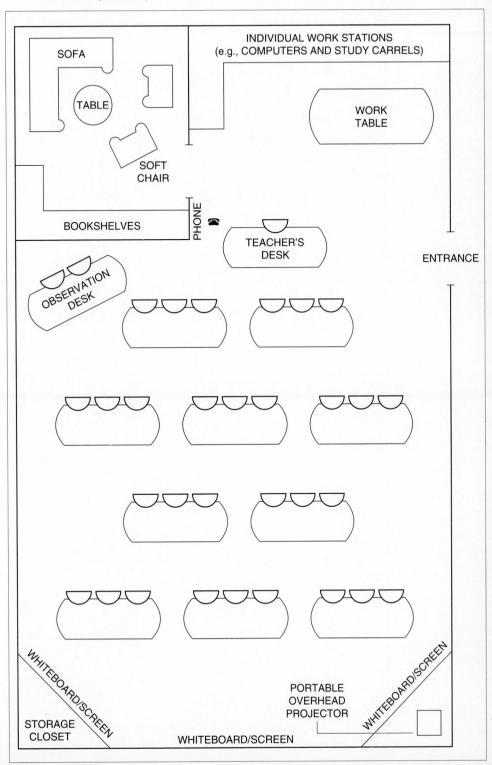

ILLUSTRATION 2.24 (Continued)

ILLUSTRATION 2.24 *(Continued)*

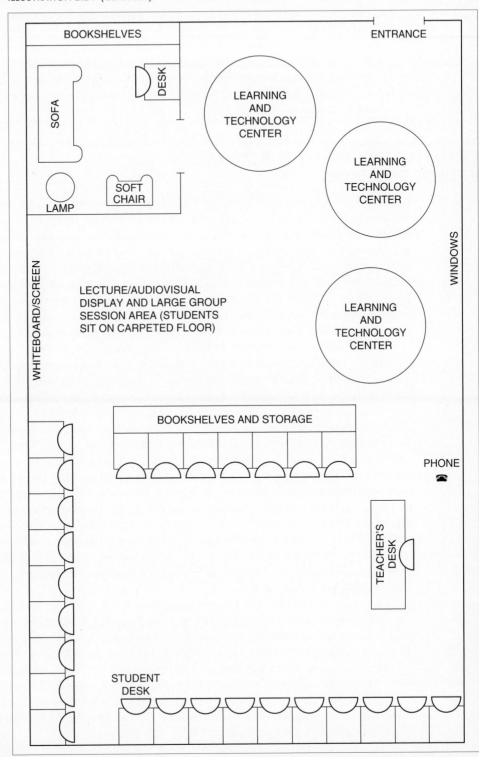

- Student-centered activities (e.g., cooperative-group work) typically provide more opportunities for feedback on what students are learning than teacher-centered activities (e.g., lectures). As Ms. Anderson supervised her students working in five cooperative-learning groups in Case 1.2, she observed multiple indicators of their progress with the objective as she heard them read paragraphs, read body language, listened to their interpretations of paragraphs, and watched the writers' reactions to hearing the interpretations. Unlike Ms. Snyer in Case 2.9, she was able to do this without having to be on stage in order for the lesson to continue.

FORMATIVE JUDGMENTS FOR MANAGING STUDENT BEHAVIORS

In Case 1.1, Mr. Chacone's pedagogically sound lesson plan could not have been successful if he had been unable to detect and deal with off-task student behaviors. Had, for example, Rosita continued to shove and displace others in line, the lesson would have gone awry. Managing student behavior involves both teaching students to supplant off-task behaviors with being on task as well as planning and conducting lessons so that students are engaged in them. A student's behavior is considered *engaged* to the degree that she or he is attempting to participate in the learning activity as directed by the teacher (Cangelosi, 1997, pp. 5–7). Besides helping him gauge students' progress toward the objective, Mr. Heaps's close observations of students in Case 2.10 helped him make formative judgments about how involved they were in the planned activities.

Because students' engagement in learning activities is inextricably interrelated to their progress with objectives, you use the same strategies to make measurements for formative judgments about how to manage students as you use for formative judgments about how to teach students. Moreover, you can hardly expect to successfully teach for academic objectives unless you also teach for classroom-management objectives. In Cases 1.4 and 2.1, you were not only concerned with students achieving history objectives; you were also concerned with them learning to show up for class on time and to complete homework assignments. Thus, strategies that you develop for monitoring students' learning with respect to academic objectives can also be applied to monitoring learning with respect to classroom management objectives. Of course, more often than not, achievement of classroom management objectives requires students to develop a willingness to behave in a certain way (i.e., an affective behavior) rather than to develop an ability or skill (i.e., a cognitive or psychomotor behavior). Your work with Chapter 12 will help you design mini-experiments for planned measurements relevant to students' affective behaviors. For now, it will be helpful for you to expose yourself to examples of teachers using information from unplanned and planned measurements for formative judgments relative to managing students' behaviors.

Cases 2.11, 2.12, 2.13, and 2.14 are such examples. As you study them, note the distinction between *disruptive off-task* behaviors (e.g., Rosita's shoving in Case 1.1) that are easy to detect and less-obvious *non-disruptive disengaged* behaviors (e.g., a student daydreaming instead of concentrating on a presentation) that are difficult to detect. It is also important for you to distinguish between *isolated incidents of behaviors* and *behavior patterns*. An isolated incident of a behavior is an event in which a student displays conduct that is not habitual for her or him. You deal with an isolated incident within a very brief teaching cycle, as did Mr. Chacone with Rosita in Case 1.1 and Mr. Holt does with Woodrow in Case 2.11 (adapted from Cangelosi, 1997, pp. 327–328).

CASE 2.11

Mr. Holt's sixth-grade class is engaged in a large-group learning activity on nutrition when Vickie responds to one of Mr. Holt's questions with, "I'm not just going to eat anything. I'm careful about what I stick in my body." Woodrow stands up and yells out, "Here's something you can stick in your body!" Woodrow momentarily grabs his crotch. Laughter erupts around the room. Because Mr. Holt has thought about handling this type of situation prior to this time and organizes his thinking in terms of teaching cycles, he is able to process the following thoughts in his mind without a moment's delay: "Woodrow has never pulled this stunt before. He's only looking for attention. It's too bad they laughed at him. That's positive reinforcement and this could be the beginning of a pattern. I need to prevent this from happening again. But how? I have numerous options. I could just laugh along and not make a big deal of it. But no, I cannot display approval. I might just ignore it and try not to focus any more attention on him. Too bad they've already laughed at him! It's too late to ignore it. I could jerk him out of his desk and give him a good tongue-lashing, but that would just call more attention to him. That's what he wants. Of course, he's left himself very vulnerable for a comeback. It would be easy for me to turn this around and embarrass him with his own words. That maybe could serve as a punishment. But that would likely have undesirable side effects; I'd never do that. It's never helpful to have a child lose face in front of peers. That could easily turn into a competitive thing between us; I can't afford that. I'm only glad no one in the class had a comeback for him. I must make sure I don't label him in any way. If I called him 'dirty' or 'rude,' he might learn to live up to that expectation. I could pretend that I did not understand the sexual connotation of his comment and respond as if he were really talking about nutrition. But that would be obvious dishonesty. No, I've got to handle this one head on."

Because Mr. Holt's mind was busy with the aforementioned thoughts in the moments immediately following the outburst of laughter, he was able to maintain a serious expression throughout. The class quickly realizes that Mr. Holt did not find Woodrow's clowning humorous. He turns to Woodrow and says, "I know you are trying to make us laugh. But I do not like to hear that kind of joke. You and I will talk about this right after the class leaves for lunch today." Turning to Vickie, Mr. Holt says, "Excuse the interruption Vickie. You were telling us that you chose your food carefully. Please continue."

Privately, Mr. Holt discusses the difference between appropriate and inappropriate ways of joking in the classroom. Woodrow's comments during the discussion (e.g., "We talk like that all the time; she knows I didn't mean it. I would never really do anything") indicates to Mr. Holt that Woodrow does understand the sexual connotations of his remark to Vickie but that he hadn't thought about how rude it was. Further exchanges convince Mr. Holt that Woodrow now understands that if a similar incident happens again, there will be serious consequences—possibly involving legal action taken against Woodrow under the safe-school/anti-harassment policy.

Anna's off-task behavior, with which Mr. Witherspoon deals in Case 2.12, is a behavior pattern. Thus, the teaching cycle is extended because he is attempting to teach her to break a habit.

CASE 2.12

Anna, one of Mr. Witherspoon's first-graders, habitually yells out to him while he is busy working with other students. Mr. Witherspoon usually responds to her by saying something such as, "Anna, please quietly wait for me to finish with Paul." On the few occasions when he tried ignoring her, she persisted, yelling more loudly until he said something to her.

After consulting with a colleague and calling to mind his knowledge of the research literature on behavior modification, he decides to apply both the principles of extinction and alternative behavior patterns in devising a scheme to deal with Anna's disruptive behavior pattern. After further thought, he judges that Anna's yelling is positively reinforced by the attention it gains her. Thus, he plans to persistently ignore her whenever she yells for him and to provide her with special attention when she acts in a more appropriate fashion. To collect information relevant to her progress, he keeps a tally sheet handy to first collect baseline data prior to implementing his plan and then continue after intervention by entering a tally mark each time Anna yells in class. After the second day of intervention, he looks at the measurement results as shown in Illustration 2.25.

He thinks, "Wow! The frequency of yelling incidents has doubled since I started the program. If I didn't know better, I'd think my plan is doing more harm than good. But I do know better. I expected the frequency to rise when I stopped reinforcing the yelling. Yelling is what worked for her in the past, so she's going to respond to being ignored with more yelling. I've got to persist. The increased yelling is driving me up the wall, and it's annoying to others. But I've got to stick with the program at least through this initial stage. Because she's yelling more, there are fewer opportunities for me to show her extra attention when she's being quiet and thoughtful of others. To speed up this process, I'll actively create more situations where she's likely to be working without yelling."

After another four school days, the tally sheet looks like Illustration 2.26.

"We've finally turned the corner," he thinks as he looks at Illustration 2.26, "I needed to see improvement to positively reinforce me to stick with the program. More and more, I'm finding ways to reward her non-yelling behaviors. As long as this trend continues, I'll stick to the plan for at least another two weeks." After 11 more school days, the tally sheet looks like Illustration 2.27. Those results influence Mr. Witherspoon to judge that the behavior pattern has changed to the point that Anna no longer needs to be positively reinforced nearly every time she displays quiet, thoughtful behavior. He decides to begin weaning her from the program and go to a less-intense intermittent reinforcement schedule.

In Case 2.13, Ms. Romberg attempts to lead most students in her class to change a behavior pattern.

CASE 2.13

Ms. Romberg, a Russian-language teacher, has been using a procedure in which each student's grade is determined by the number of points accumulated during a semester. A student has two means for gaining points: (1) Half of the total possible points are based on test scores. (2) The rest of the points are awarded for homework that, when turned in on time, is scored according to the number of correct responses.

Ms. Romberg begins to notice that increasingly more students receive high scores on homework but low scores on test papers. Under her system, these students are still able to "pass" the course. She analyzes the situation, collects some baseline information, and realizes that these students are simply copy-

3 days prior to program	2 days prior to program	1 day prior to program	1st day of program	2nd day of program
�卌 卌 /	卌 ////	卌 卌 //	卌 卌 卌 卌 /	卌 卌 卌 卌 ///
(11)	(9)	(12)	(21)	(23)

ILLUSTRATION 2.25

Tallies Indicating the Frequency of Anna's Yelling After Two Days of Intervention

3 days prior to program	2 days prior to program	1 day prior to program	1st day of program	2nd day of program
ꁍꁍꀵ ꁍꁍꀵ ꀠ (11)	ꁍꁍꀵ ꀠꀠꀠꀠ (9)	ꁍꁍꀵ ꁍꁍꀵ ꀠꀠ (12)	ꁍꁍꀵ ꁍꁍꀵ ꁍꁍꀵ ꁍꁍꀵ ꀠ (21)	ꁍꁍꀵ ꁍꁍꀵ ꁍꁍꀵ ꁍꁍꀵ ꀠꀠꀠ (23)

3rd day of program	4th day of program	5th day of program	6th day of program	7th day of program
ꁍꁍꀵ ꁍꁍꀵ ꁍꁍꀵ ꁍꁍꀵ ꀠ (21)	ꁍꁍꀵ ꁍꁍꀵ ꀠꀠꀠꀠ (14)	ꁍꁍꀵ ꁍꁍꀵ (10)	ꀠꀠꀠ (3)	ꀠ (1)

ILLUSTRATION 2.26

Tallies Indicating the Frequency of Anna's Yelling After Six Days of Intervention

ing their homework from others. Understanding that her grading system positively reinforces this habit of copying instead of actually doing homework, she decides to alter her grading procedure so that those positive reinforcers are eliminated. Under the new system, homework will still be assigned but no longer factored into the semester grade. Instead, she will use the homework strictly as a learning activity that provides students with practice and feedback relative to the skills that they will be asked to display on the tests. The tests will be the sole source of data for determining semester grades.

After explaining her new grading procedure to the class, she implements it and begins tracking the degree to which homework copying diminishes and test scores improve.

In Case 2.14, the disengaged behavior Ms. Lavaka addresses is more difficult to detect than the overt disruptive behaviors in Cases 2.11 and 2.12.

CASE 2.14

Ms. Lavaka is explaining to her high-school psychology class the difference between classical and operant conditioning. As she speaks, she looks at Le'shai who is staring directly at her, but the stare seems blank. As she moves to one side of the room, his eyes don't follow her, or at least, not right away. Then he suddenly shifts them in her direction. Judging that Le'shai is either daydreaming or finding it difficult to concentrate on the explanation, she decides to re-engage him by asking, "Do you think Pavlov believed his dogs controlled their salivating? Le'shai?" Le'shai: "Uhh, I'm sorry. What's the question?" Ms. Lavaka: "Please repeat the question for those of us who missed it, Renaldo." Renaldo: "You asked if that guy Pavlov believed his dogs knew if they were spitting." Ms. Lavaka: "Thanks, Renaldo. What do you think, Cindy?" Cindy: "Well, dogs know it when they spit." Greta: "The question wasn't if they knew they were spitting, but whether Pavlov thought they controlled their drooling." In the meantime, Ms. Lavaka is observing for signs that Le'shai and other students are attending to the discussion.

3 days prior to program	2 days prior to program	1 day prior to program	1st day of program	2nd day of program
~~HHT~~ ~~HHT~~ I ⑪	~~HHT~~ IIII ⑨	~~HHT~~ ~~HHT~~ II ⑫	~~HHT~~ ~~HHT~~ ~~HHT~~ ~~HHT~~ I ㉑	~~HHT~~ ~~HHT~~ ~~HHT~~ ~~HHT~~ III ㉓

3rd day of program	4th day of program	5th day of program	6th day of program	7th day of program
~~HHT~~ ~~HHT~~ ~~HHT~~ ~~HHT~~ I ㉑	~~HHT~~ ~~HHT~~ IIII ⑭	~~HHT~~ ~~HHT~~ ⑩	III ③	I ①

8th day of program	9th day of program	10th day of program	11th day of program	12th day of program
I ①	IIII ④	⓪	⓪	III ③

13th day of program	14th day of program	15th day of program	16th day of program	17th day of program
⓪	I ①	IIII ④	⓪	⓪

ILLUSTRATION 2.27

Tallies Indicating the Frequency of Anna's Yelling After 17 Days of Intervention

After school that day, Ms. Lavaka thinks, "More and more these kids seem to be drifting off or day-dreaming during class. I'm not sure if disengagement is increasing or I'm just getting better at detecting it. Anyway, I need to make these lessons more stimulating for them. When I called on Le'shai and then got more people involved, they seemed to perk up and pay closer attention. One thing I'll do more often is raise questions and mix their names in my explanations. That'll not only help them stay engaged, it'll also give me some indicators of how well they are staying with me."

STUDENTS' USE OF FORMATIVE FEEDBACK TO MONITOR THEIR OWN LEARNING

SELF-MONITORING

Just as you need to make formative judgments about how to teach, your students need to make formative judgments about how to learn. Although they have the advantage of your guidance as you design lessons for them, assign homework, emphasize what they need to do, and direct them into learning activities, ultimately, each student makes individual choices about what to study, when to pay attention, what questions to ask, how long to study, how to study, and how to comply with your directions. Research findings strongly support the notion that students who have access to formative feedback during lessons tend to learn more efficiently than students who are only provided with summative evaluations of their achievement after lessons (Brophy & Good, 1986; Duell, 1986; Ertmer, Newby, & MacDougall, 1996; Gagné, Yekovich, & Yekovich, 1993, pp. 192–195; McCombs, 1988; O'Malley, Russo, Chamot, & Stewner-Manzanares, 1988; Schoenfeld, 1992; Schunk, 1996). Of course, students are hardly in a position to monitor their own learning unless they understand what they are supposed to be learning. Thus, it is important for you to inform students about the goals of units and objectives of lessons.

Monitoring one's own learning is an art form students need to learn. You teach them to use formative feedback to make judgments about how to learn by the way you share the results of your own measurements with them and by the way you prompt them with questions and tasks during learning activities.

SHARING MEASUREMENT RESULTS WITH STUDENTS

In Case 1.4, you not only used the results of the test from Illustration 1.9 to provide yourself with information for summative evaluations of students' achievement and feedback for formative judgments about how to teach; you also shared those results with your students. For example, not only did you communicate the scores to students (e.g., Tonja's 10 and Salina's 40); you also used Illustration 1.11 to provide them with specific feedback on their responses relative to each of the criteria listed on the scoring form. Your review of their responses provided students with opportunities to discover connections among (1) the learning activities they engaged in prior to the test, (2) your expectations, (3) how they responded to the mini-experiments' prompts, (4) what they actually learned, and (5) how they should engage in subsequent learning activities. Tonja, for example, discovered that by doing homework she is likely to learn what you hold her accountable for learning. Salina's diligent attention to homework was positively reinforced by the feedback she received from Illustration 1.13.

In Case 2.4, Ms. Fisher developed the unit plan shown by Illustration 2.14. In Case 2.15, she uses the results of a test of progress toward that Unit's goal to provide students with formative feedback for monitoring their own learning.

CASE 2.15

On Monday of the last week of Unit 17, Ms. Fisher directs her students to complete Part I of Illustration 2.28's test document in time for Wednesday's meeting. On that Monday she administers Part II to them.

On Thursday, Ms. Fisher returns the test documents to the students along with the completed scoring forms. Illustration 2.29 shows the responses of one student, Heiko Baker; Illustration 2.30 shows the completed scorer's form Ms. Fisher gave to Heiko on Thursday. Ms. Fisher assigns the following homework to be completed for Friday's meeting:

Examine your responses to each prompt on the test. Compare your response to the criteria on the scorer's form. For each criterion, analyze why your response was marked either

U.S. History *** Unit #17 Test *** The Civil Rights Movement

<u>PART 1: TAKE HOME</u>

NOTE: Please write your responses to the following using the available space. You may use whatever resources (e.g., books, magazines, and conferences with classmates and other people) you choose to prepare your responses. Use whatever sources or suggestions you want, but ultimately the responses should be your own. In other words, you make the final decision as to what to or not to write. Part 1 of this document is available on a word processing template to make it easier for you to enter your responses with a computer.

1. What is your name?

2. (a) Recall the day about two weeks ago when we simulated segregation in our class. In what ways were the *greens'* experiences similar to those of black people living in the South in 1950?

    (b) In what ways were the blues' experiences similar to those of white people living in the South in 1950?

    (c) In what ways were the greens' experiences similar to those of black people living in the North in 1970?

ILLUSTRATION 2.28

Ms. Fisher's Test Relative to Unit 17's Goal as Stated in Illustration 2.9

(Continued)

ILLUSTRATION 2.28 (Continued)

(d) In what ways were the blues' experiences similar to those of white people living in the North in 1970?

(e) Afterwards, the class discussed different ways green people and blue people felt while the class was segregated. Describe three of the ways class members indicated they felt and explain why those feeling are or are not similar to ways people living in segregated societies today must feel.

3. Write a scenario in which a hypothetical student, teacher, or administrator here at Rainbow High School commits a crime under civil rights statutes enacted since 1964.

4. Give an example of a human activity that in 1950 was forbidden by laws in South Carolina, but which today in South Carolina is not only legal but also required under civil rights laws now in effect in South Carolina.

———————————

You have come to the end of the take-home part of this test.

ILLUSTRATION 2.28 (Continued)

U.S. History *** Unit #17 Test *** The Civil Rights Movement

<u>PART 2: IN CLASS</u>

NOTE: Unlike the take-home part of this test, you are not to use references (e.g., books or notes) or confer with anyone while taking Part 2.

5. What is your name?

6. Following is a scrambled list of events. Indicate the chronological order of the events by numbering them from 1 through 5 with "1" being the earliest and "5" being the last.

    _____ *Plessy v. Ferguson* Supreme Court decision allowing segregation of public facilities

    _____ *Brown v. Board of Education of Topeka* Supreme Court decision outlawing school segregation

    _____ Medgar Evers killed

    _____ January 1, 1970

    _____ Founding of the NAACP

7. Following is another scrambled list of events. Indicate the chronological order of the events as you did for item 6, numbering them "1" through "7."

    _____ Riots in the Watts district of Los Angeles

    _____ Absolute utopian racial equality

    _____ January 1, 3000

    _____ January 1, 1940

    _____ Civil Rights Act of 1968 prohibiting discrimination in housing

    _____ Presidential order ending segregation in the military

    _____ Rosa Parks is first arrested

8. Following is another scrambled list of events. Indicate the chronological order of the events as you did for item 6, numbering them "1" through "6."

    _____ Civil Rights Act of 1964 outlawing racial, religious, and sex discrimination in public places and by employers

    _____ Martin Luther King, Jr., assassinated

    _____ March on Washington

ILLUSTRATION 2.28 (Continued)

_____ Signing of the "Southern Manifesto"

_____ Formation of the SCLC

_____ Malcolm X assassinated

9. Following is another scrambled list of events. Indicate the chronological order of the events as you did for item 6, numbering them "1" through "8."

_____ Voting Rights Act protected Americans' right to vote

_____ The Montgomery bus boycott

_____ Douglas Wilder elected governor of Virginia

_____ "Emancipation Proclamation"

_____ U.S. Civil War between the States

_____ Martin Luther King, Jr., delivers "I Have a Dream" speech

_____ The lynching of Emmett Till

_____ Thirteenth Amendment abolishing slavery

10. What is the difference between *de jure* segregation and *de facto* segregation?

11. What is the difference between desegregation and integration?

12. In 1963, Birmingham, Alabama, police officers, under the direction of Eugene "Bull" Connors, responded to nonviolent protests with brutal arrests. How did such displays of violence by people (e.g., Bull Connors) who were fighting against the civil rights movement actually end up helping the cause of civil rights? What role did the media play in this scenario?

ILLUSTRATION 2.28 (Continued)

13. Look at the recent newspaper picture of pro-
testers against the destruction of a northwest-
ern forest. What strategies from the civil
rights movement do they appear to be using?
Explain how those strategies evolved during the
civil rights movement. In your explanation,
identify at least two individuals or groups who
argued for or used such strategies. Also identify two individuals or groups who spoke
against or refused to use such strategies.

14. Attached is an article from this week's newspaper. Explain how the
events described in this article are different as a result of the
civil rights movement.

15. Smile, you have come to the end of this test.

a "0," "1," or "2." Make notes to use in class tomorrow when you will be given an opportunity to raise questions as well as to rewrite some of your responses.

On Friday, Ms. Fisher conducts an activity in which students raise and address questions stimulated
by the homework assignment. The questions lead to productive discussions about the civil rights movement. For example:

Ms. Fisher:	"Yes, Heiko, you have something to say?"
Heiko:	"I don't get why I didn't get all the points for number 13 like Jerome did."
Ms. Fisher:	"Please read what you wrote and then we'll hear Jerome's."
Heiko:	"Just like Jerome, I told about Gandhi and that James Lawson who went to India, but you took off—"
Ms. Fisher:	"Please read exactly what you wrote, and then we'll know what we're discussing—so we can all learn from what you and Jerome wrote."
Heiko:	"I wrote, 'Gandhi, the black man,' you know, I meant James Lawson, 'who went to India, SCLC, and Martin Luther King, Jr., all believed in passive resistance. That's what the protestors in the picture are using. Malcolm X and Black Panthers were more violent, like the riots in Watts and the protest against unfair arrests in Miami, Florida.' What's wrong with that?"

```
          U.S. History *** Unit #17 Test *** The Civil Rights Movement

                            PART 1: TAKE HOME

NOTE: Please write your responses to the following using the available space. You
may use whatever resources (e.g., books, magazines, and conferences with class-
mates and other people) you choose to prepare your responses. Use whatever
sources or suggestions you want, but ultimately the responses should be your own.
In other words, you make the final decision as to what to or not to write. Part 1
of this document is available on a word processing template to make it easier for
you to enter your responses with a computer.

   1.   What is your name?      Heiko Baker

   2.   (a) Recall the day about two weeks ago when we simulated segregation in
        our class. In what ways were the greens' experiences similar to those
        of black people living in the South in 1950?
```

The greens had to do everything last. Nobody asked them what they thought.
They got crummy jobs. They were not taught as good as the blues.

```
        (b) In what ways were the blues' experiences similar to those of white
            people living in the South in 1950?
```

The were kept away from the greens. They were treated better than the greens. They had more chances to
do better things.

```
        (c) In what ways were the greens' experiences similar to those of black
            people living in the North in 1970?
```

The blacks in the North got angry. The more the class was segregated the madder the greens got. It was not
much different than for 1950 in the South except that it did not happen by law which made northern blacks
angrier because they could not blame it on the law.

ILLUSTRATION 2.29

Heiko's Responses on the Test Paper

(Continued)

ILLUSTRATION 2.29 (Continued)

(d) In what ways were the blues' experiences similar to those of white people living in the North in 1970?

In class the blues know discrimination was wrong. By 1970 everyone was being told that. In our class, the blues would be going against the authority whose the teacher. In the North that would not be true.

(e) Afterwards, the class discussed different ways green people and blue people felt while the class was segregated. Describe three of the ways class members indicated they felt and explain why those feeling are or are not similar to ways people living in segregated societies today must feel.

3. Write a scenario in which a hypothetical student, teacher, or administrator here at Rainbow High School commits a crime under civil rights statutes enacted since 1964.

The Principal only let's boys in harder math classes because he says only boys need higher math for college.

4. Give an example of a human activity that in 1950 was forbidden by laws in South Carolina, but which today in South Carolina is not only legal but also required under civil rights laws now in effect in South Carolina.

A guy that owns building and land rents an apartment to a black family in a white neighborhood. He could have been arrested for that in South Carolina before. Now if he doesn't, he could be arrested.

ILLUSTRATION 2.29 (Continued)

U.S. History *** Unit #17 Test *** The Civil Rights Movement

PART 2: IN CLASS

NOTE: Unlike the take-home part of this test, you are not to use references (e.g., books or notes) or confer with anyone while taking Part 2.

5. What is your name?   Neiko Baker

6. Following is a scrambled list of events. Indicate the chronological order of the events by numbering them from 1 through 5 with "1" being the earliest and "5" being the last.

    __1__ *Plessy v. Ferguson* Supreme Court decision allowing segregation of public facilities

    __2__ *Brown v. Board of Education of Topeka* Supreme Court decision outlawing school segregation

    __4__ Medgar Evers killed

    __5__ January 1, 1970

    __3__ Founding of the NAACP

7. Following is another scrambled list of events. Indicate the chronological order of the events as you did for item 4, numbering them "1" through "7."

    __4__ Riots in the Watts district of Los Angeles

    __7__ Absolute utopian racial equality

    __6__ January 1, 3000

    __2__ January 1, 1940

    __5__ Civil Rights Act of 1968 prohibiting discrimination in housing

    __1__ Presidential order ending segregation in the military

    __3__ Rosa Parks is first arrested

8. Following is another scrambled list of events. Indicate the chronological order of the events as you did for item 4, numbering them "1" through "6."

    __6__ Civil Rights Act of 1964 outlawing racial, religious, and sex discrimination in public places and by employers

    __5__ Martin Luther King, Jr., assassinated

    __2__ March on Washington

ILLUSTRATION 2.29 (Continued)

_3_ Signing of the "Southern Manifesto"

_1_ Formation of the SCLC

_4_ Malcolm X assassinated

9. Following is another scrambled list of events. Indicate the chronologi-
    cal order of the events as you did for item 4, numbering them "1"
    through "8."

    ___7__ Voting Rights Act protected Americans' right to vote

    _5_ The Montgomery bus boycott

    ___8__ Douglas Wilder elected governor of Virginia

    ___1__ "Emancipation Proclamation"

    __3_ U.S. Civil War between the States

    __6_ Martin Luther King, Jr., delivers "I Have a Dream" speech

    __4_ The lynching of Emmett Till

    _2_ Thirteenth Amendment abolishing slavery

10. What is the difference between *de jure* segregation and *de facto*
    segregation?

    de jure means by law. So *de jure* requires (like in the South in 1950) the races to be
    separated. *de fact* makes it illegal

11. What is the difference between desegregation and integration?

12. In 1963, Birmingham, Alabama, police officers, under the direction of
    Eugene "Bull" Connors, responded to nonviolent protests with brutal
    arrests. How did such displays of violence by people (e.g., Bull Con-
    nors) who were fighting against the civil rights movement actually end
    up helping the cause of civil rights? What role did the media play in
    this scenario?

    When they're violent acts against blacks were shown on T.V. & in magazines & videos you
    showed us, people around the country saw what was going on and put pressure on politicians in
    the government.

ILLUSTRATION 2.29 *(Continued)*

13. Look at the recent newspaper picture of pro-
    testers against the destruction of a northwest-
    ern forest. What strategies from the civil
    rights movement do they appear to be using?
    Explain how those strategies evolved during the
    civil rights movement. In your explanation,
    identify at least two individuals or groups who
    argued for or used such strategies. Also iden-
    tify two individuals or groups who spoke
    against or refused to use such strategies.

14. Attached is an article from this week's newspaper. Explain how the
    events described in this article are different as a result of the civil
    rights movement.

The picture with the article shows a black president of a university giving a degree in college to a white guy. That couldn't have happened before. Also the ~~article talks about~~ minority groups didn't have enough money to put economic pressure on companies.

→ *The graduation speaker said*

15. Smile, you have come to the end of this test.

Now's this Ms. Fisher? :)

Ms. Fisher: "I think everything you wrote is perfectly consistent with what we know about the
                  civil rights movement—"
Heiko: "Then why did you take—"
Ms. Fisher: "Wait until we've listened to what Jerome wrote and then look back at the criteria."
Jerome: "The people in the picture look like they're using passive resistance just like Dr.
                  King wanted blacks and other civil righters to use, which they did until some black
                  people got tired of being beaten down and not accomplishing enough. Then more
                  people went along with the more violent, separatist ideas of Malcolm X and the
                  Black Panthers. So after the 1960s, you had more riots, and that seemed to make
                  more of an impression on the government. So by 1970, there was more violent

protesting shown on TV than people peacefully sitting at lunch counters and stuff. Gandhi's ideas were replaced by Malcolm X's, but there were still people like in the NAACP and SCLC who would rather be more like Gandhi."

Heiko: "Jerome just wrote more than me."

Ms. Fisher: "The first criterion is that the response alludes to the nonviolent protest method in the picture. Both Heiko's and Jerome's responses did that. The second is that the response alludes to the tension between the nonviolence associated with Gandhi and the more violent methods associated with urban violence and groups such as the Black Panthers."

Jerome: "You gave me the points for that one, but I didn't put anything down about tension."

Ms. Fisher: "I think you did allude to that tension when you indicated that the more violent strategies began to dominate, but then—read your last phrase again, the one that starts with 'but.' I don't remember the exact words, but I remember something to the effect that told me you understood the tension between the two strategies."

Jerome: "'But there were still people like in the NAACP and SCLC who would rather be more like Gandhi.'"

Ms. Fisher: "Doesn't that suggest tension between two ideologies? What do you think, Ruby?"

Ruby: "But I thought the nonviolent group didn't believe in tension."

Ms. Fisher: "Okay, who wants to address Ruby's comment? Melanie."

Melanie: "There was tension all over the place. Tension between the peaceful protestors and the segregationists, between the Black Panthers and the integrationists, and between African Americans who wanted to follow Dr. King and those who wanted to follow Malcolm X."

Ms. Fisher: "Maybe we need to clarify what we mean by the word 'tension'."

Heiko: "I just looked it up in the dictionary. It says, 'the act of stretching or straining.' But that's not the one we want. We want, 'a strained relationship between individuals, nations, etc.' But you didn't ask us to talk about tension in Question 13 on the test."

Ms. Fisher: "I didn't use the word 'tension.' But by asking you to explain how strategies evolved during the movement, I hoped to get you to think about this struggle between two competing strategies. Didn't that struggle or tension lead to the competition between nonviolent methods and violent methods, with the violent methods becoming more dominant in the latter stages of the movement?

Heiko: "So we didn't have to use the word 'tension' in our answer."

Ms. Fisher: "Of course not. That's just the word I used to remind me of an idea that was part of the change from the dominant strategy being nonviolent to it becoming violent. In the response you just read to us, you identified the two different strategies. That's what I was hoping you would do. When you rewrite your response, you should keep everything you have now. What you need to add is a sentence or two indicating that the civil rights movement got off the ground through nonviolent strategies, but soon dissatisfaction with what the movement was achieving caused at least some people to turn to the competing strategies of groups such as the Black Panthers. Give sort of an explanation of how the earlier strategies were taken over by the later strategies. That's the idea of evolving."

The discussion continues, centering more and more on the civil rights movement and less on the test itself. The specific scoring form with criteria serves as an advanced organizer for students' to clarify thoughts, reconceptualize misconceptions, reinforce understanding, recall information, and most importantly, learn how to learn. For example, later in the discussion, in reference to the scoring rubric for mini-experiment 11 on the test, the following exchange takes place:

Wanda:	"I thought desegregation and integration were the same thing. How were we supposed to know the differences?"
Ms. Fisher:	"There are of course many opportunities. Here's one study tip. Everybody, grab your textbook. Wanda, open your book to any page. What page is it?"
Wanda:	"667."
Ms. Fisher:	"Okay, everybody else open your books to page 667. Oh, good choice, Wanda. This page will help us make the point. What words on the page stand out from the rest, Judy?"
Judy:	"Dulles and the Battle Against World Communism."
Ms. Fisher:	"Okay, that's a section heading. What about words from the body of the text?"
Judy:	"The word 'rollback' is one, and also 'massive retaliation.' They're in blue."
Ms. Fisher:	"Words or phrases printed in blue are technical terms or expressions that you should pay careful attention to. When you come across a blue word, jot it down and look how its special meaning is used in the book. It may be defined in the glossary in the back of the book. Don't just read over the words in blue. Study their special meanings."

The discussion takes longer than Ms. Fisher anticipated. Hurriedly, she passes out blank copies of the original test document (i.e., Illustration 2.28) and directs the students as follows: "Use this copy to rewrite your responses to any of the prompts you like. I assume you won't choose to rewrite responses that received maximum points. You have until the end of the period to finish these. I'll score your rewrites with the same scoring form. I'll adjust your score upward depending on how well your rewrites match the criteria." The students know from prior tests that Ms. Fisher will rescore each response, divide any amount above the original score by two, and add the result to the original score. But before they have a chance to begin, several students raise their hands and initiate the following exchange:

Ms. Fisher:	"Yes, Wanda."
Wanda:	"Ms. Fisher, I know how I want to change some of my answers. But I also want to read up on some things and go over my notes before redoing some others."
Percell:	"Yeah, me too. We just learned a better way to study. Let us practice what we learned before we do the rewriting."
Ms. Fisher:	"We really need to begin Unit 18 on Monday and I told you I'd give you an opportunity to rewrite today. Hmmm, your argument is compelling. If everyone agrees, we'll do the rewriting for homework and you can turn your papers in on Monday. Raise your hand if you favor that plan. Looks like it's unanimous."

Of course, the more measurement results you share with your students, the more formative feedback they have to guide their learning activities. Even more important than the amount of feedback is the specificity of that feedback. The criteria on Ms. Fisher's scoring form helps clarify for students what they are supposed to be learning. Furthermore, they have access to diagnostic information about their responses, whereas a more traditional test score only indicates how well they did. Imagine yourself as the fourth-grade student in Case 2.16.

Scores for _Heiko Baker_ 's Responses on the Unit 17 test:

NOTE: For each criterion listed for all items except for 6-9, points are awarded as follows:

+2 if the criterion in question is clearly met
+1 if it is unclear as to whether or not the criterion is met
+0 if the criterion is clearly not met

For items 6-9, the points are awarded as follows:

+2 if all events are in exact chronological order
+1 if all but one of the events is in order (adjusting for the domino effect)
+0 if more than one is out of order (even after adjusting for the domino effect)

Rubric for Prompt 2(a):

Parallels one of the _greens'_ experiences from
the simulated segregation with one for 1950s
blacks in the South & the parallel is consistent
with historical records ----------------------------------- 0 1 ②

Parallels another of the _greens'_ experiences from
the simulated segregation with one for 1950s _blacks_
in the South & the parallel is consistent with
historical records ----------------------------------- 0 1 ②

Rubric for Prompt 2(b):

Parallels one of the _blues'_ experiences from the
simulated segregation with one for 1950s <u>whites</u> in
the South & the parallel is consistent with
historical records ----------------------------------- 0 1 ②

Parallels another of the _blues'_ experiences from
the simulated segregation with one for 1950s <u>whites</u>
in the South & the parallel is consistent with
historical records ----------------------------------- 0 ① 2

Rubric for Prompt 2(c):

Parallels one of the _greens'_ experiences from the
simulated segregation with one for 1970s _blacks_ in
the North & the parallel is consistent with
historical records ----------------------------------- 0 1 ②

ILLUSTRATION 2.30

Scoring Form Ms. Fisher Completed for Heiko's Responses

(Continued)

ILLUSTRATION 2.30 *(Continued)*

Parallels another of the *greens*' experiences from the
simulated segregation with one for 1970s *blacks* in the
North & the parallel is consistent with historical
records --- (0) 1   2

Rubric for Prompt 2(d):

Parallels one of the *blues*' experiences from the
simulated segregation with one for 1970s *whites*
in the North & the parallel is consistent with
historical records ------------------------------------- 0   1 (2)

Parallels another of the *blues*' experiences from
the simulated segregation with one for 1970s *whites*
in the North & the parallel is consistent with
historical records ------------------------------------- 0   1 (2)

Rubric for Prompt 2(e):

Parallels one of the feelings expressed in class
and provides a tenable explanation as to why that
feeling is either similar or dissimilar to parallel
feelings resulting from today's real-world segregated
or discriminatory societies ---------------------------- 0 (1) (2)

Parallels another of the feelings expressed in class
and provides a tenable explanation as to why that
feeling is either similar or dissimilar to parallel
feelings resulting from today's real-world segregated
or discriminatory society ------------------------------ 0   1 (2)

Parallels yet another of the feelings expressed in
class & provides a tenable explanation as to why
that feeling is either similar or dissimilar to
parallel feelings resulting from today's real-world
segregated or discriminatory society ------------------- 0   1 (2)

Rubric for Prompt 3:

The scenario includes an incident or event in a high
school setting --- 0   1 (2)

The scenario includes an incident or event in which
one person violates the civil rights of another -------- 0   1 (2)

Rubric for Prompt 4:

The example is of an activity that was illegal in
South Carolina in 1950 (e.g., a public swimming pool
manager allows blacks and whites to swim
in the same pool) -------------------------------------- 0   1 (2)

ILLUSTRATION 2.30 (Continued)

The example is of an activity that is required
by legal statutes in South Carolina today as with
the swimming pool incident -------------------------------- 0 1 (2)

Rubric for Prompt 6:

"2" for 2, 3, 4, 5, 1; "1" if order would be
correct if either one or two of the selections are
removed; otherwise "0" ------------------------------------- 0 (1) 2

Rubric for Prompt 7:

"2" for 4, 7, 6, 1, 5, 2, 3; "1" if order would
be correct if either one or two of the selections
are removed; otherwise "0" -------------------------------- 0 (1) 2

Rubric for Prompt 8:

"2" for 4, 6, 3, 1, 2, 5; "1" if order would
be correct if either one or two of the selections
are removed; otherwise "0" --------------------------------(0) 1 2

Rubric for Prompt 9:

"2" for 7, 5, 8, 2, 1, 6, 4, 3; "1" if order
would be correct if either one or two of the
selections are removed; otherwise "0" -------------------- 0 (1) 2

Rubric for Prompt 10:

Response indicates that both distinguish & separate
two groups and that *de facto* can be *de jure*, but
not necessarily ---(0) 1 2

Indicates *de jure* is segregation supported by
legal statute --- 0 1 (2)

Indicates *de facto* is segregation as a consequence
of factors other than legal statute --------------------(0) 1 2

Rubric for Prompt 11:

Response indicates that desegregation is a process by
which either *de facto* or *de jure* segregation is reduced ---- (0) 1 2

Response indicates that integration is a process by
which two groups mix freely and enjoy the same rights ---- (0) 1 2

Rubric for Prompt 12:

Response includes a tenable explanation of at least one
way actions of segregationists "backfired" on them -------- 0 1 (2)

ILLUSTRATION 2.30 (Continued)

Response at least implicitly alludes to the relation
of violent responses to passive protest & its influence
on the national consciousness --------------------------- (0) 1 2

Alludes to the role of media coverage (e.g., national
coverage of brutal replies to nonviolent protests) -------- 0 1 (2)

<u>Rubric for Prompt 13</u>:

Response alludes to the nonviolent protest method pictured ---- 0 1 (2)

Explanation alludes to the tension between the nonviolence
associated with Gandhi and the more violent methods
associated with urban violence & groups e.g., the Black
Panthers -- (0) 1 2

Alludes to the role of media coverage (e.g., national
coverage of brutal replies to nonviolent protests) --------(0) 1 2

Identifies at least two groups or individuals associated
with nonviolent methods -------------------------------- 0 1 (2)

Identifies at least two groups or individuals associated
with violent methods ------------------------------------ 0 1 (2)

<u>Rubric for Prompt 14</u>:

Explains how one event in the article or accompanying
photo was made possible via gains attributable to the
civil rights movement ---------------------------------- 0 (1) 2

Explains how a second event in the article or accompanying
photo was made possible via gains attributable to the
civil rights movement ---------------------------------- 0 (1) 2

Explains how a third event in the article or accompanying
photo was made possible via gains attributable to the
civil rights movement ---------------------------------- 0 1 (2)

TOTAL SCORE FOR RESPONSES (Maximum 70) ___*45*___

CASE 2.16

As a fourth-grader in Mr. Yengish's class, you are making progress relative to the following objective:

Students compute the product of any two-digit whole number by any one-digit whole number.

Mr. Yengish administers a test to you and returns the scored test document as you see it in Illustration 2.31.

From your examination of Illustration 2.31, what did you learn about your achievement of the objective from Case 2.16? What information does it provide to help guide your learning activities relative to the objective?

Now, imagine yourself as the fourth-grade student in Case 2.17.

CASE 2.17

As a fourth-grader in Ms. Arroya's class, you are making progress relative to the following objective:

Students compute the product of any two-digit whole number by any one-digit whole number.

Ms. Arroya administers a test to you and returns the scored test document as you see it in Illustration 2.32.

From your examination of Illustration 2.32, what did you learn about your achievement of the objective from Case 2.17? What information does it provide to help guide your learning activities relative to the objective?

PROMPTING STUDENTS TO USE FEEDBACK AS THEY LEARN

In Case 2.10, Mr. Heaps continually raised questions and employed other prompts for students to respond throughout his presentation. Besides providing him information for formative judgments, it also provided feedback to students about their own understanding, level of

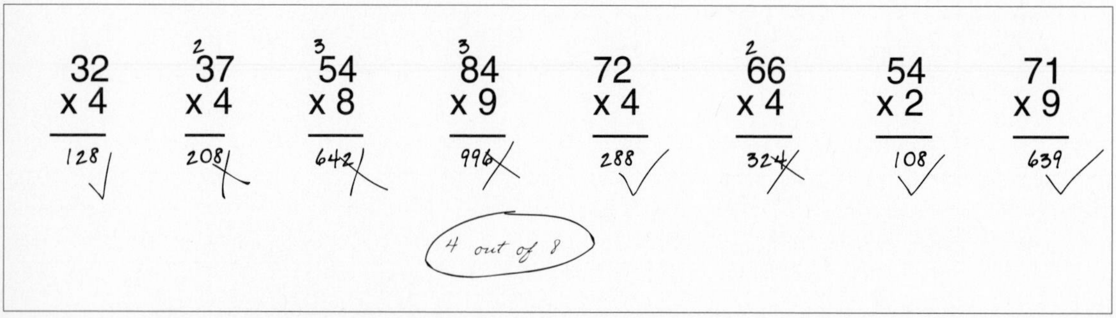

ILLUSTRATION 2.31

The Test Paper You Received Back from Mr. Yengish

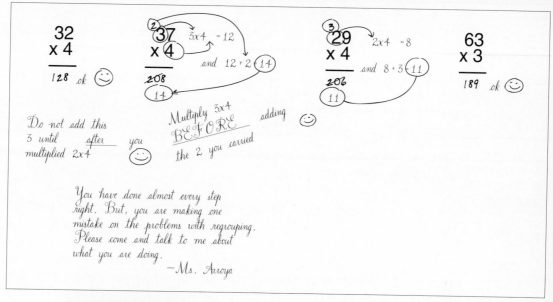

ILLUSTRATION 2.32

The Test Paper You Received Back from Ms. Arroya

engagement, progress, and what they should be doing from moment to moment. Being confronted with a prompt during a learning activity focuses students on what they should be doing and thinking.

During learning activities, seize opportunities to model learning strategies and guide students' thinking. Imagine yourself as the middle-school science teacher in Case 2.18.

CASE 2.18

Using the Punnett squares in Illustration 2.33, you explain that for eye color, brown is a dominant trait and blue is recessive. During the session, Susan says, "I have blue eyes like my dad. But my mom has brown eyes. So she could be pure brown or hybrid brown. Is that right?" You respond to Susan's question. Later in the activity, Dale asks, "Why do we call that chart 'Punnett squares?' What's a Punnett? Sounds like something you do in football!" You respond to Dale's question.

In Case 2.18, Susan and Dale provided you with opportunities to teach the class how to learn, or in other words, to lead them to make formative judgments that guide their learning activities. Note that Susan raised a question that is addressed through a reasoning process, not simply by remembering the answer. One must take a moment to figure out whether or not her mom's eyes are pure brown or hybrid brown. Dale, on the other hand, asked about why the squares in your diagram are called "Punnett squares." To answer Dale's question, one needs only to remember or look up a historical fact; there's no need to figure anything out. Suppose that in Case 2.18, you wanted to take advantage of the opportunities Susan and Dale provided in order to teach students strategies for addressing questions requiring reasoning to answer and

	B	b
B	BB	Bb
b	Bb	bb

ILLUSTRATION 2.33

Diagram of Punnett Squares You Use in Case 2.18 Discussion on Inherited Traits

strategies for addressing questions requiring only recall of information. How do you respond to Susan's question in Case 2.18? How do you respond to Dale's question? With a colleague, discuss your responses.

In Case 2.19, Kisha and Elwin discuss their responses to the prompt of putting themselves in the role of the teacher in Case 2.18.

CASE 2.19

Elwin: "For Susan's question, the easiest and quickest thing for me to do is directly answer the question myself. But because the question is reasoning-level, I should explain the reasoning leading to the answer. For example, I could display Illustration 2.33's Punnett squares and say, 'Since you have blue eyes and blue is recessive in comparison to brown, you carry two little *b* genes as indicated in the bottom right corner of this diagram. You only got one of those little *b*'s from your father, so the other one had to come from your mother. Meaning she had to have one to give. Thus, she must be a hybrid brown, not pure brown.'"

Kisha: "Rather than directly explaining the answer, I thought I'd spend more time demonstrating what goes through my mind when formulating a solution. I wanted to model the application-level reasoning I want the students to learn. So I used a think-aloud strategy by saying, 'Your question presents an interesting problem. You have blue eyes and there's no such thing as hybrid blue; so you're pure blue. Your dad's also pure blue. But your mother has brown eyes, and brown can be either pure or hybrid.' Hmmm, let's look at that diagram again. Susan has two little *b*'s and her father has two little *b*'s, so she could have gotten both of them from her father, making it possible for her mother to be pure brown. I guess that's . . . Oh, no! That can't be, because she can't get both of the genes from the same parent. That's right! What was I thinking? Susan inherits one gene from each, so her mother has to have at least one little *b* to pass on to her. Thus, Susan's mother must be hybrid! She can't possibly be pure brown or else Susan would have brown eyes."

Elwin: "So you'd put on a real show, dramatizing thinking aloud."

Kisha: "Right, but I also thought about getting Susan actively involved in the thinking."

Elwin: "By asking probing questions to her. But what about involving other students also? You'd have to probe and redirect to others also."

Kisha: "Right. Why don't I develop a probe-back-to-the-student dialogue while you do one for probe and redirect to another student?"

Kisha develops the following dialogue:

Kisha: "Your mother has brown eyes, so what are the two possibilities again?"

Susan: "Hybrid brown or pure brown."

Kisha: "Let's take the cases one at a time. Suppose your mother is hybrid brown. How could you end up with blue eyes?" (Kisha displays Illustration 2.33.)

Susan:	"If I only got one little *b* from my dad, the other could come from my mother, since she has one to give."
Kisha:	"You said if you only got one little *b* from your dad. Is it possible to get more than one or none from your dad?"
Susan:	"Yeah, he's got two little *b*'s to give, since he's pure blue."
Kisha:	"If your Dad passes two little *b*'s, how many do you get from your mother?"
Susan:	"Well,—wait! Oh! Each one has to give just one or else I'd have too many. Mother can't be pure brown because—oh, never mind! I see!"

Elwin writes the following as an example of probing and redirecting to other students as a means of prompting students to address reasoning-level questions:

Susan:	"I have blue eyes like my Dad. But my Mom has brown eyes. So she could be pure brown or hybrid brown. Is that right?"
Elwin:	"Susan raises an interesting problem—figuring out the genes of her parents from just knowing her and their eye colors. Can we tell from the information at hand whether Susan's mother has pure brown or hybrid brown eyes, Grant?"
Grant:	"Well, she has blue eyes so she carries two little *b*'s. I don't know about her parents."
Elwin:	"What did Susan tell us about the colors of her parents' eyes, Allen?"
Allen:	"She said they were . . ."

Susan and Elwin then turn their attention to Dale's memory-level question:

Elwin:	"I really don't know the answer to Dale's question, so I would tell him I don't know and then suggest how we might look up the answer."
Kisha:	"I didn't know either, so I looked up 'Punnett squares' in a biology book and it said that Reginald C. Punnett was a British geneticist who invented this type of diagram to help predict traits. It's named after him. So as the teacher, I could just answer Dale directly and say that."
Elwin:	"But since I want Dale to learn how to look things up himself—trying to teach him how to learn—we should use a how-might-we-find-that-out strategy."

Elwin produces the following dialogue:

Elwin:	"I'm glad you raised that question, Dale. Where should we go to look it up?"
Dale:	"Is it in the textbook?"
Elwin:	"I'm not sure. Check the index. If it's not there, we could try one of our life science books or maybe one of our science encyclopedias over on the shelf."

PORTFOLIOS AS A FORMATIVE FEEDBACK MECHANISM

Recall from a previous section of this chapter that an *individualized student portfolio* is a collection of products, artifacts, and demonstrations of the student's schoolwork assembled for the purpose of providing a representative sample of the student's achievement. Similar to the way professional artists, writers, models, photographers, craftspersons, architects, and researchers build a collection of their works as evidence of their accomplishments, you can guide your students to build portfolios that reflect what they learn. The purpose of so-called "portfolio assessment" (which is mandated in some school districts) is to provide a means of communicating students' school achievement that is more flexible, qualitative, individualized, and in-depth than traditional report cards. Thus, student portfolios are typically associated more with communicating summative evaluations than they are with making formative judgments. However, the ongoing process by which your students collaborate with you to produce, develop, maintain, revise, and expand individualized portfolios is a grand mechanism for focusing formative judgments on "what we should do next" ("we" referring to your students and you).

Using portfolios to communicate summative evaluations of what students learned is a topic for Chapter 3. The focus of this section is using the process of building those portfolios as a mechanism for making formative judgments—judgments you make about how to teach and judgments your students make about how to learn. How portfolios are used, what they look like, how they are packaged, and how they are managed vary considerably among classrooms. Case 2.20 provides an example that should stimulate your ideas about using portfolios with your students.

CASE 2.20

In preparation for the upcoming school year with her 24 fourth-graders, Ms. Ragusa organizes some of the bookcases and utility shelves in her classroom as follows:

- One set of shelves is set aside for student portfolios. Each of 24 spaces is labeled with a student's name and filled with a cubicle container, open at the top, that is 67 cm wide, 45 cm deep, and 25 cm high. Six hard plastic, color-coded, portable file boxes fill the container. One box is yellow and is labeled "[student's name]'s Science Portfolio," a maroon box is labeled "[student's name]'s Mathematics Portfolio," a black box is labeled "[student's name]'s Language Arts Portfolio," an orange box is labeled "[student's name]'s Art, Music, & Physical Education Portfolio," a blue box is labeled "[student's name]'s Social Studies Portfolio", and a red box is labeled "[student's name]'s Miscellaneous Portfolio and Index of Portfolios."
- A second set of shelves is reserved for print and written materials (e.g., a group report about recent discoveries in the area of nutrition and a multistudent-authored book of poems) students will be producing during the year that don't fit in individual portfolios. However, references to these materials will be contained in the individual portfolios of students who had a hand in producing them. These shelves are labeled for alphabetical filing.
- A third set of shelves is reserved for bulky artifacts of work students produce during the year. As with the print and written materials, each display will be referenced in the portfolios of the students who will be responsible for it.

As the school year begins, the portfolios serve as a focus for much of the year's work. Each student's science portfolio, for example, is organized by units. Cross referencing among science units as well as among the portfolios for the different subjects is particularly important because Ms. Ragusa interlinks units and integrates curricula among courses. Illustration 2.34, for example, is a copy of a letter Eldon wrote for a process-writing activity that he inserted in his language arts portfolio. However, the letter is evidence of some of what Eldon achieved during the science unit on magnetism. Thus, Ms. Ragusa gives Eldon the following cross-reference note to insert under "Unit 9: Magnetism" in his science portfolio:

> "Please see a copy of the letter wrote to Kiera Johnson, a third grader, in Eldon's Language Arts Portfolio under 'Unit 4.' Eldon explains magnetism to Kiera in the letter."

In January of the school year, Ms. Ragusa requires each student to identify an "area of specialization" which she or he will explore in greater depth than the rest of the class and, thus, serve as the class "expert." Eldon, for example, chose plant care, whereas Kimberley continues to read about and investigate ecological issues long after the science unit focusing on ecology was completed by the class. Each

1/26/00

Eldon Drasovich
Fourth Grade, Room 17
Eugene Elementary School

Kiera Johnson
Third Grade, Room 11
Eugene Elementary School

Dear Kiera:

Magnets are made up of tiny tiny little pieces. We learned the pieces are molecules. Molecules are like how a cheerio is made of crumbs. But molecules are too small to see them. The molecules are all lined up in rows.

Some magnets have a S and an N on the sides. The S stands for south the N stands for north. So when you put an S side with a N side they come together because there different molecules. But if you put an S with S they don't come together because there the same molecules. Its the same thing if you put a N and a N together the molecules are the same. But a N and a S will go together because there different molecules.

When you try to put a N and a N or a S and a S together you feel like something makes it hard to push them close. When you put a N and S close the two magnets touch all by themselves. That's because of the molecules. So they touch when one is north and one is south. And there both the same means they don't come together.

And sometimes when you put north and south together one of them mite spin around and come together. They spin cause the two different sides want to be together. I think what make them spin is force. There is different force on the sides of the magnet trying to go different ways so it make the magnet spin. And the other magnet is pulling its different side over to it but I am not sure about that that's just what I think.

Magnets also pull things out of medal like iron and steal but not to wood, plastic, paper, copper and other things. A N side will stick to the same things as a S side. So N and S can stick when there different sides and stick to steal and iron. I still do not know why they stick to some things. But I think I will do some research and try to find out. I also want to make more things with magnets like we did in fourth grade. I made a truck that can go up a hill by itself.

I hope I made you like magnets and hope you will do research like me. I think it is good to find out a lot about magnets. And it mit be fund for you cause it is fun for me.

SINCERELY,

Eldon Drasovich

Eldon Drasovich

ILLUSTRATION 2.34

A Letter Eldon Included in His Language Arts Portfolio

student inserts material in her or his "Area of Specialization" slot in the appropriate subject-matter portfolio as she or he develops that personal specialization.

Each student, in collaboration with Ms. Ragusa, selects materials for the portfolios that are indicative of accomplishments. Not only are additions continually being made, but as the student refines ideas and supplants previously held misconceptions with freshly constructed concepts and discoveries, the contents of the portfolios are altered and replaced. For example, as the year progresses, Eldon is likely to improve his writing skills and expand and refine what he understands about magnets (e.g., during a unit on electricity); thus, he may choose to rewrite Illustration 2.34's letter to Kiera. He may either choose to replace the old letter with the updated one or decide to keep them both in the portfolio as evidence of how his understanding of magnets and writing skills evolved.

Exactly what's included in portfolios varies considerably among students as well as from unit to unit and course to course; they are individualized. At the end of the science unit on magnetism, Eldon's slot for that unit contains the following items: (1) A copy of the report submitted by a cooperative working group of which Eldon was a member during the unit, (2) a select sample of tasksheets Eldon completed during the unit (e.g., a homework tasksheet for which he formulated a hypothesis about magnets), (3) cross-reference notes, a reference to a segment on a videotape showing Eldon conducting an experiment with magnets, and a reference to a mechanical device Eldon made that demonstrated an application of magnetism, and (4) a note from Ms. Ragusa expressing her evaluation of what Eldon learned from the unit, accompanied by a copy of the original unit test Eldon completed and a copy that Eldon reworked in light of feedback from the first administration of the test.

Throughout the year, Ms. Ragusa engages in conferences with students individually and in groups to make decisions about what they need to do to modify and expand their portfolios. These discussions stimulate considerable feedback about what they've done, what they need to do, and how to get to where they need to go. In other words, students gain feedback for decisions about how to learn as Ms. Ragusa does about how to teach.

Ms. Ragusa is required by her school administration to assign grades for periodic reports. She used to include these grade reports in students' portfolios. However, after discovering that some parents and school administrators tended to focus on the grades instead of the more information-rich materials, she sends the grade reports home but no longer makes them part of the portfolios.

Individualized student portfolios can preserve more details of what is learned than traditional grades, test scores, and what one recalls from memory. Incorporating portfolios in your teaching helps students reflect on their progress and take responsibility for monitoring their own learning. However, as suggested by Case 2.20, effective use of portfolios in the complex classroom environment requires considerable planning, organization, and decision-making on your part. Furthermore, you must teach students to work with their portfolios; Spandel and Culham (1995, p. 14) state, "Portfolios offer students a whole new set of challenges: planning, time management, comparing, analyzing, learning to understand how to learn. What is equally true is that students can potentially gain great insight from the experience—insight equivalent to the effort they put into it."

To design a portfolio system for you and your students, you first need to determine how the portfolios will be used. A portfolio should tell a story. But what type of story should it tell? If the story is to be a chronological account of what the student learned, then it might be designed somewhat like a scrapbook filled with representative work samples, products, test documents, and descriptions by which one could chart progress from the beginning to the end of the year or course. Or should the portfolio be designed to showcase selected accomplishments? McMillan (1997, p. 232) states, "The showcase portfolio includes student selection of his or her best work. Because the student chooses the work, each profile of accomplishment is unique and individual profiles emerge. This encourages self-reflection."

Relative to how, if at all, you incorporate portfolios in your teaching, you have a myriad of other decisions to make (e.g., who will have access to portfolios). Such questions are addressed in subsequent sections of this book.

A CLASSROOM ENVIRONMENT CONDUCIVE TO FORMATIVE FEEDBACK

FOCUSING ON WHAT STUDENTS DO, NOT ON WHO THEY ARE

The success of portfolios and other formative feedback mechanisms depends on how well you establish a classroom atmosphere in which students feel free to experiment, try and fail, make mistakes, raise questions, interact with you and their classmates, and expose their thinking processes without fear that they are risking embarrassment, harassment, or having their self-worth evaluated. But to establish such a classroom atmosphere requires you to counter years of tradition that (1) emphasizes summative evaluations over formative judgments, and (2) associates a person's value with her or his accomplishments. From their preschool days, most children are inundated with storybook tales, television programs, poems, songs, and talk from adults that leave them with the following unfortunate message: "The degree to which a person is loved, appreciated, and respected depends on that person's accomplishments." Rudolph the Red-Nosed Reindeer, for example, was an object of scorn for his peers until he achieved an act of heroism one Christmas Eve, after which they began to love and respect him.

This tradition, coupled with the typical emphasis on summative evaluations, influences most students to arrive for a new school year with the idea that the teacher is there to evaluate them. When students fear being devalued if they fail, they will tend to hide their failings from you and, consequently, make it more difficult for you to obtain information useful for formative judgments.

One strategy for countering this tradition and establishing that desirable classroom atmosphere is to demonstrate that you do not make judgments about the students themselves. Instead, you consistently focus on what they do and achieve without ever associating the behaviors or achievements with their self-worth or what you think of them as people. The key is how you use language (Cangelosi, 1997, pp. 31–34, 126–154). Consider Case 2.21.

CASE 2.21

Upon returning a student's science test paper with a high score, Ms. Johnson remarks, "Whitney, you proved you are quite a scientist. Thank you for being such a good student!" Whitney feels proud being praised in front of his peers. Jana, hearing Ms. Johnson's remark, thinks, "Since I had a low test score, I must be a bad student who can't do science."

Later, Whitney gets nervous, fearing that he won't score high enough on subsequent science tests to live up to Ms. Johnson's label. When science gets difficult for him, he is tempted either not to try, lest he fail to live up to the label, or to cheat on tests to maintain his status in the class.

Instead of labeling Whitney as "quite a scientist" and a "good student," Ms. Johnson should have focused on the work by describing his accomplishment. For example, she could have said, "Whitney, your response to the third prompt clearly illustrates Newton's second law of motion." Many teachers, as well as many teaching-methods textbooks, routinely refer to "bright students," "overachievers," "underachievers," and other such labels that reaffirm the tradition. Notice how Mr. Ramirez, in Case 2.22, manages to communicate judgments about students' achievements and behaviors without labeling the students themselves (adapted from Cangelosi, 1997, pp. 128–129).

CASE 2.22

Mr. Ramirez is a fifth-grade teacher who distinguishes between a student's accomplishments and the value of that student. He does not view a student's display of off-task behavior as a reflection of character flaws. Mr. Ramirez believes that he is responsible for teaching each student to be on task and to achieve learning goals. He does not include judgments of a student's character among his responsibilities. His use of descriptive language helps students realize that he focuses on learning tasks, not on personalities.

Upon returning a student's science test paper with a high score, Mr. Ramirez remarks, "Mickey, this paper indicates that you understand the dependence of animal respiration on plant respiration."

While orally giving directions to his class, Mr. Ramirez notices Mary Frances talking to a neighbor instead of paying attention. Mr. Ramirez tells her, "Mary Frances, I would like for you to stop talking and listen to these directions."

In a parent-teacher conference, Mr. Ramirez tells Nettie's father, "Nettie grasped the idea of multiplication right away. However, she does not have all of the multiplication facts memorized because she sometimes does not take the time to complete the drills that I assign in class."

To begin establishing the classroom atmosphere she wanted on the very first day of school, Ms. Elabiad, in Case 2.5, devised Illustration 2.15 so that there's no hint of labeling or judging people. She had students, for example, indicate what they like to do, not what they are good at. She avoided questions like, "Who is your best friend?" Whenever you're tempted to label a student, stop and think what the student has done that brings that label to mind. Then instead of using the label, use words that describe what the student did or accomplished. For example, four-year-old Justin shows one of his paintings to you. You would be communicating a judgment about Justin if you said, "You are a wonderful artist; that's a great picture." Your response would descriptively focus on the picture without labeling Justin if, instead, you said, "You drew the sun shining really bright. The trees are full of green leaves. Your picture reminds me of a warm summer day."

FOCUSING ON FORMATIVE JUDGMENTS

In Case 2.20, Ms. Ragusa discovered that some parents and school administrators tend to emphasize the importance of grades more than the importance of exactly what is being learned and what should be done in order to learn. The grade consciousness that many students and their parents display can interfere with how well teachers are able to communicate formative judgments to students. Consider Case 2.23.

CASE 2.23

Mr. Wedington wants to find out exactly which steps in a long-division process his fifth-graders can do and on which steps he needs to provide help. To find this out, he meets with each student individually and has the student think aloud while working out a long-division computation. It is Stephanie's turn to demonstrate her skill with the process. Mr. Wedington: "Stephanie, I want to watch you divide 753 by 12. As you work it out here on your paper, tell me what you are thinking as you go through the steps." Stephanie writes down the following:

$$12\overline{)753}$$

But quickly she stops and says, "I don't know the answer." Mr. Wedington: "Neither do I. But I do know how to find the answer. I'd like you to begin to find the answer." Stephanie: "I can't while you're watching me!" Mr. Wedington: "Why not?" Stephanie: "Because I'll make a mistake and you'll count off." Mr. Wedington: "This has nothing to do with your grade. I just want to see how you divide, so I can help you divide better." Stephanie writes "6" as a partial quotient above the "5" in "753." Quickly, she puts down her pencil and asks, "Is that right?" Mr. Wedington: "Tell me why you decided to put '6' there." Stephanie begins to erase the "6" as she exclaims, "Oh! It's not right!" Mr. Wedington gently touches the pencil, stopping her from erasing her correct response. Stephanie: "Oh! We're not allowed to erase."

All Mr. Wedington wanted to do was to diagnose Stephanie's skill with long division so he would be in a better position to help. But Stephanie was so used to having teachers grade the outcomes of her efforts that she just doesn't understand that Mr. Wedington is trying to help her, not grade her.

How can you help students overcome their defensiveness regarding "being evaluated" and gain the cooperation you need to conduct ongoing formative judgments? Here are three suggestions: (1) Use descriptive rather than judgmental language. (2) Clearly distinguish for your students those relatively infrequent tests that you use to make summative evaluations from the nearly continual observations and tests used for formative judgments. (3) Do not collect data for summative evaluations during learning activities.

Descriptive language helps convince students that you evaluate only their levels of achievement of specific learning goals and you do not evaluate them. Frequent assessments that are used to keep students apprised of their progress throughout learning units, but that do not influence their grades, help students to understand, and thus cooperate in, formative evaluations. Those less frequent evaluations that do influence students' grades should be distinguished as extraordinary events for which their engagements in your learning activities and formative judgments have prepared them.

You, like many teachers, may value student-centered learning activities in which students respond to your questions (e.g., with Socratic methods), solve problems, or have discussions. Sometimes, students are reluctant to engage in such activities because they feel they're being graded. A comment of one seventh-grader is typical: "Sure, Mr. Burke says, 'We learn by our mistakes.' But when we make mistakes, he's right there to take off points!" When performance during learning activities influences grades, students may not feel free to ask questions, try out answers, and risk making mistakes.

You should, but may not always be able to, depend on help from students' parents to help secure students' cooperation. Often, you may want to discuss formative judgments with parents to help them understand what you're trying to get their children to accomplish and how they can help. Sometimes communications are thwarted by parents who interpret nearly anything teachers say as reflecting a summative evaluation. In Case 2.24, Mr. Perkins attempts to gain Rolando's mother's cooperation. To do so, he must assertively steer the conversation away from summative evaluations and toward formative judgments.

CASE 2.24

Mr. Perkins does not have the time to confer with his fifth-graders' parents as frequently as he would like. He does, however, maintain contact by routinely phoning one or two parents each school day. In this way, he is able to speak with a parent of each student at least once every three weeks. It normally takes two conversations before parents understand that Mr. Perkins's intentions are to inform them about what their children are doing and not to either praise or criticize students. Here is an account of Mr. Perkins's first telephone conversation with Rolando Mitchell's mother:

Mr. Perkins:	"Hello, Ms. Mitchell. This is Sal Perkins, Rolando's teacher. I hope you are doing well."
Ms. Mitchell:	"Oh, yes. And what about you?"
Mr. Perkins:	"Just great! I'd like to take five to six minutes to let you know what Rolando's working on in fifth grade. If this is an inconvenient time, I can call back later."
Ms. Mitchell:	"I can talk now, but what kind of trouble is that boy giving you?"
Mr. Perkins:	"Rolando's not giving me any trouble. I just wanted to let you know about some things Rolando is working on in school."
Ms. Mitchell:	"I'm glad he's not troubling you. Is he going to pass? How are his grades?"
Mr. Perkins:	"We're just beginning a lesson on how to use mathematics to find the best prices when shopping."
Ms. Mitchell:	"That's interesting. Do you think he'll learn it?"
Mr. Perkins:	"Yes, and he should improve both his reading and mathematical skills as we start examining newspaper ads."
Ms. Mitchell:	"It'd be good for him to do more reading. He'd rather watch TV. I'm always telling him to turn off that boob-tube and go do some reading. But he just keeps watching."
Mr. Perkins:	"You've just given me an idea! Let's use his affinity for TV to build his interest in relating mathematics and reading to shopping. I'll assign Rolando to make a record of price-related information that is communicated in TV commercials. We'll use his notes during our mathematics lessons."
Ms. Mitchell:	"I'll make sure he has a pad and pencil with him when he's in front of the television."
Mr. Perkins:	"That'll be a help. Thank you."
Ms. Mitchell:	"Anything else?"
Mr. Perkins:	"He'll be working on expanding his writing vocabulary and using dictionaries for another week."
Ms. Mitchell:	"How's his writing?"
Mr. Perkins:	"Each day this week, I'll give him a list of between five and 10 new words and ask him to write sentences using them for homework. It should take him about 20 minutes a night to look up the words in his dictionary and write the sentences."
Ms. Mitchell:	"I'll see that he does it."
Mr. Perkins:	"Thank you. I'll call again in about three weeks and we can further discuss what Rolando is doing in school."
Ms. Mitchell:	"That would be very nice. Thank you for calling."

The strategy is to engage students and their parents in conversations emphasizing formative judgments about how to learn. Also, continually conducting mini-experiments with students in class for purposes of formative feedback helps students feel comfortable about responding to prompts. As in Mr. Heaps's class in Case 2.10, they can use those mini-experiments as opportunities to learn, not as performances on which they will be evaluated.

SYNTHESIS ACTIVITIES FOR CHAPTER 2

1. Reread Case 1.1. Mr. Chacone made a number of decisions. Some were formative judgments, others summative evaluations. Identify two formative judgments he made and two summative evaluations.

2. Compare your response to Prompt #1 to that of a colleague. Also compare your and your colleague's responses to the following one (which you shouldn't think of as the correct response—only an example of an accurate response):

> Mr. Chacone made a formative judgment by deciding that his students needed to construct the concept of circle for themselves. We know this is formative because he used the judgment to determine the objective for a lesson, not to judge success. On the other hand, he made a summative evaluation by determining how well students achieved the objective. The judgment that Rosita would prefer to play the game than stand by him was also formative, since it influenced his decision to apply the principle of negative reinforcement. Within this same teaching cycle, he made a summative evaluation by deciding that Rosita learned to comply with the rules.

3. Review Cases 1.4 and 2.1. Identify the formative judgments and two summative evaluations you made in those cases.

4. Compare your response to Prompt #3 to that of a colleague. Explain your rationale for the way you classified the decisions. In a discussion, resolve any discrepancies between your and your colleague's responses.

5. Get together with a colleague whose teaching specialty is the same as yours. Begin designing a course to teach by developing a sequence of units using a format similar to Illustrations 2.5–2.8. Now, reflect back on the information sources you and your colleague used to decide on which units to include and how to sequence them.

6. In collaboration with your colleague, select one of the units from your response to Prompt #5 and define the goal for that unit with a sequence of objectives. Use a format similar to Illustrations 2.9–2.12. Now, reflect back on the information sources you and your colleague used to formulate the objectives.

7. In collaboration with your colleague, select one of the objectives from your response to Prompt #6 and develop a lesson plan for that objective. Now, reflect back on the information sources you and your colleague used to design the lesson.

8. After you studied Cases 2.5, 2.6, and 2.7 and just before you studied Case 2.8, you designed an activity to help you set the tone for a school year or course. You exchanged and discussed your plans with a colleague. Since then, you considered other suggestions for creating a classroom environment that's conducive to using formative feedback to guide both learning and instruction. With your colleague, revisit your plans and, as you see fit, modify them in light of your work since you originally developed them.

9. Resurrect the lesson plan you developed in response to Prompt #7. Select one of the learning activities from that lesson and work out the details for conducting that activity so that you maximize your opportunities to use unplanned and planned measurements for ongoing formative judgments—judgments that guide the activity. As you develop the details, keep in mind the seven ideas listed at the very end of this chapter's section "Formative Judgments During Learning Activities."

10. Spend about an hour observing in an elementary, middle, or secondary school classroom. Spend about 10 minutes each to complete the first three of the following tasks and the rest of the time on the fourth:
    A. Note one student who appears to be on task. Describe what you empirically observed that leads you to believe the student was on task. Speculate as to whether the on-task behavior you observed is an isolated incident or part of an on-task behavior pattern.
    B. Note one student who appears to be off task without being disruptive. Describe what you empirically observed that leads you to believe the student was off task. Speculate as to whether the off-task behavior you observed is an isolated incident or part of an off-task behavior pattern.
    C. Note one student who appears to be off task and disruptive. Describe what you empirically observed that leads you to believe the student was disruptively off task. Speculate as to whether the off-task behavior you observed is an isolated incident or part of an off-task behavior pattern.

    D. Record the results of unplanned measurements you made while in the classroom that would be useful to the teacher as she or he makes formative judgments. For each measurement you list, note whether you would have been able to make it if you had been actually teaching, rather than simply observing the class.

11. Get together with a colleague. Have your colleague role-play one of your student's parents you are engaging in a conference similar to the conference in Case 2.24. Of course, play the role so that you are teaching in your own specialty area. Before you begin, put yourself in the context of a realistic classroom situation and determine the message you want to convey to the parent. To send the intended message, you will need to steer the focus of the conversation toward formative judgments and away from summative evaluations.

TRANSITIONAL ACTIVITY FROM CHAPTER 2 TO CHAPTER 3

In discussion with two or more of your colleagues address the following questions:

1. What purposes do the summative evaluations of our students' achievement serve?

2. To whom should we communicate our summative evaluations of students' achievement? Who should be privy to those evaluations?

3. How, if at all, should students' participation in cooperative-group activities, class activities, and homework influence their grades?

4. How, if at all, should individualized student portfolios be used to communicate summative evaluations of student achievement?

5. What are some effective ways for communicating summative evaluations of achievement to students and their parents? What role should periodic reports play?

6. How, if at all, should measurement results (e.g., test scores) be converted to grades?

Communicating Your Summative Evaluations of Student Learning

◆ GOAL OF CHAPTER 3

Chapter 3 is designed to lead you to develop strategies for communicating summative evaluations of student achievement in a professional and varied manner, the objectives are as follows:

A. You will distinguish between examples of evaluations of students themselves and examples of summative evaluations of their achievement and explain why it is important for teachers to make that distinction (construct a concept)[1] 18%[2].

B. You will distinguish between examples of unprofessional and professional use of summative evaluations of student achievement (construct a concept)[1] 18%[2].

C. You will want to clearly define the purpose of summative evaluation reports (appreciation)[1] 05%[2].

D. You will develop strategies for communicating summative evaluations in a way that encourages students to engage in learning activities, especially activities involving cooperative groups, class participation, and homework (application)[1] 18%[2].

E. You will explain a variety of methods for reporting student evaluations, converting measurement results to grades, and compiling grades for periodic reports (comprehension and communication skills)[1] 18%[2].

F. You will develop strategies and techniques for communicating summative evaluation of student learning that are appropriate for your unique teaching situation (application)[1] 18%[2].

G. You will incorporate the following technical phrases in your working professional vocabulary: "norm-referenced evaluation," "criterion-referenced evaluation," "portfolio assessment," "scoring," "traditional percentage grading," "checking-off objectives," "classical curve grading," "visual inspection grading," "compromise grading," "weighted-averaging method," and "percentage-averaging method" (comprehension and communication skills)[1] 05%[2].

---

[1]Indicates the learning level of the objective as defined in Chapter 5 of this text. (It is not necessary for you to be concerned with this scheme for categorizing learning levels until you've reached Chapter 5.)
[2]Indicates the relative importance assigned to the objective as explained in Chapter 5 of this text. (It is not necessary for you to be concerned with this weighting method until you've reached Chapter 5.)

EVALUATE STUDENTS' LEARNING, NOT STUDENTS

Examine the two columns of teachers' comments listed in Illustration 3.1. How are the comments in Column A like one another but different from those in Column B? How are those in Column B alike but different from the ones in Column A?

The teachers' comments in Column A of Illustration 3.1 communicate evaluations about the students themselves. Column A's comments characterize students, indicating the type of people the teachers have judged them to be. In contrast, Column B's comments communicate evaluations of what students have learned, not who they are. Comments about Abu's comprehension skills, Martha's need to follow directions, Katie's need to apply herself in class and do her homework, Nadine's insightful statements, Alexis's disruptive behavior pattern, how Betty writes, and the level of Julian's work in health science focus the communication on the business of teaching and learning. The business of professional teachers is to affect students' abilities, skills, attitudes, and behaviors. Thus, as a teacher, you are responsible for making evaluations about students' abilities, skills, attitudes, and behaviors. Not only is characterizing students *not* one of your teaching responsibilities, but it actually interferes with your working relationship with students and makes it difficult to focus on the business of teaching and learning (Brophy, 1998, pp. 91–100; Cangelosi, 1997, pp. 31–34, 127–131; Ginott, 1972).

As suggested in Chapter 2's section "Focusing on What Students Do, Not Who They Are," students and their parents are less defensive about and more open to evaluations of achievement when the evaluations are communicated in a way that does not reflect on the worth of students themselves. By consistently attending to even subtle differences in how you express summative evaluations, you chip away at that link between achievement and self-worth. For example, compare the last comment in Column B of Illustration 3.1 to the last one in Column A. The comment from Column A equates the grade to the student, whereas the comment from Column B attaches the grade to the student's work rather than the student himself.

WHO SHOULD KNOW WHAT ABOUT A STUDENT'S ACHIEVEMENT?

VIOLATIONS OF PROFESSIONAL TRUST

What, if anything, bothers you about the behaviors of the teachers in Cases 3.1, 3.2, and 3.3.

CASE 3.1

In a parent-teacher conference with Jan's father, Mr. Spivey says, "Jan's work habits are exceptional, and now all her hard work is paying dividends. What you see in her social studies portfolio is just a sample of what she's produced. I only wish some of my other fourth-graders, like Riley and Patricia, would do half of what Jan does!"

CASE 3.2

Walt Brousseaux, a high school science teacher, meets one of his friends, Clio Clark, in a grocery store:

Mr. Brousseaux: Well, what a pleasant surprise! Clio, I haven't seen you for months. What's been going on?

A	B

A

"Jessica is an excellent reader."

"Clarence is an at-risk student."

"Ruben is an underachiever. He has all the natural talent in the world, but he's lazy."

"Sateki is the type of young man any teacher would love to have in class. Not only is he a real scholar, but he's also thoughtful of his classmates who aren't as quick to learn as he is. They think of him as a real leader."

"Kristina has become the biggest behavior problem I have. She is a disruptive influence on the class."

"For her age, Beverly is an average writer -- nothing to worry about."

"Charlotte is a B student in health science."

B

"Abu has developed his comprehension skills to the point where he's ready for more advanced reading selections."

"Martha will not be ready for high school until she learns to follow directions."

"Whenever Katie applies herself in class and does the homework, she makes great progress. But more often than not, she doesn't do the necessary classwork and homework."

"I enjoy working with Nadine. In class, she makes insightful statements and raises stimulating questions. Other students learn quite a bit from her."

"Alexis has developed a habit of disrupting the class at least once a day."

"Betty writes in a style that's pretty typical for her age."

"Julian is doing B-level work in health science."

ILLUSTRATION 3.1

How Do the Teachers' Comments in Column A Differ from Those in Column B?

Ms. Clark: "Hi, Walt; it's great to see you! I'm getting some things for tonight. My daughter, Lavina, is having her new boyfriend over for dinner. She just broke up with Timmy Dantin, and now she's got this new guy, Wellington something."

Mr. Brousseaux: "I'll bet it's Wellington Staples! Super guy! He was in my chemistry class; made all A's. Lavina's making a good move. I also had that Dantin kid in my class—just barely passed."

CASE 3.3

Ms. Smith, a high school mathematics teacher, receives a phone call from a local bank where one of her students, Medgar, has applied for a job. Although neither Medgar nor his parents authorized her to provide a reference, she relates Medgar's mathematics grades to the bank representative over the phone.

In Case 3.1, Jan's father has no need to hear Mr. Spivey's evaluations relative to Riley, Patricia, or any student other than Jan. Mr. Brousseaux, in Case 3.2, is just trying to be friendly, but isn't he violating a professional trust by revealing evaluations about Timmy's and Wellington's achievement for nonprofessional purposes? In Case 3.3, Ms. Smith's conveyance of information about Medgar's grades was for professional purposes. However, does not Medgar have a right to control who outside of the school has access to his academic records?

Trust between you and your students is an important ingredient for a classroom climate that is conducive to learning. Do not violate that trust by communicating your summative evaluations of student achievement to people who lack either the need or the authorization to be privileged to those evaluations.

PRIVILEGED INFORMATION

Of course, there are times when you should communicate summative evaluations of students' achievement and behaviors. Who should be privileged to those communications? Typically, the following are considered to have a right and need to know:

- In most cases, the student needs to be kept apprised of her or his own status regarding achievement of learning goals.
- The student's parents need to be aware of their child's level of achievement and behaviors for two reasons:
  - Parents who are informed about just what their children are and are not accomplishing in school are in an advantageous position to serve as partners to teachers to help their children cooperate and achieve.
  - Parents are legally responsible for their children's welfare. They do, after all, delegate and entrust some of their responsibilities to teachers. They have a right to know how the school is impacting their children.
- Professional personnel (e.g., a guidance counselor or another of the student's teachers) who have instructional responsibilities for that student sometimes need to know about the student's achievement so that they are in a better position to help that student.
- Professional personnel who supervise and evaluate the teacher's performance or provide the teacher with formative feedback on instruction sometimes need to understand specifics about individual students to meet their responsibilities to the teacher (see, e.g., Cangelosi, 1991, pp. 3–14).
- Professional personnel (e.g., the principal, subject-area supervisor, or curriculum director) whose judgments impact curricula and conduct of the school sometimes need to be aware of an individual student's achievements so that they will be in an advantageous position to make school-level decisions.
- Because a school often acts as an agency that qualifies students for occupations, as students at other institutions, or for other privileges (e.g., scholarships), it may sometimes be necessary for a representative of an institution to which a student has applied to have knowledge of evaluations of that student's achievement. However, school personnel should seriously

consider following a policy that they release information on an individual student's achievement to such representatives only with that student's and his or her parents' authorization.

PERIODIC REPORTS

CLEARLY DEFINED PURPOSE

What is the purpose of the periodic reports, commonly known as "report cards," that are recorded and given to students and parents in the vast majority of schools? Here is a sample of answers from teachers, students, parents, and school administrators:

Teachers:

> "To let students and their parents know how well they've learned what they were supposed to learn."
> "Grades should motivate students to learn and reward those who try."
> "Actually, we'd be better off without report cards and grades. They categorize our students as 'winners' and 'losers.' No useful purpose is served."

Students:

> "Tell parents how their kids are doing."
> "To show who's smart and who's dumb."

Parents:

> "For the records—to show who should go to college and what vocations students should pursue."
> "To let us know how our children are doing."

School administrators:

> "You have to have grades and reports; it's part of the accountability system."
> "To provide a means for students, parents, teachers, and instructional leaders to gauge progress."

Such comments suggest rather varied agendas for simplistic periodic reports. Simplex reports can hardly be expected to serve multiple purposes such as communicating evaluations of achievement, motivating learning, reflecting progress, and identifying areas of competence.

If the purpose involves either motivation or progress, then grading would have to be individualized. If, for example, Illustration 3.2 accurately reflects Mindy's and Allison's entry and exit achievement levels, then Mindy's performance should merit a higher grade than Allison's. Otherwise, Mindy would not be motivated, realizing that her achievement level is unlikely to

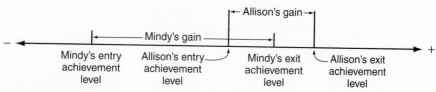

ILLUSTRATION 3.2

Which Student Displays Greater Achievement?

Grade Level Five's Six-Week Report

Student's Name ___Foster J. Simpson___ Report No. __4__ Period _1/24_ to _3/6_
Teacher Completing Report__ Mr. Jorge Perales __ Subject: __Area Language Arts__

Key to Symbols:
   A : Significantly Exceeds Minimum Standards
   B : Exceeds Minimum Standards
   C : Meets Minimum Standards
   D : Below Minimum Standards
   F : Significantly Below Minimum Standards

Reading Comprehension	Rating
Level of Achievement	C
Rate of Progress	C

Reading Vocabulary	Rating
Level of Achievement	D
Rate of Progress	C

Speaking Vocabulary	Rating
Level of Achievement	B
Rate of Progress	C

Listening Comprehension	Rating
Level of Achievement	B
Rate of Progress	B

Process Writing	Rating
Level of Achievement	B
Rate of Progress	A

Writing Mechanics	Rating
Level of Achievement	C
Rate of Progress	B

ILLUSTRATION 3.3

Report with Multiple-Grade Format

"catch" Allison's. If the grade is to reflect progress, the difference between exit and entry achievement is more relevant than exit achievement level.

In any case, grades and reports do not convey their purpose unless that purpose is spelled out and made known. Furthermore, multiple purposes can hardly be served unless multiple-grade formats (e.g., Illustration 3.3) or detailed narratives (e.g., Illustration 3.4) replace the traditional report formats (e.g., Illustrations 3.5 and 3.6).

In Case 3.4, teachers struggle with the problem of determining just what grade reports are supposed to communicate.

CASE 3.4

Rainbow High School currently uses a grade report format similar to Illustration 3.6's; several teachers have expressed dissatisfaction with the form. Denise Agular, Jamal Bond, Ludell Sims, and Entu Unitoa are appointed to a faculty committee that is to make a recommendation for either developing a

Sumac Hills Middle School
Summative Evaluation Report

Student: Erica Grotage
Grade Level: 7th
Teacher: Ivory Jackson

Course: Prealgebra
Term: 2nd 9 weeks
Class Period: 4th

Mr. Jackson's Report
(1/13/00)

The prealgebra course is designed to lead students to progress toward 16 learning goals. During the second 9-week period, the 4th-period prealgebra class worked toward accomplishing Goals 5, 6, 7, and 8:

Goal 5 (Modeling Linear Relationships):

Students will develop narrative and concrete models for linear relationships they encounter in their other Sumac Middle School courses (e.g., art, community living, healthy life-style, language arts, music, physical education, science, and Spanish). They will apply their models to describe, explain, and predict linear relationships.

Goal 6 (Using Algebra to Build Linear Models):

Students will use algebraic language and algorithms to analyze, refine, and demonstrate linear models they developed while working toward Goal 5. They will describe the behavior of linear functions algebraically and geometrically.

Goal 7 (Solving Systems of Linear Equations):

Students will apply their knowledge of modeling to build systems of linear equations and then invent and apply algorithms for solving them.

Goal 8 (Solving Systems of Linear Inequalities):

Students will extend their work toward achievement of Goal 7 to systems of linear inequalities.

ILLUSTRATION 3.4

One of the Narratives One Teacher Used to Report Summative Evaluations of a Student's Achievement

(Continued)

ILLUSTRATION 3.4 (Continued)

With respect to Goal 5:

Erica began working toward Goal 5 by identifying a number of relationships relevant to her studies in other courses. For example, stimulated by her language arts and Spanish courses, she hypothesized that it takes fewer words to say something in Spanish than it does to say that same thing in English. She immediately recognized the value of collecting numerical data to test her hypothesis as well as to address a variety of other questions raised by the class. As with almost all the other relationships brought up by students, the relationship suggested by Erica's hypothesis is not linear. I was concerned that these non-linear relationships would not serve us well as we progressed toward linear modeling. However, Erica helped out everyone in class by displaying data from an experiment she conducted that matched the number of words used in a message expressed in Spanish to the number of words used to express that message in English. She explained that although for some messages, more words are used in Spanish than in English and for others the opposite is true, her data showed a trend favoring her hypothesis. Thus, she got the class to focus on overall patterns in their data rather than details. Please see Item 5-2 in Erica's prealgebra portfolio for a record of this experiment.

Portfolio-Item 5-2 demonstrates Erica's insights into how non-linear bivariate data can be used to identify linear trends. Of course, she does not use words like "bivariate," "linear," and "non-linear" in Portfolio-Item 5-2's description of the experiment. But the way she visualized a trend in those data demonstrates a sophisticated grasp of some important relationships for which she'll learn names later in her career as a student of mathematics. In fact, two weeks after she shared her analysis of her Spanish-English experiment with the class, I used her analysis to introduce the idea of the slope of a function.

Note that Portfolio-Item 5-5 contains Unit-5 posttest documents with Erica's responses and my completed scoring form. Those results suggest to me that she has developed an advanced (for a seventh-grader) ability to develop narrative models of relationships particularly for relationships in the area of arts and languages. She can also apply modeling to address problems in the social and hard sciences, but she seems to prefer to work with problems from arts and languages. Also, she seems more comfortable expressing models as narratives more than as concrete models. My observations of her work throughout the nine-week period are consistent with the results of the posttest.

With respect to Goal 6:

In her pursuit of Goal 6, Erica began translating models from the narrative and concrete forms to algebraic expressions. This

ILLUSTRATION 3.4 (Continued)

required her to comprehend and communicate with the rudimentary language of functions. She became quite competent in using conventional graph modes (e.g., histograms and line graphs) as well as creative in designing graph modes to fit particular tasks. See, for example, Portfolio-Item 6-3.

Erica is able to express linear models as functions in tabular, equation, and graphical form; however, she resists using the shortcuts to express these functions. For example, she seems to prefer plotting coordinates and building tables to using characteristics of linear functions such as intercepts and slopes to build equations. The advantage of her "hands-on" approach is that it helps build a solid conceptual base for her to learn more mathematics. The disadvantage is that it is also important for her to become skilled with some of the basic algorithms. Skill with the algorithms will allow her to apply what she's learned to more complex problems.

Note that Portfolio-Item 6-4 contains Unit-6 posttest documents with Erica's responses and my completed scoring form. Those results suggest to me that her development of conceptual understanding of applications of algebraic methods to linear modeling is more advanced than her skill with relevant algebraic algorithms (e.g., an algorithm for building an equation from a slope and a point).

With respect to Goal 7:

Erica began her work toward Goal 7 by taking functions with which she previously worked (e.g., $y = 3x - 1$) and comparing solutions to solutions (e.g., (2, 5) to (0, -1)), solutions to non-solutions (e.g., (2, 5) to (2, 8)), and non-solutions to non-solutions (e.g., (2, 8) to (-4, 0)) to discover why given a pair of linear equations that the pair either shares exactly one solution, no solutions, or the two equations are equivalent. She not only made this discovery for herself, but explained them to others during several cooperative learning activities.

She quickly invented the substitution algorithm for solving pairs of linear equations and used it quite efficiently. However, consistent with earlier observations of her work, she insisted on using the algorithm only when the coefficients were such that reasoning or trial-and-error methods were far too time consuming. I see no disadvantage to Erica's attitude in this regard. However, she still doesn't seem to proficiently solve systems of linear equations by the elimination method, nor does she seem to be interested in understanding why it works. This will put her at a disadvantage in solving some, but not most, systems.

ILLUSTRATION 3.4 (Continued)

Erica has become quite adept at setting up linear systems that
model problems to be solved. Again she succeeds with art and
language related problems more often than she does with problems
in other areas.

Note that Portfolio-Item 7-2 contains Unit-7 posttest documents
with Erica's responses and my completed scoring form. I am very
pleased with her level of achievement with Goal 7.

With respect to Goal 8:

With Erica's conceptual-understanding relative to Goals 5, 6,
and 7, she experienced little difficulty applying her work with
systems of equations to systems of inequalities. She did struggle with rules for graphing solutions to systems of linear
equalities and keeping the direction of the inequality signs
straight. But this is a matter of needing more practice, not a
need for more depth of understanding.

Erica produced some dramatic illustrations of solutions to a
pair of inequalities based on an extension of her experiment
with Spanish and English words. Please see Portfolio-Item 8-2
for those illustrations with her own annotations.

Note that Portfolio-Item 8-3 contains Unit-8 posttest documents
with Erica's responses and my completed scoring form. I am very
pleased with her level of achievement with Goal 8. I am also
looking forward to working with her as she continues to progress
with these four goals as she applies what she's learned in the
second half of prealgebra.

new report form or retaining the current one. The four teachers engage in the following conversation during the initial meeting of the committee:

Ms. Agular: "If we decide to stick with letter grades, we are at least going to have to do a better job of defining each symbol."

Mr. Bond: "The scale is right here on the bottom of the report: A is superior, B is good, C is average, D is poor, and F is failure. It's there for anybody to read."

Ms. Agular: "It may be there for everybody to read, but what do we mean by 'superior'? Superior to what?"

Mr. Bond: "It means more than satisfactory, competent work. Good is like satisfactory—so it's superior to satisfactory."

Ms. Agular: "So average is unsatisfactory?"

Mr. Bond: "Average is just what it says—what most students do—typical work is average."

Ms. Unitoa: "So you're saying that most of our students' work is unsatisfactory."

Mr. Bond: "No, work or achievement that is typical is average—below average is unsatisfactory."

Ms. Unitoa: "But you said good is satisfactory, so anything below good is unsatisfactory."

Mr. Bond: "Okay, I changed my mind. Below average is unsatisfactory, and on the scale that's called 'poor.' Poor is unsatisfactory."

Ms. Unitoa: "By definition of 'average,' isn't half of all achievement levels above average and the other half is below average? That means half of our students' achievement is below average—which Jamal defines to be unsatisfactory or poor."

Mr. Bond: "So maybe we have an above average student body. We could say, the average is the average of all high school students and most of Rainbow's students achieve above the national average."

Ms. Unitoa: "Wow! You're really stretching things just to retain the old wording."

Ms. Agular: "One of the reasons we're going in circles is because these categories, superior, good, average, poor, and failure, aren't levels of the same variable. They should not be on the same scale. 'Average' is clearly a word that compares students' achievement to that of a group. 'Good' and 'poor' on the other hand tend to make us think of a comparison to some performance standard like 'able to do the job' or 'competent' or 'literate' or whatever that doesn't compare one student's achievement to others'. It's a difference between what evaluation specialists call 'norm-referenced' standards and what they call 'criterion-referenced' standards. Our scale defining grades has to be one or the other, not both. That's why we're going around in circles trying to compare average to good or poor."

Ms. Unutoa: "Ludell, you've been awfully quiet. What are you thinking?"

Mr. Sims: "I've been sitting here listening to all this crap about norm-reference or whatever versus the other one Denise said and all of you going back and forth when the answer is as simple as the nose on your face. What we need to do is get back to simple percentages. Everybody knows exactly what we mean by making an A 94 percent or more, a B 86 to 93 percent, and so forth down to F is below 70 percent. That's the way we used to do it. It's simple and everybody understands it."

Ms. Agular: "I, for one, don't understand it."

Mr. Sims: "What? It's just simple arithmetic. You compute the percentage by—"

Ms. Agular: "My question isn't about the arithmetic. What does it mean for a student to get 80 percent?"

Mr. Sims: "It means he's a C student because you get a C if you're between 78 and 85 percent."

Ms. Agular: "80 percent is 80 percent of what?"

Mr. Sims: "That means he learned 80 percent of the material."

Ms. Agular: "Are you trying to tell us if a student's score on a 50-point unit test is 40—that's 80 percent—then she learned 80 percent of the goal for that unit."

Mr. Sims: "That's right, Denise."

Ms. Agular: "Ludell, do you agree that for any one of your chemistry units you could make up more than one unit test so that they both relate to the goal of your unit but so that one is harder than the other?"

Mr. Sims: "Of course."

Ms. Agular: "Okay. Suppose you had a student, call her Mary, and she took your easier test and scored 95 percent. And another student, George, took the harder one and scored 40 percent. Who do you give the higher grade to, Mary or George?"

Mr. Sims: "Well 40 percent has to be failing and 95 percent is near mastery. But then if George's test is harder than Mary's—that's not fair! You have to give them the same test for this to work."

Ms. Unitoa: "I see what Denise is driving at. Because a student gets 80 percent of the points on a test doesn't mean that person achieved 80 percent of the goal. There are too many other variables—like the difficulty of the tests. Also you can't put a percentage figure on learning; learning is on a never-ending continuum. No one, not even Ludell, our resident chemistry expert, could possibly understand 100 percent of any one chemistry topic. The same goes for all our subjects. Jamal is a history expert. But the most knowledgeable person on any historical topic can't know everything about that topic. Also, everyone has some rudimentary sense of virtually any topic—so you can't say anyone understands zero percent of a topic either. And if zero percent and 100 percent aren't really meaningful, then 80 percent can't be either. That's why Denise asks 80 percent of what."

Mr. Bond:	"You've got me thinking, Entu. It gets even more complicated when you try to factor in things like attendance, homework, effort, and all those other things some of our teachers build into their grades."
Ms. Unitoa:	"Some teachers put more weight on improvement. Others count off for misbehaviors and so forth."
Ms. Agular:	"The first thing we have to decide is what grades are supposed to communicate. Is it just the level of students' achievement or what?"
Mr. Bond:	"Just let each teacher decide for herself or himself."
Ms. Unitoa:	"If we do that, we're back to where we are now. Grades in one teacher's class are not comparable to grades in another teacher's class."
Ms. Agular:	"If we can't decide on meaningful, well-defined criteria for A, B, C, D, and F, then we have two options. Either we move completely away from grades and develop some innovative system, or we take Jamal's suggestion and let each teacher decide for her or himself. But if we leave it open so that the meaning of grades varies from teacher to teacher, we need to make that known. We'll have to inform students, parents, and other users of our grade reports, warning them not to compare one grade to another."
Mr. Sims:	"But that means we can no longer say that because a student got an A in history and a C in chemistry that he did better in history than he did in chemistry."
Ms. Unitoa:	"Nor can we say, if he got a D in math last year and a B this year, that he showed improvement in math from last year to this year. Maybe we should just admit publicly that grades cannot be the tell-all mechanism we'd like for them to be."

Later in the meeting, the following exchange takes place:

Ms. Unitoa:	"I have a question that doesn't really fit into the committee's work with the grade reports. It relates more to a problem individual teachers work out for themselves, rather than involving schoolwide policies. But it's about grading, so I'd like to bring it up."
Mr. Bond:	"Go ahead, Entu, maybe it's something we could all learn from."
Ms. Unitoa:	"I have my students do a lot of cooperative group work—where they learn from each other. They do group projects and reports and stuff. My question involves how accomplishments of groups should be factored into the individual grades of students."
Mr. Sims:	"I know what you mean. Some kids do all the work, while others just tag along or even interfere with what others are doing. I've tried basing a percentage of students' individual grades on what their groups have done. But that's not really fair. I know some teachers who have each member of a group grade the contributions of the other participants, but I don't like that. Then kids are competing for the favor of the group."
Ms. Agular:	"It doesn't' really foster the kind of cooperation you need for productive collaboration. I resist ever grading engagement in any kind of learning activity—sure they should be getting formative feedback all along—but they should feel free to

Eugene Street Elementary School 1999–2000

Name: Darnell Witherspoon
Teacher: Judith Druh-Heinz
Grade 1 ② 3 4 5
Reporting Period 1/30
Promotion to Grade

A check shows that school work is adversely affected by frequent absences and tardiness.

Attendance ☐   Punctuality ☐

Action to be taken by:
(signatures)
Student: Dayne/l
Teacher: J. Druh-Hne
Parent: BW

Achievement Level: Excellent / Satisfactory / Effort needed

READING
- Recognizes differences in sounds
- Word attack skills
- Vocabulary development
- Reads with understanding
- Enjoys reading
- Vocabulary
- Comprehension
- Independent reading

LANGUAGE
- Expresses ideas orally
- Expresses ideas in written work
- Understands language concepts

SPELLING
- Applies spelling skills
- Spells assigned words correctly

HANDWRITING
- Style (form)
- Spacing
- Size (uniformity)
- Slant
- Applies handwriting skills

ART
- Participation

MUSIC
- Participation

PHYSICAL EDUCATION
- Participation
- Sportsmanship

MATHEMATICS
- Understands concepts
- Computational skills
- Problem solving

SCIENCE AND HEALTH
- Understands concepts
- Has scientific inquisitiveness

SOCIAL STUDIES
- Participates in class
- Knowledge of subject matter

WORK STUDY SKILLS
- Follows directions
- Works independently
- Works well in a group
- Listens attentively
- Uses time effectively
- Takes care of materials

SOCIAL GROWTH
- Observes school rules
- Respects authority
- Respects rights of others
- Developing self control
- Accepts responsibility
- Has positive attitude toward work

ILLUSTRATION 3.5

Example of a Traditional Elementary School Grade Report

experiment, question, make mistakes, and take the chances that lead to learning without worrying that their efforts are being graded. Concern with grades in those situations stymies openness and creativity."

Mr. Sims: "Grading on class participation of any kind interferes with a collegial classroom atmosphere. Another problem is how to factor homework into grading. The more weight for grades I put on homework, the more I encourage them to copy the right answers rather than actually treating the assignment like a learning activity."

Ms. Unitoa: "So are you guys going to give me any answers?"

The first meeting continues with more questions raised than answered.

Case 3.4 illustrates the need to specify exactly what report-card symbols are intended to convey. But it also illustrates the problems teachers face when attempting to agree on what that intent should be. Your responsibility for communicating summative evaluations of student learning presents some complex problems for you to address:

- If grades or other scales are used, how should they be defined?
- To use Ms. Agular's words from Case 3.4, should evaluations be norm-referenced or criterion-referenced?
- How, if at all, should cooperative group work be graded?
- How, if at all, should class participation be graded?
- How, if at all, should homework be graded?
- In what format should summative evaluations be reported?

GRADING SCALES

To be meaningful, a single scale (e.g., A, B, C, D, F) can reflect levels relative to only one variable at a time. If "C" is defined as "average," then a single C can only represent either (1) average level of achievement relative to a specified set of goals, (2) average difference between current level of achievement and entry-level of achievement relative to a specified set of goals, (3) average amount of effort put forth in working toward a specified set of goals, (4) average level of cooperation in working toward a specified set of goals, or (5) any other average level of performance the C is used to communicate. Of course, the questions of "average of what?" must also be addressed. The scale in Illustration 3.5 doesn't refer to an average, but it seems to suffer from the problem of mixing multiple variables. Note that in the top left corner, there are three "achievement levels": "Excellent," "Satisfactory," and "Effort Needed." Does not "effort needed" refer to a different variable than the other two?

In Case 3.4, Ms. Agular pointed out the need for a grading scale to be constructed so that the different levels all related to the same standard. For example, if C is defined as equivalent to the average performance of some specified group (e.g., all students in that same course or grade level), then the other symbols must also be defined relative to that same average. For example:

"A" indicates a level of achievement that is well above the average range of performance in the comparison group.

"B" indicates a level of achievement that is somewhat above the average range of performance in the comparison group.

"C" indicates a level of achievement that is within the average range of performance in the comparison group.

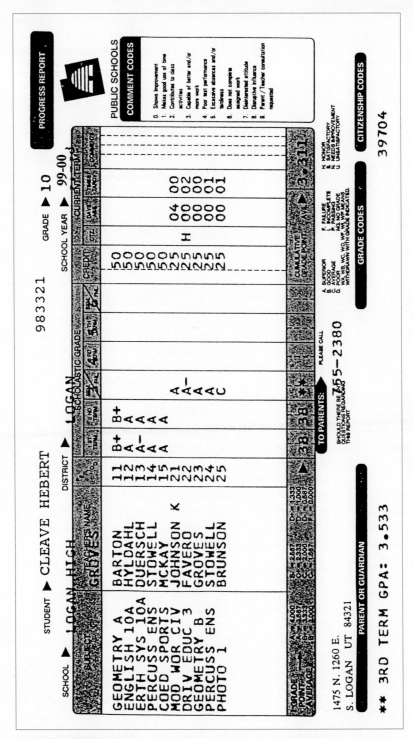

ILLUSTRATION 3.6

Example of a Traditional High School Grade Report

"D" indicates a level of achievement that is somewhat below the average range of performance in the comparison group.

"F" indicates a level of achievement that is well below the average range of performance in the comparison group.

Similarly, if C is defined as what you and other experts in your teaching specialty consider acceptable performance relative to course standards, then the scale might appear as follows:

"A" indicates a level of achievement that far exceeds the minimum standards for this course.

"B" indicates a level of achievement that somewhat exceeds the minimum standards for this course.

"C" indicates a level of achievement that meets the minimum standards for this course.

"D" indicates a level of achievement that falls somewhat below the minimum standards for this course.

"F" indicates a level of achievement that falls far short of the minimum standards for this course.

This is not to suggest that these are ideal ways of defining a letter-grade scale. These are only examples of scales with levels defined with the same reference point in mind. Avoid mixing reference points as they are mixed in Illustration 3.6.

NORM-REFERENCED EVALUATIONS OR CRITERION-REFERENCED EVALUATIONS?

As with any other type of decision or judgment, a summative evaluation is influenced by measurement results. Thus, to make a summative evaluation, you need to interpret the measurement results. Suppose, for example, Jeff, a fifth-grader, tells you, "I got a 37 on my fitness test." What information does that 37 provide regarding how well Jeff did on the fitness test? It doesn't tell me anything. Now suppose that Jeff says, "It was the second to the highest score in the whole class." Now, you at least have some basis for telling Jeff, "I'm so happy you performed so well on the fitness test!" Jeff provided you with something to which the 37 could be compared. In this case, you interpreted the 37 in light of its rank in the class's scores. Thus, to use one of Ms. Agular's phrases from Case 3.4, you just made a *norm-referenced evaluation*. A summative evaluation of a student's achievement is *norm-referenced* if the evaluation is influenced by how the measurement results relevant to that student's achievement compare to results obtained from others. The following teachers' comments are indicative of norm-referenced evaluations. (Note that the statements reflecting summative evaluations are italicized; those reflecting measurement results are underlined.)

> "Anna leg pressed 150 lb.; fewer than 10 percent of all girls her age can do 100 lb. *Her legs are very strong.*"
> "*I can hardly justify assigning a 'B' for Mayra's achievement in this course;* her exam score was 30 points less than the test average."
> "*I wish Rasheed would be more decisive about what he wants to do.* He was the last one in class to select a topic for the project and the first one to tell me he couldn't decide which report to put in his portfolio."
> "Melvin's score on the posttest for the nutrition unit was two standard deviations greater than the average score for the class. *His grasp of nutritional principles is exceptional.*"
> "*I didn't realize Jermain had learned to spell so well* until I heard he won that spelling bee yesterday."

Standards to which measurement results are compared for purposes of summative evaluations are not always norm-referenced. Suppose, for example, Jaylyn, a fourth-grader, tells you, "I got a

43 on my writing test." What information does that 43 provide regarding how well Jaylyn did on the writing test? It doesn't tell me anything. Now suppose that Jaylyn says, "It was 43 out of 45 possible." Now, you at least have some basis for telling Jaylyn, "I'm so happy you performed so well on the writing test!" Jaylyn provided you with something to which the 43 could be compared. In this case, you interpreted the 43 in light of the maximum possible score. Thus, to use one of Ms. Agular's phrases from Case 3.4, you just made a *criterion-referenced evaluation*. A summative evaluation of a student's achievement is *criterion-referenced* if the evaluation is influenced by how the measurement results relevant to that student's achievement compare to a standard that is not dependent on results obtained from others. The following teachers' comments are indicative of criterion-referenced evaluations. (Note that the statements reflecting summative evaluations are italicized; those reflecting measurement results are underlined.)

> "<u>Edmond bench pressed 150 lb.; that's more than he weighs.</u> *He has very good upper-body strength.*"
> "*I can hardly justify assigning a 'B' for Lavern's achievement in this course;* <u>her exam score was only 10 percent of the maximum possible score.</u>"
> "*I wish Craig would be more decisive about what he wants to do.* <u>He missed the deadline for selecting a topic for the project. When I asked him to select one of his six essays for his portfolio, he hemmed and hawed until I eliminated four myself and left him only two from which to choose.</u>"
> "<u>According to my observer's rubrics, Thyra's responses to every prompt on the test requiring her to use reasoning received a high score, whereas every one requiring recall of information received a low score.</u> *While she seems adept with reasoning tasks, she seems to resist memorization.*"
> "*I didn't realize Margo had learned to spell so well* until <u>I heard her spell 'idyllic' and 'misfeasance' at the spelling bee.</u>"

By making the distinction between norm-referenced and criterion-referenced evaluations, you are better able to define standards by which you will interpret measurement results. Such standards need to be defined in order to specify just what a summative evaluation report is supposed to communicate. This, of course, was one of the major problems with which the teachers in Case 3.4 struggled.

GRADES AND COOPERATIVE LEARNING

Reread Case 1.2; note the cooperative-learning activity as well as the posttest Ms. Anderson administers near the end of the 10-day unit. Case 3.5 takes place during the time when Ms. Anderson was designing that post test.

CASE 3.5

Ms. Anderson thinks to herself, "Some of the objectives for this creative writing unit involve interactions among writers and readers. My cooperative group activities provided major opportunities for the students to demonstrate how well they interact for purposes of clarifying what they write and comprehending what they read. Somehow, I need to design this test so that at least part of it reflects the quality of those interactions in the cooperative groups. But I don't want to be walking around with an observation rating scale or checklist making them nervous while they're engaged in these learning activities. That would stifle the open exchange of ideas. I could do what so many teachers do, which is to have the students in each group rate the others on how well they contributed to the process. But I don't like that; learning activities should be for learning, not evaluating. I know Frank has his English students rate their own level of participation in cooperative groups—sort of grade themselves. But I don't like that either. That would seem to discriminate more on how hard they are on themselves and how honest they are with me. Seems like asking them to do that presents them with an unnecessary predicament. No, I've got to develop a few mini-experiments that prompt them to reflect back on just what they did in those group activities and respond in some way that indicates something about the quality of those interactions. The emphasis should be on what they gained as writers and what they contributed as readers. That's right in line with my objectives."

After considerably more thought, Ms. Anderson develops her posttest. Illustration 3.7 displays two of its mini-experiments.

In Case 3.5, Ms. Anderson recognized that participation in the cooperative group's activities increased the chances of students achieving objectives to which her posttest was supposed to be relevant. Thus, instead of awarding "points" for participation, she used Illustration 3.7's mini-experiments to directly link the cooperative learning activities with achievement. The teacher in Case 3.6 uses a similar approach for using work produced by cooperative groups in a measurement for a summative evaluation without the measurement process interfering with the cooperative learning process.

CASE 3.6

As part of a physical science unit on heat and temperature, Ms. Bohrer designs a lesson to lead her sixth-graders to achieve the following objective:

> When confronted with a real-life problem, students determine how, if at all, the concepts
> of heat conduction, convection, and radiation can be used to help solve that problem.

Besides the science unit, the lesson is also part of art, health, and mathematics units. Her plans for the lesson include the cooperative learning activity described in Illustration 3.8.

She thinks about the design of a measurement to be used for a summative evaluation of what students learned from the unit: "This designing and building the dog shelters is going to be a major part of this unit. What can their shelters tell me about their abilities to apply their understanding of heat conduction, convection, and radiation? Of course, after all the effort they'll have put into the projects, they'd be awfully disappointed if it somehow didn't impact the grade for the unit. But how do I build the measurement so that their group work is reflected by individual posttest scores? One idea is to use an observer's rubric to score how well their individual responsibilities were met while they worked on the project. I'd have to come up with a rubric for the project managers, another for the materials supervisors, another for the cooling specialists, another for the heating specialists, and another for the draftspersons. That's not a bad idea—really holds them accountable for their individual roles. But knowing they'll be 'tested' that way, might inhibit them pitching in and working as a team on all aspects of the project. What I'll do is have one or two product-examination mini-experiments that produce a score for the whole group; that'll be part of each member's individual posttest. Then, I'll also have another mini-experiment in which each individual has an opportunity to demonstrate her or his understanding of the designs of the group's shelters."

Illustration 3.9 shows the two product-examination mini-experiments Ms. Bohrer developed. One of the mini-experiments she developed for individual student response is displayed by Illustration 3.10.

GRADES AND CLASS PARTICIPATION

The strategy employed in Cases 3.5 and 3.6 for linking measurements for summative evaluations to cooperative group work can, of course, be applied to reinforce other types of class participation. In Case 2.15, for example, Ms. Fisher uses posttest results as a basis for summative evaluations of achievement. Note that the posttest, shown in Illustration 2.28, includes

1. <u>Prompt for Students</u>:

   Attach a copy of the paragraph you read to your group of collaborators during the class meeting of September 7.

   Also attach a copy of the revised version of that paragraph that
   you shared with me on September 8.

   Now, use the areas below to write responses to the following
   three prompts:

   A. Explain how the paragraph you read on September 7 differs
      from the one you shared with me on September 8.

   B. Describe what you learned about the paragraph you read from
      listening to your collaborators discuss it on September 7.

   C. Explain your rationale for the changes you made in the
      paragraph you read on September 7 to produce the one you
      shared with me on September 8.

   <u>Scoring Rubric</u>:

   (Maximum points possible: 8) Score +1 for each of the following
   8 criteria that is met by the response:

   _____ The Sept. 7th draft is attached.
   _____ The Sept. 8th draft is attached.

ILLUSTRATION 3.7

Two Mini-Experiments Ms. Anderson Included on the Posttest Alluded to in
Cases 1.2 and 3.5

(Continued)

ILLUSTRATION 3.7 (Continued)

```
_____  The response for "A" is an explanation about differ-
       ences in the two drafts.
_____  The response for "A" highlights the principal differ-
       ences in the two drafts (according to my reading of the
       two drafts).
_____  The response for "B" describes at least something that
       could have been reasonably learned about the paragraph
       during the cooperative group activity.
_____  The response for "B" describes points relative to read-
       ers' interpretations of the paragraph.
_____  The response for "C" is an explanation of a rationale
       that supports the modifications reflected by the Sep-
       tember 8th draft.
_____  The response for "C" suggests that the writer at least
       considered what he/she said (in the response to "B")
       that he/she learned by listening to the collaborators
       discussing the paragraph.

2. Prompt for Students:

    Call to mind the work you and your collaborators did discussing
    one another's paragraphs on September 7.

    Now, think of one of the paragraphs, besides your own, that was
    read.  Whose paragraph did you think of (one only)?

    _____

    Now, call to mind the discussion you and your collaborators had
    about that particular paragraph.  Use the area below to list two
    points that were made during the discussion that you think would
    be especially useful to the writer when modifying the paragraph.

      1)



      2)



    Now, explain why you think the two points you just listed could
    be particularly useful to the writer.
```

ILLUSTRATION 3.7 (Continued)

```
Scoring Rubric:

    (Maximum points possible: 5) Score +1 for each of the following
    5 criteria that is met by the response:

    _____   Specifies another student in the group who read a para-
             graph.
    _____   Response displays a degree of knowledge about the
             selected student's paragraph.
    _____   Lists one point about the paragraph that it's reason-
             able to believe came out of the discussion.
    _____   Lists a second point about the paragraph that it's rea-
             sonable to believe came out of the discussion.
    _____   Final part of response connects the two points listed
             to ways the paragraph might have been modified.
```

mini-experiments that refer students to activities they engaged in while in class. If, as it should, participation in class leads students to achieve objectives to which measurements are relevant, then students are better equipped to respond to the measurements' prompts because they engaged in classroom activities. However, because students may come to you with experiences in other teachers' classrooms in which classroom activities did not prepare them for tests, you may need to highlight the link by using measurements similar to Ms. Fisher's in Illustration 2.28.

Students quickly discover the link between class participation and their performance on measurements influencing their grades when prompts on tests mimic classroom learning activities. For example, look back at the tasksheet Mr. Heaps had his students use during the classroom demonstration described in Case 2.10. The tasksheet appears in Illustration 2.22. To highlight the link between engagement in that class activity and success on tests, Mr. Heaps might include prompts on a measurement for summative evaluation purposes that are identical to those on the tasksheet, with the exception that they relate to a different demonstration. Or he might direct students to attach their completed tasksheets to the test documents and then include prompts requiring them to use data from the tasksheets.

Students engaging in Case 2.10's classroom activities are continually responding to prompts and receiving formative feedback on their responses. If that feedback helps students perform on tests for summative evaluations, they discover the link for themselves. In other words, you need not "award points" for class participation—a practice that confounds the meaning of grades, suppresses formative feedback, and interferes with learning activities. Instead, manipulate learning activities and design measurements so that students discover, "If I participate, I learn; if I learn, I'll get better grades."

GRADES AND HOMEWORK

Similarly, there is no need to artificially manipulate "points toward grades" for doing homework. Ms. Romberg discovered that in Case 2.13. The link between engaging in homework

Students will be organized into collaborative work groups of five. Individual assignments in each group will be as follows:

The Project Manager will be responsible for organizing the group, chairing meetings, and overseeing the group's work.

The Materials Supervisor will be responsible for acquiring materials and tools from Ms. Bohrer, distributing them, supervising their use, and returning tools and unused materials.

The Draftsperson will be responsible for creating the blueprints for the group's designs and keeping them updated and in a comprehensive form.

The Cooling Specialist will serve as the group's resource person on applications of scientific principles relative to cooling. This includes acquiring information from outside sources.

The Heating Specialist will serve as the group's resource person on applications of scientific principles relative to heating. This includes acquiring information from outside sources.

Each will be directed to design a shelter for the dog in the first picture. Ms. Bohrer explains that they can choose any available materials and can plan the shelter for any reasonable size for the yard. However, they have no artificial power source (e.g., electricity for air conditioning) nor can shelter be supplied with ice or any kind of cooling substance (although the dog is supplied with regular meals and fresh drinking water). The purpose of the shelter is to help keep the dog cool on hot, sunny summer days.

ILLUSTRATION 3.8

Ms. Bohrer's Plan for a Cooperative Learning Activity in One of Her Lessons on Heat Conduction, Convection, and Radiation

(Continued)

ILLUSTRATION 3.8 (Continued)

Once the designs are approved by Ms. Bohrer, the group is to build the
shelter.

Similarly, each group is also directed to design a shelter for the dog
in the second picture, the one who must stay in the yard on cold wintry days. Ms. Bohrer explains that the rules are the same; again
there is no artificial power source to supply heat. Also, they cannot
build fire just as they couldn't bring in ice for the first dog.

Once the designs are approved by Ms. Bohrer, the group is to build
the shelter.

assignments and grades should be the same as the link between engagement in class activities
and grades. In Case 1.4, you assigned homework the first day of class and administered a test
on the second day that linked the homework to success with tests.

A RECOMMENDATION

The recommendation here is that if you want to use a grade to communicate your evaluation
of a student's achievement of specified learning goals, then you should base that grade only on
measurement results that are relevant to those learning goals. To positively reinforce engagement in learning activities (e.g., with collaborative working groups, in-class participation, and
doing homework), apply strategies demonstrating the link between engagement and achievement as was done in Cases 3.5, 3.6, 2.15, 2.10, 1.4, and 2.13. Your school faculty might also
consider using a multiple-grade report format (e.g., Illustration 3.3) that sets aside symbols for
effort as well as achievement.

Of course, summative evaluation reports can hardly be meaningful unless they are based
on measurement results that are actually relevant to what students have learned. Such relevant
measurements depend on the quality of the mini-experiments that are used. Chapters 7–13
address ways of designing relevant mini-experiments.

1. Prompt for the groups:

    The students are directed to produce the blueprint and shelter for the dog on the hot day as described in Illustration 3.8.

    Observer's rubric:

    Ms. Bohrer examines both the blueprint and the shelter. For each of the following criteria she displays her judgment by using the following checklist to mark "1" if the criterion is met and "0" if it is not:

    _____ The shelter is likely to produce an overall cooler environment for the dog than outside the shelter.

    _____ At least one aspect of the design uses heat radiation in a way that will cool the dog.

    _____ There is no aspect of the design that will use heat radiation in a way to warm the dog.

    _____ At least one aspect of the design uses heat convection in a way that will cool the dog.

    _____ There is no aspect of the design that will use heat convection in a way to warm the dog.

    _____ At least one aspect of the design uses heat conduction in a way that will cool the dog.

    _____ There is no aspect of the design that will use heat conduction in a way to warm the dog.

    Ms. Bohrer uses the following space for comments about the design relative to how the design applies the concepts of heat radiation, convection, and conduction:

    _____

    _____

2. Prompt for the groups:

    The students are directed to produce the blueprint and shelter for the dog on the cold day as described in Illustration 3.8.

ILLUSTRATION 3.9

Product-Examination Mini-Experiments Ms. Bohrer Developed

(Continued)

ILLUSTRATION 3.9 (Continued)

Observer's rubric:

Ms. Bohrer examines both the blueprint and the shelter. For each of the following criteria she displays her judgment by using the following checklist to mark "1" if the criterion is met and "0" if it is not:

_____ The shelter is likely to produce an overall warmer environment for the dog than outside the shelter.

_____ At least one aspect of the design uses heat radiation in a way that will warm the dog.

_____ There is no aspect of the design that will use heat radiation in a way to cool the dog.

_____ At least one aspect of the design uses heat convection in a way that will warm the dog.

_____ There is no aspect of the design that will use heat convection in a way to cool the dog.

_____ At least one aspect of the design uses heat conduction in a way that will warm the dog.

_____ There is no aspect of the design that will use heat conduction in a way to cool the dog.

Ms. Bohrer uses the following space for comments about the design relative to how the design applies the concepts of heat radiation, convection, and conduction:

_____

_____

REPORT FORMATS

Hundreds of different summative evaluation report formats are used in schools. Most schools use traditional formats (e.g., Illustrations 3.5 and 3.6), but it is now quite common for these reports to be used in conjunction with student-parent-teacher conferences as well as individualized student portfolios.

STUDENT-PARENT-TEACHER CONFERENCES

You improve opportunities for parents and students to understand your summative evaluations by supplementing written reports with face-to-face conferences. Most school calendars reserve several days spread over the year for parent conferences. Besides these periodic conferences, it is to your advantage to schedule additional time with parents. Consider the following suggestions for planning a conference with parents:

Prompt for students:

Ms. Bohrer orally explains the following directions using words familiar to the fourth-graders:

Call to mind how you and your collaborators designed the shelter you made for the dog during the hot summer months. Following are a list of statements about the shelter. Determine which are true and which are false. Put a "T" in the blank for the true ones and an "F" for the false ones.

For each statement you marked with a "T," explain how your group designed the shelter so that the statement is true. Use the space under the statement to write your explanation.

For each statement you marked with an "F," explain how your group might have designed the shelter differently so that the statement would have been true. Use the space under the statement to write your explanation.

_____ The dog will be cooler with the shelter than without the shelter.

_____ The shelter is built so that heat radiation will help cool the dog.

_____ The shelter is built so that heat convection will help cool the dog.

_____ The shelter is built so that heat conduction will help cool the dog.

Scorer's rubric:

(maximum possible points: 24) Scores for each of the four explanations depend on how well the explanations meet the criteria listed below. The scale for each criterion is as follows:

+2 if the criterion is clearly met.
+1 If it is unclear as to whether or not the criterion is met.
+0 If the criterion is clearly not met.

ILLUSTRATION 3.10

Mini-Experiment Ms. Bohrer Developed for Individual Student Responses

(Continued)

ILLUSTRATION 3.10 (Continued)

Criteria for the first explanation:

1) The explanation indicates that the student generally understands the features of the shelter that relate to keeping
   the dog cool.
2) The explanation demonstrates an understanding of how heat-
   energy transfer principles can be applied.
3) The explanation includes nothing that's erroneous regarding
   the design of the shelter or about heat-energy transfer
   principles.

Criteria for the second explanation:

1) The explanation indicates that the student generally understands features of the shelter that are relevant to heat
   radiation.
2) The explanation demonstrates an understanding of how heat
   radiation might be used to cool the dog.
3) The explanation includes nothing that's erroneous regarding
   the design of the shelter or about heat-energy transfer
   principles.

Criteria for the third explanation:

1) The explanation indicates that the student generally understands features of the shelter that are relevant to heat
   convection.
2) The explanation demonstrates an understanding of how heat
   convection might be used to cool the dog.
3) The explanation includes nothing that's erroneous regarding
   the design of the shelter or about heat-energy transfer
   principles.

Criteria for the fourth explanation:

1) The explanation indicates that the student generally understands features of the shelter that are relevant to heat
   conduction.
2) The explanation demonstrates an understanding of how heat
   conduction might be used to cool the dog.
3) The explanation includes nothing that's erroneous regarding
   the design of the shelter or about heat-energy transfer
   principles.

- Prepare an agenda for the conference that specifies (1) the purpose of the meeting (e.g., to communicate summative evaluations relative to achievement of learning goals for the previous nine weeks), (2) a sequence of topics to be discussed, and (3) beginning and ending times for the conference.
- Except for special situations, invite the student to attend and participate in the conference. (Healthier, more open attitudes are more likely to emerge when the student is included.)
- Schedule the meeting in a small conference room or other setting where distractions (e.g., a telephone) are minimal and there is little chance for outsiders to overhear the conversation.
- Provide a copy of the agenda to each person in attendance. During the meeting, direct attention to the topic at hand by referring to the appropriate agenda item and by using other visuals (e.g., material from the student's portfolio).
- During the conference, concentrate remarks on descriptions of events, behaviors, and circumstances. Focus on needs, goals, achievement of goals, and plans for accomplishing goals. Completely avoid characterizations and personality judgments.
- During the conference, be an active listener so that you facilitate communications and, thus, increase the likelihood that you (1) get your planned message across and (2) learn from the others at the meeting and pick up ideas for more effectively working with the student.

Due to time constraints, face-to-face conferences cannot be held as frequently as needed. However, if you use other means of keeping parents informed about their students' work with you, parents are more likely to be receptive to discussing summative evaluations with you during these report periods. One of many mechanisms you might consider using is a periodic newsletter. Some teachers send home weekly or monthly newsletters that are designed to apprise parents of what their children's classes are doing. Illustration 3.11 is an example.

By taking the time to write such communiques, you foster the goodwill and understanding of parents. Their understanding of what you are trying to accomplish with their children will serve you well when you need to communicate summative evaluations or seek their cooperation.

PORTFOLIOS FOR COMMUNICATING SUMMATIVE EVALUATIONS OF STUDENT ACHIEVEMENT

THE COMPLEXITY OF STUDENT LEARNING

One point on which virtually everyone seems to agree is that meaningful evaluations of student achievement should be based on multiple measurements (American Psychological Association, American Educational Research Association, & National Council on Measurement in Education, 1985; National Council of Teachers of English & International Reading Association, 1996; National Council of Teachers of Mathematics, 1995; National Research Council, 1996). In other words, no one type of measurement (e.g., written-response test or performance observation) sufficiently provides the relevant and reliable data that reflect what students have actually learned; a variety of measurements are needed. At least some of the measurements should be individually tailored to students' characteristics, tendencies, and learning styles. Furthermore, a letter grade or other set of symbols can hardly reflect complex learning outcomes (O'Hagan, 1997). Many even suggest that grades interfere with learning (see, e.g., Bauman, 1997).

Case 3.7 (adapted from Cangelosi, 1996, pp. 334–335) demonstrates the dilemma teachers face in trying to report their summative evaluations of students' achievements and the need for alternatives or supplements to traditional grade reports.

DOING SCIENCE

A Newsletter for Parents of the Scientists
of
Fourth Grade, Room 119, Cedar Ridge Elementary School
Vol. 1, No. 11, March 4 18

From: Tearsa Lincoln, Teacher *J.L.*

Looking Back

The last letter mentioned that we had begun a unit entitled "The Air Around Us" and that the scientists in our class would be constructing a number of instruments to measure variables such as temperature, humidity, air pressure, wind speed, and wind direction. At least one of these instruments spent a night outside your residence as your scientist measured an air-related variable in your neighborhood. Your scientist along with the other scientists in the class used data from these measurements to form some insightful hypotheses about the air around (and in) us. Before the end of March, you will be receiving a letter from your scientist explaining how she or he collected data and made inferences leading to discoveries about our air. Personally, I found some of their hypotheses and insights to be quite intriguing and instructive. They are developing the letter to you as part of process writing activity in our language arts course.

During the "Air Around Us" unit, we constructed a very small greenhouse to trap heat for some of our classroom plants. But for reasons we have yet to discover, it didn't work and our plants got too cold and we had to bring them back into the classroom. Investigations into what went wrong are continuing and we'll update you in upcoming newsletters. I would also appreciate you routinely asking your scientist about that investigation as well as about other specific things we're doing in class. Your scientist gains insights by talking about such things with you.

<u>Some painful news to report</u>: Sophie, the northwestern garter snake that resided in Room 119, died overnight, March 1-2. Sophie was a native of the Vancouver, Washington, area and has been helping my students do science ever since I joined the Cedar Ridge faculty three years ago. We don't know the cause of her death. Some scientists in our class suggested we investigate how she died by performing an autopsy. However, the class voted to simply give Sophie a quiet burial. The question led to a discussion on the topic "Science, Society, and Ethics." None of our scientists suggested that performing an autopsy on Sophie would be unethical.

ILLUSTRATION 3.11

Example of a Newsletter One Teacher Used to Help Maintain Open Lines of Communications with Parents

(Continued)

ILLUSTRATION 3.11 (Continued)

However, the majority felt that we wouldn't likely find out why she died and, thus, the gain wouldn't be worth, as one of your scientists put it, "not giving a good good-bye to a friend."

Looking Forward

Over the next two weeks, we will be completing a unit entitled "Our Solar System." Your scientists won't be performing as many first hand experiments to make discoveries about our solar system the way they did to make discoveries about our air. However, they will be constructing and experimenting with some models in the classroom. These models at least mimic some of the physical properties of heavenly bodies. Also, we will be setting up a telescope for night viewing in the field just behind the parking lot on the west side of the school. Your scientist will be bringing you a note about scheduling observations. How conveniently we can successfully do this depends on a number of factors, not the least of which involves weather conditions. More information on this will be forthcoming.

Special thanks: K.C.'s Books located at 39 West Decker Street generously donated nine copies of Atlas of Stars and Planets: A Beginner's Guide to the Universe, a colorfully illustrated book by Ian Ridpath that provides up-to-date information about our solar system. Having such books for this unit is particularly important since many of the currently available books do not reflect recent discoveries about planets resulting from various space-probe expeditions. If you would like to express your appreciation for this generosity, please drop by the store and tell the owner and manager, Joseph Chung, or call Mr. Chung at 563-9944.

Following "Our Solar System," our scientists will briefly study some of the technological advances in space travel. Thereafter, they'll engage in a full health science unit studying the working of their own bodies. The brief unit on space travel technology will serve as a transition between the study of our solar system and the study of human physiology. Please raise the following question with your scientist and get her or him to think about the answer: "Why must space-travel technology be concerned with how the human body works?"

Please continue to check your scientist's assignment book as well as her or his daily journal. Thank you for working with me.

CASE 3.7

Their students having just departed for the day, Hadezza Robinson and Tyler Longley engage in the following conversation in the faculty workroom of Greystone High School:

Ms. Robinson: "You don't look happy, Tyler. Did you have one of those days?"

Mr. Longley: "Actually, I'm really pleased with the way the day went; the kids really got into their work. But thanks for asking."

Ms. Robinson: "Well, you don't appear very pleased, sitting there grimacing and moaning to yourself."

Mr. Longley: "Because my students had such a productive day, I feel worse about having to boil down all their accomplishments in mathematics to a grade and some check marks. It's distressing!"

Ms. Robinson: "So it's about one of those times of year again when we have to get grade reports out. I'm not looking forward to it either, but I'd think your students' successes would make grading a more pleasant chore. It's always easier to report successes than failures."

Mr. Longley: "I would've thought so too, but that's not the way things are working. Let me give you an example of my dilemma. You know Rebecca Powell?"

Ms. Robinson: "Sure, I have her brother T.J. for precalculus."

Mr. Longley: "Rebecca really got turned on to mathematics in our unit on probability. She began to see applications of mathematics she's been exposed to for the past couple of years—something she's never recognized before. She demonstrated such creativity in that unit, coming up with all kinds of ways to apply the relationships and algorithms."

Ms. Robinson: "I'm trying to figure out why all this is distressing you. I'd think you'd be jumping at the chance to report her successes!"

Mr. Longley: "I am, but the report-card business has me hamstrung because the grade period covers four units. She got an A for the probability unit, and an A for a unit on sequences. But for the descriptive statistics unit and another on special functions, she didn't learn much of anything. When I average out her grades, she'll end up with a B– at best. B– just doesn't reflect her enthusiasm for what she did with probabilities. If only I had made a more concerted effort to relate real-life situations in the statistics and special functions unit the way I did for the other two units, she might have gotten turned on to those also."

Ms. Robinson: "I understand what you're saying. You want to highlight her accomplishments without having them blended with and played down by her lack of success in other areas."

Mr. Longley: "And that's only one example that's bothering me. Sawyer Bond's scores on my written-response tests are really low. But now and then when I catch him in a one-on-one situation and ask him to explain concepts, relationships, and algorithms, he shows sophisticated insights. I think his test performances in mathematics are affected by some major learning gaps relative to reading comprehension. On top of that, he doesn't demonstrate his understanding in large-group class activities because he acts shy in large-group situations. But I think this kid has learned a lot about doing mathematics; it just doesn't show up on conventional tests and demonstrations. If I give him a mathematics achievement report based on the usual measures, it's going to send him and his parents the wrong message. On the other hand, I've got to grade equitably."

Ms. Robinson:	"To compound the problem, I bet you've got students whose test scores exceed their true levels of achievement."
Mr. Longley:	"You've got that right! I can think of several who are really test-wise, plus they have exceptional language arts skills."
Ms. Robinson:	"What we need is to keep an individualized file for each student—one that reflects their special accomplishments and interests as well as reports of more general achievement levels."
Mr. Longley:	"Which one of us is going to propose that at the next faculty meeting?"

INDIVIDUALIZED STUDENT PORTFOLIOS

How can you efficiently maintain and manage a file on each student? Ms. Ragusa in Case 2.20, as many other teachers, does so with individualized portfolios. Case 2.20 describes an example of how portfolios can be organized, packaged, and used as an integral part of instruction. Besides being a mechanism for learning and formative feedback, portfolios can be used to communicate some of the details of what students have learned that are missing from grade reports. In the professional literature, *portfolio assessment* refers to using individualized student portfolios to communicate summative evaluations of student achievement. Portfolio assessment is commonly used in many language arts and English courses that emphasize students' writing skills (see, e.g., Gallagher, 1998, pp. 302–320; Jones, 1997; Wolff, 1995) and is a mandated component of the grading and reporting systems in some school districts.

In Case 3.8, mathematics teachers, Tyler Longley and Hadezza Robinson, act on the need to incorporate portfolio assessment in the grade-reporting system that they discussed in Case 3.7.

CASE 3.8

Greystone High School's students have been dismissed for the summer break, and Tyler Longley and Hadezza Robinson have just completed their work assigning students' final grades. Their conversation turns toward plans for the next school year:

Mr. Longley:	"You know how the English faculty went to portfolio assessment this year; they seemed pretty pleased with the way it worked out."
Ms. Robinson:	"Portfolio assessment—that's where you save examples of students' work in folders or boxes and use them to demonstrate what they've learned and accomplished. Wouldn't that address the problem that upsets you every 10 weeks when grade reports are due? You remonstrate having to boil all students learn to a single symbol. Why don't you have your students get some folders and stick the best samples of their work in them and create the displays? Maybe you could even convince our principal, Sarah, to let you experiment with supplanting letter grades with portfolios."
Mr. Longley:	"First of all, I don't think we should think of the portfolios as simply containers to stick in samples of work students would do whether or not we employ portfolio assessments. I'd like to see us do something that significantly impacts the way we teach and students learn."
Ms. Robinson:	"What do you mean?"
Mr. Longley:	"Well, we're always saying we should do a better job of addressing the NCTM *Standards*" (National Council of Teachers of Mathematics, 1989). "You know, we talk about getting students to apply mathematics to address real-life problems, communicate mathematics, use technology, see mathematics from a historical perspective, and most importantly, to make connections among different mathematical subtopics

as well as connections between mathematics and other school subject-content areas. But then we complain that we're so busy covering material and preparing students to take traditional tests that we don't have time to emphasize these more important aspects of learning mathematics."

Ms. Robinson: "So how would portfolios help?"

Mr. Longley: "If we do it right, individualized portfolios could provide a vehicle for stimulating students to take the mathematics they learn in class and relate it to their special interests, reflect on the connections and history, and do some expository work on topics that peak their interest. But if we do go in this direction, it should also be reflected in our summative evaluations of their achievement—in the grade reports."

Ms. Robinson: "So why don't you run this idea by Sarah and try it?"

Mr. Longley: "I was hoping that it would be something we might develop and try as a department. Sometimes it's tough to be the only one attempting something new. Parents and students start to wonder, 'Why is goofy Mr. Longley doing this if nobody else is?' Then if we're all involved, we'll support one another and share ideas. Also, although Sarah can be pretty persuasive with the school board, I don't think we're ready to go to the school board with a request to supplant grades completely with portfolios."

Ms. Robinson: "Not until we've tried it out for a couple of years and gotten the bugs out of the program."

Mr. Longley: "Right. But to show that the portfolios are an integral, significant part of our mathematics curriculum, we need to tie them to grades somehow. I'd like to see us factor the portfolios into the grading scheme—maybe make the students' portfolio projects 30 percent of the 10-week term grades; 70 percent of each grade can be calculated in the traditional way using test scores, homework, or whatever teachers are doing now."

Ms. Robinson: "But shouldn't samples of students' test papers and homework be included in their portfolios?"

Mr. Longley: "Not the way I'm visualizing the portfolio projects."

Ms. Robinson: "Okay, so maybe you should tell me what you mean by a portfolio project'"

Mr. Longley: "I'm not completely sure I know myself. But it should be something that gets students to synthesize, extend, and expound upon from the mathematical content we're teaching them in our regular lessons and on which we evaluate their learning. I need you to brainstorm with me. Could we get together and collaborate on a proposal to present to the rest of the department?"

Ms. Robinson: "Yes, but don't expect everybody in the department to go for the idea. Scott will object to anything that deviates from following his religion."

Mr. Longley: "What religion?"

Ms. Robinson: "His beloved, blessed mathematics textbooks. His religion is to get students through the textbooks page-by-page and follow the commandment, 'Thou shalt not deviate from the sacred textbooks.' To him mathematics doesn't exist outside of textbooks."

Mr. Longley: "You're right, but at least we might be able to get the majority of the department to contribute their ideas and agree to try something like this."

Ms. Robinson: "What time tomorrow should we meet?"

Several days later, Mr. Longley and Ms. Robinson draft the proposal displayed by Illustration 3.12. Illustration 3.13 shows a scoring rubric for portfolio assessment, and Illustration 3.14 shows a planning form for a portfolio project.

If you decide to incorporate individualized student portfolios into your grading system as was done in Case 3.8, then either the portfolio itself or each portfolio item (e.g., a videotape production or a reflection paper) will need to be treated as a mini-experiment with a prompt for students and an observer's rubric. Strategies for designing such mini-experiments are dealt with in Chapters 7–13.

ASSIGNING GRADES TO MEASUREMENT SCORES

SCORING AND GRADING

Scoring a student's measurement responses is the process of adhering to the observer's rubric for each of the measurement's mini-experiments and compiling the results into a single measurement score (e.g., Tonja's test score of 10 from Illustration 1.15). *Grading* the measurement is the process of assigning a qualitative value to the score. Typically, grades reported on summative evaluation reports are compiled from grades assigned to measurement scores.

If you choose to report summative evaluations in the form of grades or if such reports are mandated by your school's policies, then you need to be familiar with some of the advantages and disadvantages of commonly used methods for converting measurement scores to grades.

CRITERION-REFERENCED GRADING

The Traditional Percentage Method

Among laypersons and teachers who are uninitiated in summative evaluation principles, the most familiar method for converting measurement scores to grades is the traditional percentage method. The "percentage," of course, refers to the score's percentage of the maximum possible points for the measurement. However, as Ms. Unitoa argued in Case 3.4, the percentage is not indicative of the percent of content a student has learned or objectives achieved. Consider Case 3.9.

CASE 3.9

Mr. Nelson, a high school history teacher, uses the following scale for percentage grading:

94–100% for an A
86–93% for a B
78–85% for a C
70–77% for a D
00–69% for an F

The students and their parents are comfortable with his seemingly "objective" scheme. They think they understand exactly what it takes to make a certain grade in the class.

On the first test of the semester, over half the students' scores are less than 77 percent of the maximum. Mr. Nelson, holding fast to his "standards," assigns the majority of the scores D's and F's. However, either consciously or not, he constructs the next test so that it is much easier than the first. The grade distribution for the second test is more in line with what he had anticipated for the first test. Mr. Nelson commends the class for their efforts, commenting that they must have studied harder for the second test than they did for the first.

Because Mr. Nelson thinks of C as average and because of his grading scale, he tends to design tests so that the average percentage score will be between 78 and 85. This causes his tests to be so easy that they fail to measure higher levels of achievement. If he includes enough mini-experiments

Proposed Provisions for Greystone High School
Mathematics Department's Portfolio Assessment

1. Each student enrolled in a mathematics course at Greystone High School will be required to develop and maintain an individualized mathematics portfolio for the purpose of exhibiting her/his portfolio projects.

2. For each of the four 10-week-long grading terms in the school year, the student will complete a combination of one to five projects inclusive.

3. The purpose of the combination of projects is for the student to extend and exhibit her/his ability to do the following:

   A. Connect mathematics learned during the 10-week school term to mathematics learned in previous school terms or in previous mathematics courses. In the first 10-week term, the connection should be between a mathematical topic (e.g., rational functions) from one of the first term's units to a mathematical topic from a previous mathematics course (e.g., rational numbers). In a subsequent term, the connection should be between a topic from a mathematical topic from one of the current term's units (e.g., theorems about similar triangles) to a mathematical topic from the prior term (theorems about parallel lines).

   B. Connect mathematics learned during the school term (e.g., non-linear functions) to subject content learned in other non-mathematics Greystone High School courses the student is currently taking (e.g., ecological systems in biology).

   C. Apply mathematics learned during the school term (e.g., non-linear functions) to address real-life situations the student faces outside of her/his work at Greystone High School (e.g., personal health and physical fitness questions).

   D. Explain mathematics learned during the school term from a historical perspective (e.g., the pursuit of perfect numbers).

   E. Use technology to discover, invent, or communicate mathematics related to what is learned during the school term (e.g., use *Geometer's sketchPAD* to compare relationships in hyperbolic geometry to those in Euclidean geometry).

ILLUSTRATION 3.12

Portfolio Assessment Proposal Mr. Longley and Ms. Robinson Drafted for Consideration by Greystone High's Mathematics Department

(Continued)

ILLUSTRATION 3.12 (Continued)

4. The combination of projects should be designed so that all five parts (i.e, listed "A" through "E" above) of the purpose as stated in #3 above are realized. This could be accomplished by five separate projects with each project addressing a different part or, preferably, by incorporating the parts in fewer projects (e.g., two). The following is an example of a possible project combination that accomplishes all five parts of the purpose:

One of the topics ninth-grader Allison studies during the second term of a geometry course is features of triangles in Euclidean geometry (e.g., the sum of the three degree measures of any triangle is 180). One of the topics she studied in the first term was parallel lines. Allison is also taking world history and one of the second-term topics is 19th century philosophy. Allison completes three second-term portfolio projects; one is as follows:

i)   Using *Geometer's sketchPAD*, she develops a computerized simulation demonstrating how the parallel postulate is applied to prove that the sum of the degree measures of the angles of a triangle is 180. This project fulfills the requirements of parts "A," "D," and "E" listed above.

ii) She writes a library paper explaining how the development of non-Euclidean geometries in the 19th century shook the foundations of classical logic and changed the face of philosophy. This project fulfills the requirements of parts "B" and "D" listed above.

iii) She develops a detailed floor plan for her "dream house" with a brief narrative explaining how she applied her knowledge of features of triangles in the design. This project fulfills the requirement of part "C" listed above.

5. Each combination of term projects should produce concrete artifacts that demonstrate what the student accomplished. The artifacts which are stored in the student's portfolio can employ a combination of the following modes:

- Videotaped presentation
- Expository essay
- Computer-based presentation

ILLUSTRATION 3.12 (Continued)

- Poster display illustration
- Other presentation mode mutually agreed to by the student and her/his teacher

6. The combination of portfolio projects should be scored by the teacher using the attached rubric (see Illustration 3.13).

7. The score for the combination of portfolio projects should influence the term grade by 30%.

8. By the middle of the term, the student in collaboration with the teacher should complete the attached planning form (see Illustration 3.14).

---

with very challenging prompts requiring sophisticated responses, too many students would "fail." Since the students who reach sophisticated achievement levels don't' find his tests particularly challenging, they are unlikely to learn at the levels they are capable of achieving (Stiggins, 1988).

Case 3.10, a continuation of Case 3.9, illustrates another weakness of traditional percentage grading.

CASE 3.10

Mr. Nelson administers a test consisting of 60 prompts, each with a simple scoring rubric so that +1 is awarded the "correct" response and 0 otherwise. Three students' number of correct responses and percentage scores are as follows:

Milan:	51 correct responses	→ 85%
Albin:	52 correct responses	→ 87%
Joyce:	56 correct responses	→ 93%

As shown by Illustration 3.15, Mr. Nelson uses his scale to convert Milan's score to a C, Albin's to a B, and Joyce's to a B.

Surely measurement error is a likely explanation for the difference of one between Albin's 52 and Milan's 51, yet in Case 3.10 they received different grades. On the other hand, Joyce's score received the same grade as Albin's although the difference between 56 and 52 is greater than the difference between 52 and 51.

Checking-Off Objectives

Measurements used for criterion-referenced evaluations of goal achievement are sometimes designed to produce a subscore for each objective rather than only one score for the overall goal. For example, if the goal is defined by eight objectives, the measurement might consist of eight clusters of five mini-experiments, with each cluster relevant to a different objective. A

Scoring Form for _____'s
(student's name)

_____ Term Mathematics Portfolio
(1st, 2nd, 3rd, or 4th)

Note: For each criterion listed, points are awarded as follows:

+2 if the criterion is clearly met
+1 if it is unclear as to whether or not the criterion is met
+0 if the criterion is clearly not met

Each encircled numeral (either 0, 1, or 2) indicates the number of points received for the given criterion.

A. The combination of projects clearly demonstrates that the student has made insightful associations between the following two mathematical topics:

_____

from the current term

and

_____

from the prior term or (if the current term is the 1st, then a previous mathematics course)

0   1   2

B. The combination of projects clearly demonstrates that the student has made insightful associations between the following mathematical topic:

_____

from the current term

and the following topic from the _____ course that the student is also taking:

_____

from the current term

0   1   2

C. The combination of projects clearly demonstrates that the student has applied the following mathematical content:

_____

from the current term

ILLUSTRATION 3.13

Proposed Scoring Rubric for Portfolio Assessment

(Continued)

ILLUSTRATION 3.13 (Continued)

```
         to the following situation from her/his own real-life:

     _____

     _____

                               0    1    2

  D.  The combination of projects clearly demonstrates that the student
      possesses insights into the historical foundations of the follow-
      ing mathematical topic:

      _____

      from the current term

                               0    1    2

  E.  The combination of projects clearly demonstrates that the student
      has applied the following class of technology:

      _____

         to accomplish the following mathematical task related to
the current term:

      _____

      _____

                               0    1    2


Score for the combination of portfolio projects (10) _____
```

criterion, such as "four out of five," is set to define "pass" of each objective. A student's score would indicate the number of objectives "passed" or "checked off."

Criteria for passing an objective, the number of objectives defining the goal, and the number of mini-experiments per objective vary. The idea is to identify which objectives were met according to the criterion for each. Scores from this type of measurement are typically converted to grades by one of two methods:

- A checklist indicates which objectives the student "passed."
- Grades are defined as the percentage of objectives "passed." For example, the achievement of a student who "passed" at least 90 percent of objectives is graded "highly competent," at least 80 percent but less than 90 percent is graded "competent," at least 70 percent but less than 80 percent is graded "marginally competent," and less than 70 percent is graded "incompetent."

My name is _____. The date is _____.

I plan to accomplish the following tasks via a combination of mathematics portfolio projects during this the _____ term of the school year:

A. Demonstrate that I have made insightful associations between the following two mathematical topics:

_____

      from the current term

and

_____

from the prior term or (if the current term is the 1st, then a previous mathematics course)

My plan for accomplishing this is to do the following:

_____

_____

_____

_____

using the following mode of communication (circle one):

| Videotaped presentation | Expository essay | Computer-based presentation | Poster display illustration |

Other (explain) _____

B. Demonstrate that I have made insightful associations between the following mathematical topic:

_____

      from the current term

and the following topic from the _____ course that I am taking:

_____

      from the current term

My plan for accomplishing this is to do the following:

_____

_____

_____

_____

ILLUSTRATION 3.14

Proposed Student-Planning Form for a Term's Portfolio Project

(Continued)

ILLUSTRATION 3.14 (Continued)

using the following mode of communication (circle one):

Videotaped	Expository	Computer-based	Poster display
presentation	essay	presentation	illustration

Other (explain) _____

C. Demonstrate that I have applied the following mathematical content:

_____

from the current term

to the following situation from my own real-life:

_____

_____

My plan for accomplishing this is to do the following:

_____

_____

_____

_____

using the following mode of communication (circle one):

Videotaped	Expository	Computer-based	Poster display
presentation	essay	presentation	illustration

Other (explain) _____

D. Demonstrate that I possess insights into the historical foundations of the following mathematical topic:

_____

from the current term

My plan for accomplishing this is to do the following:

_____

_____

_____

_____

using the following mode of communication (circle one):

Videotaped	Expository	Computer-based	Poster display
presentation	essay	presentation	illustration

Other (explain) _____.

ILLUSTRATION 3.14 (Continued)

E. Demonstrate that I have applied the following class of technology:

_____

to accomplish the following mathematical task related to the current term:

_____

_____

My plan for accomplishing this is to do the following:

_____

_____

_____

_____

using the following mode of communication (circle one):

| Videotaped presentation | Expository essay | Computer-based presentation | Poster display illustration |

Other (explain)   _____

Thus, I will be conducting _____ portfolio projects this term.

Signed by me _____ and my teacher:

_____ / _____ (date)

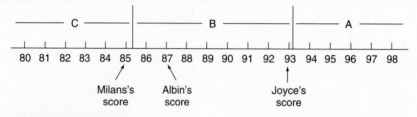

ILLUSTRATION 3.15

Comparison of Three Grades Determined by the Traditional Percentage Method

NORM-REFERENCED GRADING

Classical Curve Grading

Classical curve grading has been somewhat popular in postsecondary schools since the 1930s. This method is based on the assumption that grades should reflect how scores rank in comparison to all scores from the measurement. However, it is tenable only for extremely large groups of students (e.g., 500 or more). If the distribution of scores follows a bell-shaped, normal curve, the scores are ranked from lowest to highest and the following criteria are used (see Illustration 3.16):

A's are assigned to the highest 7 percent of the scores.
B's are assigned to the next 24 percent of the scores.
C's are assigned to the middle 38 percent of the scores.
D's are assigned to the next 24 percent of the scores.
F's are assigned to the lowest 7 percent of the scores.

The Visual Inspection Method

One of the more commonly recommended processes for assigning letter grades to measurement scores is the visual inspection method (Smith & Adams, 1972). The process is as follows:

1. Draw a number line that encompasses the range of the scores. For example, if the lowest score is 5 and the highest is 44, the segment of the number line in Illustration 3.17 would suffice.
2. Graph the frequency distribution of the scores onto the line as shown in Illustration 3.18.
3. Identify gaps or significant breaks in the distribution.
4. Assign a letter grade to each cluster of scores appearing between gaps. If, for example, you choose to define C as average, the cluster containing the middle score might be assigned the grade C. Or you may choose to sample some of the students' responses from a particular cluster and decide the grade for that cluster based on the quality of the responses in the sample. In this method, every score within the same cluster is given the same grade. Illustration 3.19 depicts one possible assignment of grades to scores from Illustration 3.18.

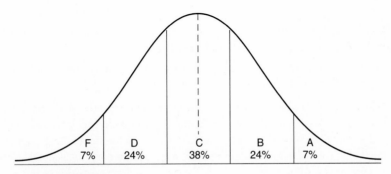

ILLUSTRATION 3.16

Classical Curve Grading Scale for Extremely Large Number of Normally Distributed Scores

ILLUSTRATION 3.17

Segment of Number Line for Use with Visual Inspection Grading
for Score Between 5 and 44

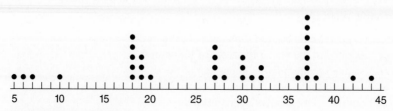

ILLUSTRATION 3.18

Sample Scores and Frequency Distribution

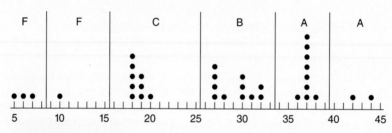

ILLUSTRATION 3.19

Example of Scores from Illustration 3.18 Assigned Grades Via Visual
Inspection

COMPROMISE GRADING

A Conflict Between the Theoretical and the Practical

Teachers who are introduced to the visual inspection method readily recognize the following
advantages it has over the traditional percentage method:

- Measurements can be designed to include challenging prompts for students with more
  sophisticated levels of achievement without fear that too many students will receive low
  grades. The difficulty of the measurement can be factored into the grading scheme.
- Scores that are not markedly different from one another are not assigned different grades;
  measurement error is recognized.

However, teachers tend to reject the visual inspection method because of the following:

- Establishing criteria for A, B, C, D, and F after a measurement has been administered does
  not seem to be as objective as having predetermined cutoff points (e.g., 70 percent for passing), which students can be aware of before being subjected to the measurement.

- Norm-referenced grading methods encourage competition and discourage cooperation among students more than do criterion-referenced methods.
- Scores often fail to fall into convenient clusters with significantly large enough gaps between different groupings as required by the visual inspection method. The distribution in Illustration 3.20 is a possibility.

A Resolution

The method I suggest has the two advantages of the visual inspection method while obviating its three weaknesses. This method is a *compromise* between the traditional percentage and the visual inspection methods and is implemented as follows:

1. As with traditional percentage grading, establish cutoff points for each letter grade before administration of the measurement. However there are two differences:

   A. To allow for the use of a measurement that includes some prompts that will challenge students with sophisticated achievement levels, you are free to set unconventionally low the cutoff points for A, B, C, D, and F. Illustration 3.21, for example, presents possible criteria for a measurement designed to produce an average score of 40 out of a possible 80.

   B. The cutoff point for each letter grade is established with the understanding that there is a buffer or in-between zone between each letter grade category. For example:

   > In Illustration 3.22, to be assigned a definite B, a score would have to be at least 54 and no greater than 66. For a definite C, the score would be between 34 and 46 inclusive. Scores greater than 46 but less than 54 would fall in the "C or B" category.

   > You decide the cutoff points and the size of the in-between zones. A statistical routine for determining the size of these zones is explained in Chapter 16. However, just creating a little distance to account for at least some measurement error is recommended here.

2. Assign in-between grades to scores that fall between the definite grade intervals. For example:

   > Using Illustration 3.22, a score of 51 falls in the "C or B" category. Final determination of whether the higher or lower grade prevails depends on results from other measurements (e.g., an interview in which the student is prompted to elaborate on some of her or his responses from the original measurement). You may also have the option of simply letting the grade remain in limbo between the two letter grades and then factoring the in-between grade into your final assignment of a grade on the periodic report.

Point and Counterpoint

The compromise method is criticized for two reasons:

- Some teachers are uncomfortable with scores falling within the buffer zones. They want clear lines of demarcation between grades.
- Unconventionally challenging prompts may lead students to be frustrated, because students' scores will be lower than with tests used in conjunction with traditional percentage grading.

It would be convenient to have clear lines of demarcation between letter grades with no scores falling within buffer zones. However, the state of the art of evaluating student achievement is not advanced to the point where precision measurement is possible. Small differences

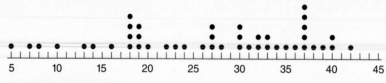

ILLUSTRATION 3.20

Inconvenient Score Distribution for Use with Visual Inspection
Grading

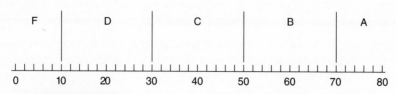

ILLUSTRATION 3.21

Example of Letter-Grade Cutoff Points Used with Compromise
Grading

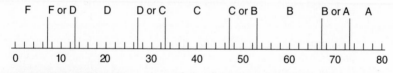

ILLUSTRATION 3.22

Example of Letter-Grade Cutoff Points with In-Between Zones
for Compromise Grading

between scores are simply not meaningful; measurement error is too great. The educational community needs to recognize this fact.

Regarding the second criticism, there may be some pedagogical disadvantages to including challenging prompts, and in some circumstances they should not be included. However, once your students become accustomed to responding to challenging prompts, you can use such mini-experiments as tools to lead them to more advanced achievement levels. This is especially true once they have experiences with challenging prompts for purposes of formative feedback. In other words, they get used to these challenges in situations where the results aren't used for summative evaluations. Then when it is time for a measurement for purposes of making summative evaluations, they are accustomed to struggling with challenging prompts.

ASSIGNING GRADES FOR A SCHOOL TERM

CONDENSING INFORMATION

Put yourself in Ms. Fisher's position in Case 2.15. When you looked at Illustration 2.29 and analyzed Heiko's responses to the Unit–17 test prompts, you used Illustration 2.30's scoring form to take the information you gained from the analysis and reduce it to a single number, namely 45. Much of the knowledge about what Heiko learned from Unit 17 that you gained from analyzing his responses is not retained by that score. When the memory of exactly what Heiko wrote fades and you're left with the number 45 in your roll book or computer file, you no longer have a detailed record of Heiko's learning. At best, you have a number you can compare to other numbers. For example, Jerome's score of 67, Linda's score of 47, and Dawnette's score of 31 provide some indication that Jerome achieved Unit 17's goal to a greater degree than did Heiko, Heiko achieved it to about the same degree as Linda, and Heiko achieved it to greater degree than did Dawnette. The disadvantage of this quantifying process is that more measurement information is lost than retained; the advantage is that measurement results become more manageable.

Continuing in Ms. Fisher's role, if you take Heiko's score of 45 and convert it to a letter grade such as a C (e.g., by the compromise method), now you've condensed the information even further. For example, if you assigned scores between 40 and 50 the grade C, then the fact that Linda's score was slightly higher than Heiko's is lost in the conversion from scores to grades. Furthermore, information is condensed even more when you derive a single report-card grade by combining the C from Heiko's Unit–17 posttest with grades converted from other measurement results.

A wealth of information about students' learning is squeezed out and discarded in the process of converting empirical observations to measurement results to scores to grades and then finally grades to a single report-card grade.

This information-destroying process is necessary if term grades are to be reported. A question for you to address is how should you convert grades derived from measurement scores to a single grade to be included on a periodic report card.

WEIGHTING GOALS AND WEIGHTING MEASUREMENT RESULTS

First of all, you need to decide what variables you want to consider in determining the grade you will report for a student's achievement. If the grade is supposed to reflect achievement of the learning goals for the units you taught during the reporting period, then I suggest that the grade should be influenced only by your summative evaluations of her or his achievement of each one of those learning goals. Consider Case 3.11, which takes you back to the time when Ms. Fisher planned the U.S. history course for which unit titles are listed in Illustration 2.8.

CASE 3.11

Before the school year begins, Ms. Fisher develops a syllabus for her U.S. history course. She plans to use the syllabus to communicate expectations for the course to students on opening day. She views the syllabus as somewhat of a contract between her and the students by which she agrees to help them achieve certain goals and they agree to cooperate by complying with certain standards of conduct and engaging in planned lessons. She also wants to publicize the bases by which she'll assign grades for achievement of learning goals. Thus, in one part of the syllabus she includes the three sections shown in Illustration 3.23.

Ms. Fisher devoted considerable thought to developing the formula for addressing the question "How will your grade be determined?" as shown in Illustration 3.23. School grading policy requires her to assign U.S. History grades for both the first and second semesters. The two semester grades are not to be combined into a single course grade. But she determines how to assign the semester grades. She decided, for example, that only scores from measurements relevant to student achievement of course goals would influence grades. She would not factor in other variables such as attention to homework, class participation, or cooperation. Besides unit tests, she also decided to have midsemester and semester tests that

WHAT WILL YOU LEARN FROM THIS CLASS?

Each unit will either introduce you to a new historical topic or extend your understanding of a previous topic. During the unit you will:

- Discover an idea or relationship

- Add to your ability to use historical methods

- Acquire new information or add depth of understanding to previously acquired information

- Extend your ability to use the lesson of history to address today's problems

The course is organized into the following 22 units:

1. Looking Ahead in Light of Past Lessons; Historical Methods
2. The First Americans, Exploration, and Colonization
3. A New Nation
4. The U.S.Constitution and the New Republic
5. Expansion
6. The Civil War and Reconstruction Eras
7. Emergence of Industrial America, New Frontiers
8. Urban Society and Gilded-Age Politics
9. Protests and the Progressive Movement
10. Expansionism
11. World War I
12. The Roaring Twenties
13. The Great Depression and the New Deal
14. A Search for Peace and World War II
15. A Cold Peace
16. The Politics of Conflict and Hope
17. The Civil Rights Movement
18. The Vietnam War
19. Dirty Politics
20. Toward a Global (and Cleaner) Society
21. The New Nationalism
22. Extending What You've Learned Into a New Century

Units 1-12 are planned for the first semester. Units 13-22 are planned for the second semester.

HOW WILL YOU KNOW WHEN YOU'VE LEARNED HISTORY?

Everyone knows as least some history, but no one ever learns it completely. History is being discovered. You will use what you

ILLUSTRATION 3.23

Three Sections Taken from the U.S. History Course Syllabus Ms. Fisher Distributed on the First Day of Class

(Continued)

ILLUSTRATION 3.23 (Continued)

learn in this course to further develop your ability to apply the lessons of history to everyday decision-making.

The question is not whether or not you've learned history, but how well you are learning it. During this course, you will be given feedback on your progress through comments Ms. Fisher makes about work you complete, scores you achieve on brief tests, and the grades you achieved based on unit, midsemester, and semester tests.

HOW WILL YOUR GRADE FOR THE COURSE BE DETERMINED?

Your grade for the first semester will be based on the results of 12 unit tests, a midsemester test scheduled between the sixth and seventh units, and a semester test. Your scores on these tests will influence your first semester grade according to the following scale:

- The 12 unit tests 60%

    distributed as follows:
    ```
    Unit  1 ....... 3%
    Unit  2 ....... 9%
    Unit  3 ....... 5%
    Unit  4 ....... 8%
    Unit  5 ....... 5%
    Unit  6 ....... 5%
    Unit  7 ....... 3%
    Unit  8 ....... 3%
    Unit  9 ....... 5%
    Unit 10 ....... 3%
    Unit 11 ....... 4%
    Unit 12 ....... 7%
    ```

- The midsemester test 15%

- The semester test 25%

Your grade for the second semester will be based on the results of 10 unit tests, a midsemester test scheduled between the seventeenth and eighteenth units, and a semester test. Your scores on these tests will influence your second semester grade according to the following scale:

- The 10 unit tests 60%

    distributed as follows:
    ```
    Unit 13 ....... 6%
    Unit 14 ....... 6%
    Unit 15 ....... 6%
    Unit 16 ....... 6%
    Unit 17 ....... 9%
    ```

ILLUSTRATION 3.23 *(Continued)*

```
                        Unit 18 ....... 8%
                        Unit 19 ....... 3%
                        Unit 20 ....... 3%
                        Unit 21 ....... 3%
                        Unit 22 .......10%


    ■   The midsemester test ................ 15%


    ■   The semester test ................... 25%
```

would encourage students to synthesize learning from the different units. She believes these high school students need a midsemester check on how well they interrelate content from various units, rather than waiting for over 18 weeks to think about more than one unit at a time. Furthermore, she believes these synthesis measures are more important than any one measure of a single unit goal. Thus, she weighted the midsemester and semester test more than any one of the unit tests. Because she plans for the semester test to be more comprehensive than the midsemester one, and because she wants to emphasize end-of-the semester achievement more than beginning-of-the-semester achievement, she weights the semester test more than the midsemester one.

Because she considers some unit goals to be more important than others, she weighted the unit tests differently. For example, when determining the percentage figures for the second semester's unit tests, she thought, "I have 10 units, 13 through 22. The 10 unit grades are to influence the semester grade by 60 percent; thus, if all the units were equally important, I'd weight each unit grade 6 percent (since $0.60 \div 10 = 0.06$). But some of these units are more critical to what I want them to accomplish in the second semester than others. Unit 22 on extending lessons from the past into the twenty-first century is the most important one. I should weight that one about twice as much as most of the rest. If I put Unit 22 up to 10 percent, I'll have to find 4 percentage points from the rest. Units 19, 20, and 21 really go together—we'll be taking less time with each of those—they're almost transitional units—I could half the weight for each one of those, make them 3 percent each. That gives me the 4 percent extra for Unit 22 and 5 percent more to play with. Unit 17 is really a big deal; I want to weight that heavily—but still less than Unit 22. Okay, . . ."

After deciding on the weights shown in Illustration 3.23, Ms. Fisher made some decisions about how she would convert test scores to test grades and the set of test grades to a single semester grade. She decided to use the compromise method to convert each test score to the possible 12 letter grades specified by the school's grading policy (i.e., A, A–, B+, B, B–, C+, C, C–, D+, D, D–, and F). Then she uses the weights published in her syllabus as shown in Illustration 3.23 to reduce the test grades to a single semester grade by the following process (displayed for the second semester):

To do computations with the 12 possible letter grades, she substitutes numerical values as follows:

A	→ 11	B–	→ 7	D+	→ 3
A–	→ 10	C+	→ 6	D	→ 2
B+	→ 9	C	→ 5	D–	→ 1
B	→ 8	C–	→ 4	F	→ 0

For each student, the numerical values for the grades from the 10 unit tests as well as from the midsemester and semester tests are multiplied by the respective percentages shown in Illustration 3.23. For example, Heiko's second-semester test grades are D for Unit 12, B– for Unit 14, C– for Unit 15, C– for Unit 16, C for Unit 17, C+ for the midsemester test, A– for Unit 18, B for Unit 19, C+ for Unit 20, C+ for Unit 21, B– for Unit 22, and B- for the semester test. She computed his second semester grade as follows:

Unit 13 test:	D $\rightarrow$ 2	$\rightarrow$	2 $\times$ .06	=.12
Unit 14 test:	B- $\rightarrow$ 7	$\rightarrow$	7 $\times$ .06	=.42
Unit 15 test:	C- $\rightarrow$ 4	$\rightarrow$	4 $\times$ .06	=.24
Unit 16 test:	C- $\rightarrow$ 4	$\rightarrow$	4 $\times$ .06	=.24
Unit 17 test:	C $\rightarrow$ 5	$\rightarrow$	5 $\times$ .09	=.45
Midsemester test:	C+ $\rightarrow$ 6	$\rightarrow$	6 $\times$ .15	=.90
Unit 18 test:	A- $\rightarrow$ 10	$\rightarrow$	10 $\times$ .08	=.80
Unit 19 test:	B $\rightarrow$ 8	$\rightarrow$	8 $\times$ .03	=.24
Unit 20 test:	C+ $\rightarrow$ 6	$\rightarrow$	6 $\times$ .03	=.18
Unit 21 test:	C+ $\rightarrow$ 6	$\rightarrow$	6 $\times$ .03	=.18
Unit 22 test:	B- $\rightarrow$ 7	$\rightarrow$	7 $\times$ .10	=.70
Semester test:	B- $\rightarrow$ 7	$\rightarrow$	7 $\times$ .25	=1.75

Sum   6.22

The sum of the far right column is 6.22, which converts to a C for the semester, because 6.22 rounded to the nearest whole number is 6.

Ms. Fisher records "C" for the second-semester U.S. History on Heiko's report card. Of course, she used her computer for the computations.

The CD-ROM disk that accompanies this textbook includes a program that facilitates employing a process similar to the one Ms. Fisher used in Case 3.11. By following the instructions from the CD-ROM, you can direct your computer to do the computations and display the resulting grades based on the weights you choose for the various measurements and test grades.

DERIVING ONE GRADE FROM A SET OF GRADES

In Case 3.11, Ms. Fisher derived Heiko's second semester grade from the set of 12 test grades using what is known as the *weighted-averaging method*. By using the *weighted-averaging method*, you control the relative emphasis of each unit and each measurement on the report-card grade. Of course, with the weighted-averaging method, you could choose to weight all units and all measurements results equally; then the final grade is determined by the simple average of the numerical values of the grades. As the teacher responsible for designing curricula, courses, units, lessons, and measurements and for making and communicating summative evaluations, you are in the best position to decide the relative importance of each unit and the relative weights of each measurement.

More commonly used than the weighted-averaging method is the *percentage-averaging* method. The *percentage-averaging* method is not recommended here, but as a professional educator you should be familiar with commonly practiced methods. In Case 3.12, Ms. Barton uses the percentage averaging method.

CASE 3.12

During the semester, Ms. Barton administers nine unit tests and one final to her French class; the maximum possible score on the tests are 40 for Unit 1, 35 for Unit 2, 56 for Unit 3, 60 for Unit 4, 40 for Unit 5, 44 for Unit 6, 30 for Unit 7, 25 for Unit 8, 55 for Unit 9, and 85 for the final. Furthermore, students can earn up to 60 points for homework and 50 points for class participation. She wants all of these results, including the points for homework and points for class participation, to be equally weighted in the derivation of the final grade, with the exception of the final test. She wants to put twice as much emphasis on it as she does on any other one measurement. Thus, she plans to count the final score twice in her computations of the final grade. The scores for one of her students, Marcos, are as follows:

Measurement	Score/MaxPossible	% Score
Unit 1	35/40	88%
Unit 2	33/35	94%
Unit 3	44/56	79%
Unit 4	55/60	92%
Unit 5	33/40	83%
Unit 6	37/44	84%
Unit 7	30/30	100%
Unit 8	20/25	80%
Unit 9	48/55	87%
Homework	45/60	75%
Participation	50/50	100%
Final (once)	66/85	78%
Final (twice)	66/85	78%
	Sum	1118%

Average of the 13 percentage scores = 1118% ÷ 13 = 86%

As shown by the computation, Ms. Barton averaged the 13 percentage scores to obtain an overall percentage of 86 percent. Using a traditional-percentage grading scale of 94–100% for A, 86–93% for B, 78–85% for C, 70–77% for D, and 0–69% for F, Ms. Barton reports a B for Marcos's French grade for the semester.

With the percentage-averaging method, you choose which variables to plug into the process; for example, unlike Ms. Barton, you choose not to include "points" for homework or participation. You may want to weight the final differently (i.e., counting it three times instead of twice) and the percentage-averaging method does not require you to use traditional percentage grading as Ms. Barton used. However, if you use a norm-referenced score-to-grade conversion (e.g., visual inspection) or one that is only partially norm-referenced (e.g., the compromise method), then note that converting test scores to percentage scores will not equalize the relative weights of the different test scores on the final grade. As explained in Chapter 14, when you make norm-referenced evaluations, test scores with greater variability will be more influential on grades than test scores with less variability. By converting test scores to percentage scores, differences in variability are usually exaggerated rather than diminished. At this point in time, you need not understand why all this is true. However, keep in mind that there are some major drawbacks to the percentage-averaging method for assigning report grades.

DEVELOPING A SYSTEM THAT WORKS FOR YOU AND YOUR STUDENTS

There seems to be no completely satisfactory system for reporting summative evaluations of student achievement. Working within the parameters of your school's grading policy, you need to decide what is best for your unique situation. Whatever you decide, consider incorporating a variety of communication mechanisms, including regular conferences with students and their parents, individual student portfolios, and periodic reports. But no combination of methods for communicating summative evaluations can be any better than the accuracy of the evaluations themselves. To be accurate, evaluations need to be based on valid measurements. Subsequent chapters of this book are devoted to helping you develop your talent for designing, selecting, and interpreting valid measurements of students' learning.

SYNTHESIS ACTIVITIES FOR CHAPTER 3

1. The following list of teachers' comments communicate evaluations of students rather than summative "evaluations of students' achievement:

   "Arnell is antisocial."

   "Tabrina is a happy child."

   "Adreth is the most coordinated athlete I've ever coached."

   "Hector is quite gifted."

   "Gwen isn't scientifically inclined; she must be right-brained."

   Reword each of the statements in the above list so that instead of reflecting an evaluation of the student, it reflects a summative evaluation of what the student achieved, learned, or did. To focus these statements on what students do rather than who they are, you will need to use your imagination and include something about what students did or accomplished that are not in the original statements. For the first statement, for example, you might ask yourself, "What behaviors might Arnell have exhibited to lead the teacher to say he is antisocial?" One possible response is, "Arnell assaulted classmates at least twice this year, and he was caught breaking into lockers in the hall." That information suggests that Arnell exhibited antisocial behavior. Possible comments reflecting summative evaluations of Arnell's behavior rather than Arnell himself might be, "Arnell exhibited antisocial behaviors" or "Arnell needs to demonstrate that his behavior no longer poses a threat to the safety of me or other students before I will allow him to enroll in any of my classes."

   Exchange your reworded statements with those of a colleague. Discuss issues stimulated by your shared work.

2. Reconsider the following statement from this book's section "Violations of Professional Trust":

   "Trust between you and your students is an important ingredient for a classroom climate that is conducive to learning. Do not violate that trust by communicating your summative evaluations of student achievement to people who lack either the need or the authorization to be privileged to those evaluations."

   With a colleague, discuss why you agree or disagree with that statement. Think of examples in which a teacher's gossiping about students' achievements or communicating summative evaluations of students' work to unauthorized persons led students to mistrust the teacher and, consequently, interfered with how well that teacher was able to collect formative feedback during learning activities.

3. Interview at least five teachers. Ask each to explain (1) what he or she does to communicate summative evaluations of students' achievement to the students and to their parents, (2) the grade reporting system used in the school and what he or she likes and dislikes about it, (3) the purposes for which grades are used by teachers, by parents, by students, and by school administrators, (4) what the purposes of grades

should be, and (5) how, if at all, he or she converts test scores to letter grades. With colleagues who interviewed other teachers, share and discuss the responses obtained from the interviews.

4. Interview at least five students and five parents. Ask each to explain (1) the grade reporting system used in the school and what he or she likes and dislikes about it, (2) the purposes for which grades are used by teachers, by parents, by students, and by school administrators, and (3) what the purposes of grades should be. With colleagues who interviewed other students and parents, share and discuss the responses obtained from the interviews.

5. In Case 3.4, a committee from the Rainbow High School faculty began meeting for the purpose of developing recommendations for the school's grade-reporting system. With four of your colleagues, form a committee to develop recommendations for the summative-evaluation reporting system for a school with which you and your colleagues are familiar.

6. Write an essay, about one page long, explaining the relative advantages and disadvantages of using the visual inspection method of converting scores to grades instead of the traditional percentage method, and the relative advantages and disadvantages of using the compromise method instead of the visual inspection method. Exchange your essay with that of a colleague and discuss issues stimulated by reading one another's explanations.

7. Following is a list of teachers' comments reflecting summative evaluations of students' achievements; distinguish the comments reflecting norm-referenced evaluations from those reflecting criterion-referenced evaluations:

"Brooks types as efficiently as any seventh-grader I've ever had in class."
"Clarence's behavior patterns are not yet to the point where I think it's safe for him to return to class."
"Marlene has learned to work with linear equations well enough to begin work with quadratic equations."
"Charlotte gets out of the blocks quicker than any sprinter we have. She should run the first leg of the relay."
"I didn't think a score that's almost a full standard deviation below the average of all the scores justified a grade higher than C."
"No score greater than 75 percent of the maximum possible score should be assigned a failing grade."

Exchange your responses categorizing the above statements with those of a colleague. In a discussion, resolve differences between the two sets of responses.

8. If you already incorporate individualized student portfolios in your teaching, write an essay, about one page long, explaining how you use them for purposes of formative feedback and for communicating summative evaluations. If you don't yet use individualized student portfolios in your teaching, but you plan to, write an essay, about one page long, explaining your plans for using them and how they'll be used for purposes of formative feedback and for communicating summative evaluations. If you do not use or plan to use individualized student portfolios in your teaching, write an essay, about one page long, explaining why you are choosing not to use them. If you are undecided about using individualized student portfolios in your teaching, write an essay, about one page long, explaining the advantages and disadvantages of using them in your teaching situation.

Exchange your essay with that of a colleague and discuss issues stimulated by the reading of one another's explanations.

9. Reconsider the following statement from this book's section "A Recommendation":

> "The recommendation here is that if you want to use a grade to communicate your evaluation of a student's achievement of specified learning goals, then you should base that grade only on measurement results that are relevant to those learning goals. To positively reinforce engagement in learning activities (e.g., with collaborative working groups, in-class participation, and doing homework), apply strategies demonstrating the link between engagement and achievement as was done in Cases 3.5, 3.6, 2.15, 2.10, 1.4, and 2.13."

With a colleague, discuss why you agree or disagree with that recommendation. Make sure to discuss the strategies employed by the teachers in Cases 3.5, 3.6, 2.15, 2.10, 1.4, and 2.13.

10. Write an essay, about one page long, explaining the relative advantages and disadvantages of using the weighted-averaging method for deriving one grade from a set of grades instead of the percentage-averaging method. Exchange your essay with that of a colleague and discuss issues stimulated by the reading of one another's explanations.

11. Get together with three colleagues. Have one of your colleagues role-play one of your student's parents with whom you will be engaging in a conference for the purpose of communicating summative evaluations of the student's achievement. Have a second colleague play the role of the student. Plan for the conference, keeping in mind the six suggestions from this chapter's section "Student-Parent-Teacher Conferences." Now, hold the conference while your fourth colleague videotapes it. Afterwards, use the videotape recording to analyze the way you communicated. Discuss with your colleagues how the way you communicated adhered to the last two suggestions from the section "Student-Parent-Teacher Conferences."

12. Insert the CD-ROM disk that accompanies this textbook into the CD-ROM drive of your computer. Follow the instructions for engaging the "grading" tutorial.

TRANSITIONAL ACTIVITY FROM CHAPTER 3 TO CHAPTER 4

In discussion with two or more of your colleagues, address the following questions:

1. The following statement is included in this chapter's section "Developing a System that Works for You and Your Students":

> "To be accurate, evaluations need to be based on valid measurements."

What is the difference between a valid and invalid measurement?

2. Can't a measurement that's valid for one situation be invalid for another? Why or why not?

3. What is the relationship between measurement validity and measurement error?

4. What factors should be considered when designing or selecting measurements to use with students?

The Art of Making Informed Decisions About Student Learning

◆━ GOAL OF CHAPTER 4

Chapter 4 is designed to provide you with a framework for analyzing the quality of measurements and to lead you to develop criteria for designing and selecting measurements you use with your students. More specifically, the objectives are as follows:

A. You will explain why the value of a measurement depends on the validity of its results and its usability (discover a relationship)[1] 15%[2].

B. You will explain why the validity of measurement results depends on the measurement's relevance and reliability (discover a relationship)[1] 15%[2].

C. You will explain why the relevance of a measurement depends on its content relevance and its learning-level relevance (discover a relationship)[1] 15%[2].

D. You will explain why the reliability of a measurement depends on the internal consistency of its results, multi-measurement consistency, and its observer consistency (discover a relationship)[1] 15%[2].

E. You will develop criteria for designing and selecting planned measurements and using unplanned measurement results (application)[1] 15%[2].

F. You will consider the influence of measurement error as you use measurement results for formative judgments and summative evaluations (application)[1] 15%[2].

G. You will incorporate the following technical phrases in your working professional vocabulary: "measurement usefulness," "measurement validity," "measurement usability," "measurement relevance," "subject-content relevance," "learning-level relevance," "measurement reliability," "internal consistency," "observer consistency," "intra-observer consistency," "inter-observer consistency," "dichotomous scoring," "weighted scoring," "analytical scoring," "global scoring," "achievement test," "commercially produced test," "standardized test," and "government-mandated core-curriculum test" (comprehension and communication skills)[1] 10%[2].

---

[1]Indicates the learning level of the objective as defined in Chapter 5 of this text. (It is not necessary for you to be concerned with this scheme for categorizing learning levels until you've reached Chapter 5.)
[2]Indicates the relative importance assigned to the objective as explained in Chapter 5 of this text. (It is not necessary for you to be concerned with this weighting method until you've reached Chapter 5.)

INFORMED BY WHAT?

VALID MEASUREMENT RESULTS

Although the teachers in Cases 4.1, 4.2, and 4.3 are faced with nearly identical decisions to make, the measurements they employ to help them make the decisions are quite different. Compare the three cases and decide whether you prefer the measurements used in Case 4.1, 4.2, or 4.3.

CASE 4.1

In December, David transfers into Ms. Camacho's fourth-grade class. "I'm very happy you're joining our class," she says. David replies, "I is too. We gotten a new house and I be gotten new friends." Later, Ms. Camacho is deciding how to integrate David into her existing student working groups in language arts. Recalling her conversations with him, she thinks, "David doesn't seem to apply conventional sentence mechanics in his speech. If that carries over into his writing mechanics, then we need to attend to some basic sentence-structure rules. I'll make a measurement to help me assess how well he applies our sentence-mechanics rules to his writing."

Ms. Camacho has the following rules in mind:

1. Every sentence should begin with a capital letter.
2. Sentences should be punctuated so that (a) questions end with question marks, (b) sentences that are not questions end with periods or exclamation points, and (c) commas are used to separate the words or phrases in a series.
3. Complete sentences with a subject and verb should be used instead of fragments.
4. Do not use run-on sentences.
5. The subject and verb should be in agreement with respect to number.
6. The verb's tense should be consistent with the rest of the sentence.
7. Use the correct form of personal pronouns.

For the measurement, Ms. Camacho selects one of the written-response tests from the instructor's supplemental package that accompanies the writing textbook adopted for her class. The test, titled "Sentence Mechanics Test," consists of the following fill-in-the-blank prompts:

1. Every sentence should begin with a _____ letter.
2. A sentence that is a question should end with a _____ _____.
3. A sentence that is not a question should end either with a _____ or an _____ _____.
4. To be complete, a sentence must have a _____ and a _____.
5. A sentence with a plural subject should have a _____ verb.
6. A sentence with a _____ subject should have a singular verb.
7. A sentence telling about something that will happen should be in the _____ tense.
8. A sentence telling about something that is happening should be in the _____ tense.
9. A sentence telling about something that already happened should be in the _____ tense.
10. The plural form of the personal pronoun "I" is _____.

CASE 4.2

In December, Azuma transfers into Ms. De La Hoya's fourth-grade class. "I'm very happy you're joining our class," she says. Azuma replies, "I is too. We gotten a new house and I be gotten new friends." Later, Ms. De La Hoya is deciding how to integrate Azuma into her existing student working groups in language arts. Recalling her conversations with him, she thinks, "Azuma doesn't seem to apply conventional sentence mechanics in his speech. If that carries over into his writing mechanics, then we need to attend to some basic sentence-structure rules. I'll make some measurements to help me assess how well he applies our sentence-mechanics rules to his writing."

Ms. De La Hoya has the same seven rules in mind as did Ms. Camacho in Case 4.1.

For one of her mini-experiments, Ms. De La Hoya directs Azuma as follows: "Please take this paper and pen. Use them to write a letter to me. In the letter, tell me how it feels to move from one city to another—the way you moved from New Orleans to here in Reno. Make the letter about one page long. Take your time. Don't rush so you can write very carefully. Thank you."

After school that day, Ms. De La Hoya analyzes Azuma's letter using an observer's rubric for which she makes notes about the writing sample and also records the following data:

1. The number of complete sentences that begin with a capital letter.
2. The number of complete sentences that do not begin with a capital letter.
3. The number of fragments that begin with a capital letter.
4. The number of fragments that do not begin with a capital letter.
5. The number of complete sentences with appropriate ending punctuation.
6. The number of complete sentences without appropriate ending punctuation.
7. The number of series of words or phrases properly separated with commas.
8. The number of series of words or phrases not properly separated with commas.
9. The number of run-on sentences.
10. The number of subject-verb pairs that agree with respect to number.
11. The number of subject-verb pairs that do not agree with respect to number.
12. The number of verbs expressed in the appropriate tense for the sentence or fragment.
13. The number of verbs expressed in the inappropriate tense for the sentence or fragment.
14. The number of personal pronouns expressed in the correct form.

CASE 4.3

In December, Moses transfers into Ms. Webb's fourth-grade class. "I'm very happy you're joining our class," she says. Moses replies, "I is too. We gotten a new house and I be gotten new friends." Later, Ms. Webb is deciding how to integrate Moses into her existing student working groups in language arts. Recalling her conversations with him, she thinks, "Moses doesn't seem to apply conventional sentence mechanics in his speech. If that carries over into his writing mechanics, then we need to attend to some basic sentence-structure rules. I'll make some measurements to help me assess how well he applies our sentence-mechanics rules to his writing."

Ms. Webb has the same seven rules in mind as did Ms. Camacho in Case 4.1.

She decides that it is important to study how Moses' application of the sentence-mechanics rules have developed within the past year. Thus, from Moses and his parents, she requests examples of his writing from the past year. Having just moved from across the country, they are unable to locate any such samples. So she contacts his previous two teachers from his former city, requesting them to send copies of Moses' writing samples they still might have on file. If and when she obtains them, she plans to use the same observer's rubric with them that Ms. De La Hoya used in Case 4.2. In the meantime, she administers a commercially produced, standardized writing-diagnostic test to Moses. It costs $25; Moses spends two hours taking it over a three-day period. Ms. Webb spends 90 minutes scoring his responses.

In Case 4.4, Kisha and Elwin discuss their comparisons of the measurements from Cases 4.1, 4.2, and 4.3.

CASE 4.4

Elwin:	"First of all, all three teachers used the unplanned measurement of hearing the students' responses to 'I'm very happy you're joining our class.' Hearing how the students spoke influenced them to suspect a need."
Kisha:	"Then all three decided to make formative judgments regarding the students' application of the seven rules. The case differed at that point—with differences in how they tried to measure the students' application of the seven rules in their own writing."
Elwin:	"And that's the point where the comparisons become a no-brainer. Ms. De La Hoya's measurements are a lot more useful than the other two teachers."
Kisha:	"What do you mean by 'useful'?"
Elwin:	"That test Ms. Camacho used doesn't seem like it measures what she really wanted to measure. She wanted to make a judgment about how well David applied the rules to his writing. Yet the 'Sentence Mechanics Test' didn't even prompt him to write sentences—only to recall words from the rules. That's not a measure of applying the rules. On the other hand, in Case 4.2, Ms. De La Hoya prompted him to produce a writing sample that gave Azuma an opportunity to respond with written sentences. She analyzed his sentences with a rubric that was relevant to how he applied the rules—not memorized the wording of the rules."
Kisha:	"I agree. You know, David might be able to apply the rules in his own writing without actually knowing which words to fill in those blanks. Or he could have those rules memorized without being able to apply them. I definitely go with Case 4.2's measurement over Case 4.1's. But tell me why you preferred Case 4.2's over Case 4.3's. Ms. Webb planned to collect even more extensive writing samples for Moses than Ms. De La Hoya did for Azuma."
Elwin:	"Yea, great! But don't you think that was a bit of overkill? Who has the time to do all that—writing to another city and then giving the expensive, time-consuming standardized diagnostic test! What she did just isn't practical. I'm not saying it wouldn't give good information; it's just too much trouble."
Kisha:	"Of course, Webb's agenda was a little different from the other two teachers'; she was the only one who mentioned the student's development of application skill over time. But you're absolutely right; what she was trying is way too impractical for me. Also, we don't know if that reading diagnostic test is even relevant to her objective about application of the seven rules. Okay, let me see if I can sum up your points. You think the test Ms. Camacho used would fail to provide meaningful information relevant to how well David applies the rules, whereas the other two teachers' measurements have the potential of providing meaningful information for their purposes. However, no matter how on-target Ms. Webb's measurements are, they're not worth all the time, trouble, and money they take."
Elwin:	"Just not cost effective."
Kisha:	"So we both prefer to do what Ms. De La Hoya did in Case 4.2."

Elwin and Kisha appear to favor the measurement in Case 4.2 over the one in Case 4.1 because they judged Ms. De La Hoya's measurement to be *more valid* than Ms. Camacho's. A measurement is more or less *valid* depending on how well the measurement's results provide accurate information pertinent to the particular decision to be made. In Cases 4.1, 4.2, and 4.3, the teachers planned to use the measurement results to influence their judgments about how well students applied certain rules in their writing. Elwin and Kisha thought Ms. De La Hoya's measurement would produce more accurate, pertinent information than Ms. Camacho's.

As explained in Chapter 1's section "Measurement Error," the results of a measurement are dependent on both (1) the correct answer to the question which the measurement is being used to decide, and (2) measurement error. In Case 4.1 for example, David's responses to the prompts on the Sentence Mechanics Test are influenced by (1) how well he can actually apply the seven rules in his writing (i.e., the correct answer to the question Ms. Camacho is addressing) as well as (2) measurement error. Elwin and Kisha suggested that a major source of measurement error in the Sentence Mechanics Test is that it did not prompt David to produce a writing sample that Ms. Camacho could analyze with respect to application of the seven rules. Now, Azuma's responses to Ms. De La Hoya's prompt in Case 4.2 are also influenced by (1) how well he can actually apply the rules as well as (2) measurement error. Possible sources of measurement error might include the following:

- Azuma may only include declarative sentences in his letter, thus not providing Ms. De La Hoya with an opportunity to observe an appropriate or inappropriate application of a question mark or an exclamation point.
- Azuma may not have included any sentences with words or phrases in a series, thus failing to provide Ms. De La Hoya with an opportunity to observe his application of commas to separate the elements in a series.
- Azuma may have had a headache or been too nervous to write the letter so that it produced a representative sample of his writing.

Of course, there are a myriad of other possible sources of error. However, in Case 4.4, Elwin and Kisha must have thought that measurement error would be less of an influence on Azuma's responses than measurement error would be on David's responses because they predicted that Case 4.2's measurement would be more valid than Case 4.1's. In other words, the *validity of a measurement* depends on the degree to which its results are influenced by measurement error. The greater the influence of measurement error, the less valid the measurement.

USABLE MEASUREMENTS

Elwin and Kisha preferred Case 4.2's measurement to Case 4.1's because they think Case 4.2's will produce more valid results. But why did they prefer Case 4.2's measurement to Ms. Webb's in Case 4.3? When Kisha raised that question in Case 4.4, Elwin did not base his preference on differences in validity but rather on differences in what we will refer to as differences in *usability*. A measurement is *usable* to the degree that it is inexpensive, does not consume time, is easy to administer and score, is safe for students and other personnel, and does not interfere with other activities.

According to Elwin, the cost in terms of time and money was too great for Ms. Webb's measurements to be usable. On the other hand, the Sentence Mechanics Test from Case 4.1 is more usable than Ms. De La Hoya's measurement from Case 4.2 because it was ready-made as well as easier to score and less time consuming for the student to take than Ms. De La Hoya's. Of course, no measurement is perfectly usable. There are always some costs in time, money, and other resources. Similarly, no measurement is perfectly valid. In designing or selecting a measurement for you to use in a particular situation, you have to consider both degree of validity and degree of usability. To be *useful* for the situation, the measurement must have a satisfactory degree of both.

MEASUREMENT VALIDITY

A measurement is *valid* to the same degree that it is both *relevant* and *reliable*. A measurement is *relevant* to the same degree that it provides information that is pertinent to the decision influenced by the measurement's results. A measurement is reliable to the same degree that it can be depended upon to provide non-contradictory information. See Illustration 4.1.

MEASUREMENT RELEVANCE

SUBJECT-CONTENT RELEVANCE

School curricula are typically organized by *subject* areas such as art, health and physical education, foreign language, language arts, mathematics, music, science, social studies, and technology. These broad subjects are often associated with courses. This course structure is even typical for self-contained classrooms with integrated curricula in elementary schools. Look back, for example, in Chapter 2's section "Planning and Organizing for the School Year." In Case 2.2, Ms. Kimura organized the curriculum for her first-graders by the courses and units displayed by Illustration 2.3. Each unit focuses on a particular *subject-content* area of the course. The unit titles are suggestive of the subject-content foci of the units (e.g., according to Illustration 2.3, the subject-content of the first art and music unit is the art in our school; for Unit 10 of the physical education unit, it's fitness games; and for Unit 14 of the science unit, it's rocks).

Whenever you make either a formative judgment or summative evaluation about students' achievement, the achievement about which you are making a decision involves some specific subject-content. The subject-content is identified by the learning goal the student is supposed to achieve. Thus, for a measurement of students' achievement of a learning goal to be *relevant*, the measurement must involve the *subject-matter* identified by the learning goal. Of course, the set of objectives defining a learning goal spells out the subject-matter more clearly than the learning goal alone. Unless the subject-matter is clearly delineated (as it should be by a set of objectives), you are hardly in a position to design or select a measurement that is relevant to student learning.

Re-examine the goal and objectives for Ms. Fisher's U.S. History Unit 17 as listed in Illustration 2.9. With what subject-contents are her students to work as they achieve these objectives? They include the civil-rights related concepts (e.g., de jure segregation), relationships

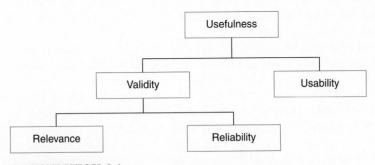

ILLUSTRATION 4.1

Measurement Usefulness Depends on Measurement Validity and Usability; Measurement Validity Depends on Relevance and Reliability

(e.g., effects of segregation on lives), events (e.g., lynching of Emmett Till), legislative acts (e.g., Voting Rights Act of 1965), personalities (e.g., Thurgood Marshall), strategies (e.g., non-violent resistance), organizations (e.g., NAACP), and so forth. Now, re-examine the prompts and observer's rubrics from Ms. Fisher's test appearing in Illustrations 2.28 and 2.30. How well does her test pertain to the subject-content specified by the objectives for Unit 17? Obviously, the test does not attend to all of the subject-contents specified by the objectives. But at least are all the subject-content areas touched upon by the test's prompts and rubrics included in the objectives? The match between the subject-contents of the objectives and the subject-contents of the test is not perfect. Is the disparity so great that it prevents the test from being relevant to students' achievement of the learning goal? That is a question for Ms. Fisher to decide.

The degree to which a measurement's mini-experiments involve students in the subject-contents specified by learning objectives is the degree to which that measurement has *subject-content relevance* for those objectives. *Subject-content relevance* is a necessary, but insufficient condition for measurement relevance. Subject-content relevance is one of two characteristics a measurement must have in order to be relevant. The other is *learning-level relevance*.

LEARNING-LEVEL RELEVANCE

In Case 4.1, Ms. Camacho wanted to make formative judgments regarding how well David *applied* the seven sentence-mechanics rules in his writing. Thus, the subject-content of the implied learning objective is the seven sentence-mechanics rules. Look once again at the prompts on the Sentence Mechanics Test Ms. Camacho planned to use to help her make the formative judgment about David's achievement of that objective. Is there not a reasonably good match between the subject-content with which David must deal on the test and the subject-content of the objective? Both the test and the objective pertain to the seven sentence-mechanics rules. However, in Case 4.4, Elwin and Kisha suggested that the test wasn't relevant to that objective. What was their rationale? They were concerned that the test required David to *recall* words from the seven rules, not *apply* them to his own writing as Ms. Camacho's objective seemed to imply. Elwin and Kisha seem to think that *recalling* a subject-content is not the same mental activity as *applying* that same subject-content. Words such as "apply" and "recall" need to be operationally defined so that we agree on exactly what they mean; we will do that in Chapter 5. For now, note that a learning objective not only specifies a subject-content, but it also specifies a way for students to think about, behave with, or interact with that subject-content. We refer to that aspect of the objective as its *learning level*.

Elwin and Kisha favored the mini-experiment Ms. De La Hoya developed in Case 4.2 because it prompted Azuma to make responses that would be indicative of his application of the sentence-mechanics rules, not his recall of words from the rules.

Throughout your work with this book, you have been attending to differences in learning levels. For example, you put yourself in the place of a first-grade teacher in Case 1.7 who needed to develop mini-experiments for two objectives. Reread Case 1.7 now. Note that both Objective A and B specify the same subject-content, namely addition of one-digit whole numbers. But what is different about the two objectives? Achievement of Objective A requires students to demonstrate why sums of two one-digit whole numbers are what they are (e.g., why $3 + 5 = 8$). Achievement of Objective B, on the other hand, requires students to remember sums of two one-digit whole numbers (e.g., call to mind "8" when prompted by "3 + 5"). The two objectives have different learning levels. That is why when you designed a mini-experiment to be relevant to Objective B, it looked different from the one you designed to be relevant to Objective A. Illustration 1.17 displays the two mini-experiments Kisha designed for those two objectives. Kisha's first mini-experiment listed in Illustration 1.17 appears to be relevant to Objective B because it matches Objective B with respect to both subject-content and learning level. That same first mini-experiment is not relevant to Objective A. However, note that its subject-content does match the subject-content of Objective A; thus, it has content-relevance with respect to Objective A. It fails to be relevant to Objective A because it lacks learning-level relevance with respect to Objective A.

The degree to which a measurement's mini-experiments require students to operate at the learning-levels specified by objectives is the degree to which that measurement has *learning-level relevance* for those objectives. *Learning-level relevance* is a necessary, but insufficient condition for measurement relevance. See Illustration 4.2.

Chapter 5 introduces you to an advanced organizer that facilitates writing objectives so that they clearly specify the subject-contents and learning levels you want your lessons to target.

MEASUREMENT RELIABILITY

INTERNAL CONSISTENCY

Imagine yourself in Case 4.5.

CASE 4.5

You're at a party where a friend of yours, Elija, introduces you to Ramon. While making small talk, Ramon asks you, "Did you see the Starzz-Liberty game on TV last night? It was awesome—double overtime victory for the Starzz on a last-second jump shot by Palmer!" You reply, "No, I missed it. But I wish I had; I love basketball." "Not me," Ramon says, "I find it boring." As you leave the party, you notice Ramon driving away in a car with a bumper sticker announcing, "I'd rather be playing basketball." Curious, you ask Elija, "How well do you know Ramon?" Elija: "We're good buddies—we go way back." You: "Does he like basketball?" Elija: "Not that I know of." Several days later, you receive the following voice-mail message from Ramon: "Hi, this is Ramon. Elija introduced us at the party the other night. I'm going to the Starzz-Comets basketball game on Wednesday. It should be a good one. I have an extra ticket. Care to join me? Let me know if you can make it."

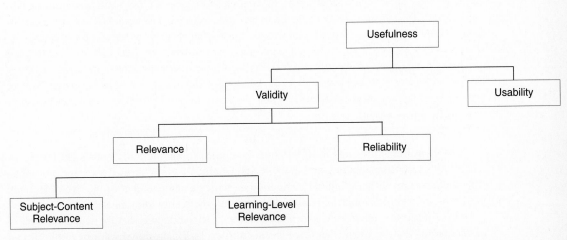

ILLUSTRATION 4.2

Measurement Relevance Depends on Subject-Content Relevance and Learning-Level Relevance

Does or does not Ramon like basketball? Surely, the unplanned measurements you made (i.e., hearing what Ramon said at the party about basketball, seeing his bumper sticker, and listening to his voice-mail message) as well as your planned measurement (i.e., asking Elija about Ramon's interest in basketball) are relevant to the question of whether or not Ramon enjoys basketball. Relevant or not, the results of those measurements leave you perplexed about Ramon's opinion of basketball. The results of the measurements contradict themselves; they are *internally inconsistent*.

A measurement's validity not only depends on its relevance; it also depends on its *reliability*. As previously stated, a measurement is *reliable* to the same degree that it can be depended upon to provide *non-contradictory information*. To be reliable, a measurement must produce *internally consistent* results and have *observer consistency*. The results from your measurements of Ramon's attitude about basketball lacked internal consistency. Consider Case 4.6.

CASE 4.6

Boa, Eddie, and Nancy are students in Ms. Conine's first grade. She needs to make a summative evaluation of their achievement of the goal of a mathematics unit on addition of whole numbers. Two of the five objectives for the unit are as follows:

A. Given two one-digit whole numbers, x and y such that $x + y = z$, students demonstrate why $x + y = z$ (e.g., explain why $3 + 5 = 8$ or $9 + 2 = 11$).

B. Given any two one-digit whole numbers, students recall the sum of those two numbers.

She plans several measurements to help her with the evaluations. One of the measurements is intended to be relevant only to Objectives A and B. She has her classroom aide, Mr. Papunu, administer it individually to the three students; its mini-experiments appear in Illustration 4.3. The resulting scores from the mini-experiments are reported in Illustration 4.4.

Examining Illustration 4.4's results, Ms. Conine thinks, "Boa appears to have progressed nicely with Objective B. He only missed 8 plus 9; that's the most difficult addition fact for most people to remember. He really seems to have achieved Objective A very well. Once students discover why these addition facts work the way they do, they can consistently demonstrate them whether it's 3 plus 1 or 9 plus 6. Okay, now for Eddie. Eddie's results are quite consistent. He got the two easier facts, B–1 and B–2, and missed the more difficult ones for Objective B. His scores for all three of the mini-experiments for Objective A are quite consistent. I don't think Eddie has made much progress toward Objective A. Now for Nancy. These results are too inconsistent to suggest much of anything about Nancy's achievement with Objectives B or A. It's baffling for her not to remember the relatively easy facts from B–1 and B–2 and then remember the more difficult ones for B–3 and B–4. Her scores for the mini-experiments relevant to Objective A are even more perplexing. How could she have scored so high on A–2 and so low on the other two? These results lack internal consistency. I won't let them influence my evaluation of Nancy's achievement of Objectives A and B.

The measurement results in Illustration 4.4 appear to be internally consistent for Boa's and Eddie's responses, but not for Nancy's. Ms. Conine displays shrewd awareness of measurement error by withholding her evaluation of Nancy's achievement of the two objectives until more reliable information is obtained. Overall, the results of a measurement administered to a group of students are internally consistent to the degree that there are more pairs of data points in agreement than there are in conflict. In Illustration 4.4 for example, Boa's score of 9 for A–1 and 9 for A–2 form a consistent, non-contradictory pair. Eddie's scores of 2 for both A–1 and A–2 are also consistent. On the other hand, Nancy's score of 2 for A–1 and 9 for A–2 form an inconsistent, contradictory pair.

Four mini-experiments, B-1, B-2, B-3, and B-4, are intended to be relevant to Objective B. For each prompt, oral directions are given by Mr. Papunu, Ms. Conine's classroom aide, with written response by students:

Directions: Write the number in the box that makes the statement true:

Prompt B-1:

$2 + 1 = \boxed{}$

Prompt B-2:

$6 + 6 = \boxed{}$

Prompt B-3:

$4 + 5 = \boxed{}$

Prompt B-4:

$8 + 9 = \boxed{}$

Observer's rubric for each:

Score +1 for correct numeral, otherwise score +0 (B-1: 3, B-2: 12, B-3: 9, B-4: 17)

Three mini-experiments, A-1, A-2, and A-3, are intended to be relevant to Objective A. The three prompts are delivered by Mr. Papunu in a one-to-one interview with each student. For each, Mr. Papunu shows the student a set of 20 plastic cubes. Then he directs the students to use the cubes to show why x plus y is z with the appropriate numbers substituted for x, y, and z for A-1, A-2, and A-3 respectively. If the student hesitates or asks for help, Mr. Papunu only clarifies directions without actually helping the student perform the task.

Prompt A-1: Show why 3 plus 1 is 4.

Prompt A-2: Show why 4 plus 6 is 10.

Prompt A-3: Show why 9 plus 6 is 15.

Observer's rubric for each:

Note: For each criterion listed for Prompts A-1, A-2, and A-3, points are awarded as follows:

+2 if the criterion is clearly met
+1 if it is unclear as to whether or not the criterion is met

ILLUSTRATION 4.3

Mini-Experiments Ms. Conine Conducted with Boa, Eddie, and Nancy

(Continued)

ILLUSTRATION 4.3 (Continued)

```
      +0 if the criterion is clearly not met

       Each encircled numeral (either 0, 1, or 2) indicates the num-
   ber of points the response received for the given criterion.

   The student counts out x cubes from the
      set and separates them from the rest ------------ 0   1   2
   The student counts out y cubes from the
      set and separates them from the rest ------------ 0   1   2
   The subsets of x and y cubes
      have no object in common ----------------------- 0   1   2
   The student joins the two subsets and
      displays to me (e.g., by counting) that
      the joined subsets have z objects  -------------- 0   1   2
   The words the student uses to explain
      what she/he is doing are consistent
      with the above criteria  ----------------------- 0   1   2

                                              (10) _____
```

When measurement results are such that the non-contradictory pairs far outweigh the contradictory ones, the overall measurement has the potential for being reliable. But to be reliable it must also have observer consistency.

OBSERVER CONSISTENCY
Intra-Observer Consistency

In most cases, teachers are the observers or scorers as they conduct mini-experiments. That is, they use the rubrics to record measurement results (often by producing scores). In Case 4.6, Ms. Conine's classroom aide, Mr. Papunu, acted as the observer or scorer rather than Ms. Conine herself. Re-examine the prompts and observer's rubrics from Illustration 4.3. Note that the rubrics for Mini-Experiments B–1, B–2, B–3, and B–4 leave virtually no room for judgment for the person scoring the responses. If a "3" appears in the box for B–1, the scorer records "1"; if not, a "0" is recorded. Hardly any judgment is required. The result from such a "cut-and-dried" rubric hardly depends on who does the scoring, when it is scored, or the mood of the observer. The rubrics for Illustration 4.3's other mini-experiments (i.e., A–1, A–2, and A–3) require the observer to make some judgments. For example, when conducting Mini-Experiment A–1 with Boa, Mr. Papunu needs to be quite attentive to see whether or not Boa counts out 3 cubes, separates out a fourth cube from the remaining 17, and combines the 4 cubes together. He also needs to hear Boa's explanation and judge whether or not it is consistent with Boa's demonstration.

Whenever you use mini-experiments with rubrics that leave some room for judgment by you or whoever serves as the observer, you need to be concerned with *intra-observer consistency*. A mini-experiment has *intra-observer consistency* to the degree that the observer

Student	B-1	B-2	B-3	B-4	A-1	A-2	A-3
Boa	1	1	1	0	9	9	9
Eddie	1	1	0	0	2	2	1
Nancy	0	0	1	1	2	9	4

Scores from Mini-Experiments

ILLUSTRATION 4.4

Boa's, Eddie's, and Nancy's Scores from Illustration 4.3's Mini-Experiments

faithfully follows the rubric so that the results are not influenced by fluctuations in the mood of the observer or in the way the observation is conducted.

In Case 4.7, Ms. Conine examines the intra-observer consistency of one of the mini-experiments in Illustration 4.2.

CASE 4.7

To examine the intra-observer consistency of Mini-Experiment A–1 from Illustration 4.3, Ms. Conine has Mr. Papunu videotape himself conducting the mini-experiment with 12 students. The videotape and initial scores are put aside for a week or so. Then Mr. Papunu, without looking at his original results, views the tape, reusing the rubric as he observes the students' responses. The original scores are retrieved and compared for consistency to the ones from the observations of the videotape.

Ms. Conine thinks, as she examines Illustration 4.5, "Except for Pauline's and Dilbert's, the intra-observer consistency looks okay. The rescores tend to be lower than the original. I wonder why. Maybe Joe [Papunu] read more into what students said and did when he was face to face with them than when he viewed this on videotape. Not surprisingly, the scores are more consistent at the extremes, like 10–10, 2–3, and 0–0, than they are nearer the middle, like 6–4 and 7–4. I think we can do better than this. I'll go over the rubric again with Joe and also see if I can't spell it out in a bit more detail. Joe and I could analyze the tape together and discuss why he recorded different scores."

In Case 4.8, Ms. Fisher from Cases 2.3, 2.4, and 2.15 checks on the intra-observer consistency of results from the test displayed by Illustrations 2.28 and 2.30.

CASE 4.8

After school on the Monday she administered the Unit 17 test as described in Case 2.15, Ms. Fisher takes a random sample of eight papers with students' responses (e.g., Heiko's in Illustration 2.29) and duplicates them with a copy machine. She then puts the copies aside. She scores all the test papers as indicated in Case 2.15. Several weeks later, without referring to the original scores, she retrieves the eight copies and, with blank scoring forms, uses the rubrics to rescore those eight tests. Afterwards, she pulls up the original eight scores from her computer and compares them to the rescores shown in Illustration 4.6. She thinks, "Close enough. I don't seem to have observer-consistency problems with this test. I'm sure glad I took the time to write detailed rubrics."

Mr. Papuna's Scores and Re-Scores for Mini-Experiment A-1

Student	Score	Re-Score
Angel	8	7
Barbara	10	10
Camary	2	3
Davalon	0	0
Dilbert	6	4
Fin-Lo	7	7
Khaled	10	10
Linda	10	9
Megan	8	7
Nioshi	10	10
Pauline	7	4
Ulrich	7	7

ILLUSTRATION 4.5

Ms. Conine's Check on Intra-Observer Consistency for Mini-Experiment A–1 of Illustration 4.3

Ms. Fisher's Sample Scores and Re-Scores for the Unit 17 Test

Student	Score	Re-Score
Melanie	40	40
Heiko	45	43
Judy	64	64
Percell	56	56
Armond	58	60
Trevor	58	58
Rolando	48	48
Wanda	60	59

ILLUSTRATION 4.6

Ms. Fisher's Check on Intra-Observer Consistency for the Test Displayed by Illustrations 2.28 and 2.30

Inter-Observer Consistency

Inextricably related to intra-observer consistency is its complement for observer consistency: *inter-observer consistency*. A mini-experiment has *inter-observer consistency* to the degree that different trained observers faithfully follow the rubric so that the results are not influenced by who makes the observation. "Trained observer" refers to a teacher who is familiar with the subject-content, learning levels, and students involved in the measurement or to some other person (e.g., Mr. Papunu in Cases 4.6 and 4.7) who has been trained in the use of the observer's rubric.

To check on inter-observer consistency, Ms. Conine could use a procedure similar to the one she used to check for intra-observer consistency in Case 4.7. The one difference would be that she, instead of Mr. Papunu, would use the observer's rubric to produce the rescores from the videotape. Similar to Case 4.8, Ms. Fisher could check on inter-observer consistency of the Unit 17 test results by having another history teacher, familiar with Unit 17, do the rescoring from those copies of the test papers with the eight student responses.

A measurement has *observer-consistency* to the degree that it has both intra-observer consistency and inter-observer consistency. See Illustration 4.7.

DESIGNING AND SELECTING VALID MEASUREMENTS

DESIGNING MEASUREMENTS

Designing Relevant Measurements

You build relevant measurements from relevant mini-experiments. Designing mini-experiments with learning-level relevance for objectives that specify complex learning levels (e.g., construct-a-concept, discover-a-relationship, application, and appreciation as defined in Chapter 5) is an especially challenging task you face as a teacher. Chapters 7–13 are devoted to helping develop your talent for designing relevant mini-experiments.

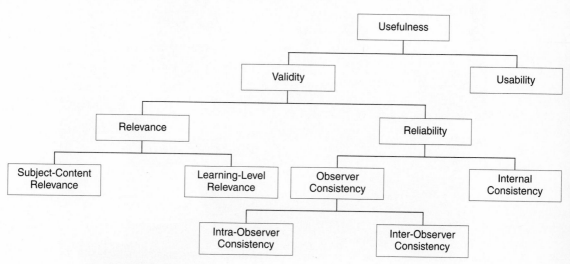

ILLUSTRATION 4.7

Measurement Reliability Depends on Internal Consistency and Observer Consistency; Observer Consistency Depends on Intra-Observer Consistency and Inter-Observer Consistency

With relevant mini-experiments in hand, you synthesize relevant measurements by assembling the mini-experiments so that what you as the teacher judge to be the more important objectives are emphasized more than the less important objectives. Procedures for doing this are explained in Chapter 6.

Designing Measurements That Produce Internally Consistent Results

As reflected by Illustration 4.4, measurement results from Nancy's responses in Case 4.6 lacked internal consistency. Case 4.9 takes you back to the administration of that measurement.

CASE 4.9

Mr. Papunu sits with Nancy as shown in Illustration 4.8. For Mini-Experiment A–1 from Illustration 4.3, Mr. Papunu says, "Use these blocks to show me why 3 plus 1 is 4." But as soon as Nancy hears, "Use these blocks to show me why" she thinks he means to show the letter "Y" with the blocks. Thus, she grabs 5 cubes and forms the letter "Y." The "Y" faces Nancy, so Mr. Papunu does not notice that she has formed a letter with the cubes. He asks, "And what next?" Nancy picks up one more cube and uses it to lengthen the leg of the "Y." She says, "There, that shows it." Mr. Papunu circles "0" for four of the five criteria on the observer's rubric form. He circles "2" for "The student counts out 1 cube from the set and separates it from the rest."

For Mini-Experiment A–2, Mr. Papunu says, "Use the blocks to show me why 4 plus 6 is 10." Nancy counts out 10 blocks, then hesitates and says, "No, put these back!" Separating 4 of the blocks from the 6, she says, "Here are the six and here's the four." Mr. Papunu: "And how does that show that 4 plus 6 is 10?" Pushing the six cubes together with the four, she says, "This is why. I don't know." Mr. Papunu, circles "2" for each criterion except for the last, for which he circles "1."

ILLUSTRATION 4.8

With Nancy, Mr. Papunu Conducts Mini-Experiments A–1, A–2, and A–3 from Illustration 4.3.

For Mini-Experiment A–3, Mr. Papunu says, "Use the blocks to show me why 9 plus 6 is 15." Nancy quickly counts out 6 blocks and then 9 blocks. But then she notices some of her classmates across the room making colorful spinners with Ms. Conine. Mr. Papunu is facing Nancy with his back to the activities that have caught Nancy's attention. He doesn't notice that she's distracted. He says, "Go on; keep showing me why 9 plus 6 is 15." Nancy, with her mind on the spinners, abruptly says, "Oh, you know what it is." She pulls the set of 9 cubes and the set of 6 cubes back into the original pile. Mr. Papunu, circles "2" for the first two criteria and "0" for the others.

In Case 4.9, Nancy's misinterpretation of Mr. Papunu's directions for Prompt A–1 and her lack of attention to the task for A–3 influenced the results of those two mini-experiments to be inconsistent with the results of Mini-Experiment A–2. Misinterpretation of directions and distractions are two common factors that tend to interfere with internal consistency of measurement results.

As with any sequence of experiments intended to reveal evidence of truth, planned measurements need to be administered under controlled conditions to minimize distractions and assure directions are followed. Directions are unlikely to be consistently followed if the mini-experiments' prompts do not clearly define tasks for students. In Case 4.9, Nancy interpreted the directions differently for Mini-Experiment A–1 than she did for Mini-Experiment A–2. Consequently, she attempted different tasks (forming a "Y" in one case and demonstrating why 4 + 6 = 10 in the other).

In Case 4.10, different students attempt different tasks although they are presented with the same prompt.

CASE 4.10

Ms. Paez includes the following essay prompt as part of a unit test on the human circulatory system:

"Discuss the passage of blood through the human heart."

One of her students, Cinnie, reads it and thinks, "It takes two to have a discussion! With whom am I supposed to discuss this? What does she want me to write? How about, 'It's a good thing blood passes through the heart or else I'd be dead.' This isn't the time to be funny; you've got to finish this test. I'll just write her a paragraph on how important it is for blood to pass through the heart."

When Ms. Paez returns the test papers to the class, she engages the students in a discussion about their responses to that prompt:

Ms. Paez:	"Three of you wrote much more than you needed. Molina filled up four pages and didn't have enough time to finish the rest of the test. But most of you didn't write enough—not even explaining why blood moves through the heart."
Matt:	"You only gave me one point out of 10 and I did what you said—wrote why blood moves through the heart!"
Ms. Paez:	"Read you answer."
Matt:	"Like the book said, 'So that oxygen-rich blood replaces oxygen-poor blood'—that is why blood passes through the heart."
Soo-Li:	"You were supposed to write more than that!"
Matt:	"I explained why blood passes through the heart, like Ms. Paez said!"
Cinnie:	"But it says 'discuss'—not 'describe how or why.' I'll bet everybody in the class 'discussed the passage of blood through the heart!'"
Ms. Paez:	"But some did so in a nice one-page essay; others just wrote a sentence."
Cinnie:	"How were we to know what to do? Whole books are written about blood passing through the heart. You didn't want us to write a book!"

Ms. Paez now realizes that the prompt's task was not clearly communicated. After class, she thinks about how to reword the directions for the next time she tests for the objective. She decides on the following:

Prompt:

> With the aid of a diagram, explain the mechanics of how venous blood, while in the heart, is transported through the human heart and to the lungs. Make sure you indicate the direction and locations of the venous blood while in the heart. Note how the action of the heart maintains the flow. Use between one and two pages for your entire response, including the diagram.

The refined version of Ms. Paez's prompt is wordier than the original one, but the task will be clearer to the students.

To be internally consistent, a measurement must also include an adequate number of mini-experiments. A measurement with a large number of mini-experiments provides a greater opportunity for consistent student response patterns to emerge than one with only a few. Illustration 4.3's measurement includes only four mini-experiments relevant to Case 4.6's Objective B. As indicated by Illustration 4.4, the results from those four experiments with Nancy are inconsistent. Nancy didn't respond correctly to the prompts for the two addition facts that Ms. Conine considers easy, but she responded correctly to the prompts for the harder ones. In Case 4.11, Nancy is given a longer test.

CASE 4.11

Ms. Conine has Mr. Papunu administer to Nancy another measurement designed to be relevant to Objective B from Case 4.6. Illustration 4.9 displays the prompts and the results.

Consistent with results from Mini-Experiments B–1, B–2, B–3, and B–4 as shown in Illustration 4.4, Nancy responded incorrectly to "$2 + 1 =$" and "$6 + 6 =$", but correctly to "$4 + 5 =$" and "$8 + 9 =$." With the additional results from eight more mini-experiments, does Illustration 4.9's scores seem to be more internally consistent than the previous results? Look again. Does a consistent pattern emerge from Illustration 4.9's results that is not apparent from Illustration 4.4?

Results from Illustration 4.9 show Nancy responding correctly to "$x + y =$" any time $x < y$ and incorrectly any time $x \geq y$. That pattern existed in Illustration 4.4, but it was hardly apparent with only four responses. With more mini-experiments, that consistent pattern was easier to detect. Of course, she can't know for sure, but at least Illustration 4.7's results can suggest to Ms. Conine that she should check on whether or not Nancy somehow acquired some process or mnemonic device whereby she recalls addition facts only when the first addend is less than the second.

To increase the likelihood that your measurements will produce internally consistent results, you need to make sure you design them so they include an adequate number of mini-experiments with unambiguously presented prompts. Then, of course, the measurements must be administered under controlled conditions free of distractions. In some situations in which results are to be used for making summative evaluations, you also need to control the experiments to prevent internal consistency from being contaminated by student cheating. Student cheating tends to affect internal consistency because in typical cases where students cheat, they don't cheat consistently. Case 4.12 is a case in point.

CASE 4.12

During a test with multiple-choice prompts, Angee gets up from her desk, walks over to the classroom pencil sharpener, and returns to her desk to continue responding to the test prompts. During her walk,

Directions: Write the number in the box that makes the
              statement true:

B-1:   B-2:   B-3:

   2 + 1 = [21]   6 + 6 = [8]   4 + 5 = [7]

B-4:   B-5:   B-6:

   8 + 9 = [17]   2 + 6 = [8]   5 + 4 = [8]

B-7:   B-8:   B-9:

   9 + 5 = [11]   8 + 8 = [10]   6 + 1 = [6]

B-10:   B-11:   B-12:

   3 + 7 = [10]   7 + 6 = [6]   5 + 1 = [15]

Scores from Mini-Experiments with Nancy

B-1	B-2	B-3	B-4	B-5	B-6	B-7	B-8	B-9	B-10	B-11	B-12
0	0	1	1	1	0	0	0	0	1	0	0

ILLUSTRATION 4.9

Prompts, Responses, and Results from Measurement Mr. Papunu Administered to Nancy

Angee looked at two other students' papers. Noticing that they both selected "B" and "D" in response to Prompts 7 and 8 respectively instead of "C" and "C," which she selected, Angee changes her answers to "B" and "D."

Because Angee only obtained the unauthorized "help" with responses to two prompts and not all the prompts, her cheating tends to create inconsistencies in her responses. For example, Prompts 9 and 10 might have been relevant to the same objective as Prompts 7 and 8, but because she didn't cheat on 9 and 10, she may miss those two, while her unauthorized responses might be correct.

Chapter 6 provides suggestions for developing and administering measurements in order to control experimental conditions so that factors (e.g., distractions and cheating) do not contaminate internal consistency. Chapters 7–13 provide suggestions for designing mini-experiments with unambiguously presented prompts.

Designing Measurements with Observer Consistency

Compare the eight mini-experiments displayed by Illustration 4.10. Which ones do you think are more likely to have comparatively high degrees of observer consistency? Which ones are more likely to have lower degrees of observer consistency?

1. Mini-Experiment Designed to Be Relevant to the Following Objective:

   For each sentence students write, they will use the verb tense that is consistent with the rest of the sentence (comprehension and communication skills)[1].

   Written-Response, Multiple-Choice Prompt:

   The verb is missing from the following sentence:

   Next Monday at this time, Wil and Terri
   _____ me move.

   Select the correct form of the verb from the following list and then write it in the blank to complete the above sentence:

   help   have helped   helped   will help

   Observer's Rubric:

   Score +1 for "will help" in the blank; +0 otherwise.

2. Mini-Experiment Designed to Be Relevant to the Following Objective:

   Students will state the definition of "rational number" (simple knowledge)[1].

   Written-Response, Short-Answer Prompt:

   Write the definition for "rational number."

   _____

   _____

   Observer's Rubric:

   Score +1 for a definition equivalent to the following one: "A number is rational if and only if it can be expressed as the ratio of two integers." Otherwise, score +0.

3. Mini-Experiment Designed to Be Relevant to the Following Objective:

   Students will state the definition of "rational number" (simple knowledge)[1].

ILLUSTRATION 4.10

Which of These Mini-Experiments Are More Likely to Suffer from Observer Consistency Problems?

(Continued)

ILLUSTRATION 4.10 *(Continued)*

Written-Response, Short-Answer Prompt:

Write the definition for "rational number."

_____

_____

Observer's Rubric:

(2 points possible) Score +2 for completely accurate definition, +1 for nearly accurate definition, or +0 otherwise.

4. Mini-Experiment Designed to Be Relevant to the Following Objective:

Students will state the definition of "rational number" (simple knowledge)[1].

Written-Response, Short-Answer Prompt:

Write the definition for "Rational Number."

_____

_____

Observer's Rubric:

4 points possible distributed as follows: (1) Score +1 for indicating that the number can be expressed as a ratio. (2) Score +1 for indicating that the expression is the ratio of two integers. (3) Score +1 for making it clear that to be rational, the number must be expressible as a ratio but it is still rational when it is expressed in another form (e.g., as a decimal). (4) Score +1 if the statement has the attributes of a definition (e.g., uses "if and only if").

5. Mini-Experiment Designed to Be Relevant to the Following Objective:

Students will explain the mechanism by which blood is moved through the human heart (comprehension and communication skills)[1].

Written-Response, Essay Prompt:

With the aid of a diagram, explain the mechanics of how venous blood, while in the heart, is transported through the human heart and to the lungs. Make sure you indicate the direction and locations of the venous

ILLUSTRATION 4.10 (Continued)

blood while in the heart. Note how the action of the heart maintains the flow. Use between one and two pages for your entire response, including the diagram.

Observer's Rubric:

5 points possible to be based on the degree to which the essay displays an understanding of (a) the mechanics of how the heart causes venous blood to circulate through the heart and (b) the path that venous blood takes through the heart. The following rating scale is to be used:

+5 for understanding well above the common level of understanding in the class

+4 for understanding slightly above the common level of understanding in the class

+3 for a level of understanding that is fairly common in the class

+2 for understanding slightly below the common level of understanding in the class

+1 for understanding well below the common level of understanding in the class

6. Mini-Experiment Designed to Be Relevant to the Following Objective:

Students will explain the mechanism by which blood is moved through the human heart (comprehension and communication skills)[1].

Written-Response, Essay Prompt:

With the aid of a diagram, explain the mechanics of how venous blood, while in the heart, is transported through the human heart and to the lungs. Make sure you indicate the direction and locations of the venous blood while in the heart. Note how the action of the heart maintains the flow. Use between one and two pages for your entire response, including the diagram.

Observer's Rubric:

8 points possible with points distributed as follows:

+1 for each of the following the student indicates in the essay: (1) venous blood enters through the superior and inferior venae cavae; (2) venous blood gathers in the right atrium; (3) proper role of the valves in the right side of the heart; (4) venous blood gathers in the right ventricle; (5) venous blood exiting the heart through

ILLUSTRATION 4.10 *(Continued)*

the pulmonary arteries; (6) the heart's pumping motion; (7) how the heart's pumping motion causes the venous blood to flow.

+1 if the essay does not indicate venous blood anywhere that it does not actually reside.

7. Mini-Experiment Designed to Be Relevant to the Following Objective:

Students employ proper mechanics when executing the following weight training exercises: Flat bench press, incline bench press, lat pull down, leg curl, leg extension, leg press, lat pull-down, and standing press, (psychomotor-skill performance)[1].

Performance-Observation Prompt:

The student, stationed in front of a barbell with only a weight that offers little resistance, is directed to demonstrate a two-arm standing press.

Observer's Rubric:

22 points possible based on the following 11 criteria; for each criterion, score +2 if the criterion is clearly met, +1 if there is a question as to whether or not it is met, or +0 if the criterion is clearly not met:

____   Feet properly positioned under the bar throughout the entire lift
____   Proper grip and hand spread throughout the lift
____   Back straight throughout the lift
____   Head facing forward throughout the lift
____   Clean initiated with knees flexed
____   Clean initiated with elbows extended
____   Clean properly executed
____   Pauses with bar just above the chest
____   Executes press properly
____   Returns bar to position just above chest and pauses
____   Gently returns bar to floor, flexing knees on the way down

8. Mini-Experiment Designed to Be Relevant to the Following Objective:

Students employ proper mechanics when executing the following weight training exercises: Flat bench press, incline bench press, lat pull down, leg curl, leg extension, leg press, lat pull-down, and standing press, (psychomotor-skill performance)[1].

ILLUSTRATION 4.10 (Continued)

<u>Video-Based Performance-Observation Prompt</u>:

While being videotaped, the student, stationed in front of a barbell with only a weight that offers little resistance, is directed to demonstrate a two-arm standing press.

<u>Observer's Rubric</u>:

The rubric is identical to the one for Mini-Experiment 7 above except that the observation is made from viewing the videotape. The tape may be played back as necessary to check on criteria.

[1] Indicates the learning level of the objective as defined in Chapter 5 of this text. (It is not necessary for you to be concerned with this scheme for categorizing learning levels until you've reached Chapter 5.)

Mini-Experiments 1 and 2 from Illustration 4.10 have observer's rubrics with *dichotomous scoring*. A rubric has *dichotomous scoring* if there are only two possible categories for students' responses. The observer classifies a response as either meeting a criterion or not. Examples of dichotomies include (1) "correct" or "incorrect," (2) "+1" or "+0," (3) "present" or "absent," and (4) "checked" or "not checked." The general idea of dichotomous scoring is the response either receives "full credit" or "no credit"; there is no "partial credit." Mini-experiments with dichotomous scoring typically have better observer consistency than mini-experiments with *weighted scoring*.

Mini-Experiments 3–6 from Illustration 4.10 have observer's rubrics with *weighted scoring*. A rubric has *weighted scoring* if there are more than two possible categories for students' responses. The observer classifies a response in terms of the degree to which it meets a criterion. Mini-experiments with weighted scoring typically leave more room for observers' judgments than those with dichotomous scoring.

Although both Mini-Experiments 1 and 2 from Illustration 4.10 use dichotomous scoring, doesn't one present more of a concern for observer consistency than the other? With Mini-Experiment 1's rubric, the observer needs to make no judgment at all in scoring responses. If "will help" appears in the blank, mark "+1"; if not, mark "+0." Whereas with Mini-Experiment 2, the observer has to judge whether or not what is written in the blank is equivalent to the given definition of "rational number." Thus, although slight, there is some element of judgment.

If the only feature you needed to build into your measurements was observer consistency, then you should only use multiple-choice prompts. However, measurement relevance is a major concern, and multiple-choice prompts can hardly be relevant to all of your learning objectives.

Now, compare the observer's rubrics of Mini-Experiment 3 to that of Mini-Experiment 4. Both use weighted scoring. However, with Mini-Experiment 3, the observer rates the accuracy of the response on a 3-point scale (i.e., +2, +1, or +0). Whereas with Mini-Experiment 4, the observer is directed to look for four specific attributes in the response. If an attribute is detected, the observer records "+1"; otherwise "+0" is recorded. This rubric provides more specific directions for the observer.

Mini-experiments with weighted scoring rubrics that specify how each single point should be distributed use *analytical scoring*. Mini-Experiment 4 from Illustration 4.10 uses *analytical scoring* because each of its possible 4 points is tied to a specific feature of the response. Mini-experiments with weighted scoring rubrics that allow the observer the leeway to rate the response use *global scoring*. Mini-Experiment 3 from Illustration 4.10 uses *global scoring*.

In general, do you think that mini-experiments with analytical scoring or global scoring tend to have better observer consistency?

From Illustration 4.10, compare the rubric for Mini-Experiment 5 to that for Mini-Experiment 6. Note that 5 uses global scoring (and, by the way, a norm-referenced one), whereas 6 uses analytical scoring. Which of the two will tend to have more observer-consistency problems?

Mini-Experiments 7 and 8 use a mix of analytical and global scoring. The 11 criteria are spelled out so specifically that there is virtually no room for judgment on the part of an expert observer. However, each characteristic of responses is marked on a 3-point instead of a 2-point scale as required for analytical scoring. The two mini-experiments are identical except that with 8, the observer has the advantage of being able to play back the student's performance on videotape. Do you think the videotape playback feature tends to enhance observer consistency?

Additional ideas for designing observer's rubrics that tend to have observer consistency are demonstrated in Chapters 7–13.

SELECTING MEASUREMENTS

Most decisions you make are best informed by the results of measurements you design and develop yourself. You are in the best possible position to design measurements tailored to the unique needs of your students and your specific learning goals. Furthermore, by virtue of having worked your way to this point in this book, you have already developed a talent for designing mini-experiments that is superior to those of most people who "write tests." However, there are times when you may choose to make use of existing measurement instruments. Also, it is very likely for supervisors to require you to administer commercially produced standardized tests or government-mandated core-curriculum tests.

Besides measurements you develop yourself, four types of measurement instruments are likely to play a role in your instructional activities: (1) *Measurements developed by other teachers*, (2) *Non-standardized commercially produced tests*, (3) *Commercially produced standardized achievement tests*, and (4) *government-mandated core-curriculum tests*.

Measurements developed by other teachers provide a rich source of ideas for mini-experiments. When you and other teachers are teaching for similar learning goals, you may decide to share measurements or use collaboratively designed ones. Teachers are now sharing measurement instruments and ideas for mini-experiment from around the world via the Internet. In any case, the selection of an existing measurement instrument should be based, first of all, on the relevance of the mini-experiments to your learning objectives. You need to go through the measurement to determine how well the mini-experiments match both the subject-contents and learning levels specified by your objectives. If you are satisfied with the match, then you need to examine the measurement to predict whether or not it will produce reasonably reliable results for your situation. In other words, to decide whether or not to use an existing measurement, analyze it for the same features you try to build into measurements you design yourself: subject-content relevance, learning-level relevance, internal consistency, observer consistency, and usability.

Non-standardized commercially produced tests are measurement instruments that can be purchased from publishers of instructional materials. Such tests often are included in the supplementary packages that accompany textbooks and adopted instructional programs. Sometimes these tests can be a rich source of ideas for mini-experiments you may choose to incorporate in measurements you design yourself. However, the vast majority of these tests do not have learning-level relevance for objectives specifying complex reasoning (e.g., construct-a-concept or discover-a-relationship) (Cangelosi, 1996, p. 316). Most of them are more relevant to how well students can recall verbiage from a textbook than they are to meaningful learning of subject-content. Case 4.13 relates an experience I had that illustrates the point.

CASE 4.13

Mr. Call administered the "Chapter 1 Test" that accompanied the life science textbook he uses with his eighth-grade class. He used the results in making summative evaluations of students' achievement of the goal of Unit 1 of the course, "What Is Life Science?" Ten of the 26 eighth-graders in the class scored 30, the maximum possible score for the test. The average score was 26.8.

Mr. Call showed me the test document. Most of the prompts seemed to be devised by taking sentences from the textbook and replacing one or two words with blanks. For example:

Prompt: Complete the following sentence so that it makes a true statement:
Man has been studying living things for thousands of years in an attempt to

_____.

Rubric: Score +1 for "better understand themselves," otherwise score +0.

With Mr. Call's permission, I administered the test to four biology professors at a university. All four hold PhDs and are internationally recognized for their research accomplishments in biology. However, their scores on the test are 20, 20, 22, and 26, all below the average for the eighth-grade class.

Does Case 4.13 lead you to believe that the four professors' understanding of the meaning of life science is not as advanced as most of Mr. Call's eighth-graders'? Or are you more inclined to believe that the Chapter 1 test that accompanied the textbook is more relevant to how well one recalls specific sentences from the textbook rather than to how well one understands the meaning of life science? Again, you need to examine the validity of existing test instruments before considering how, if at all, to incorporate them in your decision-making activities.

A test is *standardized* if it has been field-tested to assess its reliability and to establish normative standards to be used in interpreting scores from subsequent administrations of the test. An *achievement test* is a test that is used in the evaluation of what students have learned. *Commercially produced standardized achievement tests* are administered at least once a year in most elementary, middle, junior high, and senior high schools. Some of the more popularly used standardized test batteries include *California Achievement Tests, Comprehensive Tests of Basic Skills, Iowa Tests of Basic Skills, Iowa Tests of Educational Development, Metropolitan Achievement Tests, Sequential Tests of Educational Progress, Stanford Achievement Tests, Tests of Achievement and Proficiency*, and *The 3-Rs Test*. There are also single, subject-specific standardized achievement tests that can be purchased (e.g., *Gates-McGinitie Reading Tests*). Although capable of providing some evidence of what students have learned in some broad general areas, these once-a-year tests are not relevant to specific achievements of individual students. They are simply not designed to be aligned to the specific learning goals for which you teach (Neill, 1997).

However, in some school districts, scores from commercially produced standardized tests are used to determine the academic standing of students, evaluate the effectiveness of their teachers, and rate the quality of schools. Such practices are counter to the purposes for which standardized tests were developed, but such practices are not out of the ordinary. Chapter 14 presents an in-depth treatise of standardized tests—what they are, how they should be used, how their scores should be interpreted, and how to counter common misuses of them.

For now, keep in mind that commercially produced standardized achievement tests are generally not a useful source of information for monitoring your students' learning. However, depending on how standardized tests are used in your area, you might consider teaching your students the type of test-taking skills that will help their performances on commercially produced standardized tests (Taylor & Walton, 1997).

Some state offices of education, school district offices, and other government-run educational agencies produce tests intended for use in evaluating how well schools are meeting broad curriculum standards (e.g., standards established by a state office of education's core curriculum). Unlike standardized achievement tests in which scores are interpreted using norm-referenced standards, these *government-mandated core-curriculum achievement tests* are used with criterion-referenced standards. With many of these tests, the prompts are keyed to specific standards or goals in a curriculum guideline. Some criterion is established, such as "a student must respond correctly to 2 out of 3 prompts," in order to "pass" that standard. Students' scores indicate how many standards were "passed." Schools might be "graded" by the percentage of standards "passed." If you find yourself in a situation where these tests are mandated and the results are going to affect evaluations of your students' learning, then you need to take measures to prepare students for these tests. Along with standardized achievement tests, government-mandated core-curriculum tests are dealt with in Chapter 14.

USING UNPLANNED MEASUREMENTS

Your mind is continually processing results from unplanned measurements. Since you don't design unplanned measurements, you have no control over their validity. However, as your mind processes results, you can be conscious of validity factors in deciding what, if any, decisions will be impacted by those surges of information. You informally assess relevance and reliability in your head before allowing unplanned measurement results to influence your decisions. You factor measurement error into your decision-making. You don't control reception of unplanned measurement results, but you do control how much weight you afford them. Consider, for example, Case 4.14.

CASE 4.14

Having just completed a lesson to lead her sixth-grade mathematics students to construct the concept of rational numbers, Ms. Mahe defines the term "rational number" as "a number that can be expressed as a fraction so that both the numerator and denominator are integers." After reviewing the definition using examples of rational numbers, the students discuss why the following numbers are rational:

$$\frac{9}{4}, \frac{32}{65}, .5, -33, -\frac{4}{3}, 0, \sqrt{4}, \text{ and } \sqrt{9}$$

To lead into a discussion about numbers that are not rational, Ms. Mahe says, "We agreed that the principal square root of 4 is rational because it can be expressed as the fraction 2 over 1. And also that the principal square root of 9 is rational because it can be expressed as the fraction 3 over 1. But what about the principal square root of 5? Is the principal square root of 5 rational? What do you think, Candace?" Candace: "Well, since the square root of 4 is 2 and the square root of 9 is 3, the square root of 5 has got to be some fraction. A fraction like that can't be rational." The following thoughts race through Ms. Mahe's mind: "After all we've just been through, constructing the concept of rational number and then explaining the definition as a number expressible as a fraction, Candace says a number is not rational because it's a fraction! She must have misconceptualized rational numbers, so now she's not comprehending our definition." Ms. Mahe starts to correct what Candace said by pointing out that if a number is a fraction, then by definition it must be rational. But before finishing the first word, Ms. Mahe stops herself and says instead, "Let's all just stop and silently think to ourselves about what Candace said. I need to think for about 30 seconds." She thinks, "Maybe Candace really has constructed the concept of rational number, but she just used the word 'fraction' differently than I was expecting. Maybe she means that the square root of 5 is between two whole numbers rather than it is expressible as a fraction." Thus, instead of jumping to a formative judgment about Candace's concept of rational number and comprehension of the definition, Ms. Mahe decides to prompt Candace to explain herself further.

In Case 4.14, Ms. Mahe made an unplanned measurement by hearing Candace's comment that ended with, "a fraction like that can't be rational." Initially, Ms. Mahe was inclined to use those results to make a formative judgment about Candace's understanding of rational numbers. But then, Ms. Mahe questioned the learning-level relevance of the unplanned measurement. She considered the possibility that Candace said a fraction isn't rational, not because she held a misconception of rational numbers, but rather because she simply misused the word "fraction." Thus, she withholds judgment about Candace's conception of rational numbers until more measurement results are available.

In Case 4.15, Ms. Mahe informally assesses intra-observer consistency before deciding to allow the results of an unplanned measurement to influence a decision.

CASE 4.15

Ms. Mahe's sixth-graders are independently working on textbook exercises where they employ an algorithm to determine whether or not a number is rational. She moves around the classroom, responding to requests for help with the work. As she turns away from Reyes and moves toward Jessica, who has her hand raised, Ms. Mahe hears the sound of a pencil being tapped on a desktop. She glances behind her to see Reyes suddenly stop tapping. While helping Jessica, she hears the noise again. Once more, it stops when she glances at Reyes. She thinks, "Reyes must be entertaining himself by trying to annoy me. He needs to stop the disruptive behavior right away. I hate it when students are sneaky. If he wants to tap his pencil, why does he have to wait until I'm helping someone else with my back turned to do it! He must resent me giving attention to others. On the other hand, I'm not having such a great day. I've got a headache and am a bit more touchy than I normally am. With this mood I'm in, I just might be imagining that his tapping is related to what I'm doing. He might be tapping from nervous energy, not because he wants to annoy me."

Having questioned that the reception of the unplanned measurement was colored by her mood, she decides to conduct an informal planned measurement to see if the results are consistent with those from the unplanned one. Each time she turns her back to Reyes to help someone, she listens for the tapping and waits to see if it continues until she turns back toward Reyes. The results are consistent with the earlier ones. Thus, she decides that Reyes intends for his behavior to be disruptive. This decision triggers the beginning of a teaching cycle in which she deals with Reyes's misbehavior.

THE NEED FOR PINPOINTING WHAT STUDENTS ARE TO LEARN

Valid measurements are built from relevant mini-experiments. But you are hardly in a position to design or select mini-experiments relevant to students' learning unless what is to be learned is pinpointed with clearly defined learning goals. Chapter 5 presents an advanced organizer to help you pinpoint the subject-content and learning level of each objective you use to define learning goals.

SYNTHESIS ACTIVITIES FOR CHAPTER 4

1. Select the one best response for each of the following multiple-choice prompts that either answers the question or completes the statement:

   A. A reliable test may not be valid because it lacks _____.
      a) usefulness
      b) inter-observer consistency
      c) usability
      d) internal consistency
      e) subject-content relevance

   B. Which one of the following qualities of a measurement depends on the objective about which the measurement's results are used to make a formative judgment or summative evaluation?
      a) internal consistency
      b) usability
      c) learning-level relevance

   C. Which one of the following types of prompts is most likely (everything else being equal) to have intra-observer consistency?
      a) one-to-one interview with the student
      b) multiple-choice
      c) product rating
      d) essay
      e) performance observation

   D. Which one of the following types of prompts is most likely (everything else being equal) to have an observer's rubric that uses global scoring?
      a) multiple-choice
      b) product rating
      c) fill in the blank with the missing word

   E. A measurement could be valid, but *not* _____.
      a) have intra-observer consistency
      b) have inter-observer consistency
      c) useful
      d) produce internally consistent results
      e) relevant

   F. Every relevant measurement _____.
      a) has learning-level relevance
      b) has intra-observer consistency
      c) has usability
      d) produces internally consistent results

   G. A relevant measurement may not be valid because it lacks _____.
      a) usability
      b) intra-observer consistency

    c) learning-level relevance
    d) subject-content relevance

H. Every valid measurement is _____.
    a) usable
    b) reliable
    c) standardized
    d) useful

I. If a test is standardized, then _____.
    a) it has subject-content relevance
    b) it produces internally consistent results
    c) its prompts are multiple-choice
    d) its reliability has been assessed

J. Summative evaluations based on scores from commercially produced standardized tests are typically _____.
    a) norm-referenced
    b) criterion-referenced

K. The results from a mini-experiment are used to make decisions about how well students achieve an objective that specifies a learning level that involves sophisticated reasoning. However, the results actually only depend on how well students recall information. Therefore, the mini-experiment lacks _____.
    a) subject-content relevance
    b) learning-level relevance
    c) usability
    d) internal consistency
    e) intra-observer consistency

L. Which of the following influences the relevance of a measurement?
    a) The match between what the measurement actually measures and what it's used to evaluate.
    b) The importance of the goal that the measurement is supposed to measure.
    c) The validity of the measurement.

2. Compare and discuss your and a colleague's responses to the multiple-choice prompts from Synthesis Activity 1. Also, check your choices against the following key: A-e, B-c, C-b, D-b, E-c, F-a, G-b, H-b, I-d, J-a, K-b, and L-a.

3. State a learning objective for which one day you might design and teach a lesson. Make sure that you clearly understand both the subject-content and the learning level targeted by the objective. Label your objective "Objective X." Now develop three mini-experiments labeled "1," "2," and "3," so that the following three statements are true:
    A. Mini-Experiment 1 is relevant to Objective X.
    B. Mini-Experiment 2 has subject-content relevance for Objective X but is not relevant to Objective X.
    C. Mini-Experiment 3 has learning-level relevance for Objective X but is not relevant to Objective X.

4. Use Illustration 4.11's scoring form to score your responses to the prompt from Synthesis Activity 3. Exchange your responses and results with those of a colleague. Discuss issues and questions stimulated by the exchange.

5. Examine Case 4.16 and then respond to the prompts listed A–L that follow.

CASE 4.16

Mr. Francisco, a social studies teacher, overhears two of his students talking:

Kimberly: "Michelle is so cool! She shoplifts all the time. She got these earrings from Shop-N-Go."

Lee: "So! She won't feel too cool when she gets caught."

| Kimberly: | "What can they do to her? The Bill of Rights says the cops have to get her a lawyer and then they've got to prove she's guilty in court and everything. They can't lock up a juvenile for something like that!" |
| Lee: | "Yeah, I guess you're right." |

After several other episodes indicating that students misunderstand how the juvenile justice system in the state functions, Mr. Francisco decides to extend an upcoming unit, previously titled "The Bill of Rights," and retitle it "Juvenile crime, juvenile courts, and the Bill of Rights."

He defines the goal of the modified unit with 12 objectives: (1) a construct-a-concept[1] one on the differences between criminal and civil crimes, (2) a construct-a-concept[1] one on the differences between rights of adults and rights of juveniles, (3) a comprehension and communication skills[1] one on some key

---

Observer's rubric:

Note: For each criterion listed, points are awarded as follows:

    +2 if the criterion is clearly met
    +1 if it is unclear as to whether or not the criterion is met
    +0 if the criterion is clearly not met

Each encircled numeral (either 0, 1, or 2) indicates the number of points the response received for the given criterion.

    Objective X is stated so you clearly understand both
        the subject-content and the learning level -------- 0 1 2

    Mini-Experiment 1 is given so that it includes both
        a clearly-communicated prompt and rubric ---------- 0 1 2

    Mini-Experiment 1 has a reasonable degree of
        subject-content relevance for Objective X ---------- 0 1 2

    Mini-Experiment 1 has a reasonable degree of
        learning-level relevance for Objective X ---------- 0 1 2

    Mini-Experiment 2 is given so that it includes both
        a clearly-communicated prompt and rubric ---------- 0 1 2

    Mini-Experiment 2 has a reasonable degree of
        subject-content relevance for Objective X ---------- 0 1 2

    Mini-Experiment 2 does not have a reasonable degree
        of learning-level relevance for Objective X -------- 0 1 2

    Mini-Experiment 3 is given so that it includes both
        a clearly-communicated prompt and rubric ---------- 0 1 2

    Mini-Experiment 3 has a reasonable degree of
        learning-level relevance for Objective X ---------- 0 1 2

    Mini-Experiment 3 does not have a reasonable degree
        of subject-content relevance for Objective X ------ 0 1 2

ILLUSTRATION 4.11

Scoring Form for Synthesis Activity 4

legal statutes, (4) a simple-knowledge[1] one on terminology, (5) four process-knowledge[1] ones dealing with legal procedures, (6) a comprehension and communication skills[1] one on the Bill of Rights, (7) two comprehension and communication skills[1] ones on state statutes dealing with juvenile crime, and (8) an application[1] one on predicting consequences of certain juvenile criminal behaviors.

Based on students' responses to questions he raises on the second day, Mr. Francisco judges that most of his students are getting so focused on what they perceive as injustices in the system that they're having difficulty engaging in the inquiry lessons he's conducting for the two construct-a-concept objectives. Thus, he decides to insert a lesson on an affective objective to lead students to take a more pragmatic and less idealistic view of the unit's content.

On the next-to-the-last day of the unit, Mr. Francisco administers a unit test; he applies the visual-inspection method to the results to assign grades. While examining the test results, he takes special note of how students responded to the four prompts designed to be relevant to the application-level objective. Each of the four prompts, numbered on the test as 7, 11, 12, and 20, has a rubric so that the maximum possible score is 2. Illustration 4.12 provides data on the average score for the 28 students in the class for each of these four mini-experiments. Illustration 4.12 also provides the individual results from five students for Mini-Experiments 7, 11, 12, and 20.

Prompts:
A. Identify one formative judgment Mr. Francisco made that influenced his social studies curriculum.
B. Identify an unplanned measurement Mr. Francisco made that influenced the formative judgment you listed for A just above.
C. Identify a formative judgment Mr. Francisco made after the unit commenced.

Scores from Mini-Experiments

	7	11	12	20
Average for Class	1.9	1.2	1.1	0.5
Calvin	2	2	2	0
Brian	0	1	0	2
Mitsuko	2	1	1	0
Jill	1	0	0	0
Rosalie	2	2	2	1

ILLUSTRATION 4.12

Scores from Five Students' Responses to Four Prompts on Mr. Francisco's Unit Test

---

[1]Indicates the learning level of the objective as defined in Chapter 5 of this text.

    D. Identify a measurement Mr. Francisco made that influenced the formative judgment you listed for C on page 206.

    E. Identify a summative evaluation Mr. Francisco made.

    F. Identify a measurement Mr. Francisco made that influenced the summative evaluation you listed for E just above.

    G. Was Mr. Francisco's method of converting scores to grades norm-referenced or criterion-referenced? Explain why your answer is correct.

    H. Identify one measurement that *you* made that influenced how you decided to respond to G just above.

    I. According to Illustration 4.12, to which of the four prompts from the unit test (7, 11, 12, or 20) was it easiest for the 28 students to respond? Which of those four appears to have been the most difficult for the class?

    J. Based only on data presented by Illustration 4.12, are the results from Calvin's responses to Prompts 7, 11, 12, and 20 internally consistent? What about for Brian's? For Mitsuko's? For Jill's? For Rosalie's?

    K. What evidence is provided in Illustration 4.12 that supports the idea that the results from Mr. Francisco's unit test are reliable.

    L. What evidence is provided in Illustration 4.12 that supports the idea that the results from Mr. Francisco's unit test are not reliable.

6. Use Illustration 4.13's scoring form to score your responses to Prompts A–J from Synthesis Activity 5. Exchange your responses and results with those of a colleague. Discuss issues and questions stimulated by the exchange.

7. With a colleague, recall examples in which instructional decisions you or your colleague made were influenced by the results of unplanned measurements. Discuss how consideration of measurement error affected the weight you afforded those measurement results.

8. Re-examine the observer's rubrics from Illustrations 1.11, 2.30, 3.7, 3.9, 3.10, and 4.3. For each rubric, indicate whether it uses dichotomous scoring, analytical scoring, global scoring, or some combination of these scoring methods. With a colleague, discuss features of each rubric that will influence its observer consistency.

TRANSITIONAL ACTIVITY FROM CHAPTER 4 TO CHAPTER 5

In discussion with two or more of your colleagues, address the following questions:

1. The objectives listed for Chapters 1–4 have labels such as "discover a relationship," "construct-a-concept," "comprehension and communication skills," "application," and "appreciation." What are those labels supposed to indicate about the objectives?

2. A percentage figure is tagged on to each objective listed for Chapters 1–4. What purpose do those percentages serve?

3. What are some of the terms used in the professional literature to refer to different types of subject-content?

4. What does the professional literature offer to help teachers focus their thinking on different learning levels targeted by their lessons?

Observer's rubric for Prompts A-L:

Note: For each criterion listed, points are awarded as follows for
   Prompts A-H and K-L:

  +2 if the criterion is clearly met
  +1 if it is unclear as to whether or not the criterion is met
  +0 if the criterion is clearly not met

Each encircled numeral (either 0, 1, or 2) indicates the number of
points the response received for the given criterion.

A. Identifies a judgment Mr. Francisco made (e.g.,
   "Students misunderstand how the juvenile
   justice system works"), not a measurement (e.g.,
   "Hears what Kimberly and Lee said") -------------- 0 1 2
   The judgment cited influenced his decisions to
   revise plans for the upcoming unit ---------------- 0 1 2

B. Identifies a measurement Mr. Francisco made (e.g.,
   "Hears what Kimberly and Lee said") -------------- 0 1 2
   The measurement cited was unplanned --------------- 0 1 2
   The measurement cited influenced the
   formative judgment listed for "A" ---------------- 0 1 2

C. Identifies a judgment Mr. Francisco made (e.g.,
   "Students are getting so focused on what they
   perceive as injustices in ... "), not a
   measurement (e.g., "Hears students' responses
   on the second day") ----------------------------- 0 1 2
   The judgment cited influenced instructional
   decisions during the unit ----------------------- 0 1 2

D. Identifies a measurement Mr. Francisco made (e.g.,
   "Hears students' responses on the ... ") ---------- 0 1 2
   The measurement cited influenced the
   formative judgment listed for "C" ---------------- 0 1 2

E. Identifies an evaluation Mr. Francisco made (e.g.,
   "He assigns grades"), not a measurement
   (e.g., "He administers a unit test") -------------- 0 1 2
   The evaluation cited is summative ------------------ 0 1 2

F. Identifies a measurement Mr. Francisco made (e.g.,
   "He administers the unit test") ------------------ 0 1 2
   The measurement cited influenced the
   summative evaluation listed for "E" -------------- 0 1 2

G. Responds "norm-referenced" and notes that
   visual inspection methods were used -------------- 0 1 2

ILLUSTRATION 4.13

Scoring Form for Synthesis Activity 6

(Continued)

ILLUSTRATION 4.13 (Continued)

```
        Explanation points out that with visual inspection
           grades depend on relative standing of scores ------ 0   1   2

   H. Identifies a measurement you made (e.g., "Read
         Case 4.16" or "Recalled the definition of
         visual inspection")  --------------------------- 0   1   2
      The measurement cited could have reasonably
         influenced your response to Prompt "G" ------------ 0   1   2

   I. Identifies "7" as the easiest ----------------------- 0   1
      Identifies "20" as the most difficult   ------------- 0   1

   J. Indicates internally consistent for Calvin's  -------- 0   1
      Indicates internally inconsistent for Brian's   ------ 0   1
      Indicates internally consistent for Mitsuko's   ------ 0   1
      Indicates internally consistent for Jill's  ---------- 0   1
      Indicates internally consistent for Rosalie's   ------ 0   1

   K. Cites the internally consistent results from
         Calvin's, Mitsuko's, Jill's, or Rosalie's
         responses as shown in Illustration 4.12   ---------- 0   1   2
      Provides reasonable explanation as to why
         the cited results are internally consistent  ------ 0   1   2

   L. Cites the internally inconsistent results from
         Brian's responses as shown in Ill. 4.12   ---------- 0   1   2
      Provides reasonable explanation as to why
         the cited results are internally inconsistent ------ 0   1   2
```

Pinpointing What Students Are to Learn

⟨≋ GOAL OF CHAPTER 5

Chapter 5 is designed to lead you to construct an advanced organizer for specifying the subject-content and learning level of the objectives you want your students to achieve. More specifically, the objectives are as follows:

A. You will explain the rationale for using the advanced organizer for specifying subject-contents and learning levels that is introduced in this chapter (comprehension and communication skills)[1] 10%[2].

B. You will distinguish between examples and non-examples of each of the following types of subject-contents: specific, concept, discoverable relationship, relationship of convention, and process (construct a concept)[1] 20%[2].

C. You will distinguish between examples and non-examples of each of the following types of learning levels: simple knowledge, process knowledge, construct a concept, discover a relationship, comprehension and communication skills, application, creative thinking, appreciation, willingness to try, physical fitness, and psychomotor-skill performance (construct a concept)[1] 25%[2].

D. You will specify the subject-content and the learning level of each objective you set for your students (application)[1] 30%[2].

E. You will define each of your learning goals with a set of weighted objectives—weights that reflect your judgment of the relative importance of each objective (application)[1] 05%[2].

F. You will incorporate the following technical terms and phrases in your working professional vocabulary: "specific," "concept," "subordinate concept," "superordinate concept," "parallel concepts," "discoverable relationship," "relationship of convention," "process," "cognitive domain," "affective domain," "psychomotor domain," "memory-level cognition," "reasoning-level cognition," "simple knowledge," "process knowledge," "construct a concept," "discover a relationship," "comprehension and communication skill," "real-life problem," "application," "creative thinking," "divergent reasoning," "convergent reasoning," "appreciation," "willingness to try," "physical fitness," "psychomotor-skill performance," and "weighting objectives" (comprehension and communication skills)[1] 10%[2].

---

[1]Indicates the learning level of the objective as defined in this chapter.
[2]Indicates the relative importance assigned to the objective as explained in this chapter.

MEANINGFUL LEARNING

Ask yourself, "What is the difference between meaningful learning and learning that is not meaningful for students?" Address the question in a discussion with one or more colleagues. Develop a description of meaningful learning.

Now, read Cases 5.1 through 5.7 and decide which ones include examples of what you and your colleagues consider meaningful learning.

CASE 5.1

Ms. Su uses direct instructional strategies almost exclusively for the language arts lessons she conducts for her fifth-graders. Considerable emphasis is placed on the technical skills of writing, such as writing sentences that adhere to the seven rules enumerated in Case 4.1 (e.g., every sentence should begin with a capital letter). On the other hand, hardly any attention is given to students' writing for the purpose of communicating ideas, thoughts, and feelings that are personally important to them. Ms. Su believes students need to develop writing-mechanics skills well before they attempt to write for a particular purpose or to gear their writing for different audiences.

Most students learn to follow the rules to write sentences. But because they are not taught to write in any context except for Ms. Su's writing-mechanics exercises, they don't apply their writing skills for the purpose of communicating their own messages. Consequently, many students' mechanical skills diminish shortly after they "pass" Ms. Su's test on writing mechanics.

CASE 5.2

Mr. Powell uses inquiry instructional strategies almost exclusively for the language arts lessons he conducts for his fifth-graders. Considerable emphasis is placed on students expressing themselves in their own personal writing style. Mr. Powell does not stress conventional writing or the development of technical mechanical skills because he does not want to suppress students' creativity of expression as they write. Most students develop an affinity for expressing themselves with colorful, creative language; they are motivated to write for their own purposes.

However, as they write, they continue to practice unconventional mechanics that don't adhere to accepted rules of grammar. One student, Jonathan, enthusiastically writes a letter to the editor of the local newspaper in an attempt to persuade drivers to attend to school-crossing zones. Unhappily, the newspaper staff returns his letter with a note indicating that the letter does not meet minimum writing-quality standards for publication.

CASE 5.3

Ms. Fontenot mixes inquiry and direct instructional strategies for the language arts lessons she conducts for her fifth-graders. Considerable emphasis is placed on students expressing their own ideas, thoughts, and feelings in writing for reasons they consider important. Ms. Fontenot does not want to stifle students' creativity of expression by burdening them with detailed writing-mechanics rules. However, she also realizes that for students' writing to be understood by targeted readers and for the writing to be considered acceptable outside of the classroom, certain writing conventions and writing-mechanics rules need to be applied. Thus, she teaches technical writing mechanics in parallel with teaching students to write expressively for their own purposes. Students then learn to edit drafts of their writing creations so that ultimately acceptable rules of writing mechanics are followed without losing any of the thoughts, ideas, feelings, and creative expressions that serve their purposes.

Because they learn to enjoy writing and are positively reinforced for adhering to writing-mechanics rules (e.g., by having their works understood and accepted by targeted readers), their creative writing talents as well as their writing-mechanics skills continue to develop as they write long after Ms. Fontenot's writing unit has been completed.

CASE 5.4

Ms. Gomez conducts a mathematics unit on surface area for her sixth-graders. The goal is defined by the following objectives:

   A. Students state the formula for finding the area of a rectangle (i.e., Area = lw where l is the length and w is the width of the rectangle) (simple knowledge)[1].
   B. Given two of the following three measures of a rectangle, length, width, and area, students compute the third (process knowledge)[1].
   C. Students state the formula for finding the area of a square (i.e., Area = s^2 where s is the length of a side of the square) (simple knowledge)[1].
   D. Given the length of one side of a square, students compute the area of the square, or given the area of a square, students compute the dimensions of the square (process knowledge)[1].
   E. Students state the formula for finding the area of a triangle (i.e., Area = $\frac{1}{2}bh$ where b is a base of the triangle and h is the corresponding altitude) (simple knowledge)[1].
   F. Given two of the following three measures of a triangle, a height, its corresponding base, and the area, students compute the third (process knowledge)[1].
   G. Students state the formula for finding the lateral surface area of a right cylinder (i.e., Lateral surface area = $2\pi rh$ where r is the radius of the right cylinder and h is the height) (simple knowledge)[1].
   H. Given two of the following three measures of a right cylinder, height, radius, and lateral surface area, students compute the third (process knowledge)[1].
   I. Students state the formula for finding the surface area of a cube (i.e., Surface area = $2lw + 2lh + 2hw$ where l is the length of a base, w is the width of that base, and h is the height corresponding to that base) (simple knowledge)[1].
   J. Given three of the following four measures of a cube, height, length, width, and surface area, students compute the fourth (process knowledge)[1].

([1] Indicates the learning level of the objective as defined in this chapter.)

For each objective, Ms. Gomez uses direct instruction to conduct a lesson. For example, for Objective G, she opens the lesson by announcing to the class, "Today, we're going to learn how to compute the lateral surface area of a right cylinder." On an overhead transparency, she displays Illustration 5.1.

She explains, "As you can see by the formula, to find the lateral surface area of a right cylinder, you multiply 2π times the radius of the base times the height." Students write and repeatedly say, "Lateral surface area of a right cylinder = $2\pi rh$ where r is the radius of the right cylinder and h is the height."

She begins the lesson for Objective H by explaining the steps in an algorithm for computing lateral surface areas of right cylinders and then demonstrating the process with examples using specific values for r and h. The students practice the computation with other examples. Later, she explains how to compute the height when the lateral surface area and radius are known, as well as how to compute the radius when the lateral surface area and the height are known. Students also practice with these algorithms.

Most students remember the five formulas as specified by Objectives A, C, E, G, and I and execute the algorithms implied by Objectives B, D, F, H, and J well enough to compute unknown measures for rectangles, squares, triangles, right cylinders, and cubes. However, they don't discover any of the relationships leading to the formulas, nor do they see that the formulas for area of squares, triangles, and right cylinders are nothing more than an application of the formula for computing the area of a rectangle. Because the skills are taught in isolation, students don't use the skills they developed beyond this unit. In a few weeks, their memories of the formulas fade and their skills deteriorate.

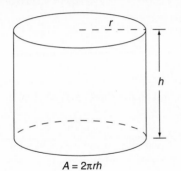

$A = 2\pi rh$

ILLUSTRATION 5.1

Ms. Gomez's Overhead Transparency Display

CASE 5.5

Mr. Eubanks realizes that depth of learning depends on students constructing knowledge for themselves from their own interactions and experiences. Thus, he uses inquiry instructional strategies almost exclusively as he conducts a mathematics unit on surface area for his sixth-graders. The goal is defined by the following objectives:

A. Students will discover and explain why the area of a rectangle is the product of the rectangle's length and width (discover a relationship)[1].

B. From their knowledge of the relationship $A = lw$ (where A is the area of a rectangle, l is the length, and w is the width), students will construct formulas for finding the surface areas of other geometric shapes, including triangles, right cylinders, and cubes (discover a relationship)[1].

([1] Indicates the learning level of the objective as defined in this chapter.)

Mr. Eubanks begins one activity during a lesson for Objective B by telling students, "With the permission of Mr. Parker-Sanchez [the head custodian for the school], I've asked Izar and Elaine to bring in one of the trash barrels from the school grounds." The two students, Izar and Elaine, stand the barrel up in front of the classroom. Mr. Eubanks continues, "Mr. Parker-Sanchez told me he plans to repaint all these barrels. He thought instead of using this drab gray again, he'd try to make them a bit more decorative this time. Yes, Parisa, you have the floor."

Parisa:	"What has this got to do with us?"
Mr. Eubanks:	"Mr. Parker-Sanchez thought you might have some ideas on what colors he should use. Yes, Izar?"
Izar:	"Could we have pictures and stuff drawn on them?"
Mr. Eubanks:	"Mr. Parker-Sanchez said each of the three sections of the barrels could be different colors, but nothing fancier than that. He also said he'd let us choose the colors in exchange for providing him with an estimate of the amount of paint he has to buy. If he's going to use colors other than the gray he has now, it's going to be expensive and he doesn't want to buy more than he needs."

Further discussions lead the students to recognize the need to find the lateral surface area of the barrels. No one has a formula for computing it, but Mr. Eubanks continues, "We may not know how to figure the area of this barrel, but there are some shapes with areas we can compute. Everyone, please write down the names of three shapes for which you have area formulas." Observing that everyone has written something, he continues, "In the order I call your names, read your lists: Elaine, Mark, and Eli."

Elaine:	"Square, rectangle, triangle."

Mark:	"Rectangle, triangle, and other polygon."
Eli:	"Rectangle, square, triangle."
Mark:	"But a square is a rectangle, so you didn't also need to list square."
Mr. Eubanks:	"Isn't that also true for this barrel?"
Michelle:	"No, a barrel isn't a type of rectangle."
Mr. Eubanks:	"Hmm, maybe that's so. I was just thinking about the part of this barrel that needs to be painted."
Izar:	"Well, we said only the outside needs to be painted."
Mr. Eubanks:	"What if we just covered the outside of the barrel with colorful contact paper?"
Michelle:	"That would never hold up."
Mr. Eubanks:	"Yeah, too bad! It's just that seeing our butcher paper over here in the corner gave me that idea. It seemed so simple just to wrap paper around the barrel. Too bad it wouldn't hold up!"
Ebony:	"Mr. Eubanks, may I try something with our butcher paper?"

Ebony wraps a section of the paper around the barrel, cuts it, unwraps it, and then displays the rectangular-shape to the rest of the class. Eyes light up around the room as students begin to understand what Ebony demonstrated: The lateral surface area of the barrel is equivalent to the area of a rectangle whose dimensions can be obtained from the barrel. See Illustration 5.2.

The lesson continues with Mr. Eubanks playing upon Ebony's discovery to lead students to associate the circumference of the base of a right cylinder with a rectangle's width and the height of the cylinder with the rectangle's length. By the end of the class period, most students understand why the lateral surface area of a barrel is $2\pi rh$.

They understand how they can construct new knowledge from what they already understand; they develop a real feel for how mathematics is discovered and invented. However, Mr. Eubanks doesn't use direct instruction to help them develop their skills using the formula they discovered to solve for unknown quantities. Thus, students don't make practical use of their discoveries.

CASE 5.6

Ms. Gaston realizes that depth of learning depends on students constructing knowledge for themselves from their own interactions and experiences. She also realizes that students need to develop certain mechanical skills and be able to recall certain information so that their discoveries have practical utility for them. Thus, she uses both inquiry and direct instructional strategies as she conducts a mathematics unit on surface area for her sixth-graders. The goal is defined by the following objectives:

A. Students discover and explain why the area of a rectangle is the product of the rectangle's length and width (discover a relationship)[1].

B. Students state the formula for finding the area of a rectangle (i.e., Area = lw where l is the length and w is the width of the rectangle) (simple knowledge)[1].

C. Given two of the following three measures of a rectangle, length, width, and area, students compute the third (process knowledge)[1].

D. From their understanding of the relationship A = lw (where A is the area of a rectangle, l is the length, and w is the width), students construct formulas for finding the surface areas of other geometric shapes, including triangles, right cylinders, and cubes (discover a relationship)[1].

E. Students efficiently access area formulas they discovered by recalling them or knowing where to find them (e.g., from a computer file or notebook) (simple knowledge)[1].

F. Given the necessary dimensions for computing the surface area of a geometric figure from a formula to which they have access, students compute the surface area of that figure (process knowledge)[1].

ILLUSTRATION 5.2

Ebony Demonstrates That the Lateral Surface Area of a Right Cylinder Is the Area of a Rectangle

G. Given all but one of the necessary dimensions for computing the surface area of a geometric figure from a formula to which they have access and given the surface area of that figure, students compute the missing dimension (process knowledge)[1].

H. Confronted with a real-life problem, students decide how, if at all, they can use one or more of their surface-area formulas to address that problem (application)[1].

([1] Indicates the learning level of the objective as defined in this chapter.)

Her lessons for Objectives A and D employ instructional strategies similar to Mr. Eubank's in Case 5.5. Lessons for Objectives B, C, F, and G employ instructional strategies similar to Ms. Gomez's in Case 5.4. To teach for Objective E, Ms. Gaston directs students to set up and use a system by which they can efficiently look up formulas as needed. Her lesson for Objective H employs inquiry strategies that promote deductive reasoning (as explained in Chapter 10). The inquiry strategies she employed in lessons for Objectives A and D promoted inductive reasoning (as explained in Chapter 7).

Because students achieved Objective H, they continued to make use of their discoveries and skills with their area formulas long after completing this unit. Their achievement of Objective H, however, was dependent on their achievement of Objectives A–G.

CASE 5.7

As she plans for the opening of the school year with her third-grade class, Ms. Hyder thinks about how she will begin teaching students to comply with the following standards of classroom conduct:

1. Respect the rights of others.

2. Respect your own rights.

3. Give everyone a chance to learn.

4. Follow procedures.

She thinks, "They need to comprehend exactly what each of these standards means, and then they need to apply them to all the different situations that crop up during the year. They also need to simply remember them. But some of these children won't have constructed the concept of respecting rights; that is, they need to discriminate between examples of respecting rights and disrespecting rights. So that means I need to have some inquiry activities for that. Also, even after they've constructed the concept of respecting rights, they still need to learn how to protect rights—especially their own. I'll probably have some students like Cito last year. Cito understood very well when his rights were being disrespected, and he even knew that he should hold on to his rights by being assertive rather than passive or hostile. But he just never developed the communication skills to pull it off. He just lacked the mechanics of being assertive although he understood he should be. I hope he has a better year in fourth grade than he did in third. Okay, I should stop regretting the past and start learning from it. This year I'm going to be more diligent about teaching students all the aspects needed to comply with these standards—the conceptual stuff, the comprehension, the mechanical, the affective, and the application."

Ms. Hyder decides to organize the teaching of classroom behavior standards just as she would organize a unit for teaching for an academic goal. This behavior-standards unit will be conducted concurrently with academic units and will extend throughout the year. In previous years, she was less formal in her plans for teaching classroom behavior standards, but in an attempt to cover all bases, she defines a goal with a set of objectives:

Goal: Students comply with the four classroom behavior standards.

A. Students discriminate between examples of rights being respected and rights being disrespected (construct a concept)[1].

B. Students explain how the quality of life within the classroom community is affected by community members respecting one another's rights, as well as their own rights, as opposed to those rights being disrespected (discover a relationship)[1].

C. Students explain the meaning of Classroom Behavior Standards 1 and 2 (comprehension and communication skills)[1].

D. Students state the four classroom behavior standards (simple knowledge)[1].

E. Students explain how Classroom Behavior Standard 3 relates to Classroom Behavior Standards 1 and 2 (e.g., the opportunity to learn is a right) (discover a relationship)[1].

F. Students explain how Classroom Behavior Standard 4 relates to Classroom Behavior Standard 3 (e.g., procedures are necessary to provide opportunities to learn) (discover a relationship)[1].

G. Students explain the meaning of Classroom Behavior Standards 3 and 4 (comprehension and communication skills)[1].

H. Students value the classroom behavior standards, judging them to be important for their own well-being and the well-being of the classroom community (appreciation)[1].

I. Students discriminate among examples of assertive, passive, and hostile communications (construct a concept)[1].

J. Students develop the assertive communication techniques necessary to comply with the classroom behavior standards (process knowledge)[1].

K. Confronted with a problem relative to classroom behavior, students determine how assertiveness techniques should be employed to address the problem (application)[1].

L. Confronted with a classroom event, students determine whether or not a classroom behavior standard was violated (application)[1].

M. Students choose to comply with classroom behavior standards (willingness to try)[1].

([1] Indicates the learning level of the objective as defined in this chapter.)

Over the past 20 years, professional education associations for virtually every teaching specialty have sponsored reports suggesting curriculum and evaluations standards. The vast majority of these reports suggest that for learning to be meaningful, students need to be able to apply what they learn in situations that are important to them (see, e.g., National Center for History in the Schools, 1997; National Council of Teachers of English & International Reading Association, 1996; National Council of Teachers of Mathematics, 1989; National Research Council, 1996; New Jersey Department of Education, 1997). For students to build upon what they learn and apply it in meaningful ways, they need to construct knowledge as exemplified in Cases 5.2 and 5.5, but they also need to acquire skills as exemplified in Cases 5.1 and 5.4. Cases 5.1 and 5.4 are examples of what many consider traditional instruction emphasizing memorization and mechanical skills, whereas Cases 5.2 and 5.5 are examples of teachers who are following suggestions from curricula reformers who tend to refer to themselves as "constructivists." But many of the more renowned constructivist researchers acknowledge that some memory-level and mechanical learning needs to complement knowledge construction in order for learning to be applicable to realistic situations (von Glasersfeld, 1995). Likewise, many hardcore proponents of direct instruction, who refer to students "mastering" very specific objectives, recognize that depth of understanding depends on students also constructing knowledge from their own experiences (Woolfolk, 1993, pp. 480–500).

The teachers in Cases 5.3, 5.6, and 5.7 incorporate both inquiry and direct instructional strategies with the intent of leading students to make their learning meaningful.

RATIONALE FOR THE ADVANCED ORGANIZER FOR SPECIFYING SUBJECT-CONTENT AND LEARNING LEVEL

NEEDED ABILITIES, ATTITUDES, AND SKILLS

The purpose of any advanced organizer for specifying subject-contents and learning levels is to help clarify learning objectives in a way that provides some direction as to how lessons for those objectives should be designed (e.g., to decide whether a particular lesson should employ inquiry or direct instructional strategies). But more to the point of this book, clarification of subject-contents and learning levels is necessary in order for you to design mini-experiments that are relevant to your objectives.

The particular advanced organizer to which you are about to be introduced is designed with the idea that you want to formulate sequences of objectives that, if achieved, result in meaningful learning. Thus, you will see learning level categories (e.g., "construct-a-concept") that suggest a constructivist perspective, while others (e.g., "process knowledge") suggest direct teaching strategies (often associated with a behaviorist approach). You, of course, retain the option of using whatever advanced-organizer categories fit your situation and rejecting the others.

SIMPLIFYING OBJECTIVES BY OPERATIONALLY DEFINING WORDS

No Need for Behavioral Objectives

Since Robert Mager (1961) published his popular book *Preparing Instructional Objectives*, many teachers have been encouraged, directed, or taught in their teacher-preparation programs and by administrative supervisors to clearly explicate their objectives in "well-stated behavioral" terms. According to Mager, for an objective to be "well-stated," it has to include four elements: (1) a *performance*, indicating what students are expected to do, (2) a *product*, indicating what students are to produce by their performance, (3) a *condition*, indicating the circumstances under which students are to perform, and (4) the *criterion*, indicating the standard of performance for the objective to be considered achieved. The following are given as examples of "well-stated" objectives by Moore (1992, p. 55):

A. "Given a set of pictures, the student will be able to place pictures in proper sequence with no more than one error."

B. "Given the necessary materials and the dimensions, the student will construct a polygon with all dimensions being within 5 percent."

C. "The student will be able to identify (select letter) on a multiple-choice test the subplots of the poems read in class with 100 percent accuracy."

D. "After completing a series of Spanish-language tapes, the student will orally recite a given Spanish dialogue with no errors in pronunciation."

E. "The student will write a 300-word essay on a given social studies topic with no sentence fragments and no more than two errors in grammar."

The *performances* for these five "well-stated" objectives are indicated by the following phrases:

A. "the student will be able to place pictures in proper sequence"

B. "the student will construct a polygon"

C. "the student will be able to identify (select letter) on a multiple-choice test the subplots of the poems read in class"

D. "the student will orally recite a given Spanish dialogue"

E. "the student will write a 300-word essay on a given social studies topic"

The *products* for these five "well-stated" objectives are indicated by the following phrases:

A. "pictures in proper sequence"

B. "a polygon"

C. "selections of letters on a multiple-choice test"

D. "oral recitation of a given Spanish dialogue"

E. "a 300-word essay on a given social studies topic"

The *conditions* for these five "well-stated" objectives are indicated by the following phrases:

A. "given a set of pictures"

B. "given the necessary materials and the dimensions"

C. "a multiple-choice test"

D. "after completing a series of Spanish language tapes"

E. prompt to write "a 300-word essay"

The *criteria* for these five "well-stated" objectives are indicated by the following phrases:

A. "with no more than one error"

B. "within 5 percent"

C. "with 100 percent accuracy"

D. "with no errors in pronunciation"

E. "with no sentence fragments and no more than two errors in grammar"

While I applaud Mager's work and the work of others who focused attention on the need for specifically stated objectives, I do not recommend that you should write your objectives in this behavioral, four-element style. First of all, this style does not efficiently accommodate the objectives that are intended to have sophisticated learning levels. Unless you are willing to state objectives as descriptive paragraphs, this style doesn't pinpoint complex subject-contents or learning levels. Achievement of Objective A from Moore's list, for example, requires students to place pictures in a proper sequence. I assume the intent is for the student to use some sort of reasoning, but what form of reasoning? What's the proper sequence? The way Objective A is stated, complex questions are left unanswered that need to be answered before a lesson and relevant mini-experiments are designed. More words are needed to clarify the statement. Consequently, while behavioral objectives tend to be embraced by proponents of mastery-learning models, they are perceived as a hindrance to meaningful learning by many who value constructivist approaches.

Personally, I do not believe criterion elements should be included in the statement of most objectives. Most objectives should target subject-contents and learning levels that are not either absolutely achieved or absolutely not achieved. They are achieved in degrees. Furthermore, I don't want my objectives to limit me in the ways I can measure my students' achievement of them. I want the option of using a variety of mini-experiments, so the statement of my objectives doesn't include phrases such as, "on a multiple-choice test." Typically, the criteria are meaningless anyway. For example, how difficult is that multiple-choice test and how complex is the Spanish dialogue alluded to in the statements of Objectives C and D respectively?

A Suggestion for Writing Objectives

Except for Moore's Objectives A–E, the objectives appearing in this book do not meet Mager's standards for being "well-stated." Instead of "well-stated" behavioral objectives, consider using just enough words to clarify the subject-content you want your objective to specify and then specify the learning level using one of the labels operationally defined in the advanced organizer explained in subsequent sections of this chapter. For example, in Case 5.6, Ms. Gaston wrote the following objective:

> A. Students discover and explain why the area of a rectangle is the product of the rectangle's length and width (discover a relationship).

Her words are specific enough that she understands that the subject-content is the relationship, area of a rectangle = length × width. But what exactly does she mean by "will discover and explain?" She knows because she comprehends the operational definition of "discover a relationship." Because of that label, it wasn't necessary for her to expand the statement to explain the rather complex and sophisticated process implied by "discover a relationship."

SUBJECT-CONTENT SPECIFIED BY AN OBJECTIVE

SPECIFICS

Understanding learning-level categories depends on understanding of subject-content. Thus, the advanced organizer includes subject-content categories as well as categories for learning levels. The least abstract type of subject-content is a *specific*. A *specific* is any unique entity. Thus, a single thing (whether it be a substance, creature, thought, event, phenomenon, activity, observation, document, topic, or whatever) can be appropriately referred to as a "*specific*," providing that the reference is made to one and only one thing. Examine the items in Illustration 5.3. Which are entities of which one and only one exists? Exchange and discuss responses with a colleague.

In Case 5.8, Kisha and Elwin discuss their responses to Illustration 5.3's question.

A. the copy of the book you are now reading

B. book

C. belief about the past

D. the belief that strategies for gaining civil rights espoused by Martin Luther King, Jr., and James Lawson were influenced by their knowledge of Mohandas Gandhi's policies of nonviolent resistance

E. The *Civil Rights Act of 1964*

F. Congressional act

G. Martin Luther King, Jr.

H. Nobel Peace laureate

I. speed of a moving object

J. 34 meters per minute

K. persons named "George"

L. The very last person to whom you spoke whose name is "George"

M. proper noun

N. the name "George"

O. the following rectangle:

P. rectangle

Q. mini-experiment

R. Mini-Experiment 8 from Illustration 4.10

S. Rosita from Case 1.1

T. Student

ILLUSTRATION 5.3

Which Words Refer to Specifics?

CASE 5.8

Kisha: "The specifics from Illustration 5.3 I listed are A, D, E, G, J, L, N, O, and S. R might be a specific also; that's one I want to discuss with you."

Elwin: "My list is a lot like yours. I labeled R as a specific. Let's see where mine differs from yours. Let's talk about A. Why did you think 'the copy of the book you are now reading' is a specific?"

Kisha: "When I was doing this exercise by myself, I had no doubt it was a specific because A referred to one and only one thing, namely the copy of the book I was reading at the time. But now I see that from your perspective, A refers to the book you were reading at the time, not the book I was reading at the time. Wow, this is confusing!"

Elwin: "So, since A refers to one copy of the book when you're reading it and another copy of the book when I'm reading mine, A must refer to a variable, not something that's unique."

Kisha: "So something can be one thing at one point in time and another later. It's very ambiguous. Some of these others, like E and G, aren't ambiguous; there is only one Civil Rights Act of 1964 and only one Martin Luther King, Jr."

Elwin: "What if someone else's name is Martin Luther King, Jr.; then wouldn't G refer to more than one thing?"

Kisha: "No. I think G refers to *the* Martin Luther King, Jr., not just anyone with that same name."

Elwin: "Don't you think we're trying to read too much into this exercise? We could drive ourselves crazy looking at all the possible nuances."

Kisha: "Actually, I think it's good for us to do this—at least as an exercise. It teaches us to be analytical with the subject-content of our objectives. It's not necessary for us to come to closure on all of these, but it's important that we start analyzing subject-content—just to get us to understand it better."

Elwin: "Okay, so maybe we don't agree on some of these, not because we have a different conception of the meaning of 'specific,' but because we're interpreting these expressions A through T differently. That's okay. The idea is that we understand that one-of-a-kind things are specifics."

Kisha: "I agree, but there are still some I want to discuss."

Elwin: "I do too. How about K, L, and N. We agree that K is not a specific because more than one person is named 'George.' So by that same reasoning, isn't there more than one name 'George'?"

Kisha: "Many people go by the name 'George,' but the name 'George' is only one name. The reason 'George' is in quotes for N is because the name 'George' is being referred to, not George the person—without quote marks."

Elwin: "Okay, I understand now. What about L? You marked that one a specific; I didn't."

Kisha: "L is confusing for the same reason that A is confusing. 'You' means Elwin when you're the reader and 'you' is Kisha when I'm the reader."

Elwin: "So it's unique to us as individuals but then varies as readers vary."

Kisha: "Hey, I like the way you put that! I'm going to consider A, L, and O to be specifics as long as the reader of Illustration 5.3 is unique. When more than one reader comes into the picture, A, L, and O are no longer specifics."

Elwin: "Why did you include O in that ambiguous category?"

Kisha: "Because the rectangle in your copy of the book is a different rectangle than the one in my copy. Sure, they are the same size and shape, but they are two different rectangles. So O is a specific in the context of one and only one book but not in the context of two or more books. Let's talk about R."

Elwin: "I called it a specific because the reference isn't to just any mini-experiment, like Q, but to a very specific mini-experiment, namely 8 from Illustration 4.10. It has a specific prompt and observer's rubric."

Kisha: "I absolutely agree. But here's why I have a question. What appears in Illustration 4.10 is sort of a blueprint for how to carry out a specific mini-experiment, rather than the mini-experiment actually being carried out. If Mini-Experiment 8 is conducted with one group of students and then later with another, are those two administrations the same experiment? The process was identical, but the subjects and conditions are not. I guess it's another perspective problem. If a mini-experiment can be conducted more than once, than I agree R is a specific. If not, then R isn't a specific."

Elwin: "So if R had clearly indicated that it referred to exactly one administration of a mini-experiment like—let me find it . . . Case 4.6 and Illustrations 4.3 and 4.4 relate not only the prompt and scoring rubric for Mini-Experiment B–1; they also refer to a specific administration of Mini-Experiment B–1 with results. That's clearly a specific event."

Case 5.8 suggests that Kisha and Elwin have successfully constructed the concept of *specific* and comprehend the meaning of the subject-content category "specific." Their confusion seems to be born out of different ways Illustration 5.3's expressions can be interpreted rather than from disagreement about the meaning of "specific." Technically, two administrations of Mini-Experiment 8 from Illustration 4.10 are not the same experiment. So, in one sense, R is not a specific. However, it is convenient to use the term "mini-experiment" in both ways: (1) as a process for presenting a prompt and observing responses to the prompt and (2) as a single administration of that process. The context in which "mini-experiment" appears should clarify the meaning. The term was presented out of context by Illustration 5.3; thus Kisha was confused. Her display of confusion was an indicator that she has a sophisticated grasp of the concept of a mini-experiment as well as the concept of a specific.

The subject-content of the following objective is the Preamble to the Constitution of the United States, a specific:

Students will explain the message expressed in the Preamble of the Constitution of the United States (comprehension and communication skills)[1].

Specifics are not one of the more common types of subject-contents for objectives. Curricula typically focus more on abstractions, relationships, and processes than on specifics. However, specifics form the building blocks of all the other types of subject-contents.

CONCEPTS

Examine Illustration 5.4's 35 items. Group the 35 specifics into seven sets so that each of the specifics belongs to at least one of the seven sets. Assign a name to each set.

Kisha and Elwin engaged in this activity and produced the groupings in Illustration 5.5.

If each of your seven categories, like Kisha's and Elwin's, includes at least two specifics, then each category is a *concept*. A *concept* is a category people mentally construct from a set of two or more specifics that have some common *attributes*. Thus, a concept is an abstraction.

Subject-content from Ms. Fisher's objectives from Illustration 2.12, numbers, people, words, former state governors, former U.S. presidents, whole numbers, organizations, congressional legislation, humans, Spanish words, proper names, and English words except for proper nouns are examples of concepts. However, when Kisha and Elwin engaged in the categorizing activity that produced the concepts listed in Illustration 5.5, they weren't so much constructing new concepts as much as they were simply identifying specific examples of concepts they constructed years ago and have learned to associate with conventional names

A. *Thirteenth Amendment to the Constitution*	R. American Civil Liberties Union (ACLU)
B. Harry Truman	S. -91
C. *Civil Rights Act of 1866*	T. "dig"
D. "congraciamiento"	U. "jump"
E. *Fourteenth Amendment to the Constitution*	V. National Association for the Advancement of Colored People
F. Ronald Reagan	W. "George"
G. George Wallace	X. $\frac{2}{3}$
H. Elijah Muhammad	Y. "window"
I. *Fifteenth Amendment to the Constitution*	Z. *Civil Rights Act of 1957*
J. "amor"	AA. Ku Klux Klan
K. Orville Faubus	BB. Rosa Parks
L. $\sqrt{5}$	CC. $\sqrt{9}$
M. Medgar Evers	DD. *Voting Rights Act of 1965*
N. 33	EE. "Jesse"
O. $\frac{5}{8}$	FF. Lyndon Johnson
P. "beetle"	GG. Ross Barnett
Q. 2.391	HH. Martin Luther King, Jr.
	II. .044

ILLUSTRATION 5.4

Specifics

(e.g., "whole numbers" and "congressional legislation"). In Cases 5.9 and 5.10, Josh and Terri construct concepts.

CASE 5.9

Josh is an infant who feels the warmth and movement of his mother when she nurses him. He hears the sounds emanating from her. Josh's father holds him and Josh experiences some of the same sensations as when he is near his mother. The house cat rubs by Josh and Josh notices that the cat is motile and re-acts to Josh's touch in a fashion similar to his parents' reactions. Josh has contact with his toys, but none

Kisha's Groupings

1. Subject-content from Ms. Fisher's objectives from Illustration 2.12:

   A   B   C   E   G   H   I   K   M

   R   V   Z   AA   BB   DD   GG   FF   HH

2. Numbers:

   L   N   O   Q   S   X   CC   II

3. People:

   B   F   G   H   K   M   BB   FF   GG   HH

4. Words:

   D   J   P   T   U   W   Y   EE

5. Former state governors:

   F   G   K   GG

6. Former U.S. presidents:

   B   F   FF

7. Whole numbers:

   N   CC

Elwin's Groupings

1. Numbers:

   L   N   O   Q   S   X   CC   II

2. Organizations:

   R   V   AA

3. Congressional legislation:

   A   C   E   I   Z   DD

4. Humans:

   B   F   G   H   K   M   BB   FF   GG   HH

5. Spanish words:

   D   J

6. Proper names:

   W   EE

7. English words except for proper nouns:

   P   T   U   Y

ILLUSTRATION 5.5

Kisha's and Elwin's Groupings of Illustration 5.4's Specifics

of them feels warm and vibrating the way his parents and cat feel. His toys do not move by themselves, nor do they breathe. In time, Josh encounters numerous other entities, including humans, dogs, furniture, spiders, clothing, food, paper, and plants. Although Josh does not know conventional names for his categories, he categorizes and classifies what he encounters in many ways. For example, he associates humans, cats, dogs, and possibly some other creatures together and places clothes, toys, furniture, and some other things in another separate category. Thus, Josh is developing a concept of living things.

When Josh begins to discriminate between things that are alive and things that are not, he is constructing the concept of an animate being. Josh constructs a myriad of concepts long before he knows conventional names for the concepts. While Josh is still very young, he may only classify his mother, father, and cat as being alive. A few years will pass before he discovers that a tree or oyster has the attributes of being alive.

CASE 5.10

Over the past month, Terri has encountered variables in her seventh-grade science, social studies, and prealgebra courses. During that time, she noticed differences and similarities among those variables. Although she never made a conscious effort to do so, she has begun to create a dichotomy between two types. The first type includes variables such as temperature fluctuations, length of wars, and all real numbers between two specific real numbers (e.g., -2 and 14.2448). The second type includes variables such as atomic numbers of chemical elements, memorable dates in history, and all the whole numbers between two specific whole numbers (e.g., 4 and 117).

Terri thinks of the first type as more difficult to deal with because, as she says, "It's too packed in to list two things that are next to one another." Terri is apparently constructing the concept of continuous data and the concept of discrete data. She does not, however, know the concepts by those names.

People, such as Josh and Terri, have experiences with specifics that lead them to identify similarities among some of those specifics. They use abstract reasoning to realize that those similarities (i.e., *concept attributes*) distinguish specifics that are examples of the concept from specifics that are not examples of the concept (i.e., *non-examples of the concept*) (Cangelosi, 1996, pp. 79–84; Kelley, 1988, pp. 263–367; Metz, 1995).

Return to the seven categories you abstracted from Illustration 5.4's list of specifics. Categorize those seven categories so that you've collapsed them into three categories. Kisha's and Elwin's responses to this prompt appear in Illustration 5.6.

Note that by grouping concepts together, you construct a new concept. In Illustration 5.6, for example, Kisha's new concept that she labeled "subject-content of mathematics or language-arts curricula" subsumes the three concepts: numbers, words, and whole numbers. A concept that subsumes another is a *superordinate concept* with respect to the concept it subsumes. The subsumed concept is *subordinate* to the superordinate concept. Note from illustration 5.6, not only is subject-content of mathematics or language-arts curricula superordinate to the three concepts of numbers, words, and whole numbers, but there is also a superordinate-subordinate relationship between numbers and whole numbers (since every whole number is also a number).

If two concepts are such that one is not subordinate to the other, then the two concepts have a *parallel relationship*. Thus, the concept of words and the concept of numbers are *parallel concepts*.

These distinctions will be helpful to you as you design mini-experiments relevant to objectives that specify concepts for subject-contents.

RELATIONSHIPS

Discoverable Relationships

Look at Illustration 5.7. Place an "s" by each item that designates a specific, a "c" by each designating a concept, and an "r" by each of the rest.

Illustration 5.8 displays Kisha's classifications of the items from Illustration 5.7. Hopefully, any differences between the way she labeled these items and the way you labeled them are due to differences in how the two of you interpreted the way the items are worded, not due to differences between your and her conceptions of specifics and concepts.

<u>Kisha's 3 Categories for Her 7
Concepts from Illustration 5.5</u>

1. <u>Subject-content from Ms. Fisher's
   objectives from Illustration 2.12</u>:

   1. Subject-content from Ms. Fisher's
      objectives from Illustration 2.12

2. <u>Subject-content of mathematics
   or language-arts curricula:</u>

   1. Numbers
   2. Words
   7. Whole numbers

3. <u>People</u>:

   3. People
   5. Former state governors
   6. Former U.S. presidents

<u>Elwin's 3 Categories for Her 7
Concepts from Illustration 5.5</u>

1. <u>Numbers:</u>

   1. Numbers

2. <u>People or their creations:</u>

   2. Organizations

   3. Congressional legislation

   4. Humans

3. <u>Words:</u>

   5. Spanish words

   6. Proper names

   7. English words except for proper nouns

ILLUSTRATION 5.6

Kisha and Elwin Categorized the Concepts They Listed in Illustration 5.5

Note that the items from Illustration 5.7 that Kisha labeled with an "r" are not simply designations of specifics or concepts. Item D, for example, associates a specific (i.e., the Thirteenth Amendment) with a concept (i.e., slavery) using a second concept (i.e., an act of abolishing). Such associations establish *relationships*. A *relationship* is a particular association between either (1) concepts (e.g., a bear is a mammal), (2) a concept and a specific (e.g., alcohol boils at 78°C), or (3) specifics (e.g., Isaac Newton was born in 1642).

The three previously listed examples of relationships, as well as the six relationships listed in Illustration 5.7, are *discoverable relationships*. A relationship is *discoverable* if one can use

---

A. *Thirteenth Amendment to the Constitution*

B. an act of abolishing

C. slavery

D. The *Thirteenth Amendment to the Constitution* abolished slavery.

E. "George" is a popular name.

F. popular name

G. Case 1.1 from this book

H. Rosita from Case 1.1

I. In Case 1.1, Rosita displayed disruptive behavior.

J. display of disruptive behavior

K. rectangle

L. the rectangle in Item O of Illustration 5.3 from your copy of this book

M. The sum of the measures of the 4 angles of any rectangle is 360°

N. sum of the measures

O. 4

P. angle

Q. 360°

R. rate of motion

S. time

T. distance

U. rate × time = distance

V. A body continues in a state of rest or uniform motion in a straight line unless it is acted upon by an external force.

ILLUSTRATION 5.7

Three Types of Subject-Content

A-s	B-c	C-c	D-r	E-r	F-c	G-s	H-s	I-r	J-c	K-c
L-s	M-r	N-c	O-s	P-c	Q-s	R-c	S-c	T-c	U-r	V-r

ILLUSTRATION 5.8

Kisha Categorized the Items in Illustration 5.7

reasoning or experimentation to find out that the relationship exists. For example, Illustration 5.7's relationships are discoverable because of the following:

Item D. By reading the Thirteenth Amendment and comprehending its message in the context of their knowledge of the era in which it was written, students can conclude that the Thirteenth Amendment abolished slavery. They can figure that out for themselves.

Item E. Whether or not "George" is a popular name is a question students can address by conducting a survey or looking up records and then making a decision about the name's popularity.

Item I. From reading Case 1.1 and applying their concept of disruptive behavior, students can decide for themselves whether or not Rosita displayed disruptive behavior.

Item M. Students can measure the four angles of each of many different rectangles to discover that the sum for each rectangle is 360°. Then they might use inductive reasoning to decide that the relationship is going to be true for any rectangle. Or students might simply reason, "By definition of rectangle, each of the four angles measures $90 \times 4 = 360$."

Item U. To discover the relationship rate × time = distance, students might engage in an activity similar to the one in which Mr. Heaps engaged his students in Case 2.10.

Item V. By applying concepts they previously constructed and relationships they previously discovered, students can engage in experiments to discover Newton's first law of motion (i.e., the relationship stated in Item V of Illustration 5.7).

Relationships of Convention

All the relationships you want your students to learn are not discoverable. Examine the relationships appearing in Illustration 5.9. Which ones are not discoverable?

In Case 5.11, Kisha and Elwin discuss their responses to Illustration 5.9's prompt.

CASE 5.11

Kisha:	"I said they are all discoverable except for B, C, and G."
Elwin:	"What about E? Isn't that just a definition, just like C?"
Kisha:	"No. C gives the definition of 'rational number.' E on the other hand is a relationship students can use reasoning to figure out for themselves, providing they comprehend the definition of 'rational number' and have constructed the concept of whole number. In mathematics, it's a provable truth—a theorem, in other words—rather than a definition based on a convention."
Elwin:	"The other one I want to discuss is G. It seems to me that students can discover those laws were called 'Jim Crow laws' on their own. They can study historical records and find that out for themselves. So doesn't that make G discoverable?"

A. A body continues in a state of rest or uniform motion in a straight line unless it is acted upon by an external force.

B. The following principle is called "Newton's first law of motion":

A body continues in a state of rest or uniform motion in a straight line unless it is acted upon by an external force.

C. A number which can be expressed as a fraction so that both the numerator and denominator are integers is called a "rational number."

D. $\sqrt{9}$ is a rational number.

E. Any whole number is a rational number.

F. $\sqrt{5}$ is not a rational number.

G. State and local laws passed in the 1800s in support of racial segregation were known as "Jim Crow laws."

H. Jim Crow laws helped perpetuate a system of injustices.

ILLUSTRATION 5.9

Which of These Relationships Are Not Discoverable?

Kisha: "You just got at the heart of the difference between discoverable relationships and relationships that exist because of conventions to which people agree. Sure students can study records and find for themselves that those segregation laws were known as 'Jim Crow.' But they would still be informed that was the name; they wouldn't need to go through some deductive or inductive reasoning process to conclude the name. Granted, they may have to do some major reasoning and problem solving to figure out how to locate their sources of information. That would be a higher-level process than just reading the name 'Jim Crow' out of a single textbook or hearing it from a teacher's mouth. But it would still be finding out rather than reasoning out."

Elwin: "Okay, your argument makes sense when I compare the relationship H to relationship G. For G, students could apply their comprehension of Jim Crow laws and their concept of injustices to deduce the relationship that Jim Crow laws helped perpetuate a system of injustices."

Kisha: "Good point. Unfortunately, in many history courses, students are not stimulated to discover relationship H for themselves. They are just told about it or read about it."

Elwin: "It would be much better understood if students discovered that relationship by appealing to their own reasoning rather than the typical appeal to authority—it's true because the book or teacher said so."

Associations that have been formed as a matter of convention (e.g., agreement within a community of scientists to refer to the principle stated for A in Illustration 5.9 as "Newton's first law of motion") are *relationships of convention*. A *relationship of convention* is a

relationship that exists because it has been established through tradition or agreement. Vocabulary, for example, exists because of the invention of conventional relationships between words and their meanings.

Obviously, the way you teach and design mini-experiments for objectives that specify discoverable relationships should be different than for objectives that specify relationships of convention.

PROCESSES

A *process* is a systematic, step-by-step method by which a task is accomplished. *Processes* depend on relationships. For example, a process for measuring temperature with a thermometer is based on two relationships, one conventional, the other discoverable. The relationship of convention is the following: A centigrade thermometer is scaled so that the freezing point of water is labeled "0°C" and the boiling point is labeled "100°C".

The discoverable relationship is as follows: Mercury expands when heated.

Illustration 5.10 lists a variety of objectives. Examine each to identify its subject-content and then label that subject-content as either a "specific," "concept," "discoverable relationship," "relationship of convention," or "process."

Kisha's responses to Illustration 5.10's prompts are displayed in Illustration 5.11. Keep in mind that differences between her responses and yours may be due to differences in how you interpreted the way the objectives are stated. The advanced organizer presented in this chapter is designed to help teachers write their own objectives, not analyze the objectives of other teachers. The exercise in which you and Kisha just engaged is simply to help you clarify different subject-content categories, not to provide practice using the advanced organizer. That comes when you formulate your own objectives. When you state your own objectives, the advanced organizer helps you think about your subject-contents and learning levels. For your own objectives, ambiguities in how the objectives are expressed are not a problem, because you know what you intend.

OTHER WAYS OF CLASSIFYING SUBJECT-CONTENT

Six subject-content categories (e.g., specific, concept, discoverable relationship, relationship of convention, and process) may be insufficient for some teaching specialties. Each teaching specialty (e.g., language arts, health and physical education, and social studies) contains its own specialized content-related terminology. Draw from your own teaching field's specialized language to expand the six-category scheme presented herein.

THE LEARNING LEVEL SPECIFIED BY AN OBJECTIVE

THE NEED TO CLASSIFY LEARNING LEVELS

Reread Chapter 4's section "Learning-Level Relevance" on pages 182–183.

LEARNING DOMAINS

Familiarity with one of the published schemes for classifying objectives according to their specified learning levels will help you design relevant mini-experiments. The scheme for classifying learning levels for the advanced organizer presented herein is adapted from a variety of sources (Bloom, 1984; Cangelosi, 1992, 1996; Guilford, 1959; Harrow, 1974; Krathwohl, Bloom, & Masia, 1964; Safrit & Wood, 1995).

Learning levels are traditionally classified into three domains: *cognitive*, *affective*, and *psychomotor*.

If the intent of an objective is for students to be able to do something mentally (e.g., construct a concept or remember the statement of a relationship), the learning level falls within the *cognitive domain*.

If the intent of the objective is for students to develop a particular attitude or feeling (e.g., a desire to read or willingness to attempt a task), the learning level falls within the *affective domain*.

If the intent of the objective is for students to develop some physical attribute (e.g., muscle flexibility) or physical skill (e.g., manipulate a pencil well enough to form legible manuscript letters), the objective falls within the *psychomotor domain*.

Much of what is taught in schools targets student behaviors that fall within all three domains. Case 5.12 is an example.

CASE 5.12

Ms. Dorsey is helping Jorge, one of her kindergarten students, to print the uppercase letter "A" accurately. She must teach him the cognitive process skill of knowing how to form the "A." Jorge will not learn to print the letter unless he is willing to try to form the "A" correctly. But even if he knows how and wants to do so, he won't be able to print the letter unless he possesses the necessary psychomotor skill to control the pencil.

Because Ms. Dorsey realizes that Jorge's development of the cognitive, affective, and psychomotor aspects of printing manuscript letters requires her to employ different teaching strategies, as well as different measurements to monitor learning, she delineates three objectives:

A. Students remember the steps for printing the uppercase letter "A" (process knowledge).
B. Students attempt to follow directions for printing the uppercase letter "A" (willingness to try).
C. Students manipulate a pencil well enough to follow the steps for printing the uppercase letter "A" (psychomotor-skill performance).

COGNITIVE OBJECTIVES

MEMORY-LEVEL AND REASONING-LEVEL COGNITION

There are two classes of learning levels in the cognitive domains: (1) *memory levels* and (2) *reasoning levels*. An objective requiring students to remember some specified subject-content (e.g., the statement of a relationship or a process) is *memory level*. There are two memory levels: *simple knowledge* and *process knowledge*. An objective requiring students to use reasoning to make judgments relative to specified subject-content is *reasoning level*. There are five reasoning levels: *construct a concept*, *discover a relationship*, *comprehension and communication skills*, *application*, and *creative thinking*.

MEMORY-LEVEL COGNITIVE OBJECTIVES
Simple Knowledge

In Case 5.6, Ms. Gaston defined the goal of a unit on surface area with eight objectives, A–H. The "simple knowledge" label on Objective B suggests she decided that students should remember certain information (e.g., the formula for area of a rectangle). Whereas achievement of

A. Students compute the product of any two-digit whole number by any two-digit whole number (process knowledge)[1].

B. When confronted with a real-life problem, students determine how, if at all, the concepts of heat conduction, convection, and radiation can be used to help solve the problem (application)[1].

C. For each sentence students write, they use the verb tense that is consistent with the rest of the sentence (comprehension and communication skills)[1].

D. Students state the definition of "rational number" (simple knowledge)[1].

E. Students explain the mechanism by which blood is moved through the human heart (comprehension and communication skills)[1].

F. Students employ proper mechanics when executing the following weight training exercises: Flat bench press, incline bench press, lat pulldown, leg curl, leg extension, leg press and standing press (psychomotor-skill performance)[1].

G. Students discover and explain why the area of a rectangle is the product of the rectangle's length and width (discover a relationship)[1].

H. Students state the formula for finding the area of a rectangle (i.e., Area = lw where l is the length and w is the width of the rectangle) (simple knowledge)[1].

I. Given two of the following three measures of a rectangle: length, width, and area, students compute the third (process knowledge)[1].

J. Students efficiently access area formulas they discovered by recalling them or knowing where to find them (e.g., from a computer file or notebook) (simple knowledge)[1].

K. Students discriminate between examples of rights being respected and rights being disrespected (construct a concept)[1].

L. Students explain how the quality of life within the classroom community is affected by community members respecting one another's rights, as well as their own rights, as opposed to those rights being disrespected (discover a relationship)[1].

M. Students explain the meaning of Classroom Behavior Standards 1 and 2 (comprehension and communication skills)[1].

N. Students state the four classroom behavior standards (simple knowledge)[1].

ILLUSTRATION 5.10

For Each Objective, Identify the Subject-Content and Label It

(Continued)

ILLUSTRATION 5.10 (Continued)

O. Students explain how Classroom Behavior Standard 3 relates to Classroom Behavior Standards 1 and 2 (e.g., the opportunity to learn is a right) (discover a relationship)[1].

P. Students value the classroom behavior standards, judging them to be important for their own well-being and the well-being of the classroom community (appreciation)[1].

Q. Students explain how segregation of black people from white people whether *de jure* segregation in the South or *de facto* segregation virtually everywhere in the U.S. affected the lives of all citizens both collectively and individually (discover a relationship)[1].

R. Students differentiate between examples and nonexamples of *de jure* segregation as well as between examples and nonexamples of *de facto* segregation (construct a concept)[1].

S. Students discriminate between speed and acceleration (construct a concept)[1].

T. Students state definitions for "speed," "acceleration," "force," "mass," and "distance" (simple knowledge)[1].

U. Students measure the speed of moving objects (process knowledge)[1].

V. Students state Newton's First Law of Motion (simple knowledge)[1].

W. Students explain the effects of friction and gravity on the speed of a moving body (discover a relationship)[1].

X. Students approach a writing task via the following procedure:

   1) Describes the targeted readers
   2) Summarizes the principal message to be communicated
   3) Outlines a plan for writing
   4) Writes the piece
   5) Reads the piece
   6) Edits the piece
   7) Rewrites
   (process knowledge)[1].

Y. Students accept constructive criticism about their own writing (willingness to try)[1].

Z. Students write with a specified purpose in mind (application)[1].

AA. Students utilize writing mechanics appropriate to the writing task (application)[1].

[1] Indicates the learning level of the objective as defined in this chapter.

Objective	Subject-Content	Type of Subject-Content
A	computation of the product of any two-digit whole numbers	process
B	heat conduction, convection, and radiation	three concepts
C	rules for verb tenses	relationships of convention
D	association between "rational number" and its definition	relationship of convention
E	mechanism by which blood flows	process
F	weight training mechanics	processes
G	Area of a rectangular region = length × width	discoverable relationship
H	Area of a rectangular region = length × width	discoverable relationship
I	algorithms for computing an unknown measure of a rectangle	processes
J	methods for looking up area formulas	processes
K	Respectfulness of rights	concept
L	effects of classroom community members respecting rights on quality of classroom life	discoverable relationship
M	Classroom Behavior Standards 1 and 2	two specifics
N	Classroom Behavior Standards 1-4	four specifics
O	Relationships among Standards 1-3	discoverable relationships
P	Classroom Behavior Standards 1-4	four specifics
Q	effects of segregation on lives	discoverable relationship
R	*de jure* and *de facto* segregation	two concepts
S	speed and acceleration	two concepts
T	definitions for terms related to motion	relationship of convention

ILLUSTRATION 5.11

Kisha's Responses to Illustration 5.10's Prompt

(Continued)

ILLUSTRATION 5.11 (Continued)

U	methods of measuring speed	processes
V	Newton's first law of motion	discoverable relationship
W	effects of friction and gravity on the speed of a moving body	discoverable relationship
X	steps in a writing procedure	process
Y	constructive criticism about writing	concept
Z	writing with a specified purpose	concept
AA	writing mechanics	processes

objectives at the reasoning levels are the bases for meaningful learning, it is also practical for students to remember conventional names for concepts they've constructed and statements of relationships they've discovered. Furthermore, they should be informed of and remember certain relationships of convention. Of course, only a minute subset of information to which you expose your students can be or should be realistically committed to memory. You, like Ms. Gaston in Case 5.6, need to decide what information your students need to know for meaningful learning.

An objective requiring students to remember a specified response (but not a step-by-step process) to a specified stimulus is at the *simple-knowledge learning level.*

The teachers who formulated the following objectives intended for them to specify the simple-knowledge learning level, as indicated by the "(simple-knowledge)" label they attached to each.

A. Students associate each vowel with its sounds (simple knowledge).
B. Students match each of the following elements with its atomic numbers and its chemical symbol: hydrogen, helium, lithium, beryllium, boron, carbon, nitrogen, oxygen, fluorine, and neon (simple knowledge).
C. Students name and identify the five empirical senses (simple knowledge).
D. Students list five fundamental water-safety rules (simple knowledge).
E. Students match each of the three schematic symbols shown in Illustration 5.12 with its appropriate electronic device (simple knowledge).

These five simple-knowledge objectives, like all the other objectives in this book labeled "(simple knowledge)," indicate responses for students to remember when presented with certain stimuli. For example, the stimuli for Objective E, stated just above, are the three symbols shown in Illustration 5.12. The targeted responses are the names of the electronic devices represented by those symbols.

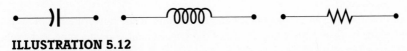

ILLUSTRATION 5.12

Three Schematic Symbols for Electronic Devices

Process Knowledge

An objective requiring students to remember the sequence of steps in a procedure is at the *process-knowledge learning level*. The subject-contents of *process-knowledge* objectives are always processes.

The teachers who formulated the following objectives intended for them to specify the process-knowledge learning level, as indicated by the "(process knowledge)" label they attached to each.

A. Students describe the procedures for safely lighting a Bunsen burner in the science lab (process knowledge).

B. Given the values of two of three variables, rate of motion, time, and distance, the students compute the missing value using the formula: rate × time = distance (process knowledge).

C. Given a description of an example of interlinking food chains, the students sketch the simplified food web (process knowledge).

D. Students prepare slides and set up science-lab microscopes for examining tiny objects (e.g., a grain of salt or spider leg) (process knowledge).

E. Given the recipe from a cookbook, students describe how to adjust the amount of ingredients according to the number of people to be served (process knowledge).

F. Students spell-check their writing using word-processing software (process knowledge).

G. Students describe the proper steps for executing a leg-extension exercise in the weight room (process knowledge).

Process-knowledge objectives are concerned with students knowing how to execute the steps in methods for finding answers or accomplishing tasks. You know the answer to the question, "What is 9 + 3?" without figuring it out, so you have achieved a simple-knowledge objective dealing with addition facts. However, unless you are quite unusual in this regard, you don't know the answer to the question, "What is 378 + 85?" What you do know is how to execute the steps in a process for finding the sum of any two whole numbers such as 378 and 85. This latter skill is indicative of your achievement of a process-knowledge objective. As suggested by Cases 2.16 and 2.17, the process, not the final outcome, is the focus of strategies for designing mini-experiments relevant to process-knowledge objectives.

REASONING-LEVEL COGNITIVE OBJECTIVES
Construct a Concept

An objective requiring students to use inductive reasoning to distinguish between examples and non-examples of a concept is at the *construct-a-concept learning level*. The subject-contents of *construct-a-concept* objectives are always concepts. The stipulation that students use inductive reasoning is explained in Chapter 7. For now, keep in mind that the reasoning employed by Josh in Case 5.9 and Terri in Case 5.10 is inductive and is indicative of how students construct concepts.

The teachers who formulated the following objectives intended for them to specify the construct-a-concept learning level as indicated by the "(construct a concept)" label they attached to each.

A. Students distinguish between verbs and other types of words in sentences (construct a concept).

B. From a description of policies and operations of the government of a hypothetical state, students determine whether or not the government is democratic and explain why (construct a concept).

C. Students discover the existence of friction (construct a concept).

D. Students distinguish examples of food webs from other mechanisms within an ecosystem (construct a concept).

E. Students distinguish between examples of animal and plant respiration and examples of other physiological activities of organisms (construct a concept).

F. Students develop their descriptions of a healthy lifestyle (construct a concept).

Discover a Relationship

As explained in Chapter 7, students use inductive reasoning to *discover relationships* as they do to construct concepts. An objective requiring students to use inductive reasoning to discover that a particular relationship exists or why the relationship exists is at the *discover-a-relationship learning level*. The subject-content of a discover-a-relationship objective is necessarily a discoverable relationship. Objectives for students to discover why relationships exist (e.g., discover *why* water expands when it freezes) are usually far more ambitious than objectives for students to discover that relationships exist (e.g., discover *that* water expands when it freezes).

The teachers who formulated the following objectives intended for them to specify the discover-a-relationship learning level, as indicated by the "(discover a relationship)" label they attached to each.

A. Students discover that plants need water (but not too much) (discover a relationship).

B. Students discover that water freezes at 32°F (discover a relationship).

C. Students discover that the behavior of air is influenced by changes in temperature (discover a relationship).

D. Students discover why drug abuse interferes with a productive life (discover a relationship).

E. Students explain why the product of two negative numbers is positive (discover a relationship).

F. Students explain why the price of a product depends on the demand for that product (discover a relationship).

G. Students explain how the principle of negative reinforcement affects human behavior patterns (discover a relationship).

Comprehension and Communication Skills

Objectives at the *comprehension-and-communication-skills learning level* focus on students' being able to use language to communicate as well as to extract and interpret meaning from expressions. The subject-content of an objective at the *comprehension-and-communication-skills learning-level* can be either a *particular message* (e.g., Article I of the U.S. Constitution or the definition of "rational number") or a *mode of communication* (e.g., weather charts from newspapers or an aspect of a foreign language).

Comprehension-and-communication-skills objectives specifying *messages* for subject-content are concerned with students being able to translate or interpret those messages. The teachers who formulated the following objectives want their students to translate or interpret messages.

A. Students explain the general provisions of the Bill of Rights (comprehension and communication skills).

B. Students explain in their own words the four standards for conduct posted on the classroom wall (comprehension and communication skills).

C. Students summarize the major points expressed in the videotape program "Crack Cocaine and Your Life" (comprehension and communication skills).

D. Students explain the Euclideans' classic proof that the set of prime numbers is infinite (comprehension and communication skills).

Comprehension-and-communication-skills objectives specifying *modes of communication* as subject-contents are concerned with students being able to use the particular mode of communications to both receive and send messages (i.e., use the mode as a language). The teachers who formulated the following objectives want their students to become fluent with certain modes of communication or translate messages expressed in those modes.

A. From watching a person expressing two or more thought units in signed English, students translate the thought into conventional spoken English (comprehension and communication skills).

B. Students express their own thoughts using signed English (comprehension and communication skills).

C. For each algebra textbook word problem they read, students (1) identify the question posed by the problem, (2) clarify the question in their own words, (3) specify the variables to be solved, and (4) list facts or data provided in the statement of the problem (comprehension and communication skills).

D. After reading a simple computer program written in BASIC, students illustrate the logic of the program with a flowchart (comprehension and communication skills).

Application

As previously stated in the section "Meaningful Learning," for learning to be meaningful, students need to be able to apply what they learn in situations that are important to them. In Cases 5.13, 5.14, 5.15 (adapted from Cangelosi, 1996, p. 158), and 5.16, students demonstrate that at least some of what they learned in school was meaningful.

CASE 5.13

Nine-year-old Terrence thinks about what he can do to cheer up his sister, who is sick. He decides to write a story to "make her laugh." With pencil in hand, Terrence stares at a blank sheet of paper, not knowing how to start. Frustrated by his lack of progress, he gives up on the idea. As he goes about his business, he continues to experience a nagging feeling that his sister, Naomi, really would enjoy a funny story he wrote himself. Having practiced several processes for different writing tasks in Ms. Foreman's classroom, he thinks, "Writing to make Naomi laugh is writing for a purpose, so I should try that same thing we did in school when we had to tell about something that surprised us." Terrence tries again to compose a story for Naomi, but this time he begins with steps in what Ms. Foreman calls the "prewriting phase" in her "framework for focused writing."

CASE 5.14

Gary is planning an exercise program for himself. It is his understanding that for heart and lung health, he should do an aerobic exercise at least every other day. He thinks: "A rhythmic, sustained exercise that elevates heart and respiratory rates continually for at least 20 minutes is aerobic. I plan to lift weights for strength. Can that count for my aerobic exercise? No, because it isn't a sustained exercise. I like soccer and flag football; I could join teams—that can be quite vigorous. But they're more stop-and-go rather than sustained. Bicycling? If I bike vigorously for a half an hour, then I would sustain elevated heart and respiratory rates. I'll plan on biking at least four times a week."

CASE 5.15

Anna is building a playhouse with her children. She has the problem of figuring how to precut the rafter ends so that they will be vertical to the ground when in place. She sketches a diagram with her planned dimensions of the rafters, as shown in Illustration 5.13.

Looking at her diagram, she thinks, "What should α and β be? $\alpha = \beta$ because they're opposite angles of a parallelogram. Okay, so how do I solve for one of them? β has got to be the same as this angle right here; I'll call it θ." She inserts "θ" as shown in Illustration 5.14.

Anna begins to doubt that $\beta = \theta$, thinking, "Or does it? Let's see, these two lines are parallel, so we have ... Okay, that's right, $\beta = \theta$! All right, I should be able to find θ, since it's part of this triangle—in fact, a right triangle! A right triangle with two known sides, that means I can use a little trig here. Okay, I know θ's opposite side and its adjacent side. So tangent is the operable function here. Tangent θ is 8 over $1\frac{1}{2}$ so—get this calculator working, arctan, open parenthesis, 8, divide by 1.5, close parenthesis, equals 1.38544. That's not right! Oh, no wonder, the calculator is set for radians. Okay, switch to degrees and try again. Ahh, 79.38—that's more like it! Okay, so I cut these two angles at almost 80°."

CASE 5.16

Michelle and Tawny are debating whether or not smoking tobacco should be restricted by law even further than it is now. To help make her point, Tawny decides to draw a parallel between restricting tobacco use today with what she and Michelle learned in Ms. Fisher's U.S. history class about the prohibition of intoxicating liquors in 1919 and its repeal in 1933.

Students apply what they learn in situations that are important to them by addressing *real-life problems*. A *real-life problem* is a perplexing or puzzling question, issue, or task an individual is motivated to address.

An objective requiring students to use deductive reasoning to decide how, if at all, to utilize the subject-content specified by the objective to address real-life problems is at the

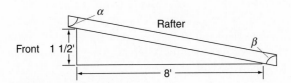

ILLUSTRATION 5.13

Anna's Initial Diagram

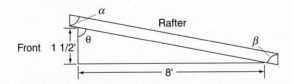

ILLUSTRATION 5.14

Anna Inserts "θ"

application learning level. The subject-content of *application* objectives can be specifics, concepts, discoverable relationships, relationships of convention, or processes. The stipulation that students use deductive reasoning is explained in Chapter 10. For now, keep in mind that the reasoning employed by Terrence, Gary, Anna, and Tawny in Cases 5.13, 5.14, 5.15, and 5.16 is deductive. The teachers who formulated the following objectives intended for them to specify the application learning level, as indicated by the "(application)" label they attached to each.

A. Given an example of a food web, students predict the impact of a number of possible disruptions to that web (application).

B. From observing the symptoms of a plant in distress, students design a program for caring for the plant to improve its health (application).

C. Students use both direct observation and second-hand information (e.g., televised weather reports) to predict weather and to make prudent decisions regarding weather safety (e.g., whether or not to go swimming or continue a softball game) (application).

D. Given a real-life problem, students determine how, if at all, using the relationship "rate × time = distance" will help solve the problem (application).

E. When the solution to a problem requires the measurement of length, students select a measurement unit (e.g., millimeter or kilometer) that is convenient for the given situation (application).

F. During oral discourses, students adjust their use of language to the audience so that listeners find expressions palatable rather than offensive (application).

G. From observing symptoms of a person in distress, students determine whether or not cardiopulmonary resuscitation (CPR) should be initiated (application).

Sometimes, teachers confuse process-knowledge objectives with application objectives. Compare Object G, stated just above, to the following objective:

H. Students demonstrate appropriate procedures for administering CPR to a person displaying a need for CPR (process knowledge).

Both Objectives G and H deal with the administration of CPR, but Objective G requires students to *decide when* to use the process, whereas Objective H requires students to *remember how* to use the process. As explained in Chapters 8 and 10, designing mini-experiments that are relevant to application objectives requires different strategies than designing mini-experiments relevant to process-knowledge objectives.

Creative Thinking

Students *think creatively* by using divergent reasoning to originate ideas, hypotheses, procedures, or problem solutions. *Divergent reasoning* is atypical reasoning that deviates from the norm of a specific population; thoughts that reflect unanticipated and unusual, but reasonable, responses are divergent. People tend to produce divergent ideas in response to dissatisfaction with available hypotheses, ideas, beliefs, and problem resolutions for dealing with perplexing situations. Consider Case 5.17.

CASE 5.17

Mr. Clemente displays the picture in Illustration 5.15 to Rosalie, one of his fourth-grade students.

Mr. Clemente: "In what ways does having such a long neck help a giraffe?"

Rosalie:	"Let's see. They can eat the leaves from the top of trees, and . . . oh, yeah! They can see higher than other animals, so a giraffe could spot a lion or something from up high."

Rosalie, like the vast majority of her classmates, responds to Mr. Clemente's question in a way that emphasizes the advantages of the giraffe being taller than other animals. Giraffes' heads high above those of other animals are apparent in Illustration 5.15. But a few students' responses diverge from those of most of their classmates.

Mr. Clemente:	"In what ways does having such a long neck help a giraffe?"
Emily:	"Hmmm . . . it makes it easier for a giraffe to reach the ground."
Mr. Clemente:	"Explain to me what you mean."
Emily:	"Look how long their legs are. If they had short necks, they'd have to bend their knees way down every time they wanted to pick something off the ground."

To most people, the most obvious advantage of giraffes having long necks is that their heads are higher. Thus, most of Mr. Clemente's students used *convergent reasoning* to produce expected, popular answers to his questions. *Convergent reasoning* is reasoning that is typical and usual for the majority of the people of a specific population. Emily's answer, on the other hand, was unusual, but no less reasonable than those of most of her classmates. Thus, Emily's response reflected divergent reasoning. Emily's divergent reasoning justifies her unexpected response, "It makes it easier for them to reach the ground," just as convergent reasoning justifies responses such as "They can reach higher." Do not confuse divergent reasoning with just any "off-the-wall" thinking. Consider Case 5.18.

ILLUSTRATION 5.15

In What Ways Does Having Such a Long Neck Help a Giraffe?

CASE 5.18

Mr. Clemente displays the picture in Illustration 5.15 to Vincent, one of his fourth-grade students.

Mr. Clemente:	"In what ways does having such a long neck help a giraffe?"
Vincent:	"Well, it makes them run faster."
Mr. Clemente:	"Explain to me what you mean."
Vincent:	"I don't know. Is it because of the spots on their necks?"

Vincent's response is unusual, so it does not appear to be the result of convergent reasoning. However, since Vincent didn't seem to have thought out his answer, the response did not appear to be a product of divergent reasoning either.

An objective requiring students to use divergent reasoning to originate specifics, concepts, relationships, or processes is at the *creative-thinking learning level*. The stipulation of originality is met as long as the creation is novel to the student. A student, for example, displays achievement at the creative-thinking learning level by originating an unusual strategy for proving a mathematical theorem even if that strategy had been previously employed. However, the student must design the strategy without knowledge of the earlier work.

The teachers who formulated the following objectives intended for them to specify the creative-thinking learning level, as indicated by the "(creative thinking)" label they attached to each.

A. Students originate novel games for their second-grade classmates so that (1) each game is dissimilar to any games students have previously played, and (2) winning depends on how well teammates cooperate with one another (creative thinking).

B. Given a collection of various words, students categorize the words in unconventional ways and formulate a rule for each category (creative thinking).

C. Students generate novel hypotheses to explain why water expands when it freezes (creative thinking).

D. Students develop ideas for designing simple machines that do not fall in any of the following categories: lever, wedge, inclined plane, screw, pulley, or wheel-and-axle (creative thinking).

AFFECTIVE OBJECTIVES

APPRECIATION

Unlike cognitive and psychomotor objectives, *affective* objectives are not concerned with students' abilities with respect to subject-content but rather with attitudes about subject-content. The affective domain includes two learning levels: (1) *appreciation,* and (2) *willingness to try.*

Students achieve an objective at the *appreciation learning level* by believing that the subject-content specified by the objective has value.

The teachers who formulated the following objectives intended for them to specify the appreciation learning level, as indicated by the "(appreciation)" label they attached to each.

A. Students want their classmates to succeed in their efforts to learn (appreciation).

B. Students believe the Constitution serves a valuable purpose (appreciation).

C. Students believe that learning how to read will be personally beneficial and rewarding (appreciation).

D. Students prefer to formulate their own algebraic sentences when solving word problems rather than having the sentences set up by someone else (appreciation).

E. Students would like to maintain a healthy diet (appreciation).

WILLINGNESS TO TRY

Achievement of an appreciation-level objective requires students to hold certain beliefs but does not require them to act upon those beliefs; objectives specifying *willingness-to-try learning levels* do. Students achieve a *willingness-to-try* objective by choosing to attempt a task specified by the objective.

The teachers who formulated the following objectives intended for them to specify the willingness-to-try learning level, as indicated by the "(willingness to try)" label they attached to each.

A. When presented with opportunities to help classmates learn, students attempt to provide the needed help (willingness to try).

B. Students regulate their eating habits in an attempt to maintain a healthy diet (willingness to try).

C. When presented with opportunities to abuse drugs, students refuse to abuse drugs (willingness to try).

D. When presented with opportunities to communicate with Spanish-speaking persons, students attempt to communicate using the Spanish they have learned to that point in time (willingness to try).

E. Students attempt to formulate algebraic open sentences to solve word problems before turning to someone else for assistance in setting them up (willingness to try).

Sometimes, teachers mistakenly think that they cannot develop relevant measurements for affective objectives as they can for cognitive or psychomotor objectives. Chapter 12 will help you develop your talent for designing mini-experiments that are relevant to your students' achievement of affective objectives.

PSYCHOMOTOR OBJECTIVES

PHYSICAL FITNESS

Designing curricula leading students to improve their physical fitness is the responsibility of health and physical education teachers. Without special preparation in health and physical education, you are not in a position to design mini-experiments relevant to objectives specifying the physical-fitness learning level. However, your students' levels of physical fitness may affect their progress with objectives specifying other learning levels for which you are responsible. Thus, it is important for you to be aware of physical fitness as a learning level although you may never teach for physical-fitness objectives.

Herein, physical-fitness learning level is defined and is alluded to in Chapter 13 as it relates to monitoring students' psychomotor skills. However, designing mini-experiments relevant to physical-fitness objectives is not within the purview of this book.

Objectives at the *physical-fitness learning level* are concerned with students improving their physical states of well-being so that they are able to "perform daily activities with vigor, reduce the risk of health problems related to lack of exercise, and establish a fitness base for participation in a variety of physical activities" (McSwegin, Pemberton, Petray, & Going, 1989, p. 1). The subject-content of physical-fitness objectives can be processes, concepts, and relationships relative to cardiovascular endurance, body composition, flexibility, muscular strength and endurance, agility, balance, coordination, power, speed, and reaction time (Pangrazi, 1998, pp. 236–237; Safrit, 1995).

The health and physical education teachers who formulated the following objectives intended for them to specify the physical-fitness learning level, as indicated by the "(physical fitness)" label they attached to each.

A. When using correct techniques, each student completes eight repetitions of (1) flat bench press with 75% of own body weight, (2) military press with 33% of own body weight, (3) leg press with 125% of own body weight, (4) calf raise with 150% of own body weight, (5) triceps pulldown with 15% of own body weight, (6) biceps curl with 10% of own body weight, (7) lat pulldown with 60% of own body weight, and (8) behind the neck press with 5% of own body weight (physical fitness).

B. Students increase flexibility in hands to maximize the distance between points that can be simultaneously reached by the thumb and little finger of the same hand (e.g., on a piano keyboard) (physical fitness).

C. Students increase cardiovascular endurance so that a two-mile jog can be sustained (physical fitness).

PSYCHOMOTOR-SKILL

I *know* how to shoot a basketball as well as anyone in the world. None of the great professional players, present or past (e.g., Michael Jordan), *knows* how to shoot any better than I do. I've studied the mechanics of basketball shooting and learned the techniques great shooters use to be accurate. My achievement of the following objective is quite sophisticated:

Students explain how to shoot a jump shot (process knowledge).

Although I know how to shoot jump shots and can describe to others how to shoot them, I lack the necessary *psychomotor skills to consistently execute* what I know how to do. The great shooters don't know more than I know about shooting, but their muscles and neural networks are better conditioned to carry out what their minds know to do.

Psychomotor-skill objectives focus on students' abilities to execute physical tasks as they cognitively know how the tasks should be executed. Apparently, the physical education teacher who formulated the unit goal defined by the objectives listed in Illustration 5.16 recognized the importance of distinguishing between teaching for process knowledge and teaching for psychomotor-skill performance.

Students achieve a *psychomotor-skill* objective by executing a specified physical process. The subject-contents of *psychomotor-skill* objectives are, of course, processes.

The teachers who formulated the following objectives intended for them to specify the psychomotor-skill performance learning level, as indicated by the "(psychomotor skill)" label they attached to each.

A. Students manipulate pencils well enough to follow the steps for printing manuscript letters (psychomotor skill).

B. Students execute legal tennis serves without faulting (psychomotor skill).

C. Students focus their eyes on printed lines of text (e.g., from a primary reader) so that one line at a time is viewed from left to right followed by the next line, again moving from left to right (psychomotor skill).

D. Students execute a back dive from a 3-meter springboard (psychomotor skill).

The advanced organizer for specifying the subject-contents and learning levels of objectives is outlined in Illustration 5.17.

Goal: Students plan and follow a weight training program for maintaining muscle strength

Objectives:

A. Upon hearing the name of a major muscle group, students point to the location of that group on their own body (simple knowledge).

B. Students describe the steps for executing a flat bench press, military press, leg press, calf raise, triceps pulldown, standing curl, seated lat pulldown, and behind-the-neck press (process knowledge).

C. Students demonstrate the correct procedures for executing a flat bench press, military press, leg press, calf raise, triceps pulldown, standing curl, seated lat pulldown, and behind-the-neck press (psychomotor skill).

D. In the weight room, students display consideration of other students, use the equipment in a safe manner, and put weights in their proper place after using them (willingness to try).

E. Students explain the fundamental relationships among (1) weight work, (2) rest, (3) nutrition, and (4) muscle strength (discover a relationship).

F. Students design a personal weight training program for maintaining overall, balanced muscle strength (application).

G. Students follow a plan for maintaining their overall, balanced muscle strength (willingness to try).

H. When using correct techniques, each student completes eight repetitions of (1) flat bench press with 75% of own body weight, (2) military press with 33% of own body weight, (3) leg press with 125% of own body weight, (4) calf raise with 150% of own body weight, (5) triceps pulldown with 15% of own body weight, (6) biceps curl with 10% of own body weight, (7) lat pulldown with 60% of own body weight, and (8) behind the neck press with 5% of own body weight (physical fitness).

ILLUSTRATION 5.16

Example of a Goal and Objectives for a High School Physical Education Unit

Subject-Content

A Specific: Any unique entity

Concept: A category people mentally construct from a set of two or more specifics that have some common attributes.

Relationship: A particular association between either (1) concepts, (2) a concept and a specific, or (3) specifics.

> **Discoverable Relationship:** A relationship that can be determined by reasoning or experimentation.

> **Relationship of Convention:** A relationship that exists because it has been established through tradition or agreement.

Process: A systematic, step-by-step method by which a task is accomplished.

Learning Level

Cognitive Domain: If the intent of an objective is for students to be able to do something mentally, the learning level falls within the cognitive domain.

> **Memory Level:** An objective requiring students to remember some specified subject-content is memory level.

>> **Simple Knowledge:** An objective requiring students to remember a specified response (but not a step-by-step process) to a specified stimulus is at the simple-knowledge learning level.

>> **Process Knowledge:** An objective requiring students to remember the sequence of steps in a procedure is at the process-knowledge learning level.

> **Reasoning Level:** An objective requiring students to use reasoning to make judgments relative to specified subject-content is reasoning level.

>> **Construct a Concept:** An objective requiring students to use inductive reasoning to distinguish between examples and nonexamples of a concept is at the construct-a-concept learning level.

>> **Discover a Relationship:** An objective requiring students to use inductive reasoning to discover that a particular relationship exists or why the relationship exists is at the discover-a-relationship learning level.

>> **Comprehension and Communication Skills:** Objectives at the comprehension-and-communication-skills learning level focus on

ILLUSTRATION 5.17

Advanced Organizer for Specifying Subject-Contents and Learning Levels.

(Continued)

ILLUSTRATION 5.17 (Continued)

students' being able to use language to communicate as well as to extract and interpret meaning from expressions.

Comprehension-and-communication-skills objectives specifying messages for subject-content are concerned with students being able to translate or interpret those messages.

Comprehension-and-communication-skills objectives specifying modes of communication as subject-contents are concerned with students being able to use the particular mode of communications to both receive and send messages (i.e., use the mode as a language).

Application: An objective requiring students to use deductive reasoning to decide how, if at all, to utilize the subject-content specified by the objective to address real-life problems is at the application learning level.

Creative Thinking: An objective requiring students to use divergent reasoning to originate ideas, hypotheses, procedures, or problem solutions is at the creative-thinking learning level.

Affective Domain: If the intent of the objective is for students to develop a particular attitude or feeling, the learning level falls within the affective domain.

Appreciation: Students achieve an objective at the appreciation learning-level by believing that the subject-content specified by the objective has value.

Willingness to Try: Students achieve a willingness-to-try objective by choosing to attempt a task specified by the objective.

Psychomotor Domain: If the intent of the objective is for students to develop some physical attribute or physical skill, the objective falls within the psychomotor domain.

Physical Fitness: Objectives at the physical-fitness learning level are concerned with students improving their physical states of well-being that allow them to "perform daily activities with vigor, reduce the risk of health problems related to lack of exercise, and establish a fitness base for participation in a variety of physical activities" (McSwegin, Pemberton, Petray, & Going, 1989, p. 1).

Psychomotor Skill: Psychomotor-skill objectives focus on students' abilities to execute physical tasks as they cognitively know the tasks should be executed.

DEFINING THE GOAL WITH A SET OF WEIGHTED OBJECTIVES

Examine Case 5.19.

CASE 5.19

Ms. Parino believes that some of her fourth-grade students need to be more respectful and considerate of their classmates. Thus, she establishes the following learning goal:

> While at school, students will act in a manner that displays respect and consideration for the rights and feelings of classmates.

She defines the goal by the following objectives:

A. Students refrain from littering the classroom floor (willingness to try).
B. If classmates express a need for help, students attempt to help if able and if such help is acceptable to the teacher (willingness to try).
C. Students refrain from interrupting others who are speaking in the classroom (willingness to try).
D. Students are careful not to waste or damage the property of classmates (willingness to try).
E. Students refrain from stealing from classmates (willingness to try).
F. Students attempt to minimize borrowing from classmates (willingness to try).
G. Students express their appreciation to classmates who are helpful to them (willingness to try).
H. Students refrain from making physical contact with others in a manner that would cause pain, injury, or discomfort (willingness to try).
I. Students want their classmates to have positive feelings about themselves (appreciation).

One of Ms. Parino's students, Sandra, almost always says "thank you" to her classmates when they help. Thus, she demonstrates advanced achievement of Objective G. On the other hand, Bernadine hardly ever says "thank you" and generally does not express appreciation when someone is helpful. Regarding Objective A, Sandra hardly ever litters the floor, whereas Bernadine frequently does. However, regarding Objective E, Sandra seizes opportunities to steal from her classmates, whereas Bernadine never steals.

Regarding all of the nine objectives, Sandra displays satisfactory achievement of seven of the objectives, A, B, C, D, F, G, and I, but not the other two. Bernadine satisfactorily achieves four of the nine objectives: D, E, F, and H.

Since Sandra achieved seven of the nine objectives, whereas Bernadine achieved only four, do you agree that Sandra's progress toward Ms. Parino's goal is more advanced than Bernadine's? Why not? Discuss the issue with a colleague.

Kisha and Elwin discuss the question in Case 5.20.

CASE 5.20

Kisha:	"Since Sandra achieved more of the objectives than Bernadine, do you agree Sandra's achievement of the goal is greater than Bernadine's?"
Elwin:	"Of course not. Look at which objectives Sandra achieved compared to which ones Bernadine achieved. Don't tell me you think littering or not saying 'thank you' are more serious offenses than stealing!"
Kisha:	"Are you making a quality versus quantity argument?"

Elwin:	"Yes. Ms. Parino's goal has to do with classroom citizenship. Refraining from steal-ing and assaulting is far more important to showing good citizenship than the other seven combined. Of course Sandra doesn't borrow from her classmates; she does-n't need to because she steals! And why would she want to waste or damage prop-erty she plans to steal?"
Kisha:	"I get your point. Some of Ms. Parino's objectives are more important for goal achievement than others."

If Ms. Parino believes her objectives vary in importance with respect to students' achieve-ment of her classroom-citizenship goal, then those differences should influence how she de-signs measurements to be relevant to that goal. By *weighting your objectives according to relative importance*, as Ms. Fernandez does in Case 5.21, you take the first step in designing measurements so that greater priority is placed on mini-experiments relevant to more impor-tant objectives than on mini-experiments relevant to less important objectives.

CASE 5.21

Ms. Fernandez plans a unit on Newton's first law of motion she will soon be conducting for her fourth-grade students. She thinks, "My goal is for them to discover Newton's first law of motion and apply it in meaningful ways. Let's see. How does the textbook state it? Here it is on page 193. 'Bodies at rest stay at rest, and bodies in motion stay in motion in a straight line at constant speed, unless a force acts on them to move them or change their motion.' Okay, so it's critical that they discover the existence of that rela-tionship for themselves before concerning themselves with how to state it and know it by the name 'New-ton's first law of motion.' But what concepts might they need to construct before discovering the relationship itself? Physical bodies and motion are needed, but they've already constructed those. The differences between speed and acceleration are something they need. I should begin with a construct-a-concept lesson on those. Oh! But even before that, they'll need to construct the concept of force. So . . ."

After more thought, Ms. Fernandez defines her goal with the following objectives:

A. Students construct the concepts of force, speed, and acceleration (construct a concept).
B. Students explain definitions for "force," "speed," and "acceleration" (comprehension and commu-nication skills).
C. Students measure the speed of moving bodies (process knowledge).
D. From either observations of a moving object or utilizing sufficient data, students determine whether the object is or isn't accelerating (process knowledge).
E. Students explain Newton's first law of motion (discover a relationship).
F. Students associate the statement of Newton's first law of motion with the name "Newton's first law of motion" (simple knowledge).
G. Given a real-life problem, students determine how, if at all, Newton's first law of motion can be used to address the problem (application).

She thinks, "Okay, so I've got seven objectives. Now, which are the more important ones? Better weight them so when I design the unit test, I'll put the emphasis where I think it should be. If I thought all seven objectives were equally important, then each should be emphasized on the test by 1/7. As a per-centage 1/7 is—where's my calculator—1 divided by 7 is 0.1428 and so forth, or about 14%. But I don't think all of these objectives are equally important, so let's see which ones should be weighted more than 14% and which should be weighted less. Objective G is the most important one since all the rest lead up to it. Objective G is the synthesis of the rest. I'll rank Objective G above any other. Now which are the next in importance? Objectives A, B, C, and D are included so they can discover Newton's first law of motion—that's E. Objective E is nearly as important as Objective G because that's the foundation, not only for Objective G, but for what we'll be doing in science units for the rest of the year. Now that I think about it, Objective E is just as important as Objective G. So I've got a tie for first place between Objectives E and G. Knowing the name of the law is important, but it's not nearly as important of the process and reasoning stuff that's going to be the foundation for further understanding. So Objective F ranks seventh. Okay, E and G are first with A, B, C, and D next and equally important—their purpose is to make Objective E possible—and then last is Objective F.

"Objectives E and G are as important as the rest combined, so I'll weight each of them 25%. That leaves 50% to split up among the other remaining five objectives. That's 10% a piece, except that Objective F should be worth less than the other four. If I drop the weight for Objective F to 2%, then I can make each of the remaining four 12%. That works! Then I'll have the two most important objectives emphasized about twice as much as any one of the others."

Ms. Fernandez labels Objectives A–G as follows:

$$A \rightarrow 12\%, B \rightarrow 12\%, C \rightarrow 12\%, D \rightarrow 12\%, E \rightarrow 25\%, F \rightarrow 2\%, \text{ and } G \rightarrow 25\%.$$

Near the end of the unit, she selects mini-experiments for the unit test so that about 12% of the maximum possible points are relevant to Objective A, about 12% to Objective B, about 12% to Objective C, about 12% to Objective D, about 25% to Objective E, about 2% to Objective F, and about 25% to Objective G.

By weighting your objectives as Ms. Fernandez did in Case 5.21, you guard against haphazardly designing measurements without consideration of how you believe emphases should be distributed. Weighting objectives provides a mechanism for enhancing the relevance of measurements you design.

SYNTHESIS ACTIVITIES FOR CHAPTER 5

1. Select the one best response for each of the following multiple-choice prompts that either answers the question or completes the statement:
   A. Which one of the following is a concept?
      a) August 7, 2001
      b) birthday
      c) 14 hours, 17 minutes, 12 seconds
      d) the day Barbara Rice was born
   B. Which one of the following is a specific?
      a) the letter "Q"
      b) communication symbol
      c) "Q" is a communication symbol.
      d) a consonant sound
   C. Which one of the following is a relationship from a specific to a concept?
      a) a relationship from a specific to a concept
      b) Bill Clinton succeeded George Bush in the White House.
      c) Books are written by people.
      d) Ernest Hemingway wrote books.
   D. Which one of the following is a relationship between two specifics?
      a) Groceries can be quite expensive.

      b) Many people enjoy living in a trailer park.

      c) Angel Enriques doesn't live in a trailer park.

      d) Fangduo Len lives at 821 Main Street.

E. Which one of the following is a discoverable relationship?

      a) The weight-training exercise shown by Illustration 5.18 is called a "close-grip bench press."

      b) The triceps is the muscle group of the back of the upper part of the arm.

      c) The close-grip bench press helps strengthen the triceps.

      d) a muscle group with three heads

F. Which one of the following is a process?

      a) the close-grip bench press

      b) The triceps extends the elbow.

      c) You extend your elbows when executing the close-grip bench press.

      d) "Elbow extension" refers to straightening the arm.

G. Which one of the following is a relationship of convention?

      a) Aerobic exercise increases cardiovascular endurance.

      b) Tobacco contains nicotine.

      c) The first letter of the first word of a sentence should be capitalized.

      d) The phrase "such that" is frequently used in the statement of mathematical theorems.

H. A learning goal is a concept that is subordinate to which one of the following concepts?

      a) what students achieve if the unit targeting the goal is successful

      b) one of the things teachers determine while designing a teaching unit

      c) teaching unit

      d) fundamental pedagogical principles upon which the design of teaching units should be based

I. The results from a mini-experiment are used to make decisions about how well students achieve a comprehension-and-communication-skills objective. However, the results actually only depend on how well students recall information. Therefore, the mini-experiment _____.

      a) is too easy for its intended purpose

      b) lacks internal consistency

      c) lacks subject-content relevance

      d) lacks learning-level relevance

ILLUSTRATION 5.18

Close-Grip Bench Press

J. The results from a mini-experiment are used to make decisions about how well students achieve an objective that specifies a subject-content that is a process and process knowledge as the learning level. To respond correctly to the mini-experiment's prompt, students must recall the steps in a process, but it is not the same process specified by the objective. Therefore, the mini-experiment has _____.
   a) intra-observer consistency
   b) learning-level relevance
   c) subject-content relevance
   d) internal consistency

K. The results from a mini-experiment are used to make decisions about how well students achieve an objective that specifies a subject-content that is a process and process knowledge as the learning level. To respond correctly to the mini-experiment's prompt, students must recall the steps in a process, but it is not the same process specified by the objective. Therefore, the mini-experiment lacks _____.
   a) relevance
   b) learning-level relevance
   c) reliability
   d) usability

L. Which one of the following is *not* a possible subject-content of a comprehension-and-communication-skills objective?
   a) definition of a concept
   b) statement of a discoverable relationship
   c) information as presented on a CD-ROM
   d) discoverable relationship

M. Students learn the meaning of a short-hand symbol by _____.
   a) using inductive reasoning
   b) using deductive reasoning
   c) using divergent reasoning
   d) being informed

N. Students construct concepts by using _____ reasoning.
   a) inductive
   b) deductive
   c) divergent
   d) convergent

O. Students achieve application objectives by using _____ reasoning.
   a) inductive
   b) deductive
   c) divergent
   d) convergent

P. Students achieve creative-thinking objectives by using _____ reasoning.
   a) inductive
   b) deductive
   c) divergent
   d) convergent

Q. Process-knowledge objectives are _____.
   a) affective
   b) memory level
   c) reasoning level
   d) psychomotor

R. By accurately measuring the size of an angle with a protractor, Antoine demonstrates learning at which one of the following levels?
   a) process knowledge

b) appreciation
c) application
d) construct a concept

S. By accurately measuring the size of an angle with a protractor, Antoine demonstrates learning at which one of the following levels?
a) comprehension and communications skills
b) willingness to try
c) discover a relationship
d) creative thinking

T. By accurately measuring the size of an angle with a protractor, Antoine demonstrates learning at which one of the following levels?
a) reasoning level
b) psychomotor-skill performance

U. Antoine could hardly be expected to learn to accurately report the number of degrees in an angle from measurements he makes with a protractor unless he _____.
a) appreciates the value of mathematics
b) has constructed the concept of an angle
c) has knowledge of a relationship of convention
d) has discovered a relationship between angles and their complements

V. One purpose of weighting objectives is to enhance the _____ of measurements used to make summative evaluations of how well students have achieved the goal those objectives define.
a) usability
b) internal consistency
c) learning-level relevance
d) intra-observer consistency

W. One purpose of weighting objectives is to enhance the _____ of measurements used to make summative evaluations of how well students have achieved the goal those objectives define.
a) subject-content relevance
b) inter-observer consistency
c) grading methods
d) diagnostic value

X. One purpose of weighting objectives is to enhance the _____ of measurements used to make summative evaluations of how well students have achieved the goal those objectives define.
a) reliability
b) validity
c) observer consistency
d) intent

Y. When a teacher conducts a lesson targeting an affective objective, that teacher is attempting to lead students to _____.
a) understand their own values
b) understand the values of others
c) embrace a value
d) be open to varying belief systems

Z. If a student achieves an objective requiring her to use reasoning to extend what is remembered, then that objective targets which one of the following learning-levels?
a) reasoning
b) memory
c) process knowledge
d) comprehension and communication skills

AA. If the intent of a teacher's lesson doesn't include improving students' abilities of some kind, then the lesson's objective must fall into which one of the following domains?
a) cognitive

    b) affective
    c) psychomotor

BB. Which one of the following pairs of concepts is a pair of parallel concepts?

    a) number, whole number
    b) pronoun, word
    c) animal, plant
    d) mammal, coyote

2. Compare and discuss your and a colleague's responses to the multiple-choice prompts from Synthesis Activity 1. Also, check your choices against the following key: A-b, B-a, C-d, D-d, E-c, F-a, G-c, H-b, I-d, J-b, K-a, L-d, M-d, N-a, O-b, P-c, Q-b, R-a, S-b, T-b, U-c, V-c, W-a, X-b, Y-c, Z-a, AA-b, and BB-c.

3. If you are currently responsible for teaching a group of students, begin designing a teaching unit for your students by formulating a learning goal and defining it by a set of *weighted* objectives. Make sure you label each objective's learning level according to the advanced organizer outlined by Illustration 5.17. If you do not now have your own group of students, then complete this task for a hypothetical group of students with respect to your own teaching specialty.

4. Examine each objective you listed in response to the prompt for Synthesis Activity 3 and label the subject-content specified by the objective as either "specific," "concept," "discoverable relationship," "relationship of convention," "process," or "other."

5. Explain in two paragraphs why you decided to assign weights to objectives as you did in response to the prompt for Synthesis Activity 3. Make sure your rationale is based on pedagogical concerns. You do not need to say things like, "I weighted Objective C 20% and Objective D 10% because I think Objective C is twice as important to goal achievement." That's obvious from your percentages. Instead relate thoughts such as the following: "More weight is placed on Objective C than D because unless students construct the concept indicated by Objective C, they will be unable to achieve the application objectives later in the unit. Objective D, on the other hand, is only needed so that students will use conventional expressions as they communicate with one another."

6. Exchange your responses to the prompts for Synthesis Activities 3, 4, and 5 with those of a colleague. Discuss one another's work; raise and address questions and issues stimulated by your reviews of each other's responses.

7. With two or three colleagues, discuss why you agree or disagree with the following statement:

> By applying the advanced organizer outlined in Illustration 5.17, teachers increase the chances that their instruction will lead to meaningful learning.

TRANSITIONAL ACTIVITY FROM CHAPTER 5 TO CHAPTER 6

In a discussion with two or more of your colleagues, address the following questions:

1. What are some strategies and techniques we can apply to develop measurements that are relevant to our learning goals?

2. In what ways can computer technology be used to develop useful measurements?

3. How is the validity of a measurement influenced by the way in which the measurement is administered to students?

4. Besides what we've already discussed based on reading Chapters 2 and 3, what other uses can we make of individualized student portfolios?

5. What are some sound strategies for preventing and dealing with students cheating on tests?

Systematically Developing Measurements

▰ GOAL OF CHAPTER 6

Chapter 6 is designed to lead you to develop a practical system for developing valid and usable measurements. More specifically the objectives are as follows:

A. You will systematically develop measurements for monitoring your students' learning rather than follow the more common practice of developing measurements haphazardly (willingness to try) 8%.

B. You will organize a computerized system for mini-experiments to facilitate the efficient development of relevant measurements (application) 30%.

C. You will explain the need for mini-experiments of varying levels of difficulty (discover a relationship) 10%.

D. You will make use of measurement blueprints when designing measurements for the purpose of making summative evaluations of your students' achievement (application) 20%.

E. When administering measurements for the purpose of making summative evaluations of your students' achievement, you will make provisions for accommodating students with special needs (e.g., students with learning disabilities) (application) 10%.

F. When administering measurements for purposes of making summative evaluations, you will employ strategies for minimizing potential contaminants to reliability (e.g., misunderstanding of directions, distractions, and student cheating) (application) 12%.

G. You will decide how, if at all, you plan to incorporate individualized student portfolios into your system for monitoring student learning (application) 5%.

H. You will incorporate the following technical phrases in your working professional vocabulary: "mini-experiment file," "computerized folder of mini-experiment files," "mini-experiment format," "mini-experiment difficulty," "measurement blueprint," "showcase portfolio," "working portfolio," and "record-keeping portfolio" (comprehension and communication skills) 5%.

WHY NOT FOLLOW COMMON PRACTICE?

Is the method for developing a measurement employed by Ms. McArdle in Case 6.1 familiar to you?

CASE 6.1

It's Wednesday night; the next day, Ms. McArdle plans to complete a unit on the U.S. Constitution she's been conducting for her eighth-grade social studies class. The unit test is scheduled for Friday. Sitting in front of her computer, she thinks to herself, "Okay, time to put this test together. Let's see. I'll make this mostly short-answer questions so it won't take me the entire weekend to score—well, maybe I need at least one essay to see if they can write about what they know. Okay, I'll start with some completion items. What would be good for the first one? Anybody who listened in class would know about the seven articles." She enters the following in a word processing file: "1. There are _____ articles in the Constitution. 2. The fifth article deals with _____." "Good, now I'm rolling!" she thinks. "I need one that'll really tell me who studied." She enters on the keyboard, "3. Write the first 15 words of the Preamble to the Constitution." "Now, what should I ask them next? Ahhh . . . Oh, yeah!" she thinks as she enters, "4. How many delegates signed the Constitution?"

She looks through the assigned textbook chapter for the unit. "Here's a sentence in bold print; anyone who read the chapter should remember it." She reads, "Our government is based on a system of representation," and enters, "5. Our government is based on a system of _____."

Thirty-five minutes later, after entering "20. Explain the importance of the Constitution to your life today," Ms. McArdle decides that the unit test document is ready to be printed.

Measurements developed in the way Ms. McArdle developed her test in Case 6.1 are unlikely to be valid because they are unlikely to be satisfactorily relevant. Unfortunately, this ill-advised, haphazard method is commonly practiced (Cangelosi, 1998; Plake & Impara, 1997; Stiggins & Conklin, 1992).

Apparently, Ms. McArdle's summative evaluations of what her students learned from the unit on the Constitution will be influenced by the results of the test she developed in Case 6.1. However, she never appeared to even look at the objectives for the unit while designing the test. She seemed more concerned with judging who listened in class, who studied, and who read the textbook than evaluating how well the learning goal was achieved.

Why should you not use Ms. McArdle's commonly used measurement-development method? First of all, mini-experiments can be relevant only if they reflect stated learning objectives. Thus, don't expect them to be relevant unless you design them so that they specifically target the subject-contents and learning levels pinpointed by your objectives.

Even if Ms. McArdle had objectives in mind as she developed her test, she should not be attempting to design mini-experiments (i.e., what she calls "questions" or "items") as she is assembling the test. Mini-experiments are components from which measurements are assembled. To be relevant, those mini-experiments should be designed ahead of time for each objective and then assembled into a measurement. The recommended method makes it easier to focus on the subject-contents and learning levels of objectives one at a time. Furthermore, by thinking up these prompts for mini-experiments as she assembles the measurement, Ms. McArdle is likely to overemphasize objectives that are easy to measure and underemphasize objectives that are more difficult to measure. For example, consider the following two objectives:

A. Students state with what each of the seven articles of the Constitution deals (simple knowledge).

B. Given a description of a current event, students explain what, if any, bearing the Constitution has on the resolution of that issue (application).

Is it easier to design a relevant mini-experiment for Objective A or Objective B? Most teachers answer that Objective A is easier to measure than Objective B (Cangelosi, 1998). Thus, with Ms. McArdle's method of thinking up prompts off the top of her head as she's assembling the test, easier to measure objectives (e.g., Objective A) are going to be emphasized more in the test than more difficult to measure objectives (e.g., Objective B). Keeping in mind that memory-level objectives are typically easier to measure than reasoning-level objectives, it's not surprising that the vast majority of tests in schools emphasize memory-level learning more than reasoning-level learning (Cangelosi, 1998; O'Hagan, 1997; Rowley, 1996). Weighting your objectives as you did while engaged in Synthesis Activity 3 of Chapter 5 is a mechanism for designing measurements so that more important aspects of learning are emphasized more than less important aspects of learning.

A SYSTEMATIC PROGRAM

Of course, before systematically developing a measurement that's relevant to a learning goal, you need to have that goal defined by a set of weighted objectives, with each objective specifying a subject-content and learning level. Then for each objective, you need relevant mini-experiments—the components from which you'll assemble your measurement. Designing or acquiring relevant mini-experiments is a very challenging task. Of all the talents this textbook is intended to help you develop, the most difficult to develop is the talent for designing relevant mini-experiments. The sole focus of Chapters 7–13 is leading you to develop that talent. In the meantime, assume you can produce these measurement components.

Once you have a means for generating relevant mini-experiments, you need a system for organizing, managing, refining, and generating more of them. Then you need an efficient way to design your measurement, assemble mini-experiments in compliance with your design, administer the measurement in a way that controls for contaminants to reliability and accommodates students with special needs, and makes use of the results for informed decision-making. Developing such a system is what you'll be working on throughout this chapter.

COMPUTERIZED FOLDER OF MINI-EXPERIMENT FILES

ORGANIZING AND SETTING UP THE FOLDER

A computer file containing a set of prompts and observer's rubrics for mini-experiments intended to be relevant to the same objective is a *mini-experiment file*. *Mini-experiment files* are organized into a folder stored on a computer disk in Case 6.2.

CASE 6.2

Ms. Fisher organizes and stores the prompts and observer's rubrics for the mini-experiments she has developed and acquired over the years on computer disks so that each disk is devoted to a course. Illustration 2.8 lists the 22 units for her U.S. history course. The storage space on the disk for the U.S. history course is partitioned into 22 folders (or directories), with each folder containing the mini-experiment files for a unit. See Illustration 6.1.

As listed by Illustration 2.9, the goal of Unit 17 of the U.S. history course is defined by eight objectives (A–H), thus the folder for Unit 17 contains eight files. File A contains the prompts and observer's rubrics for mini-experiments she considers relevant to Objective A, as do Files B–H for Objectives B–H respectively. Besides directions for the mini-experiments' prompts and rubrics, the files also include other information about the mini-experiments (e.g., cross-references to other files, prior uses of measurements,

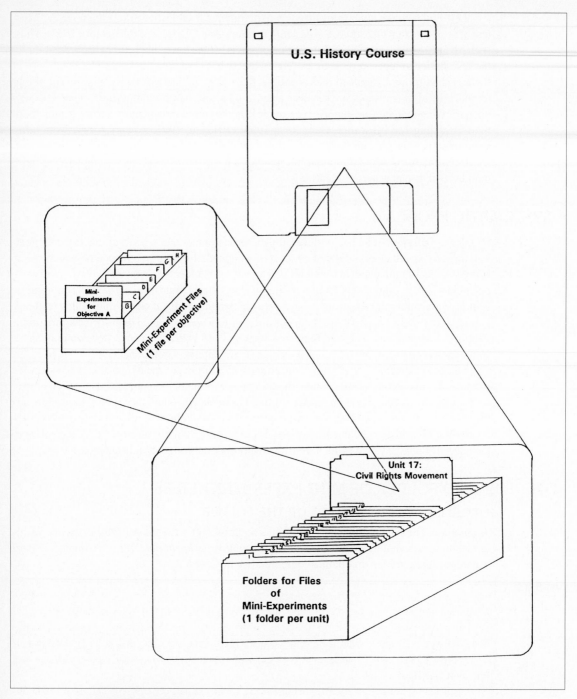

ILLUSTRATION 6.1

Space on Ms. Fisher's U.S. History Course Disk Organized into Folders with Mini-Experiment Files for Each Unit

and difficulty levels). Presently, File A includes prompts and rubrics for six mini-experiments for Objective A. Illustration 6.2 is a printout of the part of File A pertaining to the first two mini-experiments. Keep in mind that Ms. Fisher intends for these two mini-experiments to be relevant to Objective A as listed in Illustration 2.9.

MINI-EXPERIMENT FORMATS

Note from Illustration 6.2 that Ms. Fisher labeled the prompt for #1 "written-response essay" and the prompt for #2 "short-answer written-response." These labels identify the *format* of the mini-experiment. *Mini-experiment format* is the mode by which the prompt is presented and students are expected to respond. Commonly used mini-experiment formats include multiple-choice, performance observation, essay, oral discourse, matching, interview, product examination, and short-response. The formats for the mini-experiments you design yourself need not be limited to the conventional formats you've experienced on traditional tests. For some objectives, you may need to exercise your creativity and develop a never-before-seen format.

Having a variety of formats in a mini-experiment file gives you flexibility in the ways you measure students' achievement of the objective. How well a student's responses to prompts reflect his or her achievement of an objective varies according to mini-experiment formats. Some students, for example, are comfortable with essay prompts but struggle with multiple-choice prompts; for others the opposite is true. A variety of mini-experiment formats provides students with multiple ways to display learning.

DIFFICULTY LEVELS

Examine Case 6.3.

CASE 6.3

Objective J of Ms. Curry's sixth-grade mathematics unit on surface area is as follows:

When confronted with a real-life problem, students determine how, if at all, computing a surface area will help solve that problem (application).

Ms. Curry's mini-experiment file for Objective J includes the three entries shown in Illustration 6.3.

Note from Illustration 6.3 that Mini-Experiments 11, 12, and 13 are all relevant to Ms. Curry's Objective J but that they vary with respect to difficulty levels. The difficulty levels of mini-experiments depend on the percentage of students whose responses have high scores. For mini-experiments with rubrics with dichotomous scoring (e.g., Illustration 6.3's three mini-experiments), the percentage of students with correct responses is a measure of difficulty level. According to Ms. Curry's notes under "Difficulty Level for Students," #11 is the easiest of the three, since about 90% of the students responded correctly, whereas #13 was the most difficult, since only about 10% responded correctly.

For a mini-experiment with a weighted-scoring rubric, percentage of total points scored by all the students out of the maximum possible total is indicative of the difficulty level. Thus, if Ms. Fisher from Case 6.2 administered a test that included Mini-Experiment #1 from Illustration 6.2 to 30 students in her third-period class, then she could compute the difficulty-level

<u>#1</u>

<u>Written-response brief-essay prompt</u>:

(a) Recall the day about two weeks ago when we simulated segregation in our class. In what ways were the *greens'* experiences similar to those of black people living in the South in 1950?

(b) In what two ways were the *blues'* experiences similar to those of white people living in the South in 1950?

(c) In what ways were the *greens'* experiences similar to those of black people living in the North in 1970?

(d) In what ways were the *blues'* experiences similar to those of white people living in the North in 1970?

ILLUSTRATION 6.2

Printout of the Part of File A Pertaining to Ms. Fisher's First Two Mini-Experiments for Objective A (Listed in Illustration 2.9)

(Continued)

ILLUSTRATION 6.2 (Continued)

(e) Afterwards, the class discussed different ways *green* people and *blue* people felt while the class was segregated. Describe three of the ways class members indicated they felt and explain why those feeling are or are not similar to ways people living in segregated societies today must feel.

Observer's Rubrics:

NOTE: For each criterion listed, points are awarded as follows:

+2 if the criterion in question is clearly met
+1 if it is unclear as to whether or not the criterion is met
+0 if the criterion is clearly not met

Maximum possible points: 22

Rubric for Prompt 2(a):

Parallels one of the *greens*' experiences from the simulated segregation with one for 1950s *blacks* in the South & the parallel is consistent with historical records ------------------------------------- 0 1 2

Parallels another of the *greens*' experiences from the simulated segregation with one for 1950s *blacks* in the South & the parallel is consistent with historical records ------------------------------------- 0 1 2

Rubric for Prompt 2(b):

Parallels one of the *blues*' experiences from the simulated segregation with one for 1950s whites in the South & the parallel is consistent with historical records ------------------------------------- 0 1 2

Parallels another of the *blues*' experiences from the simulated segregation with one for 1950s whites in the South & the parallel is consistent with historical records ------------------------------------- 0 1 2

ILLUSTRATION 6.2 (Continued)

Rubric for Prompt 2(c):

Parallels one of the *greens*' experiences from
the simulated segregation with one for 1970s <u>blacks</u>
in the North & the parallel is consistent with
historical records   ------------------------------------- 0 1 2

Parallels another of the *greens*' experiences from
the simulated segregation with one for 1970s *blacks*
in the North & the parallel is consistent with
historical records   ------------------------------------- 0 1 2

Rubric for Prompt 2(d):

Parallels one of the *blues*' experiences from the
simulated segregation with one for 1970s *whites*
in the North & the parallel is consistent with
historical records   ------------------------------------- 0 1 2

Parallels another of the *blues*' experiences from
the simulated segregation with one for 1970s *whites*
in the North & the parallel is consistent with
historical records   ------------------------------------- 0 1 2

Rubric for Prompt 2(e):

Parallels one of the feelings expressed in class
and provides a tenable explanation as to why that
feeling is either similar or dissimilar to parallel
feelings resulting from today's real-world
segregated or discriminatory societies   ------------------ 0 1 2

Parallels another of the feelings expressed in
class and provides a tenable explanation as to
why that feeling is either similar or dissimilar
to parallel feelings resulting from today's real-
world segregated or discriminatory society   -------------- 0 1 2

Parallels yet another of the feelings expressed
in class & provides a tenable explanation as to
why that feeling is either similar or dissimilar
to parallel feelings resulting from today's real-
world segregated or discriminatory society   -------------- 0 1 2

Notes:

Cross references to other files:

    none

History:

    Used once as the second prompt on the take-home part of the
unit-17 test administered to both the 3rd and 4th period sections. In review session following administration, students

ILLUSTRATION 6.2 (Continued)

appeared to have comprehended the directions. Also, the discussion stimulated by review of responses proved to be a very productive learning experience. Discussion also suggested that the prompts should have been spelled out better.

<u>Difficulty level for students</u>:

Designed to be moderately difficult. However the mean score for the 3rd period class was 18.3 and 17.8 for 4th period. Thus, the response scores were higher than I anticipated.

<u>Evaluation of mini-experiment</u>:

After considering some refinements of the observer's rubric, I definitely plan to use this one again.

#2

<u>Short-Answer Written-Response Prompt</u>:

(a) Suppose you are a black high school student living in Atlanta, Ga. In 1950, your black grandfather was also a high school student living in Atlanta, Ga. Name one thing you can *legally* do in Atlanta today that he could not *legally* do in Atlanta in 1950. In about two sentences, explain why the activity you named is legal in Atlanta today but not in 1950.

   The activity:

   The explanation:

(b) Suppose you are a white high school student living in Atlanta, Ga. In 1950, your white grandfather was also a high school student living in Atlanta, Ga. Name one thing you can *legally* do in Atlanta today that he could not *legally* do in Atlanta in 1950. In about two sentences, explain why the activity you named is legal in Atlanta today but not in 1950.

   The activity:

   The explanation:

<u>Observer's Rubrics</u>:

For Part A:

3 points possible distributed as follows:

+1 if the activity was illegal for a black high school student in Atlanta in 1950 (e.g., to drink from a "whites only" water fountain)

ILLUSTRATION 6.2 (Continued)

+1 if the activity is legal for a high school student in Atlanta today.

+1 if the explanation reflects changes in Atlanta's laws since
1950.

For Part B:

3 points possible distributed as follows:

+1 if the activity was illegal for a white high school student
in Atlanta in 1950 (e.g., to attend a school with black
classmates)

+1 if the activity is legal for a high school student in Atlanta today.

+1 if the explanation reflects changes in Atlanta's laws since
1950.

Note: A response could meet the above criteria that did not involve
the ending of *de jure* segregation (e.g., it was illegal for an
18-year-old to vote in 1950, but not now). Such responses
should be scored as would the more desirable responses that
reflect changes in segregation laws. However, a note should be
made that a "correct" response was made that doesn't reflect
achievement of the objective.

Notes:

Cross references to other files:

History:

Developed on 4/18/00 but never used.

Difficulty level for students:

Designed to be difficult for students prior to Unit 17 and easy
for them by the end of the first week of the unit.

Evaluation of mini-experiment:

There is history to base an evaluation on or to know if
students will give "correct" responses that are unrelated
to *de jure* segregation. Also, I am concerned that by the end
of the unit students could respond correctly simply by remembering an example presented in class, thus it would only tap the
simple-knowledge level. On the other hand, if they have
to use reasoning for a correct response, the reasoning may be
deductive and reflect more an application learning level than
discover a relationship. However, I'm not going to fret over the
fine difference between the two.

#11

Multiple-Choice Prompt:

  Carpet is to be bought for the rectangular-shaped floor of a room.
  The room is 8 feet high, 12 feet wide, and 15 feet long. Which of
  the following computations would be the most helpful
  in deciding how much carpet to buy?

  a) 12' + 8' + 15'
  b) 2' x (12' + 15')
  c) 12' x 8' x 15'
  d) 12' x 15'

Observer's Rubrics:

  +1 for d only; otherwise +0

Notes:

  Cross references to other files:

    The prompt for #3 in Mini-Experiment File D is similar to this
    one except that students are directed to find the size of the
    floor to be covered and the choices are in simplified form
    (e.g., 180 square feet is the answer). Pairing the stem of this
    prompt with the response choices of #3 from File D would produce
    a prompt requiring both application (Objective J) and process
    knowledge (Objective D).

  History:

    Used at least 10 times but with different dimensions

  Difficulty level for students:

    Intended to be easy. On unit tests, about 90% of the responses
    have been correct no matter what dimensions are used.

  Evaluation of mini-experiment:

    Only problem detected is that a few students selected the
    correct response because it was the only alternative that had
    exactly two feet-marks (') and they deduced that area had
    to be in square feet.

#12

Multiple-Choice Prompt:

  Suppose we want to build book shelves across one wall of our classroom. The shelves are to be 18 inches apart. Which one

---

ILLUSTRATION 6.3

Three Prompts and Rubrics in One of Ms. Curry's Mini-Experiment Files

(Continued)

ILLUSTRATION 6.3 (Continued)

of the following numbers would be most helpful in figuring out how many shelves we can fit on the wall?

    a)   area of the wall
    b)   width of the wall
    c)   height of the wall
    d)   perimeter of the wall

<u>Observer's Rubrics</u>:

+1 for c only; otherwise +0

<u>Notes</u>:

<u>Cross references to other files</u>:

<u>History</u>:

Used at least 5 times but with different values for the distance between shelves.

<u>Difficulty level for students</u>:

Intended to be moderately difficult. On unit tests, about 70% of the responses have been correct.

<u>Evaluation of mini-experiment</u>:

A student interpreted "18 inches apart" to be lateral instead of vertical distance. They typically don't think of "apart" as up and down. However, I think that this misinterpretation is related to their not applying area to more complex problems. I don't see any reason to discontinue or modify this mini-experiment.

<u>#13</u>

<u>Multiple-Choice Prompt</u>:

The 13 steps of a staircase are to be painted. Each step is 36 inches wide, 12 inches deep, and 7 inches high. Which of the of following computations would be most helpful in determining how much paint will be needed?

    a)   [(12" x 13) x (7" x 13)] ÷ 2
    b)   36" x [13 x (12" x 7)"]
    c)   (13 x 7") x (36" + 12")
    d)   13 x [(36" x 7") + (36" x 12")]

<u>Observer's Rubrics</u>:

+1 for d only; otherwise +0

<u>Notes</u>:

ILLUSTRATION 6.3 (Continued)

```
Cross references to other files:

    #14 from this file is identical to this mini-experiment
    except that a diagram of the staircase is given. Thus, #14
    is an easier alternative to this one -- but shouldn't be used in
    the same measurement.

History:

    Used at least 5 times but with different values for the
    dimensions.

Difficulty level for students:

    Intended to be very difficult. On unit tests, about 10% of the
    responses have been correct.

Evaluation of mini-experiment:

    This mini-experiment seems to work well for more advanced
    achievement of Objective J. Discussions when responses are re-
    viewed are reinforcing to students with advanced achievement lev-
    els and instructive to students who need to learn to illustrate
    the given data with an accurate drawing.
```

percentage by adding up the 30 scores from the mini-experiment, dividing the sum by 660, and converting the result to a percentage. Why 660? Because as indicated by the scoring rubric, the maximum possible score is 22 and there are 30 students who responded to the prompt. If every student scored the maximum, the sum of their scores would be 30×22, or 660. Suppose the sum of the scores for the mini-experiment from the third-class was 549. What is the difficulty-level percentage? Check your computation against the following:

$$549 \div 660 = .83 = 83\%$$

You may already have noted that Illustration 6.2 provides information that would allow you to compute the 549 total for all 30 students in Ms. Fisher's third-period class. Find it if you haven't already done so. Note that $30 \times 18.3 = 549$.

For a given population of students, the greater the difficulty-level percentage, the easier the mini-experiment is for those students. What are the advantages of having mini-experiments of varying difficulty-levels in a mini-experiment file?

As suggested by Ms. Curry's notes in Illustration 6.3, you need easy mini-experiments to measure rudimentary achievement of an objective, moderately difficult mini-experiments to measure the achievement of most of your students, and very difficult mini-experiments to measure advanced achievement levels among your students. As suggested in Chapter 3's section "The Traditional Percentage Method," for students to reach advanced achievement levels with objectives, they need to be engaged in challenging mini-experiments (i.e., difficult mini-experiments).

CROSS-REFERENCING THE MINI-EXPERIMENTS
Examine Case 6.4.

CASE 6.4

The goal of Mr. Rose's unit on writing persuasive essays is defined by seven objectives. Objective C is concerned with students presenting a rational argument with conclusions based on evidence. He states Objective C as follows:

> C. Students write persuasive essays so that it is clear that they distinguish between facts and conclusions and that conclusions they make are supported by relevant evidence (application).

One mini-experiment Mr. Rose designs to be relevant to Objective C prompts students to develop a persuasive essay; the observer's rubric focuses on the distinctions between facts and opinions as presented in the essay and how well conclusions are supported by evidence.

Objective D is concerned with the structure of the essays; Mr. Rose states Objective D as follows:

> D. Students structure essays so that they begin with an introductory paragraph, make transitions between ideas, and end with summary or concluding paragraphs (application).

One of Mr. Rose's mini-experiments for Objective D prompts students to write an essay; the rubric focuses on how the essays are structured.

Objective E is concerned with the students' use of grammar, punctuation, and sentence structure rules; Mr. Rose states Objective E as follows:

> E. Students will employ conventional rules of grammar, punctuation, and sentence structure when writing persuasive essays (application).

One of Mr. Rose's mini-experiments for Objective E prompts students to write an essay; the rubric focuses on how well students follow rules of grammar, punctuation, and sentence structure.

For a measurement of students' achievement of the goal, Mr. Rose includes all three of the aforementioned mini-experiments. But rather than prompt them to write three different persuasive essays, he directs them to spend several days developing only one. Then he employs the three different rubrics to each student essay. Illustration 6.4 shows how he stored the three mini-experiments in separate mini-experiment files.

The cross-reference notes Mr. Rose inserts in his mini-experiment files help him use different mini-experiments in conjunction with one another when he synthesizes measurements.

CREATING A COMPUTERIZED FOLDER

Computer software designed especially for setting up, maintaining, expanding, modifying, and using computerized folders of mini-experiment files are readily available from commercial and noncommercial outlets. "Measurement and Analysis Tool," the CD-ROM that accompanies this textbook, is one such software utility. Professional journals, web sites for teachers, software companies' web sites, educational software catalogues, instructional materials catalogues, school-district resource centers for teachers, instructional resource centers on university campuses, computer retail stores, and computer magazines have information on how such software can be obtained. Of course, special software for mini-experiment files is not absolutely necessary. Many teachers use standard word-processing programs to set up mini-experiment files or prefer to write their own programs.

<u>One of the Entries in Mr. Rose's</u>
<u>Mini-Experiment File for Objective C</u>

<u>#4</u>

<u>Essay Prompt</u>:

Spend some time thinking about controversial issues about which you
have strong opinions. Identify three such controversial issues
about which you might write a persuasive essay. Meet with Mr. Rose
to discuss and decide on the topic for a persuasive essay you will
write that you will share with Mr. Rose on __[insert date]__. Using
word processing, write the essay on the topic to which you and Mr.
Rose agree. It should be approximately two single-spaced pages
long. Use the editorial advice of others as you please and use references as needed.

<u>Observer's Rubric</u>:

<u>For making distinctions between facts and opinions</u>:

Read the essay.

Use a green pen to circle each expression of an opinion. Record
the number of opinions expressed, call that number p. Now for
each of the p opinions, rate the expression of that opinion according to the following scale:

+2   if it is clear from the writing that the writer recognizes
     that the opinion is an opinion rather than a fact.
+1   if it is unclear from the writing whether or not the writer
     recognizes that the opinion is an opinion rather than a
     fact.
+0   if it is clear from the writing that the writer does not
     recognize that the opinion is an opinion rather than a
     fact.

Take the sum of the p ratings and divide that sum by p; call the
resulting ratio R_o.

Use a red pen to circle each expression of a fact. Record the
number of facts expressed, call that number f. Now for each of
the f facts, rate the expression of that fact according to the
following scale:

+2   if it is clear from the writing that the writer recognizes
     that the fact is a fact rather than an opinion.
+1   if it is unclear from the writing whether or not the

ILLUSTRATION 6.4

Mr. Rose Cross-References Three Related Mini-Experiments

(Continued)

ILLUSTRATION 6.4 (Continued)

writer recognizes that the fact is a fact rather than an opinion.

+0 if it is clear from the writing that the writer does not recognize that the fact is a fact rather than an opinion.

Take the sum of the f ratings and divide that sum by f; call the resulting ratio R_f.

The score for making distinctions between facts and opinions is $R_o + R_f$.

<u>For supporting opinions with facts</u>:

For each of the p opinions, rate the expression of that opinion according to the following scale:

+2 if it is clear from the writing that the opinion is supported by one or more facts.

+1 if it is unclear from the writing whether or not the opinion is supported by one or more facts expressed in the essay.

+0 if it is clear from the writing that the opinion is not supported by at least one fact presented in the essay.

<u>Notes</u>:

<u>Cross references to other files</u>:

The prompt is identical to prompts for Mini-Experiment #7 in File D as well as #10 in File E. Use those two mini-experiments in concert with this one.

<u>History</u>:

Never before used in this form.

<u>Difficulty level for students</u>:

Intended to be moderately difficult.

<u>Evaluation of mini-experiment</u>:

No history to base an evaluation.

<u>One of the Entries in Mr. Rose's</u>
<u>Mini-Experiment File for Objective D</u>

<u>#7</u>

<u>Essay Prompt</u>:

(See prompt for #4 from Mini-Experiment File C.)

<u>Observer's Rubric</u>:

(6 maximum possible points)

ILLUSTRATION 6.4 (Continued)

Use the following scale for the introductory paragraph:

+2 if the essay clearly contains an introductory paragraph.

+1 if there is some question as to whether or not there is an introductory paragraph.

+0 if the essay clearly does not contain an introductory paragraph.

Use the following scale for the summary or concluding paragraphs:

+2 if the essay clearly contains at least one summary or concluding paragraph.

+1 if there is some question as to whether or not there is a summary or concluding paragraph.

+0 if the essay clearly does not contain a summary or concluding paragraph.

Use the following scale for transitions between ideas:

+2 if for most consecutive expressions of different ideas, the writer has inserted a logical transition expression.

+1 if for some, but not most, consecutive expressions of different ideas, the writer has inserted a logical transition expression.

+0 if there are no logical transition expressions inserted between any of the consecutive expressions of different ideas.

<u>Notes</u>:

<u>Cross references to other files</u>:

The prompt is identical to prompts for Mini-Experiment #4 in File C as well as #10 in File E. Use those two mini-experiments in concert with this one.

<u>History</u>:

Never before used in this form.

<u>Difficulty level for students</u>:

Intended to be moderately difficult.

<u>Evaluation of mini-experiment</u>:

No history to base an evaluation.

ILLUSTRATION 6.4 (Continued)

One of the Entries in Mr. Rose's
Mini-Experiment File for Objective E

#10

<u>Essay Prompt</u>:

(See prompt for #4 from Mini-Experiment File C.)

<u>Observer's Rubric</u>:

Record the number of sentences in the essay; call that number s. Now for each of the s sentences, determine whether or not the sentence is grammatically correct with no punctuation errors nor violations of sentence structure rules. Record the number of such correctly structured sentences; call that number c.

The score is c/s.

<u>Notes</u>:

<u>Cross references to other files</u>:

The prompt is identical to prompts for Mini-Experiment #4 in File C as well as #7 in File D. Use those two mini-experiments in concert with this one.

<u>History</u>:

The rubric has been frequently used with a wide variety of essay prompts.

<u>Difficulty level for students</u>:

This mini-experiment tends to be very difficult for students the first few times they encounter it; with experience, their scores improve considerably.

<u>Evaluation of mini-experiment</u>:

Appears to work well, but it is very time-consuming for lengthy essays.

In Case 6.5, Mr. Johnson uses the CD that accompanies this book to create folders for mini-experiment files on his personal computer.

CASE 6.5

Mr. Johnson inserts the disk into his CD-ROM drive and clicks on the "Start" button for "Mini-Experiment Builder Application" that appears on the application control panel. Following directions appearing on the screen, he inserts into the floppy disk drive a blank, formatted disk that he has labeled "Social Studies 5," the name of one of the courses he teaches. Following directions, he downloads the program for setting up folders for a single course onto the disk. Because he plans 17 units for the social studies course, he creates 17 folders on the disk, entering the names for each unit in response to prompts that appear on the screen.

Within each of the 17 folders, Mr. Johnson will create mini-experiment files—one for each of the unit's objectives. He will do that as he decides the objectives. He opens the folder for Unit 1; the following prompt appears on the screen: "How many objectives do you want to include for Unit 1?" He types, "9." Automatically, nine files are created, each with a template for Mr. Johnson to enter the statement of the objective and prompts, rubrics, and notes for a large number of mini-experiments. See Illustration 6.5.

For each mini-experiment he wants to store, Mr. Johnson enters the necessary text, figures, or graphics into the appropriate rectangular regions shown in Illustration 6.5. The regions expand to accommodate the size of his entries. The program also creates a table of contents for the folder as well as for each file; the table of contents is automatically updated as Mr. Johnson adds, modifies, and deletes mini-experiments.

Of course, to make use of the software that accompanies this book or any other software for setting up computerized folders for mini-experiments, you need to try it out for yourself, following the step-by-step directions appearing on your screen.

MODIFYING MINI-EXPERIMENTS AND EXPANDING THE FILES

Even with the aid of computer software, the process of setting up a systematic measurement program is initially more time-consuming than the haphazard approach Ms. McArdle used in Case 6.1. However, once you get your system up and running, you not only have a process by which you develop and use more valid measurements than you would with a haphazard approach, but you also save considerable time by building on previous work and having the computer take care of the routine chores.

In Case 6.6, Mr. Johnson's systematic measurement program is up and running.

CASE 6.6

As Mr. Johnson develops measurements during the school year, he expands his mini-experiment files. He also learns from each measurement he administers and applies those lessons to his design of new mini-experiments and to modify prompts and rubrics of mini-experiments already stored in his computerized folders.

Mr. Johnson inserts the disk with the folders for his Social Studies 5 course units. He then engages the computer in the following dialogue:

Computer: "Click on the function you want: Insert new mini-experiment, modify existing mini-experiment, delete existing mini-experiment, move mini-experiment, create new folder, alter folder structure."

Mr. Johnson: Clicks on "Insert new mini-experiment."

Computer: Displays the table of contents for the folders and displays the following prompt: "Click on the folder you want to open."

Mr. Johnson: Clicks on "Unit 7: The Constitution."

Computer: Displays the table of contents for the Unit 7 folder and displays the following prompt: "Click on the mini-experiment file you want to open."

Mr. Johnson: Clicks on the file for Objective D.

Computer: Displays a template for inserting a new mini-experiment as shown by Illustration 6.5, but with Objective D printed out at the top.

Mr. Johnson enters the type of format he wants in the first dialogue box, the prompt in the second, the rubric in the third, and finally the notes as indicated by Illustration 6.5. The computer stores the new

Objective:

Mini-Experiment #

Prompt:

Observer's Rubric:

Notes:

Cross references to other files:

History:

Difficulty level for students:

Evaluation of mini-experiment:

NEXT

ILLUSTRATION 6.5

Computer Template for Entering Prompts, Rubrics, and Notes for Mini-Experiments

prompt-rubric-notes combination and then prompts Mr. Johnson with a list of options. He selects "mod-ify existing mini-experiment" and calls up the prompt-rubric-notes combination he wants to modify. He then modifies the prompt, rubric, or notes in the dialogue boxes, just as he would when modifying a text file with word processing.

As with most software for mini-experiment files, you can use the software that accompa-nies this book to quickly format and print out a measurement document from the prompts stored in the mini-experiment files. You, of course, need to direct the computer to follow your *blue-print* for the measurement. Illustration 6.6 is an example of a measurement blueprint that Mr. Johnson, from Cases 6.5 and 6.6, developed for one of his unit tests.

DEVELOPING THE MEASUREMENT BLUEPRINT

AN EXAMPLE OF A BLUEPRINT

A *measurement blueprint* is an outline specifying the features you want to build into a mea-surement you plan to develop from the prompts stored in your mini-experiment files. Typically, the *blueprint* indicates (1) the goal to be measured or the name of the measurement, (2) antic-ipated administration dates and times, (3) provisions for accommodating students with special needs, (4) types of mini-experiment formats to be used, (5) approximate number of mini-ex-periments to be included, (6) the targeted mix of difficulty levels for mini-experiments, (7) an approximation of the maximum possible score for the measurement, (8) how points should be distributed among the objectives that define the goal (based on the weights of the objectives), (9) the overall structure of the measurement, and (10) for summative evaluations, the method for converting scores to grades.

The blueprint serves as a guide for building the measurement the way you want it built.

ADMINISTRATION TIME AND DATES

A traditional group-administered test consisting solely of written-response prompts with direc-tions read by the students is simpler and less time-consuming than one with prompts that are presented individually (e.g., for mini-experiments with interview or performance-observation formats). Although convenient, the more usable, simpler measurements often lack relevance for complex learning goals emphasizing reasoning level or affective learning; this is especially the case for students without advanced reading and writing skills (e.g., primary-grade students). Thus, the complexity of your blueprint and the time allotted to the administration of the mea-surement depends on the learning goal and students with whom you work.

Validity considerations must be compromised with usability considerations. Generally speaking, measurements with many complex mini-experiments tend to be more valid than ones with only a few simple mini-experiments. However, the shorter, simpler measurements tend to be more usable. You cannot, of course, take more time administering and scoring a measure-ment than you have available. In deciding how much time to devote to the administration of a measurement, keep two other ideas in mind that are somewhat contrary to the traditional wis-dom that simpler is more usable:

- When measurements are used for making formative judgments, they can be integrated with learning activities, as you did in Case 1.4 and Mr. Heaps did in Case 2.10. Mini-experiments that are part of learning activities are more complex than most traditional ones on conven-tional paper-and-pencil tests, but instead of taking time away from learning, they contribute

<u>NAME</u>: Unit 7: The Constitution

<u>ADMINISTRATION TIME AND DATES</u>:

<u>Prompts Presented in Three Sessions</u>:

1. Section I of the test is a "take-home" to be assigned to students on Mon., 1/23, and due on Wed., 1/25.
2. Sections II and III on Wed., 1/25, from 1:10 to 2:00.
3. Sections IV and V on Thurs., 1/26, from 1:10 to 1:40.

<u>Time for Scoring with the Rubrics</u>:

1. Part II to be scored by aide on Wed. between 2:45 and 3:15.
2. Part III to be scored by me as administered.
3. Parts I, IV, and V scored by me on Thurs. between 3:15 and 5:00.

<u>Provisions for Accommodating</u>
<u>Students with Special Needs</u>

1. I meet with Ms. Mueller to (a) explain the directions for Sections II, IV, and V and (b) schedule Chad and Antonio to be administered Part II under her supervision on Wednesday from 1 p.m. to 3:15 and then Parts IV and V on Thursday from 1 p.m. to 3:00.

2. I meet with Mr. Isley-Vaughn to arrange to have a Spanish version of the measurement documents developed for Lupe and Rosanna as well as a Tongan version for Charlotte. At the meeting, I also need to schedule a Spanish translator to help me administer Part III to Lupe and Rosanna and a Tongan translator to help me interview Charlotte.

3. I administer Part III to Chad on Wednesday between 3:15 and 3:25 and to Antonio between 3:30 and 3:40.

4. I administer Part III to Lupe, Rosanna, and Charlotte on Thursday or Friday depending on when the translators are available to help me.

<u>Types of Mini-Experiment Formats</u>:

<u>Objective</u>	<u>Mini-Experiment Format</u>
A	multiple-choice & short-answer
B	multiple-choice & short-answer
C	multiple-choice
D	multiple-choice
E	multiple-choice & interview

ILLUSTRATION 6.6

Example of One of Mr. Johnson's Measurement Blueprints

(Continued)

ILLUSTRATION 6.6 (Continued)

```
        F                 multiple-choice
        G                 essay
        H                 multiple-choice
        I                 essay
```

Number of Mini-Experiments: 40-45

Difficulty Levels:

   Average score should be about 2/3 the maximum with approximately 40% of the mini-experiments easy, 40% moderately difficult, and 20% very difficult.

Maximum Number of Points: 60

Maximum Number of Points Per Objectives
as Indicated by Objectives' Weights:

Objective	Weight	Points
A	15%	9
B	15%	9
C	4%	2 or 3
D	4%	2 or 3
E	15%	9
F	12%	7 or 8
G	9%	5 or 6
H	18%	10 or 11
I	8%	4 or 5

Measurement Outline:

   Session 1:   Section I: take-home essay relevant to Objective I

   Session 2:   Section II: 38 multiple-choice mini-experiments (1 point each) distributed among the 9 objectives as follows: 5 for A, 5 for B, 3 for C, 3 for D, 5 for E, 7 for F, 0 for G, 10 for H, and 0 for I.

                 Section III: One 4-point interview relevant to Objective H, individually administered one to one while rest of group works on Section II.

   Session 3:   Section IV: Two 4-point short-answer mini-experiments, one relevant to Objective A, the other to Objective B.

   Section V: One 5-point essay relevant to Objective G.

ILLUSTRATION 6.6 (Continued)

<u>Method for Converting Scores to Grades</u>:

Compromise method with approximate midpoints for grade intervals
as follows: 55 → A, 45 → B, 35 → C, 25 → D, 15 → F

to learning. Thus, for formative purposes, more complex measurements can be more us-able than simpler measurements administered separately from learning activities.

- As suggested in Chapter 3, the administration of measurements used for making summa-tive evaluations shouldn't be integrated with learning activities, because students tend to be guarded and fearful of making mistakes when they think their responses are being "graded." However, as exemplified by Case 2.15, reviewing responses with students after their scores are recorded can be an extremely productive learning experience. Having a larger number of complex mini-experiments included on a measurement may provide richer learning experiences when responses are reviewed than you would expect from a simpler test. Thus, additional complexity and time spent for even measurements used for summative evaluations may pay dividends during subsequent learning activities.

Another factor influencing the time you allot to administering a measurement is the im-portance of students making rapid responses to prompts. In general, students' responses to prompts for mini-experiments that are relevant to simple-knowledge or process-knowledge ob-jectives should be made rapidly. They don't require reasoning, and students should be expected to respond quickly. However, reasoning is a deliberate process for which students shouldn't be hurried to exhibit. Thus, mini-experiments relevant to reasoning-level objectives should allow unhurried time for responses to prompts. For a measurement that includes both mini-experi-ments relevant to memory-level learning and mini-experiments relevant to reasoning-level learning, consider having a timed session that includes only the memory-level prompts and an-other session in which students have ample time to respond to the reasoning-level prompts.

Note from Illustration 6.6 that Mr. Johnson administered his Unit 7 measurement in three different sessions. Keep in mind that you need not confine the administration of a measure-ment to a single class period or to one school day. A number of short sessions, sometimes with take-home sections, is often preferable to one extended "sit-down" grind.

Just as you must limit the time your students have for responding to prompts, you must also consider the time you can reasonably devote to using rubrics to score their responses. The "Time for Scoring with the Rubrics" slot in your blueprint serves as a reminder that you must factor your time into the design of a measurement.

ACCOMMODATION FOR STUDENTS WITH SPECIAL NEEDS

The purpose for employing systematic measurement-development strategies is, of course, to produce valid measurement results relative to specified learning goals. However, the validity of a measurement varies according to individual differences among your students. For example, in Case 4.9, while Mr. Papunu is presenting Nancy with prompts in an interview format for a mea-surement intended to be relevant to Nancy's achievement of a mathematics objective, Nancy be-comes distracted by the activities of some of her classmates in another part of the classroom.

The results of the measurement did not reflect her achievement of the objective as well as they would have if she had not been distracted. What turned out to be a source of measurement error in Case 4.9 may not have contaminated the validity of that same measurement when administered to another student who is not as easily distracted by the activities of classmates as is Nancy. Reading skills, writing skills, motivation to succeed in school, self-confidence, willingness to follow directions, ability to focus on a task, psychomotor skills, tolerance for perplexity, and visual perception are only a minute subset of the myriad of characteristics with which students differ that influence their scores on measurements. Ideally, the results of a measurement used to evaluate students' achievement of a goal should only be sensitive to differences among students relative to how well they achieved that goal. Of course, the complexities of classroom-based measurements make such perfectly valid measurements unrealistic.

Although, we can hardly control for all the sources of measurement error due to individual differences among our students, we must concern ourselves with accommodating students with special needs or disabilities that influence the way they are able to respond to mini-experiment prompts. Not only are such accommodations necessary to improve the validity of measurements, but they are accommodations that we, as professional teachers, are legally required to make. Referring to the Individuals with Disabilities Education Act (IDEA), initially enacted by Congress in 1975 as Public Law 94–142 and expanded extensively since then, Turnbull and Turnbull (1998, p. 119) state:

> tests are to be selected and administered to students with impaired sensory, manual, or speaking skills so that the test results accurately reflect the student's aptitude or achievement level—or whatever other factor the test purports to measure—rather than the student's impaired skill, except when those skills are the factors the test seeks to measure. Section 300.35(b) drives home the point that tests should not be misinterpreted, that undue reliance on general intelligence tests is undesirable, and that tests should be administered in such a way that their results will not be distorted because of the student's disability.

Each student with a special-education classification is required to have an individualized education program (IEP) collaboratively developed by a committee that includes the regular classroom teacher (i.e., you), a special-education teacher, a parent of the student, and the student. The IEP serves as a written contract between the school and the student or parent that includes "a statement of present educational performance, instructional goals, educational services to be provided, and criteria and procedures for determining that the instructional objectives are being met" (Hallahan & Kauffman, 1997, p. 34). For students with disabilities that will impair their opportunities to respond to prompts on measurements in a way that accurately reflects what they have learned, IEPs should spell out accommodations for modifying measurement administration procedures to mitigate the effects of the disability contaminating the validity of the measurement. Case 6.7 is an example involving Mr. Johnson from Cases 6.5 and 6.6.

CASE 6.7

Several students with various special-education classifications are included in Mr. Johnson's Social Studies 5 course. For example, Chad has been diagnosed as having a condition that impairs his ability to process information presented verbally and to concurrently focus on multiple tasks. Chad comprehends messages as well as most students, but often word sequences become distorted by his reception mechanisms. This presents a particular problem when Chad attempts to comprehend directions as presented in the prompts of mini-experiments. Often the problem can be solved simply by having the directions rephrased and presented in a second format (e.g., having written directions rephrased orally) and allowing Chad more time to interpret and respond to prompts than most students need. The inability to focus on multiple tasks prevents Chad from doing such things as listening to a lecture and taking notes at the same time. Chad's concentration while responding to mini-experiments is easily disturbed by the presence of classmates in the classroom.

When Chad and a special-education teacher first explained this condition to Mr. Johnson, Mr. Johnson recognized the need to accommodate Chad's needs during learning activities as well as for administrations of measurements for purposes of making summative evaluations of Chad's achievement of learning goals. However, Mr. Johnson worried that modifying the administration of measurements for Chad would be "unfair" to other students for whom special accommodations would not be provided. Then the special education teacher had Mr. Johnson view the videotape program "Understanding Learning Disabilities: How Difficult Can This Be? The F.A.T. City Workshop" (Lavoie, 1989). The program led Mr. Johnson to experience what students with perceptual disabilities suffer in classrooms. Mr. Johnson realized that failing to make special accommodations for some students is what is truly unfair. For purposes of evaluating students' learning, he recognized that measurement validity is improved by making such accommodations.

Thus, Mr. Johnson took the lead in adding a provision in Chad's IEP that spelled out provisions for modifying the administration of measurements when used in making summative evaluations of Chad's achievement of learning goals. By including this in the IEP, Mr. Johnson increased the chances that he would receive support and resources from the school administration for providing the necessary accommodations. The IEP specified that the school would provide an area in which Chad could take tests in an extended time period, with a supervisor who would be available to clarify directions for prompts without influencing Chad's responses to those prompts once the directions were understood.

Note the "Provisions for Accommodating Students with Special Needs" section of Mr. Johnson's measurement blueprint shown by Illustration 6.6. He uses this section of his blueprints to plan how to modify the administration of measurements not only for students with special education classifications, but also for students with limited English proficiency. The bilingual-education program at Mr. Johnson's school provides translators on tests for students whose first language is not English—at least until those students become proficient enough in English so that they can take tests with prompts presented in English without seriously contaminating the validity of the results.

DISTRIBUTION OF POINTS AND WEIGHTS OF OBJECTIVES

The maximum possible score for a measurement is, of course, the sum of the maximum possible scores for the individual mini-experiments from which the measurement is composed. If all the rubrics are dichotomously scored as either +1 or +0, then the maximum possible score for the measurement is equal to the number of mini-experiments. With weighted scoring (i.e., either global or analytical), the number of points possible is greater than the number of mini-experiments. In any case, you need to estimate the maximum possible score in order to compute the number of points you will draw from each of the mini-experiment files.

Once you've estimated the maximum possible score, you select mini-experiments from your computerized files and make transformations of the points from the rubrics so that scores are influenced more by mini-experiments relevant to heavily weighted objectives and less by mini-experiments relevant to lightly weighted objectives. In Case 6.8, Mr. Johnson demonstrates how he accomplished this, resulting in his entries under "Maximum Number of Points Per Objective as Indicated by Objectives' Weights" in his blueprint shown in Illustration 6.6.

CASE 6.8

After looking at the weights for the nine objectives for his unit on the Constitution and surveying the mini-experiments he could access from his computerized folder for that unit, Mr. Johnson estimated that the maximum possible score for the unit test should be about 60. He then calculated the number of points he needs from each mini-experiment file, as shown in Illustration 6.7.

Thus, Mr. Johnson plans to select mini-experiments from File A that contribute approximately 9 points to the measurement's anticipated 60-point maximum. He realizes he can accomplish this task in many ways, for example, by either (1) selecting 9 dichotomously scored mini-experiments from File A, (2) selecting 1 mini-experiment from File A with a 9-point global scoring, (3) selecting 1 mini-experiment from File A with a 3-point global scoring and then multiplying the points described in the rubric by 3, (4) selecting 1 3-point mini-experiment and 6 1-point mini-experiments from File A, (5) selecting 1 2-point mini-experiment and multiplying the points in the rubric by 4, and 1 1-point mini-experiment from File A, or (6) selecting any one of a number of other possible combinations from File A and adjusting the scoring so that the total number of points on the measurement from File A's mini-experiments is 9. A similar process is followed for selecting mini-experiments from the other 8 files.

FINAL ELEMENTS OF THE BLUEPRINT

After deciding the overall structure of the measurement, you still have two more questions to address before completing a blueprint: (1) How do you want to mix the easy, moderately difficult, and very difficult mini-experiments? (2) If the measurement's results are to influence grades, what method should you use for converting scores to grades?

Objective	Weight	Computation	Points
A	15%	.15 x 60 =	9
B	15%	.15 x 60 =	9
C	4%	.04 x 60 ≈	2 or 3
D	4%	.04 x 60 ≈	2 or 3
E	15%	.15 x 60 =	9
F	12%	.12 x 60 ≈	7 or 8
G	9%	.09 x 60 ≈	5 or 6
H	18%	.04 x 60 ≈	10 or 11
I	8%	.04 x 60 ≈	4 or 5
	100%		About 60

ILLUSTRATION 6.7

Mr. Johnson's Computation to Determine the Maximum Number of Points Per Objective

When you address the first question, consider ideas presented in this chapter's section "Difficulty Levels." When you address the second question, consider ideas from Chapter 3's section "Assigning Grades to Measurement Scores."

SYNTHESIZING THE MEASUREMENT

You synthesize the measurement from mini-experiments selected from your computer folders by following the directions from your measurement blueprint. As you do this, keep in mind that one mini-experiment may interact with another; Case 6.9 is an example.

CASE 6.9

Following Illustration 6.6's blueprint, Mr. Johnson selects mini-experiments for the unit test on the Constitution from his computerized folders. Multiple-choice prompts 3 and 4 on Section II of the test appear as follows:

3. How many people signed the Constitution at the Constitutional Convention?
   a) 40   b) 42   c) 43   d) 45
4. George Mason was one of the three authors of the Constitution who refused to sign it. According to his statements, he probably would have signed the document if it had included which one of the following?
   a) the twentieth through the twenty-fifth amendments
   b) a more clearly stated preamble
   c) the first ten amendments
   d) assurances that the delegates would be paid fairly for their work

During Session 2 of the test, Judith, one of Mr. Johnson's students, thinks when she gets to multiple-choice Prompt 3, "I don't remember how many signed it, but 43 wrote it, so the answer must be 'c.'" For Prompt 4, Judith thinks, "I don't have a clue about which of these is right. But, oh look! It says three authors didn't sign it, so I'll change my answer for number 3 to 'a.'"

On Friday, when Mr. Johnson reviews responses with the class, Judith reveals her method for correctly responding to multiple-choice Prompt 3. Mr. Johnson thinks to himself, "I'd better be more careful in the future to select prompts that don't interact. I'll make note of this in my 'Notes' for those two mini-experiments."

Besides concern for interactions among mini-experiments, you also need to decide how to sequence the prompts. Look at the measurement outline section of Illustration 6.6's blueprint. Prompts are grouped by format. The test is organized so that students can respond to prompts that have less time-consuming formats (e.g., multiple-choice) before responding to those that are more time-consuming (e.g., essay). Grouping prompts together with the same format simplifies the directions to students and prevents students from having to reorient their thinking frequently due to changes in format.

For timed sections of a measurement (e.g., in which all mini-experiments are relevant to knowledge-level objectives), prompts using the same format should usually be sequenced from less difficult to more difficult. With this arrangement, students avoid spending so much time responding to difficult prompts that they don't have time to respond to easier ones. The easy-to-hard arrangement is unnecessary for untimed sections emphasizing reasoning-level learning.

You include directions to students as part of the prompts you design for mini-experiments. But when synthesizing the measurement, you collapse directions from mini-experiments with the same format so that students need only to hear or read them once. For example, turn to Chapter 1's section "Synthesis Activities for Chapter 1." Note that I gave you only one set of directions to cover short-answer Prompts A–N for the first activity and only one set of directions to cover multiple-choice prompts A–F for the third activity.

ADMINISTERING THE MEASUREMENT

Please reread "Designing Measurements That Produce Internally Consistent Results" from Chapter 4 on pages 190–193.

Proper control of measurement conditions is a function of how the measurement is administered. In Case 6.10, failure to manage the classroom environment leads to distractions that threaten internal consistency.

CASE 6.10

Mr. Johnson is administering Session 2 of the unit test whose blueprint appears in Illustration 6.6. He is seated at his desk in the front of the room, just finishing a one-to-one interview for Section III with Marjorie as the other students respond to multiple-choice prompts from Section II. Dan is selecting a response to multiple-choice Prompt 11, related to Objective C, as Mr. Johnson announces, "Okay, next let me have Kevin up here. The rest of you continue." The announcement breaks Dan's trend of thought about Prompt 11, and he chooses an incorrect response. However, he is not distracted as he thinks about Prompt 12, also relevant to Objective C, to which he selects the correct alternative.

As Kevin walks to the front to respond to the interview prompt at Mr. Johnson's desk, he jabs Kristine with his pen as she is about to circle the incorrect choice for Prompt 23. This rude act disrupts her so much that she inadvertently circles the correct response instead. Prompts 23 and 27 are both relevant to Objective F. Kristine fails to circle the correct choice to Prompt 27.

Nine students have completed Section II with 15 minutes remaining for Session 2. Some of them entertain themselves with talking and movements that are distracting to those still responding to the prompts.

Distraction-caused inconsistencies in Dan's, Kristine's, and other students' measurement results tend to contaminate measurement reliability. Had Mr. Johnson applied some very basic classroom management strategies to the administration of the test, distractions could have been avoided. To minimize distractions while measurements are being administered, consider the following suggestions:

- Anticipate times and locations when interruptions (e.g., public address announcements, building construction, and band practice outside your classroom) are likely to interfere with the quiet, undisturbed conditions needed for some mini-experiments. Work out compromises between your measurement program and the scheduling of potentially disruptive events.
- Establish and enforce standards of classroom conduct and procedures that minimize disruptive behaviors when you're administering measurements (see Cangelosi, 1997, pp. 159–173).
- Proofread measurement documents before distributing them to students. You do not want to disturb students during the administration to correct errors (e.g., typographical).

- Have constructive activities planned for students who complete their responses to prompts ahead of schedule. Students should be conditioned to begin these activities (e.g., homework assignments) without disturbing those still involved with the measurement. In Case 6.10, Mr. Johnson, for example, might put a note at the end of Section II of the test document directing each student to (1) quietly remain seated, (2) turn the test paper over and place it on her or his desk, and (3) work on Exercises 7, 8, 9, and 12 from page 188 of the social studies textbook until Mr. Johnson announces that Session 2 of the test has ended.
- Model non-disruptive, thoughtful behaviors yourself during administrations of measurements. Emphasize the serious, businesslike nature of experimental conditions. In Case 6.10, Mr. Johnson repeatedly disturbed the whole class by asking students to come up to his desk for the interview prompt. Instead, he could have organized a less disturbing system such as the following:

> The student who sits in the first desk of the first row is interviewed first. When she finishes, she quietly walks over to the second student in the row and gently taps him on the shoulder. He recognizes this as the cue to be interviewed. The procedure continues until the whole class has responded to the interview prompt.

In Case 6.11, Mr. Johnson models appropriate, businesslike behavior for students.

CASE 6.11

During Session 3 of the Unit 7 test, students are responding to Sections IV and V, as indicated by Illustration 6.6's blueprint. The school principal arrives at the doorway of the classroom and says to Mr. Johnson in a voice the students can hear, "I need to speak with you about arrangements for tonight's meeting." Instead of speaking from his station in the room, Mr. Johnson frowns and silently gestures with his hands that he doesn't want the students disturbed. He then quickly writes the principal a note indicating times he'll be available to confer with her. Quietly he brings it to her at the door and returns to his station.

You design mini-experiments to be administered in a particular fashion. Deviations from the administration plan threaten measurement reliability. For example, if the multiple-choice prompts on Section II of Mr. Johnson's unit test outlined in Illustration 6.6 were designed to be presented without the benefit of outside help, he would be risking the internal consistency of measurement results by responding to students' queries during the administration with hints and information about the Constitution. However, I'm not suggesting he shouldn't respond to questions about directions. By clarifying directions as the need arises, he might actually enhance measurement validity.

Students need to be supervised while responding to prompts, just as they should be during any other classroom activity. Supervision is essential to protect students from being disturbed by others and to prevent some from cheating. Besides being an unethical, distasteful practice, cheating contaminates reliability.

STUDENT CHEATING

NINE INCIDENTS

Some students are quite resourceful in devising ways to cheat; consider Cases 6.12 through 6.20 (adapted from Cangelosi, 1997, pp. 314–316).

CASE 6.12

Angee gets out of her desk, walks over to the classroom pencil sharpener, and returns to her desk to complete the multiple-choice science test she and the rest of her sixth-grade classmates are taking. During her walk, Angee looked at several other students' papers to find out how they responded to certain prompts to which she did not know how to respond.

CASE 6.13

Calculus teacher, Mr. Kruhl, scores test papers by writing down the number of "points off" by each prompt a student doesn't respond to correctly. Mr. Kruhl does not mark anything by correct responses; he simply subtracts the number of points for incorrect responses from the maximum possible score of 100. Jack, one of Mr. Kruhl's students, realizes this after his first calculus test is returned. When Jack is about to begin taking the second calculus test, he thinks, "I'll never have time to complete this 12-page monster in the 90 minutes Kruhl's allowing us. I'll just rip out pages 6 and 9 and discard them. He'll probably just pass over them and not realize they're missing. If he does catch it, I'll just say they were never there." Several days later, Mr. Kruhl returns Jack's paper with a score derived by subtracting the number of points off for incorrect items from 100. Jack's score is the same as it would have been if Jack had correctly responded to all of the prompts on pages 6 and 9.

CASE 6.14

June did not study for the history exam that Ms. Tolbert is giving today. Instead, June memorized the answers to an old unit test that Ms. Tolbert had administered to one of June's friends in a previously held class. June is overjoyed when Ms. Tolbert hands her a test identical to the one her friend shared.

CASE 6.15

Twelfth-graders Kraemer, Tom, and Arthur engage Ms. Hubert in a lively conversation before school as their co-conspirator, Mary Ellen, steals four copies of the final physics exam scheduled for that afternoon off of Ms. Hubert's desk. During the morning study hall, the four students jointly figure out the correct responses and each fills out a copy of the test. To avoid suspicion, they make sure that there are some discrepancies among their papers. When Ms. Hubert administers the test, the four carefully substitute their completed copies for the ones distributed by Ms. Hubert.

CASE 6.16

Sonia, an eighth-grade student, runs a popular service for her schoolmates at Abraham Lincoln Middle School. Sonia searches trash containers for test materials that have been discarded in the faculty work room or school office. From her growing "test file," she provides test information to her many "friends." Sonia feels very popular with her peers.

CASE 6.17

"May I please be excused to go to the restroom?" Mickey asks Mr. Green during a fourth-grade spelling test. Mr. Green: "Yes, but hurry so you will have plenty of time to finish your test." Mickey: "I will. Thank you very much." In the restroom, Mickey extracts his spelling list that earlier in the day he had hidden under a toilet. He quickly checks the spelling of the four words from the test that he does not know.

CASE 6.18

Freda takes a lengthy psychology test and leaves several short-answer, written-response prompts blank. Her teacher, Mr. Zabriski, scores the test and returns them to the class the following day. The prompts Freda left blank are marked with zeroes, but she quickly fills in the responses and approaches Mr. Zabriski. Freda: "Mr. Zabriski, don't I get any credit for these? I thought they were at least partially correct!"

CASE 6.19

As Mr. Duetchman supervises a large group of high-school students taking a chemistry final exam, he finds it curious that Donna seems to frequently contort her body and turn her head oddly. Not knowing what to do, he dismisses her behavior as a reflection of adolescent self-consciousness. Actually, Donna has formulas, definitions, facts, and other chemistry notes written on her body and on the inside of her clothes.

CASE 6.20

Ms. Bolden instructs her first-graders to keep their test papers covered and not to let classmates see their answers while taking a mathematics test. Ashley and Monica are sitting at the same table, taking the test, when Monica turns to Ashley and, pointing to one of her test prompts, says, "I forgot what this one is." Ashley: "Ms. Bolden said you weren't supposed to show me your paper! Cover it up." Monica: "Sorry! But I need some help on this one." Ashley: "Okay, don't show me your paper. Just read it to me." Monica: "What's this called?" Monica draws a rectangle in the air with her finger. Ashley: "Let me see what I just put for that. But don't look on my paper while I look. It's not allowed." Ashley turns back to Monica, still carefully covering her paper, and says, "It's a rectangle."

PREVALENCE AND CAUSES OF CHEATING

How prevalent is cheating in elementary, middle, and secondary school classrooms? Estimates of the ratio of test-taking behaviors involving cheating and test-taking behaviors free of cheating vary considerably from study to study, but the vast majority of studies examining the prevalence of cheating (most using self-report techniques, but some using direct observations) indicate cheating is commonplace. For example, Schab's (1991) studies suggest that more than two-thirds of high-school students are likely to admit on a questionnaire (in which their identities are protected) to having cheated on tests and that the frequency of cheating increased dramatically between 1968 and 1989. Evans and Craig (1990) indicate 50.1% of middle-school teachers, 61.4% of middle-school students, 70.0% of high-school teachers, and 71.3% of high-school students perceive cheating to be a serious problem in their schools. Cheating is observed at all grades K–12, but its practice appears to increase with grade level (see, e.g., Brandes, 1986).

It would seem that students would have no inclination to cheat on tests if they believed that *accurate* information about their achievement in the hands of their teachers is more beneficial to them than is misinformation that deceives their teachers. Why then do many of them cheat? Studies examining school conditions associated with student cheating and reasons for cheating professed by students begin to address this question (see, e.g., Evans & Craig, 1990).

Whether or not students attempt to cheat appears to be more a function of teacher-controlled factors and students' perceptions of classroom situations than a function of personality and demographic characteristics of the students themselves (see, e.g., Bushway & Nash, 1977). In general, students are more inclined to cheat when they have the following perceptions (Cangelosi, 1993):

- They need to compete for high grades to gain or retain self-esteem, approval, or other rewards extrinsic to learning itself (e.g., a scholarship or an academic letter).
- There is little or no value in the subject-content about which they are tested.
- The opportunity to cheat exists with only a low probability of being detected.
- The teacher lacks awareness of what students are doing during everyday classroom activities.

- A classroom climate has not been established in which the teaching and learning are considered serious, important business.
- Students perceive that the school's administrators value test performance as more important than learning.

Think of the message students get when regular learning activities are disrupted for several weeks to prepare for an upcoming standardized test battery to "make our school look good" or "outscore a 'rival' school." What attitudes do students learn when they are directed to make extraordinary preparations for these testing events (e.g., they're directed to get more sleep and visitors are barred from the building during the week of the test battery)? It's quite similar to the way coaches prepare teams for championship games. Keep in mind that some forms of "cheating" are an acceptable part of many sports (e.g., basketball players are taught to fall to the floor to deceive referees into thinking they've been fouled).

STRATEGIES FOR PREVENTING AND DEALING WITH CHEATING

Students would have no inclination to cheat on a test if they believed that *accurate* information about their achievement in the hands of their teachers is more beneficial to them than is misinformation that deceives their teachers. Once again, three vital principles become apparent:

- The self-worth students perceive and the respect, love, and esteem others (including teachers) feel for them should never be dependent upon their achievements.
- Formative judgments of students' achievements should be emphasized to a far greater degree than should summative evaluations.
- Grades should only be used to communicate summative evaluations; they should not be used as a reward for achievements.

Given the unfortunate fact that there is almost universal violation of these principles, you are virtually assured of encountering students with inclinations for cheating on tests. But even with these students, cheating is unlikely when you adhere to the following suggestions:

- You set a businesslike tone and display an attitude that communicates that students are expected not to cheat.
- Measurement administrations are closely supervised. Please note, however, that, as indicated by Case 6.20, the concept of cheating is not well-developed in young children. Primary-grade children do not differentiate between obtaining a correct response with unauthorized aid and obtaining it without unauthorized aid (Pulaski, 1980; Rogoff, 1990, pp. 42–61). Teachers should observe whether or not young children respond on their own or with unauthorized aid. Steps should be taken so that such aid is not attainable. However, warning young students not to cheat or to punish them for behaviors that adults consider to be cheating is, for them, a frustrating experience that only teaches them they are not trusted. Even with older students, warnings "not to cheat" are futile and should be avoided. However, students should not be given reasonable opportunities to cheat.
- The same form of a measurement document is not used repeatedly for the purpose of making summative evaluations.
- You account for each copy of a measurement document that is duplicated (copies can be numbered) and materials, such as duplicating masters, are secured. Only you control access to your computer files.

- You mark test papers so that points are added for correct responses, rather than subtracting points for incorrect ones.
- You annotate, as well as score, test papers. Not only does this practice provide helpful feedback to students, but it also helps you remember why you scored responses as you did. Students are less likely to manipulate responses after papers are returned if you have already commented on their responses.
- Students are directed to check on whether or not their test copies contain all pages and are properly collated prior to beginning.
- Students are not tested on their recall of subject-content that seems unnecessary to memorize. When obtaining a grade on a measurement is the sole perceived purpose students have for memorizing what they know will be forgotten after the test, using cheat-sheets seems like a sensible thing to do.)

Because a student cheats on a test is not a reason for recording a low score. Cheating does not reflect learning-goal attainment (except in the rare case in which the learning goal is for the student to be honest). Thus, if a teacher knows that a student has cheated on a test, then the test results are not valid and no score should be recorded, as if the student never took the test. A student's understanding of biology, for example, should not be judged by whether or not that student cooperated with the test-taking procedures. Judgments of how well learning goals are achieved should be withheld until after the student no longer displays the dishonest behavior and a valid measurement of achievement can be obtained (Cangelosi, 1982, pp. 237–238). Teachers in Cases 6.21 through 6.23 (adapted from Cangelosi, 1996, pp. 319–320) deal with some sticky situations.

CASE 6.21

While scoring a unit test he had administered to his tenth-grade first-aid class, Mr. Broussard notices some inconsistencies in Joe's test responses. Joe's responses to a couple of the more difficult prompts are correct, while he incorrectly responded to prompts for mini-experiments relevant to simple rudimentary knowledge. Mr. Broussard asks himself, "How could he get these correct without knowing this?" Later, while scoring Remy's paper, Mr. Broussard notices that Remy correctly responded to the same difficult prompts, using words very similar to those in Joe's responses. Mr. Broussard then compares their two sets of responses and notices some improbable similarities. On the multiple-choice portions of the test, Joe's choices nearly always agree with Remy's. He finds it curious that the two would consistently choose the same alternatives for multiple-choice prompts that they both missed.

Highly suspicious that Joe copied from Remy's paper, Mr. Broussard thinks about how to deal with the situation: "I should confront them both with this. Read the riot act to them! But if I'm wrong, I'll only teach them they're not trusted. That could be damaging. They just might cheat from now on because they figured there'd be no trust to lose. But I really can't put any stock in Joe's measurement results, and I need to know what he got out of this unit. I need an accurate score on his achievement. Also, I don't want Joe to get away with this. I don't think he's cheated before. I should block any positive reinforcement so this doesn't become a pattern. I'll just disregard his test paper and schedule a retest for him with an equivalent form."

The next day, Mr. Broussard distributes the scored and annotated test papers. Joe from his desk: "Mr. Broussard, you didn't give my test back." Mr. Broussard: "No, I didn't. Please come up here." Joe arrives and Mr. Broussard says softly, "You didn't get your paper back. What do you think happened?" Joe: "I don't know. I took the test." Mr. Broussard: "Yes, I know. I remember going over it." Mr. Broussard pulls out Joe's test record and says, "Here, Joe, let's see if I recorded a score for this test for you. No, there's no score here. Look." Joe sees the empty square. Mr. Broussard: "We'll just schedule a retest. How about tomorrow? I'll give you a test tomorrow." Joe: "That's not fair for me to have to take another test." Mr. Broussard: "Things don't always seem fair. Now, let's see when we can schedule it."

CASE 6.22

Mr. Stoddard validates (as explained in Chapters 15–17) each sociology test that he administers to his classes before allowing the test results to influence summative evaluations he makes regarding students' achievement levels. From analysis of one set of test results and from his observations of some curious student behaviors during the administration of that test, Mr. Stoddard suspects that student cheating contaminated the accuracy of the test results. At the next class meeting, Mr. Stoddard announces, "The results I received from the test are invalid. There are some major discrepancies among the scores. Statistical analyses indicate the test was too unreliable to accurately indicate your levels of achievement. Therefore, I discarded the results and we will take a refined version of the test under more controlled conditions on Wednesday."

CASE 6.23

Ms. Maggio administers a measurement on problem solving to her fourth-graders in which they are directed to work out in their heads a sequence of tasks that are presented on pages 39 and 40 of one of their textbooks. She directs them to look at only those two pages in their books while working out the solutions and expressing answers on a sheet of paper. Ms. Maggio notices Nettie, one student, keeping an eye on her during the administration of the measurement. Nettie seems to manipulate her book suddenly whenever Ms. Maggio comes near or looks at her. Ms. Maggio suspects that Nettie has surreptitiously turned to the back of the book, where answers to the problems are given.

After the test, Ms. Maggio examines Nettie's answer sheet. Most of the responses are correct. She then engages Nettie in a private conference in which she presents one of the problems that Nettie answered on the test and asks her to solve it. Nettie is unable to come up with a solution this time. Nettie fails twice more to reproduce answers which she had written on the test document earlier in the day. Ms. Maggio: "Nettie, I do not understand why you cannot figure out these answers now if you solved the problems during the test." Nettie: "I don't know." Ms. Maggio: "I will not check off that you can do these types of problems until you demonstrate to me that you can."

INCORPORATING INDIVIDUALIZED STUDENT PORTFOLIOS IN YOUR SYSTEM

In Chapters 2 and 3, the use of individualized student portfolios was illustrated as mechanisms for (1) reflecting what students' learn, (2) formative feedback, and (3) communicating summative evaluations of achievement. As you develop and tailor your system for monitoring student learning to fit your and your students' unique needs, you will have to decide what role, if any, portfolios will play. Keep in mind the three types of portfolios explained by Alleman and Brophy (1997, p. 341):

There are several types of portfolios that teachers can consider (Fischer & King, 1995). The most common include the *working portfolio*, the *showcase portfolio*, and the *record-keeping portfolio*. The *working portfolio* is the one that the student and teacher assess and evaluate together. Work samples are entered as evidence of learning and growth. Students and teachers select and add samples and records. Parents are encouraged to add comments. The intent is that the working portfolio will serve as a living document of the student's ongoing progress.

The *showcase portfolio* is parallel to an artist's portfolio and thus represents the student's best work. In this portfolio, the student usually has sole ownership of selections to be included. The showcase portfolio is less useful for assessment purposes because it does not illustrate day-to-day performance.

A third type of portfolio is known as the *record-keeping portfolio* and usually is used along with the showcase portfolio. Its purpose is to provide a record of the completed assessment and evaluation samples not included in the showcase portfolio. The record-keeping portfolio provides documentation for all completed assignments.

SYNTHESIS ACTIVITIES FOR CHAPTER 6

1. Set up a computerized system for mini-experiments using either the software on the CD-ROM that accompanies this book, other software for setting up mini-experiment files, or word processing software.

2. Retrieve the goal defined by a set of weighted objectives you developed for Synthesis Activity 3 for Chapter 5. Use the computer setup from Synthesis Activity 1 just above to designate a folder for that unit and mini-experiment files for the objectives.

3. For each of the objectives you developed for synthesis Activity 3 for Chapter 5, design one mini-experiment. Insert the prompt and rubric for each of the mini-experiments in the appropriate computer file you set up for Synthesis Activity 2 just above.

4. Develop a blueprint for a measurement that is to be relevant to your students' achievement of the goal you defined by a set of weighted objectives when you engaged in Synthesis Activity 3 for Chapter 5.

5. In an essay of one-half to three-quarters of a page, explain why student cheating tends (in general) to be more of a threat to measurement reliability than to measurement relevance.

6. Exchange the essay you wrote for Synthesis Activity 5 just above with that of a colleague. Use Illustration 6.8's observer's rubric to score each other's papers. Then explain to one another why you scored the papers as you did. Address questions and issues stimulated by the explanations.

```
Quickly read through the essay one time. Then go back through it and
judge whether or not each of the 5 criteria listed in the scoring
form appearing below is met. For each criterion that is clearly met,
circle "2." For each that is clearly not met, circle "0." For each
one that it is not either clearly met or not met, circle "1."

                          Scoring Form

  Approximately .5 to .75 page essay addressing
  the question posted by the prompt ------------------------- 0 1 2

  Essay displays writer's comprehension of reliability  ------ 0 1 2

  Essay displays writer's comprehension of the effects
  of cheating on reliability  ------------------------------- 0 1 2

  Essay displays writer's comprehension of the effects
  of cheating on relevance  -------------------------------- 0 1 2

  Essay includes nothing that is erroneous or extraneous  ---- 0 1 2
```

ILLUSTRATION 6.8

Observer's Rubric for Synthesis Activity 6's Prompt

7. With two or more of your colleagues, discuss how each of you would plan to incorporate individualized student portfolios in your systematic program for monitoring student achievement.

8. With two or more of your colleagues, discuss the pros and cons of the way the teachers in Cases 6.21, 6.22, and 6.23 handle the episodes of students' cheating.

TRANSITIONAL ACTIVITY FROM CHAPTER 6 TO CHAPTER 7

In a discussion with two or more of your colleagues, address the following questions:

1. As students engage in our lessons for construct-a-concept objectives, how do we manage to monitor their progress?

2. How do we design mini-experiments that are relevant to construct-a-concept objectives?

3. As students engage in our lessons for discover-a-relationship objectives, how do we manage to monitor their progress?

4. How do we design mini-experiments that are relevant to discover-a-relationship objectives?

Monitoring Students' Progress as They Construct Concepts and Discover Relationships

◆ GOAL OF CHAPTER 7

Chapter 7 is designed to lead you to design mini-experiments that will help you monitor students' construction of concepts and discovery of relationships. More specifically the objectives are as follows:

A. You will explain the stages through which students progress as they construct concepts (discover a relationship) 5%.

B. You will design mini-experiments for gauging students' progress as they engage in lessons for construct-a-concept objectives (application) 20%.

C. You will design mini-experiments relevant to how well students have achieved construct-a-concept objectives (application) 18%.

D. You will explain the stages through which students progress as they discover relationships (discover a relationship) 5%.

E. You will design mini-experiments for gauging students' progress as they engage in lessons for discover-a-relationship objectives (application) 20%.

F. You will design mini-experiments relevant to how well students have achieved discover-a-relationship objectives (application) 18%.

G. You will explain fundamental principles for using a variety of mini-experiment formats, including performance observation, product examination, oral discourse, interview, essay, short-response, and multiple-choice (discover a relationship) 9%.

H. You will incorporate the following technical phrases in your working professional vocabulary: "inductive reasoning," "example of a concept," "concept attribute," "example noise," "non-example of a concept," "performance observation format," "essay format," "oral discourse format," "multiple-choice format," "multiple-choice stem," "multiple-choice distractor," "parallel alternatives," "interview format," "product examination format," and "short-response format" (comprehension and communication skills) 5%.

HOW STUDENTS CONSTRUCT CONCEPTS

CONCEPT ATTRIBUTES

To be able to design mini-experiments relevant to your students' progress with respect to construct-a-concept objectives, you need to be familiar with how students construct concepts. From Chapter 5, reread the section "Concepts" and the section "Construct a Concept."

Whether or not a particular specific is an example of a particular concept depends on whether or not that specific possesses the defining *attributes* of the concept. For example, are you an example of the concept "preservice teacher"? By definition, a preservice teacher is a human being who is currently enrolled in a professional teacher-preparation program for the purpose of becoming qualified and certified as a classroom teacher. Once a person completes such a program and takes a position as a classroom teacher, she or he is no longer classified as a "preservice teacher" (but rather an "inservice teacher"). Thus, the attributes of preservice teacher are (1) human being, (2) enrolled in a professional teacher preparation program, and (3) not an inservice teacher. If you possess all three of these characteristics, you are an example of the concept "preservice teacher." An *attribute of a concept* is any characteristic that is common to all examples of that concept. Moreover, a specific must possess all attributes of a concept in order to be an example of that concept.

EXAMPLE NOISE

Although you are a teacher (either preservice or inservice), you possess a myriad of other characteristics that are not attributes of a teacher. Not all teachers have the same color eyes as you, nor are they all your same age, nor do they all have your same likes and dislikes. To enhance your concept of concept attributes and example noise, pair with a colleague and engage in the activity that is explained in Illustration 7.1.

In Case 7.1, Elwin and Kisha discuss their analyses stimulated by their engagement in Illustration 7.1's activity.

CASE 7.1

Kisha:	"Unless this is supposed to be some kind of trick, looks like pictures of two cats to me."
Elwin:	"Agreed. Even though they look quite different, they both look like cats. Let's make a list."
Kisha:	"Here's what I came up with: They're both four-legged with paws, have hair, whiskers, appear to have backbones—I don't know, they just look like cats."
Elwin:	"If we could actually examine the cats themselves and not just look at these photographs, we could verify that they're both mammals."
Kisha:	"Yeah, verifying that they're warm-blooded, have mammary glands, and so forth. We're so familiar with cats, we recognize one right away without consciously making a list of cat-attributes."
Elwin:	"What do you have for differences between the two?"
Kisha:	"Otis is much larger than Pepper. He's two-toned—looks to be mostly black with a distinct splash of white."
Elwin:	"Pepper, on the other hand seems to be a solid color—I think gray. She kind of looks like a Russian blue. They both have medium-length hair."

When you, like Elwin and Kisha, listed Otis and Pepper's characteristics that identify them both as cats, you were of course listing attributes with respect to the concept "cat." When you

With a colleague examine the following two photographs:

Otis   Pepper

Do you both agree that two cats (refer to them as Otis and Pepper)
appear in the photographs? If so, complete the following tasks:

1. List what you observed from the pictures that led you to believe
   that both Otis and Pepper are cats?

2. List characteristics of Otis that make him different from
   Pepper.

3. List characteristics of Pepper that make her different from
   Otis.

ILLUSTRATION 7.1

Activity to Enhance Your and a Colleague's Concept of Concept Attributes and
Example Noise

listed Otis's other characteristics (e.g., larger, black and white, and medium-length hair), you
were identifying the *noise* in this particular example of the concept "cat." For Pepper, single-
colored, female, small, and medium-length hair are characteristics which help distinguish her
from other cats. Thus, these are part of the *example noise* relative to Pepper being an example
of the concept "cat." *Example noise* is a characteristic of an example of a particular concept
that is not an attribute of that concept.

The noise in the examples to which you expose your students when you're leading them
to construct concepts plays a key role in how well they conceptualize. As you will soon see,
the way example noise is used in the design of prompts for mini-experiments plays a major
role in how relevant mini-experiments are to construct-a-concept objectives.

In Case 7.2, Ms. Martinez conducts a lesson to lead students to construct the concept
of density.

CASE 7.2

As part of a unit on physical properties of matter, Ms. Martinez conducts a lesson for her class of 28 fourth-graders for the following objective:

Students distinguish between examples of density and examples of other properties of matter (construct a concept).

She begins the lesson by displaying two identical-looking sealed cardboard boxes, each with dimensions 60 cm × 37 cm × 30 cm. Unknown to the students, Ms. Martinez has tightly packed one box with a neat stack of newspapers. The other box she filled with loosely crumpled balls of newspaper.

Students examine the two boxes without touching them, agreeing that the boxes appear to have the same capacity. Ms. Martinez announces that both boxes are filled from top-to-bottom and side-to-side with newspapers. After instructing them on how to carefully lift heavy objects (e.g., back straight, knees bent), she directs students to lift one box and then the other. They agree that one is much heavier than the other, but they don't understand why, if Ms. Martinez told them the truth about the boxes' contents.

Ms. Martinez then partitions the class into four cooperative groups. She has the classroom arranged so that each group is able to perform its individual task out of sight of the other three. The tasks are as follows:

* Group I is provided with two identical boxes, 100 soft rubber balls, a roll of packaging tape, and a scale for weighing the boxes. Each member of the group is assigned a very specific role. As directed, they fill one box with 25 balls (completely filling the box) and cram the remaining 75 balls into the second box, necessitating the balls to be squeezed nearly flat to fit into the box. The students are motivated to keep their voices low as they work with one another because Ms. Martinez's directions indicated that they are to keep their activities secret from the other three groups in the room. They seal both boxes and weigh each. The cooperative group member in charge of recording the procedures and results of the experiment completes the group's written report.
* Group II operates similarly, except one of its boxes is one-third the size of the other and students are directed to completely fill both boxes with the exact same number of balls, thus having to cram them into the smaller box. Both boxes are sealed and weighed, and a brief report is written.
* Group III operates much like Group I, but instead of filling boxes with balls, they fill two garbage bags of equal capacity, one with empty round aluminum cans, the other with flattened aluminum cans. The bags are sealed.
* Group IV operates much like Group III but fills one large garbage bag with unaltered aluminum cans and one small garbage bag with the same number of flattened aluminum cans. The bags are sealed.

The class returns to a large-group arrangement, and the products of each group's experiment are examined (without unsealing the containers) by the other three groups. Ms. Martinez conducts a large-group questioning session, in which students make inferences about what groups did to create the observed phenomena (e.g., two objects with equal volume, but different mass). Using probing questions, Ms. Martinez leads students to discover the concept of density. No one uses the word "density," but the students agree to name the idea "squishiness." The students formulate a definition of "squishiness" in terms of volume and mass. They apply their newly formulated concept to explain the mystery of the discrepant event confronting them in the initial phase of the lesson (i.e., two boxes of equal capacity, both filled with newspaper, but of unequal weight).

List the examples with which Ms. Martinez involved her students that led them to develop the concept of density. With a colleague, describe the attributes of density that make each of these examples an illustration of the concept of density. For each of Ms. Martinez's examples, list at least three characteristics that are noise with respect to the concept of density.

Case 7.3 reflects how Kisha and Elwin responded to the prompts to which you just responded.

CASE 7.3

Here are the examples from Case 7.2 that Kisha and Elwin listed:

1. The two 60 cm × 37 cm × 30 cm sealed boxes, a heavy one filled with a stack of newspapers and a light one filled with loosely crumpled newspaper balls
2. The two identical boxes, one filled with 25 rubber balls and the other crammed with 75 flattened rubber balls
3. Two boxes, one three times as large as the other, both filled with the same number of same-size balls
4. Two identical garbage bags, one filled with empty, unaltered aluminum cans, the other filled with flattened aluminum cans
5. Two garbage bags, one larger than the other, both filled with the same number of aluminum cans

Elwin and Kisha discuss the attributes of the five examples, causing each to illustrate the concept of density:

Elwin:	"In the first example, students need to explain why two same-size containers, each filled to capacity with the same type of material, differ dramatically in weight."
Kisha:	"Since the difference in weight can't be attributed to difference in volumes or that one container was filled up more than the other, the difference must be due to how crammed-in the material was in the containers. That's the idea of density."
Elwin:	"What you just said for the first example can be said for the other four examples also."
Kisha:	"But the examples differ from one another in other ways. The first example uses cardboard boxes full of newspapers. Others use garbage bags with cans, and—"
Elwin:	"Now you're getting into example noise. Let's list three bits of noise for each example."

Here's what they listed for the first two examples:

Example 1: The containers are 60 cm × 37 cm × 30 cm boxes, the material inside includes newspaper neatly stacked in one of the boxes.
Example 2: The containers are boxes, the material consists of rubber balls, and the balls are soft.

Kisha:	"I see why Ms. Martinez wouldn't want to use only boxes or only newspaper. If the noise in the examples was all the same, students might develop a very limited concept of density."
Elwin:	"And only recognize the role of density in situations involving boxes filled with newspapers.
Kisha:	"I'd also think the students need to be exposed to some non-examples of density to better construct the concept of density."
Elwin:	"What would be a non-example of density?"
Kisha:	"That's a good question; let's think. We'd need to have students explain why one container is heavier than another for reasons other than differences in density."
Elwin:	"I got it! Just use two different size boxes—like a large one filled with a neat stack of newspapers and a small one filled in the same manner."
Kisha:	"Or same-size boxes, one full and one half-full."

Students need to be exposed to specific examples and non-examples of a concept in order to construct that concept in their own minds.

INDUCTIVE REASONING

To construct a concept, students use *inductive reasoning* to distinguish examples from non-examples of a particular concept. *Inductive reasoning* is generalizing from encounters with specifics. Moreover, *inductive reasoning* is the cognitive process by which a person groups specifics into categories to either construct a concept or discover a relationship.

Recall the experiences of the infant Josh in Case 5.9 and the student Terri in Case 5.10. Persons have experiences with specifics that lead them to identify similarities among some of those specifics. They use inductive reasoning to realize that those similarities (i.e., attributes) distinguish examples of the concept from non-examples (Cangelosi, 1996, pp. 79–98; Kelley, 1988, pp. 263–367; Metz, 1995).

An inductive learning activity is one that stimulates students to reason inductively. Such activities are used in a four-stage lesson for construct-a-concept level learning: (1) sorting and categorizing, (2) reflecting and explaining, (3) generalizing and articulating, and (4) verifying and refining.

SORTING AND CATEGORIZING

In the sorting and categorizing stage, students are presented with a task requiring them to sort and categorize specifics. The teacher orchestrates the activity by managing the environment and providing guidance, but students are to complete the task themselves.

One aspect of designing lessons for construct-a-concept objectives that can be particularly trying for teachers is producing appropriate examples and non-examples for students to categorize. As you determine examples and non-examples of a concept to present to students, your attention to concept attributes and example noise is critical. Case 7.4 demonstrates how example noise can be used to facilitate rather than hinder concept formation.

CASE 7.4

Mr. Corbin is raising leading questions with individual first-grade students to help each one construct the concept of *animals-with-the-same-number-of-legs*.

He displays Illustration 7.2 to Maggie and asks her, "Which two animals are alike?" Maggie, pointing to animals B and C, replies, "These." Mr. Corbin: "Why?" Maggie: "Because they're white, not black like the others." Mr. Corbin: "Thank you. Now (pointing to animal *A*), do you see a way that this animal is like one of the other two?" Maggie: "No, it's different."

Showing Maggie Illustration 7.3, Mr. Corbin says, "Which of these two animals are alike?" Maggie points to A and C and says, "Because they have eight legs." Mr. Corbin: "Thank you. Now, let's go back and look at this one again." Mr. Corbin displays Illustration 7.2 again and the activity continues.

Note how Mr. Corbin manipulated examples and non-examples to control for noise. Had Maggie immediately categorized by number of legs upon seeing Illustration 7.2, Mr. Corbin would have moved to a noisier situation (e.g., Illustration 7.4) where the noise varies more among the examples. But since she experienced difficulty with Illustration 7.2, he reduced the noise by moving to Illustration 7.3. In any case, Maggie eventually needs to recognize similarities and differences in number of legs even in high-noise situations because real-world examples of animals are quite noisy.

In general, how well students construct a concept is dependent on how well they learn to focus on concept attributes instead of example noise. Distinguishing between examples and non-examples in high-noise situations is indicative of a higher conceptual achievement level than when the distinction is made in low-noise situations.

REFLECTING AND EXPLAINING

In the reflecting and explaining stage, students explain their rationales for categorizing the specifics as they did. The teacher raises leading questions, stimulates thought, and clarifies students' expressions.

GENERALIZING AND ARTICULATING

Students describe the concept in terms of attributes (i.e., what sets examples of the concept apart from the non-examples). They may also develop a definition for the concept; however, it isn't necessary for the conventional name for the concept to be used.

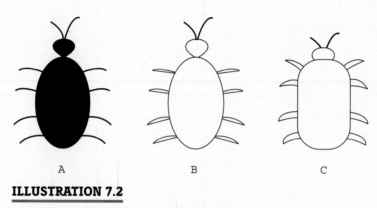

A   B   C

ILLUSTRATION 7.2

Which of the Two Animals Are Alike?

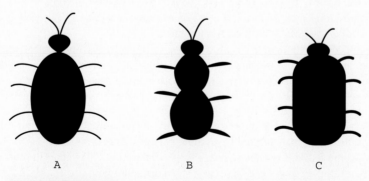

A   B   C

ILLUSTRATION 7.3

Examples and Non-Examples Mr. Corbin Used with Less
Variability of Example Noise Than Illustration 7.2

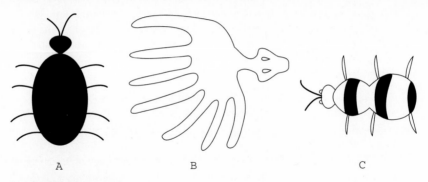

ILLUSTRATION 7.4

Examples and Non-Examples with Greater Variability of Noise than Figure 7.2

VERIFYING AND REFINING

The description or definition is tested with additional specifics that the students already know to be examples and thus should fit and with additional non-examples (which students know shouldn't fit). Further verification is pursued depending on the teacher's judgment of the situation. The description or definition of the concept is modified in light of the outcome of the tests. Prior stages are revisited as judged necessary by the teacher.

INDICATORS OF PROGRESS AS STUDENTS ENGAGE IN CONSTRUCT-A-CONCEPT LESSONS

Decisions you make while you teach depend on your formative judgments about students' progress as they engage in lessons. As illustrated by Ms. Anderson in Case 1.2 and Mr. Heaps in Case 2.10, the results of unplanned measurements are major indicators of students' progress during learning activities. But you cannot depend solely on unplanned measurements; they occur unpredictably and out of your control. Thus, you need to deliberately gather information by conducting relevant mini-experiments as students learn. Mini-experiments used to make formative judgments do not need to be designed to produce numerical scores. They do not affect grades; but they still include prompts and rubrics.

The first stage of construct-a-concept lessons is typically very student centered, thus providing ample opportunities for you to observe their responses to prompts. Case 7.5 is an example.

CASE 7.5

Ms. Fisher from Case 2.4 is in the process of planning the lesson that will begin on the third day of U.S. History Unit 17 on the civil rights movement; the lesson's objective is as follows:

B. Students will differentiate between examples and non-examples of de jure segregation as well as between examples and non-examples of de facto segregation (construct a concept).

Her unit plan as shown by Illustration 2.14 includes the following outline for the lesson:

"For the construct-a-concept lesson for Objective B, I'll engage them in four types of activities: (1) A sort-and- categorize exercise in which they'll discriminate among examples of de jure segregation, examples of de facto segregation, and non-examples of segregation, (2) a question-discussion session leading them to reflect and explain their categories from the prior activity, (3) a question-discussion session in which they develop definitions of the two types of segregation, and (4) a cooperative-group session in which they verify and re-fine their definitions."

To begin designing of the first stage, sorting and categorizing, she thinks, "After going through the colored-armband segregation experience for Objective A, they'll be ready to approach the idea of racial segregation from an academic perspective. I need to come up with some examples and non-examples of de jure segregation and de facto segregation for them to analyze. I don't think any of them know those words yet, and I won't introduce them until we're into the third stage of this lesson. I'd better generate some examples and non-examples. First of all, there are the examples of de jure segregation about which they'll learn later in this unit—like consequences of Jim Crow laws, such as blacks and whites having to attend different schools and live in different neighborhoods. Then, the textbook examples of de facto seg-regation like neighborhood settlement patterns leading to racially segregated schools although not man-dated by laws. I'll include some examples like those, but also I should put in some that are not the classic examples—ones that'll get them to really think about the subtle differences between de jure and de facto and between segregation and integration. I should try to match examples and non-examples so that the noise in the examples is similar to characteristics of the non-examples."

After further thought, Ms. Fisher produces the list shown in Illustration 7.5.

She thinks as she looks over Illustration 7.5's list, "It took me a while to come up with these, but they will not only help students construct the concepts; they'll also provide the bases for prompts that'll help me gauge students' progress as they conceptualize first segregation and then the subconcepts of de jure and de facto segregation. I did a good job of building in the right amount of example noise. There are the three all dealing with segregated schools, the three about high school teams, the three with the restaurants, and the three with the university. That gives them four different situations to discriminate between segre-gation and non-segregation and between de jure and de facto. It would be easier for them to just look at one situation at a time, like with school segregation only, but I don't want to lead them to construct these concepts too narrowly. I think by having the noise in the examples to be characteristics of the non-exam-ples, they'll be able to tease out the attributes more easily. But on the other hand, I really worry about these four non-examples of segregation. Almost anything you come up with actually segregates some group from another. Like the track team one—sure it doesn't segregate the boys from the girls like the volleyball ex-ample, but it does somewhat segregate the track athletes from the rest of the student body. One way to han-dle that would be to label each one with a 'reference to groups' note—like 'with respect to boys and girls' or 'with respect to blacks and whites' or 'with respect to economic advantage.' That would solve the prob-lem of these examples and non-examples joining one pair of groups while segregating another pair. On the other hand, these problems should come out in the discussions when we get into Stage 2 of the lesson, and maybe it would be productive to have the students bring out that subtlety—how when we refer to segre-gation, we need to refer to 'segregation of whom from whom.' This sure is complicated!

"Now, I need to figure out how I should present these examples and non-examples to them. I don't think I should give them these headings—after all, they're supposed to sort and categorize by the de-scriptions, not the labels. So I guess I should just randomly mix all 12 and have them sort them in coop-erative groups. I prompt them with, 'examine the list of 12—' Oh-oh! What should I call them? 'Descriptions'? 'Events'? 'Examples'? 'Facts'? I don't know. I'll just use 'items' unless I can think of something more descriptive for them. So, I prompt them with 'examine the 12 items and organize them into three different categories of 4 each according to some things they have in common.' But the trouble with that is that they're likely to come up with something more obvious than ones I'm hoping for—like

<u>Example of De Jure Segregation</u>

In the 1950s, some states had laws making it illegal for black students and white students to attend the same schools. Thus, blacks and whites did not attend the same school-sponsored social functions, athletic events, or classes. Schools served to keep blacks and whites apart from each other.

<u>Example of De Facto Segregation</u>

In one city, as in most cities today, it is illegal to prevent a person from attending a public school or live in a neighborhood because of her/his race, ethnic background, gender, or religion. However, because of economic and social factors many neighborhoods are either all African American, all white, all Mexican American, all Asian American, or all of some other ethnic composition.

City school board policy requires students who attend public school to attend the public school nearest to where they live.

Consequently, some of the public schools in the city have only African American students, others have only white students, others have only Mexican American students, and others are predominately attended by students from only a few minority groups.

<u>Non-Example of Segregation</u>

School district officials in one county have set up schools to serve different areas of the county so that the student body of each public school includes students from diverse ethnic backgrounds. Together these students attend and participate in a variety of school-sponsored academic, social, and civic activities.

<u>Example of De Jure Segregation</u>

Only female students are eligible to try out for the school volleyball team. The eighth-grade, ninth-grade, junior-varsity, and varsity volleyball teams consist of approximately 60 students who spend considerable time apart from the rest of the student body practicing, attending team social events, traveling to games, and participating in volleyball clinics.

<u>Example of De Facto Segregation</u>

Each year, the debate team consists of about 150 students. Tryouts for the school debate team are held in September. All regularly

ILLUSTRATION 7.5

The Initial List of Examples and Non-Examples Ms. Fisher Developed for Herself as She Plans the Sorting and Categorizing Stage of the Lesson

(Continued)

ILLUSTRATION 7.5 (Continued)

enrolled students are eligible to try out. During tryouts, students are selected for the team by a panel of debate specialists who judge (1) how well they use a volume of evidence, (2) their knowledge of fundamental philosophies of ethics and politics, (3) their familiarity with either Lincoln-Douglas debate strategies or policy debate strategies, and (4) their public-speaking skills.

Opportunities to acquire these competencies are limited to summer debate camps for which students spend at least $1500 each for two weeks at a debate camp.

It is very rare for students who are not fluent with English or who cannot afford the time or money to go to summer debate camps to be selected for the team.

Members of the debate team form a closely knit group as they practice together, help one another prepare their cases, travel to tournaments, and attend debate-sponsored social functions.

Non-Example of Segregation

Only male students are eligible for the school's boys' track team and only female students are eligible for the girls' track team. Approximately 75 boys and 60 girls compete on the ninth-grade, junior-varsity, and varsity girls' and boys' teams. The boys' and girls' teams practice together, travel to meets together, and have the same team social gatherings (e.g., end-of-the-season awards banquet).

Example of De Jure Segregation

In some parts of the country in the 1950s, it was illegal for African Americans and people of other ethnic backgrounds to eat in the same restaurants. Thus, there were "whites-only" restaurants that could legally serve anyone except for African Americans and others of African descent and "colored-only" restaurants that could legally serve only black people.

Example of De Facto Segregation

A particular restaurant serves only Mexican food. Although the Mexican American family who owns and operates the restaurant welcomes customers from all ethnic backgrounds, people who live outside its neighborhood do not patronize the restaurant because the neighborhood has the reputation of being dangerous to outsiders. The news media often report on criminal activities in which the neighborhood gangs "protect" their turf from outsiders.

Non-Example of Segregation

A particular restaurant serves only Mexican food. It is owned and operated by a Mexican American family. Most of its employees are Mexican American. The restaurant is very successful. Almost every night it is full of customers that include a mix of people from

ILLUSTRATION 7.5 (Continued)

---

diverse ethnic backgrounds such as Asian Americans, Mexican Americans, African Americans, South-Sea-Island Americans, Euro Americans, Native Americans, Non-Mexican Latinos, and non-Americans.

Example of De Jure Segregation

The charter of State University's African American club permits only African American students to be members. About 15,000 students are enrolled at State University, of which about 4,000 are African American. There are nearly 1,800 members of the African American club. The club's activities dominate the social lives of most of its members. Non-members do not attend those social events.

Example of De Facto Segregation

State University's basketball coaches and swimming and diving coaches do not discriminate with respect to ethnic background when recruiting players for their teams. They attempt to recruit the best student-athletes available to them. However, only African Americans are on the basketball team and only whites are on the swimming and diving team. At the training table in the dormitory where all State University's scholarship athletes eat, the basketball players all sit together and the swimmers and divers sit together.

Non-Example of Segregation

State University's baseball coaches do not discriminate with respect to ethnic background when recruiting players for their teams. They attempt to recruit the best student-athletes available to them. The baseball team includes a mix of African Americans, whites, Latinos, and Asian Americans. At the training table in the dormitory where all State University's scholarship athletes eat, the baseball players all sit together.

---

school related and non-school related—or something really creative and far out than segregation-related ideas. I know! I'll begin with grouping them two ways for them: examples of segregation and non-examples of segregation, but without using those labels—something completely abstract like 'Group A' and 'Group B.' Then, when they show they've discriminated between segregation and non-segregation, I'll split the eight examples of segregation and have them distinguish between de jure and de facto."

Mr. Fisher develops the initial tasksheet shown in Illustration 7.6.

She plans to go through all four stages of a construct-a-concept lesson to lead students to construct the concept of segregation and then to repeat the stages to lead them to distinguish between the two subconcepts of segregation: de jure and de facto. It helps her to realize that while de jure segregation and de facto segregation are subconcepts of segregation, they are parallel concepts with respect to each other. She develops Illustration 7.7's tasksheet for the first stage of the part of the lesson for discriminating between de jure and de facto segregation.

On the first day of the lesson (i.e., the third day of Unit 17), Ms. Fisher engages the class in a cooperative-learning activity in which groups of four or five students each respond to Illustration 7.6's tasksheet. As they do, Ms. Fisher circulates about the classroom, making mental notes to herself to help

Directions: Together examine the eight items in Group A and the four items in Group B. Then decide among yourselves how the items in Group A are alike that is different from the way the items in Group B are alike. Write your response in the blanks at the bottom of this sheet.

Group A

A-1. In the 1950s, some states had laws making it illegal for black students and white students to attend the same schools. Thus, blacks and whites did not attend the same school-sponsored social functions, athletic events, or classes. Schools served to keep blacks and whites apart from each other.

A-2. In one city, as in most cities today, it is illegal to prevent a person from attending a public school or live in a neighborhood because of her/his race, ethnic background, gender, or religion. However, because of economic and social factors many neighborhoods are either all African American, all white, all Mexican American, all Asian American, or all of some other ethnic composition. City school board policy requires students who attend public school to attend the public school nearest to where they live. Consequently, some of the public schools in the city have only African American students, others have only white students, others have only Mexican American students, and others are predominately attended by students from only a few minority groups.

A-3. Only female students are eligible to try out for the school volleyball team. The eighth-grade, ninth-grade, junior-varsity, and varsity volleyball teams consist of approximately 60 students who spend considerable time apart from the rest of the student body practicing, attending team social events, traveling to games, and participating in volleyball clinics.

A-4. Each year, the debate team consists of about 150 students. Tryouts for the school debate team are held in September. All regularly enrolled students are eligible to try out. During tryouts, students are selected for the team by a panel of debate specialists who judge (1) how well they use a volume of evidence, (2) their knowledge of fundamental philosophies of ethics and politics, (3) their familiarity with either Lincoln-Douglas debate strategies or policy debate strategies, and (4) their public-speaking skills. Opportunities to acquire these competencies are limited to summer debate camps for which students spend at least $1500 each for two weeks at a

ILLUSTRATION 7.6

The First Tasksheet Ms. Fisher Plans to Use in the Initial Stage of Her Lesson

(Continued)

ILLUSTRATION 7.6 (Continued)

debate camp. It is very rare for students who are not fluent with English or who cannot afford the time or money to go to summer debate camps to be selected for the team. Members of the debate team form a closely knit group as they practice together, help one another prepare their cases, travel to tournaments, and attend debate-sponsored social functions.

A-5. In some parts of the country in the 1950s, it was illegal for African Americans and people of other ethnic backgrounds to eat in the same restaurants. Thus, there were "whites-only" restaurants that could legally serve anyone except for African Americans and others of African descent and "colored-only" restaurants that could legally serve only black people.

A-6. A particular restaurant serves only Mexican food. Although the Mexican American family who owns and operates the restaurant welcomes customers from all ethnic backgrounds, people who live outside its neighborhood do not patronize the restaurant because the neighborhood has the reputation of being dangerous to outsiders. The news media often report on criminal activities in which the neighborhood gangs "protect" their turf from outsiders.

A-7. The charter of State University's African American club permits only African American students to be members. About 15,000 students are enrolled at State University, of which about 4,000 are African American. There are nearly 1,800 members of the African American club. The club's activities dominate the social lives of most of its members. Non-members do not attend those social events.

A-8. State University's basketball coaches and swimming and diving coaches do not discriminate with respect to ethnic background when recruiting players for their teams. They attempt to recruit the best student-athletes available to them. However, only African Americans are on the basketball team and only whites are on the swimming and diving team. At the training table in the dormitory where all State University's scholarship athletes eat, the basketball players all sit together and the swimmers and divers sit together.

Group B

B-1. School district officials in one county have set up schools to serve different areas of the county so that the student body of each public school includes students from diverse ethnic backgrounds. Together these students attend and participate in a variety of school-sponsored academic, social, and civic activities.

B-2. Only male students are eligible for the school's boys' track team and only female students are eligible for the girls'

ILLUSTRATION 7.6 (Continued)

track team. Approximately, 75 boys and 60 girls compete on
the ninth-grade, junior-varsity, and varsity girls' and boys'
teams. The boys' and girls' teams practice together, travel
to meets together, and have the same team social gatherings
(e.g., end-of-the-season awards banquet).

B-3. A particular restaurant serves only Mexican food. It is owned
and operated by a Mexican American family. Most of its
employees are Mexican American. The restaurant is very successful. Almost every night it is full of customers that include a
mix of people from diverse ethnic backgrounds such as Asian
Americans, Mexican Americans, African Americans, South-Sea-
Island Americans, Euro Americans, Native Americans, Non-Mexican
Latinos, and non-Americans.

B-4. State University's baseball coaches do not discriminate with
respect to ethnic background when recruiting players for their
teams. They attempt to recruit the best student-athletes available to them. The baseball team includes a mix of African Americans, whites, Latinos, and Asian Americans. At the training
table in the dormitory where all State University's scholarship
athletes eat, the baseball players all sit together.

<u>Your Response</u>

How are Group A's items like one another but different from
Group B's?

How are Group B's items like one another but different from
Group A's?

<u>Directions</u>: Together examine the four odd-numbered items from Group A and the four even-numbered items from Group A. Then decide among yourselves how the items from the even-numbered group are alike that is different from the way the items from the odd-numbered group are alike. Write your response in the blanks at the bottom of this sheet.

<u>Odd-Numbered Group</u>

A-1.   In the 1950s, some states had laws making it illegal for black students and white students to attend the same schools. Thus, blacks and whites did not attend the same school-sponsored social functions, athletic events, or classes. Schools served to keep blacks and whites apart from each other.

A-3.   Only female students are eligible to try out for the school volleyball team. The eighth-grade, ninth-grade, junior-varsity, and varsity volleyball teams consist of approximately 60 students who spend considerable time apart from the rest of the student body practicing, attending team social events, traveling to games, and participating in volleyball clinics.

A-5.   In some parts of the country in the 1950s, it was illegal for African Americans and people of other ethnic backgrounds to eat in the same restaurants. Thus, there were "whites-only" restaurants that could legally serve anyone except for African Americans and others of African descent and "colored-only" restaurants that could legally serve only black people.

A-7.   The charter of State University's African American club permits only African American students to be members. About 15,000 students are enrolled at State University, of which about 4,000 are African American. There are nearly 1,800 members of the African American club. The club's activities dominate the social lives of most of its members. Non-members do not attend those social events.

<u>Even-Numbered Group</u>

A-2.   In one city, as in most cities today, it is illegal to prevent a person from attending a public school or live in a neighborhood because of her/his race, ethnic background, gender, or religion. However, because of economic and social factors many neighborhoods are either all African American, all white, all Mexican American, all Asian American, or all of some other ethnic composition. City school board policy requires students who attend public school to attend the public school nearest

ILLUSTRATION 7.7

The Second Tasksheet Ms. Fisher Plans to Use in Her Lesson

(Continued)

ILLUSTRATION 7.7 (Continued)

to where they live. Consequently, some of the public schools in the city have only African American students, others have only white students, others have only Mexican American students, and others are predominately attended by students from only a few minority groups.

A-4. Each year, the debate team consists of about 150 students. Try-outs for the school debate team are held in September. All regularly enrolled students are eligible to try out. During tryouts, students are selected for the team by a panel of debate specialists who judge (1) how well they use a volume of evidence, (2) their knowledge of fundamental philosophies of ethics and politics, (3) their familiarity with either Lincoln-Douglas debate strategies or policy debate strategies, and (4) their public-speaking skills. Opportunities to acquire these competencies are limited to summer debate camps for which students spend at least $1500 each for two weeks at a debate camp. It is very rare for students who are not fluent with English or who cannot afford the time or money to go to summer debate camps to be selected for the team. Members of the debate team form a closely knit group as they practice together, help one another prepare their cases, travel to tournaments, and attend debate-sponsored social functions.

A-6. A particular restaurant serves only Mexican food. Although the Mexican American family who owns and operates the restaurant welcomes customers from all ethnic backgrounds, people who live outside its neighborhood do not patronize the restaurant because the neighborhood has the reputation of being dangerous to outsiders. The news media often report on criminal activities in which the neighborhood gangs "protect" their turf from outsiders.

A-8. State University's basketball coaches and swimming and diving coaches do not discriminate with respect to ethnic background when recruiting players for their teams. They attempt to recruit the best student-athletes available to them. However, only African Americans are on the basketball team and only whites are on the swimming and diving team. At the training table in the dormitory where all State University's scholarship athletes eat, the basketball players all sit together and the swimmers and divers sit together.

<u>Your Response</u>

How are the items from the odd-numbered group like one another but different from the items in the even-numbered group?

_____

_____

ILLUSTRATION 7.7 (Continued)

```
_____

_____

How are the items from the even-numbered group like one another but
different from the items in the odd-numbered group?

_____

_____

_____
```

her decide when the groups are ready to move into Stage 2 of the lesson for the first part of Objective B (i.e., constructing the concept of segregation). The tasksheet not only helps lead students to reason inductively, but it also serves as a prompt for the mini-experiment Ms. Fisher conducts. The rubric she follows in her mind as she listens to students' discussions and sees what they write on Illustration 7.6's tasksheet is displayed by Illustration 7.8.

Based on results from unplanned measurements as well as from the mini-experiment with Illustration 7.6's tasksheet serving as the prompt and Illustration 7.8's rubric in her head, Ms. Fisher decides to move on to Stage 2 of the first part of this lesson. Later in the class period, she uses Illustration 7.7's tasksheet and Illustration 7.9's rubrics during Stage 1 of the part of the lesson for students to construct the concepts of de jure and de facto segregation.

In Case 7.6, Ms. Ragusa conducts mini-experiments during all four stages of a construct-a-concept lesson.

CASE 7.6

Ms. Ragusa intends for Unit 9 of the science course for her fourth-graders to help her students achieve the goal, and thus the objectives, listed in Illustration 7.10.

She thinks, as she begins designing the initial lesson for Objective A, "Construct the concept magnet. That means inductive learning activities beginning with sorting and categorizing with examples and non-examples of magnets. But these kids already know the word 'magnet' and some things about magnets from playing with them and having them around their homes. They don't need to discover the existence of magnets; they need to refine their understanding of magnet attributes. I doubt that many understand exactly what materials magnets attract—most think any metal, not just the magnetic ones like iron, steel, cobalt, and nickel. They don't realize metals like aluminum, brass, tin, silver, stainless steel, copper, bronze, and gold aren't magnetic. Moreover, I doubt they understand that a magnet sets up a magnetic field. So what should be the initial experience for them? I'll start them with some magnets and non-magnets with similar example noise regarding shape and material and . . ."

Seventy minutes later, Ms. Ragusa has worked out the lesson plan displayed by Illustration 7.11. Illustration 7.12 shows the related homework tasksheet.

The lesson begins smoothly as planned. As Ms. Ragusa circulates among the five cooperative groups working through the sorting-and-categorizing task, she observes students perform the experiment, listens to their discussions, and reads what they write on the tasksheet; in her mind she follows a rubric patterned after the ones shown by Illustrations 7.8 and 7.9 that Ms. Fisher used in Case 7.5.

She soon notes that due to Edgardo's and Kimberleigh's prior experiences with magnets, Group IV is progressing through the task much faster than the others. In less than 10 minutes, Group IV has already determined that objects 1 and 3 are magnets that either attract or repel each other (though the students don't use the words "attract" and "repel") depending on which parts of the magnets are near one another. They also conclude that the other objects don't affect one another, but object 5 is attracted to the two magnets.

From the results of unplanned measurements and her mini-experiment, she infers that Group IV has discovered the most fundamental attributes of magnets before any of the other groups. Ms. Ragusa decides to intervene and introduce a demonstration that might lead them to discover a magnet-attribute that is more difficult to detect than attributes discovered through the sorting and categorizing stage in the original lesson plan. She thus takes a piece of cardboard, a jar of iron filings, and two bar magnets, joins Group IV, and says, "Excuse me, but I see you've gotten far enough along with your work to try another experiment." She then demonstrates the experiment that is explained by Illustration 7.13. She directs them to discuss their observations and to extend their list of things they know about magnets.

As students engage in discussions in their collaborative groups, I listen for comments and exchanges as well as read their responses at the bottom of the tasksheet to help me address the following questions:

1. Are most students associating Group A's items with situations in which people are being separated from one another?

2. If the answer to Question 1 is "Yes," do most of them see the variables (i.e., race for A-1, ethnicity for A-2, gender for A-3, economic advantage and native language for A-4, race for A-5, ethnicity for A-6, ethnicity for A-7, and ethnicity for A-8) upon which the separations occur?

3. Are most students associating Group B's items with situations in which people are coming together in spite of differences in variables that separated people in the situations from Group A (i.e., ethnicity for B-1, gender for B-2, ethnicity for B-3, and ethnicity for B-4).

When I feel strongly that the answer to all three questions is "Yes," it is time to move on to Stage 2 of the lesson. However, if a group appears to be moving in another direction and time begins to run short, I will ask probing questions to highlight attributes of the concept of segregation -- possibly using additional examples and non-examples in which the noise in the examples matches characteristics of the non-examples.

ILLUSTRATION 7.8

Rubric Ms. Fisher Follows in Her Mind as She Listens to Students Discussion and Sees What They Write on Illustration 7.6's Tasksheet

During the reflecting-and-explaining stage, Ms. Ragusa uses Illustration 7.14's mini-experiment as she conducts the planned questioning session.

Following the group reports during the reflecting-and-explaining stage, Ms. Ragusa conducts a questioning session as planned. From previous experiences in such sessions under Ms. Ragusa's supervision, the students have learned that whenever she calls on someone and says "Keep it going," the following procedures are in effect until Ms. Ragusa interrupts with "Excuse me": One student at a time has the floor; anyone wanting to speak raises a hand to request the floor from the student who is speaking.

Here is part of the dialogue from that session:

Ms. Ragusa: "Everyone take 20 seconds to think of two things reported by all five of our groups. Okay, what was one thing, Haeja? Tell me slowly so I can write what you say on the overhead."

Haeja: "When you put the two magnets close, they'll pull together on their own sometimes. And sometimes they push away by themselves."

Ms. Ragusa: "I see by the number of raised hands that others have something to say. Haeja, keep it going as I try to capture what people say on the overhead."

Haeja: "Eldon."

Eldon: "Sometimes the ends that are close, come together, but if you turn one around then . . ."

As students engage in discussions in their collaborative groups, I listen for comments and exchanges as well as read their responses at the bottom of the tasksheet to help me address the following questions:

1. Are most students associating the odd-numbered items with situations in which people are being separated because of laws or rules from some governmental-sanctioned body?

2. Are most students associating the even-numbered items with circumstances in which people are being separated because of existing conditions, behaviors, attitudes, or circumstances that are not a direct consequence of governmental-sanctioned laws or rules?

When I feel strongly that the answer to both questions is "Yes," it is time to move on to Stage 2 of the lesson. However, if a group appears to be moving in another direction and time begins to run short, I will ask probing questions to highlight attributes of the concept of de jure segregation and the concept of de facto segregation -- possibly pairing examples of each in which the noise in the example of de jure segregation is identical to the noise in the example of de facto segregation.

ILLUSTRATION 7.9

Rubric Ms. Fisher Follows in Her Mind as She Listens to Students Discussion and Sees What They Write on Illustration 7.7's Tasksheet

```
Unit: Magnetism (Fourth Grade)

   Goal: Students increase their understanding of magnets,
         explore their properties, and use magnets to solve real life
         problems.

   Objectives:

      A.  Students discriminate between examples and non examples
          of magnets and discover attributes of magnets (construct
          a concept).

      B.  Students list attributes of magnets (simple knowledge).

      C.  Students discover that a magnet can be used to make tempo-
          rary magnets out of objects made of magnetic materials
          (e.g., iron and steel) and that some materials (e.g., soft
          iron) are easier to magnetize than others (e.g., steel),
          but the more difficult-to-magnetize materials retain their
          magnetism longer than the easier-to-magnetize materials
          (discover a relationship).

      D.  Students state relationships discovered as a result of
          achieving Objective C (simple knowledge).

      E.  Students know how to make and care for magnets (process
          knowledge).

      F.  Students develop novel hypotheses and models for explaining
          magnetic phenomena (creative thinking).

      G.  Students know how to make a compass (process knowledge).

      H.  Students explain how the earth acts as a giant magnet (com-
          prehension and communication skills).

      I.  In general terms, students explain the rudiments of mag-
          netic theory (comprehension and communication skills).

      J.  Given a real life problem, students decide how, if at all,
          their understanding of magnetism can be used to solve the
          problem (application).
```

ILLUSTRATION 7.10

Goal and Objectives for Ms. Ragusa's Unit on Magnetism

NOTE #1: During the sorting and categorizing stages, the class will be organized in cooperative groups as follows:

Group I
Student - Role*
Monica - mgr/org
Juan L. - material sup
Chen - comm
Pauline - timer/rec
James - reporter

Group II
Student - Role*
Eldon - mgr/org
Haeja - material sup
Eiko - comm
Willard - timer/rec
Cynthia - reporter

Group III
Student - Role*
Greg - mgr/org
Adam - material sup
Brenda - comm
Sun-li - timer/rec
Bryce - reporter

Group IV
Student - Role*
Ellen - mgr/org
Edgardo - material sup
Juan T. - comm
Paige - timer/rec
Kimberleigh - reporter

Group V
Student - Role*
Wanda - mgr/org & material sup
Suzanne - comm
Salinda - timer/rec
Brookelle - reporter

* - Roles are defined as follows:

"mgr/org"
    designates the <u>manager & organizer</u> who chairs the meeting for the group and is responsible for maintaining group focus and reminding people to stay on-task.

"material sup"
    designates the <u>material supervisor</u> who takes custodial care of, distributes, collects, and returns the group's materials.

"comm"
    designates the <u>communicator</u> who communicates and clarifies the directions for the group.

"timer/rec"
    designates the <u>timer/recorder</u> who keeps track of time, making sure the group keeps to the schedule. He/she also maintains a record of data collected by the group.

"reporter"
    designates the <u>reporter</u> who summarizes the group's findings and conclusions in writing and presents them to the rest of the class.

ILLUSTRATION 7.11

Ms. Ragusa's Lesson Plan for Objective A of Illustration 7.10

(Continued)

ILLUSTRATION 7.11 (Continued)

NOTE #2: Each group's recorder/timer will use a copy of the
following tasksheet during the sorting and categorizing
stage of the lesson:

Recorder/Timer's Tasksheet

Pair of objects	Observations
1 & 2	
1 & 3	
1 & 4	
1 & 5	
1 & 6	
1 & 7	
2 & 3	
2 & 4	
2 & 5	
2 & 6	
2 & 7	
3 & 4	
3 & 5	
3 & 6	
3 & 7	
4 & 5	
4 & 6	
4 & 7	
5 & 6	
5 & 7	
6 & 7	

NOTE #3: The seven objects labeled 1-7 referred to in the tasksheet
as well as the lesson plan are as follows:

Object 1: A steel, bar-shaped magnet (without poles labeled)
Object 2: A bar-shaped piece of wood
Object 3: A steel, disk-shaped magnet (without poles labeled)
Object 4: A horseshoe-shaped rubber object
Object 5: A bar-shaped, non-magnetized piece of steel
Object 6: A bar-shaped piece of aluminum
Object 7: A disk-shaped piece of tin

The Four-Stage Lesson Plan

1. Sorting and Categorizing: I'll direct the students to take each
   possible pair of the seven objects and to slowly bring each surface of one object in contact with each surface of the other and
   then to record what is observed on the tasksheet.

ILLUSTRATION 7.11 (Continued)

Inferences from the facts recorded on the tasksheet are to be made, summarized, and reported.

To engage the students in the sorting and categorizing task, I'll first organize the class into five cooperative groups with each group's manager & organizer designating the roles that I've indicated to her/him and distributing materials. In the meantime, I'll take the five communicators aside to demonstrate the process for bringing the various surfaces together using Objects 4 and 5; I'll explain the directions to them so they can explain them to their respective groups. It should take the manager & organizers five minutes to get their groups set up while I explain the directions to the communicators.

The communicators explain the directions to the groups and the groups complete the task culminating in the preparation of a brief report to be presented to the class in a large-group session. This cooperative-group session should take about 20 minutes. My job will be to monitor for student engagement in the learning activity and to be making formative judgments, but not to get involved in groups' decision-making.

2. Reflecting and Explaining: For this stage, students will remain in their groups, but the session will have a whole-class, large-group focus as each group's reporter explains what the group's members observed and inferred from the facts.

Upon completion of the reports, I'll conduct a large-group questioning session to stimulate students' reflection on the experiments they just conducted.

3. Generalizing and Articulating: Continuing with the large-group questioning session, I'll stimulate inductive reasoning by my questions, leading students to classify Objects 1 and 3 together (i.e., the magnets) and possibly separating Object 5 from Objects 2, 3, 6, and 7 (i.e., magnetic versus non-magnetic materials).

Briefly interrupting the large-group questioning session, I'll direct each student to write out why we classified the seven objects as we did and to describe what other objects (i.e., not in the original list of seven) would have to be like to fit in a category. As they write, I'll circulate among them, reading a sample of the responses, and selecting ones to be read to the class as a whole.

Returning to a large-group questioning session, I'll direct several students to read what they wrote and use their replies to stimulate the class to articulate a response that is agreeable to the majority.

ILLUSTRATION 7.11 (Continued)

4. <u>Verifying and Refining</u>: I'll then distribute and assign the homework tasksheet (see Illustration 7.7) to be completed for tomorrow's class. I'll explain the directions to them and also suggest that they ask a parent, older sibling, or other person to help them with the directions and to sign the bottom of the tasksheet. As they leave for the day, I'll distribute the magnets (one horseshoe magnet and one bar magnet for each student) alluded to on the tasksheet.

The following day, we'll return to the same five cooperative groups with each member of each group reporting findings from the homework tasksheet.

Based on the individual reports from the homework, each cooperative group either proposes modifications to the class's original statement (as written at the top of the homework tasksheet) or agrees to maintain the original.

I then reorganize the class into a large-group session to hear group reports and engage in a discussion leading to a refined version of our statement about magnets and magnetic materials.

Before concluding this lesson, I need to make it clear that as we use our agreed-to statement on magnets and magnetic materials we may want to continue to refine it, updating it in light of new discoveries we might make.

After 13 minutes, Ms. Ragusa has the list shown in Illustration 7.15 displayed. She calls a halt to the discussion with, "Excuse me. Let's look at what we've listed to this point and group together the ones that say the same thing. What are two you'd put together, James? Keep it going." During the ensuing discussion, Ms. Ragusa color-codes the statements on the overhead to keep track of and display how the students are grouping them. The resulting grouped statements are shown in Illustration 7.16.

Having run rubrics through her head as she had done before, Ms. Ragusa judges that the discussions leading to Illustrations 7.15 and 7.16 were quite productive. She allowed the session to extend beyond the time she originally allotted for it. She thinks, "We're not going to have time to complete the generalizing and articulating stage today, so we won't have the statement about magnets we need to start the tasksheet (Illustration 7.12) I'd planned to assign for homework. The way this is working out, we'll delay articulating that initial generalization, but when we do tomorrow, the statement is going to be more advanced than I had anticipated. That's good!"

Thus, she deviates from the original plan outlined in Illustration 7.11 and directs the class as follows: "Copy the categorized lists from the overhead (Illustration 7.16) right now." When she sees they've completed the task, she continues, "For homework, analyze the list and how we categorized the statements. Then describe each category in one or two sentences and invent a name for the category."

The following day, she engages the class in a questioning session in which they discuss the descriptions and names they invented for homework. Led by Ms. Ragusa's probing questions, the class decides to collapse some categories so that no two statements are listed more than once. The result is

1. What is your name? _____ What is the date? _____

2. Copy the statement about magnets to which our class agreed today.

    _____

    _____

    _____

3. Choose six objects you find near or in your home. Try to pick ob-
    jects that are different from those with which we experimented in
    class today. Make sure no two of them are made from the same kind
    of material. From what materials are the objects made?

    (1) _____ (2) _____

    (3) _____ (4) _____

    (5) _____ (6) _____

4. Take the two magnets loaned to you in class today. Now experiment
    with the magnets and the six objects as we did in class today.
    Which objects are affected by the magnets?

    _____

5. Do you now think we should rewrite the statement from class (#2)?

    _____ If so, how would you rewrite it? _____

    _____

    _____

    Note to
    Parents: Please help your child with the directions for this home-
                work activity. Sign below when your child has completed
                the assignment. Thank you.

                    Ms. Ragusa

    Signature: _____

ILLUSTRATION 7.12

The Homework Tasksheet Used in the Verifying and Refining Stage of the Lesson
Plan from Illustration 7.11

PROCEDURE:

Lay one of the magnets on a table (making sure the other is out of range) and lay the cardboard over the magnet covering it completely. Carefully sprinkle iron filings on the cardboard (making sure the iron filings don't actually contact the magnet as they're difficult to clean off). Lightly tap the cardboard and observe how the iron filings line up as shown in the picture below:

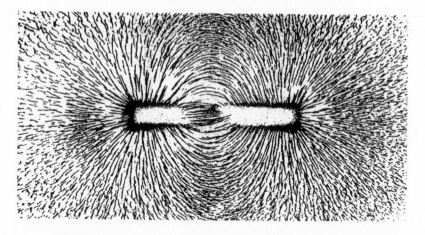

Carefully return the filings to the container. Now line up the two magnets side-by-side parallel to one another about five millimeters apart and facing opposite directions (i.e., opposite poles together). Now use the cardboard and iron filings as before. How do the iron filings line up?

ILLUSTRATION 7.13

Experiment Ms. Ragusa Demonstrated for Group IV

(Continued)

ILLUSTRATION 7.13 (Continued)

Once again, clean up the iron filings and repeat the activity with the two magnets, but this time, face the magnets in the same direction (i.e., like poles together) How do the iron filings line up now? Compare what you get to the following picture:

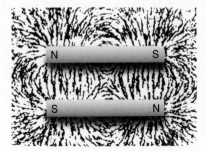 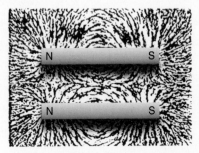

Prompt and Rubric:

I direct each of the five groups' reporters to summarize the group's findings and conclusions for the class. As the report is given, I make judgments about the following:

1. Is the oral report consistent with what I had observed during the group's engagement in the cooperative activity of Stage 1? If not, I interject probing questions, such as, "Didn't I hear Juan mention that ... ?"

2. Are the conclusions reported supported by the observations recorded on the tasksheet? If not, or if the reporter doesn't tie the conclusions to the observations, I interject with questions to other members of the group such as, "What did you observe that led you to believe that ... ?"

3. As the report is being given, I will observe for facial expressions, under-the-breath comments, and other indicators of students from within the reporting groups as well as other students who disagree, agree, misunderstand, or understand what is being reported. As needed, I will raise specific questions with those students to attempt to get at their comprehension of the report.

ILLUSTRATION 7.14

Mini-Experiment Ms. Ragusa Used During the Reflecting-and-Explaining Stage of Her Lesson

When two magnets are close, they push away sometimes. (Haeja)

If the magnets are turned one way they pull together; if they're another way, they push away. (Eldon)

Some magnets reach out farther than others. (Salinda)

Objects 1 and 3 are magnets. (Suzanne)

The magnets didn't push away other objects except the other magnet. (Juan)

One magnet was straight, the other one bent. (Adam)

Objects 1, 3, 5, 6 and 7 are metal. (Cynthia)

Object 2 is wood and Object 4 is rubber. (Cynthia)

One of our magnets was stronger than the other. (Paige)

Magnets work through cardboard. (Kimberleigh)

The magnets pulled Object 5, but not the others. (Salinda)

Magnets pull metal things. (Brenda)

The magnets didn't pull Objects 6 and 7 and they're metal. (Eiko)

Magnets pull some metal things. (Brenda)

The magnets pull hardest by their ends. (Ellen)

They form kind of a pattern like this when they pull. (Edgardo)

They pull harder the closer they get to certain things – like Object 5. (Brookelle)

Our magnets are metal. (Willard)

All magnets are metal. (Greg)

Some magnets are metal. (Chen)

Some magnets are not metal. (Wanda)

Everything is a magnet, but some are too weak to tell. (Ellen)

Everything can't be a magnet. (Greg)

Magnets are fun. (Monica)

Magnets are little. (Bryce)

One end of a magnet is different from the other end. (Pauline)

Magnets have to be bigger than what they pick up. (Chen)

Magnets reach out to things in curves around their ends. (Juan)

ILLUSTRATION 7.15

Statements about Magnets Displayed on the Overhead

Category A

When two magnets are close, they pull together sometimes. *

When two magnets are close, they push away sometimes. *

If the magnets are turned one way they pull together; if they're another way, they push away.

The magnets didn't push away other objects except the other magnet.

Magnets work through cardboard.

The magnets pulled Object 5, but not the others. *

Magnets pull metal things. *

The magnets didn't pull Objects 6 and 7 and they're metal. *

Magnets pull some metal things. *

The magnets pull hardest by their ends.

They form kind of a pattern like this they pull. (Edgardo)  when

They pull harder the closer they get to certain things - like Object 5.

Magnets reach out to things in curves around their ends.

Category B

Objects 1 and 3 are magnets.

Objects 1, 3, 5, 6 and 7 are metal.

Object 2 is wood and Object 4 is rubber.

Our magnets are metal.

All magnets are metal.

Some magnets are metal.

Some magnets are not metal.

Everything is a magnet, but some are too weak to tell.

Everything can't be a magnet.

Category C

One magnet was straight, the other one bent. *

ILLUSTRATION 7.16

Students Grouped Illustration 7.15's Statements

(Continued)

ILLUSTRATION 7.16 (Continued)

Category D

When two magnets are close, they pull together sometimes. *

When two magnets are close, they push away sometimes. *

The magnets pulled Object 5, but not the others. *

Magnets pull metal things. *

The magnets didn't pull Objects 6 and 7 and they're metal. *

Magnets pull some metal things. *

Category E

One magnet was straight, the other one bent. *

Some magnets reach out farther than others.

One of our magnets was stronger than the other.

Category F

Magnets are fun.

Category G

Magnets are little.

Category H

One end of a magnet is different from the other end.

Category I

Magnets have to be bigger than what they pick up.

———

* - indicates statement is in two categories

displayed by Illustration 7.17. The empty category, "How Magnets Work," was included in response to Ms. Ragusa's persistent questions beginning with "Why" and "How." Although none of the present statements fits that category, she worked it into the discussion as a set up for some subsequent lessons (e.g., for Objectives F and I as listed in Illustration 7.10 in the unit).

The following day, Ms. Ragusa plays off of students' responses to the homework assignment in a questioning and discussion session leading to the following statement:

"A magnet is a special piece of metal. It has a field of power. The field of power pulls some things to the magnet. But the field can't pull other things. Also, one end of a magnet will pull and be pulled by one of the ends of another magnet. The other end will push away and be pushed away by that same end of the other magnet."

Having agreed to this initial draft of a "definition" of magnet, Ms. Ragusa moves to the verifying-and-refining stage of the lesson by assigning the tasksheet from the original lesson plan shown in Illustration 7.12. The tasksheet, of course, serves as the prompt for a mini-experiment to help her make formative evaluations. The following day she completes this stage as originally planned. The class spent one more day than she had originally allocated for the lesson. However, the following refined version of the generalization identifying magnet attributes she judges to be more sophisticated than she originally anticipated:

"A magnet is a special piece of metal. It has a field of power around one end and a field of power around the other end. The two fields of power pull certain things to the magnet. The certain things are made of metal. The metal has to be like iron, steel, or nickel. But 'nickels' don't work because they're really copper mostly. One end will pull and be pulled by one of the ends of another magnet. The other end will push away and be pushed away by that same end of the other magnet."

Follow the influence of Ms. Ragusa's lesson described in Case 7.6 on one student's concept of magnets by reading Case 7.7.

CASE 7.7

Prior to the lesson, Chen's concept of magnets was based on experiences playing with a small horseshoe magnet and the magnet clip used to attach notes to the refrigerator in his apartment. Although he had engaged in brief lessons about magnets in both second and third grades, he didn't really comprehend the textbook illustrations nor the teachers' explanations. He hadn't really thought much about how magnets work nor even recognized that he was continually using magnets (e.g., in the door latches of the cabinets in his apartment and in the compass that he enjoyed so much). Had anyone asked Chen, "What is a magnet?" before Ms. Ragusa's lesson, Chen would have replied, "A U-shaped thing you can stick to metal things."

As he served the role of communicator for Group I during the first stage of Ms. Ragusa's lesson, Chen began dramatically altering and broadening his concept of magnets. As he experimented with the seven objects, he discovered that magnets can affect other objects without actually touching them. Because the shape of some of the non-magnets (e.g., Objects 2 and 6 listed in Illustration 7.11) that Ms. Ragusa had carefully selected for the activity and mini-experiment were the same as the magnets (i.e., Objects 1 and 3) and because another non-magnet (i.e., Object 4) was shaped like the magnet with which Chen was already familiar, Chen quickly realized that shape is not the principal way magnets are distinguished from non-magnets. Chen was surprised to discover that although Objects 1 and 5 looked alike, one behaved like a magnet but the other didn't. He was also surprised that the experiments didn't support his prior belief that magnets did not stick to all metal objects.

During the reflecting-and-explaining and generalizing-and-articulating stages, Chen struggled to find words to describe the discoveries he and his classmates were making about magnets. At first, he resisted responding to Ms. Ragusa's probes for him to explain what he was thinking when he himself wasn't sure what he was thinking. But she persisted and the struggle stimulated him to analyze his experiences with magnets, clarify his thinking, and ultimately reconstruct his concept of magnets.

Unless Chen one day studies to be a teacher or studies cognitive science in depth, he is unlikely to ever encounter the term "example noise." However, Ms. Ragusa's attention to the noise in the examples and non-examples she chose for this lesson played a critical role in how Chen constructed and refined his concept of magnetism and how Ms. Ragusa was able to monitor his progress.

What Magnets Do

When two magnets are close, they pull together sometimes.

When two magnets are close, they push away sometimes.

If the magnets are turned one way they pull together; if they're another way, they push away.

The magnets didn't push away other objects except the other magnet.

Magnets work through cardboard.

The magnets pulled Object 5, but not the others.

Magnets pull metal things.

The magnets didn't pull Objects 6 and 7 and they're metal.

Magnets pull some metal things.

The magnets pull hardest by their ends.

They form kind of a pattern like this when they pull. (Edgardo)

They pull harder the closer they get to certain things – like Object 5.

Magnets reach out to things in curves around their ends.

What Magnets Are Like

Objects 1 and 3 are magnets.

Objects 1, 3, 5, 6 and 7 are metal.

Object 2 is wood and Object 4 is rubber.

Our magnets are metal.

All magnets are metal.

Some magnets are metal.

Some magnets are not metal.

Everything is a magnet, but some are too weak to tell.

Everything can't be a magnet.

ILLUSTRATION 7.17

Students Re-Group and Name the Statements from Illustration 7.16

(Continued)

ILLUSTRATION 7.17 (Continued)

<u>Differences in Magnets</u>

One magnet was straight, the other one bent.

Some magnets are reach out farther than others.

One of our magnets was stronger than the other.

<u>How Magnets Work</u>

? ?

<u>Other Things About Magnets</u>

Magnets are fun.

Magnets are little.

One end of a magnet is different from the other end.

Magnets have to be bigger than what they pick up.

As he was completing Illustration 7.12's tasksheet for homework during the verifying and refining stage of the lesson, Chen tried sticking magnets to virtually everything in his apartment. By observing that the magnets stuck to objects according to what they are made of rather than what they are (e.g., the magnets adhered to a steel table leg, but not an aluminum table leg), Chen hypothesized that an object had to contain certain materials to be magnetic (although he didn't use the term "magnetic"). Chen was quite pleased the next day that his hypothesis was incorporated into the refined version of the class's generalization about magnets. Because he mentally constructed the concept of magnets for himself, it's meaningful and he'll use it. The lesson won't be lost as were the prior lessons from other teachers in which he was only exposed to what "experts" had to say about magnets.

As was true for Ms. Fisher in Case 7.5 and Ms. Ragusa in Case 7.6, the mini-experiments you conduct as you teach are virtually indistinguishable from the learning activities themselves. But for these mini-experiments to be relevant to the formative judgments you need to make as you teach, you need to plan for them and make them consciously. Although you may be the only one aware that you are making them, they are a necessary complement to the unplanned measurements that occur as you teach.

INDICATORS OF STUDENTS' ACHIEVEMENT OF CONSTRUCT-A-CONCEPT OBJECTIVES

MINI-EXPERIMENTS RELEVANT TO CONSTRUCT-A-CONCEPT OBJECTIVES

Designing mini-experiments relevant to students' achievement of construct-a-concept objectives typically requires more creative thought on your part than mini-experiments relevant to most other types of objectives. In collaboration with a colleague design two mini-experiments for student achievement of Objective B listed in Illustration 7.10. Then design two more mini-experiments for Objective A listed in Illustration 7.10.

In Case 7.8, Kisha and Elwin complete the task you and your colleague just completed.

CASE 7.8

Elwin:	"Why are we starting with Objective B instead of Objective A?"
Kisha:	"My guess is because it should be easier to come up with mini-experiments for B than for A since B is simple knowledge. For students to respond to prompts for simple-knowledge objectives, they should only have to remember content."
Elwin:	"Like for Objective B, to remember the attributes of a magnet. So our first chore is to come up with a list of magnet attributes."
Kisha:	"Let's assume we're in Ms. Ragusa's shoes and we want to test these students on how well they remember the attributes they came up with during Case 7.6's lesson for Objective A. That's all we have to go on to this point; we haven't read about her lesson for Objective B yet."
Elwin:	"Okay, let's find the statement about magnets that was articulated near the end of Case 7.6. Here it is:

'A magnet is a special piece of metal. It has a field of power around one end and a field of power around the other end. The two fields of power pull certain things to the magnet. The certain things are made of metal. The metal has to be like iron, steel, or nickel. But "nickels" don't work because they're really copper mostly. One end will pull and be pulled by one of the ends of another magnet. The other end will push away and be pushed away by that same end of the other magnet.'

"So the concept attributes we want to measure students' memory of are (1) metal substance, (2) field of power around each of its opposite ends, (3) the power fields attract objects made of certain metals, and (4) opposite poles of magnets attract one another, but like poles repel one another."

Kisha:	"They really didn't say your part 4."
Elwin:	"I know, but that's what they meant."
Kisha:	"So to observe how well students remember those things about a magnet, we could just ask them, 'What are four things special about all magnets?' That would be our prompt."
Elwin:	"And the rubric would be to see if the four things they list are consistent with the four attributes we listed. They wouldn't have to use the same words, but they should mean the same thing. How about a second mini-experiment for Objective B?"
Kisha:	"We could give them identical-looking pieces of metal, one that's been magnetized and one that's not. Then we could ask them to figure out which one is the magnet and see if they begin testing it for attributes."
Elwin:	"That's a great idea; I love it! But I think it goes beyond just Objective B. Isn't that requiring more than just remembering the attributes?"
Kisha:	"I think you're right. Do you think it's a mini-experiment for Objective A? The hard part of this exercise is to come up with two mini-experiments for Objective A."
Elwin:	"I don't know. Let's get one more for Objective B that we're sure of and then worry about Objective A. How about a multiple-choice prompt that asks students to pick out the magnet attributes from a list of characteristics?"

Kisha:	"We could have them pick the choice that makes a sentence true, like 'All magnets _____.' And give them a choice of possibilities, like 'have two fields of force' and 'are made of wood.'"
Elwin:	"That'll work; let's move on to Objective A.
Kisha:	"Objective A is for students to discriminate between examples and non-examples of magnets and discover attributes of magnets—construct-a-concept learning level."
Elwin:	"Now that I've thought about it more, I think your mini-experiment where you prompt students to figure out which of two pieces of metal is a magnet is relevant to Objective A."
Kisha:	"It's going to depend on whether the students have been previously exposed to a process for determining if something has been magnetized. By originating a test for magnetism, they'd surely be displaying they can discriminate between examples and non-examples of magnets."
Elwin:	"So with the stipulation that the students haven't been yet exposed to such a process, let's count that as our first mini-experiment for Objective A."
Kisha:	"I'm not completely convinced, but let's go on to the second one anyway."
Elwin:	"If they've constructed the concept of magnet and discovered the attributes for themselves, they'd be able to list them. But they might just be remembering them from class, so we can't just ask them to make a list as we did for Objective B."
Kisha:	"We could ask them to explain the attributes in their own words. That's beyond simple knowledge."
Elwin:	"Yes, but even if they expressed them in their own words, they might be just showing us that they comprehended someone else's explanation. That would be comprehension and communication skills."
Kisha:	"So let's focus on the first part of Objective A and give them the task of discriminating between examples and non-examples."
Elwin:	"But we've got to be careful to use examples that can't simply identify from previous exposure."
Kisha:	"Example noise! We have to play with example noise like that teacher with the first-grader where the concept was 'animals with the same number of legs.' It's Mr. Corbin in Case 7.4. Do you remember?"
Elwin:	"Yes, but go on—you're onto something."
Kisha:	"Kids think of magnets as shaped like horseshoes and bars and stuff. We should pick some non-examples that look like magnets and maybe include some unusual shapes for magnets."
Elwin:	"I see what you're driving at! That way we'd be seeing if the students discriminated based on attributes and if they can tease out the noise."
Kisha:	"Exactly."
Elwin:	"I just thought of an engaging way of confronting students with just such a prompt. You could play a game with teams. One team's job is to come up with descriptions of 'fake magnets' and 'strange magnets.' What do you think?"
Kisha:	"What's a fake magnet?"
Elwin:	"In our language, it's a non-example of a magnet that has characteristics that are example noise in many commonly seen of magnets."
Kisha:	"Like being horseshoe-shaped and so forth."
Elwin:	"Right. And a strange magnet would be something that didn't look like what kids expect magnets to look like but had all the attributes of a magnet."

Kisha:	"So you're going to have students come up with examples and non-examples them-selves to play this game in which other students have to discern the magnets from the non-magnets. The teams try to fool one another. Maybe one team would say, 'I've got this iron pipe that pulls certain things to it, but if you cut it in half the two ends that were cut would push one another away. Is my iron pipe a magnet?' And then maybe the other team would have to explain their answer. I like this idea."

Illustration 7.18 displays the two mini-experiments Kisha and Elwin designed to be relevant to Objective A.

PERFORMANCE-OBSERVATION MINI-EXPERIMENTS RELEVANT TO CONSTRUCT-A-CONCEPT OBJECTIVES

The format of Mini-Experiment #1 from Illustration 7.18 is *performance-observation*. A *performance-observation* format is also used for the second part of Illustration 7.18's Mini-Experiment #2 (i.e., the part in which the teacher observes *during* the game using the 3-part scale for Team B's responses). A *performance-observation mini-experiment* is one in which the teacher (or other designated observer) uses the rubric as students are responding to the prompt so that what the students do is the focus of the observation rather than the end product of the response.

By contrast, the first part of Mini-Experiment #2 from Illustration 7.18 does *not* use a performance-observation format because the teacher examines Team A's pictures and descriptions after they are produced. Students' methods for producing these products are not the focus of Part 1 of the rubric for that mini-experiment as they are for Part 2.

Performance observations are particularly valuable for providing information for formative judgments as students construct concepts. Ms. Fisher in Case 7.5 and Ms. Ragusa in Case 7.6 observed what students did to gauge their progress. However, as a tool for diagnosing how well students perform after learning has taken place (e.g., for purposes of making summative evaluations), performance observations are typically better suited for achievement of other learning levels besides construct a concept—particularly process knowledge, psychomotor-skill performance, comprehension and communication skills, willingness to try, and application.

ESSAY MINI-EXPERIMENTS RELEVANT TO CONSTRUCT-A-CONCEPT OBJECTIVES

Essays Prompting Students to Reflect on Concept Construction

A mini-experiment that prompts students to write a composition of at least one paragraph, but normally not more than several pages, has an *essay* format. In Case 7.9, Ms. Fisher develops an *essay* mini-experiment to prompt students to resurrect the process by which they constructed the concepts of de jure and de facto segregation.

CASE 7.9

Ms. Fisher is in the process of designing a mini-experiment to insert in her computer file for the following objective which was targeted by the lesson in Case 7.5:

B. Students will differentiate between examples and non-examples of de jure segregation as well as between examples and non-examples of de facto segregation (construct a concept).

She thinks to herself, "My observations of their activities and my discussions with them as they moved through the four stages of the lesson leave me with the impression that most of the students have

Mini-Experiment #1:

Prompt:

The prompt is administered to students one at a time. The student is given two identical-looking pieces of metal. One is magnetized; the other is not. The student is then asked to determine which one of the two is a magnet and which one is not.

Observer's Rubric:

The teacher observes what the student does with the two objects. The following is an example of a student's action that would be a positive indicator that the student has constructed the concept of a magnet:

The student asks for or locates a piece of magnetic material (e.g., the steel leg of a table) and one at a time brings each object near the magnetic material to see if the object and the magnetic material pull together. Then the student identifies the object that attracted the magnetic material as the magnet.

Other actions may be negative indicators of objective achievement (e.g., checking to see which object is heavier, bringing the two objects together to see if they attract each other, or bringing the objects near non-magnetic material (e.g., a wooden desk top)).

Mini-Experiment #2:

Prompt:

The class is divided into teams of four students each. Each team working independently and in secret from the other teams is directed to design three different fake magnets. The students are told that a fake magnet is not really a magnet but an object that their team will use to try to fool the other teams into thinking it's a magnet. For each fake magnet it designs, the students are to draw a picture and develop a written description of what it looks like.

Similarly, each team is directed to design, draw pictures, and write descriptions for three different strange magnets. The students are told that a strange magnet is a magnet that doesn't look the way most people think magnets look. The team is told to design the strange magnets so that they can use them to fool the other teams into thinking they aren't really magnets.

ILLUSTRATION 7.18

Two Mini-Experiments Kisha and Elwin Designed to Be Relevant to Objective A Listed in Illustration 7.10

(Continued)

ILLUSTRATION 7.18 *(Continued)*

The game is played between two teams, A and B, as follows:

1. Team A selects one of its six pictures and descriptions to show and read to Team B.

2. Team B is then allowed to ask up to five "yes" or "no" questions to Team A about the object it has designed. Team B may not ask any questions that are equivalent to the following: "Is the object a magnet?" "Does the object attract certain metals like steel, iron, and nickel to it?"

3. After the questions, Team B judges whether or not the object is a magnet.

4. Team B must explain why they think they are correct.

5. The game continues using Team A's other five picture-description combinations.

Observer's Rubric:

1. The teacher examines Team A's six picture-description combinations. For each, the teacher uses the following scoring scale with +2 indicating the criterion is clearly met, +1 that it is not clear whether or not the criterion is met, and +0 indicating that the criterion is clearly not met:

For each of the three fake magnets:

The object is not a magnet -------------------- 0 1 2

The object has characteristics that people tend to associate with magnets but aren't attributes of magnets (e.g., it is a bar-shaped piece of metal with "N" or "+" on one end and "S" or "-" on the other end ------ 0 1 2

For each of the three strange magnets:

The object is a magnet ---------------------- 0 1 2

The object has characteristics that people tend to disassociate with magnets (e.g., it is covered with paper or a plastic coating) -- 0 1 2

2. As the game is played the teacher listens to the questions Team B asks and the explanations given for their judgments as to whether or not objects are magnets. For each round of five questions and each explanation, the teacher uses the following scoring scale with +2 indicating that the criterion is clearly met, +1 that it is not clear whether or not the criterion is met, and +0 indicating that the criterion is clearly not met:

ILLUSTRATION 7.18 (Continued)

```
For each of the six rounds of questions asked:

The questions seem to be directed at determin-
ing if the object has magnet attributes   ------  0   1   2

For each of the six explanations:

The explanation was consistent with the decision
as to whether or not the object is a magnet  --  0   1   2

The explanation centers on whether or not
the object displays magnet attributes  --------  0   1   2
```

constructed a solid concept of de jure and de facto segregation. But I need a better basis for my summative evaluations relative to their individual achievement of Objective B. By now, they all have impressive responses to the two questions at the bottom of the second tasksheet." (See Illustration 7.7.) "From their cooperative group work and the subsequent class discussions, all of them could at least parrot seemingly insightful answers to those two questions. But I need to know how well they can explain why the odd-numbered items from that tasksheet are examples of de jure segregation and why the even-numbered items are examples of de facto segregation."

Six minutes later, Ms. Fisher inserts the prompt and rubric shown by Illustration 7.19 into her mini-experiment file for Objective B.

Time for Essays

Essay mini-experiments are typically time-consuming for students to respond to and for you to score. Consequently, it is rarely efficient to try to include more than one or two on a single measurement. Mr. Johnson planned for only one when he developed Illustration 6.6's blueprint. Of course, most essays don't need to be as long as the one required by Ms. Fisher's prompt in Illustration 7.19. Brief, focused essays in which students write only a paragraph or two (e.g., #1 from Illustration 6.2) can be usable and still provide opportunities for students to express descriptions, explanations, or reflections. Highly structured rubrics help you to cut down on the time needed to score essay responses.

You can also ease your burden of scoring essays by administering essay mini-experiments so that students use word processing when writing them. Look at Heiko's test paper in Illustration 2.29. Note how much easier it is to read his responses to "Part 1: Take Home" for which he used word processing than for Prompt 14 of the in-class part for which you must decipher his handwriting. If you don't have enough computers in your classroom for students to use them for essays, then you may at least be able to arrange to administer measurements in a writing lab or other computer facility. Of course, students should only use computers for mini-experiments if they are used to working on computers during your learning activities.

Essay Prompt:

Written directions to students:

A. Retrieve your copy of the second tasksheet you and your collaborators completed during our lesson on the differences between de jure and de facto segregation. It's the one with the odd-numbered examples of de jure segregation and the even-numbered examples of de facto segregation.

B. Read your answers to the two questions at the bottom of the tasksheet. If you are satisfied with your answers leave them alone. If you would like to change them, please write your new and improved answers in the area below before moving to C of these directions; otherwise move directly to C.

How are the items from the odd-numbered group alike but different from the items in the even-numbered group?

_____

_____

_____

_____

How are the items from the even-numbered group alike but different from the items in the odd-numbered group?

_____

_____

_____

_____

C. When you and your collaborators first worked with the tasksheet, we didn't use the words "de jure" and "de facto;" however, you still managed to see how the examples of de jure segregation were different from the examples of de facto segregation. Describe the history of how you learned the differences between de jure and de facto segregation from the time you first saw this tasksheet until right now. Include only descriptions of your own thinking and the events and experiences you had that stimulated those thoughts. Write this description in an essay about 1 page long. Use the labels (e.g., "A-1" and "A-6") from the tasksheet to refer to specific examples that influenced

ILLUSTRATION 7.19

Essay Mini-Experiment Ms. Fisher Inserts in Her Computer File for Objective B for U.S. History Unit 17

(Continued)

ILLUSTRATION 7.19 (Continued)

your thinking. Make sure to include descriptions of your thoughts so that I am convinced that you really do understand the differences between de jure and de facto segregation.

Rubric:

(Maximum points possible: 14) Ms. Fisher reads the essay focusing on the criteria listed in the following scoring scales (for each criterion +2 indicates the criterion is clearly met, +1 indicates that it is not clear whether or not the criterion is met, and +0 indicates that the criterion is clearly not met):

1. The essay is about 1 page long and it addresses the question posed by the prompt   ------ 0 1 2

2. A thought process is described that is suggestive of inductive reasoning with the student identifying attributes of de jure segregation ---- 0 1 2

3. A thought process is described that is suggestive of inductive reasoning with the student identifying attributes of de facto segregation -- 0 1 2

4. The description includes specific references to experiences, tasksheet examples, or other events that display concept construction -------- 0 1 2

5. The essay makes it apparent that at the very least the student comprehends the differences between de jure and de facto segregation -------- 0 1 2

6. Nothing is included in the essay that suggests the student holds a misconcept of de jure segregation ------------------------------------- 0 1 2

7. Nothing is included in the essay that suggests the student holds a misconcept of de facto segregation ------------------------------------- 0 1 2

Flexibility of Expression but Taxing Writing Skills

Essay prompts allow students considerable flexibility in how they express responses. Such flexibility, not available with multiple-choice and short-answer formats, is essential for measuring objectives that focus on students' abilities to structure and organize ideas. Unlike simple knowledge and process learning levels, structuring and organizing ideas is critical to concept construction.

The premium essay prompts place on students' writing skills is advantageous when writing ability is important to objective achievement as it would be for the following objective:

Students describe in writing a personal experience that evokes a feeling of frustration (comprehension and communication skills).

But for some objectives, students' level of writing skill may prevent them from demonstrating with an essay their achievement. Consider Case 7.10.

CASE 7.10

By the time Tyrone reached ninth grade, he had acquired a keen understanding and interest in history. Tyrone's ninth-grade history teacher, Ms. Dearborne, used tests with essay prompts almost exclusively. Although Tyrone achieved Ms. Dearborne's objectives at an advanced level, he never scored well on her achievement tests, which taxed his writing skills. Consequently, both Tyrone and Ms. Dearborne became convinced that he understood little about history. In time, he became discouraged and lost interest in the subject.

Daydream with me for a few minutes and imagine that Tyrone had a different ninth-grade teacher and that Case 7.11 supplants Case 7.10.

CASE 7.11

By the time Tyrone reached ninth grade, he had acquired a keen understanding and interest in history. Tyrone's ninth-grade history teacher, Ms. Bernstein, used tests with a variety of mini-experiment formats, including essay, oral discourse, multiple-choice, short-answer, interview, performance observation, and product examination. Although Tyrone achieved Ms. Bernstein's objectives at an advanced level, neither he nor Ms. Bernstein were certain about his achievement because his measurement results were inconsistent.

Ms. Bernstein's analysis of measurement results revealed that Tyrone's responses to prompts requiring him to write more than several words received low scores, whereas the scores for responses to other types of prompts were much higher. To check on her suspicion that Tyrone needed help with writing skills, Ms. Bernstein used an essay mini-experiment designed to be relevant to writing skills rather than history objectives. The results influenced Ms. Bernstein to recommend that Tyrone enroll in a program for improving writing skills.

In the meantime, Ms. Bernstein found ways of measuring Tyrone's achievement of history objectives that did not depend on sophisticated writing skills. As his writing skills improved, she gradually reintroduced Tyrone to history tests with essay prompts.

Tyrone's case is particularly pertinent to our concern for measuring achievement at the construct-a-concept learning level for two reasons: (1) As demonstrated by the infant Josh in Case 5.9 (concept of living thing) and by the lessons described in Cases 1.1 (concept of circle), 7.2 (concept of density), and 7.7 (concept of segregation), students' construction of concepts does not depend on their use of the conventional terminology associated with those concepts. (2) Concept construction is a vital prerequisite for subsequent learning that is meaningful for students.

Overcoming Common Weaknesses of the Essay Format

Gronlund (1982, p. 72) relates the following anecdote illustrating how differential writing skills among students can contaminate the relevance of essay mini-experiments so that, unlike Tyrone, some students who have failed to achieve the objective still score well:

> A college bureau selected a student with special skills and sent him into a midsemester examination in place of a regular student in order to determine how well he could do on an essay test without preparation. The main question called for critical evaluation of a novel that the student had not read. His answers started with something as follows: "This is not the best novel I have

ever read, but neither is it the worst. It has some real strengths, such as the detailed attention given in the development of main characters. On the other hand, some of the minor characters have not been developed as they might be. . . ." His evaluation continued along this vein. The paper was returned the next class meeting along with this comment by the professor: "This is the best evaluation of this novel I have ever read."

Older students have been exposed to so many poorly designed essay prompts and scoring procedures that those who are confident with their writing tend to think of essays as something to "fake my way through by impressing the teacher with how well I write." Students with less confidence in their writing cringe at the thought of an essay prompt.

Hundreds of studies point out that typically designed essay mini-experiments tend to have poor intra-observer and inter-observer consistency. Conclusions drawn from some of the classic studies include the following:

"The passing or failing of forty percent [of students] depends, not on what they know, but on *who* reads the papers. . . . the passing of about ten percent ... on *when* the papers are read." (Ashburn, 1938, pp. 1–3)

"a C paper may be graded B if it is read after an illiterate theme, but if it follows an A paper . . . it seems to be of D caliber." (Stalnaker, 1936, p. 41)

"Scorer unreliability tends to increase when one attempts to capitalize on the essay test's unique characteristics—flexibility and freedom of choice. This factor, no doubt, accounts for the great disparity in reader [scorer] reliability values reported in the literature; the disparity ranges from as low as .32 to as high as .98. It is not difficult to obtain high scorer reliability if essay questions are narrow and carefully structured." (Stanley & Hopkins, 1972, p. 199)

Unfortunately, there is little evidence that the quality of essay mini-experiments appearing on typically constructed tests has appreciably improved since these studies were conducted (Cangelosi, 1998).

Note that the essay prompts and rubrics displayed by Illustrations 3.7, 4.10 (#5 & #6), 6.2 (#1), and 6.4 are not typical of those appearing on most tests. For one thing, the prompts in these illustrations describe the tasks for students to perform in greater detail than do typical essays. In Case 4.10, Ms. Paez learned that the prompt "Discuss the passage of blood through the human heart" does not provide students with the focused directions provided by the following prompt:

"With the aid of a diagram, explain the mechanics of how venous blood, while in the heart, is transported through the human heart and to the lungs. Make sure you indicate the direction and locations of the venous blood while in the heart. Note how the action of the heart maintains the flow. Use between one and two pages for your entire response, including the diagram."

"Describe," "compare," "contrast," "explain," and "summarize" are just a few of the terms used in essay prompts that provide students with a better direction for the intended task than do terms like "discuss" and "tell about."

As discovered from your work with Chapter 4, detailed scoring rubrics are needed for intra-observer and inter-observer consistencies. Of course, essay mini-experiments with rubrics employing analytical scoring tend to have greater observer consistency than those employing global scoring.

As Ms. Paez discovered in Case 4.10, students need prompts that provide guidelines for how much to write. Phrases like "in the area provided below" and "from one to two pages" help define the task. They also help you control the length of the papers you will have to score.

Normally, when a person writes—at least outside of schools—he or she writes to a particular reader or for a specific audience. By designing essay prompts that direct students to write for a specific audience, you more clearly define the task for them. Ms. Fisher from Case 7.9, for example, might consider including the following prompt for a mini-experiment she inserts in her file for Objective B:

> Suppose a high school friend of yours who has not yet taken U.S. history says to you, "I hear people in Ms. Fisher's U.S. history class talking about de jure and de facto segregation. I know what segregation is, but what's this de jure and de facto stuff? Are they just fancy words that mean the same thing?" Develop an explanation to your friend to help her or him understand what de jure and de facto segregation are. In a paragraph, write your explanation.

The strategy helps the students determine the level at which they should write; after all, they know that you already understand what they are being asked to explain. So it is somewhat more realistic to have them write to someone who doesn't already understand rather than writing it directly to you. As you will see from your work with Chapter 9, this strategy is particularly useful when designing essay prompts for mini-experiments relevant to comprehension-and-communication-skills objectives.

ORAL-DISCOURSE MINI-EXPERIMENTS RELEVANT TO CONSTRUCT-A-CONCEPT OBJECTIVES

A mini-experiment that prompts students to give a talk or speech that is more complex than a simple recitation has an *oral-discourse* format. For some types of objectives (especially comprehension and communication skills), *oral-discourses* can serve different purposes than essays, but for construct-a-concept objectives, mini-experiments with oral-discourse formats are nearly equivalent to those with essay formats. Of course oral-discourse mini-experiments tax students' speaking skills in the way essays tax their writing skills.

The same principles for designing prompts and rubrics for essay mini-experiments apply to oral-discourse mini-experiments. At least three advantages are gained by having students record one another's oral-discourse presentations on videotape:

- You can apply the rubric when viewing the presentation on tape, thus allowing you to use the rubric at your own pace, rewinding and fast-forwarding the tape as needed, just as you reread some parts and skim through other parts of an essay.
- By having oral presentations recorded, students can present them concurrently without you having to view each one "live" while using the rubric.
- You and your students can use the recordings when going over the presentations after they have been scored. Students can view the tape to see and hear exactly why you scored the presentation as you did. Thus, the presentations better serve as formative feedback tools for students to monitor their own learning. Recall Case 2.15 in which Ms. Fisher led her students to use the results of mini-experiments as formative feedback for monitoring their own learning.

MULTIPLE-CHOICE MINI-EXPERIMENTS RELEVANT TO CONSTRUCT-A-CONCEPT OBJECTIVES
Prompting Students to Select the Example from the Alternatives

A mini-experiment that prompts students to select a response from a given list of alternatives has a *multiple-choice* format. A *multiple-choice* prompt is presented in two parts: (1) a *stem* that asks a question, gives a direction, or provides an incomplete statement, and (2) a number of *alternatives* from which students are to select the one that answers the question, follows the directions, or correctly completes the statement presented in the stem. The alternatives, except for the correct one, are referred to as *"distractors"* or *"foils."*

To be relevant to a construct-a-concept objective, multiple-choice prompts can be designed so students are directed to select the example of a concept from among a list of alternatives. In Case 7.12, Ms. Fisher develops such a mini-experiment.

CASE 7.12

Ms. Fisher is in the process of designing a mini-experiment to insert in her computer file for the following objective which was targeted by the lesson in Case 7.5:

> B. Students will differentiate between examples and non-examples of de jure segregation as well as between examples and non-examples of de facto segregation (construct a concept).

She thinks to herself, "I'll make this a multiple-choice prompt so that the stem directs them to pick out an example of de jure segregation from a list of alternatives. The distractors should be non-examples of de jure segregation; examples of de facto segregation and of non-segregation should work. That's what they worked with in the sorting-and-categorizing stage of the lesson."

She looks at the tasksheets used during the lesson (i.e., Illustration 7.6 and 7.7) and thinks, "I should come up with alternatives that are similar to these examples and non-examples on the tasksheets, but the situations need to be completely new to them. If I use any of these or any others they discussed in class, I'd just be tapping their memories rather than their conceptualization of de jure segregation. These descriptions are a bit long for multiple-choice alternatives, so I need to keep the number of alternatives down—well, no more than four anyway. So I need one example and as many as three non-examples. I think I'll try to keep the noise in the examples similar to characteristics in the non-examples so they won't have to sift through so much noise that this will become too time-consuming for them. After all, it's only one multiple-choice prompt among many on a test. Okay, so what should the general circumstance be that's common to all the alternatives? On the tasksheets, I used ones from states in the 1950s and ones involving schools and restaurants. What could I do differently here, something unlike examples we've discussed in class? The problem is that we really don't have de jure segregation in this country today and it would be too complex to get into the laws of existing countries today. I need to be a bit creative. I know! I'll come up with a hypothetical country—but what circumstances in that country should be the focus? Segregation occurs as a consequence of housing patterns, employment practices, differences in education, and—I've got to keep this simple. Okay, I'll use employment in my hypothetical country; I'll call it 'Country X.' Since students who only remember to associate government laws with de jure segregation but don't have a solid concept of de jure versus de facto segregation might go for a distractor where there's segregation and the government is in charge, I'll make the government the employer in my alternatives." Ms. Fisher then formulates her initial draft of a distractor that becomes "Alternative a" shown in Illustration 7.20.

"For the correct alternative," she thinks, "I better come up with an example that isn't going to stand out from the others. My students know I think of de jure segregation as something bad. So I need to couch this example of de jure segregation in something that has some good-sounding things in it. I could say something like the law was a result of a democratic process—they think I think democracy is good. But that won't work, because this is a country in which the government owns all the factories. I don't want them being distracted by questions like, 'Can a democracy also be socialistic?' That would end up penalizing students for thinking too deeply. I don't want to do that."

After spending more time than she normally does to create a multiple-choice mini-experiment, Ms. Fisher inserts the one shown in Illustration 7.20 into her computer file for Objective B. Although, the process took more time than a single multiple-choice prompt was worth, Ms. Fisher realizes that the experience taught her quite a bit about developing examples and non-examples, a lesson that will pay dividends the next time she designs both lessons and mini-experiments for construct-a-concept objectives.

Multiple-Choice Prompt:

Suppose there is a country in which all of its factories are government owned. Call the country "Country X." Which one of the following true statements about Country X describes a situation that is an example of de jure segregation?

a) Ten years ago when the agricultural machines factory in Country X first opened, it employed 12 workers eight of which were brown-skin people who had migrated from Country Y. Since then the factory has expanded and now has hundreds of employees. Over 80% of those employees are brown-skin people who have migrated from Country Y. This happened because as job openings occurred, employees at the factory contacted their relatives and friends living in Country Y and urged them to seek employment at the agricultural machines factory in Country X.

b) Due to their success, Country X's factories employ many migrants from other countries. Because many natives of Country X are concerned that their traditions and culture are in danger of being lost with increased migration, the government maintains a few neighborhoods in each of its two largest cities where only natives who follow Country X's traditions can live.

c) Cultural traditions of Country X's native population are such that most females are taught intricate weaving skills by their mothers. Among natives, weaving is considered "women's work." The textile factories in Country X employ workers primarily for their weaving skills. Over 97% of Country X's thousands of textile workers are female.

d) Country X's constitution contains a provision that all government-owned factories and other businesses will follow non-discriminatory hiring practices so that all people regardless of ethnicity or gender have equal opportunities for employment.

Observer's Rubric:

+1 for selecting "b" only; otherwise, +0.

ILLUSTRATION 7.20

Multiple-Choice Mini-Experiment Ms. Fisher Inserts in Her Computer File for Objective B for U.S. History Unit 17

The Role of Example Noise

In Case 7.12, Ms. Fisher designed Illustration 7.20's prompt so that the example noise in the correct response, "Alternative b," matched characteristics of distractors' non-examples. This made it easier for students to focus on the attributes of the concept. In Case 7.13, a teacher uses example noise to control the difficulty of mini-experiments.

CASE 7.13

Mr. Boudreaux is designing mini-experiments for the following objective:

> Students group examples of animals according to whether or not they are mammals (construct a concept).

He thinks, "If I give them the task of discriminating among familiar animals—like identifying the mammal from a group containing a cat, snake, frog, bird, and fish—they're likely to select the cat just because they remember cats are mammals and the others aren't. I need to see if they discriminate based on the attributes of mammals. I know! I'll create some hypothetical animals—ones with mammal attributes and some lacking mammal attributes. For easier mini-experiments, I'll make the examples clearly stand out from the non-examples—not many differences in example noise, that'll make the attributes stand out on the mammals. For harder ones, the distinctions won't be as obvious—more noise—sort of like a duckbill platypus."

As an easy mini-experiment, he develops the first one shown in Illustration 7.21; the second one in Illustration 7.21 is intended to be harder for students.

Mr. Boudreaux manipulated the noise in his examples and non-examples to vary the difficulty level of the mini-experiments. With fewer differences in characteristics (e.g., having or not having horns) to distract students, Mr. Boudreaux's students will find similarities and differences between the example and the non-examples easier to detect in the first of Illustration 7.21's mini-experiments than for second. To measure more advanced achievement levels of a construct-a-concept objective, prompts are used with examples with high levels of noise. Lower levels of achievement of construct-a-concept objectives are measured with prompts requiring students to discriminate among examples with little interference from noise.

Parallel Alternatives

Put yourself in the place of one of Ms. Fisher's students who is in the process of responding to Illustration 7.20's multiple-choice prompt. When you read Alternative a, what question do you ask yourself? Ms. Fisher designed the mini-experiment to prompt you to ask yourself, "Is this alternative an example of de jure segregation? In other words, is it an example in which people are segregated from one another as a matter of governmental law?"

When you read Alternative b from Illustration 7.20, what question do you ask yourself? Ms. Fisher intends for you to ask yourself, "Is this alternative an example of de jure segregation? In other words, is it an example in which people are segregated from one another as a matter of governmental law?"

Similarly, she designed the prompt so that you should ask yourself that same question when you get to Alternatives c and d as well. She designed the stem and alternatives so that the question remains the same for all the alternatives—a question that taps your conceptualization of de jure segregation.

Multiple-choice prompts should be designed so that the alternatives are all *parallel*. Two alternatives are *parallel* if they pose the same question to students—a question about a specific subject-content.

Less-Difficult Mini-Experiment

Multiple-Choice Prompt:

Circle the picture of the mammal:

Observer's Rubric:

+1 for circling the third one only; otherwise +0

More-Difficult Mini-Experiment

Multiple-Choice Prompt:

Circle the picture of the mammal:

Observer's Rubric:

+1 for circling the first one only; otherwise +0

ILLUSTRATION 7.21

Less-Difficult and More-Difficult Mini-Experiments Mr. Boudreaux Designed for a Construct-a-Concept Objective That Specifies Mammal as the Subject-Content

Examine the two multiple-choice prompts in Illustration 7.21. For each, are the alternatives all parallel? Mr. Boudreaux thinks that they are because he designed them so that each asks the same question, namely, "Does this animal display the attributes of a mammal? In other words, does this animal appear to belong to a class in which the members (1) have mammary glands, if female, that secrete milk to feed their young, (2) have hair or fur at some point in their lives, and (3) are warm-blooded?"

Contrast Illustrations 7.20's and 7.21's multiple-choice prompts with all parallel alternatives to those in Illustration 7.22.

A single multiple-choice mini-experiment should prompt students to address a single question relevant to a single objective. All of Prompt #1's alternatives from Illustration 7.22 are not parallel. Alternatives a and b are somewhat parallel because they both tap students' comprehension of civil rights acts. However, to judge Alternative a to be false, students must also apply their understanding of the relationship between de jure and de facto segregation; they would need to reason that ending de jure segregation does not end de facto segregation. Alternative c is the only alternative that prompts students to address the question, "What was the purpose of Malcolm X's movement in the early 1960s?" Thus, Alternative c is not parallel to any of the others. To judge Alternative d's statement to be true, students must ask themselves a question about the attributes of de jure segregation. If the other three alternatives were parallel to Alternative d, then Mini-Experiment #1 from Illustration 7.22 might be relevant to how well students had constructed the concept of de jure segregation. In its present form it is not.

Only Alternatives c and d of Illustration 7.22's Prompt #2 are parallel. They both prompt students to address the question, "In the taxonomy of living things, within what category does 'mammal' fall?" The other three alternatives are all over the place. Alternative a deals with students' knowledge of the relative size of the mammal population. Alternative b touches on their construction of the concept mammal, whereas Alternative e involves them in a question about history based on fossil evidence.

The alternatives for Prompt #3 of Illustration 7.22 are all parallel because each raises the question, "In the taxonomy of living things, within what category does 'mammal' fall?"

Regarding Prompt #4 from Illustration 7.21, at least all of the alternatives deal in some way with de jure segregation. To judge Alternative a to be false, students need to know that de jure segregation of schools is not possible in the United States today. This taps their understanding of current civil rights laws as well as their conceptualization of de jure segregation. To judge Alternative b to be false, students need to understand that de jure and de facto segregation are not mutually exclusive, so this alternative does involve their conceptualization of de jure segregation as does Alternative a. To judge Alternative c to be true, students need to recognize that the ordinance leads to an example of de jure segregation. To judge Alternative d to be false, students need to recall that de jure segregation in the military ended with President Truman's executive order of 1948. If they recall this fact, then Alternative d requires them to apply their understanding of de jure segregation. Thus, Alternatives a, b, c, and d are at least reasonably parallel. However, the parallelism could be improved by modifying a and d so that they do not depend on students' recall of historical events.

Number of Alternatives, Guessing, and Number of Prompts

How many alternatives should you include in a multiple-choice prompt? Keep in mind that the more alternatives you include, the less likely it is for students to select the correct response simply by guessing. On the other hand, the fewer the number of alternatives, the more usable the mini-experiment. Also keep in mind that multiple-choice mini-experiments provide a means to prompt students to use reasoning to compare various alternatives. This makes the format especially valuable for construct-a-concept objectives. However, unless the alternatives are extremely short to read and simple to think about (e.g., for Prompt #3 in Illustration 7.22), it is unreasonable to expect students to compare more than four or five alternatives. For complex alternatives such as Ms. Fisher included in Illustration 7.20, four may actually be too many for most students.

At least two alternatives are required for a prompt to be multiple-choice; more than two are generally needed to reduce the impact of random guessing. Four or five alternatives are often optimal.

#1

<u>Multiple-Choice Prompt</u>:

Which one of the following statements is true?

a) The Civil Rights Act of 1964 ended segregation of blacks from whites in the United States.

b) The Civil Rights Act of 1968 made it illegal to prevent citizens of the United States from voting because of the color of their skin.

c) In the 1960s, Malcolm X led a movement to end segregation of blacks from whites in the United States.

d) If a city enforces an ordinance restricting where non-native citizens can live, then de jure segregation exists in that city.

<u>Observer's Rubric</u>:

+1 for d; otherwise +0.

#2

<u>Multiple-Choice Prompt</u>:

Which one of the following statements is true?

a) Mammals are the most common form of animals living on earth today.

b) A bird is not a mammal because it is coldblooded.

c) "Mammal" refers to a *class* of life forms.

d) "Mammal" refers to a *kingdom* of life forms.

e) Fossil evidence suggests that mammals first appeared on earth about 400 million years ago.

<u>Observer's Rubric</u>:

+1 for c; otherwise +0.

ILLUSTRATION 7.22

Which of These Prompts Have All Parallel Alternatives?

(Continued)

ILLUSTRATION 7.22 (Continued)

#3

Multiple-Choice Prompt:

The category "mammal" is an example of a _____ of life forms:

    a) species

    b) genus

    c) family

    d) order

    e) class

    f) phylum

    g) kingdom

Observer's Rubric:

+1 for e; otherwise +0.

#4

Multiple-Choice Prompt:

Which one of the following statements is true?

    a) Today, de jure segregation keeps black and white people from attending the same schools in some of the larger southern cities of the United States.

    b) De jure segregation of blacks from whites and de facto segregation of blacks from whites cannot both exist in the same community at the same time.

    c) If a city enforces an ordinance restricting where non-native citizens can live, then de jure segregation exists in that city.

    d) De jure segregation in the military existed until Congress passed the Civil Rights Act of 1964.

Observer's Rubric:

+1 for c; otherwise +0.

By using nothing more than random guess, a student has one chance in four of selecting the correct response to a multiple-choice prompt with four alternatives. It is not unlikely for students to guess the correct alternative to one prompt and guess an incorrect alternative to another although both prompts are relevant to the same objective. Thus, guessing tends to contaminate the internal consistency of measurement results.

To combat this threat to measurement reliability, some commercial test publishers and some teachers are inclined to use a *correction-for-guessing* technique. When such a technique is employed, students are directed to select only alternatives to multiple-choice prompts that they are reasonably certain to be correct. If they are unsure about which alternative to select, they are directed either not to select any of the alternatives or to select an alternative with wording equivalent to "I don't know." Measurement scores are then computed using one of several correction-for-guessing formulas. One popular formula is the following:

$S = C - (W \div (A - 1))$ where S is the score received for the measurement, C is the number of prompts to which the student responded correctly, W is the number of prompts to which the student responded incorrectly (not including those not answered or for which an "I don't know" alternative was selected), and A is the number of alternatives per prompt.

Obviously, this formula applies only when the entire measurement includes only multiple-choice mini-experiments with the same number of alternatives.

The issue as to whether or not correction-for-guessing techniques should be employed was quite a controversial issue at one time (Nunnally, 1978, pp. 641–658). Since the early 1980s, measurement specialists tend to agree that it is a mistake to use correction-for-guessing techniques (Cangelosi, 1982, pp. 130–131). The practice, while discouraging some students from guessing, contaminates measurement relevance. When students are warned against guessing, students are forced to make decisions for each prompt that is not related to their achievement of the objective. They must decide whether or not to record their responses to the prompt. Consequently, measurement results are influenced by students' propensities to take chances. Students expend time and energy on a behavior that is not relevant to objective achievement. Furthermore, students should be encouraged to compare alternatives using their progress toward the objectives to eliminate some alternatives even if they are unable to eliminate all but one.

The way to control for the influence of guessing on measurement reliability is by increasing the number of prompts in the multiple-choice section of a measurement. Generally speaking, by having at least 15 such prompts with at least four alternatives each, the influence of guessing becomes predictable and tends to influence all students' results equally.

Additional suggestions for designing multiple-choice mini-experiments are included in subsequent chapters that deal with designing prompts and rubrics relevant to objectives specifying learning levels other than construct-a-concept.

INTERVIEW MINI-EXPERIMENTS RELEVANT TO CONSTRUCT-A-CONCEPT OBJECTIVES

A mini-experiment has an *interview format* if a teacher (or other interviewer) engages a student one-to-one in a process that includes the following features:

1. A sequence of questions or directives are orally presented to the student (sometimes complemented by visual prompts).
2. The student orally responds to each question or directive as it is presented, usually with the opportunity to elaborate.
3. Subsequent questions or directives may be influenced by responses the student makes to prior questions or directives.
4. The rubric is such that the interviewer takes notes or marks a scorer's form as the student completes each response either during the interview itself or while the interviewer listens to or views a taped recording of the interview.

Interviews are similar to performance observations in that the interviewer or observer uses a rubric as students make responses; however, unlike performance observations, interviews provide opportunities for the interviewer to prompt students to elaborate or modify subsequent parts of the prompt in light of students' responses to prior parts of the prompt.

In Case 7.4, Mr. Corbin displays examples and non-examples of animals with the same number of legs to his first-graders one at a time. Had he simply asked each student which two animals are alike and recorded the response, he would have been conducting a mini-experiment with a multiple-choice format. But note that in Case 7.4 he conducted the mini-experiment so that he probed students' responses with prompts for them to clarify their choices (e.g., asking Maggie, "Why?") and then allowed students' responses to one prompt to influence his choice of subsequent prompts (e.g., he chose to show Maggie Illustration 7.3 instead of Illustration 7.4). Thus, he conducted a mini-experiment with an interview format.

PRODUCT-EXAMINATION MINI-EXPERIMENTS RELEVANT TO CONSTRUCT-A-CONCEPT OBJECTIVES

A *product-examination* mini-experiment prompts students to complete a production task; the rubric is a scheme for either judging the quality of what the students produce or detecting features of the product. The first part of Mini-Experiment #2 from Illustration 7.18 uses a *product-examination* format; note that the teacher uses the four scales of the rubric to detect features of what Team A produced.

Illustration 7.23 displays a product-examination mini-experiment that Mr. Boudreaux might include in his computer file for the construct-a-concept objective on mammals that is listed in Case 7.13.

Although, as Illustrations 7.18 and 7.23 indicate, product-examination mini-experiments can be designed to be relevant to construct-a-concept objectives, the product-examination format is typically better suited for students' achievement of process knowledge, psychomotor-skill performance, or application objectives.

HOW STUDENTS DISCOVER RELATIONSHIPS

DISCOVERING RELATIONSHIPS FOR ONESELF

To be able to design mini-experiments relevant to your students' progress with respect to discover-a-relationship objectives, you need to be familiar with how students discover relationships. From Chapter 5, reread the section "Discoverable Relationships" on pages 226–228 and the section "Discover a Relationship" on page 237.

As with constructing concepts, students need to reason inductively to discover relationships. People use inductive reasoning to perceive a general relationship from their encounters with specific events in Cases 7.14, 7.15, and 7.16.

CASE 7.14

Six-year-old Roe is playing with his four-year-old sister, Anna, in the dry dirt near the side of their apartment. Gleefully, they form dust mounds but fail to sculpture the piles into the fortress-like figures they imagine them to be. Roe drinks from a nearby garden hose, leaving a puddle of dark moist dirt that catches Anna's attention. After making a few mud balls followed by a more ambitious structure, she tells Roe, "Look what I made! Let's play over here." "Awesome!" Roe says, and the two soon exhaust the tiny mud puddle. Anna: "The dirt was better here, but it's all gone." Roe: "Let's make some more over where we were before." Roe uses the hose to wet the original dust pile. Reasoning, "if a little water makes good

<u>Product-Examination Prompt</u>:

The teacher directs the student to design a mammal — one that is unlike any actual existing animal about which people know. The student is instructed to either draw a picture of the mammal or make a statue of it (e.g., using modeling clay) and to write a detailed description of it. The description should include information about how the creature behaves. The creature should unmistakably be a mammal, but it should be as much unlike any known mammal as it can be.

<u>Observer's Rubric</u>:

(Maximum points possible: 14) The teacher examines the drawing or statue and reads the description focusing on the criteria listed in the following scoring scales (for each criterion +2 indicates the criterion is clearly met, +1 indicates that it is not clear whether or not the criterion is met, and +0 indicates that the criterion is clearly not met):

1. The description and image include evidence
   of mothers nursing babies ------------------------- 0 1 2

2. The description and image include evidence
   that the animal is warm blooded --------------------- 0 1 2

3. The description and image include evidence
   that the creature has hair or fur -------------------- 0 1 2

4. The description and image include evidence
   the creature is an animal with a backbone ------------ 0 1 2

5. Nothing is included that suggests that the
   creature is not a mammal --------------------------- 0 1 2

6. The creature possesses characteristics that are
   at least somewhat unusual for a mammal -------------- 0 1 2

7. The creature possesses characteristics that are
   highly unusual for a mammal ------------------------ 0 1 2

ILLUSTRATION 7.23

Product-Examination Mini-Experiment Designed to Be Relevant to Students' Construction of the Concept of Mammal

dirt, a lot of water will make great dirt," Roe floods the play area. Following several frustrating minutes when they try to form fortresses with dirty water, the water recedes and they're left with an ideal ratio of water to dirt for mud sculptures. Later they discover the need to periodically squirt the dirt with just the right amount of water to keep the mud "just right."

The next day, Roe explains how to make "really good" mud to some classmates as they play in the schoolyard.

CASE 7.15

After completing a homework assignment in which she used a magnet to try to pick up objects consisting of various materials such as iron, wood, aluminum, copper, steel, plastic, and cloth, Desiree thinks: "A magnet will always pick up small-enough iron and steel objects but not most other kinds of stuff."

CASE 7.16

Several years ago, when his father took him to a hospital emergency room to have a cut treated, Eric noted that the man who stitched the cut was referred to as "Doctor" and the woman who also tended to his wound was called "Nurse." From various office visits, he remembers female nurses giving him shots and taking his temperature while men called "doctors" visited with him for shorter periods of time. Now that he's in kindergarten, he hears his teacher say, "Sometimes when we get sick, we need a doctor to help us get well. *He* needs a nurse to help *him*; *she*'ll be the one to . . ." Eric thinks to himself, "A man who works with sick and hurt people is a doctor. A woman who does that is a nurse."

In Case 7.14, Roe and Anna discovered a relationship between dirt and water that they can use to their advantage. In Case 7.15, Desiree formulated a hypothesis from her experiences with a magnet, thus inducting a relationship. As illustrated by Eric in Case 7.16, sometimes inductive reasoning can lead to a generalization that can be disproved with a counter-example (e.g., an encounter with a male nurse or female physician). But disproving the conclusion does not discredit the reasoning.

The importance of leading students to discover relationships for themselves (i.e., to conduct lessons for discover-a-relationship objectives) can hardly be overemphasized. Consider the following three objectives:

a. Students explain why heating one area of the human body tends to increase circulation to that body part, whereas cooling that area tends to decrease circulation to that part (discover a relationship).
b. Students state the following rule relative to treatment of sprains in human joints: Cold packs should be applied to the sprained area during the first 48 hours following the trauma; heat should be applied after the initial 48 hours (simple knowledge).
c. Based on a description of how a joint was injured and the observable symptoms, prescribe an appropriate course of action for treating the injury (application).

By first achieving Objective A (i.e., discovering for themselves the relationship underlying the rule of Objective B), students will understand the information they're storing during a lesson for Objective B. Because they will then be learning content that they themselves discovered, Objective B's rule will be meaningful and retained in their memories (Ellis & Hunt, 1983; Gagné, 1985). Furthermore, they can hardly achieve Objective C (i.e., use the subject-content to solve real-life problems they've never before confronted) without having first achieved Objective A (Driver, 1995; Smith & Sims, 1992).

Lessons for discover-a-relationship objectives include inductive learning activities organized in four stages: (1) experimenting, (2) reflecting and explaining, (3) hypothesizing and articulation, and (4) verifying and refining.

EXPERIMENTING

In the experimenting stage, students conduct some sort of experiment to provide the facts, specifics, data, or examples they need to induct a generalization or make a hypothesis in the third stage of the lesson. Whereas in Case 7.14 Anna and Roe conducted an experiment some-what by accident, in the experimenting stage of a discover-a-relationship lesson, you orchestrate and manage activities that lead them to experiment.

In Case 2.4, Ms. Fisher planned a lesson to lead her U.S. history students to discover how segregation affects the lives of people (i.e., Objective A from Illustration 2.9). Review her over-all plan for that lesson; it is listed as "1" in Illustration 2.14. She conducted the experimenting stage of that lesson during the time students were wearing green or blue armbands and experiencing life in the simulated segregated society.

Case 2.10, in which Mr. Heaps's students recorded data from the movement of a "car" on a lined overhead transparency, is another example of the experimenting stage of a discover-a-relationship lesson.

REFLECTING AND EXPLAINING

In the reflecting and explaining stage, students analyze the results of the experiments. The teacher raises leading questions, stimulates thought, and clarifies students' inferences. In Case 2.10, Mr. Heaps made the transition from the experimenting stage to the reflecting-and-explaining stage by having students read their responses from Illustration 2.22's tasksheet. This led to a discussion in which students explained and compared the results of the different trials with the "car."

HYPOTHESIZING AND ARTICULATING

During the third stage, students articulate generalizations about possible relationships. Inferences are examined and a relationship hypothesized. The hypothesized relationship is articulated in a general statement. Students in Ms. Fisher's U.S. history class may have concluded that "Segregation negatively affects the lives of the 'favored' group as well as the 'discriminated-against' group." In Mr. Heaps's class, students may have agreed on the following statement: "The speed of an object can be told by taking how far it moves and dividing that by how long it took."

VERIFYING AND REFINING

In Stage 4, the students attempt to verify or disprove their statement about the relationship. The level of verification may range from "seems intuitively clear," to a failure to produce a case in which the generalization doesn't appear to be true (i.e., a counterexample), to a formal proof such as might be the case in a mathematics lesson. If weaknesses are found in the statement of the relationship, then the statement is modified until students agree to an acceptable proposition about the relationship.

INDICATORS OF PROGRESS AS STUDENTS ENGAGE IN DISCOVER-A-RELATIONSHIP LESSONS

In Case 7.6, Ms. Ragusa conducted a construct-a-concept lesson for Objective A listed in Illustration 7.10. Her discover-a-relationship lesson plan for Illustration 7.10's Objective C is shown by Illustration 7.24.

In Case 7.17, Ms. Ragusa designs mini-experiments for monitoring students' progress when they engage in the planned lesson, as shown by Illustration 7.24.

CASE 7.17

As Ms. Ragusa goes through her lesson plan shown by Illustration 7.24, she thinks, "To keep track of their progress as they move through these stages, I need to have some prompts and rubrics in my mind to use as needed. Okay, during the experimenting stage, I should monitor how well they're following directions and then . . ."

NOTE #1: During the experimenting stage, the class will be organized in cooperative groups as follows:

Group I	Group II	Group III
Student - Role*	Student - Role*	Student - Role*
Juan L. - mgr/org	Haeja - mgr/org	Adam - mgr/org
Chen - material sup	Eiko - material sup	Brenda - material sup
Pauline - comm	Willard - comm	Sun-li - comm
James - timer/rec	Cynthia - timer/rec	Bryce - timer/rec
Monica - reporter	Eldon - reporter	Greg - reporter

Group IV	Group V
Student - Role*	Student - Role*
Edgardo - mgr/org	Suzanne - mgr/org & material sup
Juan T. - material sup	Salinda - comm
Paige - comm	Brookelle - timer/rec
Kimberleigh - timer/rec	Wanda - reporter
Ellen - reporter	

* - Roles are defined as Illustration 7.11

NOTE #2: Each cooperative group will need the following materials for the experimenting stage: (a) a strong magnet, (b) an iron nail, (c) a container of iron filings, (d) several small straight pins, and (e) a stopwatch.

NOTE #3: Each group's recorder/timer will use a copy of the following tasksheet during the experimenting stage of the lesson:

Recorder/Timer's Tasksheet

Object	pick up filings?	# pins held	# sec. held	comments
iron nail (15 strokes)				
iron nail (30 strokes)				
iron nail (60 strokes)				
wooden stick (15 strokes)				
wooden stick (30 strokes)				

ILLUSTRATION 7.24

Ms. Ragusa's Lesson Plan for Objective C of Illustration 7.10

(Continued)

ILLUSTRATION 7.24 (Continued)

wooden stick (60 strokes)			
steel bar (15 strokes)			
steel bar (30 strokes)			
steel bar (60 strokes)			

Inferences:

_____

NOTE #4: This is the homework tasksheet in Stage 4 of the lesson:

Homework Tasksheet

DIRECTIONS: Choose three objects you think can be magnetized with the magnet Ms. Ragusa lent you. Attempt to magnetize each object and then test its power. Record your results below.

Object	# of strokes	Magnet-ized?	If so, how strong was it? How do know? What are the facts?

Refined (if at all) Hypothesis:

_____

The Four-Stage Lesson Plan

1. Experimenting: I'll direct students in groups to perform an experiment by going through the following procedures:

   A. Begin stroking the nail from one end to the other with one end of the magnet. Continue for 15 strokes, making sure to stroke in one direction only always with the same pole of the magnet. Make sure to lift the magnet

ILLUSTRATION 7.24 (Continued)

clear of the nail after each stroke. Now test if the nail has been temporarily magnetized by seeing if it will pick up some iron filings.

B. If it does, quickly test its power by seeing how many straight pins it can pick up before losing its magnetism. Don't take the time to clean off the filings before doing this. Use the stopwatch to find out how many seconds pass before all of the pins fall off.

C. Repeat the experiment, but this time use 30 strokes.

D. Repeat the experiment but this time use 60 strokes. Discuss how the number of strokes appears to influence the strength and durability of the magnetic power of the nail.

E. Repeat the procedures for A, B, C, and D, but this time with a wooden stick. Discuss what happens.

F. Repeat the procedures for A, B, C, and D, but this time with the steel bar. Discuss whether or not the steel bar was more difficult to magnetize than the iron nail. Discuss whether or not it holds its magnetism longer than the iron nail.

Inferences from the facts recorded on the tasksheet are to be made and reported.

To engage the students in the experiment, I'll first organize the class into the five cooperative groups with each group's manager & organizer designating the roles that I've indicated to her/him and getting the materials distributed. In the meantime, I'll take the five communicators aside to explain how to do the experiment. It should take the manager & organizers five minutes to get their groups set up while I'm with the communicators.

The communicators explain the directions to the groups and the groups complete the experiment, recording their results on the tasksheets. I'll allow 25 minutes.

2. <u>Reflecting and Explaining</u>: Each cooperative group will have already begun this stage as they complete the bottom of the tasksheet, but we'll continue to make inferences in a large-group session in light of all the groups' results.

To begin the session, I'll reorganize the class for a large-group session. Each group's reporter will then report the facts from the experiment. After the facts have been reported, I'll conduct a large-group discussion and ask leading questions to clarify inferences to which the class can agree.

ILLUSTRATION 7.24 (Continued)

3. <u>Hypothesizing</u>: Continuing with the large-group discussion session, I'll stimulate inductive reasoning by my questions, leading students to form a hypothesis from the agreed-to inferences.

4. <u>Verifying and Refining</u>: I'll then distribute and assign the homework tasksheet to be completed for the following day. As they leave for the day, I'll give each student a magnet with which to work.

   The following day, we'll return to the same five cooperative groups with each member of each group reporting findings from the homework tasksheet.

   Based on the individual reports from the homework, each cooperative group either proposes modifications to the class's original hypothesis or agrees to maintain the original wording.

   I then reorganize the class into a large-group session to hear group reports and engage in a discussion leading to a refined version of our hypothesis.

   Before concluding this lesson, I need to make it clear that as we use our agreed-to hypothesis we may want to continue to refine it, updating it in light of new discoveries we might make.

She develops the mini-experiments displayed by Illustration 7.25. However, she doesn't write them out or put them in her computer file as she would for mini-experiments she includes on a more formal measurement. She only jots down some notes on her lesson plan so that she doesn't forget her ideas for conducting these mini-experiments while students are engaged in the lesson.

INDICATORS OF STUDENTS' ACHIEVEMENT OF DISCOVER-A-RELATIONSHIP OBJECTIVES

MINI-EXPERIMENTS RELEVANT TO DISCOVER-A-RELATIONSHIP OBJECTIVES

Measuring students' achievement of a discover-a-relationship objective after they've experienced a four-stage lesson for that objective is a challenging responsibility. Ms. Ragusa's students, for example, will have thoroughly discussed statements of the relationship indicated by Objective C from Illustration 7.10 by the end of the lesson outlined in Illustration 7.24. Thus, even those who didn't really discover the relationship for themselves may have had enough exposure to what their classmates discovered to correctly respond to prompts such as the following:

Explain how a magnet can cause certain objects, like an iron nail, to also be a magnet.

<u>During Stage 1 of the Lesson</u>

<u>Prompt and Rubric</u>:

The five groups are directed to engage in the activities as described in the experimenting stage of the lesson plan. While keeping an eye on all five groups, I will move about the room from group to group watching each to see if the procedures are being followed as listed A-F in the lesson plan.

As they begin the experiment, I need to be especially attentive that they actually do begin stroking the nail from one end to the other with one end of the magnet about 15 times making sure they lift the magnet clear after each stroke. If I see them dragging the magnet back and forth on the nail as students have done when I tried this in the past, I'll immediately step in and remind them of the correct procedure.

I also need to see if they test the nail and other objects after stroking them quickly before the magnetic power of the object significantly diminishes.

I'll check each recorder/timer's tasksheet to see if the data and comments are consistent with the relationship I expect them to discover. If not, I will probe the group with questions or directives such as, "Show me what you did to get 6 pins for the iron nail." or "Why did you write that the steel bar is stronger than the nail? Stronger in what way?" I'll use their responses as an indicator as to whether or not unexpected results reflect (1) a failure to follow procedures, (2) simply that what they wrote down doesn't really communicate what they mean, or (3) a chance aberration. In the case of a failure to follow procedures, I'll direct them to repeat the trial using the correct procedures. In the case of a miscommunication, I'll not intervene at this point and wait for Stage 2's large-group discussion when they should clarify their meanings. Neither will I intervene in the case of a chance aberration; deviant data may help stimulate some helpful insights into scientific experimentation when we compare results from all five groups during Stage 2.

<u>During Stage 2 of the Lesson</u>

<u>Prompt and Rubric</u>:

As each group presents its facts, I'll look for expressions indicating surprise or concurrence and respond to students making such expressions with questions such as, "Are you sur-

ILLUSTRATION 7.25

Mini-Experiments Ms. Ragusa Decides to Use While She Implements Illustration 7.24's Plan

(Continued)

ILLUSTRATION 7.25 (Continued)

prised by their findings? Why? How are they different from what you expected?" I'll judge their responses for indications that they are formulating relationships among the type of material, the number of strokes, the number of pins picked up, and the number of seconds the object held at least one pin. As I detect in indications that they are making such associations, I'll probe with questions such as, "Why do you suppose it took longer for the steel bar to become a magnet than it did for the iron nail?" or "Why do you think the steel bar held the pins for a longer time?"

As their responses suggest to me that they are beginning to formulate hypotheses that will move us toward the target relationships, I'll make the transition into Stage 3.

<u>During Stage 3 of the Lesson</u>

<u>Prompt and Rubric</u>:

I continue to prompt them to formulate statements that describe their findings with directives such as, "Sun-li, repeat what you just said one more time for the class. ... Thank you. Now, once again, let's hear what Brookelle said. ... Thank you. Now, everybody take 45 seconds to silently think about what Sun-li and Brookelle just said to form a hypothesis about why the iron nails were sometimes strong magnets and sometimes weak magnets. ... Forty-five seconds are up. Raise your hand if you're ready to write out your hypothesis. ... Okay, whether you're ready or not, it's time to write them out. You've got another 45 seconds to write them down on your paper while I hurry around the room reading what you write."

At this point, I need to select statements that will contribute to hypotheses for the class to examine. Statements with elements to help us build a hypothesis such as the following are indicative of progress toward the objective:

An old magnet can be used to turn objects made of certain materials (like iron or steel, but not wood) into new magnets. The power of the new magnet doesn't last very long. It lasts longer if you stroke it with the old magnet a lot rather than just a few times. Also, it's easier to make some objects a magnet than it is others. The object that is harder to make into a magnet might become a more powerful magnet than the one that is easier to make into a magnet.

I'll have students display their statements on the board arranged by which aspect of the above hypothesis is emphasized. As we discuss and compare the statements, I'll listen for indications that students are making conclusions that are consistent with the targeted relationships.

ILLUSTRATION 7.25 (Continued)

<u>During Stage 4 of the Lesson</u>

<u>Prompt and Rubric</u>:

As I check the homework tasksheets, I'll read their refined hypotheses. For each, I'll check for which of the following relationships (in their own words, of course) they have incorporated in their statements:

A. Old magnets can be used to create new magnets.

B. All objects can't become magnets; they have to be made of certain materials.

C. Objects made of some materials are easier to make into magnets than others.

D. Objects that are easy to make into magnets do not make as strong and long-lasting magnets as objects that are hard to make into magnets.

E. The more strokes you use to make a magnet, the stronger the magnet you make.

F. The more strokes you use to make a magnet, the longer the magnet lasts.

To help me determine how to direct the rest of the lesson, I'll informally tally which of the six relationships (A–F) are frequently incorporated in their statements, which are infrequently touched on, and which are neglected.

During both the small-group and large-group discussions of the verifying and refining stage, I'll observe which of these six relationships are emphasized in the hypotheses they ultimately formulate.

A student could describe the process for making a magnet from a magnet simply by remembering what happened in class just as one might recall the definition of the name of a concept without having ever constructed the concept. Thus, it is especially important to use informal "inside your head" mini-experiments such as those in Illustration 7.25 to monitor student achievement during lessons for discover-a-relationship objectives. Watch them engaging in experiments, listen to the inferences they make, and continually ask them probing questions (e.g., "Is the magnetic pull of the nail still as powerful as it was before? Why not? What do you think might have happened to change it?").

For measurements to be used for summative evaluations, one strategy for getting an indication of discover-a-relationship level learning after a lesson is to confront students with prompts requiring them to describe their experiences leading them to discover the relationship. An example of a mini-experiment with such a prompt is shown in Illustration 7.26.

Design two mini-experiments that are relevant to a discover-a-relationship objective that specifies a subject-content within your own teaching specialty area. When you engaged in

Essay Prompt:

You know that a magnet can be used to make other magnets. Write one paragraph telling me about things you did and observed that make you know that magnets can be used to make other magnets.

Rubric:

(Maximum possible points: 6) The teacher reads the paragraph using the following scoring scale with +2 indicating the criterion is clearly met, +1 that it is not clear whether or not the criterion is met, and +0 indicating that the criterion is clearly not met:

Nothing is included in the paragraph to suggest that the student does not understand how a magnet can be used to create a new magnet   ------------------------ 0 1 2

The paragraph relates experiences that would plausibly lead one to use inductive reasoning to discover at least part of the relationship specified by Objective C: i.e., A magnet can be used to make temporary magnets out of objects made of magnetic materials (e.g., iron and steel) and that some materials (e.g., soft iron) are easier to magnetize than others (e.g., steel), but the more difficult-to-magnetize materials retain their magnetism longer than the easier-to-magnetize materials. ---------------------- 0 1 2

The paragraph relates experiences that are described specifically enough that they can easily be traced back to discovery of the relationship specified by Objective C --- 0 1 2

ILLUSTRATION 7.26

Mini-Experiment Designed to Be Relevant to Objective C from Illustration 7.10

Synthesis Activity 3 for Chapter 5, you formulated a set of objectives. If at least one of those objectives is at the discover-a-relationship learning level, you may want to design the mini-experiments to be relevant to it. Exchange your mini-experiments with those of a colleague who also engaged in this exercise. Critique and discuss one another's work.

In Case 7.18, Kisha and Elwin discuss their work from the exercise in which you and your colleague just engaged.

CASE 7.18

Elwin: "The objective I chose was for my elementary school students to discover Newton's Second Law of Motion."

Kisha: "You'll have to remind this math teacher what Newton's Second Law of Motion is."

Elwin: "It states that an object's acceleration depends on the mass of the object and the size and direction of the force acting on it."

Kisha: "Okay, so it is a discoverable relationship."

Elwin: "I tried to get at their understanding of the dependence of a body's acceleration on its mass and on the magnitude and direction of the force acting on it without using the technical terms that would be introduced in the lesson. People can discover how the strength and direction of a force on a body can propel it, stop it, or whatever without ever using words like 'magnitude,' or 'acceleration' or even having heard about Isaac Newton. I think many children discover Newton's Second Law of Motion from their experiences striking objects, throwing balls, and being hit—accidentally I hope. We learn to swing harder to hit a ball farther or to fear being struck by someone big more than by someone small. So here's what I came up with."

Elwin shows Kisha Illustration 7.27.

Kisha: "This really gets at how well the student can explain the relationship, not just parrot back what someone told him or her."

Elwin: "My biggest concern is with its usability. How practical is it for a teacher to have to interview each student individually?"

Kisha: "You could turn it into a written format. The teacher could demonstrate the ping-pong ball business and ask students to explain the behavior of the ball in writing. It wouldn't be quite as diagnostic or probing as the one-to-one interviews, but it would still be better than the more traditional ways most of us have been tested."

Elwin: "And it would even be time efficient if the teacher combined it with a writing assignment in language arts."

Kisha: "Let's see your second mini-experiment."

Elwin: "I spent so much time with the first one, I didn't get to finish the second one. I thought for the prompt I'd direct students to explain how they found out for themselves that Newton's Second Law of Motion is true. The rubric will be similar to the one in Illustration 7.26—just substitute the relationship embedded in Newton's Second Law of Motion for the ones about making magnets."

Kisha: "Makes sense to me. Here, let me show you what I came up with. My discover-a-relationship objective is for students to explain why the lateral surface area of a right cylinder equals 2

Elwin: "Oh! This is similar to some of our cases! Hold on, let me find them. Here, in Chapter 5, Cases 5.4, 5.5, and 5.6"

Kisha: "That's right. Rather than design mini-experiments only for formative feedback during the lesson, I decided to try my hand at designing them for summative evaluation purposes near the end of a unit. I decided to prompt students with a problem that had the computations already set up and laid out for them, then see if they can explain why the computations will give the lateral surface area. Here it is."

Kisha shows Elwin Illustration 7.28.

Elwin: "I like that the prompt directs students to analyze why the computation works, not to do the computation. It definitely taps a cognitive process that's not the usual focus on the answer, but rather on the relationship underlying a process for getting an answer."

Kisha: "Of course no single mini-experiment can by itself tell us if the student actually discovered the relationship, but it does give us some indicator. We just have to combine a number of relevant mini-experiments into a measurement to obtain valid results."

Elwin: "We have to keep reminding ourselves that one mini-experiment is only one piece of a big puzzle. What about your second one?"

Interview Prompt and Rubric:

1. The teacher sits across the table from the student and places a ping-pong ball on the middle of the table.

2. The teacher directs the student to gently roll the ball to him so that he can easily catch it.

3. If the student does so as directed, the teacher catches the ball and returns it to the center of the table.

4. The teacher directs the student, "Roll the ball again, but this time, make it hard for me to catch it.

5. If the student follows the direction, she/he'll push the ball to one side and/or push it with greater force than before. In such a case the teacher asks the student, "What did you do differently this time than the first time?"

6. The student is likely to say something similar to, "I made it harder for you to catch the ball." But the teacher wants the student to explain the difference in the mechanics of his actions. Thus the teacher probes with questions like, "What did you do differently with your hands to make it harder for me to catch the ball?"

7. The teacher listens to the explanations. Students' answers displaying an awareness of the direction of the applied force (e.g., "I pushed on the side of the ball instead of the back.") and magnitude of the applied force (e.g., "I moved my hand faster.") are noted as evidence of the students' grasp of the relationship.

8. If the student doesn't express this awareness, then the teacher should set up a simpler experiment. For example, the teacher could nudge the ball on one side with a pencil and ask the student why the ball didn't go straight. If the student expresses an awareness, the teacher moves to a more complex experiment. For example, have the student deflect a moving ball and explain what happened.

ILLUSTRATION 7.27

Mini-Experiment Elwin Designed to Be Relevant to How Well Students Discovered Newton's Second Law of Motion

Kisha: "After I came up with the first one, I worried that it puts too much of a premium on students being able to comprehend the directions and also on their writing skills. So instead of coming up with an entirely new idea for a second one, I concentrated on modifying the first one so that students' abilities to figure out what I wanted and to organize their thoughts in an essay aren't so critical. I wanted to allow them to concentrate more on the mathematics and less on the writing."

<u>Essay Prompt</u>:

Suppose you wanted to find how much paint would be needed to cover the outside of the tube pictured (it's open at both ends). Use from one half to one page to explain why the size of the surface to be painted can be found by the following computation:

$$2 \times 3.14 \times 3.98 \times 15$$

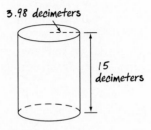

3.98 decimeters

15 decimeters

<u>Rubric</u>:

(Maximum possible points: 8) The teacher reads the paragraph using the following scoring scale with +2 indicating the criterion is clearly met, +1 that it is not clear whether or not the criterion is met, and +0 indicating that the criterion is clearly not met:

The following relationship is explained: The
cylinder can be transformed into a rectangle
without changing its lateral surface area -------- 0 1 2

The following relationship is explained: The
circumference of the right cylinder is associated
with one side of the rectangle ----------------- 0 1 2

The following relationship is explained: The
height of the right cylinder is associated
with the other side of the rectangle ------------ 0 1 2

The explanation associates the computation
with $2\pi rh$ --- 0 1 2

ILLUSTRATION 7.28

The First Mini-Experiment Kisha Designed to Be Relevant to How Well Students Discovered the Formula for Lateral Surface Area of a Right Cylinder

Kisha shows Elwin Illustration 7.29.

Elwin:	"This version should be easier for most students. You've done some of the cognitive work for them."
Kisha:	"Which one do you like better?"
Elwin:	"It depends on whether you want students to organize their explanations themselves or you want to do some of the structuring for them. The first probably taps a more sophisticated degree of objective achievement than the second. But the second one will be easier for you to score."
Kisha:	"Yeah. If this were only one of many prompts on a test and I had 35 students, I'd be happier with the second one when I was up late at night scoring responses."

A VARIETY OF FORMATS FOR MINI-EXPERIMENTS RELEVANT TO DISCOVER-A-RELATIONSHIP OBJECTIVES

As suggested in Chapter 6, having a variety of formats in mini-experiment files gives you flexibility in the ways to measure students' achievement of objectives. The same formats described in a prior section of this chapter, "Indicators of Students' Achievement of Construct-a-Concept Objectives," are used for mini-experiments relevant to discover-a-relationship objectives. Throughout the first six chapters, you've been exposed to mini-experiments for discover-a-relationship objectives with a variety of formats; for example:

- The second of the two mini-experiments in Illustration 1.17 has a performance-observation format and is relevant to the following objective:

    Given two one-digit whole numbers, a and b such that $a + b = c$, students demonstrate why $a + b = c$ (e.g., explain why $3 + 5 = 8$ or $9 + 2 = 11$) (discover a relationship).

    Discuss the following question with a colleague: Why is it actually a performance-observation instead of interview even though Kisha used the word "interview" in the prompt?

- Mini-Experiment #1 from Illustration 6.2 has an essay format and is relevant to the following objective:

    Students explain how segregation of black people from white people whether de jure segregation in the South or de facto segregation virtually everywhere in the U.S. affected the lives of all citizens both collectively and individually (discover a relationship).

SHORT-RESPONSE MINI-EXPERIMENTS RELEVANT TO DISCOVER-A-RELATIONSHIP OBJECTIVES

One very commonly used format that was not among those described in the section "Indicators of Students' Achievement of Construct-a-Concept Objectives" is *short-response*. A mini-experiment that prompts students to respond with a brief verbal expression (either orally or in writing) has a *short-response format*. With a short-response format, students might be prompted to respond with a single numeral, word, phrase, or sentence or with a few sentences, but never with the equivalent of a whole paragraph, as would be the case for an essay or oral-discourse format.

Essay Prompt:

Suppose you wanted to find how much paint would be needed to cover the outside of the tube pictured (it's open at both ends.) Use from one half to one page to explain why the size of the surface to be painted can be found by the following computation:

2 × 3.14 × 3.98 × 15

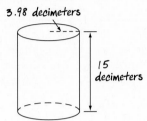

State the formula on which the computation is based.

_____

Why does the formula work for the tube in the problem? Explain why in a paragraph. Include a drawing showing how the tube has the same surface size as another more familiar figure.

Drawing:

Paragraph:

In the computation, we calculate 2 × 3.14 × 3.98 × 15. Why is there a 2?

Why is there a 3.14?

Why is there a 3.98?

Why is there a 15?

ILLUSTRATION 7.29

The Second Mini-Experiment Kisha Designed to Be Relevant to How Well Students Discovered the Formula for Lateral Surface Area of a Right Cylinder

(Continued)

ILLUSTRATION 7.29 (Continued)

<u>Rubric</u>:

(Maximum possible points: 8) The teacher reads the paragraph using the following scoring scale with +2 indicating the criterion is clearly met, +1 that it is not clear whether or not the criterion is met, and +0 indicating that the criterion is clearly not met:

The following relationship is explained: The
cylinder can be transformed into a rectangle
without changing its lateral surface area --------   0   1   2

The following relationship is explained: The
circumference of the right cylinder is associated
with one side of the rectangle   ------------------   0   1   2

The following relationship is explained: The
height of the right cylinder is associated
with the other side of the rectangle   -----------   0   1   2

The explanation associates the computation
with $2\pi rh$ ---------------------------------------   0   1   2

Examples of short-response mini-experiments relevant to discover-a-relationship objectives include (1) Mini-Experiment #2 from Illustration 6.2 and (2) the prompts on Illustration 2.22's tasksheet.

Short-response mini-experiments are particularly appropriate for objectives requiring students to furnish or provide expressions rather than select expressions from a given list (as would be the case with a multiple-choice format). More attention will be given to the short-response format in Chapter 8.

SYNTHESIS ACTIVITIES FOR CHAPTER 7

1. Read Case 7.19.

CASE 7.19

Ms. Tatkon-Coker conducts a unit for her psychology class on behavioral learning theories. Her objectives include the following:

C. Students will discriminate between examples and non-examples of classical conditioning (construct a concept).

During the unit, the students read and hear about how in the 1920s Ivan Pavlov, a Russian physiologist, noted that dogs have an automatic, involuntary response to sensing food; they salivate. Ms. Tatkon-Coker explained the following:

Dogs' salivating at the sight of food is an unconditioned response to an unconditioned stimulus. They do not normally salivate to the sound of a tuning fork. However, Pavlov demonstrated the principle of classical conditioning by sounding a tuning fork just before feeding the dogs. In time, the dogs salivated when hearing the tuning fork even when no food was presented. Classical conditioning occurs when an animal (e.g., a dog or human) associates an automatic involuntary emotional or physiological response (e.g., salivating) with a new stimulus (e.g., hearing a tuning fork). Classical conditioning is different from other types of conditioning, such as operant conditioning, in which an animal learns a response pattern because the response has been repeatedly reinforced.

Ms. Tatkon-Coker has two multiple-choice mini-experiments stored in her computer file for Objective C. They are shown in Illustration 7.30.

With a colleague, compare Illustration 7.30's two mini-experiments. Which of the two will be more difficult for Ms. Tatkon-Coker's students? Which one is more relevant to Objective C. Discuss the role of example noise in #1's prompt as compared to that in #2's prompt. Also, for each mini-experiment, discuss if all the alternatives are parallel.

2. Compare the discussion you had with your colleague when engaging in Synthesis Activity 1 to Elwin and Kisha's discussion in Case 7.20.

CASE 7.20

Elwin: "Mini-Experiment #1 seems relevant enough to Objective C. The correct alternative, b, is a perfect example of classical conditioning."

Kisha: "Mini-Experiment #1 may have subject-content relevance, but it doesn't have learning-level relevance. And if it doesn't have them both, it lacks relevance."

Elwin: "So why doesn't it have learning-level relevance?"

Kisha: "I think students who read and heard about Pavlov's experiments from Ms. Tatkon-Coker's unit will simply associate dogs, salivation, and tuning forks with classical conditioning whether or not they actually constructed the concept of classical conditioning."

Elwin: "You're saying that students would select b simply because that's the only alternative with those three elements associated with Pavlov's demonstration of classical conditioning. So they could easily use simple-knowledge rather than concept construction to get it right. If that's so, then it's a simple-knowledge mini-experiment rather than construct-a-concept.

Kisha: "Although it has subject-content relevance because it does pertain to classical conditioning as specified by the objective, it's still not relevant."

Elwin: "What about Mini-Experiment #2? Do you think it's relevant?"

Kisha: "Look how Ms. Tatkon-Coker manipulated the example noise in the example and the characteristics in the non-examples to 'foil' or 'distract' students who really haven't constructed the concept of classical conditioning even though they might associate it with tuning forks, dogs, and salivation."

Elwin: "The correct response has the attributes of classical conditioning but not the same example noise of the example most people think of when they hear the words 'classical conditioning.' Distractor a uses the words 'salivate' and 'food,' but isn't classical conditioning because the salivation is a direct response to the food. That's an unconditioned response, not one learned form classical conditioning. 'Tuning fork' is used in b. Okay, I see how the use of example noise makes #2 more relevant than #1."

Kisha: "#2 should also be harder for students. What about parallel alternatives? Do you think #1's alternative are all parallel?"

Mini-Experiment #1

Multiple-Choice Prompt:

Circle the letter in front of the one example of a situation in which a subject is displaying a response to *classical conditioning*:

a) A cat paws its owner whenever it wants to be fed.

b) A dog begins to salivate whenever the dog hears the sound from a tuning fork.

c) A man coughs involuntarily after smoking.

d) Every time a student talked out of turn in a classroom, the teacher required the student to stand and face a corner of the room for an hour. The student no longer talks out of turn in class.

Rubric:

+1 for circling "b," otherwise, +0.

Mini-Experiment #2

Multiple-Choice Prompt:

Circle the letter in front of the one example of a situation in which a subject is displaying a response to *classical conditioning*:

a) A cat salivates whenever it tastes food.

b) A man sees a tuning fork and it reminds him of the many years he spent taking music lessons.

c) A man coughs involuntarily whenever he sees the image of a cigarette on television.

d) Every time a student talked out of turn in a classroom, the teacher required the student to stand and face a corner of the room for an hour. The student no longer talks out of turn in class.

Rubric:

+1 for circling "c," otherwise, +0.

ILLUSTRATION 7.30

Two Mini-Experiments Ms. Tatkon-Coker Intends to Be Relevant to Objective C from Case 7.19

Elwin: "Yes, because they all prompt students to ask the same question: Is this a situation in which the subject is displaying classical conditioning? And the same is true for #2. Each alternative is a situation that prompts that same question."

Kisha: "I agree. Neither prompt mixes in other questions, like when or where did Pavlov demonstrate classical conditioning."

---

3. Select the one best response for each of the following multiple-choice prompts that either answers the question or completes the statement.

  A. According to advice from this chapter, which one of the following strategies should be used to control for the guessing factor when devising measurements consisting entirely of multiple-choice mini-experiments?
  a) Use a large number of mini-experiments.
  b) Use a small number of mini-experiments.
  c) Use a reputable correction-for-guess formula.
  d) Use a weighting scheme for each multiple-choice alternative.

  B. According to advice from this chapter, which one of the following strategies should be used to increase the difficulty of a construct-a-concept mini-experiment without contaminating its relevance?
  a) Raise the comprehension level of the directions.
  b) Refine the mini-experiments so that it requires a more sophisticated level of cognition.
  c) Make the noise in the examples more similar to the characteristics of the non-examples.
  d) Make the noise in the examples less similar to the characteristics in the non-examples.

  C. You are an example of a mammal. Which one of your characteristics from the following list is *not* example noise with respect to you being an example of a mammal?
  a) You are now reading from a book.
  b) You have an interest in teaching.
  c) You are a human being.
  d) You breathe air.

  D. Which one of the following mini-experiment formats would be *least* desirable for a measurement that includes only one mini-experiment?
  a) Performance observation.
  b) Essay.
  c) Multiple-choice.
  d) Product-examination.
  e) Interview.
  f) Oral discourse.

  E. Which one of the following mini-experiment formats would be *least* likely to have a rubric with global scoring?
  a) Performance observation.
  b) Essay.
  c) Multiple-choice.
  d) Product-examination.
  e) Oral discourse.

  F. For which one of the following mini-experiment formats is it easier to design a rubric that has high intra-observer consistency?
  a) Performance observation.
  b) Essay.
  c) Multiple-choice.
  d) Product-examination.
  e) Interview.
  f) Oral discourse.

G. Which one of the following mini-experiment formats is the most advantageous with respect to providing students with opportunities for clarifying their responses to prompts?
   a) Performance observation.
   b) Essay.
   c) Multiple-choice.
   d) Product-examination.
   e) Interview.
   f) Oral discourse.

4. Compare your responses to the multiple-choice prompts from Synthesis Activity 3 to those of colleagues and discuss. Also, check your choices against the following key: A-a, B-d, C-d, D-c, E-c, F-c, and G-e.

5. Retrieve the computerized folder you set up when you engaged in Synthesis Activity 2 for Chapter 6. From your work doing Synthesis Activity 3 for Chapter 6, each file contains at least one mini-experiment. Call up each of those files that is for either a construct-a-concept or discover-a-relationship objective. Now, in light of your work with Chapter 7, revise the mini-experiments in those files. For each file (i.e., files for construct-a-concept or discover-a-relationship objectives), design at least two more mini-experiments and insert them into the file.

6. With a colleague, exchange printouts of the mini-experiments you designed or revised when you engaged in Synthesis Activity 5. Discuss and critique one another's mini-experiments. Revise them as you decide they should be revised.

7. Retrieve the goal defined by a set of weighted objectives you developed for Synthesis Activity 3 for Chapter 5. Select one of the construct-a-concept or discover-a-relationship objectives from that set (if indeed the set includes at least one such objective). Now, design a four-stage lesson for leading students to achieve that objective. For each stage, design a mini-experiment to provide you with indicators of your students' progress during that stage. Note that this synthesis activity is prompting you to do something quite similar to what Ms. Ragusa did in Case 7.17 when she designed the four mini-experiments shown by Illustration 7.25. Whereas Ms. Ragusa's work in Case 7.17 relates to a discover-a-relationship objective, her work in Case 7.6, as well as Ms. Fisher's in Case 7.5, relates to construct-a-concept objectives. You may want to review these three cases before completing this synthesis activity.

8. With a colleague, share and discuss your work from Synthesis Activity 7. Revise the mini-experiments in light of your discussions.

TRANSITIONAL ACTIVITY FROM CHAPTER 7 TO CHAPTER 8

In a discussion with two or more of your colleagues, address the following questions:

1. As students engage in our lessons for our simple-knowledge objectives, how do we manage to monitor their progress?

2. How do we design mini-experiments that are relevant to simple-knowledge objectives?

3. As students engage in our lessons for our process-knowledge objectives, how do we manage to monitor their progress?

4. How de we design mini-experiments that are relevant to process-knowledge objectives?

Monitoring Students' Development of Knowledge and Process Skills

⟫ GOAL OF CHAPTER 8

Chapter 8 is intended to lead you to design mini-experiments that will help you monitor students' acquisition of information and develop process-knowledge skills. More specifically the objectives are as follows:

A. You will explain the stages through which students acquire and remember information (discover a relationship) 5%.

B. You will design mini-experiments for gauging students' progress as they engage in lessons for simple-knowledge objectives (application) 20%.

C. You will design mini-experiments relevant to how well students have achieved simple-knowledge objectives (application) 18%.

D. You will explain the stages through which students progress as they develop process-knowledge skills (discover a relationship) 5%.

E. You will design mini-experiments for gauging students' progress as they engage in lessons for process-knowledge objectives (application) 20%.

F. You will design mini-experiments relevant to how well students have achieved process-knowledge objectives (application) 18%.

G. You will extend your ability to explain fundamental principles for using a variety of mini-experiment formats, including performance observation, product examination, oral discourse, interview, essay, short-response, and multiple-choice (discover a relationship) 9%.

H. You will incorporate the following technical phrases into your working professional vocabulary: "mnemonics," "overlearning," "error-pattern analysis," "overlapping multiple-choice alternatives," "matching multiple-choice prompt," and "display-process format" (comprehension and communication skills) 5%.

HOW STUDENTS ACQUIRE AND REMEMBER INFORMATION

INFORMATION TO BE REMEMBERED

To be able to design mini-experiments relevant to your students' progress with respect to simple-knowledge objectives, you need to be familiar with how students acquire and remember information. From Chapter 5, reread the section "Simple Knowledge" on pages 231 and 235.

RETENTION OF INFORMATION

Think of an item of information that you remember well (e.g., your own name) but for which you don't specifically recall the event in which you first acquired this knowledge. Speculate on how you first learned this information and explain in a paragraph why you think you'll never forget it.

Think of another item of information you also remember well, but this time the information should be something you discovered by yourself. Reflect on the events leading you to discover this information and explain in a paragraph why you think you easily remember the information today.

Think of a third item of information that you remember well, but this time it should be information about which you recall being informed (i.e., you didn't discover it for yourself; you read or heard of it). Explain in a paragraph why you think you easily remember the information today.

Now think of a final item of information that you have difficulty remembering (e.g., the name of someone to whom you were introduced but don't recall at the moment, or a formula or date you once learned for a test in school but can't recall right now). Explain in a paragraph why you think you have difficulty remembering this information today.

Get with a colleague who is also working on this activity. Share your examples and explanations with one another. In collaboration, formulate a description of a process by which people acquire and retain information. With other pairs of colleagues, exchange and discuss your descriptions.

In Case 8.1 Elwin and Kisha discuss their responses to the four prompts to which you just responded.

CASE 8.1

Elwin: "Here; would you read mine while I read yours?"

Elwin hands Kisha his responses to the four prompts (see Illustration 8.1) in exchange for hers (see Illustration 8.2).

Kisha: "What you've written makes perfect sense to me; I especially like the part about never forgetting my name."

Elwin: "I follow what you've done also, but I have a question about the first one, about people enjoying your company more when you talk about them. Is that a form of information or is it more a matter of opinion?"

Kisha: "Good question! It's surely something I believe to be true, but it's a matter of opinion. Does that keep it from being information?"

Elwin: "Well, it's a statement of a relationship that you discovered to be true—at least for you. If nothing else, it's information that you believe in. We don't need to get hung up on the semantics."

Kisha: "Okay, the next part of the task is to formulate a description of the process by which we acquire and obtain information."

Elwin:	"In our examples, the acquisition of information part varies. For some we found out from an outside source, like hearing or reading about it. Others we figured out for ourselves."
Kisha:	"The ones we figured out for ourselves tend to stay with us longer."
Elwin:	"But look at the two lists. The information that stuck also tended to be what we continued to use repeatedly. Repetition over time seems to make it indelible."
Kisha:	"Right. Also, your use of a mnemonic device helps hold things in short-term memory."
Elwin:	"By my mnemonic device, you refer to my association of your name with a rolling cart of kiwi fruit. Is that right?"
Kisha:	"Yes. So to begin listing the steps in the process, first, we are either informed of something or we figure it out for ourselves. To get an initial grip on some hard-to-remember things—ones we didn't figure out on our own—we might need to visualize a connection between something already familiar to us and the new, unfamiliar information."
Elwin:	"That's the mnemonic device."
Kisha:	"To retain the information in long-term memory, we need to refer to it repeatedly, be exposed to it, or use it over a period of time."
Elwin:	"That's what we called 'overlearning' in our educational psychology course."

FACILITATING RECEPTION AND RETENTION OF INFORMATION THROUGH DIRECT INSTRUCTION

Students achieve construct-a-concept and discover-a-relationship objectives by engaging in inquiry lessons leading them to form generalizations based on their own work with examples and non-examples or from information they gathered through experimentation. On the other hand, students achieve simple-knowledge objectives by *receiving* and *retaining* information. Reception and retention are accomplished through a four-stage direct-instruction process: (1) exposure, (2) mnemonics, (3) reinforcement, and (4) overlearning.

EXPOSURE

In the first stage of a simple-knowledge lesson, students are exposed to the information they are to remember. Case 8.2 is an example.

CASE 8.2

From engaging in the lesson described in Case 7.6 and Illustration 7.11, Ms. Ragusa's students constructed a concept of magnets associating magnets with attributes articulated in the statement appearing at the very end of Case 7.6. Integrating her language arts and her science courses, Ms. Ragusa conducted a language arts lesson for the following objective the day after that construct-a-concept lesson on magnetism was completed:

> Students state definitions for "attract," "repel," "magnet," "magnetic field," "magnetic pole," "positive magnetic pole," and "negative magnetic pole" (simple knowledge).

For the exposition stage of this vocabulary lesson, she assigns the tasksheet shown in Illustration 8.3 for homework. The next day, she displays the definitions on the overhead screen and reads them aloud as the students check the accuracy of the copies in their glossaries.

Information I'll never forget,
but don't remember learning:

My name is Elwin Loren. Barring a traumatic event or disease
robbing me of my memory, I don't think I'll ever forget my name. I
imagine that my mother, aunt, brother, and others who were around
me continually in my first few years of life repeatedly referred
to me by my name. Gradually, I must have made the association between my name and myself. I easily remember it because nearly
every day of my life I have cause to say, write, hear, and read my
name repeatedly. The ongoing repetition makes
it "stick" in my memory.

Information I discovered myself
and am not likely to forget:

Rainbows typically appear when the sun shines shortly after a rain
storm or during a light rain. I discovered that relationship myself from direct and repeated observations. I don't think I'll
ever forget it because I discovered it myself and the belief
is reinforced every time I see a rainbow.

Information about which I remember being
informed and am unlikely to forget:

My friend Kisha's name is "Kisha Cartell." I learned Kisha's name
when she first introduced herself in class. However, even after
I began working with her in cooperative group activities, I had
trouble remembering "Kisha Cartell." Then I made this silly
association: "Kisha" reminds me of one of my favorite things
to eat, kiwi. And "Cartell" reminds me of "cart." So when I first
had trouble remembering her name, I'd picture this cart of kiwi
fruit rolling down the road. Thus, I used a mnemonic device
to initially remember her name; now, I'll never forget it.

Information I've forgotten but once knew:

A label that has stuck with me is "Doppler effect." I even remember how to spell "Doppler." I'm sure I learned what the Doppler
effect is for a number of science courses I passed with flying
colors. However, I no longer have any idea what the Doppler effect
is. I'm pretty sure I heard more than one teacher's lecture on the
Doppler effect and I've read about it in textbooks. But I don't
remember the statement of the relationship.

ILLUSTRATION 8.1

The Four Paragraphs Elwin Wrote in Response to the Same Four Prompts to Which
You Just Responded

Something I'll always remember, but
don't remember when I learned it:

> Most people enjoy my company more when I talk about them
> rather than when I talk about myself. That's something that
> I discovered to be true sometime between my pre-adolescent
> years and as a young adult. But I can't specifically put my
> finger on when I learned the relationship to be true. I won't for-
> get it because the belief is reinforced again and again
> in my contact with people.

Something I discovered on my
own and will always remember:

> What I just wrote fits this category, but since I don't recall the
> events leading to the realization, I'll select another.
> It's bees are not as likely to sting me if I stay still and don't
> flail my hands at them. I clearly remember being stung after try-
> ing to shoo bees away that were flying around me and having them
> leave me alone when I just went about my business quietly or
> calmly exited the area.

Something about which I was
informed and won't forget:

> "Direct instruction is used to inform students and help them re-
> member; inquiry instruction is used to stimulate them to reason
> and draw conclusions for themselves." That's something about which
> I was informed during this teaching methods course. I won't forget
> it because we've repeated the idea again and again. Now that I
> think about it, it's probably an idea I discovered for myself as I
> recall my own learning experiences. However, it never before stuck
> with me to use the "direct instruction" and "inquiry instruction"
> in just those ways -- although I'm pretty sure I was exposed to
> them before.

Something I no longer remember but once did:

> I memorized a massive amount of verbiage dealing with group
> theory during an abstract algebra course I recently took. "Homo-
> morphism," "ideal," "rings," "kernels," "vector spaces,"
> and on and on and on. I even did well on tests regurgitating them.
> But right know I don't remember what's "ideal" and I still think
> of a "kernel" as having to do more with corn than with algebra.
> Although I don't really understand how to apply any
> of that material from abstract algebra, I do know how to look
> it up if I ever need it.

ILLUSTRATION 8.2

The Four Paragraphs Kisha Wrote in Response to the Same Four Prompts to Which
You Just Responded

DIRECTIONS: Read each word and its definition from the list below. Copy the words and definitions into the glossary of your science notebook.

<u>attract</u>: To pull toward oneself

<u>repel</u>: To force away from oneself

<u>magnet</u>: A piece of metal that has the power to attract certain objects

<u>magnetic field</u>: The space around a magnet where the magnet's power reaches

<u>magnetic pole</u>: Either end of a magnet where the magnetic field is strongest

<u>positive magnetic pole</u>: The magnetic pole of a magnet that attracts the negative magnetic pole of other magnets and repels the positive magnetic poles of other magnets

<u>negative magnetic pole</u>: The magnetic pole of a magnet that is not the positive magnetic pole

ILLUSTRATION 8.3

The Homework Tasksheet Ms. Ragusa Used in the Exposure Stage of a Simple-Knowledge Vocabulary Lesson

She tells students what to remember when prompted by these words. She says, for example, "Anytime you see or hear the words 'magnetic field,' picture this in your mind." She displays the illustration shown in Illustration 8.4 on the overhead screen and continues, "Think these words: 'the space around a magnet where the magnet's power reaches.'"

MNEMONICS

Mnemonics is a word derived from "Mnemosyne," the name of the ancient Greek goddess of memory. The word means *aiding the memory*. For some, but not all, simple-knowledge objectives, you might consider providing students with mnemonic devices to enhance retention. Mnemonic devices have proven to be effective in helping students remember new information (Bourne, Dominowski, Loftus, & Healy, 1986, pp. 9–100; Joyce, Weil, & Showers, 1992, pp. 159–179; Woolfolk, 1993, pp. 267–270). I, for example, informed you about the derivation of "mnemonics" as an aid to helping you remember the definition. Thus, that was a mnemonic aid. However, unless you were already familiar with the goddess Mnemosyne, my mnemonic device is not likely to be very effective. The most effective mnemonic devices link the new information to be remembered to something already familiar to the student. Case 8.3 is an example.

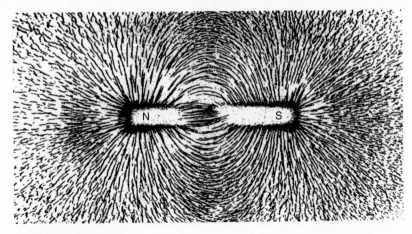

ILLUSTRATION 8.4

An Illustration Ms. Ragusa Used in a Language Arts Lesson

CASE 8.3

To help students remember that like poles of two magnets repel one another, while opposite poles attract, Ms. Ragusa displays Illustration 8.5 and says, "Think of these two elephants staying together linked by a head and a tail, while these two elephants are going away from each other with their tails pointing at each other."

To help her students associate the words "de jure" and "de facto" with the respective concepts they constructed during the lesson described in Case 7.5, Ms. Fisher might tell her students to make the following associations:

> For "de jure," think of "jury." A jury is linked to law; de jure segregation is segregation based on official law. For "de facto," think of "fact." De facto segregation exists as a matter of fact—that is, in reality, not as a matter of law.

Usually, it isn't necessary to use mnemonics for remembering definitions of concepts students have already constructed or statements of relationships they've already discovered. Mnemonic devices are more helpful for recalling conventions that are not logically connected to content students have already learned.

REINFORCEMENT

In the third stage of a simple-knowledge lesson, the accuracy with which students recall what they are supposed to have memorized is monitored. Correct responses are positively reinforced and errors corrected. Case 8.4 is an example.

CASE 8.4

Kimberleigh asks Ms. Ragusa, "What does the book mean by 'magnetic north'?" Ms. Ragusa: "Hmm, 'magnetic north,' that's an interesting expression. What's 'positive magnetic pole' mean?" Kimberleigh: "Something about the ends of magnets; I don't know." Ms. Ragusa: "Look up 'magnetic pole' in the

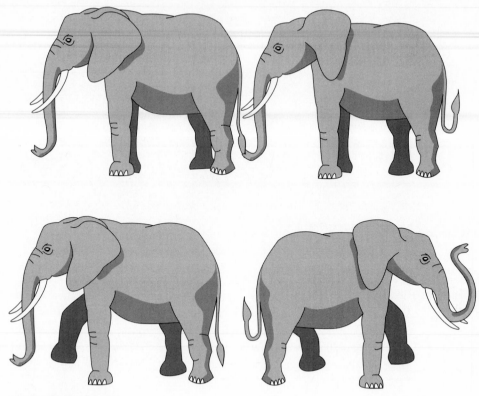

ILLUSTRATION 8.5

The Head-to-Tail Elephants Stick Together, But the Tail-to-Tail Pair Move Away

glossary in your notebook." Kimberleigh: "It says, 'Either end of a magnet where the magnetic field is strongest.' Is that right?" Ms. Ragusa: "Absolutely. Now, recite the definition to me without looking in your book." Kimberleigh: "Either end of a magnet where the magnetic field is strongest." Ms. Ragusa: "Exactly. Now, let's look at the words 'positive magnetic pole' and then we'll talk about magnetic north."

OVERLEARNING

Students *overlearn* by continuing to practice recalling subject-content even after they have memorized it. Overlearning increases resistance to forgetting and facilitates long-term retention of information (Chance, 1988, pp. 221–222). For example, even after the completion of the unit on magnets, Ms. Ragusa continues to confront students with tasks requiring them to remember definitions and statements of relationships involving magnets.

INDICATORS OF PROGRESS AS STUDENTS ENGAGE IN SIMPLE-KNOWLEDGE LESSONS

In Case 8.5, Mr. Boudreaux conducts informal mini-experiments to monitor students' progress during a four-stage simple-knowledge lesson.

CASE 8.5

Mr. Boudreaux conducts a lesson for the following objective:

Students list the defining attributes of mammals (simple knowledge).

Using Illustration 8.6's overhead transparency slide to illustrate his words, he tells the third-grade class, "A mammal is any animal which has a backbone, is warm-blooded, has some body hair, and whose females have what are called 'mammary glands' for feeding milk to their babies. I'm going to repeat the five things that are true about mammals. First, a mammal is an animal—like a snake, spider, fish, bird, bear, whale, human being, or dog, but not like a tree, weed, or rock. Second, a mammal has a backbone—like a snake, fish, bird, bear, whale, human being, or dog, but not like a spider or worm. Third, a mammal is warm-blooded—like a bird, bear, whale, human being, or dog, but not like a snake or fish. Fourth, a mammal has body hair like a bear, whale, human being, or dog, but not like a bird or fish. And fifth, mammal mothers can feed their babies milk from their bodies using mammary glands, like those of a bear, whale, human being, or dog, not like a bird, lizard, fish, and all other things that are not mammals. Now, take one more look at the overhead screen and implant these five things in your minds. Then I'm going to turn it off and check to see which ones we remember. Off we go. List one for me, Don." Don: "Warm-blooded." Mr. Boudreaux: "Another, Eva." Eva: "Milk from mothers and—" Mr. Boudreaux: "Thank you. Another, Deliah."

The recitation continues for another 30 seconds, with Mr. Boudreaux checking off a very simple rubric in his mind: The more correct responses students make to his prompts, the better indication that there is no need to dwell on this initial stage and that it is time to make the transition into the mnemonic stage.

Mr. Boudreaux displays Illustration 8.6 again and says, "Anytime you hear the word 'mammal,' I want you to think of these five things—animal, backbone, warm-blooded, hair, and mother's milk or mammary glands. Also, anytime you observe a creature that has the five characteristics, think what? Okay, all together." Most of the class: "Mammal."

For a mnemonic device, Mr. Boudreaux says, "To help me remember the word 'mammal,' I think of 'mother's milk from *mammary* glands' as I picture my cat nursing her kittens." He holds up a large picture

ILLUSTRATION 8.6

Mr. Boudreaux's Overhead Transparency for Simple-Knowledge Lesson on Mammals of a mother cat nursing kittens and then directs one student to tack it on the bulletin board. He completes this stage of the lesson with, "Three m's: mother, milk, mammary, just like in the word 'mammal.'"

Mr. Boudreaux then brings out a closed box, holds it up, and directs the class, "I've got a mammal in here. Silently think to yourself what you know about it." He then calls on different students to share their descriptions until he's reasonably convinced that they associate the five attributes with the word "mammal."

In subsequent lessons and units, the term "mammal" arises, and Mr. Boudreaux sets up prompts (e.g., "What does that mean again? Well, why do you say a fish isn't a mammal?") to lead students to recall the conventional relationship he taught in this lesson.

INDICATORS OF STUDENTS' ACHIEVEMENT OF SIMPLE-KNOWLEDGE OBJECTIVES

MINI-EXPERIMENT RELEVANT TO SIMPLE-KNOWLEDGE OBJECTIVES

Stimulus-Response

A mini-experiment relevant to students' achievement of a simple-knowledge objective presents students with the task of responding to the stimulus specified by the objective with the desired word, image, sound, symbol, name, date, definition, statement, location, or other subject-content. Typically, designing mini-experiments for simple-knowledge objectives won't tax your creative talents to the same degree as designing mini-experiments for construct-a-concept or discover-a-relationship objectives. However, there are pitfalls to avoid.

First of all, you need to maintain the same stimulus- response relationship that's defined by the objective. For example, design a mini-experiment that is relevant to the following objective taken from a middle-school science curriculum guide:

So that the student will be able to read scientific material, he or she will recall the meanings of the following terms: "hypothesis," "empirical observation," and "experiment" (simple knowledge).

Compare your mini-experiment to the curriculum guide's "sample test item" for the aforementioned objective; it is reproduced in Illustration 8.7.

Exchange your mini-experiment with a colleague's. Critique one another's work as well as the one from the curriculum guide that is displayed by Illustration 8.7.

Prompt:

  Fill in the blank with the word that makes the statement true:

    A generalization which appears to be true from a pattern
    of direct observations is a(n) _____.

Rubric:

    "Hypothesis" is the correct response.

ILLUSTRATION 8.7

"Sample Test Item" from a Middle-School Curriculum Guide

Kisha and Elwin's mini-experiments for the aforementioned objective appear in Illustration 8.8. Case 8.6 is a portion of their discussion.

CASE 8.6

Kisha: "The objective is concerned with students being able to know word meanings as they read about science. Thus, it is important for the students to *respond* with a definition upon seeing the word 'hypothesis,' not respond with 'hypothesis' upon seeing the definition. The curriculum guide's sample item reverses the objective's stimulus with its response."

Elwin: "I see you've kept the objective's stimulus-response relation intact with the item you wrote. I didn't do that with my mini-experiment, but I was trying to come up with something that would be easy to score and students wouldn't have to write a lot. But does it really make any difference? It seems to me if you can remember the definition upon seeing a word, you can remember the word when you see the definition."

Kisha's Mini-Experiment

Short-Response Prompt:

What does the word hypothesis mean? _____

_____

_____

Rubric:

(4 points possible) +1 for each of the following that's indicated about a hypothesis: (1) a generalization, (2) based on direct observations, and (3) consistency among a number of observations; +1 for nothing false included.

Elwin's Mini-Experiment

Multiple-Choice Prompt:

A generalization that appears to be true from a pattern of direct observations is which one of the following:

    a)   empirical observation
    b)   scientific law
    c)   experiment
    d)   hypothesis
    e)   conjecture
    f)   variable

Rubric:

    +1 for d; otherwise, +0

ILLUSTRATION 8.8

Kisha's and Elwin's Mini-Experiment Alternatives to Illustration 8.7's

Kisha:	"I'm thinking of a word right now; it means having an abundance of riches. What's the word?"
Elwin:	"Is it 'rich'?"
Kisha:	"That's not it."
Elwin:	"How about 'opulent'?"
Kisha:	"Nope."
Elwin:	"Ahh, I think I know the one. I just can't think of it right now."
Kisha:	"Do you know what the word 'affluent' means?"
Elwin:	"Now I see what you're driving at. I could modify my multiple-choice prompt so that the stem directed the student to select the correct definition for 'hypothesis.' Then the alternatives would be different definitions—one of which is the one for 'hypothesis.' That way, the stimulus-response order is the same as in the objective."

Although Elwin is able to remember the definition of "affluent" upon hearing or seeing it, that word didn't pop up in his mind when he heard Kisha give its definition. The suggestion here is for you to be aware of the stimulus-response sequence specified by each of your simple-knowledge objectives so that you can maintain that sequence in the mini-experiments you design for that objective.

Avoiding Responses Beyond Simple Knowledge

Students' responses to prompts for simple-knowledge objectives should depend only on how well they remember information. Mini-experiments are not relevant to simple-knowledge objectives whenever students use reasoning or higher-order cognitive processes to determine responses. But because a prompt is designed to elicit a simple-knowledge response does not guarantee that students will respond at the simple-knowledge level. Consider Case 8.7.

CASE 8.7

Ms. Blair wants to measure her students' recall of addition facts, that is, achievement of the following objective:

> Given any two one-digit whole numbers, students will recall the sum of those two numbers (simple knowledge).

To do so, she administers a five-minute test with 12 prompts similar to the following one:

$$7 + 4 = \underline{\hspace{2cm}}$$

When Casey, one of her students, confronts the prompt, he uses his fingers to count to himself, "eight, nine, ten, eleven." He scores 12 out of 12 on the test.

Casey used process-knowledge cognition to respond to Ms. Blair's prompts. If Ms. Blair is really serious about the objective being at the simple-knowledge rather than the process-knowledge learning level, then she should redesign the measurement so that students do not have time to work through a process. She could increase the number of prompts or rapidly display prompts, one at a time, on flash cards, pausing only long enough for students to respond orally or on answer sheets.

In Case 8.8, a student responds to what was supposed to be a simple-knowledge prompt with reasoning because of ambiguous wording.

CASE 8.8

In a health unit on nutrition, Mr. Brewer emphasizes that the consumption of tea interferes with the body's ability to use iron. To learn whether his students remember this fact, he includes the following true-false prompt on his test:

Circle "T" if the following statement is true; otherwise, circle "F" for false:

T   F   Drinking tea provides iron for the body.

According to the scoring rubric, the correct response is to circle "F."

Maxine remembers that tea interferes with the body's use of iron as she reads the statement. However, she moves beyond simple-knowledge level as she reasons, "Tea is not the way to get iron into the body. But the statement says, 'drinking tea provides iron.' Tea is mixed with water and most water contains traces of iron. So actually, drinking tea does provide iron. I'll circle 'T.'"

Mr. Brewer might argue that if Maxine paid attention in class, she would know what he meant by that true-false statement and she would have known to circle "F." However, a simple-knowledge prompt shouldn't contain a warning label for students "not to reason on this one." The problem is best avoided by wording prompts so that there is little room for misinterpretation.

SHORT-RESPONSE MINI-EXPERIMENTS RELEVANT TO SIMPLE-KNOWLEDGE OBJECTIVES

The stimulus-response nature of simple-knowledge objectives tends to encourage the use of mini-experiments with short-answer formats. The student is simply prompted with the stimulus part of the objective's subject-content, with the expectation for the student to express the response part of the subject-content. In Case 8.7, Ms. Blair used a short-response prompt for a simple-knowledge objective. But even with straightforward simple-knowledge objectives and straightforward short-response prompts, there are often pitfalls. As suggested in the very beginning of Chapter 1, teaching is not brain surgery; teaching is far more complex. Nothing about teaching is ever as simple as it appears on the surface. Consider Case 8.9.

CASE 8.9

Intended to be relevant to a simple-knowledge objective regarding certain facts about the discovery of the Americas, the following short-response prompt is included on a unit test:

Who discovered America? _____

According to the scoring rubric, the correct response is to write "Columbus."

When Pauline reads the question on the test, she thinks, "Christopher Columbus sailed to the New World in 1492. But Native Americans were already there. I wonder what answer she [the teacher] wants. It could be those Vikings who sailed over before Columbus. Or does she want that guy John Cabot who made it to America. Columbus only made it to the Caribbean."

Often, it is difficult to present a short-response prompt that is not open to a variety of interpretations. You want the mini-experiment to discriminate as to how well students have achieved the objective, not discriminate according to how students interpreted the question or directions. In Case 8.9, Pauline's sophisticated understanding of subject-content hindered, instead of helped, her performance relative to the mini-experiment. The wording of Illustration 8.9's two prompts is less ambiguous than that of the one in Case 8.9.

Illustration 8.9's short-response prompt is a little more complicated to read than the one in Case 8.9. The multiple-choice one maintains the simple wording of Case 8.9's question but avoids the ambiguity, because defensible responses such as "Native Americans," "Vikings," and "John Cabot" are not included among the alternatives. Note two disadvantages of the multiple-choice format in comparison to the short-response format: (1) The multiple-choice prompt is not as appropriate for objectives requiring students to provide rather than simply identify information, and (2) students are far more likely to guess the correct response to a multiple-choice prompt than to a short-response prompt.

MULTIPLE-CHOICE MINI-EXPERIMENTS RELEVANT TO SIMPLE-KNOWLEDGE OBJECTIVES
Controlling for Difficulty

The principal advantage of multiple-choice prompts for simple-knowledge objectives is that you can include many of them on a measurement and, thus, sample a large share of students' knowledge of information in a relatively short period of time. As was the case for the multiple-choice mini-experiment in Illustration 8.9, the stimulus is presented in the multiple-choice stem with directions for students to select the one correct response from a list of alternative responses.

As you understand from your work with Chapter 7, the difficulty of multiple-choice mini-experiments relevant to construct-a-concept objectives can be controlled by making the noise in examples more or less similar to characteristics of the non-examples. For simple-knowledge

---

Short-Response Prompt:

According to our history textbook, who was the first person to sail from Europe to what is now known as the Americas?

_____

Rubric:

+1 for "Columbus;" otherwise, +0.

Multiple-Choice Prompt:

Circle the letter in front of the one correct answer to the question:

Who discovered America?

a) Amerigo Vespucci
b) George Washington
c) Vasco de Balboa
d) Christopher Columbus

Rubric:

+1 for "d" only; otherwise, +0.

ILLUSTRATION 8.9

Two Mini-Experiments Relevant to a Simple-Knowledge Objective About the Discovery of America

objectives, the difficulty can be controlled by manipulating the similarity among alternatives. For example, which of the two multiple-choice mini-experiments in Illustration 8.10 appear to be the more difficult for students? They are intended to be relevant to the following objective:

> Students will identify key personalities, especially political figures, who played major roles relative to southern reconstruction in the United States between 1865 and 1900 (simple knowledge).

Do you not agree that more students would probably respond correctly to #2 from Illustration 8.10 than to #1? The alternatives for Prompt #1 are all presidents who held office between

---

```
                                    #1

Multiple-Choice Prompt:

    Circle the letter in front of the one correct answer
    to the question:

        Who was the president of the United States when the era
        of southern reconstruction was officially terminated?

            a) Rutherford B. Hayes
            b) James Garfield
            c) John Tyler
            d) Ulysses S. Grant
            e) Andrew Johnson

Rubric:

    +1 for "a" only; otherwise, +0.



                                    #2

Multiple-Choice Prompt:

    Circle the letter in front of the one correct answer
    to the question:

        Who was the president of the United States when the era
        of southern reconstruction was officially terminated?

            a) Rutherford B. Hayes
            b) Benjamin Franklin
            c) John Tyler
            d) Ralph Bunche
            e) Franklin Roosevelt

Rubric:

    +1 for "a" only; otherwise, +0.
```

ILLUSTRATION 8.10

Two Mini-Experiments Relevant to a Simple-Knowledge Objective About Southern Reconstruction

1841 and 1881. The alternatives for Prompt #2 are not all presidents, and they appear in U.S. history from colonial times well into the twentieth century. Both mini-experiments are relevant to the same simple-knowledge objective, but the first is better for measuring more sophisticated achievement of that objective, whereas the second is better for measuring less sophisticated achievement.

Correct Responses for the Wrong Reasons

The student in Case 8.10 increases her chances of selecting the correct alternative to a multiple-choice prompt, but not because of anything to do with her achievement of the simple-knowledge objective for which the mini-experiment was meant to be relevant.

CASE 8.10

Intended to be relevant to a simple-knowledge objective regarding certain facts about cultures in Afghanistan, the following multiple-choice prompt is included on a unit test:

> The majority of the people in Afghanistan today are members of which one of the following religious faiths?
>
> a) Christian   b) Protestant   c) Islam   d) Jewish   e) Catholic   f) Buddhist

According to the scoring rubric, the correct response is to select "c."

When Ruth is confronted by the prompt, she thinks, "I don't know what religions they have in Afg-whatever. I've got one chance in six of guessing this right. That's not very good. Maybe I can improve my chances. Let's see. Ah-ha! Only one answer can be right. So I can eliminate 'b' and 'e,' because if either of those are right, 'a' would be right also. That would make two correct answers. So now my chances are up to one in four."

Ruth would not have been able to use the deductive logic to improve her chance of selecting a correct response to a prompt intended to be relevant to an objective she had not achieved if the prompt had not included *overlapping alternatives*. Two *alternatives overlap* if one cannot be correct unless the other is also correct. Overlapping alternatives should be avoided unless the mini-experiment is supposed to be relevant to how well students solve logic puzzles.

Another multiple-choice design flaw to avoid is a *grammatical mismatch* between the stem and a distractor; Case 8.11 illustrates the problem.

CASE 8.11

Intended to be relevant to a simple-knowledge objective regarding the meaning of the statistical word "mode," the following multiple-choice prompt is included on a unit test:

> The modes of 7, 3, 3, 8, 4, 4, 1, 7, 5, 3, 11, and 7 are _____.
>
> a) 7   b) 1, 3, and 7   c) 4   d) 3 and 7

According to the scoring rubric, the correct response is to select "d."

When Antoine, who does not know the statistical meaning of the word "mode," is confronted by the prompt, he thinks, "Well at least I know 'c' and 'a' can't be right, because the verb in the sentence is 'are.' That's plural. I now only have to guess either 'b' or 'd.'"

Of course you want to model proper grammar, sentence structure, and spelling for your students. Unless you are using a mini-experiment to be relevant to knowledge of such writing skills, be sure all alternatives are grammatically consistent with the stem. The flaw in Case 8.11's prompt could be remedied with one minor modification in the stem:

The mode(s) of 7, 3, 3, 8, 4, 4, 1, 7, 5, 3, 11, and 7 is (are) _____.

Distractors should not only match the stem grammatically; they also need to be *plausible*. Case 8.12 illustrates the problem.

CASE 8.12

Intended to be relevant to a simple-knowledge objective regarding the historical facts about the People's Republic of China, the following multiple-choice prompt is included on a unit test:

The People's Republic of China was established in 1949 under the leadership of

_____.

a) Chou En-lai   b) Phil Smith   c) Jina Quing   d) Marlin Printer   e) Mao Tse-tung

According to the scoring rubric, the correct response is to select "e."

When Jacelyn, who does not know the name of the person in question, is confronted by the prompt, she thinks, "I don't think anyone with a name like 'Phil Smith' or 'Marlin Printer' would have ever been a political leader in China. It's got to be one of the other three with Asian names."

Incorrect Responses for the Wrong Reasons

Just as you have to be careful how short-response prompts are worded so students don't make "incorrect" responses because they use reasoning or "know too much," as illustrated by Case 8.9, so you also need to avoid this design flaw with multiple-choice prompts. Case 8.13 illustrates the problem.

CASE 8.13

Intended to be relevant to a simple-knowledge objective regarding the characteristics of human cells, the following multiple-choice prompt is included on one of Ms. Bung-Lee's biology measurements:

Human cells have _____ chromosomes.

a) 18   b) 26   c) 46   d) 58

According to the scoring rubric, the correct response is to select "c."

When Pace, who has achieved the objective, is confronted by the prompt, he thinks, "All normal human cells have 46 chromosomes except, of course, egg cells in females and sperm cells in males—they only have 23. And I'll bet there are billions of abnormal cells that have missing or extra chromosomes. So the only choice that is always correct is 18—that's 'a.' All cells have at least 18 chromosomes; all don't have 46. Is this a trick question? It must be." Pace selects "a."

The following day, when Ms. Bung-Lee reviews the measurement results with the class, Pace informs her of the dilemma that prompt presented. She apologizes and tells him to add another point to his measurement score. Later, she opens the computer file with that mini-experiment and rewords the stem so that it reads as follows:

"What is the maximum number of chromosomes that a human cell has, providing that the cell is normal and is not a sex cell?"

Ms. Bung-Lee is pleased that the revised version of the prompt is not ambiguous like the original one, nor should it discriminate against advanced achievement levels. However, she's unhappy that the new wording requires a higher level of reading-comprehension skills. She worries that some students will now incorrectly respond to the prompt, not because they haven't achieved the objective but because they have difficulty understanding the question.

Placement of the Correct Responses

Where should the correct response be placed among a multiple-choice prompt's alternatives? In most cases, the correct response should be randomly placed among the alternatives. Sometimes teachers are tempted to place correct responses among alternatives so that the answers form a pattern on the test scoring key that will make the test easier to score. Students soon realize this and waste their test-taking time searching for, and often discovering, the pattern. Correct responses to multiple-choice prompts on a measurement should appear in each alternative position about the same number of times. An inordinate number of "b" alternatives being correct, for example, will affect the guess factor.

Another temptation to resist is trying to "hide" the correct response somewhere in the middle of the alternatives. This practice is particularly tempting when alternatives are numerical, as they are in Case 8.13's prompt. When students guess on these types of prompts, they tend to select "in-between" alternatives (e.g., "b" or "c") more often than extreme ones (e.g., "a" or "d").

Matching Multiple-Choice Format

Matching prompts are a common variation of the multiple-choice format. A matching prompt presents students with two lists and the task of associating each entry of one list with an entry from the second list. Illustration 8.11 is an example.

The left-hand column of a matching prompt is a sequence of multiple-choice stems. The right column contains the responses which form a list of alternatives for each stem. Contrary to the way the prompt in Illustration 8.11 is constructed, it is usually advisable to design matching prompts so that the stems in the left column contain the longer-to-read items. Since students normally read from left to right, they will be repeatedly reading items from the right column, but only reading items from the left column once. Thus, you save them time by arranging prompts as suggested. The music teacher who designed Illustration 8.11's prompt had a sound reason for not taking this suggestion. She was more concerned about her students reading music than writing music. Thus, she wanted the musical symbols to be the stimuli in the prompt and their meanings the responses. Therefore, she knowingly compromised one prompt-design principle in favor of another (i.e., to maintain the stimulus-response order of her objective).

Illustration 8.12 is an example of a highly flawed matching prompt. Administer it to yourself and discuss its flaws with a colleague.

In Case 8.14, Elwin and Kisha discuss Illustration 8.12's mini-experiment.

CASE 8.14

Kisha: "The mini-experiment clearly has learning-level relevance for a simple-knowledge objective having something to do with learning theory, but the subject-content is all over the place. It involves personalities significant to the development of learning theory and also meanings of certain theories or principles."

Matching Prompt:

Directions: Column I is a list of standard musical symbols. For each, determine which item from Column II expresses what the symbol indicates. All but two of the items from Column II should be used once and only once. Two shouldn't be used at all. Indicate your matches by writing the letter of items from Column II in the matching blanks under Column I.

I		II
___ 1.	♭♭	a) indicates a single sharp when used after a double sharp.
___ 2.	♮	b) natural: indicates that the note it precedes is lowered one half step.
___ 3.	o	c) indicates a single flat when used after a double flat.
___ 4.	♮♭	d) sharp: indicates the note it precedes is raised one half step
___ 5.	✖	e) double sharp: indicates that the note it precedes is raised two half steps.
___ 6.	♯	f) flat: indicates that the note it precedes is lowered one half step.
		g) double flat:indicates that the lower note it precedes is lowered two half steps.
		h) whole note; semibreve.

Rubric:

(Maximum points: 6) +1 for each blank completed as follows: 1-g, 2-b, 3-h, 4-c, 5-e, and 6-d

ILLUSTRATION 8.11

A Matching Mini-Experiment Relevant to a Simple-Knowledge Objective on Musical Symbols

Elwin: "In other words, the alternatives aren't parallel. More than one question is raised by each prompt. It's also badly arranged. Unless the objective is for students to respond with the Column B's items to stimuli from Column A, the longer items should be on the left and the shorter ones on the right."

Kisha: "I agree. You know, I don't remember the right responses to hardly any of these, but when I administered this mini-experiment to myself, I scored quite high, even though I don't remember what these different people or theories are."

Elwin: "Tell me what you did."

Matching Prompt:

Directions: Match the element in Column A with those of Column B by placing the letter of your choice from Column B. Use each letter once.

A	B
_____ 1. E. L. Thorndike	A. Developed the first mechanical device for self-instruction in 1924.
_____ 2. Associationist	B. Animals tend to repeat satisfying experiences.
_____ 3. faculty psychology	C. Developed the first branching programmed-learning machine.
_____ 4. law of readiness	D. Called the "Father of Behavioristic Psychology."
_____ 5. John Watson	E. Causes students initially to enjoy teaching machines then lose interest in them over time.
_____ 6. Norman Crowder	F. Concluded in 1890 that general memory was not a faculty that could be trained.
_____ 7. pall effect	G. An individual will not be satisfied to act in a certain way until he or she is ready.
_____ 8. William James	H. Includes the belief that transfer of training could occur between disciplines.
_____ 9. Sidney Pressey	I. A student of William James who is largely responsible for connectionism theory.
_____ 10. law of effect	J. A school of thought that maintained that memory is a process by which experiences are re-excitement of a location of the brain.

Rubric:

(Maximum points: 10) +1 for each blank completed as follows:
1-I, 2-J, 3-H, 4-G, 5-D, 6-C, 7-E, 8-F, 9-A, and 10-B.

ILLUSTRATION 8.12

A Poorly Designed Matching Mini-Experiment

Kisha:	"The only thing I know about E. L. Thorndike is that he's an author of a book on measurement I once saw. I don't remember which one of those items in Column B that Thorndike did, but I know the answer to 1 has to be either A, C, D, F, or I because those are the only responses that fit the name of a person. Already I've increased my chances without remembering what I'm supposed to remember about Thorndike. So I look over the other names in the list and recognize the name 'William James' as a philosopher who had some revolutionary ideas around 1890 or so. Although I didn't know that James concluded that general memory was not a faculty that could be trained, I keyed on the 1890 and the contrariness of 'F' to put 'F' by '8.' I wouldn't think that a guy who wrote a measurement book recently enough for me to see it would be called the 'father of behavioristic psychology' or would have developed the first branching programmed-learning machine, so I eliminated those, leaving me with either A or I for Thorndike. I don't know what connectionism theory is, but I figured Thorndike must be more into measurement than mechanical devices for self-instruction, so I guessed 'I' for 1. For the other three guys, I had no clue. The only name that even seemed vaguely familiar was 'John Watson.' I don't even know why it was familiar, so I decided to associate him with the most impressive-sounding item of the remaining three possibilities."
Elwin:	"And that would have to be D, 'Father of Behavioristic Psychology.'"
Kisha:	"You got that right. For the other two, Crowder and Pressey, I just guessed—and it turns out I guessed wrong. I put 'A' for 6 and 'C' for 9—guessed 'em backwards."
Elwin:	"But without knowing what you were being tested on, you managed to get 1, 5, and 8 right. That's three out of five so far."
Kisha:	"So now I go to the list of laws and theories. I do know what faculty psychology is, so I put 'H' for 3. I have no idea about Associationist, so I skip that one and go to 4, law of readiness. I don't know that either, but as I look through the remaining items in Column B, G is the only one that contains the word 'ready.' Bang! I put 'G' in 4's blank. I look at the remaining three. I still don't know what an Associationist is, but it begins with a capital letter, so the only plausible response left is J, because that's a school of thought; a school of thought is likely to start with a capital letter. B and E are effects—they wouldn't be associated with what sounds like a group of people—'Associationists.' So now I'm just down to guessing whether 7 is E or B. I flip a coin and get E. The only thing left for 10 is B."
Elwin:	"So you get 8 out of 10 without having achieved whatever simple-knowledge objective this thing was supposed to measure."
Kisha:	"If we assume that the objective is simple-knowledge about some learning principles, theories, and effects and about some related historical figures, what could we do to refine this mini-experiment?"
Elwin:	"First of all, we should make sure the alternatives are all parallel—only deal with one question or type of subject-content at a time."
Kisha:	"That means we need to turn it into several, shorter mini-experiments, with each matching prompt dealing with only personalities or only theories or only effects."
Elwin:	"Also, we need to fix how the prompts are arranged. I don't like capital letters naming both the columns and the responses; that's confusing."
Kisha:	"Also, we ought to have more possible responses than stems, so that it isn't as easy to use a process of elimination, the way I did."

Illustration 8.13 displays Elwin's and Kisha's modified version of Illustration 8.12's mini-experiment.

As Elwin points out in Case 8.14, there should be one common basis for matching all stems with alternatives, and that basis should be specified in the directions. Elwin and Kisha attended to this suggestion when they produced Illustration 8.13.

An Ill-Advised Variation of the Multiple-Choice Format

Some commercially produced and teacher-developed tests contain prompts with an ill-advised variation of the multiple-choice format. Illustration 8.14 is an example.

Multiple-choice prompts with "all of the above," "some of the above," or "none of the above" alternatives lead students to expend greater effort and time sorting out the puzzle of directions than they spend with the task related to the subject-content specified by the objective. Illustration 8.14's variation is a very inefficient way to use measurement-administration time. Use separate true-false prompts or multiple multiple-choice prompts (as illustrated in Chapter 9) whenever you want to prompt students to select any one of a possible number of alternatives from a given list.

HOW STUDENTS DEVELOP PROCESS-KNOWLEDGE SKILLS

ACQUIRING AND POLISHING PROCESS-KNOWLEDGE SKILLS

To be able to design mini-experiments relevant to your students' progress with respect to process-knowledge objectives, you need to be familiar with how students develop process-knowledge skills. From Chapter 5, reread the first paragraph of the section "Processes" on page 230 as well as all of the section "Process Knowledge" on page 236.

Think of two procedures or processes with which you are skilled (e.g., using long division to find the quotient of two rational numbers expressed in decimal form, keyboarding, or shooting a jump shot in basketball). For each, reflect on the stages you went through that moved you from barely knowing how to execute the process to your current level of proficiency.

Get with a colleague to share your examples and reflections with one another. In collaboration, formulate descriptions of a process by which people acquire, polish, and retain process-knowledge skills. Exchange and discuss your descriptions with others who engage in this activity.

In Case 8.15, Kisha and Elwin discuss their examples.

CASE 8.15

Kisha:	"I selected keyboarding for one. Before I ever sat in front of a computer, I had seen people typing and working at computer terminals. That's where I got the general idea of what to do."
Elwin:	"I received instructions in primary school before I ever touched a keyboard."
Kisha:	"Not me, I just started playing around on our home computer using the hunt and peck method. Eventually, I got pretty good with that until my Dad showed me how to place my fingers. At first, I didn't want to do it his way; it was harder. But he kept insisting and coaching until I became comfortable with it. But it was a few years before I developed any speed."
Elwin:	"And you'll retain the skill because you kept doing it after you learned how—overlearning."
Kisha:	"What's one knowledge-process skill you picked?"
Elwin:	"Finding the sum of two fractions. In fourth grade, my teacher just started telling us a bunch of rules about the numbers on the bottom having to be the same, but none of it made any sense. I mindlessly went through some steps to get answers to make her happy, but I had no idea why they were right or wrong. Then in fifth grade, I had

#1

Matching Prompt:

Directions: Column I is a list of contributions to the development of learning theory between 1885 and 1940. For each, determine which person listed in Column II made that contribution. All but one of the persons from Column II should be used once and only once. Indicate your matches by writing the letter of items from Column II in the matching blanks under Column I.

I	II
____ 1. Developed the first mechanical device for self-instruction.	A. E. L. Thorndike
	B. John Watson
____ 2. Developed the first branching programmed-learning machine.	C. Norman Crowder
____ 3. Concluded that general memory was not a faculty that could be trained.	D. William James
____ 4. Largely responsible for connectionism theory	E. Sidney Pressey

Rubric:

(Maximum points: 4) +1 for each blank completed as follows:
1-E, 2-B, 3-D, and 4-A.

#2

Matching Prompt:

Directions: Column I is a list of ideas associated with certain principles of learning that were developed between 1885 and 1940. For each, determine the item from Column II that refers to the idea. All but one of the items from Column II should be used once and only once. Indicate your matches by writing the letter of items from Column II in the matching blanks under Column I.

I	II
____ 1. Animals tend to repeat satisfying experiences.	A. Associationist's belief
____ 2. Students initially enjoy teaching machines, then lose interest over time.	B. law of readiness
	C. principle of overlearning

ILLUSTRATION 8.13

Kisha's and Elwin's Refinement of Illustration 8.12

(Continued)

ILLUSTRATION 8.13 (Continued)

____ 3. An individual will not be
satisfied to act in a certain   D. pall effect
way until she or he feels
prepared to do so.   E. law of effect

____ 4. Memory is a process by which
experiences are re-excitement
of a location of the brain.

<u>Rubric</u>:

(Maximum points: 4) +1 for each blank completed as follows:
1-E, 2-D, 3-B, and 4-A.

<u>Prompt</u>:

Circle the letter in front of the one correct answer
to the question:

Langston Hughes wrote _____.

    a) *Mulatto*
    b) *Day of Absence*
    c) *Native Son*
    d) both a and b
    e) both a and c
    f) both b and c
    g) a, b, and c
    h) none of the above

<u>Rubric</u>:

+1 for "a" only; otherwise, +0.

ILLUSTRATION 8.14

A Flawed Variation of the Multiple-Choice Format

	this really cool teacher who had us use blocks to discover the rules for adding fractions. Then when she showed us how to do the algorithm, it made sense."
Kisha:	"So you discovered the relationship behind the process first."
Elwin:	"Exactly. Also, unlike my fourth-grade teacher, she showed us how the process generally worked before getting into the little tiny steps one at a time. I knew what I was getting at before starting."
Kisha:	"At what point did adding fractions—finding common denominators and all—become second nature to you?"
Elwin:	"Oh, it took awhile. She probably should have made us practice more. By the end of fifth grade, I was getting pretty proficient. Then I didn't use the skill over the

summer, and in sixth grade I had to relearn some of the steps, but it didn't take long to get my skill level back to where it was at the end of fifth grade."

Kisha: "What was the second process you thought of?"

Elwin: "Shooting a jump shot. I grew up watching guys shooting basketball, and I just started imitating them. I kept practicing and changing my technique according to what worked and eventually got some help from coaches."

Kisha: "Are we ready to describe how people develop process-knowledge skills?"

Elwin: "Initially, acquiring a process skill is similar to acquiring information in simple-knowledge learning. It seems to be important to first develop a big picture of the whole process."

Kisha: "We mimic what we see or hear others do and make crude attempts to accomplish what the process is supposed to accomplish."

Elwin: "Then we're introduced to the individual steps."

Kisha: "And practice and practice, polishing the steps—maybe with the help of some coaching or sometimes using only trial and error to tell us what to do differently."

Elwin: "And like in simple-knowledge learning, overlearning is necessary to retain the skill once you're doing it right."

Kisha: "Let's not forget your fifth-grade experiences compared to fourth grade."

Elwin: "That's right; we learn a process more efficiently if we first discover the underlying relationships that make the process work."

DELINEATING THE STEPS IN THE PROCESS

Return your attention to Cases 2.16 and 2.17, in which you imagined yourself first as a fourth-grader in Mr. Yengish's class and then in Ms. Arroya's class. In those cases, you were working on developing a process-knowledge skill; specifically, you were achieving the following objective:

> Students will compute the product of any two-digit whole numbers by any one-digit whole number (process knowledge).

Recall how much more informative it was for you to receive back Illustration 2.32's test paper from Ms. Arroya than it was to receive back Illustration 2.31 from Mr. Yengish.

In order for Ms. Arroya to be able to design Illustration 2.32's mini-experiments that would provide such diagnostic information on just how you were executing the process, Ms. Arroya had to have analyzed the process herself and delineated the steps.

Thus, before you are in a position to design mini-experiments for process-knowledge objectives (or, for that matter, lessons), you must analyze the process and delineate the steps for yourself. The first few times you do this, you may be quite surprised to discover that the process involves more steps than you, who are already proficient with them, had imagined. Shoenfeld (1985, p. 61) points out, "It is easy to underestimate the complexity of ostensibly simple procedures, especially after one has long since mastered them."

In Case 8.16, Ms. Ragusa delineates the steps in a process she plans to teach her students.

CASE 8.16

Ms. Ragusa thinks, "They've already discovered that a magnet can be used to create other magnets when I engaged them in the lesson for Objective C [listed in Illustration 7.10]. Now for Objective E [also listed in Illustration 7.10], I'll need to teach them how to efficiently use the process and also how to care for magnets so that they retain their power. They really haven't discovered that banging magnets around, heating them, or storing them improperly will weaken or destroy their magnetism. But

I'll go ahead and include caring for magnets as part of the process. They can work on hypotheses explaining why magnets need to be cared for in a special way when we get to lessons for Objectives F and I [listed in Illustration 7.10]. Okay, first of all I need to spell out the process so I can figure out how to teach it and monitor their learning as they develop the skill."

After several minutes of thought, Ms. Ragusa lists the steps shown in Illustration 8.15.

TO USE A MAGNET TO MAKE ANOTHER MAGNET:

1. <u>Select the object to be magnetized</u>. (The object must be made of magnetic material. Iron objects are easier than steel ones to magnetize but they don't keep their magnetic power as long. Slender objects like nails are easier to magnetize than thicker objects.)

2. <u>Select a strong magnet</u>.

3. <u>With one pole of the magnet stroke the object from one end to the other repeatedly</u>. (Make sure to lift the magnet clear of the object after each stroke. Don't stroke back and forth; always stroke in the same direction. The more strokes, the stronger the magnetic power of the object.)

4. <u>Immediately after completing Step 3, test the object to see if it is now a magnet by using it to pick up a small magnetic object (e.g., a steel straight pin)</u>.

5. <u>If the object's magnetic power is too weak for your purposes, then return to Step 3</u>.

TO CARE FOR A MAGNET:

<u>So as not to cause a magnet to lose power, do not throw, bang, hit, drop, vigorously shake, or heat the magnet</u>.

TO STORE A MAGNET:

<u>Put magnets away as shown in the diagram</u>:

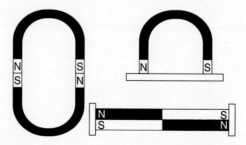

ILLUSTRATION 8.15

The Steps Ms. Ragusa Plans to Teach Her Students

Once you have the steps in the process clearly delineated in your mind, you are in a position to design mini-experiments for monitoring students as they learn that process during a four-stage, direct-instructional lesson: (1) general overview of the process, (2) step-by-step explanation, (3) trial execution of the process, error pattern analysis, and correction, and (4) overlearning the process.

GENERAL OVERVIEW OF THE PROCESS

Processes are based on relationships. If your students have already discovered the underlying relationship for the process, then explaining the purpose of the process is a trivial task. The first stage often begins with an announcement such as, "We've discovered that magnets can be used to make other magnets. Now we're going to develop our skills for creating magnets." Students are then provided with an outline of the process they'll be executing. This is particularly important for complex processes in which students are likely to get so focused on the individual steps that they lose sight of the overall task. For example, Ms. Ragusa demonstrates the procedure, generally outlining what she did to magnetize an object.

For some processes, students need to get into the habit of estimating or anticipating outcomes before executing a process. This (1) tends to add a little interest to the task as students want to check their predictions, (2) provides an informal check on the accuracy of the process, and (3) maintains some connection between the process and its underlying relationship. In Ms. Ragusa's lesson for Objective E from Illustration 7.10, she might, for example, teach her students to estimate the strength and longevity of the magnets they create based on the strength of the magnet they used, the size, shape, and material of the object to be magnetized, and how long they spend stroking the object with the magnet.

Whether or not you decide to include a predicting exercise in the first stage of a process-knowledge lesson depends on the subject-content of the objective and, of course, what you decide your students need. In Case 8.17, a teacher decides she should attend to predicting outcomes in the general-overview-of-the-process stage of one of her lessons.

CASE 8.17

Ms. Minoso teaches a lesson for the following objective:

> Given a whole number n and a percentage p, students compute p percent of n (process knowledge).

She administers a measurement relevant to students' achievement of the objective. Ms. Minoso examines students' responses, including Butch's responses to two prompts shown in Illustration 8.16.

Ms. Minoso thinks, "Butch, like so many of the others, misplaced the decimal for one of these. He really seems to know the process, but he doesn't catch careless errors—like the misplaced decimal for the first one—because he doesn't step back from the process and get an idea of what the outcome should be before diving into the individual steps." The following day, she engages Butch in the following conversation:

Ms. Minoso: "Butch, look at what you did for the first one where you computed 30% of 80."
Butch: "Oh! Is it wrong? I thought I did it like you showed us."
Ms. Minoso: "It appears to me that you completed all the steps you should have except for one mistake at the very end. Look at your final result, 240; does that seem right to you?"
Butch: "I don't know. If you said I did something wrong, it must not be right."
Ms. Minoso: "What about the second one; does your answer of 29.7 seem right?"
Butch: "I don't know. Did I mess up on that one too?"

1. What is your name? *Butch Rose*

2. Simplify each of the following; display your computations:

   a)   30% of 80   b)   30% of 99

$$
\begin{array}{r}
80 \\
\times .30 \\
\hline
00 \\
240 \\
\hline
240.0
\end{array}
\qquad\qquad
\begin{array}{r}
99 \\
\times .30 \\
\hline
00 \\
297 \\
\hline
29.70
\end{array}
$$

ILLUSTRATION 8.16

Butch's Responses to Two of Ms. Minoso's Prompts

Ms. Minoso: "29.7 is 30% of 99; your answer is correct."
Butch: "So why is the first one wrong?"
Ms. Minoso: "What number is larger, 80 or 99?"
Butch: "99."
Ms. Minoso: "Then what number should be larger, 30% of 80 or 30% of 99?"
Butch: "I guess 30% of 99."
Ms. Minoso: "Now, compare your answer to the first one to the answer on the second. What's larger, 240 or 29.7?"
Butch: "240 is. Oh! I should have moved that decimal over to the left one more place."
Ms. Minoso: "Next time, when you're working these kinds of computations, I want you to ask yourself before you even begin, 'About what should my answer be?' Your answer should make sense. When you've finished the computation, check to see if your answer is close to what you thought it should be. If it isn't, better go back and review what you did."
Butch: "Okay."
Ms. Minoso: "Let's practice that skill right now. 30% of 80 is larger or smaller than 80?"
Butch: "Smaller."
Ms. Minoso: "Is it going to be more or less than 40?"
Butch: "Uhh, less—I know! because 30% is less than half and half of 80 is 40!"

Ms. Minoso resolves to attend to estimating or predicting outcomes during the initial stage of lessons for at least some of her process-knowledge objectives.

STEP-BY-STEP EXPLANATION

The step-by-step explanation is the paramount stage of a process-knowledge lesson. You begin by explaining the first step to the students, and then having them try it. You then explain how the result of the first step triggers the second, and the second step is explained and tried. Movement to subsequent steps and the steps themselves are each explained and tried in turn.

TRIAL EXECUTION OF THE PROCESS, ERROR-PATTERN ANALYSIS, AND CORRECTION

Students respond to prompts designed to demonstrate any error patterns they may have learned by mistake. For example, see Illustration 2.32 for the prompts Ms. Arroya designed to detect error patterns in the computations. The first purpose of this stage is to obtain formative feedback on just what aspects of the process students execute correctly and which ones they do not. The correctly executed steps are reinforced, while improperly executed steps are corrected. Additional coaching and practice are provided as warranted by the formative feedback.

OVERLEARNING THE PROCESS

Just as students need extended exposure to information acquired in a simple-knowledge lesson for long-term retention, so too must students continue to practice a process so that they don't lose their newly acquired skill. The efficient way to do this is to make sure students use the process in subsequent lessons and units long after the process-knowledge objective is initially achieved.

INDICATORS OF PROGRESS AS STUDENTS ENGAGE IN PROCESS-KNOWLEDGE LESSONS

In Case 8.18, Ms. Ragusa conducts informal mini-experiments to monitor students' progress during a four-stage process-knowledge lesson.

CASE 8.18

Ms. Ragusa conducts a lesson for the following objective:

E. Students know how to make and care for magnets (process knowledge).

In a large-group session, she announces, "On Tuesday and Wednesday, we discovered that a magnet can be used to make other magnets. Now, we're going to build on that discovery to develop our skills for creating new magnets. Let's review some of the statements we agreed to on Wednesday." She flashes the list shown in Illustration 8.17 on the overhead screen and reads the statements aloud with the class.

To lead students to predict outcomes of the process and also to obtain information for formative feedback on their understanding of the statements on the transparency and of the relationships they previously discovered, Ms. Ragusa engages the class in the following dialogue:

Ms. Ragusa:	"I'm going to ask several questions. After each, I'll call on one of you to answer. When the person answers, I would like the rest of you who agree with the answer to put your hands on top your heads like this. Those of you who disagree with the answer should fold your arms like this. Okay, here we go. First question: If we want to make magnets that are going to have much strength and ones that will last for more than just a few seconds, we better start off with what? Okay, Haeja."
Haeja:	"Another magnet."
Ms. Ragusa:	"I see one, two,—most of us have our hands on top our heads. Why do you agree, Chen?"
Chen:	"Because it takes a magnet to make a magnet."
Ms. Ragusa:	"I accept that, but Willard has his arms folded. Why do you disagree with Haeja's answer, Willard?"
Willard:	"You said we wanted magnets with much strength and that last long. It takes a strong magnet to do that, not any magnet. It's got to be powerful."

😊 Magnets can turn things into magnets.

😊 Iron nails can be turned into magnets.

😊 Rubbing a magnet on a stick of wood doesn't work.

😊 Sliding a magnet the right way on a steel bar makes another magnet.

😊 Nails are easier to make into magnets than the steel bar.

😊 The steel bar was a stronger magnet than the nails.

😊 The more you work at making a magnet, the stronger the magnet.

ILLUSTRATION 8.17

Transparency Ms. Ragusa Uses in the Initial Stage of a Process-Knowledge Lesson

Ms. Ragusa: "Let's see those responses to Willard's answer. I see Cynthia, Greg, Adam, Monica, Juan, and even Haeja with their hands on their heads—okay, I see you, James—but the rest of you haven't signaled whether you agree with Willard or not. Oh! Hands are going up on the heads in a hurry now. But Sun-li is disagreeing with Willard. You've got the floor, Sun-li."

Sun-li: "I think what Willard said is right, but I don't agree that that means that Haeja's answer was wrong."

Ms. Ragusa: "Wow! A lot of hands on their heads. Sun-li, more than a few people agree with you. Why do you agree with Sun-li, Bryce?"

Bryce: "Willard is right because a powerful magnet will work better. But Haeja didn't say the magnet couldn't be powerful, so she's right too."

Ms. Ragusa: "Thank you." I see by all the hands on heads, it's time to move on to the next question. Here we go. What kinds of objects are we going to be able to magnetize? What kind will we be able to magnetize easily? Monica.

Monica: "Steel or iron."

Ms. Ragusa: "Everyone seems to agree except for Willard and Salinda. How would you answer the question, Salinda?"

Salinda: "I think we should use iron because we found out from before that iron works better."

Ms. Ragusa: "Some people don't agree. Tell us, Salinda, what do you mean by 'better'?"

Salinda: "We got the iron to be a magnet faster than steel."

Ms. Ragusa: "I agree but some of us don't. Okay, Pauline."

Pauline: "I don't know."

Ms. Ragusa: "Pauline, call on someone else who has their arms folded."

Pauline: "Brenda."

Brenda: "The steel stays a magnet longer than the iron."

Ms. Ragusa: "Steel or iron will work fine. The iron is easier to magnetize, but a steel magnet usually holds its power longer. We'll also find that small, thin objects like steel pins or iron nails are easier to turn into magnets than objects shaped like this (displaying a small iron sphere). We'll also see that the closer you follow the steps I'm about to show you and the longer you carry out the process, the stronger your new magnet will be."

Using a powerful U-shaped magnet, Ms. Ragusa magnetizes an iron nail for the class and demonstrates its power to pick up steel pins. She then demonstrates two ways to store the horseshoe magnet as well as a bar magnet, as shown in Illustration 8.18. Each step is accompanied by a brief explanation and followed by a question such as, "What did I just do? Greg." She continues to use the hands-on-head or arms-folded procedure for informal mini-experiments to indicate who is and who isn't following the steps.

Ms. Ragusa organizes the class into 12 pairs of students, supplying each pair with a box containing three magnets (1 powerful, 2 weak), a variety of materials (some good candidates to be magnetized, others poor candidates to be magnetized). Within each pair, one student attempts to create a magnet with materials from the box while her or his partner serves as coach. They reverse roles. In the meantime, Ms. Ragusa circulates among the students, noting successes and failures with various steps; she makes suggestions as warranted by the formative feedback.

The following day, she has them create and store more magnets while she again provides corrective feedback. In subsequent lessons (e.g., those for Objectives F and J listed in Illustration 7.10), students will apply their magnet-making skills.

INDICATORS OF STUDENTS' ACHIEVEMENT OF PROCESS-KNOWLEDGE OBJECTIVES

MINI-EXPERIMENTS RELEVANT TO PROCESS-KNOWLEDGE OBJECTIVES

Students achieve a process-knowledge objective by remembering how to follow the steps in a sequence or employ some technique. Thus, a mini-experiment for such an objective should prompt students to exhibit whether or not they know how to follow the procedure. For a simple-knowledge objective, only a single response needs to be remembered; but for process-knowledge, a sequence of responses is required so that each response is dependent on the

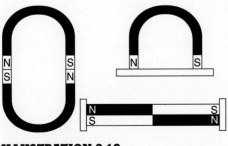

ILLUSTRATION 8.18

How to Store Magnets So They Retain Their Power

previous one. Consequently, when measuring process-knowledge achievement, you should not simply look at the final outcome as you would for simple-knowledge learning; you need to check which steps are remembered and which are not. Emphasis is on the process rather than the final outcome.

Design a mini-experiment relevant to how well Ms. Ragusa's students achieve Objective E from Case 8.18. Exchange your mini-experiment with that of a colleague; discuss and critique one another's mini-experiments.

In Case 8.19, Elwin and Kisha discuss theirs.

CASE 8.19

Elwin:	"For mine, I'd supply each student with an iron nail and a strong bar or horseshoe magnet and direct the class to magnetize the nail. They'd try it at their desks, and when each is done, she or he is to signal me with a raised hand, and then I check to see if the nail is magnetized with my own piece of iron. If it is, I check off that skill; if not, I don't."
Kisha:	"What you describe seems reasonable, but I have two concerns. First of all, I checked Illustration 8.17—the one with the steps Ms. Ragusa wanted them to learn. The first step is for them to select an object to be magnetized; the second is to select a strong magnet. You won't be prompting them to execute those two steps."
Elwin:	"Good point! Besides the nail and the strong magnet, I should supply them with some non-magnetic objects—like plastic or wooden sticks—and a couple of weak magnets. Thanks for bringing that up. What's your other concern?"
Kisha:	"Since it's a process-knowledge skill you're trying to measure, shouldn't you be looking at more than just whether or not they're successful? Should you be looking at how they attempted each step—use a performance-observation format instead of the product-examination format you suggested?"
Elwin:	"That would be better. I'd have to develop a more elaborate, detailed rubric. Oh! What about this? To save time and not have to observe each and every student, what if I use the product-examination prompt with my simple rubric—with the refinements we agreed to before—you know, supplying them with the weak magnets and so forth—to see if they could produce a magnet. Then for those that don't, I could use the performance-observation mini-experiment to diagnose what they're doing."
Kisha:	"You're assuming that if they produced a magnet, they followed the steps. Then you identify the steps for students who need the diagnosis. That makes sense to me."
Elwin:	"Let's see yours."

Kisha shows Elwin Illustration 8.19.

DISPLAY-PROCESS MINI-EXPERIMENTS RELEVANT TO PROCESS-KNOWLEDGE OBJECTIVES

A mini-experiment that prompts students to complete a task and exhibit evidence of the steps used to attempt the task has a *display-process format*. *Display-process* prompts (e.g., those in Illustration 8.16) are especially useful in diagnosing students' progress with process-knowledge skills when used in conjunction with rubrics that focus attention on the individual steps. Illustration 8.20 is an example.

Performance-Observation Prompt:

I will interview each student while the rest of the class is engaged in some independent-work activity. I'll call the student to my desk and direct him/her to magnetize one of the objects in a box containing two iron rods, an aluminum rod, and a plastic stick (each about 10 cm long) using one of the magnets in a second box. The second box will contain one weak bar magnet and one strong bar magnet. Then I'll observe what he/she does, recording my observations on the chart I developed for the rubric.

Rubric:

Check exactly one category for each of steps 1, 2, & 4, but as many as are observed for Step 3:

1. In selecting the object to magnetize:

_____ Selects one of the iron rods without first testing to see if it's made of magnetic material

_____ Selects the aluminum rod without first testing to see if it's made of magnetic material

_____ Selects the plastic rod without first testing to see if it's made of magnetic material

_____ Selects one of the iron rods after testing to see if it's made of magnetic material

_____ Selects the aluminum rod after testing to see if it's made of magnetic material

_____ Selects the plastic rod after testing to see if it's made of magnetic material

_____ Other -- explain: _____

2. In selecting the magnet:

_____ Selects the stronger one without first testing its power against the other

_____ Selects the weaker one without first testing its power against the other

_____ Selects the stronger one after testing its power against the other

ILLUSTRATION 8.19

The Mini-Experiment Kisha Designed for Ms. Ragusa's Objective E

(Continued)

ILLUSTRATION 8.19 *(Continued)*

_____ Selects the weaker one after testing its power against the other

_____ Other -- explain: _____

3. In attempting to magnetize the object:

   _____ Contacts the object with the magnet in some manner

   _____ Strokes the object with the magnet in some manner

   _____ Uses only one pole of the magnet in contact with the object

   _____ Strokes in one direction only

   _____ Repeats strokes enough times to expect reasonable magnetic power

   _____ Uses only clean strokes, clearing the magnet from the object after each stroke

   _____ Other -- explain: _____

4. In testing the object's magnetic power:

   _____ Tests the power immediately by seeing if it is repelled by the other end of the magnet or seeing if it attracts a piece of magnetic material (e.g., the other iron rod)

   _____ Does not test the power immediately

   _____ Other -- explain: _____

PERFORMANCE OBSERVATION MINI-EXPERIMENTS RELEVANT TO PROCESS-KNOWLEDGE OBJECTIVES

Examine the two mini-experiments shown by Illustration 8.21. Discuss with a colleague why the first has a performance-observation format but the second one does not.

Students' abilities to respond to performance-observation prompts for process-knowledge objectives often depend not only on how well they remember the steps in the process but also some psychomotor and affective behaviors. Consider Case 8.20.

CASE 8.20

As part of a measurement of five-year old Alex's achievement of the following objective, Ms. Bailey conducts the mini-experiment shown by Illustration 8.22:

> Students follow the steps described in the Groves-Haimowitz handwriting manual to write uppercase letters (process knowledge).

In response to the prompt, Alex wrote the figure shown in Illustration 8.23.

Mini-Experiment for the following objective:

Students simplify algebraic polynomial expressions with nested parentheses (process knowledge).

Prompt:

Simplify (display your work):

$$\frac{1}{3} (c - (c - 3c) - 6(2c + c))$$

Rubric:

12 points maximum distributed according to six 2-point scales with a criterion for each scale so that +2 is recorded if the criterion is met in all phases of the work, +1 if it is met only some of the time, and +0 if it is never met. The six criteria are as follows:

_____ 1. Computations proceed from inside out relative to parentheses.

_____ 2. Associative properties are appropriately applied.

_____ 3. Distributive properties are appropriately applied.

_____ 4. Numerical computations are accurate.

_____ 5. Final answer is simplified completely.

_____ 6. Final answer is equivalent to -5c.

ILLUSTRATION 8.20

Example of a Display-Process Mini-Experiment

Because Ms. Bailey's mini-experiment has a performance-observation format, she was able to detect that Alex appeared to know the steps in the process for forming the uppercase "A," but that he appeared to need to also achieve a psychomotor-skill performance objective before he's able to form legible letters. She also considers the possibility that Alex didn't take the task seriously and chose to joke around rather than to try to make the "A" as well as he could. To check her hypothesis that Alex has actually achieved the stated process-knowledge objective but needs to engage in a lesson for a psychomotor-skill performance objective, she decides to conduct another mini-experiment—one that is relevant to the following objective:

Students display the psychomotor skill needed to employ the steps described in the Groves-Haimowitz handwriting manual to write uppercase letters (psychomotor skill).

1. <u>Mini-Experiment for the following objective</u>:

   Students know how to perform mouth-to-mouth artificial resuscitation (process knowledge).

   <u>Performance-Observation Prompt</u>:

   The student is told to apply mouth to mouth artificial resuscitation on the practice dummy.

   <u>Rubric</u>:

   The teacher observes the student work with the dummy and records which of the following steps are executed in proper sequence with the following checksheet:

   _____1. Attempts to clear obstructions.

         Comments:

   _____2. Pinches nose.

         Comments:

   _____3. Uses proper mouth technique.

         Comments:

   _____4. Exhales into dummy's mouth.

         Comments:

   _____5. Uses proper inhale/exhale rhythm.

         Comments:

2. <u>Mini-Experiment for the following objective</u>:

   Students know how to apply a pressure wrap immediately following a lateral-ankle sprain (process knowledge).

   <u>Product-Examination Prompt</u>:

   Students work in pairs. Each student is directed to apply a pressure wrap to her/his partner as if the partner just

ILLUSTRATION 8.21

Why Is the First Mini-Experiment a Performance Observation but Not the Second?

ILLUSTRATION 8.21 (Continued)

suffered a lateral ankle sprain. As the work is completed,
students are to inform the teacher to examine the wrap.

Rubric:

The teacher examines the finished wrap and, using the
following checksheet, records which features of the wrap
are evident:

_____1. The weave is inside-out.

 Comments:

_____2. The wrap is stable, not loose.

 Comments:

_____3. The wrap is not so tight that it restricts
 circulation too severely.

 Comments:

_____4. The wrap is smooth, free of wrinkles and folds.

 Comments:

How might Ms. Bailey design a mini-experiment for the psychomotor-skill performance objective she stated? That is a question that will be addressed in Chapter 13.

In Case 8.21, a performance-observation mini-experiment is used for a process-knowledge objective with the same student twice, but with differing results.

CASE 8.21

As part of a special social studies program for students whose parents recently migrated to the United States, Mr. Palmero includes the following objective in a unit focusing on the geography of the native countries of the students' parents:

Students locate the native country of their parents on a world map (process knowledge).

Mr. Palmero uses the globe in the classroom to show students where the respective countries are located. Later, he uses the same globe to conduct the mini-experiment shown in Illustration 8.24 to Ramon, a Cuban-born six-year-old. Ramon responds by pointing directly to Cuba's location on the globe.

A week later, Ms. Fernandez visits the school site in an effort to evaluate the success of the program. At one point, she conducts Illustration 8.24's mini-experiment with Ramon. Using a globe she brought

<u>Performance-Observation Prompt</u>:

The student is given a pencil and lined paper and told to make a capital letter A.

<u>Rubric</u>:

The teacher watches the student proceed using the following 5-point checksheet:

____ 1. Uses exactly three strokes.

____ 2. Strokes are made in the designated sequence:

____ 3. Strokes are made in the designated directions:

____ 4. Letter properly spaced between lines:

____ 5. The resulting "A" is legible.

Comments:

ILLUSTRATION 8.22

Mini-Experiment Ms. Bailey Conducted with Alex

from her office, Ms. Fernandez displays it to Ramon and says, "Point to Cuba." Without hesitation, Ramon turns the globe. Frowning, Ramon looks up and down as if he knows exactly what he's looking for but can't find it. Finally, Ramon tells Ms. Fernandez, "It's not here!" Pointing to Cuba, Ms. Fernandez says, "That's okay. Cuba is right here." "Oh!" says Ramon, "I thought Cuba was yellow."

Ms. Fernandez realizes that Ramon correctly responded to the prompt when Mr. Palmero used the classroom globe not because Ramon had achieved the objective, but because he had associated Cuba with a color.

ILLUSTRATION 8.23

What Alex Wrote in Response to Illustration 8.22's Prompt

Performance-Observation Prompt:

In a one-to-one format, the teacher places a standard globe map in front of the student and spins it around randomly. Then the teacher directs the student, "Point to Cuba."

Rubric:

The teacher observes what the student does using the following checksheet:

___ 1. The student turns the globe to the Western hemisphere.

___ 2. The student at least points in the vicinity of the Gulf of Mexico, Bahamas, and Caribbean Sea.

___ 3. The student points to Cuba.

ILLUSTRATION 8.24

Multiple-Choice Mini-Experiment Both Mr. Palmero and Ms. Fernandez Used with Six-Year-Old Ramon

MULTIPLE-CHOICE MINI-EXPERIMENTS RELEVANT TO PROCESS-KNOWLEDGE OBJECTIVES

The performance-observation format is generally more conducive to process-knowledge objectives than the multiple-choice format. However, for some objectives, multiple-choice mini-experiments can be designed to help diagnose students' error patterns in a process. Case 8.22 is an example.

CASE 8.22

Mr. Chapley, a fourth-grade teacher, is expanding his computer file for the following objective:

Students compute the product of three-digit and one-digit whole numbers in cases where regrouping is necessary and no digit is 0 (process knowledge).

He attempts to design mini-experiments that will provide information not only on how well students can execute the computation but also on exactly what they are doing when they compute incorrectly. Over the years, he has identified a number of common error patterns that students make while executing the computation specified by the objective. Thus, he thinks, as he designs one multiple-choice prompt, "For the stem, I'll use 423 × 7. That fits the subject-content of the objective. If that's multiplied out correctly it's, ahh, 2961; so that'll be one of the alternatives. I'll get the distractors by using some of the common error patterns. Let's see; if I multiply from left to right instead of right to left and do the regrouping, I get, let's see, 2323. Executing the algorithm correctly except for adding the carried digit before multiplying gets, ahh, 4281. One more. Sometimes students just multiply two unit's digits and bring the rest down. That comes out to be 4221."

He enters the mini-experiment into the computer file; it's displayed by Illustration 8.25. After it is used on a measurement, Mr. Chapley records the percentage of students who select each alternative. The resulting percentages serve as formative feedback for planning subsequent lessons.

SYNTHESIS ACTIVITIES FOR CHAPTER 8

1. Retrieve the computerized folder you set up when you engaged in Synthesis Activity 2 for Chapter 6. From your work doing Synthesis Activity 3 for Chapter 6, each file contains at least one mini-experiment. Call up each of those files that is for either a simple-knowledge or process-knowledge objective. Now, in light of your work with Chapter 8, revise the mini-experiments in those files. For each file (i.e., files for simple-knowledge or process-knowledge objectives), design at least two more mini-experiments and insert them into the file.

2. With a colleague, exchange printouts of the mini-experiments you designed or revised when you engaged in Synthesis Activity 1. Discuss and critique one another's mini-experiments. Revise them as you decide they should be revised.

3. Retrieve the goal defined by a set of weighted objectives you developed for Synthesis Activity 3 for Chapter 5. Select one of the simple-knowledge or process-knowledge objectives from that set (if indeed the set includes at least one such objective). Now, design a four-stage lesson for leading students to achieve that objective. For each stage, design a mini-experiment to provide you with indicators of your students' progress during that stage. Note that this synthesis activity is prompting you to plan something similar to what Mr. Boudreaux did in Case 8.4 and Ms. Ragusa did in Case 8.18.

4. With a colleague, share and discuss your work from Synthesis Activity 3. Revise the mini-experiments in light of your discussions.

```
Multiple-Choice Prompt:

    Without using your calculator, find the product. Circle the
    letter by the number you get:

            423 × 7 = ?

        a) 2323        b) 4281      c) 4221        d) 2961

Rubric:

        +1 for d; otherwise, +0.
```

ILLUSTRATION 8.25

Mr. Chapley Designs a Multiple-Choice Prompt to Provide Information on Students' Error Patterns

TRANSITIONAL ACTIVITY FROM CHAPTER 8 TO CHAPTER 9

In a discussion with two or more of your colleagues, address the following questions:

1. As students engage in our lessons for our comprehension-and-communication-skills objectives, how do we manage to monitor their progress?

2. How do we design mini-experiments that are relevant to comprehension-and-communication-skills objectives?

Monitoring Students' Development of Comprehension and Communication Skills

⇔ GOAL OF CHAPTER 9

Chapter 9 is intended to lead you to design mini-experiments that will help you monitor students' development of comprehension and communication skills. More specifically the objectives are as follows:

A. You will explain the stages through which students learn to comprehend and communicate messages (discover a relationship) 7%.

B. You will design mini-experiments for gauging students' progress as they engage in lessons for comprehension-and communication-skills objectives (application) 40%.

C. You will design mini-experiments relevant to how well students have achieved comprehension-and-communication-skills objectives (application) 36%.

D. You will extend your ability to explain fundamental principles for using a variety of mini-experiment formats (discover a relationship) 12%.

E. You will incorporate the following technical phrases in your working professional vocabulary: "mode of communication," "literal understanding," and "interpretive understanding" (comprehension and communication skills) 5%.

HOW STUDENTS LEARN TO INTERPRET, EXTRACT MEANING FROM, AND COMMUNICATE MESSAGES

MESSAGES FOR STUDENTS TO COMPREHEND AND COMMUNICATE

To be able to design mini-experiments relevant to your students' progress with respect to comprehension-and-communication-skills objectives, you need to be familiar with how students learn to interpret, extract meaning from, and communicate messages. From Chapter 5, reread the section "Comprehension and Communication Skills" on pages 237–238.

Curricula for virtually all subject-content areas (e.g., business education, English, health and physical education, home economics, mathematics, music, science, and social studies) include certain messages for students to comprehend and communicate. For example, U. S. history teachers typically attempt to lead their students to comprehend and explain the message expressed by the Declaration of Independence. Curricula for most subject-content areas also attend to students' being able to understand and use the special or technical language of the discipline (i.e., modes of communications). For example, geography teachers typically attempt to lead their students to read maps as well as to draw maps to communicate geographical features of an area. However, curricula for some subject-content areas focus almost entirely on developing students' abilities to use certain modes of communication. These include content-subject areas such as foreign language, music, reading, signed English, speech, visual arts, and writing.

Illustration 9.1 is a sample of objectives specifying messages for subject-content and the comprehension-and-communication-skills learning level. To help clarify each objective, a mini-experiment designed to be relevant to that objective is also included. Similarly, Illustration 9.2 is a sample of comprehension-and-communication-skills objectives and mini-experiments, but the subject-contents specified by Illustration 9.2 objectives are communication modes rather than messages. To help you distinguish between these two types of subject-contents specified by comprehension-and-communication-skills objectives, please examine Illustrations 9.1 and 9.2. The mini-experiments will serve as examples in subsequent sections of this chapter.

Comprehension-and-communication-skills lessons for objectives specifying messages as subject-content proceed somewhat differently from lessons for comprehension-and-communications-skills lessons for objectives specifying modes of communication as subject-content.

LESSONS FOR COMPREHENSION AND COMMUNICATION OF MESSAGES
Literal and Interpretive Understanding

Comprehension-and-communication-skills lessons for objectives specifying messages as subject-content focus on two levels of understanding, *literal* and *interpretive*. Students *literally understand* a message if they can accurately translate its explicit meaning, as Edgardo demonstrates in Case 9.1.

CASE 9.1

Edgardo reads the following definition from the glossary of his science notebook:

> "*Magnetic field:* the space around a magnet where the magnet power reaches."

He then displays *literal understanding* of the definition by saying: "A magnetic field is like the air by the end of a magnet where something that gets in that part can—you know—be pulled in by the magnet."

Students understand a message at the *interpretive level* if they can infer implicit meaning and explain how aspects of the communication are used to convey the message, as demonstrated by Edgardo in Case 9.2.

CASE 9.2

From examining the same definition of magnetic field he read in Case 9.1, Edgardo displays *interpretive understanding* of the definition by extending his previous explanation when he says, "A strong magnet can pull things from far away because it has a big magnetic field—not like a weak magnet. The field is kinda shaped—you know—like this." Edgardo gestures with his hands, simulating the curved lines of force around a magnetic pole.

<hr>

#1

Objective (primary grade - classroom management):

Students explain in their own words the four standards for conduct posted on the classroom wall (comprehension and communication skills).

Interview Prompt and Rubric:

The student and teacher stand in front of the poster with the following four standards for conduct:

1. Take advantage of learning opportunities.

2. Cooperate with your classmates and teacher in the business of learning.

3. Help make our classroom a safe and happy place for all of us.

4. Follow your teacher's directions.

The interview is conducted for only one standard at a time. The part of the interview focusing on Standard 1 should take about 1 minute. At other times, the student is interviewed regarding Standard 2 (about 3 minutes), Standard 3 (about 3 minutes) and Standard 4 (about 1 minute).

For Standard 1:

A. The teacher reads Standard 1 aloud (pointing to each word as he/she does), then directs the student to repeat it (again pointing to each word).

B. The teacher directs the student to "think of a learning opportunity that you had today." If the student does not seem to understand the direction, the teacher clarifies but without suggesting the meaning of the phrase "learning opportunity." If the student responds with an example of a learning opportunity (e.g., "when you showed us how to make the bottles shoot up"), the teacher moves to Part C of this prompt. If not, the teacher notes that the he/she needs to reteach this standard to the student and terminates this phase of the interview.

C. The teacher directs the student to "tell me about a time when you took advantage of a learning opportunity." If the student responds with an example (e.g., "when I tried real hard to make my bottle shoot up high"), the teacher accepts the response as a positive indicator that the student comprehends Standard 1. If not, the teacher notes that the he/she needs to reteach this standard to the student.

<hr>

ILLUSTRATION 9.1

Examples of Comprehension-and-Communication-Skills Objectives Specifying Messages as Subject-Content (Each Accompanied by a Relevant Mini-Experiment)

(Continued)

ILLUSTRATION 9.1 (Continued)

For Standard 2:

A. The teacher reads Standard 2 aloud (pointing to each word as
   he/she does), then directs the student to repeat it (again pointing
   to each word).

B. The teacher asks the student, "Why do we say the business of learning?
   Why do we call learning a business?" If the student does not seem to understand the direction, the teacher clarifies but without suggesting the
   meaning of the phrase "business of learning." If the student's answer
   suggests that she/he thinks of learning as the reason why she/he, the
   teacher, and classmates come to school (e.g., by answering "because
   learning is what I'm supposed to do"), the teacher moves to Part C of
   this prompt. If not, the teacher notes that he/she needs to reteach this
   standard to the student and terminates this phase of the interview.

C. The teacher directs the student to "tell me about a time when you
   cooperated in the business of learning." If the student responds with
   an example (e.g., "when I showed Peter how to fix the fins on his bottle
   so it could go higher"), the teacher accepts the response as a positive
   indicator that the student comprehends Standard 2. If not, the teacher
   notes that he/she needs to reteach this standard to the student.

For Standard 3:

A. The teacher reads Standard 3 aloud (pointing to each word as
   he/she does), then directs the student to repeat it (again pointing
   to each word).

B. The teacher asks the student, "You just said 'all of us.' Who are all
   of us?" If the student does not seem to understand the direction, the
   teacher clarifies but without suggesting the meaning of the phrase "all
   of us." If the student's answer suggests that she/he understands that
   "all of us" refers to every student in the class as well as the teacher
   (e.g., by starting to name everybody or answering "everybody in here"),
   the teacher moves to Part C of this prompt. If not, the teacher notes
   that he/she needs to reteach this standard to the student and terminates
   this phase of the interview.

C. The teacher directs the student to "tell me about a time when you helped
   make our classroom a safe place." If the student responds with an example
   (e.g., "when I didn't shoot off my bottle until everyone was back like
   you said"), the teacher moves to Part D of this prompt. If not, the
   teacher notes that he/she needs to reteach this standard to the student.

D. The teacher directs the student to "tell me about a time when you helped
   make our classroom a happy place for one of us." If the student responds
   with an example (e.g., "I didn't make fun of Jamaki when his bottle
   didn't go up."), the teacher accepts the response as a positive indicator
   that the student comprehends Standard 3. If not, the teacher notes that
   he/she needs to reteach this standard to the student.

ILLUSTRATION 9.1 (Continued)

For Standard 4:

A. The teacher reads Standard 4 aloud (pointing to each word as
   he/she does), then directs the student to repeat it (again pointing
   to each word).

B. The teacher asks the student, "What do we mean by 'directions'?" If the
   student does not seem to understand the direction, the teacher clarifies
   but without suggesting the meaning of the word "directions." If the student's answer suggests that she/he understands the meaning (e.g., by answering "Doing like you say."), the teacher moves to Part C of this
   prompt. If not, the teacher notes that he/she needs to reteach this standard to the student and terminates this phase of the interview.

C. The teacher directs the student to "tell me about a time when you
   followed my directions." If the student responds with an example
   (e.g., "when I waited 'til everybody was back to shoot my bottle up"),
   the teacher accepts the response as a positive indicator that the
   student comprehends Standard 4. If not, the teacher notes that he/she
   needs to reteach this standard to the student.

#2

Objective (high school - U.S. History):

Students explain the salient points expressed in the *Declaration of Indepen-*
dence (comprehension and communication skills).

Multiple Multiple-Choice Prompt:

The following passage is taken from the second paragraph of the *Declaration of*
Independence (i.e., the paragraph after the Preamble):

> Prudence, indeed will dictate that Governments long established should
> not be changed for light and transient causes; and accordingly all ex-
> perience hath shown that mankind are more disposed to suffer, while
> evils are sufferable, than to right themselves by abolishing the forms
> to which they are accustomed. But when a long train of abuses and
> usurpations, pursuing invariably the same Objective evinces a design to
> reduce them under absolute Despotism, it is their right, it is their
> duty, to throw off such Government, and to provide new Guards for their
> future security.

Below is a list of 5 statements. At least some of these statements relate beliefs expressed in the above passage from the *Declaration of Independence*;
others may not. For each statement, decide whether or not it relates a belief
expressed in the above passage. If it does, write "Yes" in the blank in front
of the statement. If it does not, write "No" in the blank.

ILLUSTRATION 9.1 (Continued)

<u>The 5 statements</u>:

_____ A. Whenever a government makes mistakes, it should be overthrown.

_____ B. People will tolerate wrongdoing up to a point rather than make systemic changes in the way things are done.

_____ C. People have the right to revolt against an authority that abuses its power time and time again.

_____ D. Limitations should be imposed on the power of Government.

_____ E. The future security of a people depends on their ability to replace an existing armed force.

<u>Rubric</u>:

(maximum possible score: 5) +1 for each of the following responses: "No" for A and E, "Yes" for B, C, and D.

#3

<u>Objective (high school - mathematics)</u>:

Students explain why certain proofs of theorems presented in class are valid (comprehension and communication skills).

<u>Multiple Short-Response Prompt</u>:

Following is the Euclideans' classic proof that the set of prime numbers is infinite:

Suppose there are only finite prime numbers. Call the number of primes "n." Then we can list all the primes as follows: p_1, p_2, p_3, ..., p_n. Since primes are also integers, there exists a greatest prime. Let's call the greatest prime "p_k" with $1 \leq k \leq n$.

Now consider the number q such that

$$q = p_1 \cdot p_2 \cdot p_3 \cdot \ldots \cdot p_n + 1.$$

Note that since q is 1 more than the product of all n primes, q is greater than any one of the primes and that includes p_k which is the greatest prime.

However, if you divide q by any of the primes, you will get a remainder of 1. Thus, none of the primes is a divisor of q, and so q is itself a prime.

But it is impossible for q to be a prime that is greater than p_k, the greatest prime.

Since our supposition leads to this contradiction, the supposition must be false. Therefore, the set of prime numbers is infinite.

ILLUSTRATION 9.1 (Continued)

Following are 7 questions for you to answer about the proof or tasks
for you to complete that are related to the proof; respond to each using
the available page area:

A. Why could you <u>not</u> express all prime numbers as follows without the supposition given by the first sentence of the proof; p_1, p_2, p_3, ..., p_n?

B. From what two statements do the authors of the proof deduce that there is
a greatest prime?

C. What gives the authors the right to restrict k as follows: $1 \leq k \leq n$?

D. Demonstrate that $q > 11$.

E. Demonstrate that 11 is not a divisor of q.

F. Why is it impossible for q to be both prime and greater than p_k?

G. Explain why deducing a contradiction from the supposition leads to the
conclusion that the set of prime numbers is infinite.

ILLUSTRATION 9.1 (Continued)

Rubric:

(14 points possible) +2 for each of the following criteria clearly exhibited by the 7 parts of the response, +1 for which it is unclear if it's exhibited, and +0 for each that's clearly not exhibited:

A. The response to A indicates that the student recognizes that if there is a specific number of primes you can represent that number by "n." Also that if the supposition were not made, no such limit could be placed on the set of primes; without the supposition the listing of the primes would be open-ended (e.g., p_1, p_2, p_3, ...).

B. The response for B lists the equivalent of the following two statements: (1) There are infinitely many primes. (2) Primes are also integers.

C. The response for C indicates that the student understands that since p_k is prime that it must be one of the numbers in the list p_1, p_2, p_3, ..., p_n.

D. The response for D demonstrates that $q > 11$. For example:

"The product of the three smallest primes (i.e., 2, 3, 5) is 30 which is greater than 11. Multiplying all the primes together and adding 1 will result in an even greater number."

E. The response for E demonstrates why q is not a divisor of 11. For example:

"Suppose 11 is represented in the list of all primes used by the author as 'p_1.' Then $q \div 11 = p_2 \cdot p_3 \cdot ... \cdot p_n + 1/11$ which is not an integer."

F. The response for F indicates that the student understands that if there were a greatest prime, it would have to be unique.

G. The response for G indicates that the student understands (1) contradictions can be legitimately deduced only from false suppositions and (2) a set is either finite or infinite.

#4

Objective (fifth grade - social studies):

Students explain the meaning of vocabulary words that are used during the unit on communities (comprehension and communication skills).

Essay Prompt:

Directions explained orally - responses to be written:

Our textbook defines "community" as "a social group of people who share some common things." Write one paragraph explaining what the definition means. Do not use any of the following words in your explanation: "social," "group" "share," and "common."

ILLUSTRATION 9.1 (Continued)

```
Rubric:

  Note: Only score if the definition is limited to one paragraph without the ex-
  cluded words; otherwise clarify the directions and have the student respond to
  the prompt again.

  (6 points possible) +2 for each of the following criteria clearly exhibited by
  the paragraph, +1 for which it is unclear if it's exhibited, and +0 for each
  that's clearly not exhibited:

    A. The response indicates that the student understands how "social"
       is used in the text's definition (i.e., includes the idea of people being
       together).

    B. The response indicates that the student understands that it takes more
       than one person to have a community.

    C. The response indicates that the student understands that "share some com-
       mon things" is used to indicate that there is some degree of cooperation
       or that people depend on one another (e.g., expressions like "help" and
       "need one another" can reflect this understanding).
```

Learning Activities for Literal Understanding

Interpretive understanding depends on literal understanding. Thus, the initial phase of a lesson for a comprehension-and-communication-skills objective should promote literal understanding. To design the learning activities, you will need to analyze the message to be understood, identifying prerequisites for understanding regarding the following:

- *Vocabulary.* What general, special, and technical terms and symbols will students need to understand in order to translate the message? Meanings of words, expressions, and symbols are learned through lessons for simple-knowledge objectives. Are there any prerequisite simple-knowledge objectives that students need to achieve before being ready for the comprehension-and-communication-skills lesson?
- *Concepts.* What concepts does the author of the message assume students have constructed prior to receiving the communication? In Cases 9.1 and 9.2, Edgardo's understanding of the definition depended on his prior construction of the concept of magnet.
- *Relationships.* What relationships does the author of the message assume students have discovered prior to receiving the communication? In Cases 9.1 and 9.2, Edgardo's understanding of the definition depended on his prior discovery of the effects magnets have on other objects.
- *Modes of Communication.* What modes of communication (e.g., maps or histograms) are used to convey the message students need to understand? Students may need to achieve a comprehension-and-communications-skills objective that specifies a particular mode of communication before they are ready to receive or communicate a message employing that communication mode.

#1

<u>Objectives (advanced French language - high school)</u>:

A. Using only spoken French, students describe what happened during some event to a person who does not know about the event but understands French (comprehension and communication skills).

B. From hearing someone describe an event in French (an event about which students have no prior knowledge), students can relate fundamental aspects of the event using English (comprehension and communication skills).

<u>Oral-Discourse and Short-Response Prompts</u>:

<u>Note</u>: This mini-experiment is conducted with two students at a time, Student A and Student B. It is intended to measure Student A's achievement of Objective A and Student B's achievement of Objective B.

The teacher gives Student A a one-paragraph written (in English) description of an event. For example:

Yesterday, Charles parked his car outside the south door of Shop-N-Save. He entered the nearby door and bought some shoes. He exited the store through the west door. He panicked when he did not see his car by the door. He went back inside the store and called the police. He waited for them for 30 minutes by the west door. Charles then heard the police car drive up on the south side of Shop-N-Save. Running to meet the police officers, he spotted his car where he had left it just as he began to report his "stolen" car.

Student A is given four minutes to read the paragraph and develop a description of the event. Then, speaking only in French, Student A takes up to four minutes to describe the event to Student B (who has not seen the paragraph). Student A's presentation to Student B is tape recorded.

Right after listening to Student A, Student B is directed to write responses to the following short-response prompts:

A. Why do you think Charles felt embarrassed by what happened?

ILLUSTRATION 9.2

Examples of Comprehension-and-Communication-Skills Objectives Specifying Modes of Communication as Subject-Content (Each Accompanied by a Relevant Mini-Experiment)

(Continued)

ILLUSTRATION 9.2 (Continued)

B. Where was Charles when he first panicked?

C. Why did Charles go to Shop-N-Save?

D. How many times did Charles go into Shop-N-Save during the event just de-
    scribed to you?

E. To whom do you think Charles spoke while he was in Shop-N-Save?

F. What do you think Charles will say to the police?

Rubric:

Note: Initially the teacher reads Student B's responses to the short-response
       prompts using the B scoring scale given below. If the teacher judges
       that Student B's responses to Questions A-F indicate that she/he com-
       prehended the event as described in the paragraph that Student A read,
       then the teacher uses the results of the mini-experiment as a positive
       indicator of Student A's achievement of Objective
       A and Student B's achievement of Objective B.

       If the teacher judges that Student B's responses do not provide
       positive indicators of achievement of Objective B, then the teacher
       listens to the tape of Student A's presentation (using the A scoring
       scale given below) to determine if Student A's oral presentation
       is indicative of positive achievement of Objective A. If it is, then
       the teacher uses the results of the mini-experiment as a positive indi-
       cation of Student A's achievement of Objective A and a negative

ILLUSTRATION 9.2 (Continued)

indicator of Student B's achievement of Objective B. If it is not, then the teacher uses the results as a negative indication of Student A's achievement of Objective A and as no indication (neither positive or negative) of Student B's achievement of Objective B.

The B scoring scale:

(12 points possible) +2 for each of the following criteria clearly exhibited by the responses, +1 for which it is unclear if it's exhibited, and +0 for each that's clearly not exhibited:

A. The answer to A indicates that Student B understands that Charles realizes that he made a mistake that resulted in police and possibly store personnel wasting their time.

B. The answer to B places Charles at the west side of the building.

C. The answer to C indicates that Student B understands that Charles bought shoes.

D. The answer to D indicates that Charles went into the store twice.

E. The answer to E indicates that Charles at least spoke to someone at the police station over the phone and also probably to store personnel when buying the shoes.

F. The answer to F indicates that Student B recognizes Charles no longer needs the police to help him locate his car.

The A scoring scale:

(20 points possible) +2 for each of the following things about the event that is clearly expressed by the oral presentation, +1 for which it is uncertain if it's clearly expressed, and +0 for each that is not clearly expressed:

A. The event occurred yesterday.

B. The event occurred at Shop-N-Save.

C. Charles left his car near the south door.

D. Charles bought shoes in the store.

E. Charles exited through the west door.

F. Charles panicked when he didn't see his car where he thought he had left it.

G. Charles went back in the store to call the police.

H. Charles waited for the police by the west door for 30 minutes.

I. Charles heard the police drive up on the south side of the building.

J. Charles spotted his car just as he got to the police to report that his car was stolen.

ILLUSTRATION 9.2 (Continued)

#2

<u>Objective (primary grade - reading)</u>:

From reading a level 2.1 paragraph, students can place events described in the paragraph in a time sequence (comprehension and communication skills).

<u>Interview Prompt and Rubric</u>:

The teacher directs the student to silently read the following:

It is dark outside. The little bird waits for the sky to be bright. This morning the bird will try to fly. Her mother told her to wait for the sky to be bright. Finally, the sky is bright. She moves her wings. The bird is flying. Her Mother is not worried anymore.

A. The teacher then asks the student, "When did the little bird's mother tell her to wait for the sky to be bright?"

If the student's response indicates that he/she does not understand that the mother told her some time before the sky was bright, then the teacher accepts that as a negative indicator of objective achievement and moves to Step B of this prompt.

If the student's response indicates that he/she understands that the mother told her some time before the sky was bright, then the teacher accepts that as a positive indicator of objective achievement and then asks the student, "How do you know that the bird's mother told her that before the sky was bright?" If the student provides a tenable rationale, then the teacher accepts that as a positive indicator of objective achievement and moves to Step B of this prompt. If the student doesn't provide a tenable rationale, then the response is interpreted as neither a positive or negative indicator and the teacher moves to Step B.

B. The teacher then asks the student, "When was the little bird's mother worried?"

If the student's response indicates that he/she does not understand that the mother was worried before the little bird started flying, then the teacher accepts that as a negative indicator of objective achievement and moves to Step C of this prompt.

If the student's response indicates that he/she understands that the mother was worried before the little bird started flying, then the teacher accepts that as a positive indicator of objective achievement and then asks the student, "How do you know that the bird's mother was worried before the little bird flew?" If the student provides a tenable rationale, then the teacher accepts that as a positive indicator of objective achievement and moves to Step C of this prompt. If the student doesn't provide a tenable rationale, then the response is interpreted as neither a positive or negative indicator and the teacher moves to Step C.

ILLUSTRATION 9.2 (Continued)

C. The teacher then asks the student, "About what time of the day
do you think it was when the little bird was waiting and waiting
to try to fly?"

If the student's answer suggests a time other than in the morning near
dawn or at least shortly after dawn (e.g., 9 o'clock or earlier), then
the teacher accepts that as a negative indicator of objective achievement
and terminates the interview.

If the student's answer suggests a time in the morning near dawn or at
least shortly after dawn (e.g., 9 o'clock or earlier), then the teacher
accepts that as a positive indicator of objective achievement and then
asks the student, "Why do you think it was that time of the morning?" If
the student provides a tenable rationale, then the teacher accepts that
as a positive indicator of objective achievement and terminates the interview. If the student doesn't provide a tenable rationale, then the response is interpreted as neither a positive or negative indicator and the
teacher terminates the interview.

#3

Objective (middle school - Signed English):

From watching a person expressing two or more thought units in signed English,
students translate the expression into conventional spoken English (comprehension and communication skills).

Video-Based Multiple-Choice Prompt:

Directions: When the number of this prompt appears on the TV monitor, translate the sign language of the person on the screen. After the signing is completed, select the best interpretation that is given below and circle the
letter of your choice:

A. "Only one job is still available."

B. "Is a job still available?"

C. "A few jobs are still available."

D. "No jobs are available."

E. "How many jobs are available?"

Rubric:

+1 for circling "E;" otherwise +0

#4

Objective (science - upper elementary):

From reading a two-dimensional bar graph, students explain what the data indicate about the relationship between the two variables (comprehension and communication skills).

ILLUSTRATION 9.2 (Continued)

Multiple-Choice and Short-Response Prompt:

Oral directions: According to the graph, at what time of the day was it the coldest? Circle the letter in front of your answer. After you've made your selection, describe what you saw was in the graph that helped you answer the question.

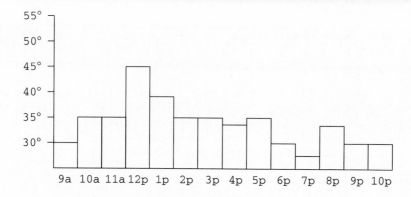

a) 9a

b) 12p

c) 3p

d) 7p

What you saw in the graph that helped you select your answer:

_____

_____

_____

Rubric:

(maximum score: 3) +1 for circling "d." For the description, score either +2, +1, or +0 depending on how clearly the student's description indicates that she/he chose "d" because the bar over "7p" is shorter than the bars over any of the other times.

Learning Activities for Interpretive Understanding

Interpretive understanding of a message is achieved with learning activities designed with inquiry instructional strategies in mind. Open-ended questions are used to stimulate students to examine the message so that they extract its main idea, facts, assumptions, and conclusions. When you get to the section "Indicators of Progress as Students Engage in Comprehension-

and-Communication-Skills Lessons" and read Case 9.4, you'll note how Ms. Ragusa shifts from direct instructional activities during the literal understanding phase to activities leading students to generate ideas during the phase for interpretive understanding.

LESSONS FOR COMPREHENSION AND FLUENCY WITH MODES OF COMMUNICATION

To comprehend and communicate messages within various subject-content areas, students need to be able to use the conventional modes of communications for those areas. A comprehension-and-communication-skills lesson for an objective specifying a mode of communication should include learning activities that (1) use direct teaching strategies to inform students about the special conventions of the mode and (2) use inquiry strategies for leading students to develop techniques for using that mode.

INDICATORS OF PROGRESS AS STUDENTS ENGAGE IN COMPREHENSION-AND-COMMUNICATION-SKILLS LESSONS

In Cases 9.3 and 9.4, teachers monitor students' learning as they engage in comprehension-and-communication-skills lessons; Case 9.3 focuses on a mode of communication, whereas Case 9.4 focuses on a message. As you study these two cases, note the prompts with which the teachers confront students throughout the lessons. For each, imagine the rubrics the teachers follow in their minds as they listen to and observe students' responses.

CASE 9.3

Mr. Scott frequently plans lessons so that during a large-group activity, he leads students to formulate hypotheses based on data that were collected during a cooperative-group activity or for homework. For some of these lessons, he believes that students would more readily recognize patterns in data if those data were expressed as histograms. Thus, he includes the following objective in an integrated mathematics and science unit:

> Given data for independent and dependent variables expressed as a histogram, students summarize what the data indicate about the relationship between the two variables (comprehension and communication skill).

To begin the lesson, Mr. Scott holds up a large jar of marbles and tells the class, "Look at this jar full of marbles. Now silently guess how many marbles are in the jar. Write your number down right now." He then flashes Illustration 9.3 on the overhead screen and directs students one at a time to read their guesses aloud. With each response, he adds an "X" to the graph until he gets Illustration 9.4's histogram upon recording the last student's number.

He engages the class in the following dialogue:

Mr. Scott:	"The type of graph you're looking at is called a 'histogram.' Along the bottom we indicated our what? Eva."
Eva:	"The numbers we guessed. But you didn't put our exact guesses down."
Mr. Scott:	"What did I do instead? Tracy."
Tracy:	"You lumped them into little groups."
Mr. Scott:	"Why do you suppose I recorded your numbers in little neighborhoods instead of having a different spot for each different number? Leona."
Leona:	"I don't know."

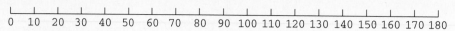

ILLUSTRATION 9.3

Mr. Scott's First Transparency for His Lesson on Histograms

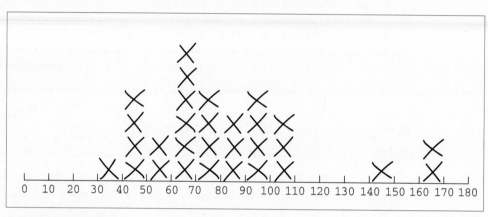

ILLUSTRATION 9.4

The Histogram Mr. Scott Used for His Comprehension-and-Communication-Skills Lesson

Mr. Scott:	"How would our graph be different if we used a spot for each number instead of grouping the numbers into neighborhoods, Leona?"

Mr. Scott demonstrates the point by beginning to draw a horizontal axis with a point for each number.

Leona:	"You'd have to make it a lot wider."
Mr. Scott:	"And what would happen to the shape of the graph? Grant."
Grant:	"It would be flatter, more even—not like those buildings you got."
Mr. Scott:	"Where's the highest building on the histogram? Lyle."
Lyle:	"Right there." (pointing)
Mr. Scott:	"I don't know where you mean, Lyle."
Lyle:	"Here, I'll show you." (starting to get up)
Mr. Scott:	"I want you to tell me from your desk, not show me."
Lyle:	"I can't."
Mr. Scott:	"Read what it says below the tallest building and then find a way to tell me where the highest building is without pointing to it."
Lyle:	"It's on top between 60 and 70."

The dialogue continues, culminating in Mr. Scott explaining how to read a histogram. Mr. Scott then distributes copies of the tasksheet shown in Illustration 9.5 and circulates about the room, providing constructive feedback as students complete it in an independent work session.

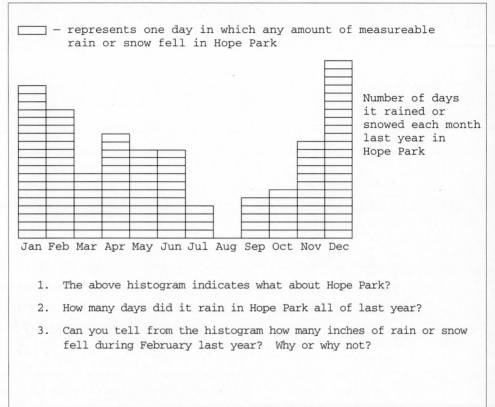

☐ — represents one day in which any amount of measureable
rain or snow fell in Hope Park

Number of days
it rained or
snowed each month
last year in
Hope Park

Jan Feb Mar Apr May Jun Jul Aug Sep Oct Nov Dec

1. The above histogram indicates what about Hope Park?

2. How many days did it rain in Hope Park all of last year?

3. Can you tell from the histogram how many inches of rain or snow
    fell during February last year? Why or why not?

4. In what month was there no rain or snow?

5. How many days did it rain or snow in September?

6. Can you conclude from the histogram that December had more rain
    than January? Why or why not?

ILLUSTRATION 9.5

Mr. Scott's Tasksheet

CASE 9.4

During the previous lessons of this unit, students experimented with magnets, made magnets, made compasses, and observed Ms. Ragusa demonstrate certain magnetic phenomena. For example:

> She carefully sawed a powerful bar magnet in half. Students tested the power of the two halves and identified which poles of the halves repel one another and which attract. Ms. Ragusa then sawed the pieces into even smaller pieces. The students experimented with them and discovered the phenomenon depicted by Illustration 9.6.

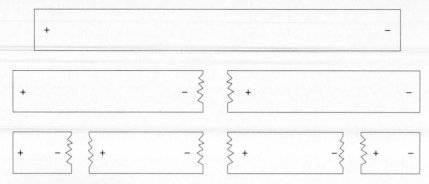

ILLUSTRATION 9.6

Magnetic Phenomenon Ms. Ragusa Demonstrated for Her Students

Students are now ready to engage in her lesson for the following objective:

J. In general terms, students explain the rudiments of magnetic theory (comprehension and communication skills).

Because the objective is at the comprehension-and-communication-skills level, she plans to explain the rudiments of magnetic theory and lead students to understand them, rather than have students discover the theory for themselves as she would for a discover-a-relationship objective. She believes it would be far too ambitious to expect her students to discover such a complex relationship for themselves.

Ms. Ragusa begins the lesson for Objective J by engaging the class in the following dialogue as she holds up a powerful bar magnet:

Ms. Ragusa: "What are some of the things I need to remember about caring for this magnet to prevent it from losing its power? Juan."

Juan: "You shouldn't throw it down on the floor or let it get too hot."

Ms. Ragusa: "Thank you. Okay, Salinda."

Salinda: "When you put it away, you ought to attach another magnet like you showed us before or hook it to a piece of steel or something."

Ms. Ragusa: "Oh, I'm glad you reminded us of that one. But why does storing magnets like Salinda said help keep magnets powerful, and why does heating or banging them cause them to lose power like Juan said? Paige."

Paige: "I don't see why, as long as you don't break them or melt them."

Ms. Ragusa: "We don't know why. But do you know that it really happens that way? Paige."

Paige: "Sure, because we did it ourselves in class. When we banged them around, they lost power. But I don't know why."

Ms. Ragusa: "I don't think anybody knows for sure why magnets work the way they do, but there is a theory that is generally accepted by scientists. Let me explain it to you. Here's another steel bar that has not been magnetized."

Ms. Ragusa displays a bar similar to the first but demonstrates with an iron nail that it is not a magnet.

Ms. Ragusa: "Remember that this piece of steel is made of tiny little what? Eiko."

Eiko: "Atoms."

Ms. Ragusa: "Yes, and billions of atoms form molecules, and millions of molecules form little tiny parts of steel. Now, imagine that the inside of this steel bar looks like this."

She flashes Illustration 9.7 on the overhead screen for the class to see.

Ms. Ragusa: "In this diagram, what do the tiny particles of steel appear to be? Sun-li."
Sun-li: "They're drawn like little magnets."
Ms. Ragusa: "With this theory, you are to think of them as little magnets, each with a positive pole and a negative pole. The theory states that when this object becomes magnetized, like this one . . ."

She holds up the bar magnet.

Ms. Ragusa: "The little tiny particles that make up the object line up like this."

She flashes Illustration 9.8 on the screen.

Ms. Ragusa: "What does the theory say about magnets that's different from non-magnets? Brookelle."
Brookelle: "That those little pieces inside it all face the same way."
Ms. Ragusa: "I agree. What does Brookelle mean by 'all face the same way,' Eldon?"
Eldon: "I don't know; ask her."

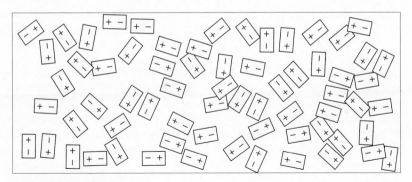

ILLUSTRATION 9.7

Ms. Ragusa's Transparency Depicting the Unmagnetized Bar

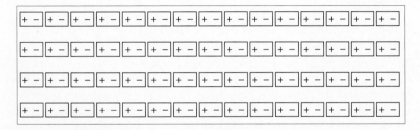

ILLUSTRATION 9.8

Ms. Ragusa's Transparency Depicting a Magnet

Ms. Ragusa:	"James, what does Brookelle mean by 'all face the same way' in this diagram?"
James:	"That the little positive poles are lined up next to the negative ones, just like with real magnets."
Ms. Ragusa:	"Oh, I like the way you said that. Come take this magnet, James. Show us which way you think it would be facing if it were the one on the screen."

James goes up to the front of the room and lines up the bar magnet so that it is parallel to the diagram on the screen (i.e., Illustration 9.8) with the "+" on the bar magnet to the left and the "−" on the right.

James:	"Like this."
Ms. Ragusa:	"Why do you suppose James decided to put the positive pole on that side and the negative on this side? Pauline."
Pauline:	"He aimed it the same way as the little magnets inside."
Ms. Ragusa:	"And that's what our theory of magnetism states, that the positive pole is over here and the negative one here. Thank you, James. If we take this magnet and bang it around real hard or heat it up real hot, what is going to happen to it? Juan."
Juan:	"It'll lose its power."
Ms. Ragusa:	"Why does this happen—according to this theory? Paige."

Paige displays a huge smile.

Paige:	"Because it causes those little magnets inside to get all jumbled up again."
Ms. Ragusa:	"Thank you for that smile. It's times like this that make me especially happy to be a teacher. Everybody, quickly draw three pictures, label them 'strong magnet,' 'weak magnet,' and 'non-magnet.' According to the theory, diagram the inside of each one."

As the students draw, Ms. Ragusa circulates about the room with a rubric in mind, checking how closely their diagrams reflect the theory of magnetism. She also selects drawings to use in the next part of the lesson (e.g., Monica's shown in Illustration 9.9).

After using their drawings to further explain the theory, Ms. Ragusa assigns the tasksheet shown in Illustration 9.10. The following day, Ms. Ragusa conducts another discussion relating students' responses on the tasksheet to the theory.

INDICATORS OF STUDENTS' ACHIEVEMENT OF COMPREHENSION-AND-COMMUNICATION-SKILLS OBJECTIVES

MODES OF COMMUNICATION FOR PROMPTS AND RESPONSES

The concern of comprehension-and-communication-skills objectives is for students to derive meanings from given messages and to communicate messages. For some of these objectives, the reception of the message is emphasized (e.g., the four objectives listed in Illustration 9.1 and Objective B from #1 of Illustration 9.2); for others, the emphasis is on delivering messages (e.g., Objective A from #1 of Illustration 9.2).

When designing mini-experiments for objectives focusing on reception of, rather than formulation of, messages, note that the objectives specify the modes of communication for prompts. For example, Objective B from #1 of Illustration 9.2 specifies that the student will receive a message by listening to someone speak in French. Thus, to be relevant, a

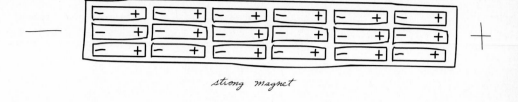

strong magnet

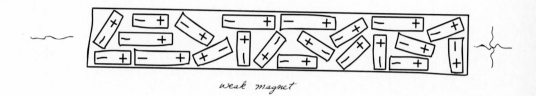

weak magnet

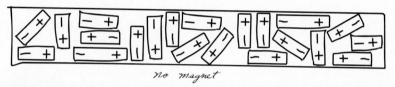

no magnet

ILLUSTRATION 9.9

Monica's Drawing

mini-experiment should prompt students with a message spoken in French. The mode of communication for students' responses is not specified by such an objective. The suggestion here is to make sure that the mode by which the prompt is communicated is consistent with the way the objective is stated. On the other hand, the modes by which students respond to these prompts are not restricted by such objectives. Thus, you can design some mini-experiments in which students display their comprehension of a message with oral explanations, written explanations, or by other modes of communication.

Of course, the converse is true when designing mini-experiments for objectives focusing on formulation of, rather than reception of, messages. For example, Objective A from #1 of Illustration 9.2 specifies that the student will deliver a message using spoken French. Thus, to be relevant, a mini-experiment should require students to respond by speaking in French. However, the mode of communication by which the student receives the message is not restricted by the objective. In the part of Illustration 9.2's mini-experiment that is relevant to Objective A, students are prompted by reading the story they are to translate. Note that the objective does not require students to receive the story via reading it. Another relevant mini-experiment for that objective could be designed in which students receive the message they are to translate into French by hearing someone tell it in English or by looking at a sequence of pictures. The suggestion here is to make sure that the mode by which students communicate their responses is consistent with the way the objective is stated.

1. You know that we should store magnets as the picture shows. Write a paragraph telling how our theory of magnetism explains why we should store magnets this way. Include your own drawing that helps you explain why.

2. Remember that we discovered that cutting a magnet in half gives us two smaller magnets each with two opposite poles. Also, we learned that banging, heating, or dropping a magnet could weaken it. Write a paragraph telling how our theory of magnetism explains why this happens. You may want to draw a picture for this one also.

ILLUSTRATION 9.10

Tasksheet Ms. Ragusa Used

INSIGHTFUL RESPONSES

As indicated by Illustration 5.17, students must use reasoning, not only their memories, to achieve comprehension-and-communication-skills objectives. Unlike memory-level prompts for simple-knowledge and process-knowledge objectives, comprehension-and-communication-skills prompts present students with tasks that are not identical to tasks they've previously encountered. Note that Illustration 9.1's mini-experiments prompt students to use their insights about messages in order to develop responses that are positive indicators of objective achievement. For example, rather than simply directing students to read or recite the four standards for classroom conduct, Mini-Experiment #1 prompts students to think of personal examples that happened that day that fit certain meanings in the standards. Students aren't prompted to explain concepts they've constructed or relationships they've discovered, but they are prompted to display that they have enough insights into the messages to make associations they haven't previously been called upon to make.

Mini-Experiment #2 from Illustration 9.1 provides another example. Students are presented with an excerpt from the Declaration of Independence. Then for each of the five statements, students are prompted to decide whether or not the passage implies that statement.

Without interpretive understanding of the passage, students are unlikely to determine that the first sentence of the passage does not imply Statement A, but that it does imply Statement B.

One common strategy for designing mini-experiments for many comprehension-and-communication-skills objectives is to reword the message or express it in a different form and then prompt students to determine how, if at all, the meaning of the new expression differs from that of the original. For other objectives, you might prompt students to express the message in some restricted way. For example, Illustration 9.1's Mini-Experiment #4 prompts students to explain the given definition of "community," but without using some of the key words from the original expression of the definition. Thus, the teacher is able to detect students' insights into what those key words contribute to the definition. You could also prompt students to explain the message with words that are less sophisticated than those in the original expression. For example, "Explain what a rational number is to someone who is three years younger than you, has never taken prealgebra, and doesn't know the meaning of 'ratio,' 'integer,' or 'whole number.'"

As you may have inferred from the examples of mini-experiments to which you've been exposed in this chapter, any of the mini-experiment formats introduced in Chapters 7 and 8 can be used for comprehension-and-communication-skills objectives. Especially note the combination of formats used with Illustration 9.2's Mini-Experiments #1 and #4.

SYNTHESIS ACTIVITIES FOR CHAPTER 9

1. Retrieve the computerized folder you set up when you engaged in Synthesis Activity 2 for Chapter 6. From your work doing Synthesis Activity 3 for Chapter 6, each file contains at least one mini-experiment. Call up each of those files that is for a comprehension-and-communication-skills objective. Now, in light of your work with Chapter 9, revise the mini-experiments in those files. For each file (i.e., files for comprehension-and-communication-skills objectives), design at least two more mini-experiments and insert them into the file.

2. With a colleague, exchange printouts of the mini-experiments you designed or revised when you engaged in Synthesis Activity 1. Discuss and critique one another's mini-experiments. Revise them as you decide they should be revised.

3. Re-examine Ms. Ragusa's tasksheet, shown by Illustration 9.10. For each of the two prompts, develop a rubric to make it easier for Ms. Ragusa to use students' responses on the tasksheet for formative judgments about their achievement of Objective J from Case 9.4.

4. With a colleague, share and discuss your work from Synthesis Activity 3. Revise the rubrics in light of your discussions. Also compare your rubrics to Illustration 9.11's.

5. Retrieve the goal defined by a set of weighted objectives you developed for Synthesis Activity 3 for Chapter 5. Select one of the comprehension-and-communication-skills objectives from that set (if indeed the set includes at least one such objective). Now, design a lesson for leading students to achieve that objective. Design one or more mini-experiments to provide you with indicators of your students' progress during that lesson.

6. With a colleague, share and discuss your work from Synthesis Activity 5. Revise the mini-experiments in light of your discussions.

TRANSITIONAL ACTIVITY FROM CHAPTER 9 TO CHAPTER 10

In a discussion with two or more of your colleagues, address the following questions:

1. As students engage in our lessons for our application objectives, how do we manage to monitor their progress?

2. How do we design mini-experiments that are relevant to application objectives?

Rubrics:

NOTE: For each criterion listed, points are awarded as follows:

+2 if the criterion in question is clearly met
+1 if it is unclear as to whether or not the criterion is met
+0 if the criterion is clearly not met

Rubric for Prompt 1:

The paragraph relates the safe storage of magnets
to the theory of magnetism   --------------------------- 0   1   2

The paragraph indicates the student recognizes the
importance of storing magnets so that the + is
to - and - is to +   ---------------------------------- 0   1   2

The paragraph indicates the student relates the lining
up of opposite poles to maintain the way the "little
magnet" particles' poles are lined up inside the
magnet   -- 0   1   2

The drawing illustrates understanding of the theory
of magnetism   -- 0   1   2

The paragraph includes nothing inconsistent with the
theory of magnetism or the way magnets should be
stored   -- 0   1   2

Rubric for Prompt 2:

The paragraph relates the safe handling of magnets to
the theory of magnetism   ---------------------------- 0   1   2

The paragraph indicates the student recognizes the
importance of not "stirring up" or "mixing up" the
particles inside of a magnet   ----------------------- 0   1   2

The paragraph indicates the student relates agitation
of a magnet with disrupting the way the "little magnet"
particles' poles are lined up inside the magnet   ------ 0   1   2

The paragraph includes nothing inconsistent with the
theory of magnetism or the way magnets should be
handled   -- 0   1   2

ILLUSTRATION 9.11

Examples of Rubrics for Illustration 9.10's Prompts

Monitoring Students' Progress with Problem Solving

✖ GOAL OF CHAPTER 10

Chapter 10 is intended to lead you to design mini-experiments that will help you monitor students' application-level learning. More specifically the objectives are as follows:

A. You will explain the stages through which students learn to solve problems (discover a relationship) 7%.

B. You will design mini-experiments for gauging students' progress as they engage in lessons for application objectives (application) 40%.

C. You will design mini-experiments relevant to how well students have achieved application objectives (application) 36%.

D. You will extend your ability to explain fundamental principles for using a variety of mini-experiment formats (discover a relationship) 12%.

E. You will incorporate the following technical phrases into your working professional vocabulary: "deductive reasoning" and "syllogism" (comprehension and communication skills) 5%.

HOW STUDENTS LEARN TO SOLVE PROBLEMS

APPLICATION-LEVEL LEARNING

To be able to design mini-experiments relevant to your students' progress with respect to application objectives, you need to be familiar with how students learn to address and solve problems, determining when and how to use what they have learned in the past. From Chapter 5, reread the section "Application" on pages 238–240.

DEDUCTIVE REASONING

In Case 5.13, Terrence was confronted with the problem of figuring out how to write a story to cheer up his sister. Perplexed, he searched through his mental file of what he had learned to decide how to address the problem. Finally, he *deduced* that the writing-for-a-purpose process he learned from Ms. Foreman's lessons would be useful.

In Case 5.14, Gary was confronted with the problem of deciding how to build aerobic activities into his exercise regimen. As he thought about each item on a menu of exercises, he *deduced* whether the item fit his concept of an aerobic exercise.

Similarly, Anna in Case 5.15 and Tawny in Case 5.16 deduced what aspects of prior learning would be useful as they addressed problems. The people in all four of these cases *applied* previously learned processes (as in Cases 5.14 and 5.15), concepts (as in Case 5.14), or relationships (as in Cases 5.15 and 5.16). Such problem solving depends on *deductive reasoning*.

Deductive reasoning is deciding whether or not a specific problem is subsumed by a generality. The use of *syllogisms* is inherent in deductive reasoning. A *syllogism* is a scheme for making a conclusion from a *major premise* and a *minor premise*. Illustration 10.1 displays examples of syllogisms.

Although syllogisms are not normally expressed in the formal terms of Illustration 10.1, people are continually using this same syllogistic or deductive reasoning as they address everyday problems. It is being emphasized in formal terms here because this is the reasoning process you need to monitor as your students engage in lessons for application objectives.

A *deductive learning activity* is one that stimulates students to reason deductively. Lessons for application objectives include deductive learning activities organized in four stages: (1) problem confrontation, (2) analysis and rule articulation, (3) subsequent problem confrontation and analysis, and (4) extension into subsequent lessons.

PROBLEM CONFRONTATION

In the problem-confrontation and analysis stage of a lesson, you confront students with problems in which they need to decide how, if at all, to use what they've learned with respect to the subject-content of the objective to address the problem. Case 10.1 is an example.

CASE 10.1

Ms. Ragusa is conducting the initial stage of a lesson for the following objective:

J. Given a real-life problem, students decide how, if at all, their understanding of magnetism can be used to solve the problem (application).

She explains and demonstrate the following three situations:

1. You're riding in a car when suddenly the driver slams on the brakes. Your body seems to be pulled forward. Only your seat belt prevents you from crashing into the windshield.
2. You're holding a compass with its needle pointing north. One of your friends walks right by you. As she passes near you, the needle on your compass spins around and points south. When your friend is gone, the needle again points north.
3. You have to push the door latch pictured on the left harder to keep it closed than the one pictured on the right (Illustration 10.2).

In collaborative working groups, Ms. Ragusa has her students address and discuss the following question about each of the three situations: What caused this to happen?

She listens to their discussions, with a rubric in her head, focusing on whether or not they decide that magnetism played a role in Situation 2, but not in Situation 1. Also, she observes to see if they suggest that the door latch on the right of Illustration 10.2 may have been designed with magnets, whereas the one on the left was not. She is influenced by the results of these mini-experiments to determine when they are ready to confront the following problem:

Take advantage of your understanding of magnets to either invent a device someone you know would find useful or invent a toy you would enjoy.

1. Question: Is this lemon a source of vitamin C?

    Syllogism:

        Major Premise: All citrus fruits are a source
                         of vitamin C.

        Minor Premise: This lemon is a citrus fruit.

        Conclusion: This lemon is a source of vitamin C.

2. Question: (From Case 5.13) How should I write a story
            to make Naomi laugh?

    Syllogism:

        Major Premise: The writing-for-a-purpose process
                         Ms. Foreman taught us works.

        Minor Premise: Writing a story to make Naomi laugh
                         is writing for a purpose.

        Conclusion: I'll use the writing-for-a-purpose
                         process Ms. Foreman taught to write
                         my story for Naomi.

3. Question: (From Case 5.14) Is bicycling an aerobic exercise?

    Syllogism:

        Major Premise: A rhythmic, sustained exercise that
                         elevates heart rate for at least
                         20 minutes is aerobic.

        Minor Premise: Bicycling is a sustained exercise that
                         elevates heart rate for at least
                         20 minutes.

        Conclusion: Bicycling is an aerobic exercise.

4. Question: (From Case 5.15) Is $\alpha = \beta$ (in Illustration 5.13)?

    Syllogism:

        Major Premise: Opposite angles of a parallelogram
                         have the same measure.

        Minor Premise: The angle with measure α and the angle
                         with measure β in Illustration 5.13 are
                         opposite angles of a parallelogram.

        Conclusion: $\alpha = \beta$.

ILLUSTRATION 10.1

Examples of Syllogisms

(Continued)

ILLUSTRATION 10.1 (Continued)

5. <u>Question</u>: (From Case 5.16) Are lessons learned from the country's experience with prohibition of intoxicating
liquors applicable to the debate about enacting laws
restricting the use of tobacco?

<u>Syllogism</u>:

<u>Major Premise</u>: Lessons about the effects of legislating
restrictions on the use of potentially
harmful substances were learned from the
country's experience with prohibition of
intoxicating liquors.

<u>Minor Premise</u>: Enacting laws restricting the use of
tobacco is an example of legislating
restrictions on the use of a potentially
harmful substance.

<u>Conclusion</u>: Lessons learned from the country's expe-
rience with prohibition of intoxicating
liquors are applicable to the debate
about enacting laws restricting the use
of tobacco.

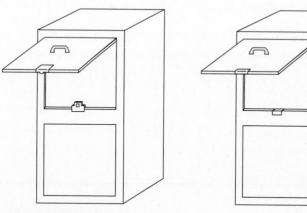

ILLUSTRATION 10.2

Two Types of Door Latches

ANALYSIS AND RULE ARTICULATION

Students analyze their solutions to the problems, explaining how, if at all, they used their understanding of the subject-content specified by the objective (e.g., magnetism). If they didn't use
the subject-content, they explain why it didn't apply. Students formulate a rule for when the
subject-content of the objective applies to the solution of problems. The rule serves as a framework for the syllogism used to deduce whether or not the subject-content applies to specific

situations. If students constructed underlying concepts or discovered critical relationships in previous lessons, they may only need to recall a statement of a relationship formulated during those earlier lessons. Statements of previously learned relationships are the major premises of syllogisms. Case 10.2 illustrates an example.

CASE 10.2

As students work in collaborative groups discussing the three situations listed in Case 10.1, Ms. Ragusa hears the following conversation:

James:	"You don't start to crash into the windshield because the windshield is a magnet."
Chen:	"Maybe it's the engine. The engine could be a magnet."
James:	"No way."
Monica:	"You start to crash into the windshield because of that thing we figured out a long time ago before we did these magnets. What's it called?"
Chen:	"Oh yeah! You mean one of those three laws of motion."
James:	"Yeah, the one where something keeps moving the way its moving 'til something stops it."
Monica:	"In the car it's the seat belt that stops you."

Ms. Ragusa recognizes that James, Chen, and Monica have just worked through the following syllogism, although they never formally stated it:

Major premise: (Newton's first law of motion discovered in previous unit.) Objects at rest stay at rest and objects in motion stay in motion in a straight line at a constant speed, unless a force acts on them to move or change their motion.
Minor premise: When a person is riding in a car, she or he is moving in a straight line at a constant speed.
Conclusion: The person will keep moving in the direction in which she or he is moving until a force acts on her or him to change the speed or direction (i.e., Newton's first law of motion applies, with the seat belt acting as the force to stop the motion of the person's body).

She then hears the following conversation about the second situation listed in Case 10.1.

Chen:	"Well, I know this next one is about magnets."
James:	"Why?"
Monica:	"A compass is a magnet."
James:	"But the person that passed by isn't a piece of iron or something."
Chen:	"They could've had a magnet in their pocket."
Monica:	"Or just been wearing a steel chain or something."
James:	"Yeah, that'd make the needle jump."

Ms. Ragusa recognizes that they have again worked out a syllogism:

Major premise: A magnet will attract and be attracted by magnetic objects (e.g., objects made of iron).
Minor premise: The needle of a compass is a magnet, and the person who walked by the compass might have been wearing a magnetic object.
Conclusion: The compass on the needle may have been attracted by a magnetic object the person was wearing.

Ms. Ragusa also notes that Paige, who is also working in the group with the other three students, did not contribute to the discussion. She plans to check on Paige's thoughts on the three situations before assigning the project of inventing a device or toy indicated in Case 10.1.

In cases in which students began the application lesson with some conceptual learning gaps relative to the subject-content, this phase may require some inductive learning activities to help them reconstruct concepts or rediscover relationships.

SUBSEQUENT PROBLEM CONFRONTATION AND ANALYSIS

Students are confronted with additional problems and analyze their solutions as in the prior phases. Students who readily succeeded with the first two stages of the lesson should be confronted with more difficult problems in this stage. On the other hand, select easier problems if the initial problem seemed too challenging.

EXTENSION INTO SUBSEQUENT LESSONS

Teaching is a complex art; one lesson does not typically end before another begins. Achievement of one application-level objective is enhanced during the first two stages of lessons for subsequent application-level objectives. For example, with Situation 1 from Case 10.1 (i.e., the one involving riding in a car when the brakes are suddenly activated), students needed to reason deductively about Newton's first law of motion (a relationship from a previous unit). In a subsequent unit on electricity, Ms. Ragusa will likely include problems students will solve by applying their understanding of magnetism. Thus, application lessons for one subject-content extend into those for subsequent subject-contents.

INDICATORS OF PROGRESS AS STUDENTS ENGAGE IN APPLICATION LESSONS

In Case 10.3, Ms. Ragusa continues the lesson begun in Cases 10.1 and 10.2; as in those two cases, she uses informal mini-experiments to help her make formative judgments.

CASE 10.3

Ms. Ragusa assigns Illustration 10.3's tasksheet for homework and explains the directions to the class.

The following day, she has the class share their proposed inventions in cooperative groups. She directs each group to analyze the list of potential gadgets and toys, describing which, if any, could be designed using their understanding of magnetism. The groups report their deductions to the whole class, and Ms. Ragusa conducts a large-group questioning-discussion session culminating with the following list of gadgets and toys to be invented: a door opener/lock for pets, various magic tricks, "Ms. Steel Head" (similar to "Mr. Potato Head"), a game in which players use a compass to locate magnets others have hidden, a remote-control device for a secret panel, and a device for sending messages using iron filings.

Each student expresses a first and second choice from the list to invent. Ms. Ragusa then assigns pairs of students to work on various inventions. The students work on these projects over a two-week period. Each day, some students discuss their plans and present a progress report. Ms. Ragusa listens to their discussions and examines the plans and products for indications of how they are using magnetism. Her supervision of the work is guided by how she answers the following questions: Do they use magnetism when it is helpful to do so? Do they recognize situations when it is not useful to try magnetism?

In the meantime, Ms. Ragusa moves ahead with her next science unit, one on electricity.

During the analysis-and-rule-articulation stage, students describe, demonstrate, and explain their inventions. Some efforts result in working prototypes that appear to be successful solutions to problems. Others produce sound theoretical designs but not working prototypes. Others had seemingly unsolvable design flaws. However, Ms. Ragusa directs the activities so that all students' efforts make equally important contributions to the class's understanding of how to use magnets. Each time she examines one of

Note: Directions are explained orally.

1. Think of a gadget that would be useful in your home. It should not now exist so it would have to be invented. The gadget should cost less than $50 to make. Draw a diagram of your gadget, explain what it would do, and give it a name.

<u>Picture</u>

<u>What My Gadget Does</u>

<u>Name</u>

2. Think of a toy that a child you know would enjoy. It should not now exist so it would have to be invented. The toy should cost less than $50 to make. Draw a diagram of your toy, explain what it is, and give it a name.

<u>Picture</u>

<u>About My New Kind of Toy</u>

<u>Name</u>

ILLUSTRATION 10.3

Homework Tasksheet Ms. Ragusa Used in the First Stage of an Application Lesson

their inventions, she conducts a product-examination mini-experiment with a rubric designed similarly to the ones in Illustration 3.9.

The class formulates the following rule near the end of the second stage of the lesson:

> "Magnets can be used to make things for bringing things together or pushing them apart. But to push them apart, you always need two magnets. Pulling them together works best with two magnets because you have two things pulling instead of just one (but they have to be facing the right way). Also, if you use one magnet to pull something toward it, the other thing has to have something in it or on it that's magnetic. Also, none of this works very well unless the magnet is pretty close to the other magnet or to the things it's supposed to pull."

For the third stage of the lesson, Ms. Ragusa confronts students with the problem of explaining various phenomena, some of which involve magnetic power (e.g., one involving a compass needle suddenly pointing the "wrong" way) and some of which don't (e.g., two objects coming together because of gravity). Since Ms. Ragusa began her unit on electricity before concluding the one on magnetism, the extension into subsequent lessons phase was immediate. She plans to continue to confront students with magnet-related problems during application lessons throughout the remainder of the school year.

Near the end of Chapter 2's section "Formative Judgments During Learning Activities" is a list of suggestions for conducting informal mini-experiments as students are engaged in lessons. Reread them now. Note that in Cases 10.1, 10.2, and 10.3, Ms. Ragusa employed most of them (e.g., her student-centered activities provided her with multiple opportunities to observe students respond to prompts).

INDICATORS OF STUDENTS' ACHIEVEMENT OF APPLICATION OBJECTIVES

DECIDING HOW TO SOLVE PROBLEMS

Ms. Ragusa's talent for listening to and observing students so that she's able to translate their words and actions into syllogisms helps her design mini-experiments that are relevant to application objectives. An application-level mini-experiment prompts students to confront a problem and respond in a way that reveals the deductions they make as they attempt to address the problem. Illustration 10.4 displays examples of mini-experiments designed to be relevant to application objectives.

AVOIDING "GIVE-AWAY" WORDS

In Case 3.6, Ms. Bohrer designed a lesson for the following objective:

> When confronted with a real-life problem, students determine how, if at all, the concepts of heat conduction, convection, and radiation can be used to solve the problem (application).

When she designed Illustration 3.9's product-examination mini-experiments, she carefully avoided using the words "conduction," "convection," and "radiation" in the prompts. After all, she wanted these mini-experiments to provide indicators of whether or not her students would deduce for themselves to make use of these concepts, thus she did not prompt them with, "Use what you know about heat convection to . . . ." Such "give-away" words can turn an intended-to-be application-level mini-experiment into one that is at the simple-knowledge level. Consider Case 10.4.

#1

Objective (high school - first aid):

From observing symptoms of a person in distress and from considering the availability of other means of help, students determine whether or not CPR (cardiopulmonary resuscitation) should be initiated (application).

Essay Prompt:

On a hot summer day, you see a middle-aged jogger grab his chest, stagger for several meters, and slowly fall to the sidewalk. When you get to him he is lying on his back seemingly unconscious and breathing with dilated pupils, rapid pulse, and very dry skin. No-one else is available to help and you have no immediate means of transporting the victim. In a one-half page essay, (1) indicate if and when you should use CPR on the man, and (2) explain the reasons for your decision.

Rubric:

(maximum possible points: 4) Score +1 if CPR is not suggested as an initial procedure, +1 if rapid pulse or breathing is given as a reason for withholding CPR, +1 for any other tenable reason for withholding CPR (e.g., victim is displaying signs of a heat stroke), and +1 for an implicit or explicit indication that symptoms that warrant the use of CPR (e.g., lack of respiration) would be considered.

#2

Objective (elementary school - integrated science and math):

Confronted with a need to measure weight, students select a convenient unit of measure for the particular situation (application).

Combination Multiple-Choice and Essay Prompt:

(Directions explained orally) Suppose you wanted to compare the weights of two ladybugs. Which one of the following units of weight would you choose? (circle one)

pounds	ounces	kilograms
grams	tons	metric tons

ILLUSTRATION 10.4

Four Examples of Mini-Experiments Relevant to Application Objectives

(Continued)

ILLUSTRATION 10.4 (Continued)

Now write a paragraph explaining why you chose the one you circled.

Rubric:

(maximum possible points: 3) +1 for circling "grams" only, +1 for indicating that he/she comprehends the size of the unit he/she selected (e.g., understood that a ladybug would only weigh a minute fraction of a pound), and +1 for not including anything erroneous in the paragraph (e.g., "I picked grams because it would make the ladybug weigh more.").

#3

Objective (high school - science):

From examining a bio-ecological system, students identify components that are necessary to the maintenance of the system (application).

Essay Prompt:

A 1,000 mile grassy plain was inhabited by a healthy, stable population of wolves and a variety of smaller animals including rabbits, birds, rodents, snakes, and insects. This self-sustaining plain existed for at least a thousand years. People then began to hunt and kill wolves that inhabited the area. Ten years after people began killing the wolves, dust storms started to plague the plain and erosion changed its face. There are no records of dust storms or erosion having ever occurred before this time.

There are, of course, a number of possible theories for the onset of the dust storms and erosion. Describe in a half-page essay one possible scenario of events that could explain a link between the erosion, dust storms, and hunting of wolves. Be as specific as you can in the one-half page.

Rubric:

(maximum possible points: 6) Score +1 for establishing a plausible link between the erosion, dust storms, and hunting wolves and +1 (up to +5) for each relevant event that would lead to that connection.

#4

Objective (art):

Students incorporate light sources in the design and production of realistic sketches of live models (application).

ILLUSTRATION 10.4 *(Continued)*

Product-Examination Prompt:

The student is provided with the necessary supplies and a live
model. The following directions are given: "Make a realistic,
shaded line drawing of the model. The model will hold the pose
for 20 minutes with a one-minute break after the first 10 minutes.
Spend the 20 minutes capturing the features you need from the
model. You are to complete the drawing at a more leisurely pace
over the next two days.

Rubric:

The teacher views the finished drawing and checks to see if it
clearly indicates a light source and the effects of the direction
of the light source on the image. For example, the image on
the left meets this criterion; the one on the right does not.

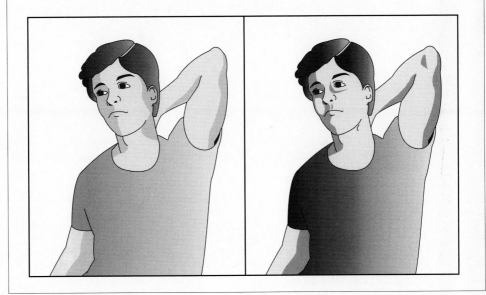

CASE 10.4

For years, Mr. Boatwright taught his second-graders to count, add, and subtract. Recently, however,
he's discovered that many of his students learn these processes but are unable to apply them to real-life situations. Thus, he redesigns his mathematics units to include application objectives such as the following:

Students distinguish between problems that can be efficiently solved using subtraction and
problems that cannot (application).

His computerized file for that objective includes the mini-experiment displayed by Illustration 10.5.

<u>Prompt</u>:

The teacher explains the directions and presents the prompts
orally as each student responds on an answer sheet with blanks numbered 1 through 4. The teacher says the following:

"I'm going to give you four problems. Some of them can
be solved by addition. Some can be solved by subtraction.
And then there are some for which you do not need to add
or subtract. Your job is to write down an add sign ('+') for
those that are addition problems, a subtract sign ('-') for
the subtraction problems, and a big 'N' if you would not either
add or subtract. Put your pencil on blank number 1 as I read the
first one:

1. Dustin has some money and Casey has some money. They
   agree to add their money together and buy a computer game.
   How much money do they have to spend on a computer game?

   Write either an add sign, a subtract sign, or a big 'N.'

2. Kate has 15 books on her shelf; she takes away 4 and
   gives them to Allison. How many books does she have left
   on her shelf?

   Write either an add sign, a subtract sign, or a big 'N.'

3. Brandon started reading a book from Page 1. He just finished
   reading Page 16. How many pages has he read?

   Write either an add sign, a subtract sign, or a big 'N.'

4. Sarah had 19 stickers in a box before she took away 7 to
   decorate her door. How many stickers are left in her box?

   Write either an add sign, a subtract sign, or a big 'N'."

<u>Rubric</u>:

(maximum possible points: 4) +1 for each of the following:
"+" for #1, "-" for #2 and #4, and "N" for #3.

ILLUSTRATION 10.5

An Intended-to-Be Application-Level Mini-Experiment in Mr. Boatwright's Computerized Files

Mr. Boatwright conducts the mini-experiment with the class. Afterward, he asks Levi, whose
responses resulted in a score of 4, to explain his choices to the class. Levi says, "It was easy! It's plus for
the first one, 'cause Mr. Boatwright said Dustin and Casey agreed to *add* their money. It's the subtract
sign for two and four, since he said '*take away*.' 'Take away' means subtract. Mr. Boatwright told us that
a long time ago." Other students chime in, "Yeah, that's how you do them!"

Mr. Boatwright now realizes that some students were simply remembering word associations—simple-knowledge learning. To rectify this weakness, he modifies the mini-experiment for subsequent use so that it now appears as shown by Illustration 10.6.

MIXING SUBJECT-CONTENT

Even before modifying Illustration 10.5's mini-experiment, Mr. Boatwright realized that measuring achievement of an application objective necessitated confronting students with two types of problems: (1) those with solutions that use the subject-content specified by the objective and

---

Prompt:

The teacher explains the directions and presents the prompts orally as each student responds on an answer sheet with blanks numbered 1 through 4. The teacher says the following:

"I'm going to give you four problems. Some of them can be solved by addition. Some can be solved by subtraction. And then there are some for which you do not need to add or subtract. Your job is to write down an add sign for those that are addition problems, a subtract sign for the subtraction problems, and a big 'N' if you would not either add or subtract. Put you pencil on blank number 1 as I read the first one:

1. Dustin has some money and Casey has some money. They agree to buy one computer game and share it. How much money do they have to spend on a computer game?

   Write either an add sign, a subtract sign, or a big 'N.'

2. Kate has 15 books on her shelf; she takes away 4 and gives them to Allison. How many books did Kate give to Allison?

   Write either an add sign, a subtract sign, or a big 'N.'

3. Brandon started reading a 30-page book. He just finished reading Page 16. How many pages does he have left to read?

   Write either an add sign, a subtract sign, or a big 'N.'

4. Sarah had 19 stickers in a box before she used 7 to decorate her door. How many stickers are still in her box?

   Write either an add sign, a subtract sign, or a big 'N'."

Rubric:

(maximum possible points: 4) +1 for each of the following: "+" for #1, "-" for #3 and #4, and "N" for #2.

ILLUSTRATION 10.6

Mr. Boatwright's Modified Mini-Experiment

(2) those with solutions that do not. That is why his mini-experiments for Case 10.4's application objective on subtraction confronted students with both problems that are solvable by subtraction as well as problems that are not solvable by subtraction.

Similarly, when Ms. Curry designed the three mini-experiments in Illustration 6.3 to be relevant to Case 6.3's application objective on surface area, she mixed problems that involve area with problems that do not. In Case 10.5, Ms. Suarez applies this strategy in a mini-experiment with an interview format.

CASE 10.5

Sitting at a table located away from the other fifth-grade students who are working on a written assignment, Ms. Suarez begins an interview mini-experiment with Lenora; it is intended to be relevant to the following objective:

When confronted with a real-life problem, students determine whether or not the following relationship is useful in solving the problem: time = distance.

Ms. Suarez: "Lenora, I am going to ask you some questions about math. I could ask you about using math when you cook or when you travel or when you shop or when you play sports. Which one do you want me to ask you about?"

Lenora: "What can I choose from?"

Ms. Suarez: "Cooking, traveling, shopping, or sports."

Lenora: "Traveling—I like to go on trips."

Ms. Suarez looks into her file and pulls out a document labeled "Traveling Prompts."

Ms. Suarez: "These questions will be about traveling. Please remember that I'm trying to find out what math you would use to solve certain problems. I will ask you questions, but I won't be discussing your answers with you until later. We'll tape this interview so you can listen to and think about your answers later. I'll be making some notes as we go. Do you have any questions for me before we start?"

Lenora: "No, ma'am."

Ms. Suarez turns on the tape recorder.

Ms. Suarez: "Here is the first one. Suppose that you are going to take a trip from here to St. Louis, and you want to know how long it will take you to get there by car. Do you know how long it will take?"

Lenora: "No."

Ms. Suarez: "How would you find out?"

Lenora: "I'd ask my mamma."

Ms. Suarez: "But what would you do if your mamma told you to try to figure it out for yourself—because she wanted you to practice figuring things out for yourself?"

Lenora: "Get a map."

Out of Lenora's view, Ms. Suarez marks "+1" in a square on her scorer's sheet as she continues.

Ms. Suarez: "And what would you learn from the map?"

Lenora: "How far St. Louis is."

She marks "+1" in a second square.

Ms. Suarez: "Then would you know how much time the trip will take?"

Lenora: "Yes."

She marks "+0" in the third square.

Ms. Suarez: "Suppose you found out St. Louis is 200 miles away. What else would you need to know?"

Lenora: "How fast my car could go."

Ms. Suarez: "Is your car going to be driven its fastest?"

Lenora: "No."

Ms. Suarez: "Then what do you need to know?"

Lenora: "I don't know."

Ms. Suarez: "Remember that you want to know how long it will take you to travel the 200 miles to St. Louis. Take 30 seconds to think about what you need to know. Then give me your best guess."

Lenora: "How fast my car would go."

She marks "+1" in the fourth square.

Ms. Suarez: "Let's suppose you average 50 miles for every hour you travel in your car. Now, how would you figure out the time the trip would take?"

Lenora: "Multiply 50 and 200."

She marks "+0" in the fifth square. Ms. Suarez then branches into a sequence of easier questions she had prepared for students whose responses up to this point led to a "+0" in the fifth square. Had Lenora responded with, "Divide 200 by 50," Ms. Suarez would have branched into a sequence of more difficult questions.

SYNTHESIS ACTIVITIES FOR CHAPTER 10

1. Retrieve the computerized folder you set up when you engaged in Synthesis Activity 2 for Chapter 6. From your work doing Synthesis Activity 3 for Chapter 6, each file contains at least one mini-experiment. Call up each of those files that is for an application objective. Now, in light of your work with Chapter 10, revise the mini-experiments in those files. For each file (i.e., files for application objectives), design at least two more mini-experiments and insert them into the file.

2. With a colleague, exchange printouts of the mini-experiments you designed or revised when you engaged in Synthesis Activity 1. Discuss and critique one another's mini-experiments. Revise them as you decide they should be revised.

3. Compare the two mini-experiments from Illustration 10.7. Which one of the two, #1 or #2, is relevant to the following objective:

   When given a real-life problem, students determine how, if at all, computing a surface area will help solve the problem (application).

   Which is relevant to the following objective:

   In a real-life problem situation, students can determine the surface areas of rectangular regions (process knowledge).

#1

Essay Prompt:

In about 1/2-page, explain how you would go about finding the surface area of the front wall of the classroom you are in right now. Use at least one diagram to illustrate how you would do it.

Rubric:

(maximum points possible: 3) +1 for each of the following criteria that is clearly met:

_____ 1. The student indicates that she/he recognizes that the front wall is a rectangular region.

_____ 2. The student indicates that she/he would measure the length and width of the front wall.

_____ 3. The student indicates that she/he would find the area by the following formula: Area = length × width.

#2

Essay Prompt:

In about 1/2-page, explain how you would go about determining how much paint would be needed to cover all the walls of the classroom you are in right now. Use at least one diagram to illustrate how you would do it.

Rubric:

(maximum points possible: 4) +1 for each of the following criteria that is clearly met:

_____ 1. The student indicates that she/he deduces that the surface area of the walls should be computed.

_____ 2. The student indicates that she/he would partition the walls into rectangular regions.

_____ 3. The student indicates that she/he would measure the length and width of each of those rectangular regions.

_____ 4. The student indicates that she/he would find the sum of the areas of the rectangular regions.

ILLUSTRATION 10.7

Which Mini-Experiment Is Relevant to an Application Objective? Which Is Relevant to a Process-Knowledge Objective?

4. With a colleague, share and discuss your responses to the prompt from Synthesis Activity 3. Make sure to touch upon the problem of "give-away" words.

5. Retrieve the goal defined by a set of weighted objectives you developed for Synthesis Activity 3 for Chapter 5. Select one of the application objectives from that set (if indeed the set includes at least one such objective). Study the subject-content of that objective. Think of a question that students who have achieved that objective could answer (e.g., a question similar to one of the five questions from Illustration 10.1). Now write out a syllogism (i.e., major premise, minor premise, and conclusion) by which a student could deduce the answer to the question.

6. Design a lesson for leading students to achieve the objective you identified when you engaged in Synthesis Activity 5. Design one or more mini-experiments to provide you with indicators of your students' progress during that lesson.

7. With a colleague, share and discuss your work from Synthesis Activities 5 and 6. Revise the mini-experiments in light of your discussions.

TRANSITIONAL ACTIVITY FROM CHAPTER 10 TO CHAPTER 11

In a discussion with two or more of your colleagues, address the following questions:

1. As students engage in our lessons for creative-thinking objectives, how do we manage to monitor their progress?

2. How do we design mini-experiments that are relevant to creative-thinking objectives?

Monitoring Students' Progress with Creative Thinking

✎ GOAL OF CHAPTER 11

Chapter 11 is intended to lead you to design mini-experiments that will help you monitor students' progress with creative thinking. More specifically the objectives are as follows:

A. You will explain principles associated with students' learning to think creatively (discover a relationship) 7%.

B. You will design mini-experiments for gauging students' progress as they engage in lessons for creative-thinking objectives (application) 40%.

C. You will design mini-experiments relevant to how well students have achieved creative-thinking objectives (application) 36%.

D. You will extend your ability to explain fundamental principles for using a variety of mini-experiment formats (discover a relationship) 12%.

E. You will incorporate the term "synectics" into your working professional vocabulary (comprehension and communication skills) 5%.

THOUGHTS ON CREATIVITY

DIVERGENT REASONING

From Chapter 5, reread the section "Creative Thinking" on pages 240–242.

Note that divergent reasoning is atypical as well as reasoned and is often motivated out of dissatisfaction with the status quo. Contrary to popular belief that aptitude for creative production is found only in rare, exceptional individuals, virtually everyone possesses creative talents (Starko, 1995, pp. 61–95; Torrance, 1988). What is rare is for that talent to be recognized and rewarded. Historically, society and its institutions (e.g., schools and churches) have frowned upon and generally discouraged creative thinking (Strom, 1969, pp. 222–236; Woolfolk, 1993, pp. 305–310). Divergent reasoning threatens common beliefs and established "truths." Irrational thought and emotionally controlled behaviors are often associated with mental instability. However, Gordon (1961, p. 6) suggests that irrational, emotionally charged thought tends to produce an environment more conducive to creative production than rational, controlled thought. Joyce, Weil, & Showers (1992, p. 220) state, "Nonrational interplay leaves room for open-ended thoughts that can lead to a mental state in which new ideas are possible. The basis for decisions, however, is always rational; the irrational state is the best mental state for exploring and expanding ideas, but it is not the decision-making stage."

Creativity thrives in an environment in which ideas are valued on their own merit, not on the basis of how they were produced nor who produced them (Strom, 1969, pp. 258–267). In such an environment, irrationally produced ideas are valued with the same regard as those resulting from a rational process. The attention afforded an idea should not depend on the eminence of the originator.

Gordon's (1961) studies challenge typical views about creativity with four ideas:

- Creativity is important in everyday circumstances; it should not only be associated with the development of great works.
- Creativity is utilized in all subject-content areas, not just the arts.
- Creative thoughts can be generated by groups as well as solitary individuals via similar processes. This is contrary to the common view that creativity must be an intensely personal experience.
- The creative process is not mysterious; it can be described and people can be taught to use it.

Gordon's points are critical to justifying attention to creative thinking in curricula. However, how best to teach for and monitor creative thinking is still not well understood. One difficulty is resolving the phenomenon that creative thought seems to rise unpredictably (Bourne, Dominowski, Loftus, & Healy, 1986, pp. 9–10).

PRESERVING CREATIVITY

Studies indicate a steady decline in most students' curiosity and creative activity during their school years (Strom, 1969, pp. 259–260):

> Given the great number of children with creative prospect and the fact that it represents a natural evolving process, the first concern among educators ought to be one of preservation. Creativity will develop if allowed to grow, if teachers permit and encourage a course already begun (see Gowan, et al., 1967). A primary clue comes from the process itself—allowing inquiry, manipulation, questioning, guessing, and the combination of remote thought elements. Generally, however, the preferred cognitive style of learning creatively is discouraged [in typical classrooms]. Studies indicate that discontinuities in creative development occur at several grade levels and that the losses are accompanied by a decline in pupil curiosity and interest in learning. At the same grade levels at which creative loss occurs, increases are noted in the incidence of emotional disturbances and egregious behavior. Among Anglo-American cultures, the greatest slump in creative development seems to coincide with the fourth grade; smaller drops take place at kindergarten and seventh grade. Children at each of these grades perform less well than they did one year earlier and less well than children in the grade below them on measures of divergent thinking, imagination, and originality. This problem was ignored, since it was judged to be a developmental phenomena instead of man-made or culture-related (Torrance, 1962). Not long ago it was first recognized that in certain cultures the development of creative thinking abilities are continuous. And, even in our own country, under selective teachers who encourage creative boys and girls and reward creative behavior, no slump occurs at grade four.

As a teacher, you can choose not to include creative-thinking objectives in your curriculum. However, simply managing to preserve students' creativity and allowing it to grow requires some conscious effort on your part.

FOSTERING CREATIVITY

Consistent with the vast majority of reports by professional education associations on curriculum and evaluations standards (see, e.g., National Center for History in the Schools, 1997; National Council of Teachers of English & International Reading Association, 1996; National Council of Teachers of Mathematics, 1989; National Research Council, 1996; New Jersey Department of Education, 1997), you may choose not only to preserve your students' creativity but also to conduct lessons that help them achieve creative-thinking objectives. Lessons for creative thinking can be efficiently interwoven with those for other types of objectives, especially construct-a-concept and discover-a-relationship. The strategy is to conduct these other lessons so that students feel free to question, make mistakes, and disagree with ideas, even yours. Particularly important is for them to be positively reinforced for depending on themselves and on their own devices for decision-making and problem solving.

Although the creative process is not well understood, strategies for teaching for creativity have been tried and studied with promising results (Bourne, Dominowski, Loftus, & Healy, 1986, p. 9; Starko, 1995, pp. 123–247). Strom (1969, p. 261) recommends students be exposed to examples of creative production (e.g., through historical accounts of inventions and discoveries and through teachers' modeling divergent thinking in "think-aloud" sessions). Beyer (1987, pp. 35–37) points out the importance of heuristic activities such as brainstorming, open-ended questioning sessions, and discussions in which ideas for consideration are critiqued regarding purpose, structure, advantages, and disadvantages.

To be able to design mini-experiments relevant to your students' progress with respect to creative-thinking objectives, you need to be familiar with how students learn to think creatively.

METAPHORS AND ANALOGIES TO STIMULATE STUDENTS TO THINK CREATIVELY

SYNECTICS

One of the more systematic and researched methods for fostering creativity is referred to by its designer, William J. J. Gordon (1961), as *synectics*. *Synectics* is a means by which *metaphors* and *analogies* are used to lead students into an illogic state for situations where rational logic fails. The intent is for students to free themselves of convergent thinking and to develop empathy with ideas that conflict with their own. Starko (1995, p. 220) states:

> The basic processes of Synectics are "making the strange familiar" and "making the familiar strange" (Prince, 1968, p. 4). To make the strange familiar you combine something familiar with a new problem or situation in order to solve the problem or come to an understanding. To make the familiar strange you also combine something new or strange with something familiar, this time to gain new insights or perspectives on the already familiar idea. These two processes are facilitated through the creation of various types of analogies.

Three types of analogies are used in learning activities based on synectics: (1) *direct analogies*, (2) *personal analogies*, and (3) *compressed conflicts*.

DIRECT ANALOGIES

Students are led to make *direct analogies* by being prompted to raise and analyze comparisons between a subject-content and some familiar specific, concept, relationship, or process. For example, they address questions such as the following:

- How is a historical event like a tossed salad?
- What is the difference between a noun-verb agreement and frozen yogurt?

- Which is rounder, a hexagon or a television show?
- What is the difference between magnetism and religion?
- What moves faster, water flowing downhill or de facto segregation?

PERSONAL ANALOGIES

Students are led to make *personal analogies* by being prompted to empathize with subject-content, losing themselves in some imaginary world. They are directed to place themselves in situations with mind-bending tasks to accomplish; the following are examples:

- You are a magnet. Describe how you feel as the temperature where you are starts to rise, hotter and hotter. Describe how you feel as the temperature drops, lower and lower.
- You have just invented a way of constructing an equilateral right triangle. How do you feel about your invention? How will this accomplishment change life on earth?
- You are the English language. You must give up either all of your verbs, all of your nouns, all of your pronouns, or all of your adjectives. You get to choose which type of words to give up. What type of words do you choose and why did you choose that type?
- You live in a world in which all people get younger with each passing year. People who live out their lives move from old age, to middle age, to young adulthood, to adolescence, to childhood, to being babies, to being embryos inside their mothers, and finally to vanishing completely. Describe what your society and life are like.
- You are the variable real number y so that $y = 1/x$ with $-1 < x < 0$. Describe how you feel as x moves from near -1 to about -0.5. Describe how you feel as x moves from -0.5 nearer and nearer to 0.

COMPRESSED CONFLICTS

Students are led to work with metaphors that bring together diametrically opposed ideas. They are prompted to engage in *compressed-conflict* tasks; the following are examples:

- Explain how to study history without any record of the past.
- Describe and illustrate two objects that take up exactly the same amount of space. One of the objects has greater mass but is less dense than the other.
- Describe how mathematics would be different if only parallel lines could be perpendicular?
- Show how an infinite set is small.

The metaphors and analogies are used to stimulate students to reconstruct old ideas, thus promoting divergent thinking.

INDICATORS OF PROGRESS AS STUDENTS ENGAGE IN SYNECTICS ACTIVITIES

In Case 11.1, Ms. Ragusa begins a synectics activity; throughout, students respond to prompts designed to stimulate divergent reasoning.

CASE 11.1

Throughout the unit on magnetism, Ms. Ragusa continually raised "why" questions (e.g., "Why are you only stroking that piece of iron in one direction?" "Why can't we make a magnet with only one pole?" "Why did you make that compass so the needle is free to spin?"). She encouraged students to try out their own ideas, raise questions, and design new experiments. From the very beginning of the school year, she established a classroom environment in which every idea was valued, trial and error encouraged, and failure was impossible by turning "mistakes" into learning experiences. Thus, her lesson for the following objective was embedded in her lessons for all the other objectives in the unit:

> F. Students develop novel hypotheses and models for explaining magnetic phenomena (creative thinking).

On a few occasions, she decides that the time is right to deviate from a lesson for one of the other objectives and engage the students in a synectics activity.

On one such occasion, Ms. Ragusa distributes a ball of clay to each student. In an independent work session, she directs them to form their clay balls into unique shapes. "Each of you has three minutes and seventeen forty-thirds of another minute to come up with a shape that's like no one else's; make a shape you think no one else would have ever before imagined," she says.

When the allotted time expires, she announces, "Everyone, close your eyes and hold your shape of clay over your head. Okay, while your eyes are shut, I'm going to wave my special 'magnetic-imaginer' over you, and when you open your eyes, you're to imagine that your shape of clay has been magnetized. Okay, it's done, open your eyes." Unfortunately, Eiko and Willard pretend their "magnets" are repelling one another, and they playfully fall out of their desks; a few others join the game and pretend their magnets are pulling them toward or repelling them away from other students. Ms. Ragusa responds, "I understand your point. But please control your 'magnets' or I will have to demagnetize them so we can continue with this lesson. Thank you. I appreciate you controlling your 'magnets.'"

Having dealt with the disruption, Ms. Ragusa engages the class in the following dialogue:

Ms. Ragusa:	"Everyone, please put your 'magnets' on your desk and take out a sheet of paper and a pencil. Thank you. Wanda, please stand up and hold up your 'magnet' so the rest of us can see it. Everyone else, quickly draw a picture of Wanda's magnet. Okay. Now, write one or two sentences explaining how Wanda's 'magnet' is like a nightlight—you too, Wanda. Wait, Brookelle has a question."
Brookelle:	"Where are the poles on her 'magnet'?"
Ms. Ragusa:	"Each of you can imagine the poles to be anywhere you want them to be. Or, if you like, imagine Wanda's 'magnet' to have more than two poles or no poles at all."
Brookelle:	"But that's impossib—"
Ms. Ragusa:	"While we're imagining things, let's stretch our thoughts beyond what we've been able to observe in the past."

Ms. Ragusa circulates among the students as they write. As she reads each answer, she keeps the following rubric in her mind:

> She asks herself the following two questions: (1) Is the student's answer reasonably related to magnets? (2) If so, does the answer put some sort of new twist on the way we have thought about magnets in the past? If the answer to both questions is "yes," then she thinks the student's response is helping set the mood for divergent reasoning about magnets.

When the allotted time expires, Ms. Ragusa makes the transition into a questioning-discussion session with the whole class:

Ms. Ragusa:	"Read what you wrote, Pauline."
Pauline:	"It's like a nightlight because a nightlight makes you feel safe and her 'magnet' pulls things safely together."
Ms. Ragusa:	"And yours, Juan."

Juan:	"The way she's got all those pointy things coming out all over, I thought if it was a magnet it would be like a nightlight because it would shoot its power field all around it like a light."

The session continues with Ms. Ragusa raising other direct analogy questions for other students' "magnets" and having students initiate the questions for the rest of the class. As she reads and listens to each of their answers, she continues to silently use the aforementioned rubric. She uses this planned, but informal, mini-experiment to help her decide whether or not to move to the next stage of the lesson involving personal analogies. If she thinks too many of the students' answers are either not reasonably connected to magnetism or do not introduce something novel, then she will abort the lesson for now and try to resurrect it on another day. If, on the other hand, students' answers are stimulating the desired mood, then she plans to continue the lesson into the next stage.

Deciding to continue with the lesson, Ms. Ragusa puts a halt to the questioning-discussion session and directs students to write responses to the prompts from Illustration 11.1's tasksheet. After reading each prompt to them, she allots three minutes and $23\frac{3}{4}$ seconds for students to write their responses.

As they write, Ms. Ragusa reads a sample of their responses with a rubric in mind that is similar to the one she used earlier for their direct analogies. For example, to the first part of Prompt א, Brookelle writes, "I feel okay, until it gets hotter and hotter. My insides are starting to jump all around and get mixed up. I'm feeling so weak now. Now my power is gone." Ms. Ragusa thinks, "That shows Brookelle is into this activity. She's clearly drawn a personal analogy that dramatizes magnetic theory in a way we haven't before done in class."

For the second part of Prompt א, Brookelle writes, "Now that it gets cold, my power is coming back. I can feel my insides being fixed. I'm a strong magnet again!" Ms. Ragusa is tempted to "correct" Brookelle's seeming misconception about magnetic theory. She thinks, "It's reasonable for Brookelle to think that since heating a magnet alters the alignment of its particles, cooling it down again will cause the particle to realign. But of course, that's not how to re-magnetize it. But during a creativity lesson is not the time to lead her to reason convergently and stick with conventional wisdom. She is reasoning about magnets, and that's what counts here. Don't dare give into the temptation to deal with the misconception now!"

After a session in which students share and discuss their responses to the tasksheet, Ms. Ragusa decides to wait until the next day to engage them in an activity involving compressed conflicts.

INDICATORS OF STUDENTS' ACHIEVEMENT OF CREATIVE-THINKING OBJECTIVES

Unless you devise very unusual curricula for students, relatively few of your objectives specify creative thinking as the learning level. Lessons fostering creative thinking tend to be integrated with other lessons and extend beyond the confines of a single teaching unit. You may, for example, include learning activities based on synectics within most teaching units, but you will detect an increase in students' inclinations to think creatively only over the course of several units. Consequently, monitoring students' progress relative to a creative-thinking objective may be more of a long-range endeavor than monitoring their progress with other types of cognitive objectives.

Numerous test instruments for measuring creativity have been developed; some are available commercially. Starko (1995, pp. 304–320 lists and describes features of 16 such tests (e.g., *Torrance Tests of Creative Thinking, Thinking Creatively in Action and Movement, Thinking*

א You are a magnet. The temperature is rising. It is getting
warmer. Describe how you feel as it gets warmer and warmer and
then hotter and hotter.

Now, the temperature starts to drop. You are finally starting
to cool down. Describe how you feel as you change from feeling
very hot, to warmer, to cooler, to being very cold.

ב Imagine that you are one of the tiny pieces of iron inside of a
powerful magnet. Suddenly, you feel a big jolt and go spinning
around facing the other way. The other pieces of iron all
around you seem to still be facing the same way they were before. Describe how you feel right now.

ה You are a nail having a good time with your three best friends
who are also nails. You are made of pure silver. All of your
friends are made of iron. Suddenly a person walks up to the
four of you and pulls out a large magnet. Tell the rest of the
story.

ILLUSTRATION 11.1

Tasksheet Ms. Ragusa Used to Prompt Students to Make Personal Analogies

Creatively with Sounds and Words, *The Remote Associates Test*, and *Group Inventory for Finding Creative Talent*). Starko notes that these assessment tools can be categorized as focusing on (1) processes associated with creativity, (2) products of creativity, or (3) characteristics of "creative persons." She states:

> Some instruments provide tasks that require individuals to use *processes* associated with creativity. They may require test takers to solve open-ended problems, pull together remote associations, or derive multiple responses for a particular question. Tasks are constructed to demand the types of thinking emphasized in the definition or theory accepted by the test constructor.
>
> Other measures focus on the *products* of creativity. These assessments are less concerned with how a creative product came to be than in the quality of the product itself. Rather than presenting subjects with an artificial task, they may assess the products of "wild," or at least authentic, creativity. Works of art, scientific experiments, pieces of writing, or other creative efforts can be evaluated. While the emphasis on this type of assessment is more on real-world products, it is similar to the process-focused assessment in that the thing to be measured is the result of someone's creative effort.
>
> Still other measures of creativity focus, not on the processes or products of creativity, but on the creative *person*. Rather than asking individuals to complete specific tasks, these measures focus on biographical or personality traits tied to creativity. Individuals may be evaluated to assess their willingness to take risks, internal locus of evaluation, past creative efforts, or other traits or activities commonly associated with creativity. The assumption is that individuals who have a high number of the personal characteristics found in creative individuals may be creative themselves. Many times these measures take the form of self-report surveys or observational checklists. (pp. 304–305)

Of course, our concern here is designing mini-experiments relevant to specific creative-thinking objectives you formulate for your students. The tests of creativity to which Starko refers are used in identifying talent for creative thinking in a given population—not for making formative judgments or summative evaluations about students' achievement of specific objectives. However, the type of prompts Starko alludes to for the first two types of creativity tests (i.e., those focusing on creative processes and products resulting from creative processes) can stimulate ideas for designing mini-experiments for specific objectives. The third type of creativity test, focusing on characteristics of "creative persons" is hardly a useful source for our purposes. As emphasized in Chapter 3 and modeled throughout this book, you should avoid characterizing students with labels such as "creative" and "not creative."

For mini-experiments relevant to creative-thinking objectives, you develop prompts by presenting them with a task that is accomplished via divergent reasoning. The rubric must be constructed to detect how well students' responses reflect divergent reasoning (i.e., reasonableness regarding the subject-content as well as novelty). Note that the rubrics for mini-experiments relevant to construct-a-concept, discover-a-relationship, simple-knowledge, process-knowledge, comprehension-and-communication-skills, and application objectives are structured so that convergent reasoning is reinforced; the opposite should be true for creative-thinking mini-experiments.

Illustration 11.2 displays three mini-experiments relevant to creative-thinking objectives.

SYNTHESIS ACTIVITIES FOR CHAPTER 11

1. Retrieve the computerized folder you set up when you engaged in Synthesis Activity 2 for Chapter 6. From your work doing Synthesis Activity 3 for Chapter 6, each file contains at least one

#1

Objective (elementary school - language arts):

Students categorize words in unconventional ways and define their categories (creative thinking).

Short-Response Prompt:

(directions given orally) The students are shown the following five words: "crutch," "clutch," "find," "seek," and "orphan." Using language familiar to them, the teacher directs the students to make five different subsets from those five words so that each subset contains exactly three of the words. No two subsets should be exactly the same (i.e., contain the same three words). For each of the five subsets, students are directed to write a rule that explains why those three words are grouped together. The rules are to be written without using any of the original five words. Students are to respond in writing using the following form:

First group of words: _____

First rule: _____

_____

_____

Second group of words: _____

Second rule: _____

_____

_____

Third group of words: _____

Third rule: _____

_____

_____

Fourth group of words: _____

Fourth rule: _____

_____

_____

Fifth group of words: _____

ILLUSTRATION 11.2

Examples of Mini-Experiments Relevant to Creative-Thinking Objectives

(Continued)

ILLUSTRATION 11.2 (Continued)

Fifth rule: _____

_____

_____

Rubric:

(maximum possible points: 5) Score +1 for each subset/rule pair that fits criterion established in the directions.

#2

Objective (high school - history):

Students generate a variety of novel scenarios illustrating nontraditional views explaining why certain historical figures behaved as they did (creative thinking).

Combination Short-Response and Essay Prompt:

For each of the following five prompts (numbered -3 through 2), answer the question or complete the task using the available page area:

-3. How would a conversation between Adolph Hitler and Martin Luther King, Jr., be like a bolt of lightning?

-2. How would the conversation be like boiled spaghetti?

-1. If you explained to Adolph Hitler how you felt about Martin Luther King, Jr., and then you explained to King how you felt about Hitler, why do you suppose someone might accuse you of being unpatriotic?

0. How were Martin Luther King, Jr., and Adolph Hitler alike?

ILLUSTRATION 11.2 (Continued)

1.   Explain why Martin Luther King, Jr., would have admired Adolph Hitler.

2.   Explain why Adolph Hitler would have admired Martin Luther King, Jr.

Rubric:

(maximum possible score: 30) Each of the five responses is read with the following criteria in mind:

A.   The response addresses the task presented by the prompt.

B.   The response is reasonable (i.e., the underlying reasoning is detectable).

C.   The response is novel (i.e., hardly predictable).

For each criterion, score either +2 if the response clearly meets the criterion, +1 if it is unclear as to whether or not the criterion is met, or +0 if the response clearly does not meet the criterion.

#3

Objective (high school - mathematics):

Students formulate propositions and prove theorems about subsets of whole numbers (creative thinking).

Combination Short-Response and Essay Prompt:

The number of dots in each of the following arrays is called a triangular number:

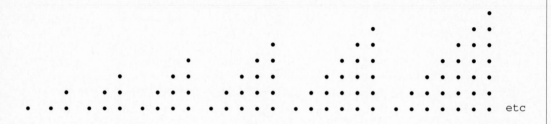

ILLUSTRATION 11.2 *(Continued)*

The set of triangular numbers is infinite. Take at least 15 minutes to examine triangular numbers. Then make three different statements you think are true about triangular numbers. These statements should be hypotheses that are not immediately apparent (e.g., "All triangular numbers are positive integers" is too obvious). Try to prove one of your statements. Display your work on the proof or the proof attempt in the indicated area below.

First statement: _____

_____

_____

Second statement: _____

_____

_____

Third statement: _____

_____

_____

Which statement did you attempt to prove? _____

Proof or work toward proof:

Rubric:

The rubric is based on a comparison of this response to those of others. First of all, blatantly obvious statements (e.g. "No triangular number is irrational") is eliminated. Then each of the remaining statements is compared to a list of statements compiled from other students who have responded to this prompt. Comparison statements are sequenced from the most frequently occurring to the least frequently occurring. The statements from this response are ranked in the sequence and scored the number of points equal to its rank. Thus, if there are 50 comparison statements, 20 of which have been made more than once, then if one of the statements from this response is equivalent to one of those first 20, it receives a score from 1 to 20 inclusive. If the statement is equivalent to one of the previously unique 30 comparison statements, it receives a score of 21. If the statement is not equivalent to any of the 50 comparison statements, it receives a score of 36 (i.e., a three-way tie for 21st place). If the display of the work on the proof demonstrates a discernible line of thought, the statement score is multiplied by 4. If the proof is valid, that score is doubled.

mini-experiment. Call up each of those files that is for a creative-thinking objective. Now, in light of your work with Chapter 11, revise the mini-experiments in those files. For each file (i.e., files for creative-thinking objectives), design at least two more mini-experiments and insert them into the file.

2. With a colleague, exchange printouts of the mini-experiments you designed or revised when you engaged in Synthesis Activity 1. Discuss and critique one another's mini-experiments. Revise them as you decide they should be revised.

3. With a colleague discuss why you think Ms. Ragusa gave such strange times for students to respond in Case 11.1, why she used Hebrew letters instead of numbers for Illustration 11.1's prompts, and why the five parts to Mini-Experiment #2 from Illustration 11.2 are numbered "−2, −1, 0, 1, 2" instead of the more conventional and expected "1, 2, 3, 4, 5."

4. With your colleague, discuss whether you agree or disagree with the following statement: "Illustration 10.4's Mini-Experiment #4 prompts students to create a drawing. That makes it relevant to a creative-thinking objective, not an application objective as stated in the illustration."

5. Retrieve the goal defined by a set of weighted objectives you developed for Synthesis Activity 3 for Chapter 5. Select one of the creative-thinking objectives from that set (if indeed the set includes at least one such objective). Now, design a lesson for leading students to achieve that objective. Design one or more mini-experiments to provide you with indicators of your students' progress during that lesson.

6. With a colleague, share and discuss your work from Synthesis Activity 5. Revise the mini-experiments in light of your discussions.

TRANSITIONAL ACTIVITY FROM CHAPTER 11 TO CHAPTER 12

In a discussion with two or more of your colleagues, address the following questions:

1. As students engage in our lessons for appreciation objectives, how do we manage to monitor their progress?

2. How do we design mini-experiments that are relevant to appreciation objectives?

3. As students engage in our lessons for willingness-to-try objectives, how do we manage to monitor their progress?

4. How do we design mini-experiments that are relevant to willingness-to-try objectives?

Monitoring Students' Attitudes

◆══ GOAL OF CHAPTER 12

Chapter 12 is intended to lead you to design mini-experiments that will help you monitor students' progress with affective objectives. More specifically the objectives are as follows:

A. You will explain principles associated with students' progress with affective objectives (discover a relationship) 10%.

B. You will design mini-experiments for gauging students' progress as they engage in lessons for affective objectives (application) 40%.

C. You will design mini-experiments relevant to how well students have achieved appreciation objectives (application) 19%.

D. You will design mini-experiments relevant to how well students have achieved willingness-to-try objectives (application) 19%.

E. You will extend your ability to explain fundamental principles for using a variety of mini-experiment formats (discover a relationship) 12%.

THE ROLE OF AFFECTIVE OBJECTIVES

From Chapter 2, reread the section "Formative Judgments for Managing Student Behavior" on pages 86–90; from Chapter 5, reread the section "Affective Objectives."

By teaching for appreciation objectives, you attempt to influence students' preferences, desires, and opinions; by teaching for willingness-to-try objectives, you attempt to influence how they choose to act. In other words, by leading students to achieve affective objectives, you are attempting to indoctrinate them into embracing the values specified by the subject-content of those objectives. Words and phrases such as "indoctrinate" and "embracing values" are more likely associated with the goals of curricula for religious schools than for public schools. However, the subject-content of the example objectives from the two sections you just reread (e.g., cooperating with classmates, benefits of reading, and benefits of healthy diets) are typically considered within the purview of public-school curricula. Even if you choose to define the goal of a unit only with cognitive and/or psychomotor objectives, you still must concern yourself with students' attitudes about the subject-content of the cognitive or psychomotor objectives as well as their willingness to work with you. In other words, cognitive and psychomotor learning cannot take place in the absence of affective learning.

Because you are compelled to teach for affective objectives, even if you do not formally state them when you define your unit goals, you are compelled to monitor your students' progress with these affective objectives. You can hardly teach students to be on-task and engaged in learning activities without making formative judgments about affective learning. But should your judgments about students' achievement of affective objectives influence the summative evaluation reports of their achievements (e.g., the grades you assign)? In my opinion, the answer to that question is no, except for units in which the definition of the goal includes one or more affective objectives. To what degree should achievement of the stated affective objectives influence your summative evaluation reports? The answer to that question depends on how you weight the objectives. For example, I defined the goal for Chapter 6 of this book with seven objectives (A–G). Objective A is affective and is weighted 8%; the other six objectives are cognitive. My blueprint for a measurement to be used for a summative evaluation of your achievement of the goal of Chapter 6 should specify that 8% of the maximum possible score on that measurement should be relevant to Objective A (which is at the willingness-to-try learning level). The remaining 92% of the maximum possible score should be distributed among the other six objectives as indicated by the weights listed. Note how Ms. Eisley addresses this issue in Case 12.1.

CASE 12.1

Ms. Eisley is defining the goal of a language-arts unit on expressing arguments, especially by writing persuasive essays. She begins her list of objectives with the following three:

A. Students distinguish between examples and non-examples of each of the following: fact, opinion, evidence, and conclusion (construct a concept).
B. Students state definitions for "fact," "opinion," "evidence," and "conclusion" (simple knowledge).
C. From reading an essay (with the sophistication level of typical articles in magazines such as *Exploring Our World* or *Rainbows Everywhere*, students summarize the author's conclusions and identify evidence used to support those conclusions (comprehension and communication skills).

Then she thinks, "If I'm going to keep them motivated to work through these lessons, they need to value being able to present sound arguments in writing. Also, it'll take some courage on their part to lay out their opinions in writing for others to read—for others to take shots at. I'd also better target a willingness-to-try objective or two. But on the other hand, I don't want their unit grade to be a reflection of their attitudes. I don't want them faking enthusiasm; I can teach them better when they're straight with me. Okay, so I guess I should only include cognitive objectives. On the other, other hand—I must be losing my mind—good thing; no sane person should teach—if I don't write out the necessary affective objectives, I'm less likely to consciously teach for them. I know! I'll include them in the list, but for the measurement blueprint for summative evaluation purposes, I'll weight them zero."

Illustration 12.1 displays the weighted objectives she determines for the unit.

Earlier in the school year, Ms. Eisley had developed an ongoing unit, a unit that runs concurrently with all her other units throughout the school year. This unit is for teaching students to follow her four standards for classroom conduct. Since the school's summative evaluation reporting system requires her to give grades for classroom citizenship, she decided in the beginning of the school year to base those classroom citizenship grades on students' achievement of the goal of that ongoing unit. For her measurements of that goal, she weighted the objectives as shown by Illustration 12.2.

As you can see, she decided to emphasize affective learning over cognitive learning for the classroom citizenship grade.

Goal:

> Students present arguments, especially by writing
> persuasive essays

Objectives:

A. Students distinguish between examples and non-examples of each
of the following: fact, opinion, evidence, and conclusion (construct a concept) 15%.

B. Students state definitions for "fact," "opinion," "evidence,"
and "conclusion" (simple knowledge) 5%.

C. From reading an essay (with the sophistication level of typical
articles in magazines such as *Exploring Our World or Rainbows
Everywhere*), students summarize the author's conclusions and
identify evidence used to support those conclusions (comprehension and communication skills) 20%.

D. Students recognize the advantages they gain by being able to
use their writing to influence what others think (appreciation)
0%.

E. Given an opportunity to write an essay for the purpose of influencing others regarding an issue about which they hold
strong opinions, students will choose to write the essay (willingness to try) 0%.

F. Students welcome suggestions about their writing and choose to
edit their writing in light of those suggestions. (willingness
to try) 0%.

G. Students write persuasive essays that articulate and defend
opinions about well-defined issues (application) 35%.

H. Students articulate both supporting and counter-arguments to
opinions expressed by others (application) 20%.

I. Students develop novel ways of presenting and countering arguments (creative thinking) 5%.

ILLUSTRATION 12.1

Goal Defined by Weighted Objectives for One of Ms. Eisley's Language Arts Units

HOW STUDENTS DEVELOP ATTITUDES CONDUCIVE TO LEARNING AND COOPERATION

CONNECTING SUBJECT-CONTENT TO EXISTING VALUES

Telling students about the importance and value of what you want to teach them is generally
ineffectual as a learning activity for an appreciation objective. Case 12.2 is an example.

Goal:

Students comply with the four standards for classroom conduct.

Objectives:

A. Students discriminate between rights being respected and rights being disrespected as well as between a safe and comfortable classroom and one that is not comfortable and safe (construct a concept) 5%.

B. Students explain how the quality of life within the classroom community is affected by community members respecting one another's rights, as well as their own rights, as opposed to those rights being disrespected (discover a relationship) 5%.

C. Students explain the meaning of the following four standards for classroom conduct:

1. Respect everyone's rights (including your own) to work in a classroom community that is safe and comfortable.

2. Cooperate with your classmates and teacher in the business of learning.

3. Take advantage of learning opportunities.

4. Follow your teacher's directions.

(comprehension and communication skills) 5%.

D. Students state the four standards for classroom conduct (simple knowledge) 0%.

E. Students value the four standards for classroom conduct, judging them to be important for their own well-being and the well-being of the classroom community (appreciation) 5%.

F. Confronted with a classroom event, students determine whether or not a standard of classroom behavior was violated (application) 5%.

G. Students choose to comply with Classroom Conduct Standard 1. (willingness to try) 30%.

H. Students choose to comply with Classroom Conduct Standard 2. (willingness to try) 15%.

I. Students choose to comply with Classroom Conduct Standard 3. (willingness to try) 15%.

J. Students choose to comply with Classroom Conduct Standard 4. (willingness to try) 15%.

ILLUSTRATION 12.2

Goal Defined by Weighted Objectives for Ms. Eisley's Ongoing Classroom Citizenship Unit

CASE 12.2

Mr. Wickware realizes that if his history students appreciate the value of understanding certain events in the history of the U.S. Congress, they will be more receptive to achieving the cognitive objectives of his unit on congressional activities between 1901 and 1935. Thus, his initial objective for the unit is as follows:

> Students recognize the advantage of being able to relate congressional activities during the first 35 years of the 20th century to today's current issues (appreciation).

In an attempt to lead students to achieve that objective, he tells the class, "Today, we're going to begin studying the extremely important work of Congress between 1901 and 1935—a fantastic period in the history of our country! By learning about the intriguing things Congress did in that era, we will be wiser in dealing with the problems and issues of today—problems and issues that affect your very lives! I know you'll enjoy debating today's issues when you can apply lessons from the past."

Generally speaking, students are not open to being told what they enjoy or find important (Cangelosi, 1997, pp. 130–133, 187–192). Rather than wasting time with lip service for his appreciation-level objective, Mr. Wickware should integrate learning activities for the appreciation objective with lessons for cognitive objectives while keeping the following three suggestions in mind:

1. The first few examples used to introduce the subject-content should involve situations in which students have already demonstrated an interest. For an example, reread Case 2.1.
2. Initial tasks to which the subject-content applies should be selected so that the value of the new specific, concept, relationship, or process is readily demonstrated. Case 12.3 is an example.

CASE 12.3

Mr. Hogan is designing a lesson to lead his fourth-graders to achieve the following objective:

> C. Students explain why they can find the area of a rectangle by multiplying its length by its width (discover-a-relationship).

The students have already constructed the concept of area and know that they can find the area of a rectangle by employing the following process:

1. Partition the interior of the rectangle into unit squares, as shown by Illustration 12.3.
2. Count the number of unit squares.

He decides to confront them with a problem in which they need to find the area of a 4 by 2 rectangle as shown in Illustration 12.3. He wants to lead them to discover the relationship (i.e., Area = length × width). But then he remembers the need to also be concerned with the following objective:

> D. Students value being able to use the area formula as a way of finding areas without going to the trouble of counting individual unit squares (appreciation).

ILLUSTRATION 12.3

The First Rectangle Mr. Hogan Thought of Using for a Discover-a-Relationship Lesson

Then Mr. Hogan thinks, "A 4 by 2 rectangle is so small that you can count the unit squares—or even just see that there's a total of 8—just as easily as you can multiply 4 and 2. The formula doesn't save them any time for such a small rectangle." He changes his plan to begin the lesson with a problem that will prompt students to count the unit squares in a rectangle such as the one in Illustration 12.4. "A 16 by 6 rectangle will be just the right size," he thinks, "just big enough to make counting up the unit squares annoying but not so big that the task overwhelms them. If the problem grabs their interest, they'll be motivated to look for a shortcut process."

3. Consistent with Chapter 5's treatise on meaningful learning, inquiry instructional strategies should be used to lead students to construct concepts and discover relationships for themselves whenever reasonably possible. The inductive learning activities of construct-a-concept and discover-a-relationship lessons lead students to feel that they own subject-content. It is part of them; thus, they are more likely to appreciate it. Surely, Ms. Fisher's strategies in Case 2.4 stimulated her students' interest in the civil rights movement. Similarly, Ms. Ragusa managed to get her students excited about magnets in Cases 7.6 and 7.17.

FREEDOM TO EXPERIMENT, QUESTION, HYPOTHESIZE, AND MAKE ERRORS

Even though students have learned to appreciate certain subject-content, they still may not attempt to work eagerly with it because they lack confidence that they will successfully use it in situations they find meaningful. Until they have accumulated experiences successfully addressing problems, students tend to be reluctant to apply what they have learned as did Terrence in Case 5.13, Gary in Case 5.14, Anna in Case 5.15, Tawny in Case 5.16, and Ms. Ragusa's students in Case 10.3.

Willingness-to-try objectives require learning experiences similar to those for appreciation objectives. However, to lead students from the appreciation level to the willingness-to-try level, you must prompt them with tasks or problems that are interesting enough to maintain their attention, but easy enough for them to experience success. Keep the following in mind:

• Until students gain confidence in their abilities and in the benefits of working on perplexing tasks, most of the tasks you prompt them to tackle should be such that they will feel successful before becoming frustrated. As their confidence builds, you should present them with tasks of gradually increasing difficulty.

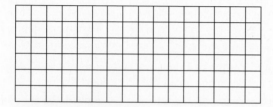

ILLUSTRATION 12.4

The Rectangle Mr. Hogan Decided to Use After Considering His Appreciation Objective

- The more the task relates to what already interests them, the more students tend to tolerate perplexity before becoming too frustrated to continue. It is quite a challenge for you to judge that fine line between interest and frustration.
- Achievement of willingness-to-try objectives requires a learning environment in which students feel free to experiment, question, hypothesize, and make errors without fear of ridicule, embarrassment, or loss of status. As emphasized in Chapter 3, students should never be judged by what they achieve or fail to achieve.
- By presenting students with problems requiring application of previously acquired skills and abilities (e.g., from prior units), students not only maintain and improve on earlier achievements, but you also provide additional opportunities for them to experience success working with subject-content. You can see the close association between achievement of application-level objectives and achievement of both appreciation and willingness-to-try objectives.

REINFORCEMENT

Students are positively reinforced for having attempted tasks when they see that their efforts have been productive. In cases throughout this text, teachers have made sure that the products of students' efforts are used in subsequent activities. For example in Case 1.1, Mr. Chacone not only used his second-graders' revisions of the rules for the ball-kicking game to replay the game, but their rules were also used in the classroom to construct the concept of a circle. In Cases 1.4 and 2.1, you positively reinforced your students' willingness to engage in classroom activities and do homework by the way you tested what they learned from their efforts. You also used information they provided in subsequent lessons. The principle to keep in mind is that students develop and retain a pattern of choosing to do assigned work if and only if they are positively reinforced for their efforts.

INDICATORS OF PROGRESS AS STUDENTS ENGAGE IN AFFECTIVE LESSONS

Unlike Mr. Wickware in Case 12.2, Mr. Rose integrates his lesson for affective objectives with those for cognitive objectives in Case 12.4.

CASE 12.4

Mr. Rose realizes that if his students appreciate the value of understanding certain events in the history of the U.S. Congress, they will be more receptive to achieving the cognitive objectives of his unit on congressional activities between 1901 and 1935. Thus, he includes the following among his objectives:

> B. Students recognize the advantage of being able to relate congressional activities during the first 35 years of the 20th century to today's current issues (appreciation).

He believes it is very important to monitor students' progress with the objective for purposes of making formative judgments throughout the unit; however, for purposes of summative evaluation near the end of the unit, he assigns a weight of 0% to Objective B.

In deciding how to lead students to achieve Objective B, he makes a number of observations of students to identify current issues that concern them. He decides to focus on the following problems: (1) Should the use of some street drugs be decriminalized? (2) What should the federal government do about unemployment? (3) What should Congress do to ensure the rights of ethnic minorities? (4) Should English be the only official language for doing business in the United States? (5) What should federal policy be regarding providing services to residents who are not registered as citizens or legal immigrants? (6) What should Congress do about right-to-life versus right-to-choose issues? (7) What should Congress do to protect the environment?

Mr. Rose designs all of the unit's lessons around these seven current problems. One sequence of learning activities is as follows:

1. Mr. Rose assigns each student to one of seven task groups (according to his perception of their individual interests and according to who tends to work cooperatively with whom). For example, one group of five students is directed to "research" the first problem, concerning the decriminalization of the use of street drugs. The group is to examine how Congress handled the prohibition of alcohol in the first 30 years of the 20th century and then relate those "lessons of history" to the current question about use of street drugs. Specifically, the group is directed to (a) explain Congress' rationale for enacting the 18th Amendment to the Constitution and then for repealing it with the 21st Amendment, (b) explain the benefits and consequences of prohibition, and (c) identify both similarities and differences between the alcohol prohibition issues in the earlier period to the problem of using street drugs today. Each of the other six task groups researches one of the other six problems, following a parallel process.

2. Mr. Rose provides each task group with an organizational structure within which to operate, a list of resources from which to acquire information, a list of deadlines for specific subtasks, and directions for reporting findings to the rest of the class.

3. To obtain an overall picture of the climate within which Congress operated from 1901 to 1935, and thus to better compare the problems of that time to those of the present, each student is directed to read a textbook chapter about the 1901–1935 period.

4. Each task group receives a schedule for making periodic progress reports.

5. After each task group presents its final report, students who were not part of the reporting group debate and vote on the task group's proposals about dealing with the current problem.

Because the learning activities are student-centered, Mr. Rose has ample opportunities to observe students respond to prompts (e.g., assignment to explain Congress' rationale); at least some rubrics depend on whether or not students meet prescribed deadlines. As Mr. Rose detects evidence of students' enthusiasm for addressing the problems (e.g., students generating their own relevant questions), he makes decisions regarding the degree of structure he imposes on the activities. For example, because the group addressing the issue of services to immigrants without "papers" is completing tasks ahead of schedule as well as making in-depth reports, he sticks with his original schedule. On the other hand, the group working on the right-to-life versus the right-to-choose issues missed an early deadline, and the quality of the work did not meet the standard Mr. Rose was expecting. Thus, he decided to break that group's tasks into smaller subtasks with more frequent deadlines than originally planned.

Of course, Mr. Rose realizes that students are at least partially motivated to apply their understanding of history and meet deadlines because he is requiring them to do this work for a grade. That he is closely supervising their activities is a possible source of measurement error in using their meeting deadlines as an indication of their willingness to engage in these activities on their own. But even if they would not now choose to apply lessons of history without Mr. Rose's guidance, he believes that the satisfaction they gain from making arguments from a knowledge base will encourage at least some of the students to use this approach once again.

At some point after this unit is completed, he plans to conduct a mini-experiment for the following objective by giving them the option of either addressing current problems by applying the process they used in this unit or by applying some process that does not build on lessons of history:

H. Given a choice of addressing current problems by applying lessons of history or addressing those problems without considering lessons of history, students choose to apply lessons from history (willingness to try).

INDICATORS OF STUDENTS' ACHIEVEMENT OF APPRECIATION OBJECTIVES

IS APPRECIATION MEASURABLE?

A mini-experiment is relevant to achievement of a cognitive or psychomotor objective when students who have achieved the objective can perform the task presented by the prompt with a higher success rate than those who have not achieved the objective. On the other hand, appreciation objectives are not concerned with students' being able to perform tasks. Achievement of appreciation objectives involves students' preferences, beliefs, desires, or values. Appreciation mini-experiments are designed to address questions such as whether or not students want to do something, not whether or not they are able to do something.

Since you cannot distinguish between students who have achieved an appreciation objective and those who have not by observing what they *can* do, how is it possible for a mini-experiment to prompt students to display indications of what they appreciate? Some argue that affective achievement isn't measurable. They are mistaken. We know affective achievement is measurable because you and I are routinely making judgments about people's attitudes. We base those judgments on empirical observations we make; those empirical observations are mini-experiments—usually informal mini-experiments.

Think, for example, of several people you know who you believe do not value cultural diversity in their communities. Now, think of a second group of people who you believe do value cultural diversity in their communities. Take your time.

Now, take some time to think of specific empirical observations you have made that influenced you to believe that some do not value cultural diversity and that the others do. Make two lists: (1) a list of empirical observations that are negative indicators of appreciation of cultural diversity and (2) a list of positive indicators of appreciation of cultural diversity.

In Case 12.5, Elwin and Kisha collaboratively respond to the prompt to which you just responded.

CASE 12.5

Elwin:	"To do this exercise well, we really need to clarify what we mean by 'valuing cultural diversity.' Don't you agree?"
Kisha:	"It's like the need to specify objectives before you attempt to monitor students' progress with them. I'm assuming that 'valuing' is used to imply appreciation learning level—especially since we're working from a section in the book on designing mini-experiments for achievement of appreciation objectives."
Elwin:	"So the learning level is appreciation and the subject-content is cultural diversity. Do we need to define 'cultural diversity,' or is it clear enough from our courses on multicultural education?"
Kisha:	"Yeah, let's agree that people who value cultural diversity in their communities welcome having people from different backgrounds and tend to celebrate and enjoy the differences rather than being threatened by them."
Elwin:	"Sounds good to me. I've got my list of bigots and non-bigots."
Kisha:	"Let's not be labeling people; although it's difficult not to for this exercise."
Elwin:	"Just kidding! Let's develop our two lists of indicators."

Illustration 12.5 displays their lists.

Negative Indicators of
Appreciation of
Cultural Diversity:

o   When someone of a cultural background different from their own
    moves into the community, they complain using comments such as,
    "The neighborhood keeps going downhill!"

o   They make remarks disparaging people's differences, for exam-
    ple, "The houses here used to have uncluttered lawns; now,
    those Mexicans have Mother Mary statues everywhere!"

o   They only rarely associate with people who are culturally dif-
    ferent from themselves.

o   They take stands in favor of "cultural purity" or push for uni-
    formity in dress and custom (e.g., speak in favor of strict
    dress codes in schools that are based primarily on the customs
    and habits of a single culture).

Positive Indicators of
Appreciation of
Cultural Diversity:

o   When someone of a cultural background different from their own
    moves into the community, they tend to celebrate the occasion
    with comments such as, "There is a greater opportunity to learn
    from a variety of people here than there used to be!"

o   They make remarks applauding people's differences, for example,
    "All the lawns here used to look the same; there are more
    things to see now. The place isn't so sterile and drab!"

o   They often associate with people who are culturally different
    from themselves.

o   They take stands in favor of "cultural diversity" or push for
    policies that accommodate differences in customs (e.g., speak
    in favor of school dress codes that provide for differences in
    customs).

ILLUSTRATION 12.5

Elwin and Kisha's Lists of Indicators of the Degree to Which People Value Diversity

The next step in designing relevant mini-experiments for appreciation of cultural diversity
is to formulate prompts that would stimulate individuals to respond either with a negative or
positive indicator. Again, we should continue to remind ourselves of the impact of measurement error on how well such indicators truly reflect what is in the minds of our students. Our
formative judgments and summative evaluations should always be tentative rather than final.

PRESENTING CHOICES

Because you are able to associate observable behaviors with differential achievement of appreciation objectives, it is possible for you to design relevant mini-experiments. The trick is to prompt students with situations in which they are confronted with choices of behaving either like a person who has achieved the appreciation objective or like one who has not.

Consider Case 12.6.

CASE 12.6

Ms. Makito is designing mini-experiments to insert in her computer file for the following objective for her health science class:

A. Students want to maintain a healthy diet (appreciation).

Keeping in mind that the objective is at the appreciation rather than the willingness-to-try learning level, she lists the names of four people she believes would like to follow a healthy diet although they may or may not actually follow a healthy diet. She lists four people and then for each makes note of at least one observation she's made that influenced her to believe that person wants to maintain a healthy diet. Next, she lists the names of four people she believes have not achieved the objective and notes for each an observation she once made to indicate that the person is not interested in maintaining a healthy diet.

Her two lists appear in Illustration 12.6. She then thinks of ways to prompt students into responding either with a negative or positive indicator. Illustration 12.7 displays two of the mini-experiments she inserts into her file.

The prompt for Mini-Experiment #1 from Illustration 12.7 is quite direct with students. It simply asks students about a belief. This direct approach can work under the condition that students are confident that they risk nothing by answering honestly. Such a condition is limited to situations in which students recognize that the measurement results will be used for formative judgments only—not summative evaluations. Unfortunately, many students have been conditioned by their experiences with some other teachers besides you to believe that teachers "test" only for grading purposes. Consequently, you will need to make a concerted effort to establish a classroom environment in which students feel it is safe to provide you with honest responses to your prompts. The teachers in Cases 2.5, 2.6, 2.7, and 2.8 from the section "Formative Judgments for Setting the Tone for the School Year" demonstrate strategies for establishing such an environment from the first day of the school year.

The prompt for Illustration 12.7's Mini-Experiment #2 is less direct with students than the prompt for #1. A more indirect approach is used in Case 12.7.

CASE 12.7

Ms. Liechty includes the following objective among those for an ongoing classroom citizenship unit for her fifth-grade students:

Students want classmates to succeed in their efforts to learn (appreciation).

As she designs a mini-experiment for the objective, Ms. Liechty considers using a direct approach by simply asking, "Do you want your classmates to learn how to do mathematics?" However, she feels

From Ms. Makito's group who
appreciate a healthy diet:

Sandra: She frequently mentions that she ought to diet. Once, before eating junk food, she said, "I really shouldn't eat this!"

Karl: He often inquires about what he should eat to maintain good health. He reads magazine articles on nutrition.

Eddie: He frequently mentions that he has to start watching what he eats. He said, "I haven't had much energy lately; I wonder if it's my diet."

Jolene: She told someone who had been eating junk food, "That stuff will kill you!" Once she said, "People ought to drink more water."

From Ms. Makito's group who do
not appreciate a healthy diet:

Phil: He said, "I don't worry about cholesterol. When you die you die! As soon as I start giving up the food I enjoy, I'll probably get run over by a truck."

Marion: He hardly ever reads or talks about nutrition.

Juanita: She said, "Listening to the health nuts makes me think if it tastes good, it's bad, and if it tastes bad, it's good! I don't care what they say; I eat the way I want. If God didn't want us to eat sugar and fat, he wouldn't have given them to us."

Mavis: She said, "You don't need to worry about what you eat as long as you exercise."

ILLUSTRATION 12.6

Ms. Makito's Lists of Observations She Made About People Who Appreciated and Didn't Appreciate Healthy Diets

such a prompt won't work for two reasons: (1) The question is ambiguous and would be interpreted differently by different students. (2) Students would tend to say what they think she wants them to say.

Consequently, she uses an indirect approach and enters Illustration 12.8's mini-experiment into her computerized file for the objective.

Ms. Liechty realizes that this mini-experiment alone is not a strong indicator of students' progress with the objective. However, she knows that if she draws on a variety of situations (e.g., softball, science projects, and oral presentations) to design and administer several similar mini-experiments, patterns may emerge from responses that do indicate progress.

<u>#1</u>

<u>Multiple-Choice Prompt</u>:

Do you think people should avoid some foods (even if they taste good) and eat others (even if they taste bad)? Check one:

Yes _____   No _____

<u>Rubric</u>:

+1 for checking "Yes" only, otherwise, +0.

<u>#2</u>

<u>Weighted-Response Multiple-Choice Prompt</u>:

Sugar-Fizz is a new candy that is being sold in grocery stores. Here are some facts about Sugar-Fizz:

1. It is not poisonous.

2. It is not known to cause any fatal diseases.

3. It has no nutritional value.

4. There is some evidence that it lowers the body's resistance to some infections.

John is a 14-year-old who has no health problems, has never tasted Sugar-Fizz, and has heard it tastes delicious. What should John do? Check only one answer:

_____ a) Eat Sugar-Fizz whenever he wants, but stop if he gets sick.

_____ b) Try Sugar-Fizz, but not very often.

_____ c) Never even try Sugar-Fizz.

_____ d) Eat as much Sugar-Fizz as he wants.

<u>Rubric</u>:

+3 for checking either "b" or "c" only, +1 for checking "a" only, and +0 for checking "d."

ILLUSTRATION 12.7

Two Mini-Experiments Ms. Makito Inserted Into Her Computer File for an Appreciation Objective on Healthy Diets

Multiple, Multiple-Choice Prompt:

The student is given an audiotape player containing a cassette on which the directions for the prompt are recorded. The student is instructed to circle either "YES" or "NO" by each letter on the following response sheet:

A. YES   NO

B. YES   NO

C. YES   NO

D. YES   NO

E. YES   NO

F. YES   NO

G. YES   NO

H. YES   NO

The script on the cassette is as follows:

"Things can happen that make us feel happy and sad at the same time. But some things make us only happy or only sad. I'm going to ask you to pretend something and ask you some questions about why you feel happy or sad about what you pretended. [pause] Pretend you are playing third base during a P.E. class softball game. The other team is batting. The batter strikes out.

A. Does seeing the batter strike out make you feel happy because it will help your team win? Answer by circling 'YES' or 'NO' next to 'A' on your answer sheet. [pause]

B. Does seeing the batter strike out make you feel sad because it will help their team win? Circle 'YES' or 'NO' next to 'B.' [pause]

C. Does seeing the batter strike out make you feel happy because the pitcher for your team did well? Circle 'YES' or 'NO' next to 'C.' [pause]

D. Does seeing the batter strike out make you feel happy because it will make their team feel sad? Circle 'YES' or 'NO' next to 'D.' [pause]

E. Does seeing the batter strike out make you feel sad because the batter will feel sad? Circle 'YES' or 'NO' next to 'D.' [pause]

ILLUSTRATION 12.8

A Mini-Experiment with an Indirect Prompt That Ms. Liechty Designed to Be Relevant to an Appreciation Objective

(Continued)

ILLUSTRATION 12.8 (Continued)

> F. Does seeing the batter strike out make you feel sad be-
> cause the game will soon be over? Circle 'YES' or 'NO'
> next to 'F.' [pause]
>
> G. Does seeing the batter strike out make you feel happy be-
> cause the batter will feel sad? Circle 'YES' or 'NO' next
> to 'G.' [pause]
>
> Rubric:
>
> (Maximum possible score: 4) If the student circled "YES" for
> A and "NO" for B, continue scoring the response. Otherwise, do not
> score the response because it appears the student did not under-
> stand the directions. Score +1 for each of the following
> that is marked as indicated: "YES" for C, "NO" for D, "YES" for E,
> and "NO" for G.

INDICATORS OF STUDENTS' ACHIEVEMENT OF WILLINGNESS-TO-TRY OBJECTIVES

OBSERVING BEHAVIORS

Since willingness-to-try objectives require students to take some sort of observable action, not only embrace unseen values, they can be easier to design mini-experiments for than appreciation objectives. However, keep in mind that trying is different from succeeding. Consider Case 12.8.

CASE 12.8

Donnelle's teacher includes the following objective for his class:

Students attempt to follow a healthy diet (willingness to try).

Chris is convinced of the value of a healthy diet and eats what he thinks is good for him. However, having yet to achieve some of the cognitive objectives of his teacher's health unit, Donnelle mistakenly believes that since fat is stored energy, he will gain energy by eating a lot of animal fat. In his enthusiasm for maintaining a healthy diet, Donnelle makes a concerted effort to consume animal fats.

Did Donnelle seem to have achieved the objective stated in Case 12.8? Because he acted on his belief about nutritious diets and was trying to follow what he thought was a healthy diet, it appears that he has achieved the objective.

Mini-experiments for a willingness-to-try objective can be designed so that students are prompted with choices of either trying to work with the objective's subject-content or not. Consider Case 12.9.

CASE 12.9

Mr. Clemente is embarking on a new school year as a middle-school social studies teacher. He plans to use a number of learning activities in which students work with partners on projects. Because one of his long-range goals is for students to increase their interest in reading about social studies topics, he wants to plan some of the projects so that students with an affinity for reading are teamed with students with an aversion to reading. He is counting on some of the enthusiasm of those who like to read rubbing off on their partners.

To implement his plan, he needs to measure his students' willingness to read so he'll know whom to team together. At this time, Mr. Clemente is not concerned with identifying reading-skill levels but rather identifying students who enjoy and advocate reading. Thus, he needs to design mini-experiments relevant to the following objective:

Students choose to read and express the merits of reading to others (willingness to try).

To design mini-experiments, he thinks about persons whom he considers to be avid readers and reading advocates. He also thinks about persons he believes dislike reading. Asking himself what he observed about these people that influenced these beliefs about their propensities toward reading, he develops the list of observable behaviors displayed by Illustration 12.9.

Mr. Clemente uses the lists in designing several mini-experiments, including the one in Illustration 12.10. The difficulty of Illustration 12.10's mini-experiment can be manipulated by varying the interest levels of the reading matter available in the guidance counselors' waiting area. For an easy prompt, sports, music, video, and teenage-oriented magazines would be available. For a more difficult prompt, only low-interest reading material would be available.

Positive Indicators of
Affinity for Reading:

- Speak about literary works they have read, are reading, or plan to read

- When confronted with problems, refer to reading material as solution sources

- Frequent libraries, bookstores, and magazine stands

- Recommend reading selections to their friends

- Often seen reading

Negative Indicators of
Affinity for Reading:

- Complain about the length of reading assignments in school

- When confronted with problems, seek solutions that do not require reading

- When given the option of going to a library or some other place associated with reading, does not go to such a place

- While spending time in a waiting room (e.g., a physician's office) does not pick up available reading material

ILLUSTRATION 12.9

Mr. Clemente's Lists of Observations for Discriminating Between People Who Enjoy and Advocate Reading and People Who Don't

Performance-Observation Prompt:

The student is directed to wait outside the guidance counselors' offices where a variety of books and magazines are prominently displayed.

Rubric:

An unobtrusive observer in the waiting room uses a watch and makes notes to record the number of minutes the student spends:

    A. waiting for the counselor

    B. looking at, thumbing through, or holding magazines but not actually reading

    C. appearing to read

The score is computed as follows:

$$Score = 2(C/A) + (B/A)$$

where A = the number of minutes the student spent waiting for the counselor, B = the number of minutes the student spent looking at, thumbing through, or holding books or magazines without appearing to actually read them, and C = the number of minutes the student appeared to be reading.

ILLUSTRATION 12.10

A Mini-Experiment Mr. Clemente Designed to Be Relevant to a Willingness-to-Try Objective

INFERRING BEHAVIORS

Willingness-to-try mini-experiments that depend on direct observation (e.g., Illustration 12.10's) often lack usability. Thus, prompts must often be designed to be incorporated into usable questionnaires. Instead of directly observing the behaviors specified by the objectives, you might prompt students to indicate how they would behave or have behaved in some relevant situations. Illustration 12.11 displays such a mini-experiment intended to be relevant to the same objective as the mini-experiment Mr. Clemente designed in Case 12.9.

Mini-experiments for willingness-to-try objectives (e.g., Illustration 12.11's) that do not depend on direct observations are of little value unless they are used in concert with other similar prompts that present a variety of situations. As with appreciation prompts with indirect approaches, a number of them are needed to identify response patterns that are indicative of students' attitudes.

The difficulty of these mini-experiments can be manipulated by varying the attractiveness of the choices. Students, for example, are more likely to select a reading activity over watching a movie if the choice of movie is one they consider boring rather than exciting.

SELF-REPORTS

In Case 12.6, Ms. Makito designed mini-experiments for an appreciation objective relative to healthy diets. She used a very direct approach with Illustration 12.7's Mini-Experiment #1 that simply prompted students to answer a question about what they believe. Simply asking students

Objective:

When provided with appropriate opportunities, students choose to read (willingness to try).

Multiple-Choice Prompt:

Suppose you find out that next week you will be meeting a visitor from Mexico. You would like to know more about life in Mexico before visiting with this person. Which one of the following would you most likely do? (Circle the letter in front of your choice.)

a) Watch the travel channel on television in hopes that you see a program about Mexico.

b) Read about Mexico in an Atlas.

c) Look up "Mexico" in an encyclopedia.

d) Phone a travel agent and ask her or him about life in Mexico.

e) Go to the library and ask the reference librarian what he or she knows about Mexico.

f) Wait for the visitor from Mexico to arrive and ask her or him.

g) Search the internet for references to read about Mexico.

Rubric:

Score +1 for any one of the following: b, c, or g. Score +0 for any of the others.

ILLUSTRATION 12.11

A Willingness-to-Try Mini-Experiment That Does Not Depend on Direct Observation

about what they appreciate or what they are willing to do is generally more usable than making direct observations of what they actually do (e.g., Illustration 12.10's mini-experiment) or inferring what they would do from a pattern of responses to a number of prompts such as the one in Illustration 12.11. In Case 12.10, Ms. Makito decides to use a direct approach for a mini-experiment relevant to a willingness-to-try objective; however, rather than simply asking students what they would or wouldn't do, she directs them to keep a record of what they did.

CASE 12.10

Including Objective A as listed in Case 12.6, Ms. Makito defines the goal of her unit on maintaining a healthy diet with nine objectives; two of them are as follows:

G. Students maintain a record of what they eat each day for a period of time, classifying their daily intake according to the five food groups of the food guide pyramid (process knowledge).
H. Students choose to maintain a healthy diet that is in accordance with the food guide pyramid (willingness to try).

Objective:

    Students maintain a record of what they eat each day for a period of time, classifying their daily intake according to the five food groups of the food guide pyramid (process knowledge).

Prompt:

    Students are directed to maintain a record of everything they eat for two weeks. The following form is to be completed for each day and is to be turned into Ms. Makito on the next school day. How to keep these records is explained in class. Directions: List each food item you eat during the 24-hour period and indicate the approximate time of the day you ate it. Also for each food item, under "Amount," circle either "L" if you consumed a large amount, "M" for a moderate amount, or "S" for a small amount. For each item, under "Food Group," circle either "G" if the food item is in the bread-cereal-rice-pasta group, "V" if it is the vegetable group, "F" if it is in the fruit group, "D" if it is in the dairy group, or "M" if it is in the meat group. The column under "Notes" is for any special circumstances you want to make note of about any of the food items in your list.

The Form

Name _____ Day of the week _____ Date _____

Time	Food Item	Amount	Food Group	Notes
		L M S	G V F P M	
		L M S	G V F P M	
		L M S	G V F P M	
		L M S	G V F P M	
		L M S	G V F P M	
		L M S	G V F P M	
		L M S	G V F P M	
		L M S	G V F P M	
		L M S	G V F P M	
		L M S	G V F P M	
		L M S	G V F P M	
		L M S	G V F P M	

ILLUSTRATION 12.12

One of Ms. Makito's Mini-Experiments Relevant to a Process-Knowledge Objective

For purposes of summative evaluation and grading, she weights Objective G 15% and Objective H 0%. However, for purposes of making formative judgments to guide her teaching as well as for providing students with formative feedback, she designs mini-experiments relevant to students' achievement of Objective H. She thinks, "I can hardly follow them around 24 hours a day to observe what they eat. But I could simply ask them if they're maintaining a healthy diet or if they plan to cut down on junk food and eat more healthy foods—or better yet, I could ask them more specifically how much they plan to eat from each of the five groups from our food guide pyramid. Oh! Even better yet, I'll use the same prompt for one of my mini-experiments relevant to Objective G." The prompt she has in mind is shown in Illustration 12.12.

She continues to think, "Some of them won't be as diligent about doing it as others, but I'll bet the ones who are more likely to keep accurate records of what they eat are more likely to watch what they eat and at least think about what they're sticking into their stomachs. In any case, those who are motivated by grades will fill it in because 15% of their unit test scores will depend on it. Of course, the rubric I use for Objective H should depend on what they eat rather than on simply whether or not they listed food—good or bad food—and correctly classified the items according to our five food groups." For objective H, she develops the rubric shown by Illustration 12.13.

She thinks, "Since their grades aren't depending on their achievement of Objective H, they have no reason to be dishonest with me regarding what they actually eat. I'll have them keep the record for two weeks. Then they can compare the first week's results to the second's as an indicator of whether or not they're moving in a healthier direction. For my own purposes, I can make the comparison for the whole class to help me assess if my unit is impacting actual eating habits.

```
Objective:

   Students choose to maintain a healthy diet that is in accordance
   with the food guide pyramid (willingness to try).

Prompt:

   Use Illustration 12.12's prompt.

Rubric:

   Rather than a total score for all 14 days, a separate score
   is given for each day. A trend of increasing scores from Day 1
   through Day 14 is considered indicative of positive achievement.
   A trend of decreasing scores is considered indicative of negative
   achievement. Each day's form is scored as follows:

      (Maximum possible score: 4) +1 if the largest amount of food
      is from the G group, +1 if the combined amounts of food from the
      V and F groups exceeds that of the combined D and M groups, +1
      if the least amount of food is from either the D group or the M
      group, +1 if the amount from the G group is twice as much as
      from each of the other four groups.
```

ILLUSTRATION 12.13

One of Ms. Makito's Mini-Experiments Relevant to a Willingness-to-Try Objective

SYNTHESIS ACTIVITIES FOR CHAPTER 12

1. Retrieve the computerized folder you set up when you engaged in Synthesis Activity 2 for Chapter 6. From your work doing Synthesis Activity 3 for Chapter 6, each file contains at least one mini-experiment. Call up each of those files that is for an affective objective. Now, in light of your work with Chapter 12, revise the mini-experiments in those files. For each file (i.e., files for appreciation or will-ingness-to-try objectives), design at least two more mini-experiments and insert them into the file.

2. With a colleague, exchange printouts of the mini-experiments you designed or revised when you engaged in Synthesis Activity 1. Discuss and critique one another's mini-experiments. Revise them as you decide they should be revised.

3. Retrieve the goal defined by a set of weighted objectives you developed for Synthesis Activity 3 for Chapter 5. Select one of the affective objectives from that set (if indeed the set includes at least one such objective). Now, design a lesson for leading students to achieve that objective. Design one or more mini-experiments to provide you with indicators of your students' progress during that lesson.

4. With a colleague, share and discuss your work from Synthesis Activity 3. Revise the mini-experiments in light of your discussions.

TRANSITIONAL ACTIVITY FROM CHAPTER 12 TO CHAPTER 13

In a discussion with two or more of your colleagues, address the following questions:

1. What should we know about the physical-fitness of our students before engaging them in lessons for psychomotor-skill objectives?

2. As students engage in our lessons for psychomotor-skill objectives, how do we manage to monitor their progress?

3. How do we design mini-experiments that are relevant to psychomotor-skill objectives?

CHAPTER **13**

Monitoring Students'
Development of
Psychomotor Skills

⟸ GOAL OF CHAPTER 13

Chapter 13 is intended to lead you to design mini-experiments that will help you monitor students' progress with psychomotor-skill objectives. More specifically the objectives are as follows:

A. You will explain the dependence of students' physical fitness on their readiness to develop psychomotor skills (comprehension and communication skills) 5%.

B. You will explain how aspects of physical fitness (i.e., cardiovascular endurance, body composition, flexibility, muscular strength and endurance, agility, balance, coordination, power, speed, and reaction time) are generally developed and measured (comprehension and communication skills) 15%.

C. You will explain the stages by which students develop psychomotor skills (discover a relationship) 15%.

D. You will design mini-experiments for gauging students' progress as they engage in lessons for psychomotor-skill objectives (application) 20%.

E. You will design mini-experiments relevant to how well students have achieved psychomotor-skill objectives (application) 25%.

F. You will extend your ability to explain fundamental principles for using a variety of mini-experiment formats (discover a relationship) 15%.

G. You will incorporate the following technical terms and phrases into your working professional vocabulary: "cardiovascular endurance," "body composition," "flexibility," "muscular strength," "muscular endurance," "agility," "static balance," "dynamic balance," "coordination," "power," "speed," and "reaction time" (comprehension and communication skills) 5%.

PREREQUISITES FOR DEVELOPMENT OF PSYCHOMOTOR SKILLS

PHYSICAL FITNESS

From Chapter 5, reread the section "Psychomotor Objectives" on pages 243–247.

Although you may not be in the business of designing mini-experiments relevant to physical-fitness objectives, you may need to be concerned with the physical-fitness levels of your students, because students' achievement of psychomotor-skills objectives is dependent on their physical fitness. Thus, it is important to be cognizant of certain physical-fitness needs of your students and to possibly have aspects of their physical fitness assessed. Aspects of physical fitness include (1) cardiovascular endurance, (2) body composition, (3) flexibility, (4) muscular strength and endurance, (5) agility, (6) balance, (7) coordination, (8) power, (9) speed, and (10) reaction time (Pangrazi, 1998, pp. 236–237; Williams, Harageones, Johnson, & Smith, 1995, pp. 18–28).

CARDIOVASCULAR ENDURANCE

Cardiovascular endurance is how well a person's circulatory and respiratory systems efficiently deliver oxygen and fuel for muscles so that the person is able to sustain an activity for an extended period of time. Cardiovascular endurance is developed through aerobic exercise, that is, through continuous rhythmic activities that require the body to use an elevated amount of oxygen for at least 15 minutes. Examples of aerobic exercises include sustained biking, rope jumping, aerobic dancing, swimming, and jogging.

Illustration 13.1 is an example of a mini-experiment designed to be relevant to cardiovascular-endurance physical fitness. Note that the prompt is classified as "product-examination" rather than "performance observation," because the rubric is such that only the distance covered by students is recorded. Had the rubric indicated that the observer should record something about students' running techniques, then the prompt would be performance observation.

Repeated applications of Illustration 13.1's mini-experiment can provide some indication of a student's progress with cardiovascular endurance by charting changes in the number of laps covered. Of course, there is no limit to the number of ways cardiovascular-endurance physical fitness can be measured. Some of the more accurate ways include stress tests on stationary bicycles or treadmills in appropriately equipped physical-fitness centers.

Product-Examination Prompt:

The student is told that she/he will be directed to run and/or walk around a standard 400 meter track for a period of 12 minutes so that she/he covers as much distance (i.e., as many laps) as reasonably possible without experiencing extreme discomfort. She/he is then directed to engage in appropriate warm-up exercises for a sustained distance run. Then the student is directed to a starting position on the track where the observer gives the signal to run and/or walk around the inside lane of the track until she/he hears the observer give the command to stop once 12 minutes have elapsed. The student is also told that the observer will yell out the number of minutes remaining after each minute elapses. The observer uses a timer.

Rubric:

The observer records the number of times the student goes around the track to the nearest 10 meter mark (i.e., the error of the measure of the distance should not be greater than 5 meters).

ILLUSTRATION 13.1

Example of a Mini-Experiment Designed to Be Relevant to Cardiovascular-Endurance Physical Fitness

BODY COMPOSITION

Body composition is the ratio of fat mass to lean body mass (Heyward & Stolarczyk, 1996). Lean body mass is composed of bone, muscle, and other body tissues exclusive of fat, except for the essential fat stored in bone marrow, the brain, spinal cord, and internal organs. What health and physical-fitness specialists consider ratios that fall within a healthy range depends on a complex of variables including age, gender, and lifestyle. The ratio of body fat to lean body mass is itself a function of a complex of variables, some of which cannot be controlled (e.g., genetics). We can exert control over others, most significantly, the balance between caloric intake and caloric expenditure (i.e., eating and exercise).

Body composition can be measured in a variety of ways. Underwater weighing and electrical impedance analysis are generally considered the two most accurate methods of estimating the percentage of body weight that is from fat (Hurd, 1998). However, because these two methods require expensive equipment, body composition is more commonly estimated via skinfold measurements. Illustration 13.2 displays an example of a mini-experiment in which skinfold calipers are used.

FLEXIBILITY

Flexibility is the range of motion for various joints and combination of joints. Flexibility is lost as a consequence of inactivity. Flexibility is gained through regular and appropriate stretching exercises; ligaments and tendons must be routinely used in order to retain their elasticity.

Mini-experiments for flexibility vary, depending on the joint or combination of joints in question. Illustration 13.3 displays a mini-experiment designed to be relevant to students' flexibility with respect to their lower back and posterior thighs; it is commonly referred to as the "sit-and-reach test."

MUSCULAR STRENGTH AND ENDURANCE

Muscular strength is the capacity of various muscle groups to exert force. The strength of a muscle group is dependent on the amount of force that group is able to exert. *Muscular endurance* is the ability of various muscle groups to repeatedly exert force. A muscle group's endurance depends on the frequency with which that group can exert a force before resting.

Muscle strength is developed through resistance exercises whereby muscle groups are pushed to exhaustion because of the amount of resistance they oppose. Strength is gained during the time period (e.g., 48 hours) in which muscle groups recover from being stressed by the exercises. Muscle endurance is increased through resistance exercises whereby muscles are pushed to exhaustion because of the frequency in which they oppose resistance. Exercises in which relatively heavy weights are lifted a relatively few times tend to build strength; whereas lifting relatively light weights many times tends to build endurance.

Illustration 13.4 is an example of a mini-experiment designed to be relevant to muscle strength; Illustration 13.5 is one designed to be relevant to muscle endurance.

AGILITY

Agility is the ability of a person to make controlled changes in body position both rapidly and accurately while moving through space. Agility is developed through exercises requiring the same type of fluid and rapid movements typically associated with sports activities such as basketball, fast-pitch softball, flag football, handball, hockey, racquetball, tennis, and wrestling.

Mini-experiments for agility are often designed with movements associated with various sports in mind. Illustration 13.6 is an example of one commonly referred to as the "zig-zag run."

Using skinfold calipers, the observer measures the thickness of skinfolds at two body sites: (1) a point over the triceps on the back of the right arm midway between the top of the shoulder and the elbow as shown in picture A and (2) a point on the medial side of the right leg between the ankle and knee over the largest part of the calf girth as shown in Picture B.

A   B

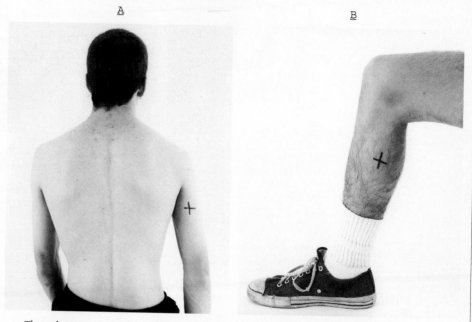

The observer marks the two sites with a grease pencil. The observer then makes the measurement at the triceps site as follows:

1. The observer creates the skinfold by grasping the skin with his/her thumb and forefinger and lifting up as shown in Picture C.

2. The contact surface of the caliper is placed 1 cm below the finger as shown in Picture D.

ILLUSTRATION 13.2

Example of a Mini-Experiment Using a Skinfold Method

(Continued)

ILLUSTRATION 13.2 (Continued)

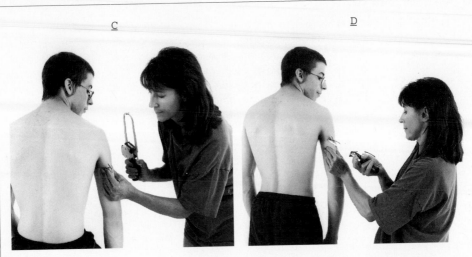

C   D

3. The caliper grip is slowly released so that the jaws of the calipers exert their full tension on the skinfold.

4. The thickness of the skinfold is read to me nearest .05 mm when the needle on the meter stabilizes (about 2 seconds after the caliper grips have been released).

5. Steps 2-4 are repeated two more times at the same site to obtain a second and third reading.

Using a similar procedure, the measurements are obtained at the site on the calf; note picture E.

E

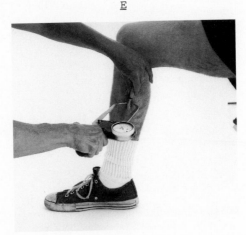

ILLUSTRATION 13.2 (Continued)

```
Rubric:

    The score is the sum of the two medians (i.e., the middle) of the
    three readings from each site. For example, if the readings from
    the triceps are 9.0 mm, 9.5 mm, and 8.0 mm, then the median is 9
    mm. If the readings from the calf are 6.5 mm, 7.0 mm, and 7.0 mm,
    then the median is 7.0. Thus, the score is 9.0 + 7.0 = 16.0.
```

STATIC AND DYNAMIC BALANCE

Static balance is the ability to maintain equilibrium in a stationary position. *Dynamic balance* is the ability to maintain equilibrium while in motion. Many gymnastic activities (e.g., practicing handstands and moving on a balance beam) are used to improve balance.

Illustration 13.7 is an example of a mini-experiment designed to be relevant to static balance; Illustration 13.8 is one designed to be relevant to dynamic balance.

COORDINATION

Coordination is the ability of the body to concurrently execute multiple motor tasks. Typically, coordination involves the integration of eye, hand, limb, and trunk movements. Coordination is learned by repeatedly practicing targeted skills (e.g., throwing, catching, and striking).

As for agility, mini-experiments for coordination are often designed with combinations of movements associated with various sports in mind. Illustration 13.9 is an example of one.

POWER

Power is the ability to generate maximum force in an explosive, nearly instantaneous way. Athletic activities such as jumping, sprinting, shot putting, rapid swimming, and fast-pitch-softball pitching require high levels of power. Students develop power by practicing explosive moves especially in conjunction with specialized resistance training.

Illustration 13.10 is an example of a mini-experiment commonly used as a measure of power with respect to the leg extensors; it is referred to as the "vertical jump test."

SPEED

Speed is the ability of the body to rapidly move between two points—especially when running a relatively short distance (e.g., 50 m). Students can increase their ability to run fast by improving their overall conditioning and refining their running technique.

Mini-experiments for running speed are often conducted by timing students in sprint races. To avoid injury, appropriate warm-up and stretching exercises are especially essential prior to sprinting.

REACTION TIME

Reaction time is how quickly the body initiates a controlled movement in response to a stimulus signaling the need to make that movement. Students may be able to improve reaction times by practicing movements in response to cues; coaching students on being alert for cues can also help.

Illustration 13.11 is an example of a mini-experiment designed to be relevant to reaction time.

<u>Prompt</u>:

The student is directed to engage in an appropriate warm-up activity in preparation for stretching. The student is then directed to remove her/his shoes and sit at the test box as shown in Pictures A and B.

<u>A</u>   <u>B</u>

The observer directs the student to place her/his feet shoulder-width apart and flat against the test box. The student then slides her/his arms forward with palms forward and one hand on top the other as shown by Picture B. As the observer places his/her hands on top of the student's knees to keep them from bending, the student reaches forward, sliding the fingertips as far forward along the rule as possible and holds that position for one second without bouncing or rocking forward.

From the scale on the box, the observer records the distance the fingertips reach to the nearest centimeter.

The procedure is repeated three more times.

<u>Rubric</u>:

The highest number from the four trials is recorded as the result of the experiment.

ILLUSTRATION 13.3

The Sit-and-Reach Test

MEASUREMENT INSTRUMENTS AND PROCEDURES RELEVANT TO PHYSICAL FITNESS

Numerous standardized tests are available commercially that focus on various aspects of physical fitness, for example, *The Prudential FITNESSGRAM test* (Institute for Aerobics Research, 1992) and the *Presidential Physical Fitness Test Battery* (President's Council on Physical Fitness

Prompt:

After appropriate warm-up, the student is directed to execute a single left-leg extension on a leg-lift bench as shown in Pictures A and B. The weight is set markedly below the student's maximum for the lift.

A   B

After adequate recuperation time (e.g., 1 minute), the weight is increased (e.g., by 3 kg) and the trial is repeated with the heavier weight. The trials and rest periods are repeated with the weight being increased with each attempt until the student is unable to perform the lift.

Rubric:

The maximum weight lifted (i.e., for the second-to-last attempt) is recorded.

ILLUSTRATION 13.4

A Mini-Experiment Designed to Be Relevant to Strength of Quadriceps

and Sports, 1991). For information about these tests, see Safrit and Wood's (1995) *Introduction to Measurement in Physical Education and Exercise Science* or other titles that focus on measurements of physical fitness.

HOW STUDENTS DEVELOP PSYCHOMOTOR SKILLS

INTEGRATION WITH PROCESS-KNOWLEDGE LESSONS

Students achieve psychomotor-skill objectives by being able to execute physical tasks as they cognitively know tasks should be executed. Thus, their abilities to learn psychomotor skills are not only dependent on how well they've developed certain aspects of physical fitness; they are also dependent on their achievement of certain process-knowledge objectives. From Chapter 8, reread the sections "General Overview of the Process," "Step-by-Step Explanation,"

Prompt:

After appropriate warm-up, the student is directed to execute as many repetitions of left-leg extension as she/he can before becoming too uncomfortable to continue. The weight on the leg-lift bench is set markedly below the student's maximum for the lift.

Rubric:

The number of times the lift is repeated without rest is recorded.

ILLUSTRATION 13.5

A Mini-Experiment Designed to Be Relevant to Endurance of Quadriceps

Prompt:

Soft cones are used to make a zig-zag or slalom-like running course on the gym floor. After appropriate warm-up, the student is directed to run the course as fast a possible having to pass between cones without knocking them over. The observer uses a stopwatch to time the run as shown by the picture below.

Rubric:

The time is recorded to the nearest .1 second and the number of cones knocked over is also noted. If the student does not run the course as prescribed (i.e., by passing between the cones as directed) that is noted without recording a time.

ILLUSTRATION 13.6

A Zig-Zag Run

Prompt:

A smooth cubic shaped stick (1" wide, 1" high, and 12" long)
is taped to the floor.

The student places the dominant foot lengthwise on the stick as
shown in the picture below. The observer instructs the student to
keep both the ball of the foot and the heel resting on the stick.
The student lifts the opposite foot from the floor and holds the
position shown in the picture as long as possible. The observer
starts the stopwatch as soon as the student achieves the position.
The watch is stopped when the student loses the position by one of
the feet touching the floor. Three trials are performed.

Rubric:

The score is the greatest time recorded (to the nearest second) for
the three trials.

ILLUSTRATION 13.7

A Mini-Experiment Designed to Be Relevant to Static Balance (Bass, 1939)

"Trial Execution of the Process, Error-Pattern Analysis, and Correction," and "Overlearning
the Process" on pages 393–395.

Lessons for psychomotor-skill objectives are typically integrated with lessons for a corresponding process-knowledge objective. The following four stages of psychomotor-skill
lessons closely parallel the four stages of process-knowledge lessons: (1) analysis of initial trials, (2) step-by-step trials with coaching, (3) practice with coaching, and (4) extended practice
for overlearning.

<u>Prompt</u>:

The student is directed to stand at one end of a balance beam and then to slowly walk to the opposite end where he/she is to pause for 5 seconds, turn around, and slowly walk back to the starting position. See the picture below. The experiment is conducted for three trials.

<u>Rubric</u>:

For each trial, the observer records if the task is completed; if not, the observer notes how much of the task the student completed.

ILLUSTRATION 13.8

A Mini-Experiment Designed to Be Relevant to Dynamic Balance

ANALYSIS OF INITIAL TRIALS

Imagine yourself attempting to teach the psychomotor skill of executing a tennis serve to a student who has never before attempted to serve a tennis ball nor witnessed anyone else executing a serve. What do you suppose you would do first? If your thinking is similar to mine, you would have the student watch someone execute a complete serve so that he or she can visualize the whole idea of a serve. Thus, you would be operating within the first stage of a process-knowledge lesson (i.e., general overview of the process). Shortly thereafter, you might direct the student to try a complete serve as a mini-experiment to gain formative feedback that will influence the design of how you'll begin instructing your student in the steps leading to a properly executed serve. Having students attempt the skill as you observe their performance to make formative judgments is the analysis-of-initial-trials stage of a psychomotor-skill lesson.

Cases 13.1 and 13.2 are examples.

Prompt:

Following an appropriate warm-up exercise, the student stands behind a line parallel to and approximately 3 meters from a gym wall
(or in a racquet ball court). A soccer ball is placed on the floor
and the student is directed to kick the soccer ball so that it rebounds off the wall to a point for the student to kick it again repeatedly from behind the line. See the picture below.

The student is given six trials. A trial consists of consecutive
kicks before the ball either does not rebound off the wall
or it rebounds to a point where the student is unable to kick
it back to the wall (e.g., the ball goes behind the student
or stops before it reaches the line).

Rubric:

For each trial, the observer counts the number of kicks.
The score is the number of kicks for the most successful trial
(i.e., with the greatest number).

ILLUSTRATION 13.9

A Mini-Experiment for Foot-Eye Coordination

CASE 13.1

As part of a language arts unit for her kindergarten students, Ms. Coco begins lessons for the following
two objectives:

A. Students know how to draw different size circles (process knowledge).
B. Students draw different size circles (psychomotor skill).

Prompt:

After appropriate warm-up, the student is given a piece of chalk and directed to stand with feet flat on the floor and the dominant arm extended as shown by Picture A. Reaching as high as possible while keeping the feet flat on the floor, the student marks the measuring board with chalk. Then from a preparatory position with both feet on the floor (as shown in Picture B), the student jumps as high as possible making a second mark on the measuring board (as shown in Picture C). Care should be taken and the marking board should be installed so that the student does not scrape him/herself against the wall. Two more trials are executed.

A   B   C

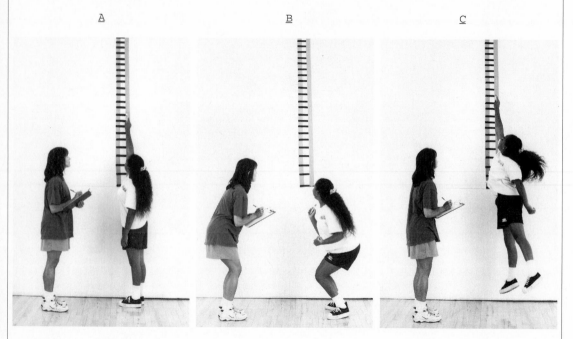

Rubric:

For each trial the difference between the second and first mark is computed. The greatest difference among the three trials is recorded.

ILLUSTRATION 13.10

The Vertical Jump Test

Ms. Coco knows the words "circle," "bigger," and "smaller," are included in the working comprehension vocabulary of all 18 students. Now she conducts an informal mini-experiment to check on how students relate different sizes of circles and can express them using physical movements. With the students standing in front of her, she tells them, "When I say 'now,' I need everyone to move her or his hand around in a circle. Marisa and Kishawn, please make a little more room between yourselves. Thank you. I don't want anyone to be touched by someone else's circle. Ready—now." Ms. Coco notes that 12 of the students make smooth circular motions; most rotate their elbows, creating small circles in front

<u>Prompt</u>:

The observer holds a meter stick just above the student's dominant hand as shown in the picture below. The objective is for the student to catch the stick with the hand as quickly as possible once the observer lets go of the stick and it begins falling between the student's thumb and fingers. Once the student catches the stick he/she keeps his/her hand in place until the observer is able to note the place on the stick where it was caught. Two more trials are repeated.

<u>Rubric</u>:

For each trial, the distance the stick fell before being caught is noted. The shortest distance from the three trials is recorded.

ILLUSTRATION 13.11

A Mini-Experiment Designed to Be Relevant to Reaction Time

of their bodies, while others rotate shoulders to make large circles on the sides of their bodies. John waved his hand in a triangular pattern. Zali lifted her hand straight up, paused, looked around at her classmates, and then abruptly brought it straight down. Bernardo rotated both his shoulders to make two sweeping arcs that collided in front of him. Dorsey made no attempt to follow the directions, choosing to stare at her feet.

Ms. Coco repeats the procedure, but this time she directs the students to make "little tiny circles" with their fingers that are smaller than their first ones. For the third trial, she directs them to give themselves plenty of room and then to make "great big circles, bigger than their first ones."

Later on in the day, students are seated at tables, each with colored pencils and handwriting paper. She directs students' attention to a white board with handwriting lines. She tells them, "I am going to draw a red circle so that it just touches three of these lines." The circle on the left-side of Illustration 13.12 is displayed. "Now, everyone take out your red pencil and get your paper ready. When I say 'start,' draw a red circle that touches three lines just like mine does on the board. Okay start." When the students finish, she repeats the process, but this time with a green circle that touches only two lines, as indicated by the center circle in Illustration 13.12. Finally, she repeats the experiment but with a large blue circle that touches four lines, as indicated by the right side of Illustration 13.12.

Quickly, Ms. Coco walks around the room, examining their responses. Illustration 13.13 displays what she sees on four students' papers. Most students' responses are similar to Marisa's.

Ms. Coco thinks to herself, "Everyone clearly relates circles to larger and smaller. That's not going to be a problem for anyone. Most, like Marisa, seem to just need practice refining their techniques. Surely they know what the different size circles should look like. On the other hand, I'm not sure John is sure what a circle looks like. I'll check on his understanding separately. I think Zali might find it difficult to control a pencil in any sort of continuous motion. With Kishawn, I may need to just check to see if he attempted to follow directions. I'd really be surprised if he's forgotten the meaning of 'circle.' Maybe he just spaced out for this activity."

Ms. Coco decides to work individually with the several students who didn't produce circles at least somewhat similar to Marisa's before moving on to the direct step-by-step instruction she plans for all students during the second stages of these two lessons. She goes over to Kishawn and draws a circle on a clean sheet of handwriting paper as he watches; she then directs him to draw a circle next to hers. Kishawn draws a circle and then begins to scribble over the top of it. Ms. Coco says, "Wait. Make another circle but do not color over it this time." He does, and she's convinced that he's ready for the second stages of the lessons.

She prompts Zali to draw the three different size circles as she had done with the whole class. As she observes her performance, she decides that Zali needs to develop coordination skills with a pencil. At this time, she appears unable to control her pencil to make a continuous arc for more than just a minute distance. She seems to know what circles look like, but she makes them using a sequence of discrete steps, producing more straight segments than arcs. To test her hypothesis, Ms. Coco engages Zali in the mini-experiment described by Illustration 13.14.

The results corroborate Ms. Coco's belief that in the second stages of the lessons, she should teach Zali a different process for drawing circles than she plans for most of the other students. Rather than

ILLUSTRATION 13.12

The Three Circles Ms. Coco Drew on the White Board

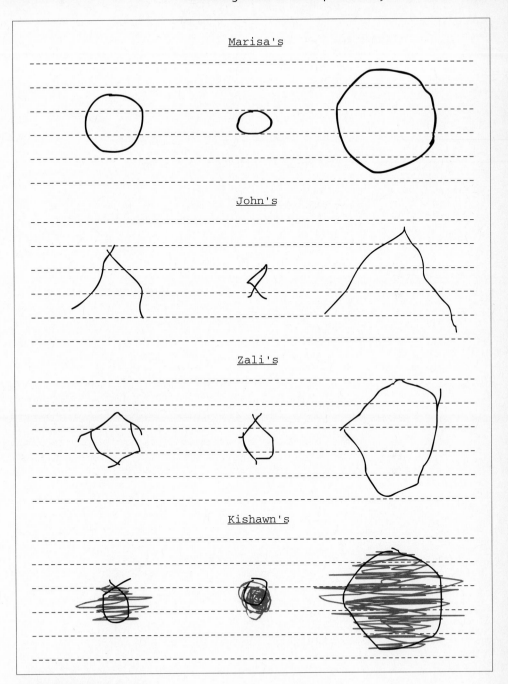

ILLUSTRATION 13.13

What Ms. Coco Observed on Four Students' Papers

<u>**Prompt and Rubric:**</u>

Ms. Coco marks two dots on a sheet of paper in front of Zali and directs her to connect them using her pencil. She watches Zali's technique to produce the following:

Because Zali's movements with the pencil were not fluid and she seemed to struggle with coordinating movements for a continuous stroke. Ms. Coco directs Zali to complete another trial, but with the dots closer together. The trial produces the following:

Ms. Coco is fairly convinced that making continuous curves will be even more difficult for Zali. However, she needs to check that hypothesis also without having Zali experience too much frustration. She decides to have Zali attempt a complete circle while following a dot-to-dot pattern. Prompted by Ms. Coco with dots arranged in a circle and the directions, "Follow these dots with your pencil to make a nice smooth circle," Zali produces the following:

ILLUSTRATION 13.14

A Mini-Experiment Ms. Coco Conducted with Zali

(Continued)

attempt to teach Zali to use one continuous motion to draw circles, she'll teach Zali to draw circles in four strokes, with each stroke producing a 45° arc.

From prior work with John, she is convinced that John knows what circles look like. To test his psychomotor skill on simply being able to control his pencil as he pleases, she conducts the mini-experiment with John that is displayed by Illustration 13.15.

ILLUSTRATION 13.14 (Continued)

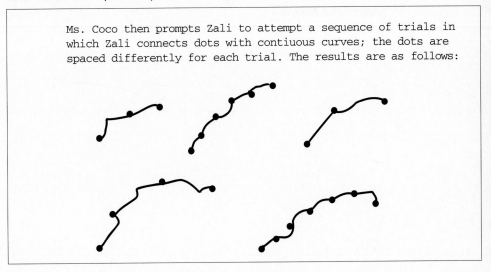

> Ms. Coco then prompts Zali to attempt a sequence of trials in which Zali connects dots with contiuous curves; the dots are spaced differently for each trial. The results are as follows:

Ms. Coco decides that John will not be ready for the second stage of the psychomotor-skill lesson although he is ready for the second stage of the process-knowledge lesson. She decides to consult with the physical-education resource specialist to develop some special small-motor coordination exercises. Until he's ready, she will just help him through the psychomotor lessons (e.g., by having him draw circles as she physically guides his hand) without really pushing to try the steps on his own. This way he can participate with the rest of the class without becoming too frustrated.

CASE 13.2

As part of a basketball unit for her students at Westdale Junior High, Ms. Andreas begins lessons for the following two objectives:

A. Students know the proper form for shooting layups from both sides of the basket (process knowledge).
B. Students shoot layups using proper form from both sides of the basket (psychomotor skill).

She demonstrates a layup from the right side and then another from the left. Then students line up on the right or left side of the basket, depending on their dominant hand. They take turns attempting layups until everyone completes five trials. During the trials, she observes using Illustration 13.16's scoresheet. The results are used to group students for the second stage of the lesson, in which she plans to have students displaying advanced skill levels and process knowledge by serving as coaches for other students.

STEP-BY-STEP TRIALS WITH COACHING

Integrated with the second stage of a process-knowledge lesson, students practice the steps in the psychomotor process to condition neural networks and muscle groups to execute the steps as the students know them. Students are prompted to attempt individual steps as they learn about them. The teacher serves as coach, giving feedback to students about how closely their body movements correspond to what students think they are doing. For example, as Ms. Coco continues the work she began in Case 13.1, she engages Kishawn in Case 13.3's dialogue.

Prompt and Rubric:

Ms. Coco marks two dots on a sheet of paper in front of John and directs her to connect them using his pencil. She watches John's technique to produce the following:

She then directs him, "Okay, let's do it again with these two dots; try to stop your pencil right on the second dot. John produces the following:

Okay, now connect these starting here,... then to here, over to here,... and then finally stop right on this dot. Try to stop your pencil on each dot. John produces the following as Ms. Coco watches:

ILLUSTRATION 13.15

A Mini-Experiment Ms. Coco Conducted with John

CASE 13.3

Students are practicing the steps Ms. Coco demonstrated. Ms. Coco watches Kishawn produce the circle shown by Illustration 13.17.

Ms. Coco:	"Where did you start and finish your circle?"
Kishawn:	"Here."

Kishawn places his pencil on the line that is supposed to be above his circle.

Ms. Coco:	"If you do that, how many times will the circle touch that line?"
Kishawn:	"One time."
Ms. Coco:	"How many times does your circle touch that line?"
Kishawn:	"Two times."
Ms. Coco:	"Draw another circle. Make sure it touches that line just one time."

Performance Observation Prompt:

The student is directed to take a position approximately 1.5 meters on the right side of the basket where she/he is directed to receive a pass thrown from the foul line, pivot, and shoot a right-handed layup from the right side.

Rubric:

The observer watches for the steps in the process, recording the results on the following score sheet by circling, for each criterion, either "Y" for clearly yes, "?" for not sure, and "N" for clearly no:

Y ? N 1. Upon receipt of the ball the student pivots and faces the basket.

Y ? N 2. With the ball, the student takes a path that splits the angle determined by the basket support and the backboard.

Y ? N 3. The student takes an elongated step on that path with the left foot.

Y ? N 4. The student jumps off the left foot flexing the right knee and right hip to swing the right side of the body into the air.

Y ? N 5. The jump is reasonably vertical, up toward the target point on the backboard.

Y ? N 6. The student brings the ball into shooting position just above and forward of the right side of the head as she/he jumps.

Y ? N 7. The student shoots the ball with the right hand, guiding it and shielding it from a possible defender with the left hand and arm.

Y ? N 8. The ball is released off the right fingertips with the right arm extended.

Y ? N 9. The ball is released near the peak of the jump.

Y ? N 10. The ball touches the right half of the inside of the rectangular target on the backboard.

Y ? N 11. The ball is released relatively free of spin and with the needed "touch" for it to rebound into or nearly into the basket.

ILLUSTRATION 13.16

A Mini-Experiment Ms. Andreas Conducted During the First Stages of Her Two Lessons

(Continued)

ILLUSTRATION 13.16 *(Continued)*

| Y ? N | 12. | The angle of release is close to the angle necessary for the ball to rebound into the basket. |
| Y ? N | 13. | After the ball is released, the student lands on the floor in a position to the right of the basket and not behind the backboard |

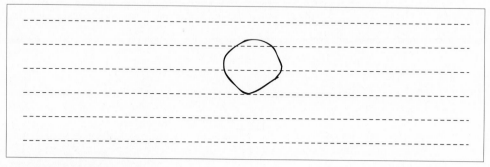

ILLUSTRATION 13.17

A Circle Kishawn Drew

In Case 13.4, continuing the lessons she began in Case 13.2, Ms. Andreas uses peer coaches to provide feedback to students who need it.

CASE 13.4

Ms. Andreas uses the results of Illustration 13.16's mini-experiment to partition her class of 33 students into five teams, with each team having one player coach. The five coaches demonstrated during the first stages of the two lessons that they are quite proficient at shooting layups. She takes the five coaches aside and explains the steps for shooting layups she wants them to teach members of their teams. She also shows them some layup drills to use and instructs them on how to give their team members constructive feedback on their techniques.

As she supervises the student coaches at work, she sees Marvin step to the left side of the basket with his left foot and make a shot using his right hand. His coach, Nancy, yells, "Way to go, Marvin, nice shot!" The next student approaching from the left side takes an elongated stride with her right leg, throws her left knee in the air, jumps vertically, and bangs the ball off the rectangular target, missing the basket. "Come on, Yen, you can do better than that!" Nancy yells. Ms. Coco calls Nancy aside and quietly says, "They don't need you to tell them whether the ball goes in the basket or not. They need you to describe their form. Next time, point out to Marvin that for a shot from the left side, he needs to take off from his right foot and shoot with his left hand. Let Yen know that she took a nice long step with the correct foot to get to the basket. Look at what they do, not whether or not the ball goes in the basket."

PRACTICE WITH COACHING

Once students know how to execute the process and have actually performed it correctly several times, they need to condition their neural networks and muscles to respond smoothly without conscious thought by correctly practicing the coordinated moves repeatedly. Coaching is critical so that they are not conditioning their bodies to incorrectly execute steps. Thus, you are there to prevent error patterns from becoming habits, just as you do during the third stage of a process-knowledge lesson. The third stage is for students to polish their skills.

EXTENDED PRACTICE FOR OVERLEARNING

If psychomotor-skill learning is to be long range, students need to continue to practice the skill long after it has been polished. Ms. Coco, for example, will make sure that she routinely prompts students to make varying size circles well after the unit she started in Case 13.1 ends. That they will be repeatedly practicing forming manuscript letters such as "d," "p," "Q," and "O" will serve this stage of the lesson. Ms. Andreas, of course, intends to interest her students enough in the game of basketball that most will choose to play it repeatedly for recreation—thus, overlearning the skill of shooting layups.

INDICATORS OF PROGRESS AS STUDENTS DEVELOP PSYCHOMOTOR SKILLS

Because performance observations are most often the format of choice for mini-experiments for psychomotor-skill objectives, monitoring progress as they learn psychomotor skills is a relatively straightforward process when compared to lessons for cognitive and affective objectives. You can see what students are doing rather than have to infer what is going through their heads. The four-stage instructional strategies employed by Ms. Coco and Ms. Andreas in Cases 13.1 through 13.4 require teachers to be continually employing the types of mini-experiments for formative decision-making that are displayed by Illustrations 13.13 through 13.17.

INDICATORS OF STUDENTS' ACHIEVEMENT OF PSYCHOMOTOR-SKILL OBJECTIVES

When designing mini-experiments relevant to psychomotor-skill objectives, you need to decide if you want to focus attention on the outcome of the execution of the skill or on how students executed the skill. Generally speaking, performance observations in which the process is examined rather than simply the outcome provide richer information on students' achievement. For example, Illustration 13.16's mini-experiment fits Ms. Andreas's purposes in Case 13.2 better than a mini-experiment with a rubric that simply recorded the number of shots students made out of so many attempts. However, mini-experiments that focus only on outcomes tend to be more usable. For some purposes, mini-experiments with product-examination formats that record only outcomes may be helpful for identifying who needs to have their performances analyzed.

For example, in Case 8.20, Ms. Bailey conducted Illustration 8.24's performance observation mini-experiment with Alex. The outcome was Illustration 8.25—not a very legible manuscript letter "A." Had Ms. Bailey simply wanted to pretest students' skills for making legible manuscript letters, she may have just directed the whole group to make an "A." Then only those producing unsatisfactory A's would be administered Illustration 8.24's mini-experiment. If a measure of psychomotor skill appeared to be warranted, as it seemed to be for Alex in Case 8.20, then the teacher might use Illustration 13.18's mini-experiment.

In psychomotor-skill competitions (e.g., gymnastics and diving), expert judges rate performances using scales (e.g., 7.3 out of a possible 10). For instructional purposes, teachers tend to use performance observations often supported by videotape for in-depth analysis of what the student is doing. Illustration 13.19's mini-experiment is designed to compare the various

<u>Performance Observation Prompt</u>:

The student is given three pencils, one that marks red, another that marks blue, and one that marks green. As the student observes, the teacher puts two colored dots on a sheet of paper (as shown below) and directs the student to draw a straight red line segment from the blue dot to the red dot.

• (blue)

• (red)

If the student succeeds in drawing a straight line segment as directed, the prompt continues; otherwise it is terminated. The teacher then puts a green dot as shown below and directs the student to draw a straight blue line segment from the blue dot to the green dot.

(blue)

(red) • (green)

If the attempt succeeds, then the student is directed to draw a straight green line segment from the *middle* of the red line segment to the *middle* of the blue line segment. The teacher points to the middle of the red line segment as she/he says "middle" and to the middle of the blue line segment as she/he says "middle." The teacher immediately removes her/his finger from the middle of the segment before the student has a chance to begin.

<u>Rubric</u>:

The following are checked as satisfactorily completed:

____ red segment   ____ blue segment   ____ green segment

ILLUSTRATION 13.18

A Mini-Experiment Relevant to the Psychomotor-Skill Objective Stated in Case 8.20

components of a performance to one another to help the student and teacher make formative judgments about relative strengths and weaknesses.

The results of mini-experiments for psychomotor-skill objectives are especially influenced by factors such as type of equipment used, students' current states of health, weather and climate conditions, students' warm-up activities, and how rested students are. Unlike mini-experiments for most cognitive and affective objectives, the reliability of psychomotor measurements can be checked by repeating experiments and comparing consistency of results. For example, it is useful to repeat Illustration 13.19's experiment and compare the consistency

Objective:

Students properly execute back dives from 3-meter spring boards (psychomotor skill).

Performance Observation Prompt:

After appropriate warm up, the student is directed to perform a back dive from a 3-meter springboard. The dive is videotaped.

Rubric:

The observer views the videotape repeatedly to complete the following ranking scale:

A. Rank the parts of the dive "1st," "2nd," and "3rd" from relatively strongest to relatively weakest:

     ____ takeoff   ____ turn   ____ entry

B. Rank the parts of the takeoff from the relatively strongest (1st) to the relatively weakest (3rd):

     ____ body position   ____ height   ____ angle

C. Rank the parts of the turn from stronger (1st) to weaker (2nd):

     ____ body position   ____ timing for entering the turn

D. Rank the parts of the entry from the relatively strongest (1st) to the relatively weakest (3rd):

     ____ timing for stopping the turn   ____ angle

     ____ body position

ILLUSTRATION 13.19

A Mini-Experiment Relevant to Back Dive Performance

of the two results, whereas repeating the same question raised by a prompt for a simple-knowledge objective hardly serves a purpose.

SYNTHESIS ACTIVITIES FOR CHAPTER 13

1. Retrieve the computerized folder you set up when you engaged in Synthesis Activity 2 for Chapter 6. From your work doing Synthesis Activity 3 for Chapter 6, each file contains at least one mini-experiment. Call up each of those files that is for a psychomotor-skill objective. Now, in light of your work with Chapter 13, revise the mini-experiments in those files. For each file (i.e., files for psychomotor-skill objectives), design at least two more mini-experiments and insert them into the file.

2. With a colleague, exchange printouts of the mini-experiments you designed or revised when you engaged in Synthesis Activity 1. Discuss and critique one another's mini-experiments. Revise them as you decide they should be revised.

3. Retrieve the goal defined by a set of weighted objectives you developed for Synthesis Activity 3 for Chapter 5. Select one of the psychomotor-skill objectives from that set (if indeed the set includes at least one such objective). Now, design a lesson for leading students to achieve that objective. Design one or more mini-experiments to provide you with indicators of your students' progress during that lesson.

4. With a colleague, share and discuss your work from Synthesis Activity 3. Revise the mini-experiments in light of your discussions.

TRANSITIONAL ACTIVITY FROM CHAPTER 13 TO CHAPTER 14

In a discussion with two or more of your colleagues, address the following questions:

1. What role should standardized tests and government-mandated tests play in schools?

2. How are standardized tests and government-mandated tests used and abused in schools?

3. How are standardized tests developed, and how are norms established?

4. What statistical models and routines are used in the test standardization process?

5. How should standardized test results reported in terms of percentiles, stanines, grade equivalents, NCEs, scaled scores, and other such scores be interpreted?

6. How should we report standardized test results to students and to their parents?

Interpreting Systemwide and Standardized Test Results

◈ GOAL OF CHAPTER 14

Chapter 14 is intended to lead you to examine some of the common uses and misuses of systemwide and standardized tests in schools, to explain how standardized tests are normed, and to interpret and communicate standardized test results. More specifically, the objectives are as follows:

A. You will explain typical uses and misuses of systemwide and standardized tests in schools (comprehension and communication skills) 15%.

B. You will explain statistical conventions for comparing an individual score to norm-group scores (discover a relationship) 10%.

C. You will use statistical conventions to compare an individual score to norm-group scores (process knowledge) 10%.

D. You will explain the process by which tests are standardized and normed (comprehension and communication skills) 10%.

E. You will interpret standardized test results reported as commonly used derived scores (comprehension and communication skills) 30%.

F. You will develop strategies for communicating systemwide and standardized test results to students, parents, and your supervisors (application) 15%.

G. You will incorporate the following technical terms and phrases into your working professional vocabulary: "systemwide test," "high-stakes testing," "test battery," "standardized test," "test item," "achievement test," "aptitude test," "norm group," "test norms," "raw score," "derived score," "student's grade level," "test level," "test form," "edition of a test," "test manual," "concurrent validity," "predictive validity," "frequency distribution," "measures of central tendency," "mode," "median," "arithmetic mean," "measures of variability," "range," "variance," "standard deviation," "*z*-score," "normal distribution," "standard score," "stanine," "percentile," "NCE," "grade equivalent score," and "scaled score" (comprehension and communication skills) 10%.

SYSTEMWIDE TESTS

SCHOOL DISTRICT TESTING PROGRAMS

Chapter 2's section "Planning and Organizing for the School Year" included a brief reference to standardized test scores as a possible data source of information relevant to achievement levels of a group of students. Otherwise, the entire focus of the first 13 chapters of this book has been on leading you to develop your talent for designing measurements for the unique needs of your own students. Even that brief reference in Chapter 2 contains the following caution: "Standardized test scores are not nearly as meaningful as most people think."

Meaningful or not, standardized tests as well as other tests that you neither design nor select yourself play a role in the operation of your school. Depending on your particular school, school district, and state, results of such tests can influence (1) your students' academic and vocational options, (2) who is promoted to the next grade level, (3) who is placed in special programs, (4) your school's funding, (5) your job status and salary, and (5) the public's impression of your school and school district. Historically, the use of such tests in schools has not been limited to the purposes for which they were designed. When properly interpreted, these tests can be useful sources of information; too often, however, misinterpreted results are a source of misinformation. As a teacher, you need to accurately interpret results from such tests for your students, their parents, and sometimes for your colleagues and supervisors. As a professional educator, you need to influence the course of schoolwide, districtwide, statewide, and possibly nationwide testing programs so that they are used appropriately rather than misused and abused. Chapter 14 is intended to lead you to develop your talents for doing just that.

Programs employing these tests vary among school districts. Case 14.1 is representative of many. Case 14.1 is lengthy, but it establishes a context for the subject-content of this chapter. As you confront technical terms (e.g., "aptitude test," or "grade equivalent score") in Case 14.1, keep in mind that you do not need to be concerned with their literal meanings until they are defined in subsequent sections of this chapter.

CASE 14.1

The South Point School District contains 36 elementary, nine middle, three junior high, eight high, one technical, and two special schools. Before 1972, the district had no policy regarding the use of standardized tests, nor were any tests administered districtwide. Most schools made room in their budgets for standardized testing programs; others did not. Practices among the district's schools varied considerably. For example:

- At Grove Street Elementary School, all students in grades 2, 4, and 6 were pretested in September and posttested in May with the *Key Math Diagnostic Arithmetic Test* and *Woodcock Reading Mastery Test*.
- No schoolwide or standardized tests were administered at Claybourne Middle School.
- All physical education classes at Parkway Middle School were administered the *Presidential Physical Fitness Test Battery*.
- At Barber Elementary School, the *Otis-Lennon School Ability Test* (*OLSAT*) was administered in August to place students in "remedial," "average," or "accelerated" tracks. Scores from a February administration of the *Metropolitan Achievement Tests* to all grades were used in conjunction with the August *OLSAT* scores to label students as "underachievers," "expected achievers," and "overachievers" for reading, mathematics, language, science, social science, and study skills.
- "College-bound" eleventh-graders at Washington High School took the *Iowa Test of Educational Development* in April.

- Most high schools helped arrange and prepare students for taking college aptitude and placement exams (e.g., *Preliminary Scholastic Aptitude Tests* (*PSAT*), *Scholastic Aptitude Tests* (*SAT*), and *Advance Placement Tests*).
- As a requirement of Third Street Elementary School's Title I funded program in reading and mathematics, all of its students were administered a Stanford Achievement Test battery in early September, and students who participated in the program were tested again in May with reading and mathematics subtests from that battery.

In 1972, responding to complaints about inefficiency and a lack of accountability, the school board established the South Point School District Department of Evaluation. The department was to be responsible for designing and implementing a uniform, districtwide standardized testing program. The new program was to be completely phased in by the beginning of the 1974–75 school year.

The evaluation department set up a committee of teachers, school administrators, parents, and a measurement consultant to (1) set the goals of the program, (2) review available standardized tests and test batteries, (3) select the tests that would provide the most cost-effective means for realizing the goals, and (4) design a plan for administering and using the test results. It took the committee three months to establish the goals. Some members wanted to use standardized test results to (1) provide end of the year pass-fail cutoff scores for each student, (2) compare achievement in one subject-content area to that in others, (3) provide data for decisions about retention of and merit pay for teachers, (4) place students in "homogeneous" groups or tracks, (5) rank schools, and (6) compare the achievement of South Point School District to "national standards." Other members, including most of the teachers and the measurement consultants, argued that standardized tests are not capable of providing valid data for those purposes. Ultimately, the committee agreed on three goals:

1. Periodically provide data on student achievement to which teachers could compare the results from their own teacher-made measurements. (The intent is for teachers to reconsider summative evaluations based on measurement results that are dramatically inconsistent with the standardized test results.)
2. Make data available for research and evaluation studies that address questions about how to improve the district's curricula, programs, and schools
3. Fulfill the need to have standardized test data for developing school improvement grant proposals and for evaluations of existing grant projects

By a split vote, the committee agreed that standardized tests would not be used for purposes other than those three goals.

In light of the goals, the committee reviewed scores of test publishers' catalogues, examined sample items (i.e., prompts) for some of the tests, interviewed test publishers' sales representatives, and studied excerpts from *Tests in Print*, the *Mental Measurement Yearbooks*, and measurement and evaluation textbooks. Unanimously, the members agreed to the following:

1. Any one of four of the 14 available standardized achievement test batteries could meet the needs of the district's program.
2. The district office should enter into competitive negotiations with the publishers of those four test batteries to contract for one of the batteries to be administered in grades K through 12 in September and April each school year.
3. No group-administered aptitude or psychological tests should be administered in the district, but a program for individually administered aptitude and psychological tests for special needs should be coordinated by the district office.

4. A second committee should be formed to design and oversee the individually administered aptitude and psychological testing program; the committee should include guidance counselors, school psychologists, special education teachers, and teachers from the original committee.

The school board approved the plan, and the program was implemented during the 1976–77 school year. The standardized achievement test battery was replaced in 1980 when a contract was negotiated with a different publisher. For the most part, the program was considered successful. Data were used in several research and evaluation studies that affected school operations. Several schools were awarded curriculum development grants as a result of needs assessments using data from the standardized tests. Most teachers compared the test scores to results from their own ongoing measurements. Whenever the standardized test results were inconsistent with their other measurements, these teachers would take a second look at the achievement levels in question.

However, by 1982, the original three goals established by the committee seemed to be forgotten. Average test results for individual schools were being publicized on television and in newspapers. Illustration 14.1 is an example. Some school administrators attempted to pressure teachers to raise scores, and some teachers "taught to the tests." Because of the implied competition among schools, some principals adjusted school schedules to suspend regular curricula for two weeks in the spring prior to the administration of the posttest batteries so classes could work on their test-taking skills. During the week in which the batteries were administered, routine interruption of classes (e.g., for

---

South Point Schools Below Par

Copper Lake Elementary Best School in District

By Claudia Schaeffer
Education Writer

South Point schools are inferior when compared to the nation's other public schools. Superintendent Brinlee Gibbons released the results from the *Comprehensive Test of Basic Skills (CTBS)* that were administered in May. The average percentile of all high school students is 42.7 or 7.3 below the national average. The district's elementary schools fared somewhat better averaging 45.1 but still significantly below the national average of 50. Gibbons expressed some optimism, "Plans for improvement are already taking shape." Dr. Delphine Ramirez, principal of Copper Lake Elementary suggested, "We must be doing something right." Copper Lake topped all other schools, finishing above the national average with 54.7.

A complete listing of scores for all South Point Schools will appear in Sunday's edition of the *Advocate*.

ILLUSTRATION 14.1

Newspaper Article About South Point Schools' Standardized Test Scores

public address announcements) were suspended, and parents were alerted that their children should be sent to school on those days well rested with a good breakfast. In some schools, the atmosphere for "test week" resembled that surrounding the football team about to enter the playoffs. This elaborate preparation led some parents to mistakenly believe these tests measured their children's intelligence and were a more important indicator of their children's knowledge than the routine results from their teachers' measurements.

In 1983, the school board enacted the following two regulations:

1. Elementary school students may be promoted to the next grade only if their reading and mathematics grade equivalent scores on the May-administered achievement test battery are within "six months" of their current grade level (e.g., a student could not be promoted from fourth to fifth grade unless her or his grade equivalent scores for each of the two subjects is at least 4.2).

2. Principals must base their recommendations for teachers' merit pay on a rationale that takes into account students' progress as reflected in the difference between the standardized test scores students received in May and the scores they received in September.

However, these regulations have yet to be implemented because of legal action initiated by the state's professional teachers' association.

In the meantime, the State Office of Education developed "core competency" tests intended to measure how well school curricula throughout the state were adhering to the statewide curricula standards in business education, health and physical education, home economics, language arts, mathematics, science, and social studies. Beginning with the 1990–91 school year, the State School Board mandated that all the state's fifth- and eighth-graders take the core competency tests, as well as high school students in business education and home economics. Minimal scores were required for promotion out of fifth and eighth grade and for receiving credit in business education and home economics. Reluctantly, South Point School District personnel added these tests to their testing program.

In 1995, the state legislature enacted a law that all public school students in third, fifth, eighth, and eleventh grade be given a common standardized test battery so that schools and school districts would be "accountable to the taxpayers who support them." The law specified that results were to be published in newspapers as a "basis for the public to judge the effectiveness of schools." The State Office of Education was charged with the responsibility of administering the statewide program and developing a system for publicizing the results.

State Office curriculum and evaluation specialist Patrick Halifia was quite concerned about the consequences of the tests being misinterpreted and misused. He was aware of the following problems that had occurred in other states that had implemented similar programs:

1. Characteristics of the communities served by schools are better predictors of average scores from group-administered standardized achievement tests than are variables over which the schools have no control (Keeves, 1988b). For example, socio-economic status (SES) variables such as average educational levels of the mothers in communities served by schools are highly correlated with school averages on such tests. Ranking schools by average test scores is not a fair indictor of those schools' accomplishments (Guskey & Kifer, 1990). Applications of statistical models by which average scores are adjusted for the influences of SES variables or attempts at leading people to interpret average scores in light of SES factors have been typically received with misunderstanding and suspicion. Parents, for example, may be misled into thinking that the relationship between SES variables and standardized achievement test scores indicates that children from less affluent communities are not as smart as those from more affluent communities. Mr. Halifia is aware that the explanation for the relationship is a complex function of a myriad of factors.

2. Although the legislation specifies that the test results were to be used only to compare schools, results are likely to be used in judging the achievement levels of individual students. If administrators attempt to pressure teachers into raising average scores, teachers may in turn attempt to motivate students to do well on these tests by using the scores in the determination of grades.

3. Standardized achievement tests emphasize simple-knowledge, process-knowledge, and comprehension-and-communication-skills achievement with virtually nothing on construct-a-concept, discover-a-relationship, application, and affective achievement. If pressure to improve scores leads school administrators and teachers to adjust curricula toward the subject-content and learning levels emphasized by standardized tests, meaningful learning will be de-emphasized (Herman & Golan, 1995).

4. Parents as well as many teachers and school administrators tended to misinterpret the derived scores in standardized reports. Grade equivalent scores were especially prone to misinterpretation—more so than stanines or scale scores (Barber, Paris, Evans, & Gadsen, 1992).

5. Because of bad publicity resulting from "below average scores" and good publicity from "above average scores," administrators tend to put pressure on teachers by untenably basing decisions affecting teachers' employment (e.g., with respect to merit pay, advancement, and retention) on their students' standardized test scores (Cangelosi, 1991, pp. 11–12, 103–105; Soar, Medley, & Coker, 1983).

In an attempt to prevent some of these problems, Mr. Halifia wrote the brief shown by Illustration 14.2 and distributed it to school district offices throughout the state. He also conducted workshops for school administrators on how these tests should be used and scores interpreted and reported.

Today, South Point District's Department of Evaluation has four times the personnel it had in 1972, but its responsibilities have increased by even more. South Point's systemwide testing program now includes the following components:

- As mandated by the State School Board, state core-curriculum test batteries are administered each April to all fifth- and eighth-grade students with subtests in language arts, mathematics, science, and social studies. State core-curriculum tests are also administered to high school classes in business education and home economics.

- Each May, nearly all students are administered the standardized achievement test batteries mandated by the State Legislature for students in fifth, eighth, and eleventh grade. The batteries are also administered in September to meet the needs of some projects funded by state and federal grants. Illustration 14.3 is an example of an "individual student's profile" report from one of these batteries. Illustration 14.4 is a grade-level report for a school that is publicized in newspapers.

- For the expressed purpose of helping kindergarten teachers plan curricula, kindergarten students are administered a "school-readiness" test during the first two weeks of each school year. The performance-based test was developed through a state-funded grant project.

- The Evaluation Department arranges for the *Stanford Diagnostic Reading Test* and the *Stanford Diagnostic Mathematics Test* to be administered in September at the option of the district's elementary school principals.

- In conjunction with various special education programs, the Evaluation Department and the Special Education Department coordinate the administration of a variety of aptitude and psychological tests.

- The *Prudential FITNESSGAM* test is administered to physical education classes at the levels of fourth, sixth, seventh, ninth, and tenth grade.

- The Evaluation Department works with counselors at the high schools to facilitate the process by which students can take a variety of vocational and college aptitude and interest tests (e.g., *Vocational Interest Inventory, Campbell Interest and Skill Survey, American College Test* (ACT), *Enhanced ACT Assessment*, and *Preliminary Scholastic Aptitude Test/National Merit Scholarship Qualifying Tests* (PSAT/NMSQT)). Advanced placement programs are also continued in the high schools.

July 3, 1995

School District Officials:

As indicated by the attached cover letter and schedule, I will be conducting workshops throughout the state for teachers, instructional supervisors, and school administrators on appropriate uses of standardized tests with respect to the new state statute, "School Testing and Accountability Act." In the meantime, please keep the following in mind:

1. Standardized tests are relevant to skills that are far more general than the goals of any one curriculum. The test items emphasize knowledge, process skills, and comprehension far more than conceptual and higher-order reasoning. Thus, standardized tests should not be a principal data source for evaluation of student achievement.

2. The validity of standardized tests are based on correlational statistics that deem the tests more appropriate for evaluations that pertain to *groups* rather than to individuals.

3. Test scores are affected by some degree of measurement error (i.e., they are not perfectly valid). Thus, it is inadvisable to use any one test (standardized or not) as the sole measure for an evaluation. Furthermore, the most fundamental professional standards for evaluating achievement and aptitude require "multiple lines of evidence" (American Psychological Association, 1985).

4. The dangers of basing judgments of teachers' effectiveness are well documented throughout the educational literature (Cangelosi, 1991, pp. 11-12, 103-105; Soar, Medley, & Coker, 1983). The following are among the many drawbacks of this practice:

   A. Student achievement is affected by many factors (e.g., students' aptitude and prior experiences) that teachers cannot control.

   B. Standardized tests are hardly relevant to the specific goals of individual courses or classrooms.

   C. Teachers are encouraged to restrict their curricula to what appears on the standardized tests even when the test items lack relevance to curricula goals.

ILLUSTRATION 14.2

Mr. Halifia's Brief Distributed to School District Offices

(Continued)

ILLUSTRATION 14.2 (Continued)

5. It is a popular myth among laypersons that standardized tests somehow measure "real intellectual ability" that teacher-developed measurements cannot measure. Because (a) standardized test score reports appear to be highly technical, using words such as "stanine," (b) scores are reported in terms of important-sounding labels (e.g., "grade equivalent"), (c) standardized tests are more impressively packaged than teacher-made measurements, and (d) some school administrators make such a "big deal" of them, people assume standardized tests are far more meaningful than they actually are.

6. Like other educational and psychological measurements, standardized tests provide gross, not precise, data. Consequently, the scores of two students suggest that their achievement levels might be different *only* if their scores are *markedly* different.

7. Standardized test results are often reported in scores (e.g., percentiles and grade equivalents) that lack properties of familiar cardinal numbers. Consequently, arithmetic computations (e.g., subtracting one score from another) may distort the meaning of results. For example, the difference between a percentile of 50 and a percentile of 40 represents a much smaller difference in test performance than the difference between a percentile of 10 and a percentile of 5. Grade equivalent scores from standardized tests are particularly misused by the misapplication of arithmetic.

8. Comparisons between scores from different standardized tests or from different subtests of the same standardized test battery are often misleading and should be avoided. The problem is inherent in the method by which the tests are normed.

9. Socio-economic-status variables (SES) have a major effect on schools' standardized test score averages. This is only one reason why standardized tests are not a fair method of comparing the effectiveness of schools or school districts (Guskey & Kifer, 1990). Unfortunately, our state legislature chose to ignore this fact when it passed the School Testing and Accountability Act. Thus, we are confronted with the dilemma of explaining to our constituents that it is unfair to compare two different schools based on these scores without leaving the false impression that SES factors determine how much children learn. At our workshops, I will be suggesting that you address this problem by some combination of the following:

    A. Hold meetings with parents and community leaders to explain the correlations between standardized test scores and various SES variables, emphasizing that the correlations don't reflect cause-and-effect

ILLUSTRATION 14.2 *(Continued)*

> relationships. For example: Standardized tests emphasize convergent rather than divergent reasoning and multicultural communities tend to foster divergent reasoning more than mono-cultural communities.
>
> B. Use the norm group option from the standardized testing company that most closely fits the SES profile of the community your school serves. To do this you will need to study the technical manual the company produces. The manual explains the characteristics of its "National" "Catholic," "Private," "High SES," and "Urban" norm groups — the group to which your students' scores are compared.
>
> C. Report the average scores from your school as a comparison to the predicted averages based on your community's SES variables. My office will provide each school in the state with a set of predicted scores based on a stepwise regression statistical model that projects what the average scores for schools with similar SES factors are expected to be. The idea is that an average that is significantly greater than the predicted average might be considered as a positive indicator of school effectiveness. Similarly, an average that is significantly less than the predicted averages might be considered as a negative indicator of school effectiveness.
>
> These methods do not solve our problem, but in concert with application of our highly developed interpersonal skills and common sense, we can mitigate the effects of misunderstandings that are sure to occur.
>
> I am looking forward to sharing ideas with you in the workshops.
>
> Sincerely,
>
> *Patrick Nalifia*
>
> Patrick Halifia
> Evaluation Specialist
> State Office of Education

A test is *systemwide* if it is administered to nearly all or a representative sample of all students in at least one grade level (e.g., third grade) or in one subject-content area (e.g., U.S. history) in a school district or state (Phelps, 1996). In Case 14.1, the standardized test battery mandated by the state legislature, the school-readiness test administered to all kindergarten students, and the state core-curriculum test batteries mandated by the state school board are examples of *systemwide tests*.

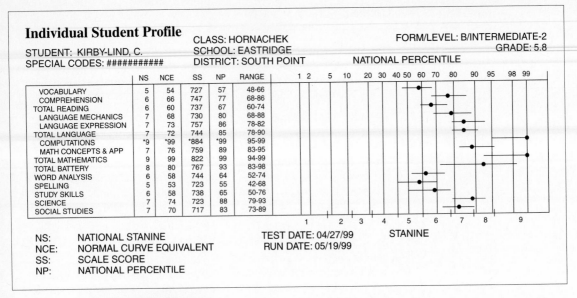

Individual Student Profile

STUDENT: KIRBY-LIND, C.
SPECIAL CODES: ##########

CLASS: HORNACHEK
SCHOOL: EASTRIDGE
DISTRICT: SOUTH POINT

FORM/LEVEL: B/INTERMEDIATE-2
GRADE: 5.8

NATIONAL PERCENTILE

	NS	NCE	SS	NP	RANGE
VOCABULARY	5	54	727	57	48-66
COMPREHENSION	6	66	747	77	68-86
TOTAL READING	6	60	737	67	60-74
LANGUAGE MECHANICS	7	68	730	80	68-88
LANGUAGE EXPRESSION	7	73	757	86	78-82
TOTAL LANGUAGE	7	72	744	85	78-90
COMPUTATIONS	*9	*99	*884	*99	95-99
MATH CONCEPTS & APP	7	76	759	89	83-95
TOTAL MATHEMATICS	9	99	822	99	94-99
TOTAL BATTERY	8	80	767	93	83-98
WORD ANALYSIS	6	58	744	64	52-74
SPELLING	5	53	723	55	42-68
STUDY SKILLS	6	58	738	65	50-76
SCIENCE	7	74	723	88	79-93
SOCIAL STUDIES	7	70	717	83	73-89

NS: NATIONAL STANINE
NCE: NORMAL CURVE EQUIVALENT
SS: SCALE SCORE
NP: NATIONAL PERCENTILE

TEST DATE: 04/27/99
RUN DATE: 05/19/99

STANINE

ILLUSTRATION 14.3

Individual Student Standardized Achievement Test Report

SCHOOL GRADE-LEVEL SUMMARY REPORT

SCHOOL: EASTRIDGE
DISTRICT: SOUTH PT

FORM/LEVEL: B/INTERMEDIATE-2
GRADE: 5.8

TEST DATE: 04/27/99
RUN DATE: 05/19/99

AVERAGE PERCENTILES

SUBJECT-CONTENT AREA	SCHOOL	SES PRE-DICTED	NATIONAL NORM
TOTAL READING	47.7	43.9	50.0
TOTAL LANGUAGE	48.4	44.0	50.0
TOTAL MATHEMATICS	50.6	49.2	50.0
WORD ANALYSIS	44.4	44.8	50.0
SPELLING	47.6	42.9	50.0
STUDY SKILLS	41.3	41.1	50.0
SCIENCE	48.4	45.3	50.0
SOCIAL STUDIES	39.4	41.2	50.0

ILLUSTRATION 14.4

1999 Fifth-Grade Standardized Achievement Test Report for Grove Street Elementary School

A *test battery* is a sequence of individual tests that are administered under a single title (e.g., "State Core-Curriculum Tests" or "*Stanford Achievement Test 9*") within a single time interval (e.g., three consecutive days with three or four *subtests* per day). An individual test in a battery is referred to as a *subtest*. For example, the standardized test report shown by Illustration 14.3 reports scores for 11 subtests: (1) vocabulary, (2) comprehension, (3) language mechanics, (4) language expression, (5) computations, (6) math concepts and applications, (7) word analysis, (8) spelling, (9) study skills, (10) science, and (11) social studies.

STATEWIDE AND DISTRICT-WIDE CORE-CURRICULUM TESTS

Almost all state offices of education publish core-curriculum guides for each subject-content area (e.g., language arts, mathematics, and music). The guides list standards or goals to be incorporated in all public school courses in the respective subject-content areas. For example, Utah State Office core-curriculum guide for sixth-grade mathematics lists 13 standards, explicating each with a statement of purpose, a list of objectives, and a list of skills and strategies. Illustration 14.5 displays one of those standards as presented in the guide (Utah State Office of Education, 1995).

Most state offices of education provide competency or core tests intended to be relevant to the core standards or goals in their respective core-curriculum guides. In most states these tests are developed by committees of teachers, state office personnel, and curriculum and testing consultants. In a few states, the tests are developed through contracts with commercial testing companies. State core tests are usually designed so that scores indicate the percentage of points each student obtained relative to each core-curriculum standard. Thus, unlike standardized tests, these tests are considered "criterion-referenced" rather than "norm-referenced" because they are intended to be used for criterion-referenced summative evaluations of students' achievements.

As explained in Chapter 3's section "Norm-Referenced Evaluations or Criterion-Referenced Evaluations," a summative evaluation of a student's achievement is *criterion-referenced* if the evaluation is influenced by how the measurement results relevant to that student's achievement compare to a standard that is not dependent on results obtained from others. Illustration 14.6 is an example of a student's score report from a state core-curriculum test for one subject-content area.

Some local school districts have their own core-curriculum standards and competencies and their own district core-curriculum tests that are administered districtwide. These tests are typically very similar to state core-curriculum tests. In fact, some of the state-level tests were developed as revisions of existing district-level tests. With the advent of statewide testing, fewer and fewer local school districts are now administering their own core-curriculum tests.

POLITICAL ACCOUNTABILITY AND HIGH-STAKES TESTING

A test is considered *high-stakes* if it is administered for the purpose of (1) accountability for student achievement or (2) evaluations affecting promotion, retention, or graduation (U.S. General Accounting Office, 1993). In Case 14.1, the state core-curriculum tests are high-stakes because the results are used to make summative evaluations that influence the lives of students. The legislative-mandated standardized test battery is high-stakes for school personnel because it is used for the expressed purpose of politicians and voters holding them accountable for student achievement.

As Mr. Halifia feared in Case 14.1, high-stakes testing can sometimes lead to undesirable consequences for school curricula (Nolen, Haladyna, & Haas, 1992). High-stakes testing hysteria in some school districts has led to events that seem to be sheer madness; Case 14.2 is an example.

| Standard 5060-<u>02</u> | **The students will show understanding and application of mathematical concepts and justification of solutions to problems by communicating in oral, pictorial, and/or written form.** |

Purpose: This standard highlights the need to involve students individually in cooperative learning groups actively doing mathematics. Exploring, investigating, describing, and explaining mathematical ideas promotes communication. Teachers facilitate this process when they pose probing questions and invite students to explain their thinking.

<u>Objectives</u>

5060-02<u>01</u>.   Model situations using oral, written, concrete, pictorial, graphical, and algebraic methods.

5060-02<u>02</u>.   Reflect on and clarify thinking about mathematical ideas and situations.

5060-02<u>03</u>.   Develop common understandings of mathematical ideas including the role of definitions.

5060-02<u>04</u>.   Interpret and evaluate mathematical ideas by using the skills of reading, listening, and viewing.

5060-02<u>05</u>.   Discuss mathematical ideas and make conjectures and convincing arguments.

5060-02<u>06</u>.   Understand the value of mathematical notation and its role in the development of mathematical ideas.

SKILLS AND STRATEGIES

1.   Represent mathematical topics studied at this grade level by making sketches, drawing diagrams, or by using objects.*

2.   Recognize that representing data in a list, table, or graph is a way of translating a mathematical idea into a new form.*

3.   Discuss, read, and write about mathematical topics presented at this grade level. (Write the steps to follow when multiplying a two-digit number by a two-digit number.)*

4.   Explain and justify solutions to a given problem.*

5.   Write about and discuss interpretations and various solutions to open-ended problems.

ILLUSTRATION 14.5

Excerpt from *Mathematics Core Curriculum: Level 6*
Source: Utah State Office of Education, 1995.

(Continued)

ILLUSTRATION 14.5 *(Continued)*

6. Employ precise language in conjunction with mathematical symbols, including algebraic notation (variables).*

7. Employ and define mathematical words and symbols appropriate to this grade level.*

8. Discuss and write about attitudes concerning mathematical topics and lessons. (Possible journal entries: What I liked best about this lesson. What was easy and what was difficult about this lesson.)*

CASE 14.2

For three days of the first week of May, the state-mandated core-curriculum test battery is administered to the students at Castle Creek Elementary School. The following week, the principal receives the results back from the State Office of Education. He and the assistant principal note that the scores for three subtests (mathematics, reading, and science) from Mr. Lorenzo's second-grade class of 25 students are greater than those from the other three second-grade classes. For reasons they explain later at a district school board hearing, they decide to readminister those three subtests to Mr. Lorenzo's class. The students take the three subtests in one day during the third week of May.

The three average scores for the retest are lower than the respective three average scores from the initial administration of the test. In July, Mr. Lorenzo is notified by the assistant superintendent of the district that his contract will not be renewed because of improper testing practices. With the help of the legal staff from the state affiliate of the National Education Association (NEA), Mr. Lorenzo appeals the firing at a hearing conducted by the district school board.

The hearing is conducted very similarly to a court trial, with the district school board president serving as judge, the school board acting as jury, the school board's lawyer presenting the case to uphold the firing, and an attorney from the legal staff of the NEA affiliate presenting the case supporting Mr. Lorenzo's appeal. The case to uphold the firing is argued on only four points:

1. Dr. Rush Thomas, the school district's special education and psychology specialist, reported "statistically significant" differences between means (i.e., averages) from the first administration of the subtests as compared to the scores from the retest. Illustration 14.7 displays his memorandum to the assistant superintendent, which was the principal evidence presented by the school board's attorney.

2. The school principal and assistant principal testified that when they were packing up the test documents to send them to the State Office of Education for scoring, they noticed a high number of erasures on Mr. Lorenzo's students' multiple-choice response bubbles.

3. The school principal testified that one of the school's teachers remarked to him that she saw Mr. Lorenzo near the filing cabinet where the tests were stored after they had been administered to the students.

4. The school board attorney argued that Mr. Lorenzo altered students' responses to the test in order to make himself look good as a teacher.

The case supporting Mr. Lorenzo's appeal was based on the following:

1. Dr. Trinity Brown, measurement and statistics specialist from a university, attempted to explain to the school board that Dr. Thomas's statistical analysis reported by Illustration 14.7's memo was to-

State Core-Curriculum Test

Mathematics Level 6
Individual Student Report

5/13/99

District: South Point
School: Parkway Middle

Student: Sarah Anderson
Teacher: Ms. C. Yanjun

	Core Standard	Sub-Score	Competency Level
3360–01	Applies math concepts and skills to solve real-life problems	3	Sufficient
3360–02	Communicates, illustrates, and justifies solutions to problems	3	Sufficient
3360–03	Uses inductive reasoning to form mathematical relationships	4	Excellent
3360–04	Recognizes connections within mathematics and to other disciplines	3	Sufficient
3360–05	Communicates with and translates among multiple number representations	2	Insufficient
3360–06	Demonstrates an understanding of various subsets of real numbers	2	Insufficient
3360–07	Explains relationship underlying computation and estimation algorithms	3	Sufficient
3360–08	Analyzes, generalizes, and represents functional relationships and patterns	3	Sufficient
3360–09	Informally explores fundamental algebraic concepts and relationships	3	Sufficient
3360–10	Organizes, translates, and represents data in useful ways	4	Excellent
3360–11	Explores real-life situations by experimenting with probability models	3	Sufficient
3360–12	Informally explores and discovers fundamental geometric relationships	4	Excellent

ILLUSTRATION 14.6

Example of a Student's Score Report from a State Core-Curriculum Test for One Subject-Content Area

(Continued)

ILLUSTRATION 14.6 (Continued)

```
3360-13    Applies appropriate measurement              4              Excellent
           tools for problem solving

           TOTAL SCORE: 41     OVERALL COMPETENCY LEVEL: Sufficient
```

tally inappropriate. The last paragraph of the memo is complete nonsense. Dr. Brown correctly pointed out that inferential statistics, such as the *t*-statistic used by Dr. Thomas, are methods for measuring the probability of a difference being attributable to random sampling error. Because the experiment conducted by the school administrators (e.g., testing and retesting the same population of students) involved no sampling (i.e., all the students in Mr. Lorenzo's class were tested), the whole idea of "statistical significance" has no meaning in this case.

2. Dr. Brown obtained the two sets of test documents from the State School Board Office and analyzed the erasure patterns. She analyzed the erasures and found that the erasure patterns were consistent with second-graders' erasure patterns on these types of tests when there is no tampering with results. She also showed that the erasure patterns on the retest were similar to those from the initial administration. Among her many displays for the school board is Illustration 14.8, showing three types of erasures students made in response to the same prompt.

3. Besides testifying that Dr. Thomas's analysis was a misapplication of statistics and her erasure analysis was relevant to the question at hand, she also pointed out that the impact of measurement error due to imperfect measurement reliability should be examined as a possible explanation for differences in test and retest scores. She computed reliability coefficients and standard error of measurements for the tests (a topic you will address in Chapter 16) and demonstrated that imperfect test reliability could account for the discrepancies between the two sets of scores.

4. Dr. Brown pointed out that the tests were administered under considerably different conditions the first time than they were the second time. The subtests the first time were administered in three days instead of one. Also, the first time, other non-test-taking school activities (e.g., public address interruptions and visitors in the building) were shut down; for the second administration, classes other than Mr. Lorenzo's conducted business as usual.

5. Dr. Brown attempted to explain that reliability of such tests for second-graders is affected by the children having to mark multiple-choice response bubbles (Gaffney & Maguire, 1971; Lassiter, 1987).

In spite of overwhelming evidence to the contrary, the school board sided with its own attorney and superintendent. The firing was upheld, and Mr. Lorenzo's teaching certificate was revoked. Several months later, the evidence presented at the school board hearing was reviewed by the state's Professional Practices Board. The board ruled in favor of Mr. Lorenzo, censured the school board, and reinstated Mr. Lorenzo's teaching certificate.

Case 14.2, like all the other cases herein, reflects an actual event. Names, of course, have been changed to protect the identities of the protagonists. Case 14.2 is one of the more extreme examples of miscarriages of justice as a consequence of big-stakes testing hysteria. However, naive statistical analyses of test scores by so-called experts in education with "EdD" or "PhD"

Crystal County Board of Education

Dr. Marlin Bishop
Superintendent
Olden Dickerson
Ass't. Superintendent

Terrence Robinson
President
Shiree Tomasola
Vice-President
Board Members:
Alice Johnson
Rodam Bishop
Parker Pickett
Antoine Martinez

June 18, 1996

To: Olden Dickerson, Assistant Superintendent
From: Dr. Rush Thomas, Ed.D.
        Director of Special Education and School Psychology
Re.:   Statistical Comparison of Scores: First vs. Second Administration
      of State Core Examinations

As per your request for a comparison of scores for first and second administration of State Core tests for Mr. Lorenzo's second grade class in Reading, Math, and Science. Because of the audience for this study, an elaborate statistical design was not attempted but rather a simple direct comparison of first and second administration test scores in the three subject areas was done using the t-test for related samples (Roscoe, 1969). The results of these three comparisons follow:

Subject	Reading	Math	Science
1st Admin. Mean	87.20	88.76	78.72
2nd Admin. Mean	75.48	75.67	72.04
Mean Difference	11.72	13.09	06.68
No. of Comparisons	21	21	25
t-statistic	6.828	5.045	5.186
degrees of freedom	20	20	24
significance level	$p<.001$	$p<.001$	$p<.001$

In each of the above cases, the probability of differences of this magnitude occurring by chance is less than 1 in 1,000 times. From a statistical standpoint, test scores from the first administration were significantly higher than test scores obtained in the second administration in Reading, Mathematics, and Science.

An Equal Opportunity Employer

ILLUSTRATION 14.7

Dr. Rush Thomas' Memorandum to the District's Assistant Superintendent

Example of an erasure trace indicating a change from a distractor to the correct alternative:

$$565$$
$$- \ 302$$

253	263	362	867
(●)	(●)	( )	( )

Example of an erasure trace indicating a change from a distractor to another distractor:

$$565$$
$$- \ 302$$

253	263	362	867
(●)	( )	(●)	( )

Example of an erasure trace indicating a change from the correct alternative to a distractor:

$$565$$
$$- \ 302$$

253	263	362	867
( )	(●)	(●)	( )

ILLUSTRATION 14.8

Dr. Brown Illustrates Three Types of Erasures Students Made to the Same Test Prompt

behind their names is not at all unusual. Furthermore, legitimate cases of teachers' and school administrators' cheating with test results appear to be related to the degree to which high-stakes testing is emphasized in school districts (Cangelosi, 1993).

One of the issues argued in the debate over nationwide testing for national curriculum standards is whether nationwide testing will further exacerbate the climate of high-stakes testing (Davey, 1992; Davey & Neill, 1991). Some claim that students in the United States are already being over-tested by traditional methods, and that schools should focus more on the types of measurements that have been emphasized in the first 13 chapters of this book (Sheppard, Flexer, Hiebert, Marion, Mayfield, & Weston, 1996). On the other hand, Phelps (1996) reports that U.S. students spend less time taking high-stakes, lengthy systemwide tests than most of their counterparts in countries with comparable schooling systems. According to Phelps's study, U.S. students spend more time taking shorter, low-stakes tests, and that systemwide tests in the U.S. are more often norm-referenced and standardized than they are in other countries.

STANDARDIZED TESTS

A test is *standardized* if it has been field-tested to (1) measure its reliability and (2) establish norm-referenced standards for use in interpreting scores from subsequent administrations of the test. Measurement of reliability is a topic for Chapter 16. The establishment of norm-referenced standards and how they should be used to interpret standardized test scores are principal foci of this chapter. At this point, turn your attention to the meanings of some of the terms and phrases commonly used in communications about standardized tests:

Test Item

"Test item" is synonymous with "mini-experiment." A test is composed of items. Each test item consists of a prompt (e.g., a question) and a scoring key (i.e., a rubric). Most group-administered standardized tests are comprised solely of multiple-choice items. However there is a growing trend to also include open-ended items. The open-ended items usually have short-response formats; some tests of writing include essay prompts. The publisher of the ninth edition of the *Stanford Achievement Test* (*Stanford 9*), for example, provides its customers with the option of an open-ended battery or a traditional multiple-choice battery. Each grade-level subtest in reading, mathematics, science, and social science of the open-ended *Stanford 9* consists of nine short-response items instead of the traditional 25 to 60 multiple-choice items. In the first 13 chapters of this book, "mini-experiment" was used rather than "test item," as a reminder that when you design prompts and rubrics yourself, you are preparing experiments to scientifically gather information. I also did not want you to limit your designs of mini-experiments to the traditional types of items that you've encountered on most tests.

Achievement Test

If the scores from a test are used to evaluate what students have learned or how well they have achieved certain goals, then the test is referred to as an *achievement test*. Illustration 14.9 lists some of the popular standardized achievement tests with references on how to obtain information on each.

Aptitude Test

An *aptitude test* is a test whose scores are used to evaluate students' potential for achieving certain goals if the students engage in reasonably appropriate learning activities. Illustration 14.10 lists some of the popular standardized aptitude tests with references on how to obtain information on each.

Norm Group

A *norm group* for a standardized test is the sample of students with whom the test is field-tested and whose scores provide the standards for interpreting scores from subsequent administrations of the test. Evaluations based on standardized test results are norm-referenced because the scores are interpreted in light of how they compare to scores from the norm group. The more popular standardized tests that appeal to a nationwide market are *nationally normed*. In other words, the norm groups for these tests are samples drawn from geographic regions widely spread across the United States. Typically, demographic information about a standardized test's *national norm group* is provided by one of the test's user's manuals. Illustration 14.11 is an example of an excerpt from a user's manual. Often, students' scores on

Sources of information regarding over 3,000 commercially available tests include the following books typically located in the reference sections of college and university libraries as well as teacher resource centers:

o *Tests in Print* (Murphy, Conoley, & Impara, 1994) provides an alphabetical listing of 3,009 commercially available test instruments. Each test's publisher and publication date are listed along with related bibliographical references. (web site address: www.unl.edu/buros)

o *The Mental Measurement Yearbooks* (Conoley & Impara, 1995) provide information and reviews on virtually every widely used commercially available test instrument. Included for each test are (1) reviews regarding validity and usability, (2) a description of the instrument and its features (e.g., (a) types and number of items, (b) levels, (c) forms, (d) whether it is a single test or part of a battery, (e) types and availability of test manuals, and (f) types of reports and derived scores used), (3) a description of the targeted test populations, (4) information about the norm group and how the test was normed (if it is standardized), and (5) information about costs and how it can be acquired. (web site address: www.library.uiuc.edu/edx/mmybgui.htm)

Several publications from Educational Testing Service (ETS) provide information on a wide assortment of both commercially available as well as non-commercial test instruments. They include a test collection index and a quarterly newsletter, *News on Tests*, accessible through the internet (web site address: www.ets.org) or by writing to the following address: Educational Testing Service, P.O. Box 6736, Princeton, NJ 08541-6736.

Test publishers provide catalogues of their products, information on individual tests, and test samples. Some are accessible through web sites.

The following is a list of a few of the more popular group-administered standardized achievement test batteries used in elementary and secondary schools:

o *California Achievement Tests* (CAT). Grades: K-12. Reviewed in the 10th *Mental Measurement Yearbook*. Publisher's address: CTB/Macmillan/McGraw-Hill, 20 Ryan Ranch Road, Monterey, CA 93940 (www.ctb.com/products.htm).

o *Comprehensive Test of Basic Skills*, 4th edition (CTBS/4). Grades: K-12. Reviewed in the 11th *Mental Measurement Yearbook*.

ILLUSTRATION 14.9

Sources of Information on Some Popular Standardized Achievement Tests

(Continued)

ILLUSTRATION 14.9 (Continued)

Publisher's address: CTB/Macmillan/McGraw-Hill, 20 Ryan Ranch Road, Monterey, CA 93940 (www.ctb.com/products.htm).

o *Iowa Test of Basic Skills* (ITBS). Grades: K–9. Reviewed in the 11th *Mental Measurement Yearbook*. Publisher's address: Riverside Publishing, 425 Springlake Dr., Itasca, IL 60143 (www.hmco.com/hmco/riverside).

o *Iowa Test of Educational Development* (ITBS)(8th edition). Grades: 10–12. Reviewed in the 10th *Mental Measurement Yearbook*. Publisher's address: Riverside Publishing, 425 Springlake Dr., Itasca, IL 60143 (www.hmco.com/hmco/riverside/6test/top.htm).

o *Metropolitan Achievement Tests*, 7th edition (MAT7). Grades: K–12. Reviewed in the 12th *Mental Measurement Yearbook*. Publisher's address: Psychological Corporation, 555 Academic Court, San Antonio, TX 78204 (www.hbem.com).

o *Stanford Achievement Tests*, 9th edition (Stanford9). Grades: K–13. 8th edition reviewed in the 11th *Mental Measurement Yearbook*, 9th edition published after publication of the 12th *Mental Measurement Yearbook*. Publisher's address: Psychological Corporation, 555 Academic Court, San Antonio, TX 78204 (www.hbem.com).

standardized tests are also compared to the scores from *local norm groups*. A local norm group is a sample of test-takers within a particular geographic region. Just how "local" a norm group is varies considerably, depending on how the sample was drawn, the standardized test administered, and the size of the school district purchasing the test. The local norm group for a rural school district in Wyoming might include students across the western one-third of the country. For a large urban school district, the local norm group may be drawn from within the school district itself.

Test Norms

Test norms are statistics computed from the norm group's scores that provide the (1) standard to which subsequent scores are compared (i.e., an average of scores from the norm group), and (2) unit of measure for making those comparisons (i.e., a measure of the variability of the scores from the norm group). You will learn about these statistics and how they are used to establish test norms as you engage in learning activities through your work with subsequent sections of this chapter.

Raw Score

The *raw score* a student obtains from a test is simply the sum of the points from the individual items composing the test. For example, if a test consists of 36 dichotomously scored items and a student responds correctly to 19 of those items, then the student's raw score is 19.

Reference sources listed in Illustration 14.9 (i.e., *Tests in Print*, the *Mental Measurement Yearbooks*, and ETS publications) provide information on aptitude tests as they do for achievement tests.

The following is a small sample of some of the more popular tests of general aptitude used in elementary and secondary schools:

o *Cognitive Abilities Test* (CogAT). Grades: K–13. Reviewed in the 10th *Mental Measurement Yearbook*. Publisher's address: Riverside Publishing, 425 Springlake Dr., Itasca, IL 60143 (www.hmco.com/hmco/riverside).

o *Culture Fair Intelligence Tests*. Ages: 4–adult. Reviewed in the 6th *Mental Measurement Yearbook*. Publisher's address: Institute for Personality and Ability Testing, P.O. Box 188, Champaign, IL 61824 (www.ipat.com).

o *Goodenough-Harris Drawing Test*. Ages: 3–15. Reviewed in the 7th *Mental Measurement Yearbook*. Publisher's address: Psychological Corporation, 555 Academic Court, San Antonio, TX 78204 (www.hbem.com).

o *Hennon-Nelson Tests of Mental Ability*. Grades: K–12. Reviewed in the 8th *Mental Measurement Yearbook*. Publisher's address: Riverside Publishing, 425 Springlake Dr., Itasca, IL 60143 (www.hmco.com/hmco/riverside).

o *Kaufman Assessment Battery for Children* (K-ABC). Ages: 2.5–12.5. Reviewed in the 9th *Mental Measurement Yearbook*. Publisher's address: American Guidance Service, Publishers Buildings, Circle Pines, MN 55014.

o *Kuhlmann-Anderson Intelligence Test*, 8th edition (KA). Grades: K–12. Reviewed in the 9th *Mental Measurement Yearbook*. Publisher's address: Scholastic Testing Service, 480 Meyer Road, Benseville, IL 60106 (www.ststesting.com).

o *Otis-Lennon School Ability Test*, 7th edition (OLSAT7) Grades: K–12. Reviewed in the 11th *Mental Measurement Yearbook*. Publisher's address: Psychological Corporation, 555 Academic Court, San Antonio, TX 78204 (www.hbem.com).

o *Slosson Intelligence Test*. Ages: 2 weeks–27 years. Reviewed in the 12th *Mental Measurement Yearbook*. Publisher's address: Slossan Educational Publications, P.O. Box 280, East Aurora, NY 14052.

ILLUSTRATION 14.10

Sources of Information on Some Popular Standardized Aptitude Tests

(Continued)

ILLUSTRATION 14.10 (Continued)

> o   *Wechsler Intelligence Scale for Children*, 3rd edition (WISC-
>   III). Ages: 6-16. Reviewed in the 12th *Mental Measurement Year-
>   book*. Publisher's address: Psychological Corporation, 555
>   Academic Court, San Antonio, TX 78204 (www.hbem.com).

Standardization The 1999 edition differs from the 1991 edition in
that it contains more up-to-date content and illustrations. For standardization purposes the subtests were administered in October, 1998,
to a sample of approximately 11,000 pupils in 63 school systems. An
attempt was made to use school systems so that their geographic and
socio-economic characteristics were comparable to the country as a
whole. Pertinent descriptive data of the norm group are given below
as well as in Section C-6 of this manual.

1. REGIONAL DISTRIBUTION OF NORM GROUP

Region	States	Number of Schools	Number of Pupils
Northeast	PA, MA, NY, NJ	128	5,950
South	LA, TX, SC	16	1,380
Central	WI, MN, MO	52	1,623
Pacific	California	78	2,052

2. POPULATION OF COMMUNITY WHERE PUPILS LIVE

Population	Number of Pupils
Above 200,000	3,645
100,000-200,000	3,912
25,000-100,000	2,441
Less than 25,000	1,007

3. APTITUDE TEST SCORES

Deviation IQ	Number of Pupils
Above 125	770
115-125	1,100
105-115	2,421
95-105	2,752
85-95	2,312
75-85	1,098
Below 75	552

ILLUSTRATION 14.11

Excerpt About a Norm Group from a Standardized Test User's Manual

Derived Score

A *derived score* is a test score that is the result of an arithmetic computation involving a raw score and other data (e.g., test norms). Note that Illustration 14.3 presents the standardized test results for C. Kirby-Lind in terms of stanines, normal curve equivalents, scaled scores, and percentiles. These are examples of scores that have been derived from C. Kirby-Lind's raw scores and the test norms. Standardized test results are commonly reported in terms of derived scores that automatically rank each student's raw score with those from the norm group. Commonly reported derived scores (e.g., percentiles, stanines, grade equivalents, deviation IQs, NCEs, and scaled scores) are defined and explained in a subsequent section.

Student's Grade Level

For purposes of standardized testing, a student's grade level is expressed in the form "*g.m*," where *g* is what grade the student is in when she or he takes the test and *m* is the month of the school year in which the test was administered. Thus, a student who takes a standardized test in October while in fifth grade is assigned a grade level of 5.2 for that test (assuming September was the first month of that school year). A student's grade level determines (1) which level of the test she or he will be administered and (2) the grade-level norms to which her or his scores will be compared.

Test Level

Recall your experiences taking or administering standardized tests. For a single test or subtest, a student is typically confronted with about 35 items. Now, instead of thinking of that test as having only about 35 items, imagine that it has about 350 items sequenced in a progression from easy items to difficult items. For example, if the subject-content area of the test is mathematics, then the first 10 or so items deal with kindergarten-level counting and grouping, subsequent items deal with addition of one-digit whole numbers, further items deal with more advanced mathematics, and finally items beyond Item #250 deal with high-school level topics from algebra, trigonometry, and precalculus. Illustration 14.12 may help you imagine the way this test is structured.

A *test level* refers to the particular subset of items from this mammoth sequence of items that appears on the part of the test taken by students at a particular grade level. Illustration 14.13 provides an example of how the association among test levels and grade levels is presented in a test manual for one standardized test battery. Note that Illustration 14.3's standardized test report indicates that C. Kirby-Lind took the Intermediate–2 level of the test.

Test Form

Illustration 14.3's standardized test report indicates that C. Kirby-Lind was administered Form B of Intermediate–2 level of the test. Most popular standardized tests are published in multiple *forms*. Two different forms of the same level of a test are designed to be equivalent. Two forms

```
Level:    I     II     III     IV        V         VI        VII       VIII      IX
Item #: 1-30  25-60  55-85  80-115  110-160  155-210  205-255  250-300  290-345
```

ILLUSTRATION 14.12

A Standardized Test Partitioned into Levels

Test Level:	PrePrimer		Primer		Prim. 1		Prim. 2		Elem		Inter.		Adv. 1		Adv.2	
Grade Range:	k.0–k.5		k.5–1.4		1.5–2.4		2.5–3.4		3.4–4.9		5.0–6.9		7.0–9.9		10.0–12.9	
Test	I*	T**	I*	T**	I*	T**	I*	T**	I*	T**	I*	T**	I*	T**	I*	T**
Reading:	60	50	37	50	55	45	55	40	60	40	60	40	55	35	50	30
Mathematics:	25	25	35	30	40	35	45	35	50	40	50	40	50	40	50	40
Language:	25	25	25	25	40	35	55	38	60	40	60	40	60	40	60	40
Science:					34	25	40	30	45	35	50	35	55	35		
Soc. Studies:					34	25	40	30	45	35	50	35	55	35		
Total Time	1hr40min		1hr45min		2hr45min		2hr53min		3hr10min		3hr10min		3hr05min		1hr50min	

*I: number of items **T: approximate administration time in minutes

ILLUSTRATION 14.13

Test Levels, Grade Levels, Number of Items, and Administration Times for One Standardized Test Battery

are *equivalent* if they have almost exactly the same number and types of items, are relevant to the same goals, and are equally difficult. By having multiple forms of a test available, publishers can provide customers with the option of retesting with equivalent rather than the exact same tests. Also, for tests administered to extremely large groups, multiple forms may be used as a strategy for reducing opportunities for students to cheat by copying from others' response sheets.

Edition of a Test

The *edition* of a test is the number of times it has been revised and normed. As with textbooks, each edition is associated with a copyright date. Until about 1985, tests were only infrequently revised and renormed. But due to adverse publicity regarding "outdated" items, "culturally biased" items, and "yesterday's" norm groups, publishers of the more popular tests are renorming and issuing new editions of their tests more often. The eighth edition of the *Stanford Achievement Test* battery carries a 1989 copyright date; the ninth was normed in 1995. As you will see from your work in a subsequent section, there are both advantages and disadvantages to using a recently normed edition of a test instead of an older one.

Test Manuals

When school personnel acquire a standardized test, usually by purchasing it from a commercial test publisher, they typically receive several *manuals* containing (1) detailed directions for how the test should be administered uniformly, (2) reliability coefficients (i.e., measures of reliability), (3) demographic information on the norm group (e.g., Illustration 14.11), (4) information on how the test was normed, (5) explanations on how scores should be interpreted, and (6) information on appropriate uses of the test. Depending on test publishers, manuals have various titles including "Administrator's Guide," "User's Manual," and "Technical Manual."

Concurrent Validity

Test manuals and advertisements for tests frequently report statistics indicating how well results from their tests correlate with results from other well-known tests. The publisher of a group-administered aptitude test that takes only an hour to administer might advertise that its results correlate highly with a less usable, individually administered, but better known test (e.g., *Stanford-Binet Intelligence Scale*). Or a test publisher may simply believe that advertising such correlations might suggest something positive about the test's validity. A test has *concurrent validity* with respect to another test to the same degree that results from the two tests positively correlate. In other words, results from administrations of both tests to the same group of students displayed a group trend in which (1) students with higher ranking scores on one test tended to have higher ranking scores on the second test, and (2) students with lower ranking scores on one test tended to have lower ranking scores on the second test. Illustration 14.14 depicts different levels of correlation.

Predictive Validity

An aptitude test has *predictive validity* to the degree that (1) students with high scores from the test of their potential for success with targeted goals actually do achieve those goals, and (2) students with low scores fail to achieve those goals. For example, the *Graduate Record Examination (GRE)* is used in screening applicants for graduate school. The *GRE* is designed to

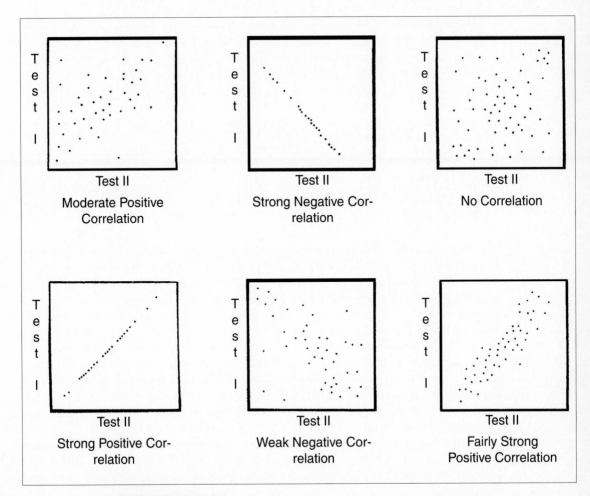

ILLUSTRATION 14.14

Graphical Representations of Varying Degrees of Correlation

discriminate according to applicants' potential for succeeding in graduate school. The following would be one way of measuring the predictive validity of the *GRE*:

> A large group of applicants for graduate school (e.g., 1,000) are administered the *GRE* prior to being admitted. Irrespective of their scores, all members of the group are admitted and begin work toward their graduate degrees. As these students matriculate through the programs with varying degrees of success—some dropping out in the early stages, others failing due to low grades, others graduating with minimal grade-point averages, and others graduating with high grade-point averages—a measure of "success in graduate school" is obtained on each. The correlation between the *GRE* scores and the measures of success is computed. The greater the positive correlation, the better the predictive validity.

If educators paid more attention to predictive validity of aptitude tests, two labels sometimes attached to students might disappear from the professional vocabulary: "underachiever" and "overachiever." Case 14.3 is an example of how students sometime acquire these labels.

CASE 14.3

Upon entry into Ms. Zilles's third-grade class, both Denise and Larry are given an aptitude test that is used in evaluating their potential for succeeding in third grade. Denise's score is very low and Larry's very high. Throughout the school year, Denise's responses to Ms. Zilles's many measurements of her achievement of learning goals are quite impressive. Larry's responses on these measurements are not nearly as successful. Ms. Zilles's summative evaluations of Denise's year-long achievements are far more positive than they are for Larry. Because of the inconsistency between each of their aptitude scores and each of their actual performances in third grade, the school psychologist refers to Larry as an "underachiever" and Denise as an "overachiever."

Instead of considering Larry as an "underachiever" and giving Denise the paradoxical label of "overachiever" (i.e., exceeded her own capability!), why not acknowledge that the aptitude test had poor predictive validity in this case?

Because standardized achievement tests are designed to be sold and widely distributed to many schools across the United States, their items target very general skills (e.g., word recognition and listening comprehension) within very broadly defined subject-content areas. They are not intended to be relevant to specific objectives, as are the mini-experiments you design for your classes. The items were developed by testing specialists, curriculum specialists, and teachers employed by the publishers.

Test publishers depend on the cooperation of school districts throughout the country to obtain their norm groups. Historically, suburban school districts have been overly represented in norm-group samples while urban and rural school districts have been under-represented. However, since about 1985, publishers have made a very deliberate effort to use norm groups that are representative of all segments of the population—especially those from urban school districts.

In order for you to understand exactly how derived scores are used to compare your students' raw scores to those from the norm-group and, thus, to be able to correctly interpret standardized test reports (e.g., Illustration 14.3), it is necessary to examine some fundamental ideas from the field of statistics.

ESTABLISHING A NORM-REFERENCED POINT OF COMPARISON

HOW LARGE IS 27?

Theresa's raw score from a test is 27. Is 27 a large score or is it a small score? Does it help answer the question to know that Eva's score from the test is 21? Now at least you know of one other score to which you can compare 27; 27 is 6 greater than 21. But is 6 a large or small difference? To make sense out of a raw score, we need a standard, either norm-referenced or criterion-referenced, to which it can be compared. The meaning of a test score is relative, not absolute.

In the world of standardized testing, the question about the relative magnitude of a raw score is addressed, not by comparing it to only one other raw score, but by comparing it to a whole group of other scores (i.e., the scores from a norm group). So using this strategy, is 27 large or small? The answer of course depends on the norm-group scores. Suppose that the norm-group's scores to which we will compare Theresa's score of 27 are the ones from Illustration 14.15.

Illustration 14.15 does not include anywhere near as many scores as a typical standardized test norm group. But 37 scores will serve our purpose of understanding how standardized test norms are established and used to attribute relative size to raw scores. Before continuing with the problem of comparing Theresa's raw score to the norm group's, note some conventional statistical shorthand notations that are used:

In Illustration 14.15, "i" is used as an index to designate students' identification numbers; "x_i" (read "x sub i") designates Student-i's raw score. For example, Cameron is Student–7 and his raw score is 10, thus $x_7 = 10$. Student–20 is Jose; thus, Jose's score is x_{20}.

i	Student	x_i	i	Student	x_i
1	A.J.	41	20	Jose	39
2	Arlene	10	21	Joy	31
3	Bill	42	22	Lucinta	43
4	Bonita	30	23	Luke	34
5	Buddy	17	24	Michael	18
6	Buhla	38	25	Melinda	12
7	Cameron	10	26	Nadine	37
8	Candice	34	27	Nettie	40
9	Celeste	16	28	Ory	23
10	Charles	37	29	Phyllis	28
11	Eloise	35	30	Quinn	33
12	Elvira	36	31	Raul	18
13	Evelyn	25	32	Ricardo	39
14	Garret	34	33	Rufus	39
15	Gilda	39	34	Sidney	14
16	Hans	32	35	Singh	21
17	Hilda	29	36	Tomaria	37
18	Ira	40	37	Zelda	40
19	Jacob	35			

ILLUSTRATION 14.15

Norm-Group Scores for the Test Theresa Took

Note that $x_{20} = 39$. There are 37 students and raw scores listed in Illustration 14.15; thus, i is used to represent either 1, 2, 3, . . . , or 37. "N" is often used to designate the number of students in a norm group. For Illustration 14.15's norm group, $N = 37$. So, in general, for any norm group, i is used to represent either 1, 2, 3, . . . , or N.

Some people find the subscripts and other shorthand notations used in statistics quite confusing. For our immediate purposes in this section, statistical shorthand conventions are not very useful. However, I am introducing them to you now because it will help you to become accustomed to using them for your work in subsequent sections of this chapter as well as in Chapters 16 and 17.

Let's return to the question about Theresa's raw score of 27. Compared to Illustration 14.15's norm-group scores, is 27 a low, medium, or high score? The comparison would be more convenient to make if the norm group scores were resequenced in descending order, as in Illustration 14.16. This is an example of how statistical manipulations are used to make it easier to obtain meaning from data.

From Illustration 14.16, it is easy to see that Theresa's 27 would fall somewhat below the middle of the pack, in between 25 and 28 or between the 26th and 27th ranked scores. Relative to Illustration 14.15's norm-group, it appears that 27 is somewhat low. On the other hand, suppose the 27 is to be compared to the norm group scores in Illustration 14.17. Note that Illustration 14.17's norm-group scores are designated by "w_i" simply to distinguish them from those in Illustration 14.16.

i	Rank	x_i	i	Rank	x_i
22	1	43	23	19	34
3	2	42	30	21	33
1	3	41	16	22	32
18	5	40	21	23	31
27	5	40	4	24	30
37	5	40	17	25	29
15	8.5	39	29	26	28
20	8.5	39	13	27	25
32	8.5	39	28	28	23
33	8.5	39	35	29	21
6	11	38	24	30.5	18
10	13	37	31	30.5	18
26	13	37	5	32	17
36	13	37	9	33	16
12	15	36	34	34	14
11	16.5	35	25	35	12
19	16.5	35	2	36.5	10
8	19	34	7	36.5	10
14	19	34			

ILLUSTRATION 14.16

Illustration 14.15's Norm-Group Scores in Descending Order

Compared to Illustration 14.17's scores, 27 is somewhat high, ranking about 9th or 10th out of 30.

Note another shorthand notation used in the remainder of this book:

Braces with subscripted terms are used to designate a sequence of scores. For example, "$\{x_i\}$" represents Illustration 14.15's sequence of scores, indicated by the following relationship of convention:

$$\{x_i\} = \{x_1, x_2, x_3, \ldots, x_{37}\} = (41, 10, 42, \ldots, 40)$$

CENTRAL TENDENCY

Collectively, the sequence of scores from Illustration 14.16 (i.e., $\{x_i\}$) is higher than the sequence from Illustration 14.17 (i.e., $\{w_i\}$). That is why Theresa's 27 is relatively low compared to $\{x_i\}$ and relatively high compared to $\{w_i\}$.

Describe in your own words what features of the two sequences, $\{x_i\}$ and $\{w_i\}$, lead you to decide that $\{x_i\} > \{w_i\}$ (i.e., that the collective sequence of scores from Illustration 14.16 is greater than the collective sequence of scores from Illustration 14.17).

In Case 14.4, Elwin and Kisha discuss how they responded to this task.

CASE 14.4

Kisha:	"It's pretty obvious that the x_i's in Illustration 14.16 run higher than the w_i's in Illustration 14.17. The average x_i is going to be greater than average the w_i.
Elwin:	"I know. If all this is just about differences in averages, I don't know why we need to make such a big deal of all this. It seems pretty trivial! The only thing hard is getting used to this new notation."

i	Rank	W_i		i	Rank	W_i
9	1	45		6	16	19
19	2	37		10	18	16
1	3	34		20	18	16
13	4.5	33		14	18	16
30	4.5	33		8	20	15
12	6	30		2	21	13
29	7	29		27	22	12
7	8	28		17	23.5	10
23	9.5	27		15	23.5	10
25	9.5	27		16	25.5	9
18	12	24		26	25.5	9
24	12	24		21	27	8
4	12	24		5	28	3
3	14.5	20		22	29.5	0

ILLUSTRATION 14.17

A Second Sequence of Norm-Group Scores to Which Theresa's Score Is Compared

Kisha:	"Besides getting used to the notation we'll need when we come to something really new, I think we're being engaged in a sort of construct-a-concept lesson. We're supposed to articulate how we compared the x_i's to the w_i's not just by saying 'on average the x_i's are greater,' but by describing what we mean by 'greater on the average.' We're being led to look in depth at the concept of average or what statisticians call 'central tendency.'"
Elwin:	"Okay, what if I say $\{x_i\}$ is greater than $\{w_i\}$ because the sum of the x_i's is greater than the sum of the w_i's?
Kisha:	"But the sum of a sequence of scores is not only affected by the magnitudes of the individual scores, but also by the number of scores. There are more x_i's than there are w_i's. In other words N_x is greater than N_w."
Elwin:	"That's why when you compute an average, you divide the sum by the number of scores—to account for the affect of the number of scores. That allows you to compare two different sequences of scores even though one has more scores than the other."
Kisha:	"You're right; adding up the scores and dividing by the number of scores is probably the best way to measure average or central tendency. That way of measuring central tendency is called the 'arithmetic mean' or just 'mean' for short. But there are other ways of measuring central tendency, like by looking at the median or the mode."
Elwin:	"Okay, here's my last try at articulating what you're telling me is called 'central tendency.' Even though some of the x_i's are greater than some of the w_i's (e.g., $w_1 \to$ is greater than x_4), $\{x_i\}$ is greater than $\{w_i\}$ because overall the x_i's are greater. That's not very well put, but you know what I mean."
Kisha:	"Sometimes, the more obviously true something is, the more difficult it is to explain. I think that the purpose of this exercise wasn't so much for us to come up with a precise description as much as it was to get us to think about the characteristics of a sequence of scores that makes one average greater than another."

As Kisha points out in Case 14.4, the central tendency of a sequence of scores is any indicator of how high the scores tend to be. Many statisticians consider "average" to be synonymous with *central tendency*. However, it is also very common for people to use the word "average" as a synonym for the best known measure of central tendency—arithmetic mean. Herein, "average" is used in the broader sense (i.e., as a synonym for central tendency.)

MEASURES OF CENTRAL TENDENCY

Median

According to Illustration 14.16, the middle score in $\{x_i\}$ is 34. The middle score is one measure of central tendency and is called the *median*. Because there is an odd number of scores in $\{x_i\}$ (i.e., $N_x = 37$), then the median of $\{x_i\}$ is one of the scores (i.e., 34). However, in a sequence with an even number of scores, the median is half the sum of the two middle scores. Note from Illustration 14.17 that the two middle scores in $\{w_i\}$ are 20 and 19. Thus the median of $\{w_i\}$ is 19.5.

Note that when suggested that Theresa's 27 is somewhat low relative to $\{x_i\}$ and somewhat high relative to $\{w_i\}$, we compared 27 to the respective medians.

Arithmetic Mean (μ)

In standardized testing, the *arithmetic mean* of the norm-group's scores is the measure of central tendency that is most often used as the standard to which raw scores from subsequent administrations of the test are compared. The Greek letter "μ" is the conventional symbol for mean of a population. As Elwin suggested in Case 14.4, the *arithmetic mean* for a sequence of scores is the sum of the scores divided by the number of scores.

Besides arithmetic means, other means (e.g., harmonic means and geometric means) are used in mathematics. But since the arithmetic mean is the only one used herein, the term "arithmetic mean" is shortened to simply "mean." For Illustration 14.15's scores, μ_x (i.e, the mean for $\{x_i\}$) is computed as follows:

$$(41 + 10 + 42 + \ldots + 40) \div 37 = 1126/37 = 30.4324324 \ldots \approx 30.43$$

The symbol "≈" is used to indicate "approximately equal" because 30.43 is rounded to the nearest 0.01. For our work with statistics in this chapter as well as in Chapters 16 and 17, we do not need more than accuracy to the nearest 0.01. Thus, feel free to express statistical results to the nearest 0.01.

Of course, you need not ever compute means or any other statistics by hand. Calculators and computers handle such computations for us.

Using shorthand symbols, the mean can be defined as follows:

$$\mu_x = (x_1 + x_2 + x_3 + \ldots + x_N) \div N$$

If we use one more conventional shorthand symbol known as the "summation notation" or "sigma notation," the definition can be restated as follows:

$$\mu_x = \frac{\sum\limits_{i=1}^{N_x} x_i}{N_x}$$

The summation notation will prove useful in subsequent sections and chapters. To familiarize yourself with its meaning, please study the explanation presented by Illustration 14.18.

Using Illustration 14.17's scores, compute μ_w.

As you expected, $\mu_w < \mu_x$, because $\mu_w = 19.7$ and $\mu_x \approx 30.43$. Note that if we use the means as standards for comparisons for Theresa's score of 27, the 27 appears to be less than average with respect to $\{x_i\}$ and greater than average with respect to $\{w_i\}$.

Mode

Another commonly used measure of central tendency is the *mode* or *modes*. Some sequences of scores have more than one mode. The *mode* is the most frequently occurring *score value* in a sequence. Note from Illustration 14.16 that $x_{18} = 40$ and $x_{27} = 40$. Thus, Student–18's and Student–27's raw scores have the same *value*. $x_{18} = 40$ and $x_{22} = 43$. Thus, Student–18's and Student–22's raw scores have different *values*. If two or more score values in a sequence are equally popular, then the sequence has more than one mode.

What is the mode or what are the modes of $\{x_i\}$ from Illustration 14.16? Four of the scores are 39; no other value appears in $\{x_i\}$ as many times as 39. Thus the mode of $\{x_i\}$ is 39.

What is the mode or are the modes for $\{w_i\}$ from Illustration 14.17? $\{w_i\}$ has two modes, namely, 24 and 16.

The summation notation is symbolized by the uppercase Greek letter "Σ" (i.e., sigma) as follows:

$$\sum_{i=1}^{M} f_i \text{ is the sum of the numbers in the sequence } \{f_i\} \text{ where } \{f_i\} \text{ has } M \text{ numbers.}$$

In other words,

$$\sum_{i=1}^{M} f_i = f_1 + f_2 + f_3 + \ldots + f_M$$

For example, suppose $\{q_i\}$ = (3, 10, 3, 0, 9). In other words, q_1 = 3, q_2 = 10, q_3 = 3, q_4 = 0, and q_5 = 9. Now, for the sake of our example, further suppose that f_i is some mathematical function that manipulates the scores of $\{q_i\}$ as follows:

$$\{f_i\} = \{(q_i - 10)^2\} = ((q_1 - 10)^2, (q_2 - 10)^2, (q_3 - 10)^2, (q_4 - 10)^2, (q_5 - 10)^2), =$$
$$((3 - 10)^2, (10 - 10)^2, (3 - 10)^2, (0 - 10)^2, (9 - 10)^2) =$$
$$((-7)^2, 0^2, (-7)^2, (-10)^2, (-1)^2,) = (49, 0, 49, 100, 1).$$

In other words, f_i forms a sequence by taking each score from $\{q_i\}$ subtracting 10 from it and squaring the result.

Thus, for our example where $\{f_i\} = \{(q_i - 10)^2\}$ and $\{q_i\}$ = (3, 10, 3, 0, 9),

$$\sum_{i=1}^{5} f_i = \sum_{i=1}^{5} (q_i - 10)^2 = 49 + 0 + 49 + 100 + 1 = 199$$

Note that in the example, index numbers (i.e., the values of i) vary from 1 to 5 (i.e., M = 5) because there are 5 numbers in $\{f_i\}$.

As an exercise, suppose $\{t_i\}$ is a sequence of 3 scores such that $\{t_i\}$ = (12, 9, 9); simplify the following expression:

$$\sum_{i=1}^{3} (2 + 5t_i)$$

Compare your results with the following:

$$\sum_{i=1}^{3} (2 + 5t_i) = (2 + 5(12)) + (2 + 5(9)) + (2 + 5(9)) = 62 + 47 + 47 = 156$$

ILLUSTRATION 14.18

An Explanation of the Summation Notation

FREQUENCY DISTRIBUTION

Sometimes it is convenient to express scores in a *frequency distribution*. A *frequency distribution* associates each possible score value with the number of scores having that value. Illustration 14.19 is a frequency distribution of $\{x_i\}$ from Illustration 14.16.

Illustration 14.19's frequency distribution is expressed in tabular form. Of course, frequency distributions can also be expressed graphically. Illustration 14.20 is Illustration 14.19's frequency distribution expressed as graphed points.

Although test scores always yield frequency distributions whose graphs are disjointed points such as in Illustration 14.20, frequency distributions for sequences of scores are often expressed as histograms or smooth curves to make reading them easier. Illustration 14.21 expresses Illustration 14.19's frequency distribution as a histogram. Illustration 14.22 expresses it also, but as a smooth curve. Why would you ever want to read a frequency distribution or graph? Relative to our immediate purposes, reading graphs helps you recognize trends in the values of scores. How do the values vary? Are they widely distributed, or do they clump together? Where do the breaks in score values occur? From your work with Chapter 3, you recall how trends in the distribution of scores can be used in converting scores to grades (e.g., with the visual inspection and compromise methods).

Two different groups of students were administered the same test, resulting in two score sequences, $\{u_i\}$ and $\{v_i\}$. Graphs for the frequency distributions for $\{u_i\}$ and $\{v_i\}$ are superimposed on the same grid in Illustration 14.23; the solid curve is the graph for the $\{u_i\}$'s frequency

Possible Score Value	Frequency	Possible Score Value	Frequency
less than 10	0	27	0
10	2	28	1
11	0	29	1
12	1	30	1
13	0	31	1
14	1	32	1
15	0	33	1
16	1	34	3
17	1	35	2
18	2	36	1
19	0	37	3
20	0	38	1
21	1	39	4
22	0	40	3
23	1	41	1
24	0	42	1
25	1	43	1
26	0	greater than 44	0

ILLUSTRATION 14.19

Tabular Frequency Distribution of Illustration 14.16's Scores

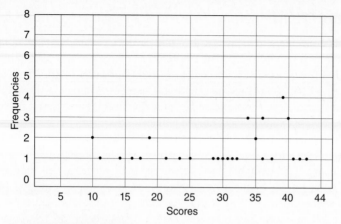

ILLUSTRATION 14.20

Frequency Distribution of Illustration 14.16's Scores Expressed as Graphed Points

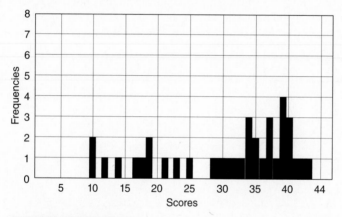

ILLUSTRATION 14.21

Frequency Distribution of Illustration 14.16's Scores Expressed as a Histogram

distribution and the dotted curve for $\{v_i\}$'s. Which of the two sequences $\{u_i\}$ or $\{v_i\}$ appears to have a greater central tendency?

Because the graph of $\{v_i\}$'s frequency distribution is shifted farther to the right on the horizontal axis, $\{v_i\}$ has a greater central tendency than $\{u_i\}$.

Graphs of two frequency functions are superimposed on the same grid in Illustration 14.24. The solid curve is from $\{p_i\}$, dotted curve from $\{s_i\}$. Which of the two sequences appears to have more scores? In other words, which of the two sequences is the result of more students being tested? In other other words, is N_p greater than or less than N_s?

Because there is a greater area under the curve for $\{p_i\}$'s frequency distribution than for $\{s_i\}$'s, $N_p > N_s$.

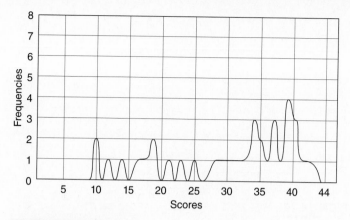

ILLUSTRATION 14.22

Smooth-Curve Graph Frequency Distribution of Illustration 14.16's Scores

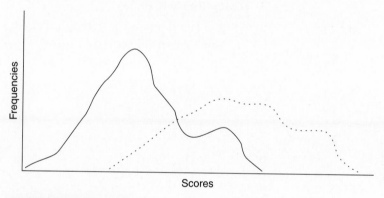

ILLUSTRATION 14.23

Which of the Two Sequences $\{u_i\}$ or $\{v_i\}$ Appears to Have a Greater Central Tendency?

ESTABLISHING A NORM-REFERENCED UNIT FOR COMPARISON

VARIABILITY

In the section "How Large Is 27?," the question was raised as to whether the difference of 6 between Theresa's raw score of 27 and Eva's raw score of 21 is a large or small difference. Readdress that question, but this time, suppose that the two scores are being compared to $\{b_i\}$ that is displayed by Illustration 14.25.

Are not the differences between pairs of scores from $\{b_i\}$ generally somewhat greater than 6? Actually, if you bothered to do the much too tedious computation to figure an average of all the differences between paired scores from $\{b_i\}$, you would find that the mean of all those differences is about 17.33. Keeping in mind that you do not need to execute that computation yourself, examine Illustration 14.26, noting how the 45 differences between paired scores were

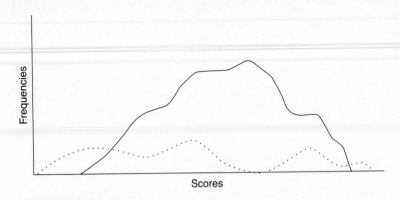

ILLUSTRATION 14.24

Which of the Two Sequences $\{p_i\}$ or $\{s_i\}$ Appears to Have the Greater Number of Scores?

b_i
46
40
38
30
24
20
16
16
10
0

ILLUSTRATION 14.25

Is a Difference of 6 Between Two Scores Large or Small When Compared to $\{b_i\}$?

46–40=6									
46–38=8	40–38=2								
46–30=16	40–30=10	38–30=8							
46–24=22	40–24=16	38–24=16	30–24=6						
46–20=26	40–20=20	38–20=18	30–20=10	24–20=4					
46–16=30	40–16=24	38–16=22	30–16=14	24–16=8	20–16=4				
46–16=30	40–16=24	38–16=22	30–16=14	24–16=8	20–16=4	16–16=0			
46–10=36	40–10=30	38–10=28	30–10=20	24–10=14	20–10=10	16–10=6	16–10=6		
46–0=46	40–0=40	38–0=38	30–0=30	24–0=24	20–0=20	16–0=16	16–0=16	10–0=10	

Illustration 14.25's 10 scores from $\{b_i\}$ can be paired in 45 ways. The 45 differences from those pairs are computed above. The median of the differences is 16; the mean is approximately 17.33. The modes are 6, 8, 10, 14, 16, and 30.

ILLUSTRATION 14.26

Computation of Differences Between Paired Scores from Illustration 14.25

computed. Of course, 17.33 is the result of dividing the sum of the 45 differences (which is 780) by 45. In light of the fact that 6 is between $\frac{1}{3}$ and $\frac{1}{2}$ the mean of the differences, the difference between Theresa's 27 and Eva's 21 seems relatively small when compared to $\{b_i\}$. Note that the median of the differences from Illustration 14.26 is 16, also greater than 6.

Suppose that instead of comparing the difference between Theresa's 27 and Eva's 21 to $\{b_i\}$, you compared it to $\{c_i\}$ from Illustration 14.27. Now does the difference of 6 appear to be relatively large or small?

The score values from Illustration 14.27's $\{c_i\}$ do not vary as much as the score values from Illustration 14.25's $\{b_i\}$. A difference of 6 appears to be greater than an average difference for $\{c_i\}$. All possible differences between paired scores from $\{c_i\}$ are as follows:

9, 8, 8, 7, 6, 6, 6, 6, 5, 5, 5, 5, 5, 5, 4, 4, 4, 4, 3, 3, 3, 3, 3, 3, 2, 2, 2, 2, 2, 2, 2, 2, 2, 2, 2, 2, 1, 1, 0, 0, 0, 0, 0, 0, 0

The mean of those 45 differences is approximately 2.34, the median is 3, and the mode is 2. Each of those three measures of central tendency is no more than half of 6. Thus, by comparison to $\{c_i\}$, the difference between Theresa's and Eva's raw scores seems large.

Compare $\{b_i\}$ from Illustration 14.25 to $\{c_i\}$ from Illustration 14.27. They are similar in that they have the same number of scores (i.e., $N_b = N_c = 10$) and the same mean (i.e., $\mu_b = \mu_c = 24$). In what way are they dissimilar—a dissimilarity that causes a difference of 6 to be small in comparison to $\{b_i\}$ and large in comparison to $\{c_i\}$?

The scores values from $\{b_i\}$ are more dispersed or varied than the score values from $\{c_i\}$. $\{b_i\}$ is the more heterogeneous; $\{c_i\}$ is more homogeneous. In the world of standardized testing, whether a difference between two scores or between a score and a norm-group mean is considered great or not depends on the dispersion or *variability* of the score values from the norm group. The greater the differences among the values in a sequence of scores, the greater the variability of that sequence. Think of a sequence of scores with no variability. Here are two examples:

$\{g_i\} = (51, 51, 51, 51, 51, 51, 51)$
$\{h_i\} = (20, 20, 20, 20, 20, 20, 20, 20, 20, 20, 20, 20, 20)$

Before developing a few measures of variability, examine the graphs of the two frequency distributions superimposed on the same grid in Illustration 14.28. Which of the two graphs, the one for $\{a_i\}$'s frequency distribution or the one for $\{e_i\}$'s, reflects a score sequence with greater variability than the other?

$\{a_i\}$ appears to have greater variability than $\{e_i\}$.

c_i
29
28
25
25
23
23
23
23
21
20

ILLUSTRATION 14.27

Is a Difference of 6 Between Two Scores Large or Small When Compared to $\{c_i\}$?

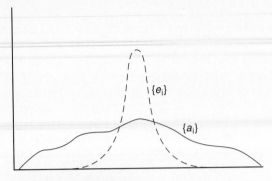

ILLUSTRATION 14.28

Which Graph Reflects the Score Sequence with the Greater Variability?

(74, 70, 70, 70, 69, 69, 69, 69, 69, 69, 69, 68, 68, 68, 68, 68, 68, 68, 3)

ILLUSTRATION 14.29

Homogeneous Sequence of Scores with a Deceptively Large Range

MEASURES OF VARIABILITY

Range

Illustration 14.28's graph for the frequency distribution of $\{a_i\}$ spans a wider horizontal distance than the one for $\{e_i\}$. The difference between the greatest and least score values in $\{a_i\}$ appear to be greater than the difference between the greatest and least score values for $\{e_i\}$. The *range* of a score sequence is a very usable measure of variability. It is simply the difference between the greatest and least score values. What is the range of $\{b_i\}$ from Illustration 14.25? What is the range of $\{c_i\}$ from Illustration 14.27?

$\text{Range}_b = 46 - 0 = 46$. $\text{Range}_c = 29 - 20 = 9$. Finding the range of $\{b_i\}$ to be greater than that for $\{c_i\}$ is consistent with our previous judgment of $\{b_i\}$ being more varied than $\{c_i\}$. However, in some cases, the range alone may be a misleading indicator of variability. Consider Illustration 14.29's score sequence. The range is 71, but 19 of the 20 scores are extremely close in value. The outlier, 3, causes the range to be deceptively large.

Mean Deviation (*MD*)

Whereas the range is the difference between only the two most extreme values in a score sequence, you looked at the differences of all possible pairs of scores when you initially compared $\{b_i\}$ to $\{c_i\}$ from Illustrations 14.25 and 14.27. By computing the mean of all those differences as shown by Illustration 14.26, you obtain a measure of variability that is influenced by the spread of all the scores rather than only the two extremes. However, computing the difference of every combination of N scores taken 2 at a time is much too time-consuming (even for a computer) for a sequence with a large N. N_b from Illustration 14.25 is only 10, but you found 45 different ways to pair 10 scores. Had we attempted Illustration 14.26's computations with the 37 scores from

$\{x_i\}$ in Illustration 14.15, we would have had to deal with 666 pairs. For $N = 50$, the number of pairs jumps to 1,225; for $N = 100$, there are 4,950 pairs.

What we need is a measure of variability that is as meaningful as the mean of all the differences of pairs of scores but is not so time-consuming to compute. Instead of computing the difference between each score and each of the other $N-1$ scores, could we not compute the difference between each score and a number that reflects the collective size of all the scores? What do you suggest?

As the measure of central tendency that is a function of every score, the mean is an excellent representative of the collective scores. Thus, instead of computing the differences between each score and every other score, we only need to compute the differences between each score and the mean. The mean of the differences between each score from Illustration 14.25's $\{b_i\}$ and μ_b is computed in Illustration 14.30. The result of this computation is the *mean deviation* of $\{b_i\}$; the shorthand symbol is "*MD*." Thus, from Illustration 14.30 we get $MD_b = 11.6$.

Note that the sum of the differences between each score and the mean is 0. Will this be true for any sequence of scores? Compute the sum of differences between each score and the mean for $\{c_i\}$ from Illustration 14.27. Once again the sum is 0. Think about the meaning of "mean" and you will understand why the sum of the N differences between each score and the mean is 0 for any score sequence. Return to your computations with $\{c_i\}$ and take the absolute value of those 10 differences (i.e., change all the negative numbers to positive numbers) and find the mean of those 10 non-negative numbers. You should get $MD_c = 2.2$. Note that the symbol "$|n|$" for any real number n means "the absolute value of n."

$$\mu_b = \frac{1}{10} \sum_{i=1}^{10} b_i =$$

$$(.1)(46 + 40 + 38 + 30 + 24 + 20 + 16 + 16 + 10 + 0) = (.1)(240) = 24$$

b_i	$b_i - 24$	$|b_i - 24|$
46	22	22
40	16	16
38	14	14
30	6	6
24	0	0
20	− 4	4
16	− 8	8
16	− 8	8
10	− 14	14
0	− 24	24
	0	116

$$MD_b = 116 \div 10 = 11.6$$

ILLUSTRATION 14.30

Computation of the Mean Difference of $\{b_i\}$ from Illustration 14.25

Consistent with our previous comparison of $\{b_i\}$'s variability to $\{c_i\}$'s, $MD_b > MD_c$. The following is a general formula for computing the mean deviation of a score sequence:

$$MD_x = \frac{\sum_{i=1}^{N_x} |x_i - \mu_x|}{N_x}$$

Variance (σ^2)

Although mean deviation is a stable, useful measure of variability, it is not the one that is commonly used in the world of standardized testing. The history of the development of statistical models for measuring variability took a slightly different turn from the one we just took. When the time came to remove the negative numbers from the second column of Illustration 14.30's computations, squaring the differences became more popular than simply taking absolute values. An alternative computation to that shown by Illustration 14.30 created a third measure of variability known as the *variance*. The shorthand symbol for variance is "σ^2" (i.e., "sigma squared"). The variance of $\{b_i\}$ from Illustration 14.25 is computed in Illustration 14.31.

The following is a general formula for computing the variance of a score sequence:

$$\sigma_x^2 = \frac{\sum_{i=1}^{N_x} (x_i - \mu_x)^2}{N_x}$$

Compute σ_c^2 for $\{c_i\}$ from Illustration 14.27.
Is $\sigma_c^2 = 7.2$? Not surprisingly, $\sigma_b^2 > \sigma_c^2$.

b_i	$b_i - 24$	$(b_i - 24)^2$
46	22	484
40	16	256
38	14	196
30	6	36
24	0	0
20	-4	16
16	-8	64
16	-8	64
10	-14	196
0	-24	576
	0	1888

$$\sigma_b^2 = 1888 \div 10 = 188.8$$

ILLUSTRATION 14.31

Computation of the Variance of $\{b_i\}$ from Illustration 14.25

Standard Deviation (σ)

The standard deviation is the most commonly employed measure of variability. In the world of standardized testing, the mean of the norm-group scores is the standard to which scores from subsequent administrations of the test are compared. The norm-group *standard deviation* is the unit of measure by which those comparisons are made. The *standard deviation* of a score sequence is the principal square root of the variance. The shorthand symbol for standard deviation is "σ" (sigma).

Compute σ_b for $\{b_i\}$ from Illustration 14.25 and σ_c for $\{c_i\}$ from Illustration 14.27.

$$\sigma_b = \sqrt{\sigma_b{}^2} = \sqrt{188.8} \approx 13.74. \qquad \sigma_c = \sqrt{\sigma_c{}^2} = \sqrt{7.2} \approx 2.68$$

Note that the standard deviations for $\{b_i\}$ and $\{c_i\}$ approximate the mean deviations you previously computed (i.e., $MD_b = 11.6$ and $MD_c = 2.2$). Think of the standard deviation as approximately the average of the differences between individual scores and the mean of all the scores. Thus, the standard deviation serves as a reasonable norm-referenced unit of measure when comparing a score to the mean.

Return to the task of comparing Theresa's raw score of 27 to $\{x_i\}$ from Illustration 14.16. Recall that $\mu_x \approx 30.43$. Thus, Theresa's raw score is about 3.43 less than μ_x. Now, if you use your calculator (look for the "σ" button) or the user-friendly statistical software on the CD that accompanies this book to compute σ_x for Illustration 14.16's scores, you'll find that $\sigma_x \approx 9.87$. The difference of 3.43 between Theresa's raw score and the mean is about ⅓ of σ_x. Thus, it is about ⅓ of the average of the differences between the norm-group scores and the mean. Theresa's raw score seems to be a relatively small number of points below the mean.

As we did once before, let's suppose that instead of using $\{x_i\}$ from Illustration 14.16 for norm-group scores, we want to use $\{w_i\}$ from Illustration 14.17. $\mu_w = 19.7$. Thus, Theresa's score is 7.3 greater than the mean. How great of a difference is 7.3? To address that question, we compute σ_w and find $\sigma_w \approx 11.10$. Thus, 7.3 is about ⅔ of an average of the differences between scores from $\{w_i\}$ and μ_w.

Z-SCORES

From the section "Standardized Tests" in this chapter, reread the definition and explanation of "Derived Score" on page 531.

In the world of standardized testing, raw scores are converted to derived scores that indicate how many standard deviations each raw score is above or below the mean. The most fundamental derived score from which other derived scores are based is the z-score. The z-score associated with a particular raw score is the number of standard deviations that the raw score falls above the mean.

For example, suppose the norm group's score sequence is $\{m_i\}$ such that $\mu_m = 70$ and $\sigma_m = 12$. A raw score of 76 would convert to a z-score of what? Because 76 is 6 greater than 70 and $6 = \frac{1}{2}$ of 12, $z_{76} = \frac{1}{2}$ or 0.5. Continuing to use $\{m_i\}$ as the norm-group's scores, compute the following: z_{82}, z_{73}, z_{70}, z_{58}, z_{64}, z_{88}, z_{46}, and z_{78}.

Because 82 is 12 greater than 70 and 12 is 1 standard deviation, $z_{82} = 1$. $z_{73} = 0.25$ because 73 is 3 more than 70 and 3 is ¼ of 12 (i.e., $.25\sigma_m$). $z_{70} = 0$ because 70 is 0 standard deviations greater than 70. $z_{58} = -1$ because 58 is 12 less than 70, which is 1 standard deviation below the mean (i.e., -1 standard deviation above the mean). $z_{64} = -0.5$. $z_{88} = 1.5$. $z_{46} = -2$. $z_{78} \approx 0.67$.

Analyze the process by which you just computed those eight z-scores. First you noted whether the raw score was greater than, less than, or equal to μ. If greater than μ, z is positive;

if less than μ, z is negative. Then you found the difference between the raw score and μ and determined how many σ's or what part of a σ that difference is. In other words, to compute the z-score for a raw score of x_i from Test x, you used the following general formula:

$$z_{x_i} = \frac{x_i - \mu_x}{\sigma_x}$$

What is the z-score associated with Theresa' raw score of 27 if you use $\{x_i\}$ from Illustration 14.16 for the norm-group scores? Recall that $\mu_x \approx 30.43$ and $\sigma_x \approx 9.87$.

$$z_{27} \approx ((27 - 30.43) \div 9.87) \approx -0.35.$$

But what would z_{27} be if the norm group scores were from $\{w_i\}$ from Illustration 14.17? Recall that $\mu_w = 19.7$ and $\sigma_w \approx 11.10$.

$$z_{27} \approx ((27 - 19.7) \div 11.10) \approx 0.66.$$

Note that although there is no theoretical bound on how small or large z-score values can be, z-score values tend to be between -2.5 and 2.5, with more nearer 0 than nearer either -2.5 or 2.5.

DISTRIBUTION OF NORM-GROUP SCORES

GRADE-LEVEL NORMS ($M_{g.m}$, $\Sigma_{g.m}$)

From the section "Standardized Tests" in this chapter, reread the definition and explanation of "Student's Grade Level" on page 531.

When a test publisher acquires the norm-group scores for one of its tests, it includes samples of scores from a variety of grade levels a few times during a school year. Test norms (i.e., μ and σ) are obtained for different grade levels (i.e., $g.m$). In other words, for each grade level represented in the norm group a mean (i.e., $\mu_{g.m}$) and standard deviation (i.e., $\sigma_{g.m}$) are computed. Mathematical interpolation and extrapolation are used to estimate $\mu_{g.m}$ and $\sigma_{g.m}$ for $g.m$'s that are not directly represented in the sample.

Suppose, for example, that Racheed is a fourth-grader who takes a standardized test in March. If March is considered the 7th month of the school year, Racheed's raw score will be converted to derived scores using $\mu_{4.7}$ and $\sigma_{4.7}$ from the norm group. If Racheed takes the test again in October when he is in fifth grade, his new raw score will be compared to the mean and standard deviation estimated for those in the norm-group who were in the 5.2 grade level when they took the test. Thus, for the fifth-grade administration, Racheed's z-score would be computed by subtracting it from $\mu_{5.2}$ and dividing the result by $\sigma_{5.2}$.

NORMAL DISTRIBUTIONS

A sequence of norm-group scores can be expressed as a frequency distribution and, thus, as a graph. Because of the way standardized tests are designed and normed, the graphs of norm-group raw scores tend to look something like Illustration 14.32.

Note that the mean, mode, and median have nearly the same value, and that the curve is roughly (but not exactly) symmetrical with respect to a vertical line that includes the apex of the curve and the point on the horizontal axis associated with the median. When the size of a norm group is very large (e.g., $N > 1,000$), as norm groups typically are for popular nationally sold standardized tests, the frequency distribution of scores can tenably be treated as if it is *normal*. The graph of a *normal frequency distribution* has a bell-shaped appearance similar to Illustration 14.33's graph.

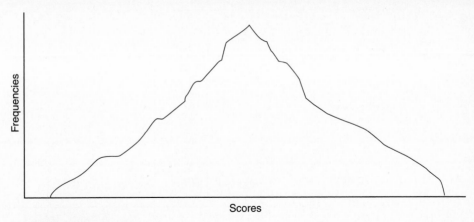

ILLUSTRATION 14.32

Example of the Graph of the Frequency Distribution of a Norm-Group's Scores

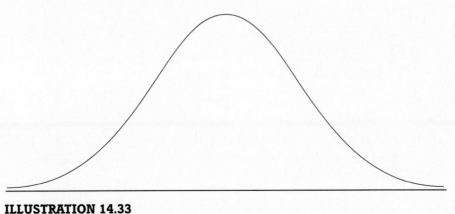

ILLUSTRATION 14.33

The Bell Shape of a Normal Curve

   Besides a bell-like shape, a normal frequency distribution has a number of other defining characteristics including the following ones which are important to the interpretation of standardized test scores:

- The curve is symmetrical with respect to a vertical line that includes the apex of the curve and the point on the horizontal axis that is associated with the mean. In other words, the left half and the right half of the curve are mirror images of each other.
- There is only one mode, and it is equal to both the mean and median.
- As suggested by the bell-like shape, the frequency of score values is greatest near the mean and tapers off symmetrically toward the extremes.
- As indicated by Illustration 14.34, approximately 68.2% of the raw scores fall within 1σ of μ (i.e., are associated with z-scores between -1 and 1). Because a normal curve is symmetrical with respect to a vertical line through the point associated with μ, about 34.1%

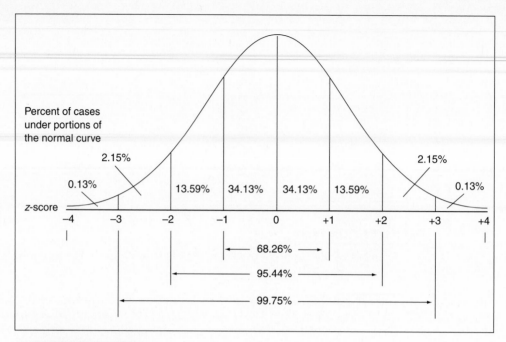

Percent of cases
under portions of
the normal curve

ILLUSTRATION 14.34

Some Attributes of a Normal Curve

of the raw scores have z-score values between −1 and 0 and about 34.1% have z-score values between 0 and 1. Illustration 14.34 indicates the percentage of raw scores falling within
different z-score intervals.

• Although the frequency of raw scores associated with z-scores either less than −3 or
greater than 3 (i.e., more than 3σ from μ) is near 0, the curve is unbounded on both the
left and the right. In other words, there is no minimum nor maximum score. At both
extremes, the frequency of scores approaches but never reaches 0. How could a test
have neither a minimum nor maximum score? It can't. However, when the actual frequency distribution of norm-group scores (which is bounded on both the left and the
right) is interpreted as if it were normal, theoretical low scores are extrapolated that are
less than the actual minimum, and theoretical high scores are extrapolated that exceed
the actual maximum.

• A well-defined function exists for generating normal distributions. This is an important
feature that facilitates interpolating and extrapolating norms for all possible grade levels
from a sample of grade-level norms. Furthermore, having such a function facilitates conversion of z-scores to more commonly used derived scores such as percentiles. For our
purposes here, it is only important to know that a formula for the function exists, not to
know what it is. However, if you are curious, the formula can be stated as follows:

$$f(x) = \frac{1}{\sigma\sqrt{2\pi}} e^{-(x-\mu)^2/2\sigma}$$

where e is Euler's constant (i.e., $e \approx 2.71828$) and μ and σ are, respectively, the mean and standard deviation of the domain.

COMMONLY USED DERIVED SCORES

STANDARD SCORES

As suggested by Illustration 14.34, the z-score scale has a mean of zero (i.e., $\mu_z = 0$) and a standard deviation of one (i.e., $\sigma_z = 1$). When raw scores are converted to z-scores, the resulting values are numbers such as the following: $-0.04, 0.32, 1.07, 0.12, -0.09$, and -1.33. About half of the z-scores reported are negative, most are near 0, and they're expressed using decimal points. Such numbers do not appeal to many standardized testing companies' customers. Many are uncomfortable with the language of mathematics and have an aversion to negative numbers and decimal points. Yet z-scores express the most fundamental information about a raw score: the number of standard deviations the raw score is above or below the mean.

Test publishers have addressed this problem by renumbering the z-score scale so that the mean is positive (thus virtually eliminating the need for negative numbers) and the standard deviation is a two-digit or three-digit whole number (thus reducing the need for decimal points). The derived score commonly referred to as a *T-score* is an example. *T-scores* are derived from z-scores by the following formula:

$$Tx_i = 10z_{x_i} + 50 \text{ where } z_{x_i} \text{ is the } z\text{-score associated with a raw score value of } x_i.$$

Thus, a z-score of 0 converts to a *T-score* of 50 because $10(0) + 50 = 50$. Compute the *T-score* equivalents of the following z-scores: $1, -1, 0.5, -0.5, -2, 0.25, -0.75$.

For $z = 1$, $T = 60$ because $(10)1 + 50 = 60$. For $z = -1$, $T = 40$ because $(10)(-1) + 50 = 40$. For $z = 0.5$, $T = 55$ because $(10)(0.5) + 50 = 55$. For $z = -0.5$, $T = 45$ because $(10)(-0.5) + 50 = 45$. For $z = -2$, $T = 30$ because $(10)(-2) + 50 = 30$. For $z = 0.25$, $T = 52.5$ because $(10)(0.25) + 50 = 52.5$. For $z = -0.75$, $T = 42.5$ because $(10)(-0.75) + 50 = 42.5$.

The *T-score* scale has a mean of 50 and a standard deviation of 10. *T-scores* provide the same information as z-scores, just in other words.

T-scores and *z-scores* are examples of a type of derived scores called *standard scores*. A *standard score*, Sx_i, is any derived score that is computed by the following formula:

$Sx_i = D(z_{x_i}) + M$ where z_{x_i} is the z-score associated with a raw score value of x_i, D is a constant (whatever the inventor of the standard score wants the standard deviation of the standard-score scale to be) and M is a constant (whatever the inventor of the standard score wants the mean of the standard score scale to be).

Thus, for *T*-scores, $D = 10$ and $M = 50$.

Illustration 14.35 displays a number of different standard score scales reported for various standardized tests.

PERCENTILES

Illustration 14.36 is an example of a standardized test report in terms of five of the more commonly used derived scores as well as a raw score for each of four subtests. Note that Sonnet's language test raw score of 33 converts to a *percentile* of 29. This indicates that 29% of the raw scores from the norm group are less than 33 and 71% are greater than 33. Interpret Sonnet's percentile score of 62 from the math test.

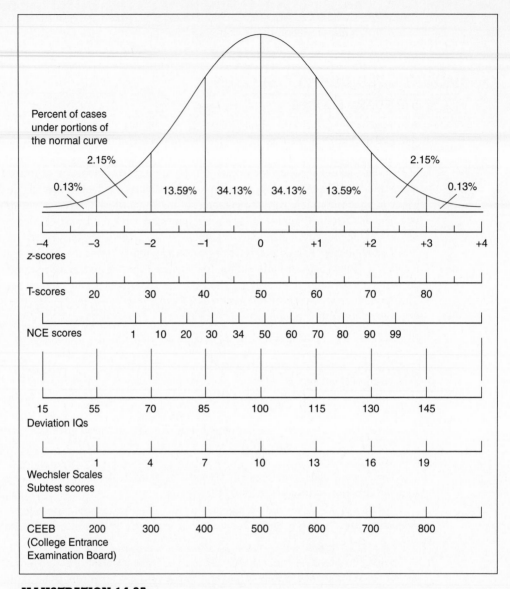

Percent of cases under portions of the normal curve

0.13% 2.15% 13.59% 34.13% 34.13% 13.59% 2.15% 0.13%

z-scores: −4 −3 −2 −1 0 +1 +2 +3 +4

T-scores: 20 30 40 50 60 70 80

NCE scores: 1 10 20 30 34 50 60 70 80 90 99

Deviation IQs: 15 55 70 85 100 115 130 145

Wechsler Scales Subtest scores: 1 4 7 10 13 16 19

CEEB (College Entrance Examination Board): 200 300 400 500 600 700 800

ILLUSTRATION 14.35

Standard-Score Scales Reported for a Variety of Standardized Tests

The 62 percentile reported for Sonnet on the math test indicates that her raw score for that test (i.e., 23 in this case) is greater than 62% of the raw scores in the norm group and less than the remaining 38%. The general meaning of *percentile* is as follows:

A raw score x_i converts to a *percentile* of p if x_i is greater than p% of the norm-group's raw scores and x_i is less than $(100 − p)$% of the norm-group's raw scores.

Note that because norm-group scores are assumed to be normal and include extrapolated scores that have no minimum value, no actual raw score can be less than every one of the norm-

Pupil Profile for Sonnet Jacoby	Grade Level: 5.7			
	Language	Math	Social Studies	Science
Percentile	29	62	27	48
NCE	38.3	56.4	37.1	48.9
Grade Equivalent	5.1	6.3	4.8	5.7
Scaled Score	323	366	348	344
Stanine	4	6	4	5
Raw Score	33	23	30	27

ILLUSTRATION 14.36

Sonnet Jacoby's Scores from a Standardized Test Battery

group scores. Thus, the percentile value derived from any actual raw score must be greater than 0. In other words, for every raw score x_i, $P_{x_i} > 0$. Also, because of the assumption of normality, extrapolated norm-group scores have no maximum. Thus, no matter how great an actual raw score is, it cannot be greater than all the extrapolated score values on the extreme right-hand side of a normal curve. For every raw score x_i, $P_{x_i} < 100$.

Keeping in mind that norm-group raw scores are assumed to have a normal frequency distribution, use Illustration 14.35 to estimate the percentiles associated with the following z-scores: 0, 1, −1, 2, and −2.

Illustration 14.35 indicates that the vertical line through the point associated with $z = 0$ divides the area under a normal curve in half. Thus, 50% of the norm-group scores are less than a raw score that converts to a z-score of 0. Therefore, the percentile associated with $z = 0$ is 50. Another 34.13% of the scores are associated with z-scores such that $0 < z < 1$, so a z-score of 1 is associated with a percentile score of about 84.13 (because 50% + 34.13% = 84.13%). A z-score of −1 is associated with a percentile of about 15.87 because 13.59% + 2.15% + 0.13% = 15.87%. You may have also associated $z = -1$ with the percentile score of 15.87 by using the following computation: 100% − (50% + 34.13%) = 15.87%.

For $z = 2$, the percentile is about 97.72 because 50% + 34.13% + 13.59% = 97.72%. For $z = -2$, the percentile is about 2.28 because 100% − 97.72% = 2.28%.

Keeping in mind that the percentile associated with a z-score of 0 is 50 and that the percentile for a z-score of 1 is about 84.13, what is the percentile associated with a z-score of 0.5? Should it be greater than, less than, or equal to the mean of 50 and 84.13 (i.e., 67.065 because (50 + 84.13) ÷ 2 = 67.065)?

According to Illustration 14.35, the percentile for $z = 0.5$ should be greater than 67.065. The curve is taller over the z-score interval between 0 and 0.5 than it is over the z-score interval between 0.5 and 1. Thus, the percentage of the area under the curve for $0 < z < 0.5$ is greater than it is for $0.5 < z < 1$. By applying integral calculus, each z-score can be paired with a percentile. Examine Illustration 14.37.

From Illustration 14.37, notice that although the z-score scale increases from −3 to 3 in equal intervals of 0.1, the corresponding percentiles increase from 0.13 to 99.87 in unequal intervals. For example, the difference between the percentile associated with $z = 3$ (i.e., 99.87) and the percentile associated with $z = 2$ (i.e., 97.72) is 2.15. But the difference between the percentile associated with $z = 2$ (i.e., 97.72) and the percentile associated with

z-score	Approximate Percentile	z-score	Approximate Percentile
-3.0	00.13	3.0	99.87
-2.9	00.19	2.9	99.81
-2.8	00.26	2.8	99.74
-2.7	00.35	2.7	99.65
-2.6	00.47	2.6	99.53
-2.5	00.62	2.5	99.38
-2.4	00.82	2.4	99.18
-2.3	01.07	2.3	98.93
-2.2	01.39	2.9	98.61
-2.1	01.79	2.1	98.21
-2.0	02.28	2.0	97.72
-1.9	02.87	1.9	97.13
-1.8	03.54	1.8	96.46
-1.7	04.46	1.7	95.54
-1.6	05.48	1.6	94.52
-1.5	06.68	1.5	93.32
-1.4	08.08	1.4	91.92
-1.3	09.68	1.3	90.32
-1.2	11.51	1.2	88.49
-1.1	13.57	1.1	86.43
-1.0	15.87	1.0	84.13
-0.9	18.41	0.9	81.59
-0.8	21.19	0.8	78.81
-0.7	24.20	0.7	75.80
-0.6	27.43	0.6	72.57
-0.5	30.85	0.5	69.15
-0.4	34.46	0.4	65.54
-0.3	38.21	0.3	61.79
-0.2	42.07	0.2	57.93
-0.1	46.02	0.1	53.98
0.0	50.00		

ILLUSTRATION 14.37

Relationship Between Norm-Group z-Scores and Norm-Group Percentiles

$z = 1$ (i.e., 84.13) is 13.59. The number of percentile values associated with z-scores near 0 is much greater than the number of percentiles values associated with more extreme z-scores. The scale for percentiles is shown parallel to the scale for z-scores by Illustration 14.38. Note how dense percentile values are in the middle compared to the ends.

Because of the unequal-spacing of percentiles, arithmetic computations can lead to deceptive results. Case 14.5 is an example.

CASE 14.5

Ms. Gunnell notes from her students' standardized test reports that Shane's percentile score for the reading-comprehension subtest is 46, Nick's is 62, Anna's is 92 and Steve's is 98. She thinks, "That's a 16

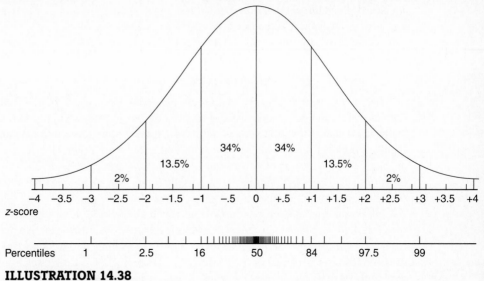

z-score

Percentiles   1   2.5   16   50   84   97.5   99

ILLUSTRATION 14.38

Percentiles Values Do Not Occur on Equally Spaced Intervals as Do z-Scores

point difference between Shane's and Nick's scores; that seems pretty significant. Maybe I should give Nick more advanced reading assignments than Shane. On the other hand, the difference of 6 points between Anna's 92 and Steve's 98 isn't all that great; they appear to be reading on nearly the same level."

If Ms. Gunnell were to examine Illustrations 14.37 and 14.38, she would see that the "difference" between a percentile of 62 and a percentile of 46 is actually less than the "difference" between a percentile of 98 and a percentile of 92. Note from Illustration 14.37 that the span of 16 percentile points between 62 and 46 is only about $0.4z$, whereas the span of 6 percentile points between 98 and 92 is about $0.7z$. Thus, there is a greater difference between Steve's and Anna's raw scores than there is between Nick's and Shane's. The point to keep in mind is that percentiles only provide rankings or ordinal numbers. Ordinal numbers should not be arithmetically manipulated as cardinal numbers. The accuracy of arithmetic operations, such as subtraction, depends on the proposition that 1=1 irrespective of whether the 1 is the result of subtracting 89 from 90 or 49 from 50. You can see from Illustration 14.38 that such a proposition is not true for percentiles.

NORMAL CURVE EQUIVALENTS (NCEs)

Percentiles are the most commonly reported type of standardized test score. However, if *gains* or *differences* between scores are to be considered (as Ms. Gunnell did in Case 14.5), percentiles are inappropriate because percentiles shouldn't be subtracted. In the past, some schools' records included standardized test results only in the form of percentiles. This poses a problem when one considers that standardized test results are often used in evaluating the effects of special programs funded by public grant monies. These evaluations usually employ some statistical methods that require arithmetic operations. For example, a *gain score*, (i.e., the difference between a posttest score and a pretest score) is often computed. In order to use such statistical procedures when only percentiles are available, *normal curve equivalent* (*NCE*) *scores* were invented (Tallmadge & Wood, 1976; Tallmadge, 1985).

As suggested by Illustration 14.35, an NCE score is a type of standard score and can be computed for a raw score x_i as follows:

$NCEx_i = 21.06z_{x_i} + 50$ where z_{x_i} is the *z*-score associated with a raw score value of x_i.

Like percentiles, NCE score values are positive numbers less than 100. But unlike percentiles, NCE values are equally spaced. Look at the percentile scale in Illustration 14.39. Imagine yourself sliding the little vertical marks on the percentiles scale sideways until they are all evenly spaced between 1 and 99. The mark associated with 50 remains in place, but in varying degrees, you slide the ones between 1 and 50 to the left and the ones between 50 and 99 to the right. The order of the numbers remains the same. When you are done, you have the NCE scale also displayed by Illustration 14.39.

NCE scores are useful for situations in which you need to use arithmetic with percentile scores (e.g., to compute gain scores or examine the differences between two means). For such cases, convert the percentiles to NCEs by either (1) reading a conversion table from a standardized test user's manual or (2) starting the "Percentile/NCE Converter Application" from the CD-ROM that accompanies this book. Do the arithmetic with the NCEs, not the percentiles.

As with any type of standard score, arithmetic computations with NCEs can be meaningful. However, using NCEs and most other types of derived scores to assess progress or differences over time can be very misleading. For example, suppose a standardized test is administered in November to Joy, a sixth-grader. Joy takes the test again the following May. The November testing yields a percentile score of 65, which converts to an NCE of 58.1; the May testing yields a percentile of 57, which converts to an NCE of 53.7. Do these results suggest that Joy's raw score from the May test is less than the raw score from the November testing? Not necessarily. The drop from November's NCE of 58.1 to May's 53.7 may have been caused by her November raw score being compared to the 6.3 grade-equivalent norms and her May raw scoring to the 6.9 grade-equivalent norms. Furthermore, it's possible that Joy took a higher level of the test in May than she did in November. There is one type of derived score by which comparisons over time can be made in a way that deals with the problems created by unequal intervals as well as differences in grade-equivalent norms and test levels: *scaled scores*.

SCALED SCORES

The derivation of *scaled scores* is considerably more complex than that for other commonly reported standardized test scores. Latent-trait scaling (Douglas, 1988; Keeves, 1988a), item-response

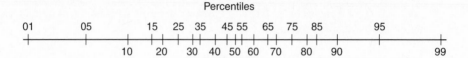

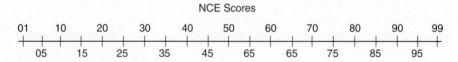

ILLUSTRATION 14.39

Percentile and NCE Score Scales

models (Hambleton & Swaminathan, 1985), and psychometric techniques originated by Thurstone (1928; Nunnally, 1978, pp. 35–85) underlie algorithms for converting raw scores to *scaled scores*. Unlike standard scores, percentiles, and NCEs, the conversion of scaled scores from raw scores in conjunction with test norms is unique to each edition of each standardized test. Thus, there is no general formula for converting between other types of derived scores and scaled scores the way there is for converting from *z*-scores to NCEs. Algorithms for deriving scaled scores utilize a complex of factors, including (1) the overlap among items from different test levels, (2) discrimination and difficulty levels of test items (topics addressed in Chapter 17), (3) probabilities of students' guessing correct responses, (4) error estimates due to imperfect reliability (a topic for Chapter 16), (5) variations in test levels, and (6) variations in grade-level norms.

Scaled score values are positive numbers less than 1,000, with raw scores from lower grade levels (e.g., 1.2) associated with lower scaled scores (e.g., 109) and raw scores from higher grade levels (e.g., 11.7) associated with higher ones (e.g., 722). But again, the particular correspondences between scaled scores and other types of scores as well as grade levels are different depending on the test and the edition of the test.

In recent years, it has become popular for scaled scores (sometimes called "scale scores") to be included in standardized test reports, as in Illustration 14.3 and 14.36. Scaled-score conversion tables are typically included in standardized test user's manuals.

Why would you ever want to use scaled scores? Scaled scores are the only type of derived scores that you should use for making comparisons over time. Scaled scores are derived in a way that accounts for differences in grade-level norms and test levels; addition and subtraction with scaled scores can also produce meaningful results. However, even two scaled scores are not comparable unless they are both from the same edition of the same test. It's okay if they are from different levels or different forms of the same test, but not from different tests. For example, Illustration 14.36 is the report of Sonnet's scores from a standardized test she took at the 5.7 grade level. Illustration 14.40 displays Sonnet's report from having been administered the same edition of that test battery but when she was in the 4.8 grade level. The difference between her most recent language-test scaled score of 323 and the previous one of 309 reflects a level of improvement between the two test performances. However, it is untenable to compare any of her language scores to any of her math scores (even the scaled scores) because the language subtest and math subtest are not the same tests. Nor should you compare two test scores from two standardized tests of the same subject-content area (e.g., two mathematics tests) produced by different publishers.

Pupil Profile for Sonnet Jacoby	Grade Level: 4.8			
	Language	Math	Social Studies	Science
Percentile	34	59	33	48
NCE	41.3	54.8	40.7	48.9
Grade Equivalent	4.2	5.4	4.1	4.8
Scaled Score	309	314	332	287
Stanine	4	5	4	5
Raw Score	33	23	30	27

ILLUSTRATION 14.40

Sonnet Jacoby's Scores from the Same Edition of the Same Standardized Test Reported in Illustration 14.36 but Administered About a Year Earlier

The comparison between Sonnet's scaled scores from Illustrations 14.36 and 14.40 for the same subject-area test is meaningful only because they came from the same edition of the same test. Thus, you've discovered a disadvantage of administering recently normed, brand-new editions of tests. You need to continue to use the same edition of a test in order to make comparisons over time.

GRADE EQUIVALENT SCORES

Grade equivalent scores are one of the more popular ways of reporting standardized test results and, in my opinion, the most widely misused and misinterpreted type of derived scores. Illustration 14.36 shows Sonnet's language test grade equivalent score to be 5.1. Many people mistakenly make the following misinterpretation:

> "Sonnet's level of achievement is about right for a student who is in the first month of fifth grade. Because she took the test when she was in grade 5.7, her language development is about six months behind."

Such an interpretation is in error; a standardized test is simply not powerful enough to provide such profound information. People are naively attracted by the impressive title "grade equivalent score"; it sounds so important and meaningful. "Grade equivalent score" sounds as if it will answer the question they want answered: "Is this student's achievement level behind, ahead, or right at what is expected for her or his grade in school?" "z-score," "NCE score," "scaled score," and "stanine" aren't as impressive sounding, but just like grade equivalent scores, they all compare the same raw score to the same test norms. The following comment made to me by a teacher reflects the misguided beliefs of many teachers, parents, and school administrators:

> I don't know what this standard deviation or norm-group stuff is all about, but grade equivalent scores make perfect sense. If a kid's grade equivalent score is 5.3, then that means he's doing the work of a student in the third month of fifth grade. If he's in a grade higher than say the middle of fifth grade, he's got some catching up to do. If he's somewhere like the fourth grade or lower, then he can handle advanced work. Some of the other scores like NCEs, stanines, and z-scores make no sense at all—maybe they would if I was a mathematician. . . . Now I can understand percentiles. A kid with a percentile of say 60 knows 10% more than average. But I still like grade equivalent scores better because they pinpoint exactly where the kid is.

Teachers cannot possibly understand grade equivalents or percentiles unless they have some critical prerequisite knowledge. Because you do understand test norms (e.g., standard deviations), you can understand how to properly interpret grade equivalent scores. Sonnet's language test grade equivalent score of 5.1 should be interpreted as follows:

> Sonnet's raw score from the language test is approximately equal to the mean of the raw scores of those students in the norm group who took the test when they were in the first month of the fifth grade.

Of course, it would be easier to simply say, "Sonnet scored at the fifth year, first month grade on the language test." But the problem with the simpler statement is that those who wouldn't understand the wordier, more accurate version read more into the simpler statement than they should. It's better for people to know they don't understand than to think they understand when they don't.

In general a *grade equivalent score* of g.m is associated with a raw score x_i if x_i is approximately equal to the mean of the raw scores of those students in the norm group who were in the g.m grade when they took the test.

As you understand from your work with this chapter's section "Grade-Level Norms ($\mu_{g.m}$, $\sigma_{g.m}$)," test publishers do not obtain actual norm-group scores for every *g.m*. Most of the grade-level means used to convert raw scores to grade equivalent scores have been interpolated or extrapolated from the sample of actual norm-group scores.

Because of the way they are derived, grade equivalent scores, like percentiles, are only ordinal and, thus, should not be used in arithmetic computations. Consider Case 14.6.

CASE 14.6

Mona was administered a language arts standardized test at the end of third, fourth, and fifth grades. Illustration 14.41 displays the grade equivalent scores from the three administrations.

Ms. Blanding, the school's principal, shows these scores to Ms. Ortego and asks why Mona was only able to make "5 months' progress" in 9 months of work while Mona had been able to "advance 1 year and 6 months" under Mr. Kitson's tutelage. Ms. Ortego, being more knowledgeable about grade equivalent scores than Ms. Blanding, displays the conversion tables from raw scores to grade equivalents that appear in the test's technical manual, as shown by Illustration 14.42.

Mona's Teacher	Mona's Grade Level	Mona's Grade Equivalent Score
Ms. Swink	3.8	2.4
Mr. Kitson	4.8	4.1
Ms. Ortego	5.8	4.6

ILLUSTRATION 14.41

Mona's Language-Arts Standardized Test Scores for Three Consecutive Years Earlier

Raw Score	Grade Equivalent	Raw Score	Grade Equivalent
30	2.4	49	3.6
31–32	2.5	50	3.7
33	2.6	51	3.8
34	2.7	52	3.9
35	2.8	53	4.0
36	2.9	54	4.1
37	3.0	55–59	4.2
38–39	3.1	60	4.3
40–42	3.2	61–70	4.4
43	3.3	71–79	4.5
44	3.4	80	4.6
45–48	3.5		

ILLUSTRATION 14.42

The Raw Score to Grade Equivalent from the Test Technical Manual Ms. Ortego Showed Ms. Blanding

Ms. Ortego points out that for this test, the "5 month gain" between the 4.1 and 4.6 grade equivalent scores reflects a 26 point difference in raw scores, whereas the "17 month gain" between the 2.4 and 4.1 grade equivalent scores reflects a 24 point difference in raw scores.

Of course, if Ms. Ortego wants to compare Mona's year-to-year progress, she should use scaled scores. In any case, it is unwise to base evaluations of a teacher's effectiveness on standardized test results (Cangelosi, 1991, pp. 11–12, 103–105; Soar, Medley, & Coker, 1983).

In Case 14.7, a teacher attempts to deal with a parent's misconceptions regarding grade equivalent scores.

CASE 14.7

Donna, a student in Mr. Shin's third-grade class, obtains a grade equivalent score of 6.3 on a standardized mathematics test. Donna's mother, Ms. Drickey, engages Mr. Shin in the following conversation:

Ms. Drickey: "Thank you so much for the wonderful work you've been doing with Donna. A grade level score of 6.3—that means you've got her doing sixth-grade math in third grade!"

Mr. Shin: "I'm really pleased with Donna's score on that test. That 6.3 indicates that she scored well above the average of the third-graders who took that test in a national sample."

Ms. Drickey: "So what accommodations will the school be making to move her into sixth-grade mathematics?"

Mr. Shin: "Pardon me; I don't follow your question."

Ms. Drickey: "There's no reason to hold her back now that we know she's capable of doing sixth-grade math. The school has an obligation to accommodate her gift."

Mr. Shin: "I'll make sure she won't be held back. I'll continue to monitor her progress in mathematics as well as in the other subject-content areas so that the third-grade curriculum is right for Donna. I'll continue to engage her in challenging work."

Ms. Drickey: "Oh, so you plan to keep her with you in third grade, but have her work out of a sixth-grade math book."

Mr. Shin: "Donna's score on this mathematics test is very high. But it tested her over math content that's in the third-grade curriculum, not the sixth-grade curriculum. The mathematics curriculum for sixth grade is mainly prealgebra. There was no prealgebra on this test. Donna is just beginning to construct the concept of division with one-digit whole numbers right now. She is very capable in mathematics, language arts, science, social studies, physical education, and citizenship, but she's not yet ready for the sixth-grade curriculum."

Ms. Drickey: "But this was a nationally normed, scientifically developed test, and it says she's capable of sixth-grade math. You people just don't think girls should be pushed in math and science! I'll bet if she were a boy, this school would make sure she reaches her mathematical potential!"

Mr. Shin: "I'd like for you to understand more about this standardized math test Donna took. First of all, it tested Donna on mathematical content that is in the third-grade book, not the sixth-grade book. Her score suggests that she did very well with this third-grade content. In fact, she did so well that according to the standardized test publisher's estimates, her score is about equal to the average of what a group of sixth-graders would have scored if they had taken the test."

Ms. Drickey: "Are you trying to tell me she's not gifted in mathematics?"

Mr. Shin:	"Personally, I believe Donna is gifted in mathematics as well as some other areas. I will continue to help her advance in mathematics and in the other areas as fast as she reasonably can, but she's got more work to do before she's ready for prealgebra."
Ms. Drickey:	"Then why would this test says she's at the 6.3 grade level? That's double third grade."
Mr. Shin:	"It would be easier for me to explain what these test results indicate if we looked at her stanine score of 8. This 8 indicates that on this test she answered many more questions correctly than the average number for third-graders in a large national sample. If we took all the scores and laid them out like this . . ."

Mr. Shin draws the figure shown by Illustration 14.43 for Ms. Drickey to see.

Mr. Shin:	"Donna's score would fall way up here in category 8."
Ms. Drickey:	"But that 8 doesn't mean as much to me as grade level 6.3. It's not nearly as precise."

STANINES

In Case 14.7, Ms. Drickey doesn't perceive *stanine* scores to be nearly as precise as grade equivalent scores. One of the great advantages of *stanines* is that they don't seem to be more precise than they are. No achievement or aptitude test is so valid that small differences in scores are meaningful. To discourage people from making the mistake that the school counselor makes in Case 14.8, stanines were invented.

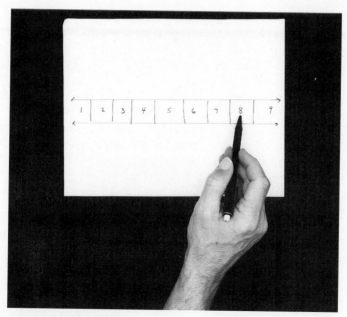

ILLUSTRATION 14.43

Mr. Shin Points to the Interval of a Stanine Scale Where Donna's Raw Score Falls

CASE 14.8

Darnell's raw score on a standardized social studies test converted to a percentile of 53 and a grade equivalent score of 10.0. On the same test, Levi's raw score of 45 converted to the 49th percentile and a 9.8 grade equivalent score. Based on these results, Ms. Benoit, a school counselor, erroneously judges that Darnell's achievement in social studies is more advanced than Levi's.

To encourage people to perceive standardized test scores for what they are—rough comparisons to norm-group scores—raw scores are collapsed into 9 categories or intervals so that each raw score is reported simply as either a "1," "2," . . . , or "9." Raw scores very near the norm-group mean (i.e., μ) are assigned to the middle interval, which is stanine 5. The length of each of the 9 stanine intervals (except for the two most extreme ones) is one-half a norm-group standard deviation (i.e., $\frac{1}{2}\sigma$). The 9 *stanines* are defined as follows:

1. If x_i is a raw score such that $z_{x_i} < -1.75$, then x_i is assigned to stanine 1.
2. If x_i is a raw score such that $-1.75 \leq z_{x_i} < -1.25$, then x_i is assigned to stanine 2.
3. If x_i is a raw score such that $-1.25 \leq z_{x_i} < -0.75$, then x_i is assigned to stanine 3.
4. If x_i is a raw score such that $-0.75 \leq z_{x_i} < -0.25$, then x_i is assigned to stanine 4.
5. If x_i is a raw score such that $-0.25 \leq z_{x_i} < 0.25$, then x_i is assigned to stanine 5.
6. If x_i is a raw score such that $0.25 \leq z_{x_i} < 0.75$, then x_i is assigned to stanine 6.
7. If x_i is a raw score such that $0.75 \leq z_{x_i} < 1.25$, then x_i is assigned to stanine 7.
8. If x_i is a raw score such that $1.25 \leq z_{x_i} < 1.75$, then x_i is assigned to stanine 8.
9. If x_i is a raw score such that $1.75 < z_{x_i}$, then x_i is assigned to stanine 9.

Respond to Illustration 14.44's prompt, and then use the rubric to score your response.

If you want to see the computations leading to the derived scores indicated by Illustration 14.44's rubric, check Illustration 14.45.

In a normal distribution, as the norm-group scores are typically assumed to form, stanines 1 and 9 each contain about 4% of the scores, stanines 2 and 8 each have about 7%, stanines 3 and 7 each have about 12%, stanines 4 and 6 each have about 17%, and stanine 5 has about 20%.

Some standardized test manuals include the suggestion that two students' scores should not be considered significantly different if they are in the same stanine or if they are in adjacent stanines. A raw score that converts to a stanine of 7 may be considered significantly greater than a raw score that converts to a stanine of 5, but it shouldn't be considered significantly greater than a raw score that converts to a stanine of 6.

Illustration 14.46 serves as an indicator of how the scales for different derived scores relate to one another.

INTERPRETING STANDARDIZED TEST SCORES FOR STUDENTS AND THEIR PARENTS

It is no trivial task for you to explain your students' standardized test reports to their parents. How do you help C. Kirby-Lind's parents understand Illustration 14.3 or Sonnet Jacoby's parents understand Illustration 14.36? Here are some suggestions:

- Keep in mind that you are a professional educator who has formal preparation and experience in the interpretation of measurement results. Parents should not be expected to understand them without your guidance—and even with your help, not with the same level of sophistication as you and your professional colleagues. Although you don't want to confuse

Prompt:

Use your calculator or the statistics software package from the CD that accompanies this book to fill in the blanks with the missing derived scores in the following example:

A standardized test is administered concurrently to the following four students who are in the same grade level: Sidna, Daryl, Camille, and Burton. The norms are as follows: $\mu = 83$, $\sigma = 11$. The raw scores are displayed in the table below.

Student	Raw Score	z-Score	Stanine	NCE
Sidna	65	_____	_____	_____
Daryl	68	_____	_____	_____
Camille	81	_____	_____	_____
Burton	103	_____	_____	_____

Rubric:

(Maximum possible score: 24) +1 for each of the following that is indicated by the response:

$z_{65} < 0$, $z_{65} \approx -1.64$, $Stanine_{65} = 2$, $NCE_{65} \approx 15.46$,

$z_{68} < 0$, $z_{68} \approx -1.36$, $Stanine_{68} = 2$, $NCE_{68} \approx 21.36$,

$z_{81} < 0$, $z_{81} \approx -0.18$, $Stanine_{81} = 5$, $NCE_{81} \approx 46.21$,

$z_{103} > 0$, $z_{103} \approx 1.82$, $Stanine_{103} = 9$, $NCE_{65} \approx 88.33$.

ILLUSTRATION 14.44

Conduct This Mini-Experiment with Yourself

parents with a lot of technical jargon, you also shouldn't oversimplify your explanations to the point that parents construct misconceptions in their minds. For example, if in your effort to simplify the meaning of the 29th percentile for Sonnet's father, you say, "Sonnet did better than 29% of those who took the test," instead of, "Sonnet's score on the test was higher than 29% of a nationwide sample of students on whom this test was tried in 1997" (or whenever it was normed). "Sonnet did better" might lead him to generalize about her overall achievement, whereas, "Sonnet's score on the test was higher" might lead him to think of this test as only one data point—which, of course, is all it is. Also the more simplified statement might lead him to think that the test was a competition with other students in Sonnet's class, rather than a comparison to externally established norms.

• As explained in Chapter 3's section "Evaluate Students' Learning, Not Students," avoid characterizing students. Discuss what students have learned and the progress they are or are not making, not how smart they are or are not. Make statements such as, "Sonnet's score in math is higher than the average of the scores from the national sample," rather than, "Sonnet did better than average in math," or even worse, "Sonnet is above average in math."

• Do not equate any single test score to a level of achievement. For example, say, "Sonnet's score on this particular social studies test is about the same as the average of the scores

The following formulas were used in computing the z-score and NCE score for raw score x_i:

$$z_{x_i} = \frac{x_i - \mu_x}{\sigma_x}$$

$$NCE_{x_i} = 21.06 z_{x_i} + 50$$

To convert Sidna's raw score of 65 to z, stanine, and NCE scores:
z_{65} = (65 − 83) ÷ 11 ≈ −1.64. Since −1.75 < −1.64 < −1.25 and z_{65} ≈ −1.64, stanine$_{65}$ = 2. NCE$_{65}$ ≈ (21.06)(−1.64) + 50 ≈ −34.54 + 50 = 15.46.

To convert Daryl's raw score of 68 to z, stanine, and NCE scores:
z_{68} = (68 − 83) ÷ 11 ≈ −1.36. Since −1.75 < −1.36 < −1.25 and z_{68} ≈ −1.36, stanine$_{68}$ = 2. NCE$_{68}$ ≈ (21.06)(−1.36) + 50 ≈ −28.64 + 50 = 21.36.

To convert Camille's raw score of 81 to z, stanine, and NCE scores:
z_{81} = (81 − 83) ÷ 11 ≈ −0.18. Since −0.25 < −0.18 < 0.25 and z_{81} ≈ −0.18, stanine$_{81}$ = 5. NCE$_{81}$ ≈ (21.06)(−0.18) + 50 ≈ −3.79 + 50 = 46.21.

To convert Burton's raw score of 103 to z, stanine, and NCE scores:
z_{103} = (103 − 83) ÷ 11 ≈ 1.82. Since 1.82 > 1.75 and z_{103} ≈ 1.82, stanine$_{103}$ = 9. NCE$_{103}$ ≈ (21.06)(1.82) + 50 ≈ 38.33 + 50 = 88.33.

ILLUSTRATION 14.45

Computation of the Missing Derived Scores from Illustration 14.44

from the national sample," rather than "Sonnet is achieving at a level that is about average in comparison to the national sample."

- Emphasize that results from any single testing should never be used as the sole basis for an evaluation of achievement. Emphasize the influence of measurement error and that standardized tests only touch on a very small part of what students are learning in school.
- Explain why the tests were administered. For example, in Case 14.1, the standardized test battery is administered for the purpose of gathering data that the State Office of Education can use in gauging the effectiveness of schools. The tests aren't really designed to indicate very much about what individual students are learning.
- Rather than trying to explain each type of derived score in the report, explain that for each test, the percentile, NCE, grade equivalent score, stanine, and the others are all different ways of saying the same thing—just as 5 feet, 60 inches, and 1,524 millimeters all indicate the same length. Then select the type of derived score in the report with which you feel most comfortable. Consider making stanines your first choice, percentiles your second choice, and grade equivalent your last choice.

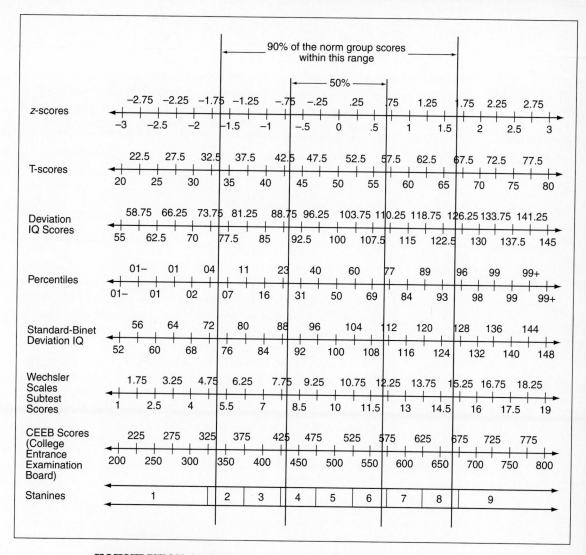

ILLUSTRATION 14.46

Relationship Among Derived Score Scales Commonly Used for Various Standardized Tests

A teacher attempts to incorporate these suggestions in a conference with a parent in Case 14.9.

CASE 14.9

Ms. Hornachek, fifth-grade teacher at Eastridge Elementary School, meets with Catherine and her dad, Mr. Kirby-Lind:

Mr. Kirby-Lind: "Thank you for meeting with us, Ms. Hornachek. We received this in the mail and would like for you to tell us what it means."

Mr. Kirby-Lind displays a copy of the standardized test report shown by Illustration 14.3.

Ms. Hornachek: "I'm pleased to be meeting with you; I have my copy of the scores right here."

Mr. Kirby-Lind: "Does all this mean Catherine is doing okay or what?"

Ms. Hornachek: "Based on my monitoring of what Catherine learns every school day, I believe Catherine is progressing exceptionally well with nearly all of our curriculum goals. Today, for example, she took a major step in discovering how airplanes are able to fly. Catherine, demonstrate how Bernoulli's principle can be applied to an air foil."

Catherine picks up the sheet with the standardized test report from the table and blows over the top of it, causing it to rise.

Catherine: "I made the air over the top of the paper move faster than the air below. That made the air pressure below it to be greater. That's what pushed the paper up."

Mr. Kirby-Lind: "Pretty neat. So that's what keeps those big airplanes from falling out of the sky. What was that principle again?"

Catherine: "Bernoulli's principle. Bernoulli was this scientist and math guy in the 1700s."

Ms. Hornachek: "Catherine's demonstration just gave us a little glimpse of her understanding of one scientific principle and a little about what she remembers from history. These standardized tests Catherine took in April emphasize more of what she remembers than what she understands in depth. Catherine, tell your Dad about some of the questions that were on the test."

Catherine: "I can't remember much about them. I know we had to fill in these little bubbles in these little books. It asked things like, uhh, what's the right word in this sentence and how many cans of paint it would take to do something. I don't know anymore."

Ms. Hornachek: "We've done so many things in class since we took those tests, it's difficult to remember what was asked. I have some examples. Excuse me; let me find them in here."

Ms. Hornachek shows Illustration 14.47 to Mr. Kirby-Lind and Catherine and explains the type of skills the items are intended to measure.

Mr. Kirby-Lind: "What about all these numbers on this report? What do they mean?"

Ms. Hornachek: "These are scores from eight different tests: reading, language, mathematics, word analysis, spelling, study skills, science, and social studies. Let's pick one of the tests and discuss what the scores mean for it."

Mr. Kirby-Lind: "How about reading—that's awfully important."

Ms. Hornachek: "We look across this line of scores for Total Reading, and we see a national stanine score of 6, an NCE score of 66, a scale score of 737, and a national percentile of 67."

Mr. Kirby-Lind: "What about this range 60–74? What is that?"

Ms. Hornachek: "This test, like any test, is not perfectly reliable. That range reminds us that we should not think of these scores as exact numbers, but rather fuzzy estimates of what the scores might be if the test were perfectly valid. The 60–74 suggests that if back in April Catherine had taken this test many times over, that national percentile score would not continue to be exactly 67. But most of the time it would be somewhere between 60 and 74."

Mr. Kirby-Lind: "I thought it might have meant the range of her intelligence."

Ms. Hornachek: "Not at all. This was not an intelligence test. It's just supposed to sample learning in a few very basic subject areas."

```
    I:   The dark sky threatened us with rain.
    II:  The storm is now beginning.
```

23.   The subject of Sentence I is _____
      A)   sky threatened
      B)   The dark sky
      C)   with rain
      D)   threatened with rain

24.   Which word in these sentences is an adjective?
      A)   beginning
      B)   with
      C)   now
      D)   dark

25.   If Sentence II is changed to a yes/no question, which word will
      come first?
      A)   is
      B)   the
      C)   storm
      D)   beginning

ILLUSTRATION 14.47

Sample Language Test Item Ms. Hornachek Shows Mr. Kirby-Lind and Catherine

Mr. Kirby-Lind: "You said before that the test is not perfectly reliable. Why does the school give Catherine a bad test?"

Ms. Hornachek: "It's not a bad test. But it is very limited in what it is capable of telling us about what Catherine has learned. No test is perfectly reliable; there is error in every test. That's why I measure Catherine's learning throughout the year—not just base evaluations of what she achieves on just a few tests. Eastridge School administers this standardized test battery because we're required to do so by legislative mandate. The legislature requires the State Office of Education to use these test results as an indicator of how schools across the state are doing in comparison to schools across the country. But let's get back to what these individual scores are supposed to mean. These four different kinds of scores are all different ways of comparing the number of questions Catherine answered correctly to the average number of correct answers from a national sample of students that took this test back in 1993."

Mr. Kirby-Lind: "Shouldn't her achievement be compared to today's standards?"

Ms. Hornachek: "That's a question that would take another half-hour conference to address. I have another conference scheduled in 16 minutes so let's save that question for another time."

Mr. Kirby-Lind: "Oh, I'm sorry. You were saying all these scores mean the same thing."

Ms. Hornachek: "No need to apologize; you raised a great question that needs to be discussed when we have more time to do so. Anyway, since all four of these scores tell us the same thing, let's pick on one and interpret it. This stanine of 6 indicates that on this reading test, the number of questions Catherine answered correctly was somewhat greater than the average number answered by the national sample of students."

Mr. Kirby-Lind: "So she's an above average reader?"

Ms. Hornachek: "I never think of my students in those terms. All these reading scores mean is that on this particular reading test, Catherine got more answers correct than the average of the sample. These stanine scores are on a 9-point scale with 5 being right around the average of the sample group and 6 being somewhat higher than the average; 7, of course, would be even higher; 4 would be slightly lower than the average of the scores. We might expect these numbers to be more precise than that, but they really aren't. We shouldn't make them out to be more than they are."

Mr. Kirby-Lind: "The last time we met, we went through Catherine's portfolio. That told me a lot more about what she's learning."

Ms. Hornachek: "I agree. On the other hand, these standardized tests do serve as a little check-point for schools."

The conference continues with the scores for each of the other tests being discussed briefly.

In Case 14.9, Ms. Hornachek briefly addressed Mr. Kirby-Lind's question about the "range 60–47." As she suggested, that interval (which is also reflected by the bars extending the per-centile scores in Illustration 14.3's chart) is a function of measurement error due to imperfect measurement reliability. From your work with Chapter 16, "Examining Reliability of Mea-surements," you will learn to compute error ranges and better understand what Ms. Hornachek tried to explain to Mr. Kirby-Lind about measurement error.

USES AND ABUSES OF STANDARDIZED TESTS

Because of their experiences attempting to interpret standardized test reports as Ms. Hornachek did in Case 14.9, Eastridge School teachers decided to conduct an annual schoolwide meeting with a large group of parents to discuss some of the more general issues related to systemwide testing programs. The teachers believe that by having such a meeting just prior to the confer-ences with individual parents, the conferences might proceed more efficiently and be less likely to get sidetracked with general issues (e.g., "Shouldn't her achievement be compared to today's standards?"). Case 14.10 is an account of one brief exchange during one such meeting.

CASE 14.10

Ms. Sedress: "Just how good are these standardized tests we're giving our children? Are they valid?"

Ms. Hornachek: "Allow me to try to address the question by asking you a question. Do you think that there are times when we should have our temperatures taken, like when we see our physicians for checkups?"

Ms. Sedress: "Sure."

Ms. Hornachek: "Then do you think measuring body temperature is a valid measure?"

Ms. Sedress: "I've always thought so."

Ms. Hornachek: "What if you went to your doctor for a checkup and she had her nurse take your temperature, resulting in a score of 98.6°? Based on that test score only, your doctor declared you to be disease-free, healthy, and very fit. How valid do you think the temperature test is now?"

Ms. Sedress: "That would be ridiculous. Having a normal temperature doesn't rule out most diseases, like cancer. Even if my temperature were elevated, it would only indicate the possibility that I have an infection; that suggests a need for further tests—such as analyzing a blood sample—to pinpoint the cause of the elevated temperature."

Ms. Hornachek: "So you're telling us that taking your temperature is only valid for a very limited purpose, like to help decide whether to conduct further tests for a possible infection. There are a myriad of other health-related factors to which taking one's temperature is not relevant."

Ms. Sedress: "Right, it's valid for the one thing but not others."

Ms. Hornachek: "The analogy works when we address the question about the validity of various standardized achievement tests. They are valid only for very limited purposes, like to compare two large groups relative to some very general skills. The standardized tests themselves aren't bad, but what is bad is misusing them to make evaluations about questions for which they are not relevant.

From Illustration 14.2, please reread the nine points listed in Mr. Halifia's memo. They should be more meaningful to you now than they were when you first read them.

SYNTHESIS ACTIVITIES FOR CHAPTER 14

1. For each of the multiple-choice prompts, select the one best response that either answers the question or completes the statement:

   A. If a test has been standardized, then it _____.
      a) has been field-tested
      b) is valid
      c) is usable
      d) is an aptitude test

   B. Results of aptitude tests are used to _____.
      a) make summative evaluations of achievement
      b) predict subsequent performances
      c) diagnose learning gaps
      d) assess mastery
      e) measure attitudes

   C. Suppose you examine the items on two different levels of the same standardized achievement test. Which one of the following would you expect to discover about the two levels of the test?
      a) They are relevant to different subject-content areas (e.g., one includes items on mathematics, the other on social studies).
      b) The items on one are relevant to more advanced subject-content than the items on the other.
      c) The items on one are relevant to higher cognitive-learning levels than the items on the other.
      d) The two levels are equivalent forms of the same test.

   D. Standardized achievement tests are best suited for providing data for _____.
      a) comparing the achievement of one large group to that of another
      b) determining which individual students have achieved and which have not
      c) diagnosing individual differences among students
      d) evaluating learning capabilities

E. Sue's report from a standardized achievement test battery includes the following results for the science subtest: National percentile → 53; Local percentile → 48. Which one of the following can tenably be deduced from those two scores?

  a) The national level of the test is harder than the local level.

  b) The local level of the test is harder than the national level.

  c) The median of the raw scores from the national norm group is greater than that from the local norm group.

  d) The median of the raw scores from the local norm group is greater than that from the national norm group.

F. Heidi's and Will's raw scores from a standardized test are 33 and 29 respectively. Which one of the following values for the norm-group standard deviation provides the best opportunity for the two scores to be converted to the same stanine?

  a) 18.4

  b) 11.3

  c) 8.9

  d) 7.5

G. Different levels of the same standardized test differ in several ways, including which one of the following?

  a) subject-content area (e.g., one social studies, the other English)

  b) geographical locations from which norm groups are drawn

  c) norms for comparing scores

  d) types of derived scores used to report the results

H. Most standardized achievement tests tend to emphasize which one of the following combinations of learning levels?

  a) construct-a-concept and discover-a-relationship

  b) creativity, appreciation, and process-knowledge

  c) creativity, comprehension-and-communication-skills, and discover-a-relationship

  d) simple-knowledge, process-knowledge, and comprehension-and-communication-skills

I. Michael's percentile score on a standardized test is 81. Which one of the following is an accurate conclusion?

  a) Michael's raw score is 19% lower than the mean of the norm group raw scores.

  b) Michael's raw score is lower than 19% of those who took the test with Michael.

  c) Michael missed 19% of the items.

  d) Michael's achievement level is 81% higher than the norm group standard

  e) Michael's raw score is greater than 81% of the raw scores from the norm group.

J. Paul took a standardized science test with his tenth-grade class in December and received a stanine score of 4. Three months later he took the same standardized science test again and received a stanine score of 3. All except one of the following is a possible explanation for the difference in the two stanines. Which one is *not* a possible explanation?

  a) The raw score Paul obtained the first time was compared to a different mean and standard deviation than was the raw score he obtained the second time.

  b) The test lacks perfect test-retest reliability.

  c) The test lacks relevance to the specific objectives Paul's teacher targeted in class.

  d) Paul took a higher level of the test the second time than he did the first.

K. Test X and Test Y both measure affective behaviors. However, Test Y measures an opinion that is more controversial than the opinion measured by Test X. Which one of the following would you anticipate about data from the two tests?

  a) $\mu_X > \mu_Y$.

  b) $\mu_X < \mu_Y$.

  c) $\sigma_X > \sigma_Y$.

  d) $\sigma_X < \sigma_Y$.

L. Which one of the following types of derived scores is *not* conducive to arithmetic operations?
   a) scaled scores
   b) NCEs
   c) T-scores
   d) z-scores
   e) grade equivalent scores

M. The norms for a standardized test are as follows: $\mu = 33.41$ and $\sigma = 9.2$. Approximately what is z_{40}?
   a) 0.72
   b) 1.04
   c) 1.24
   d) 2.92
   e) 6.59

N. The norms for a standardized test are as follows: $\mu = 33.41$ and $\sigma = 9.2$. In what stanine does a raw score of 40 on that test fall?
   a) 2
   b) 3
   c) 4
   d) 5
   e) 6

O. If $NCE_{28} = 46$, then which one of the following must be true?
   a) $z_{28} > 0$
   b) $z_{28} < 0$
   c) $z_{28} = 0$

P. If $NCE_{28} = 46$, then which one of the following must be true?
   a) $Stanine_{28} = 4$
   b) $Stanine_{28} = 5$
   c) $Stanine_{28} = 6$

Q. If $NCE_{28} = 46$, then which one of the following must be true?
   a) $z_{28} \approx -0.28$
   b) $z_{28} \approx -0.19$
   c) $z_{28} = 0$
   d) $z_{28} \approx 0.19$
   e) $z_{28} \approx 0.28$

2. With a colleague, compare and discuss your responses to the multiple-choice prompts from Synthesis Activity 1. Also, check your choices against the following key: A-a, B-b, C-b, D-a, E-d, F-a, G-c, H-d, I-e, J-c, K-d, L-e, M-a, N-e, O-b, P-b, and Q-b.

3. Below is a list of statements made by parents; each reflects a misconception about standardized tests. With a colleague, discuss how you would respond to each of these erroneous statements as if it was made to you by one of your students' parents.

A. "You said these stanines are on a 9-point scale. Since Ronald got a stanine of 6, he only got 6 out of every 9 right."

B. "Since my Erica got a 4.3 grade equivalent score in reading, you should start her on some fourth-grade readers even though she is going to stay in second grade."

C. "According to this grade equivalent score, Salvador is over 9 months behind. I think we should put him back a grade."

D. "I averaged out the percentiles for these subtests and it comes to 50.32. So I guess we can say he's above average."

E. "I don't understand how Jamali could be getting A's and B's from you and then be getting only 60 percentile. You have to get 70% to pass."

F. "I guess my girl is just an overachiever. She gets practically all A's in school but is below average on these real tests of her achievement. I guess hard work pays off even if you don't have the aptitude."

G. "These scores say Andrew is way above the average of the class. Yet you gave him a D!"

4. In a discussion with two or more colleagues, address the following question:

> Sandra and Bernice took the same biology test. Sandra's raw score is 73, Bernice's 65. From the standpoint of conventional statistical models, the difference between their two scores doesn't seem particularly important or significant. However, Rocky and Blanton took an art test and obtained raw scores of 73 and 65 respectively. From the standpoint of conventional statistical models, the difference does seem particularly important or significant. What might be different about the entire set of biology test scores as compared to the entire set of art test scores that would cause the difference between 73 and 65 to be considered "big" in one case but not in the other?

5. In a discussion with two or more colleagues, address the following question:

> Audrey took a standardized mathematics test with her eighth-grade class in December and received a stanine score of 6. She took the exact same level of the exact same test the following May. This time her stanine score is 4. Her teacher remarks, "I don't understand why Audrey's score dropped! Before sending the papers away to be scored, I looked at her answers, and she seemed to do at least as well the second time as she did the first. What's going on here?"

What might have caused the "drop" if, in fact, Audrey performed as well on the test in May as she did in December?

6. Get together with three colleagues. Have one of your colleagues role-play one of your student's parents, Ms. Twyman, with whom you will be engaging in a conference for the purpose of interpreting Illustration 14.48's standardized test score report. Have a second colleague play the role of the student, Corina Twyman. Plan for the conference, keeping in mind the suggestions from this chapter's section "Interpreting Standardized Test Scores for Students and Their Parents." Hold the conference while your fourth colleague videotapes it. Afterwards, use the videotape recording to analyze how and what you communicated. Discuss with your colleagues how you adhered to the suggestions.

Pupil Profile for Corina Twyman	Grade Level: 8.2			
	Language	Math	Social Studies	Science
National Percentile	78	55	71	49
Local Percentile	72	51	66	41
Nat. Grade Equivalent	9.9	8.2	9.0	8.2
Scaled Score	566	540	551	494
National Stanine	7	5	6	5
Local Stanine	6	5	6	5

ILLUSTRATION 14.48

Corina Twyman's Scores from a Standardized Test Battery

7. With a colleague, discuss why Illustration 14.6's score report is designed for criterion-referenced summative evaluations of achievement, whereas Illustration 14.48's is designed for norm-referenced summative evaluations of achievement.

TRANSITIONAL ACTIVITY FROM CHAPTER 14 TO CHAPTER 15

In a discussion with two or more of your colleagues, address the following questions:

1. What are some strategies we can employ to assess the relevance of the measurements we design?

2. If we design a test for a research or evaluation study or one that will be used systemwide, how should we assess its relevance before it is used?

3. How can we assess the relevance of a commercially produced or standardized test prior to recommending whether or not it should be used in our schools?

Examining the Relevance of Measurements

✎ GOAL OF CHAPTER 15

Chapter 15 is intended to lead you to develop strategies for conducting the initial stage of a measurement validation study: assessing relevance. More specifically, the objectives are as follows:

A. You will explain why measurement validation studies are conducted (comprehension and communication skills) 10%.

B. You will list the three questions addressed by measurement validation studies (simple knowledge) 02%.

C. You will explain why measurements that you design by employing systematic methods described in Chapter 6 are relevant (comprehension and communication skills) 20%.

D. Given a goal defined by a set of weighted objectives within your own teaching specialty and a measurement, you will assess the relevance of the measurement with respect to the learning goal (application) 25%.

E. Given a measurement designed for use in your own teaching specialty, you will assess to what subject-contents and learning levels that measurement is relevant (application) 25%.

F. In general terms, you will describe the steps by which formal studies of measurement relevance are conducted (comprehension and communication skills) 15%.

G. You will incorporate the following technical phrases into your professional vocabulary: "measurement validation study" and "think aloud trial" (comprehension and communication skills) 03%.

MEASUREMENT VALIDATION STUDIES

A *measurement validation study* is a systematic effort to assess the validity of a particular measurement. Given a specific decision or evaluation to be made, a study of the validity of a measurement addresses the following question: To what degree does this measurement provide *reliable* results that are *relevant* to making the decision or evaluation?

Why would you ever need to conduct a measurement validation study? Cases 15.1 through 15.5 are examples of situations in which measurement validation studies are needed.

CASE 15.1

You have just designed and administered a measurement for the purpose of making a summative evaluation of how well students have achieved the goal that you defined by a set of weighted objectives. But before you make your evaluations, you question the degree to which the evaluations should be influenced by the results of this measurement. To answer that question, you need to assess the error of the measurement. You decide to conduct a measurement validation study in order to assess measurement error.

CASE 15.2

The package of "supplemental materials for teachers" provided by the publisher of the textbook you use with one of your classes includes a set of "unit tests." To help you decide whether or not to administer one of these test instruments to your students, you assess the validity of that test.

CASE 15.3

You are part of a team of teachers who are responsible for developing a systemwide test for your school district. As you design mini-experiments for the measurement (i.e., test items) and the measurement blueprint, you conduct field tests to find out what works and what doesn't work. Results from the field tests help guide how you and your colleagues make improvements in the mini-experiments as well as the blueprint. After the measurement is developed, you assess its error so that measurement error estimates can be considered in the interpretation of the results.

CASE 15.4

You are part of a statewide committee that has been asked to make a recommendation regarding the selection of a standardized test battery. You base your recommendation on assessments of how the test batteries compare with regard to validity and usability.

CASE 15.5

For your master's thesis project, you are comparing the effects of two teaching methods, Method A and Method B. Both methods target the same learning goal. You develop a measurement of achievement of that goal, which you plan to administer to a group of students that was instructed by Method A and to another group that was instructed by Method B. You want to use the measurement results to compare μ_A to μ_B. But before you use the results, your thesis committee requires you to assess the validity of the measurement to determine if it is "good enough" to be used in the study. You plan to include the results of the validation in your final thesis report. Thus, readers of your published results will be able to consider measurement error in their own interpretations of your findings.

Re-examine Illustration 4.7. Obviously, a measurement validation study should examine the relevance and reliability of the measurement in question. How to assess relevance is the focus of this chapter. Chapter 16 deals with the assessment of reliability. But besides relevance and reliability, some situations require measurement validation studies that examine a third aspect of a measurement: the effectiveness of the individual mini-experiments from which the measurement is built. Chapter 17, "Examining the Effectiveness of Mini-Experiments," deals with that topic.

THE CASE FOR RELEVANCE OF A MEASUREMENT YOU DESIGNED

From your work with Chapters 5 and 6, you developed a procedure for designing and synthesizing relevant measurements. The procedure includes the following steps:

1. Define the learning goal to which the measurement is supposed to be relevant with a set of weighted objectives.

2. Develop a blueprint specifying, among other features, how the measurement's points should be distributed according to how you weighted the objectives.
3. Follow the blueprint to build the measurement from relevant mini-experiments from your computerized folder.
4. Administer the measurement.
5. Use the mini-experiments' rubrics to score students' responses and compile the measurement results.

By following the blueprint, you select mini-experiments from your computerized files and adjust point values so that objectives are emphasized according to their relative importance for goal achievement. This procedure practically guarantees that your measurement will be relevant, providing that one critically essential condition has been met:

> The mini-experiments you draw from your computerized folder are themselves relevant to the objectives.

That, of course, is a huge, not-so-easy-to-come-by condition. You've already worked with Chapters 7–13 to develop your talents for designing relevant mini-experiments—a talent you'll continue to foster through practice, reflective teaching, and experimentation.

To assess the relevance of a measurement you designed yourself, you need to verify that you employed the five-step procedure explained in Chapter 6 and that each of the measurement's mini-experiments matches the learning level and subject-content specified by its objective. In other words, if you are conducting the validation study alluded to in Case 15.1, the first and most difficult stage of the study (i.e., assessing relevance) is automatically completed if (1) you followed the five-step procedure, and (2) you are convinced that the mini-experiments are reasonably relevant.

Of course, if you are conducting the study for not only your benefit but for the benefit of other users of the measurement (as would be true in Cases 15.3 and 15.5), then you need to formally document that you followed the five-step procedure, and you need to have other experts besides yourself judge the relevance of the mini-experiments. Case 15.6 is an example.

CASE 15.6

In Cases 2.3 and 2.4, Ms. Fisher developed a U.S. history unit on the civil rights movement. Since conducting the unit, she has thought about the value of the simulated-segregated-society activity she used as part of the lesson for Objective A, as listed in Illustration 2.9. For her master's thesis project, she decides to compare the following two groups of students relative to their achievement of the unit's goal:

A. A group of students who experience the unit that includes the simulated-segregated-society activity.
B. A group of students who experience a similar unit but in which the simulated-segregated-society activity is supplanted by more traditional activities (e.g., viewing videotapes on and discussing the consequences of segregation).

Because the test she previously developed for that unit (see Illustrations 2.28 and 2.30) included prompts in which students had to reflect back on the simulated-segregated-society activity, she needs to develop a new measure of the unit's goal—one that could be used with both groups of students in her planned research study. Thus, her research proposal includes a section titled "Measurement Development and Validation Procedures." In this section, she indicates that she will (1) develop or select relevant mini-experiments for the measurement, and (2) follow the five-step procedure explained in Chapter 6 to synthesize the measurement. But since she will need to demonstrate for her thesis committee that the measurement is relevant, she includes the following additional steps that she would not ordinarily take for a measurement that does not have to be approved by anyone other than herself:

1. She has a panel of four experts (consisting of two other U.S. history teachers from the local schools, an educational measurement specialist from the university, and a social science education specialist from the university) to judge the relevance of the files of mini-experiments from which she plans to build the test.
2. In light of the panel's judgment, she decides which mini-experiments should be modified, which should be eliminated from consideration, and finally which should be included on the measurement.
3. She carefully documents that she, in fact, does follow the five-step procedure when synthesizing the test. Her final report will include a careful description of exactly how she followed the procedures and how the test was administered to both groups.

Using procedures with which you will become familiar when you work with Chapters 16 and 17, she also plans to field test the measurement in order to assess its reliability and the effectiveness of individual mini-experiments.

ASSESSING THE RELEVANCE OF AN EXISTING MEASUREMENT INSTRUMENT

A SYSTEMATIC ANALYSIS

To assess the relevance of an existing measurement instrument, you need to compare what it actually measures to what it is supposed to measure. How well do the mini-experiments pertain to the subject-contents and learning levels specified by the objectives? How closely does the distribution of points reflect how the objectives are weighted? In Case 15.7, a teacher is very systematic in the way he addresses those two questions.

CASE 15.7

Mr. Cocora defines the goal of one of the units for his eighth-grade consumer-education class with the following weighted objectives:

A. Students associate words and phrases commonly used in the selling of products (e.g., "sales tax" and "discount") with their respective definitions (simple knowledge) 10%.
B. Students accurately interpret the meaning of store advertisements and other commonly exhibited messages dealing with prices and sales (comprehension and communication skills) 20%.
C. Given a sequence of arithmetic operations for computing a sales-related figure (e.g., sales tax or discounted price), students accurately execute the computation (process knowledge) 20%.
D. When confronted with a purchase-related problem, students determine the sequence of arithmetic computations that help them solve the problem (application) 50%.

As a source of information to help him evaluate his students' achievement of the goal prior to the unit, he considers using the "Unit Test" included in the textbook publisher's package that is shown by Illustration 15.1.

Mr. Cocora thinks, "A test with only 10 multiple-choice items can hardly be a reliable measure of anything. But maybe if this test is reasonably relevant, I can make some use of it." From one of his computer files, he pulls up and prints out the form shown by Illustration 15.2.

He begins examining the 10 prompts, one at a time, asking himself, "To which, if any, of my four objectives is this item relevant?" His familiarity with how his students tend to think and the curriculum

CONSUMER EDUCATION TEST OVER CHAPTER 7

Name _____

Multiple-Choice: For each item, circle the letter in front of the answer.

1. A basketball has a price tag marked $32.97. There is a 4% sales tax on the ball. What does this mean?

   A. The store keeps only 97% of the $32.97 and pays 4% of the $32.97 to the government.
   B. In addition to the $32.97, a customer must pay 4% of $32.97. This additional amount goes to the government.
   C. The customer deducts 4% of the $32.97 from his/her income tax.
   D. The customer pays 2% of $32.97 and the store pays 2% of $32.97 to the government.

2. A store advertises a "dollar off on all CDs." What does this mean?

   A. The store profits $1 on each CD sold.
   B. The customer pays $1 per CD.
   C. The store raised the price of its CDs $1 over its usual retail price.
   D. The store is charging $1 less than it usually charges for a CD.

3. What is meant by a store's mark-up on a product?

   A. The amount of sales tax it pays for the product.
   B. The amount it pays for the product.
   C. The difference between the retail price for the product and the actual price the customer pays after sales tax.
   D. The difference between what the customer pays and the store pays for the product.

4. $7 + (14 - 8) \times 3 =$ _____

   A. 25   B. 39   C. 27   D. 37

5. 15% of $183 is _____

   A. $12.25   B. $274.50   C. $27.45   D. $122.50

ILLUSTRATION 15.1

"Unit Test" Included in Mr. Cocora's Supplemental Materials for Teachers Provided by the Textbook Publisher

(Continued)

ILLUSTRATION 15.1 (Continued)

---

6. 44 is 6% of what?

   A. 77.33   B. 26.40   C. 264.00   D. 733.33

7. $13.84 + .05 × $13.84 = _____

   A. $192.24   B. $14.53   C. $27.68   D. $138.40

8. A store advertises 15% off on a product that regularly
   sells for $75. Sales tax is 2%. What will the product cost
   the customer?

   A.   (15 × 75) + (.02 × 75)
   B.   (.85 × 75) + (.02 × 75)
   C.   (.85 × 75) + (.02 × (.85 × 75))
   D.   (75 × .02) + 75 - .15

9. A store pays $20 for a product which it sells for $27. Sales tax
   on the product is 2%. What is the store's mark-up on the product?

   A. $27.00   B. $20.00   C. $13.50   D. $7.00

10. A newspaper ad says that cars at Willie's Used Car Lot "start at
    $300." This means that at Willie's Used Car Lot _____

    A.   no car sells for less than $300.
    B. $300 is the most a customer will be charged for a car.
    C.   most cars sell for about $300.
    D.   None of the above.

    _____

Teacher's Scoring Key:

     1-B, 2-D, 3-D, 4-A, 5-C, 6-D, 7-B, 8-C, 9-D, 10-A

---

to which they've been exposed influence his judgments about learning-level relevance. For Item #1, he imagines himself in the role of one of his students, reads the stem and alternatives, and chooses "B." Then he thinks, "To select the correct alternative, I had to remember the meaning of 'price' and 'sales tax.' That's indicative of my achievement of Objective A. But also I had to go beyond just that simple-knowl-edge level in order to interpret the meanings in the context of the example described in the item's stem. This prompt stimulated me to operate at the comprehension-and-communication-skills level with these sales-related terms. That's Objective B. Achievement of Objective B depends on achievement of Objec-tive A. Although Item #1 is related to Objective A, it requires comprehension-level thinking. I judge it to be relevant to Objective B." He then writes "#1" in Row B under "Items" on Illustration 15.2's form.

He goes through the same process with Item #2 and decides that it is also relevant to Objective B. Thus, he writes "#2" right next to "#1" in Row B.

After working through Item #3, he thinks, "The stem prompted me to simply remember the defini-tion of 'mark-up'; that would make Item #3 relevant to Objective A if only there was a correct alterna-tive. But the supposed correct response, 'D,' is not worded properly. Other items, like #1, include sales

Relevance Assessment Form

Objective	Items	Actual Weight	Desired Weight	Comments
A				
B				
C				
D				
other				

Interpretation

ILLUSTRATION 15.2

Form Mr. Cocora Uses in Systematically Assessing the Relevance of Illustration 15.1's Test Instrument

tax in the 'amount the customer pays.' Alternative D, doesn't take sales tax into account. That's not really the right definition for mark-up. I'd better see if that's the way the definition is worded in the textbook. Let's see. Go to the index . . . page 37 . . . yep, right here the book defines mark-up as 'the difference between what the customer pays and the store pays for a product.' So, Item #3 is relevant to Objective A if that's the definition I want them to remember. But it isn't, so for my purposes, I should classify Item #3 in the 'other' category." On the form, he writes "#3" in the "other" row under "Items."

In a similar fashion, he works through and analyzes the other seven items. Illustration 15.3 reflects how he associated the 10 test items with his four objectives.

Mr. Cocora computes the percentage of the test's points devoted to each objective and then compares those percentages to the weights he previously assigned to objectives. He completes the form so that it now appears as shown by Illustration 15.4.

ITEM-BY-ITEM EXAMINATION
Content and Learning-Level Relevance

Assessing relevance is the most difficult phase of a measurement validation study, and judging the relevance of individual mini-experiments is the most difficult aspect of assessing relevance. How well you are able to judge content relevance depends on your own command of the subject-content area to which the measurement is supposed to be relevant. Your judgment of learning-level relevance depends not only on your expertise with the subject-content but also on your (1) familiarity with how the students think, (2) familiarity with their backgrounds, (3) expertise with Chapter 5's advanced organizer for specifying subject-contents and learning levels, and (4) expertise applying fundamental measurement principles (e.g., from your work with Chapters 4–13).

Relevance Assessment Form

Objective	Items	Actual Weight	Desired Weight	Comments
A				
B	#1, #2, #10			
C	#4, #5, #6, #7			
D	#8, #9			
other	#3			

Interpretation

ILLUSTRATION 15.3

Mr. Cocora Associates the Items from Illustration 15.1's Test with His Four Objectives

Relevance Assessment Form

Objective	Items	Actual Weight	Desired Weight	Comments
A		00%	10%	More points needed
B	#1, #2, #10	30%	20%	Too high, but close
C	#4, #5, #6, #7	40%	20%	Much too high
D	#8, #9	20%	50%	Much too low
other	#3	10%	00%	Item needs to be modified

Interpretation

Only 1 item is not relevant to any of the objectives and that item, #3, can be easily modified (by replacing Alternative D with a correct definition) so that it is relevant to Objective A. If that were done, the actual and desired weights for Objective A would match. The most significant mismatch is regarding Objective D. To be relevant to the goal, the test needs more emphasis on application-level achievement. If two of the items relevant to Objective C were replaced by two items relevant to Objective D and one of Objective D's items was replaced by an item relevant to Objective D, the actual weights would match the desired weights.

ILLUSTRATION 15.4

Mr. Cocora's Completed Form

In Case 15.7, Mr. Cocora's expertise in these areas was taxed as he examined each item to judge for which, if any, of the four objectives it is relevant. Of course, Illustration 15.1's 10-item test is much simpler than many of the measurement instruments for which you need to assess relevance. Naturally, you further develop your talent for assessing the relevance of mini-experiments with experience. You will gain some experience from your engagement in the synthesis activities near the end of this chapter.

Think-Aloud Trials

Throughout your work with this book, you've encountered cases of students responding to prompts with reasoning patterns that were unanticipated by the teachers who designed the mini-experiments. Cases 8.7 through 8.13 are examples. In Case 8.13, Ms. Bung-Lee refined a mini-experiment for subsequent use after hearing Pace's description of the thinking he used to respond to the prompt. Sometimes consider incorporating *think-aloud trials* in the item-by-item examination phase of an assessment of relevance. Case 15.8 is an example of a teacher using this strategy.

CASE 15.8

To help her assess the relevance of some of the items from a reading comprehension subtest from one of the older editions of the *Stanford Achievement Tests*, Ms. Kromenhoek interviews some of her students as she presents the prompts shown by Illustration 15.5.

Ms. Kromenhoek asks Noelani to read the paragraph. When Noelani is finished, she directs her as follows: "Noelani, I would like for you to choose the right answer to number 12 right here. But as you do, I would like for you to do your thinking out loud so I can learn what goes through your mind as you decide on the answer. Just speak your thoughts as you think them.

Noelani:	"Turpentine, a sweet-smelling liquid, maple syrup, pine needles . . . let's see . . . go back and find the right one in the paragraph. There! 'Turpentine' is in the second line, and there it is again, 'turpentine.' None of the others are in there. So the answer is turpentine, so I shade in the '1.' Did I get it right?"
Ms. Kromenhoek:	"Yes, you did. Explain to me how you decided the answer."
Noelani:	"I just went back over the paragraph. 'Turpentine' was the only one of the choices in it."

Ms. Kromenhoek thinks to herself, "So rather than operating at the comprehension-and-communication-skills level to select the correct alternative, Noelani used process-knowledge-level learning to go back and hunt for the word in the paragraph. The distractors in the prompt need to include words from the paragraph also, so students can't respond correctly simply by using Noelani's strategy without having to comprehend the paragraph's message. Based on this trial with Noelani, this item seems to be at the process-knowledge rather than the comprehension-and-communication-skills level."

Ms. Kromenhoek also conducts a think-aloud trial for Item 12 with another student, Sharone. From prior work with Sharone and Noelani, Ms. Kromenhoek believes that Sharone's reading comprehension skills are more advanced than Noelani's and that Sharone tends to use divergent reasoning more than most students. After reading the paragraph, Sharone thinks aloud as follows:

Sharone:	"Hmm . . . it says turpentine is a valuable product you get from pine trees, but it doesn't really say the trees are a valuable source of turpentine. That's not the same thing. I don't know if pine needles are a valuable product, but I bet pine trees are the best source of pine needles. This is kind of a trick question. If you don't read it good, you pick 'turpentine,' but the right answer is 'pine needles.' So I color in this '4' here."

Ms. Kromenhoek thinks to herself, "Wow, I never thought of it like that. Sharone is perfectly right. Sharone's sophisticated reading-comprehension and reasoning skills led him to select a more logical alternative than the one in the answer key. This item needs to be modified."

DIRECTIONS: (1) Read the paragraph. (2)Choose the word or phrase that best completes the selection or that best answers the question about the paragraph. (3) Look at the answer spaces at the right.
(4) Fill in the space which has the same number as the answer you have chosen.

From the longleaf pine, which grows abundantly in the southern United States, the valuable product turpentine is obtained during the spring by cutting and scarring the trunks of the trees. The sap which runs from the cuts is collected, placed in copper stills, and heated until the lighter products are driven off as vapors. These are condensed by means of cold water to "spirits of turpentine," which when pure is a colorless liquid with a penetrating, aromatic odor and a bitter, burning taste. "Spirits of turpentine," can be purchased in many hardware, art, drug, and even grocery stores and has several household uses as well as the main commercial use in thinning paint.

12. Longleaf pine trees are a valuable source of

     1. turpentine
     2. a sweet-smelling liquid
     3. maple syrup
     4. pine needles   12. (1)(2)(3)(4)

13. Which one of the following people might be most likely to buy turpentine at a store?

     1. cook
     2. artist
     3. photographer
     4. writer   13. (1)(2)(3)(4)

14. Pure spirits of turpentine

     1. has a sweet taste
     2. has no odor
     3. has a penetrating odor
     4. is brown in color   14. (1)(2)(3)(4)

15. Spirits of turpentine is of greatest value to

     1. farmers
     2. doctors
     3. house painters
     4. sailors   15. (1)(2)(3)(4)

ILLUSTRATION 15.5

Five Prompts from a Reading Comprehension Test with Which Ms. Kromenhoek Experimented Using Think-Aloud Trials

(Continued)

ILLUSTRATION 15.5 (Continued)

```
16. To extract turpentine from trees, it is necessary to

        1.  burn the tree
        2.  boil the wood
        3.  cut down the trees
        4.  break the bark on the trunk      16.  (1)(2)(3)(4)
```

After conducting interviews with Noelani, Sharone, and two other students regarding Items 13–16, Ms. Kromenhoek makes the following judgments:

For Item #13: "Item #13 appears to be at the comprehension-and-communication-skills level. The responses of all four students appeared to depend on how well they comprehended the last sentence."

For Item #14: "Most of the students took the phrase 'pure spirits of turpentine has a penetrating odor' directly from the third sentence and used process-knowledge cognition to select the correct alternative. They picked out those words and selected '3' without needing to comprehend much of anything."

For Item #15: "Three of the four students appeared to use their comprehension skills to select 'house painters.' But once again, Sharone's high-level comprehension and divergent thinking caused him to choose one of the distractors. He reasoned that turpentine is valuable to house painters, but its greatest value is to those who farm pine trees and whose livelihood depends on the sale of turpentine. After all, painters could use water-based paints. So Sharone chose 'farmers.' This item needs to be modified."

For Item #16: "Two students, including Noelani, missed this one, whereas Sharone and another student selected the correct alternative, 'break the bark.' According to my interpretation of their thinking aloud, this item does an excellent job of providing an indicator of how well students comprehend the first two sentences of the paragraph."

Think-aloud trials can be efficiently incorporated with the methods for assessing the effectiveness of individual mini-experiments that you will learn from your work with Chapter 17. Chapter 17's methods help identify which items need to be examined and considered for modification.

Expert Judgments

Mr. Cocora and Ms. Kromenhoek served in the roles of expert judges for the item-by-item examinations in Cases 15.7 and 15.8 respectively. Because of the special circumstances in Case 15.6, Ms. Fisher's judgments were supplemented by those of a panel of experts. You, of course, are the person to make the expert judgments during the item-by-item examination stage of assessments of the relevance of measurements you use with your own students.

COMPARING ACTUAL TO TARGETED WEIGHTS

Once the items are examined and categorized as Mr. Cocora did, as shown by Illustration 15.3, the actual weights are compared to the targeted weights as a basis for judging the relevance of the measurement. Illustration 15.4 reflects the outcome of the process.

ASSESSING TO WHAT A MEASUREMENT IS RELEVANT

You may sometimes find yourself in a situation in which you would like to assess what an existing measurement instrument measures although you do not have a pre-existing set of weighted objectives in mind. Case 15.9 is an example.

CASE 15.9

Ms. Baker, San Marcos High School principal, hands Illustration 15.6's test document to Mr. Doleac, a health science teacher. They engage in the following conversation:

Ms. Baker:	"I just received this first-aid test from some group at the state office. They want our opinion about it. Can you tell me if it's valid?"
Mr. Doleac:	"Valid for what purpose? What is it supposed to measure? Were a set of weighted objectives included with it?"
Ms. Baker:	"They didn't say; no objectives were included."
Mr. Doleac:	"I could field test it to assess its reliability, but relevance depends on what it is used to evaluate. Relevance depends on what it is supposed to measure."
Ms. Baker:	"I'd like to help out these people if possible. What can you do for them?"
Mr. Doleac:	"As I said, I could assess its reliability—but without pre-existing objectives, no one can attest to its relevance. Okay, here's what I'll do. Besides assessing reliability, I could analyze its items and assess to what it is relevant."
Ms. Baker:	"I see what you're saying. You'll identify a set of objectives to which it is relevant."
Mr. Doleac:	"That's the idea. I'll go through it to assess what learning levels it emphasizes and what first-aid-related subject-contents it emphasizes."
Ms. Baker:	"I really appreciate your help."

From his computer file, Mr. Doleac pulls up the form shown by Illustration 15.7. Quickly, he reads through the test document to identify the subject-contents on which various prompts seem to focus. From this initial examination, he lists the subject-area categories on the form, as shown by Illustration 15.8.

He carefully examines each item, asking himself two questions: To what subject-content is this item relevant? To what learning level is this item relevant? He records his judgments to those two questions as indicated by Illustration 15.9. Then he computes the total points the test devotes to each subject-content, as indicated by the second-to-last column of Illustration 15.9. He then converts those numbers to percentages of the total 25 points on the test. The last column of Illustration 15.9 shows those percentages. Thus, he obtains an indication of the relative weight for each subject-content.

Similarly, he computes the total points the test devotes to each learning level, as indicated by the second-to-last row of Illustration 15.9. He then converts those numbers to percentages of the total 25 points on the test. The last row of Illustration 15.9 shows those percentages. Thus, he obtains an indication of the relative weight for each learning level.

Mr. Doleac's report regarding the relevance of the test is displayed by Illustration 15.10.

In Case 15.9, Mr. Doleac used a systematic procedure for assessing the degree to which a measurement emphasized different subject-contents and different learning levels. Such an assessment addresses the following question: For what, if anything, should the measurement be used?

OTHER MODELS FOR EXAMINING RELEVANCE

The models for assessing relevance suggested in this chapter are designed to be useful for you and other classroom teachers. Other models presented in the psychometric literature are

```
FIRST AID TEST — DRAFT DOCUMENT — State Office of Education

                  PART A: WRITTEN RESPONSE

NAME_____DATE_____


I. MULTIPLE CHOICE (one and only one correct response for each. Cir-
cle the letter of your choice. 1 point each.)

  1.  Circulation to an injured area of the body is increased
      by _____ the area.

         a. applying heat to
         b. applying cold to
         c. applying a pressure bandage to
         d. elevating

  2.  The recommended technique for controlling most severe
      bleeding is:

         a. tourniquet
         b. hot pack
         c. cold pack
         d. direct pressure

  3.  A dangerous drop in blood pressure is known as:

         a. contusion
         b. trauma
         c. shock
         d. hemorrhaging

  4.  Contusions are caused by:

         a. shock
         b. sprains
         c. trauma
         d. poor nutrition

  5.  You are bitten by a rattlesnake. You should:

         a. capture the snake and bring it to the hospital.
         b. lie perfectly still to reduce your circulation.
         c. go directly to the hospital.
         d. cut an "X" over the wound and suck out the poison.
```

ILLUSTRATION 15.6

Test Document Ms. Baker Asked Mr. Doleac to Assess

(Continued)

ILLUSTRATION 15.6 (Continued)

6. The greatest danger from most superficial lacerations is:

    a. infection
    b. loss of blood
    c. nerve damage
    d. ligament damage

7. While playing basketball, Nancy turns her right ankle inward. There is pain and swelling. Immediate first aid procedures should include

    a. a bandage putting pressure on the outside of her right ankle.
    b. a bandage putting pressure on the inside of her right ankle.
    c. heat applied to the outside of her right ankle.
    d. heat applied to the inside of her right ankle.

8. While playing basketball, Nancy turns her right ankle inward. There is pain and swelling. Immediate first aid should include

    a. encouraging Nancy to walk and keep the ankle "loose."
    b. sit with her foot down in a bucket of ice.
    c. sit with her foot elevated with an ice pack.
    d. use a "deep heat" rub on the swollen area.

9. You witness a two car accident. There are three victims (all alive) and you are the only person who first arrives on the scene. Victim A lies motionless on the ground with no external injuries except for a mild head laceration. Victim B is conscious and sitting outside of the car bleeding from a severe leg wound. Victim C's breathing is labored and he is pinned by the steering wheel in one car. Victim C is complaining that he "can hardly breathe." Which one of the following would you do <u>first</u>?

    a. call for an ambulance
    b. take notes that would be helpful to the police
    c. attempt to solicit help from passing traffic
    d. administer first aid to the victims

II. Shari is a person who arrives on the scene described in multiple-choice item 9 above.

1. If she decides to administer first aid to the victims, which of the following should she do <u>first</u>?

    _____ (place letter of your choice here)

    a. attempt to wake up victim A
    b. attempt to control victim B's bleeding

ILLUSTRATION 15.6 (Continued)

        c. attempt to help victim C breathe (e.g., by applying
           mouth to mouth resuscitation)

        d. attempt to extract victim C from the automobile

  2. List one of the 4 things given just above that you believe
     Shari should not do at all.

      _____ (place letter here)

III. A friend of yours begins to gag and choke while eating pasta. He
stops breathing. Using 1 page, tell what technique you would use, why
you selected that technique, and describe how you would execute the
procedures of that technique. (5 points: 1 point for selecting a correct technique, 1 point for explaining why, and 1 point for each correct step in the process.)

PART B: PERFORMANCE OBSERVATION
AND PRODUCT EXAMINATION

I. The student is told to apply mouth to mouth artificial resuscitation on the practice dummy while the teacher observes with the following 5-point check sheet:

      _____1. attempts to clear obstructions

      _____2. pinches nose

      _____3. uses proper mouth technique

      _____4. exhales into dummy

      _____5. uses proper inhale/exhale rhythm

II. Each student is directed to apply a pressure bandage for a lateral ankle injury on a partner. The teacher examines each finished
wrap with the following 4-point check sheet:

      _____1. insideout weave

      _____2. not loose

      _____3. not so tight that it cuts off circulation

      _____4. smooth and stable

TEACHER'S RUBRICS OR SCORING KEY

(25 total points)

Items

  A-I (9 points): 1-a, 2-d, 3-c, 4-c, 5-c, 6-a, 7-a, 8-c, 9-d

 A-II (2 points): 1-b, 2-a

A-III (5 points): 1 point for selecting a correct technique,
                     1 point for explaining why, and 1 point for each
                     of 3 correct steps in the process.

  B-I (5 points): 1 point for each of the 5 steps that is
                     correctly executed.

  B-II (4 points): 1 point for each of the four features of the
                     finished wrap.

Subject-content	LEARNING LEVEL										point total	Weight
	simple knowledge	process knowledge	comprehension & com. skills	construct a concept	discover a relationship	application	creativity	appreciation	willingness to try	other		
point total												
weight												

ILLUSTRATION 15.7

Blank Form Mr. Doleac Prints from a Computer File

Subject-content	LEARNING LEVEL										point total	Weight
	simple knowledge	process knowledge	comprehension & com. skills	construct a concept	discover a relationship	application	creativity	appreciation	willingness to try	other		
joint injuries												
lacerations, bleeding, & circulation												
poison												
respiration												
head injuries												
other												
point total												
weight												

ILLUSTRATION 15.8

Mr. Doleac Lists Subject-Contents from His Examination of Illustration 15.6's Test Document

Subject-content	LEARNING LEVEL										point total	Weight
	simple knowledge	process knowledge	comprehension & com. skills	construct a concept	discover a relationship	application	creativity	appreciation	willingness to try	other		
joint injuries	A-I-1	B-II, B-II, B-II,B-II				A-I-7, A-I-8					7	28%
lacerations, bleeding, & circulation	A-I-2, A-I-3, A-I-3		A-I-6			A-II-1					5	20%
poison										A-I-5	1	04%
respiration		A-III, A-III, A-III, B-I, B-I, B-I, B-I, B-I				A-III, A-III					10	40%
head injuries						A-II-2					1	04%
other									A-I-9		1	04%
point total	4	12	1	0	0	6	0	0	1	1	25	
weight	16%	48%	04%	00%	00%	24%	00%	00%	04%	04%		100%

ILLUSTRATION 15.9

The Results of Mr. Doleac's Item-by-Item Examination of Illustration 15.6's Test Document

intended for use with large-scale studies—not for classroom-size populations. These psychometric models use various statistical routines such as factor analysis (e.g., see Kleinbaum, Kupper, & Muller, 1988, pp. 595–641) or cluster analysis (e.g., see Romesburg, 1984). Even with such models that require considerable data analysis, the same types of expert judgments teachers made in Cases 15.6 through 15.9 must be made to decide exactly what subject-content and learning-level variables are being measured.

SYNTHESIS ACTIVITIES FOR CHAPTER 15

1. Select about 10 mini-experiments from the computer files you built as part of your work with Chapters 6–13. Print out the documents for those mini-experiments accompanied by statements of the respective objectives. Have a colleague whose teaching specialty is the same as yours judge the relevance of those mini-experiments. Provide the same professional service for your colleague. Discuss how, if at all, the mini-experiments should be refined.

2. Interview several age-appropriate and grade-appropriate students for the purpose of conducting think-aloud trials with some of the mini-experiments from your computer files. In light of the trials, modify the mini-experiments as you see fit.

3. Obtain a test document that someone other than you designed; it should be intended to be used within your teaching specialty. Use the same procedure employed by Mr. Doleac in Case 15.9 to assess to what the test is relevant.

4. Exchange your work from Synthesis Activity 4 with that of a colleague whose teaching specialty is the same as yours. Discuss your findings as well as points of agreement and disagreement.

San Marcos High School
Faculty Memorandum

To: Marsha Baker, Principal
From: Kordel Doleac, Health Science Dept. $K.\Omega$.
Re.: Assessment of Relevance of First-Aid Test
Date: January 11, 1999

This is a progress report relative to the validity assessment of the First-Aid Test from the State Office committee. Because no objectives were stated, relevance cannot be assessed. However, I examined the items for the purpose of assessing to what the test is relevant. As indicated by the attached chart, my analysis indicates the following:

Regarding the subject-content emphasized by the items:

Relatively heavy emphasis is placed on first-aid for respiratory-distress situations (40% of the total points). To lesser degrees, joint injuries (28%) as well as lacerations, bleeding, and circulation situations (20%) are emphasized. No other first-aid situations are emphasized to a significant degree.

Regarding the learning levels emphasized by the items:

Nearly half the test focuses on process knowledge. About 1/4 of the test emphasizes applications. There is some focus on simple knowledge learning (16% of the total points). No other learning levels are significantly emphasized.

The technical quality of the items is fairly sound with one exception. Item A-I-5, the only one dealing with poisoning, presents an ambiguous prompt and should be modified.

I will be calling on you in a few days to request your help in arranging a field test with about 40 students. I'll use the results of the field test to assess the reliability of the test and the effectiveness of its items.

ILLUSTRATION 15.10

Memorandum Mr. Doleac Sends Ms. Baker Regarding the Relevance of Illustration 15.6's Test

TRANSITIONAL ACTIVITIES FROM CHAPTER 15 TO CHAPTER 16

In a discussion with two or more of your colleagues, address the following questions:

1. What are some strategies we can employ to assess the reliability of measurements?

2. How can measurement error be quantified?

3. What do reliability coefficients indicate about the quality of a measurement, and how can they be used to help us interpret measurement results?

16

Examining the Reliability
of Measurements

⬧ GOAL OF CHAPTER 16

Chapter 16 is intended to lead you to develop strategies for assessing measurement reliability and interpreting measurement results in light of measurement error. More specifically, the objectives are as follows:

A. You will explain how the internal consistency of a measurement is reflected in the measurement's mini-experiments' outcomes matrix (discover a relationship) 15%.

B. You will explain the roles of the following models in the development of useful methods for assessing reliability: test-retest, equivalent forms, split halves, odd-even, adjusted odd-even, and Kuder-Richardson (comprehension and communication skills) 15%.

C. You will explain how correlational statistics are used in the assessment of reliability (comprehension and communication skills) 05%.

D. You will explain the derivation of the standard error of measurement function, including the roles of two operational definitions of reliability (test-retest and ratio), true-score theory, and the central-limit theorem (discover a relationship) 05%.

E. You will assess the internal consistency of the results of measurements you use with your students (application) 20%.

F. You will assess the error of measurements you use with your students (application) 20%.

G. You will assess the observer consistency of measurements you use with your students (application) 15%.

H. You will incorporate the following technical phrases into your professional vocabulary: "mini-experiments," "outcomes matrix," "true score," "observed score," "obtained score," "reliability error," "scatterplot," "correlation coefficient," "test-retest method," "reliability coefficient," "equivalent form method," "split-halves method," "odd-even method," "Spearman-Brown formula," "Kuder-Richardson formulas," and "standard error of measurement" (comprehension and communication skills) 5%.

THE MINI-EXPERIMENTS' OUTCOMES MATRIX

Reread Chapter 4's section "Measurement Reliability" on pages 183–189.

Now we are concerned with developing methods for assessing measurement reliability—internal consistency as well as observer consistency. First, turn your attention to the problem of assessing internal consistency. Illustration 4.4 is a matrix indicating the item-by-item scores of three students on a measurement that included 7 items (i.e., mini-experiments). Illustration 16.1 is a similar matrix, but from a hypothetical 20-item test administered to 30 students. All 20 of

Student i	1	2	3	4	5	6	7	8	9	10	11	12	13	14	15	16	17	18	19	20	(Test Score) x_i
1	1	1	1	1	0	1	1	0	0	1	0	0	0	0	1	0	0	0	0	0	8
2	1	1	1	0	0	1	0	0	0	1	0	0	0	0	0	0	0	0	0	0	5
3	1	1	1	1	0	1	1	0	0	1	0	0	0	0	1	0	0	0	0	0	8
4	0	1	0	0	0	0	0	0	0	0	0	0	0	0	0	0	0	0	0	0	1
5	1	1	1	1	1	1	1	1	1	1	0	1	1	1	1	1	0	0	1	0	16
6	1	1	1	1	0	1	1	0	0	1	0	0	0	0	1	0	0	0	0	0	8
7	1	1	0	0	0	1	0	0	0	1	0	0	0	0	0	0	0	0	0	0	4
8	1	1	1	1	1	1	1	1	1	1	0	1	1	1	1	1	0	0	1	0	16
9	1	1	1	1	1	1	1	1	1	1	1	1	1	1	1	1	1	0	1	1	19
10	1	1	1	1	0	1	1	0	0	1	0	0	0	0	1	0	0	0	0	0	8
11	1	1	1	1	0	1	1	0	1	1	0	1	1	0	1	0	0	0	1	0	12
12	1	1	1	1	0	1	1	0	1	1	0	0	0	0	1	0	0	0	0	0	9
13	1	1	1	1	0	1	1	0	1	1	0	1	0	0	1	0	0	0	0	0	10
14	1	1	0	0	0	1	0	0	0	1	0	0	0	0	0	0	0	0	0	0	4
15	1	1	1	1	0	1	1	0	1	1	0	1	1	0	1	0	0	0	1	0	12
16	0	0	0	0	0	0	0	0	0	0	0	0	0	0	0	0	0	0	0	0	0
17	1	1	1	1	1	1	1	1	1	1	0	1	1	1	1	1	0	0	1	1	17
18	1	1	1	1	0	1	1	0	1	1	0	1	1	0	1	0	0	0	1	0	12
19	1	1	1	0	0	1	0	0	0	1	0	0	0	0	0	0	0	0	0	0	5
20	1	1	1	1	0	1	1	0	1	1	0	1	0	0	1	0	0	0	0	0	10
21	1	1	1	1	0	1	1	0	1	1	0	1	0	0	1	0	0	0	0	0	10
22	1	1	1	1	0	1	1	0	1	1	0	1	0	0	1	0	0	0	1	0	11
23	1	1	1	1	0	1	1	0	1	1	0	0	0	0	1	0	0	0	0	0	9
24	1	1	1	1	0	1	0	0	0	1	0	0	0	0	0	0	0	0	0	0	6
25	1	1	1	1	0	1	1	1	1	1	0	1	1	1	1	0	0	0	1	0	14
26	1	1	1	1	1	1	1	1	1	1	0	1	1	1	1	0	0	0	1	0	15
27	1	1	1	1	1	1	1	1	1	1	0	1	1	1	1	0	0	0	1	0	15
28	1	1	1	0	0	1	0	0	0	1	0	0	0	0	0	0	0	0	0	0	5
29	1	1	0	0	0	0	0	0	0	1	0	0	0	0	0	0	0	0	0	0	3
30	1	1	0	0	0	1	0	0	0	1	0	0	0	0	0	0	0	0	0	0	4

ILLUSTRATION 16.1

Matrix of Item-by-Item Scores from a Hypothetical Test

the items on the hypothetical test are dichotomously scored; thus, only 1's and 0's can appear in the matrix for students' individual item scores. Illustration 16.1's matrix also includes a column for students' scores on the test (i.e., the sum of each student's item scores).

What can you tell about the internal consistency of the hypothetical test results from examining Illustration 16.1? I fabricated the hypothetical test results so that they would have perfect internal consistency. Suppose we rearrange the rows and columns in Illustration 16.1's matrix in the following way:

1. Determine the difficulty level of each of the 20 items by counting the number of students with correct responses to the item (out of a possible 30). A general formula for computing the item difficulty levels is explained in Chapter 17, but for this case in which all the items are dichotomously scored, the total number of 1's suffices as an indicator of item difficulty. The sums for of the items are as follows: #1 $\rightarrow$ 28, #2 $\rightarrow$ 29, #3 $\rightarrow$ 23, #4 $\rightarrow$ 21, #5 $\rightarrow$ 6, #6 $\rightarrow$ 27, #7 $\rightarrow$ 20, #8 $\rightarrow$ 7, #9 $\rightarrow$ 16, #10 $\rightarrow$ 28, #11 $\rightarrow$ 1, #12 $\rightarrow$ 14, #13 $\rightarrow$ 10, #14 $\rightarrow$ 7, #15 $\rightarrow$ 20, #16 $\rightarrow$ 4, #17 $\rightarrow$ 1, #18 $\rightarrow$ 0, #19 $\rightarrow$ 11, #20 $\rightarrow$ 2.

2. Reorder the columns of item scores from left to right from easier items to harder items. Thus the column for Item #2's scores becomes first, because #2 $\rightarrow$ 29, and 29 is greater than any of the other totals. If we do not worry about the order of equally difficult items, the columns are arranged by item numbers from left to right as follows: 2, 1, 10, 6, 3, 4, 7, 15, 9, 12, 19, 13, 8, 14, 5, 16, 20, 17, 11, 18.

3. Reorder the rows from top to bottom from higher students' test scores to lower test scores. Thus, Student–9's row is placed first, since $x_9 = 19$, and $19 > x_i$ for i $\neq$ 9. Student–16's row is placed last, because $x_{16} = 0$, and $0 < x_i$ for i $\neq$ 16. Similarly, the rows between are arranged in descending order of test scores without concern for order of scores with equal values (i.e., ties).

Keeping in mind that I fabricated the hypothetical test results to have perfect internal consistency, where in the newly rearranged matrix do you expect the 1's to cluster? Where do you expect the 0's to fall? Should you not be able to draw a somewhat jagged diagonal (jagged because of equally difficult items and the ties in the test scores) so that all the 1's are above your line and all the 0's below?

Illustration 16.2 is the rearranged matrix resulting from the three-step procedure.

This ideal of 1's clustered in the upper left portion of the matrix and the 0's in the lower right portion provides a standard to which actual measurement results can be compared for internal consistency. Illustration 16.3 displays the item-by-item (i.e., mini-experiment by mini-experiment) results from an actual measurement. In Illustration 16.4, those results are rearranged into the mini-experiments' outcomes matrix for you to examine for internal consistency.

How does Illustration 16.4 compare to the Illustration 16.2's ideal? Although it is impossible to draw the jagged diagonal so that all the 1's fall above and the 0's below, you could draw a jagged diagonal below the vast majority of 1's and above the vast majority of the 0's. Thus, although Illustration 16.3's measurement results do not have perfect internal consistency, they do appear to have a positive degree of internal consistency.

The measurement results we've examined up to now came from tests consisting solely of dichotomously scored items. However, the process for setting up a mini-experiments' outcomes matrix with rows and columns arranged as in Illustrations 16.1 and 16.3 is also applicable to measurements that include mini-experiments with weighted scoring (i.e., the maximum score defined by the item's rubric is greater than 1). For each item with weighted scoring, the entry in the matrix for each student is the proportion of the maximum possible points obtained by

	Item Scores																				(Test Score)
Student i	2	1	10	6	3	4	7	15	9	12	19	13	8	14	5	16	20	17	11	18	x_i
9	1	1	1	1	1	1	1	1	1	1	1	1	1	1	1	1	1	1	1	0	19
17	1	1	1	1	1	1	1	1	1	1	1	1	1	1	1	1	1	0	0	0	17
8	1	1	1	1	1	1	1	1	1	1	1	1	1	1	1	1	0	0	0	0	16
5	1	1	1	1	1	1	1	1	1	1	1	1	1	1	1	1	0	0	0	0	16
27	1	1	1	1	1	1	1	1	1	1	1	1	1	1	1	0	0	0	0	0	15
26	1	1	1	1	1	1	1	1	1	1	1	1	1	1	1	0	0	0	0	0	15
25	1	1	1	1	1	1	1	1	1	1	1	1	1	1	0	0	0	0	0	0	14
11	1	1	1	1	1	1	1	1	1	1	1	1	0	0	0	0	0	0	0	0	12
18	1	1	1	1	1	1	1	1	1	1	1	1	0	0	0	0	0	0	0	0	12
15	1	1	1	1	1	1	1	1	1	1	1	1	0	0	0	0	0	0	0	0	12
22	1	1	1	1	1	1	1	1	1	1	1	0	0	0	0	0	0	0	0	0	11
21	1	1	1	1	1	1	1	1	1	1	0	0	0	0	0	0	0	0	0	0	10
20	1	1	1	1	1	1	1	1	1	1	0	0	0	0	0	0	0	0	0	0	10
13	1	1	1	1	1	1	1	1	1	1	0	0	0	0	0	0	0	0	0	0	10
12	1	1	1	1	1	1	1	1	1	0	0	0	0	0	0	0	0	0	0	0	9
23	1	1	1	1	1	1	1	1	1	0	0	0	0	0	0	0	0	0	0	0	9
1	1	1	1	1	1	1	1	1	0	0	0	0	0	0	0	0	0	0	0	0	8
3	1	1	1	1	1	1	1	1	0	0	0	0	0	0	0	0	0	0	0	0	8
6	1	1	1	1	1	1	1	1	0	0	0	0	0	0	0	0	0	0	0	0	8
10	1	1	1	1	1	1	1	1	0	0	0	0	0	0	0	0	0	0	0	0	8
24	1	1	1	1	1	1	0	0	0	0	0	0	0	0	0	0	0	0	0	0	6
28	1	1	1	1	1	0	0	0	0	0	0	0	0	0	0	0	0	0	0	0	5
19	1	1	1	1	1	0	0	0	0	0	0	0	0	0	0	0	0	0	0	0	5
2	1	1	1	1	1	0	0	0	0	0	0	0	0	0	0	0	0	0	0	0	5
7	1	1	1	1	0	0	0	0	0	0	0	0	0	0	0	0	0	0	0	0	4
30	1	1	1	1	0	0	0	0	0	0	0	0	0	0	0	0	0	0	0	0	4
14	1	1	1	1	0	0	0	0	0	0	0	0	0	0	0	0	0	0	0	0	4
29	1	1	1	0	0	0	0	0	0	0	0	0	0	0	0	0	0	0	0	0	3
4	1	0	0	0	0	0	0	0	0	0	0	0	0	0	0	0	0	0	0	0	1
16	0	0	0	0	0	0	0	0	0	0	0	0	0	0	0	0	0	0	0	0	0

ILLUSTRATION 16.2

Item-by-Item Scores from Illustration 16.1 with Rows Arranged in Descending Order of Test Scores and Columns by Ascending Order of Item Difficulty

the student's response. For example, if the rubric indicates that the maximum possible score for the item is 6, and a student's response to that item's prompt merits 4, then "0.67" is entered in the matrix (because $4 \div 6 \approx 0.67$). The point to keep in mind is that the strategy we developed for examining the internal consistency of measurement results from tests with only dichotomously scored items is applicable to other measurements as well.

Although the strategy we've developed to this point is sound, it's not very practical for routine use by busy teachers. Furthermore, comparing a matrix from actual test results to the

Student i	\multicolumn{18}{c}{Item Item Scores}	(Test Score) w_i
	1	2	3	4	5	6	7	8	9	10	11	12	13	14	15	16	17	18	
1	1	1	0	0	1	1	1	1	0	1	1	0	0	1	1	0	1	0	11
2	0	1	1	1	0	1	0	0	0	0	1	0	0	0	1	0	0	0	6
3	1	1	1	1	0	1	1	1	1	1	1	1	1	1	1	1	0	0	15
4	1	1	1	1	0	0	1	0	1	0	0	1	0	1	0	0	1	0	9
5	1	1	1	1	1	1	1	1	1	1	1	1	1	1	1	1	0	0	16
6	1	1	1	0	0	0	1	0	0	1	1	0	0	1	1	0	1	1	10
7	1	1	1	1	1	1	1	0	1	1	1	0	1	1	1	1	1	0	15
8	0	1	1	0	0	0	1	0	0	0	0	0	0	0	0	0	0	0	3
9	1	1	1	1	1	1	1	1	0	1	1	1	0	1	1	1	1	1	16
10	0	1	1	1	1	0	1	0	0	1	1	1	1	1	1	0	0	0	11
11	1	1	1	1	1	1	1	1	1	1	0	1	1	1	1	0	1	0	15
12	0	1	0	0	0	1	1	0	0	0	0	0	0	0	0	0	0	0	3
13	1	1	1	1	1	1	1	1	1	1	0	1	1	1	1	0	1	1	16
14	1	1	1	1	0	1	0	0	0	1	1	1	1	1	1	0	0	0	11
15	1	1	1	1	0	1	1	0	1	1	0	0	1	1	1	0	0	0	11
16	1	1	0	1	0	1	0	1	1	1	0	0	1	0	0	0	0	0	8
17	1	1	1	1	1	1	1	1	1	1	1	1	1	1	1	1	1	1	18
18	1	1	1	0	0	1	1	0	1	1	0	1	1	1	1	1	0	1	13
19	1	1	1	0	0	1	0	0	0	1	0	1	1	0	0	0	1	0	8
20	1	1	1	1	0	1	0	1	1	1	0	1	1	1	1	0	1	0	13
21	1	1	1	1	1	1	1	0	1	1	1	1	0	0	1	1	1	1	15
22	1	1	0	0	0	1	1	0	1	1	1	1	1	0	0	0	0	0	9
23	1	1	1	1	1	1	1	1	1	1	1	1	1	1	1	0	0	0	15
24	1	1	1	1	0	1	1	0	1	1	0	0	0	1	1	0	1	0	11
Item Sums	20	24	20	17	10	20	19	10	15	20	13	15	15	17	18	7	12	6	

ILLUSTRATION 16.3

Item-by-Item Scores from an 18-Item Test Administered to 24 Students

ideal does not easily yield meaningful information about internal consistency. Illustration 16.5 is the rearranged mini-experiments' outcomes matrix from actual test results. How does the internal consistency of Illustration 16.5's measurement results compare to those from Illustration 16.4? Which appears to be more like Illustration 16.2's ideal?

I don't think the answer is very obvious. So why did I put you to the trouble of developing this impractical strategy for assessing internal consistency of measurement results? I wanted you to make these comparisons to the ideal mini-experiments' outcomes matrix because your understanding of the practical methods for assessing internal consistency depends on your understanding of this strategy.

Now we are ready to turn our attention to the development of some usable methods.

| | Item
Item Scores | | | | | | | | | | | | | | | | | | (Test
Score) |
| Student | | | | | | | | | | | | | | | | | | | |
i	2	1	3	6	10	7	15	14	4	9	13	12	11	17	5	8	16	18	w_i
17	1	1	1	1	1	1	1	1	1	1	1	1	1	1	1	1	1	1	18
13	1	1	1	1	1	1	1	1	1	1	1	1	0	1	1	1	0	1	16
9	1	1	1	1	1	1	1	1	1	0	0	1	1	1	1	1	1	1	16
5	1	1	1	1	1	1	1	1	1	1	1	1	1	0	1	1	1	0	16
3	1	1	1	1	1	1	1	1	1	1	1	1	1	0	0	1	1	0	15
7	1	1	1	1	1	1	1	1	1	1	1	0	1	1	1	0	1	0	15
11	1	1	1	1	1	1	1	1	1	1	1	1	0	1	1	1	0	0	15
21	1	1	1	1	1	1	1	0	1	1	0	1	1	1	1	0	1	1	15
23	1	1	1	1	1	1	1	1	1	1	1	1	1	0	1	1	0	0	15
18	1	1	1	1	1	1	1	1	0	1	1	1	0	0	0	0	1	1	13
20	1	1	1	1	1	0	1	1	1	1	1	1	0	1	0	1	0	0	13
1	1	1	0	1	1	1	1	1	0	0	0	0	1	1	1	1	0	0	11
10	1	0	1	0	1	1	1	1	1	0	1	1	1	0	1	0	0	0	11
14	1	1	1	1	1	0	1	1	1	0	1	1	1	0	0	0	0	0	11
15	1	1	1	1	1	1	1	1	1	1	1	0	0	0	0	0	0	0	11
24	1	1	1	1	1	1	1	1	1	1	0	0	0	1	0	0	0	0	11
6	1	1	1	0	1	1	1	1	0	0	0	0	1	1	0	0	0	1	10
4	1	1	1	0	0	1	0	1	1	1	0	1	0	1	0	0	0	0	9
22	1	1	0	1	1	1	0	0	0	1	1	1	1	0	0	0	0	0	9
16	1	1	0	1	1	0	0	0	1	1	1	0	0	0	0	1	0	0	8
19	1	1	1	1	1	0	0	0	0	0	1	1	0	1	0	0	0	0	8
2	1	0	1	1	0	0	1	0	1	0	0	0	1	0	0	0	0	0	6
8	1	0	1	0	0	1	0	0	0	0	0	0	0	0	0	0	0	0	3
12	1	0	0	1	0	1	0	0	0	0	0	0	0	0	0	0	0	0	3
Item Sums	24	20	20	20	20	19	18	17	17	15	15	15	13	12	10	10	7	6	

ILLUSTRATION 16.4

Item-by-Item Scores from Illustration 16.3 with Rows Arranged in Descending Order of Test Scores and Columns by Ascending Order of Item Difficulty

CLASSICAL TEST-RELIABILITY THEORY

The fundamental tenets for assessing measurement reliability were laid down by the founders of psychometrics during the first quarter of the 20th century. Charles Spearman (1904) expressed the following relationship on which models for assessing reliability focus:

$x_i = T_i + E_x$ where x_i is the score Student-i obtains on Test-x, T_i is the score Student-i would have obtained if Test-x had been perfectly reliable, and E_x is the error of measurement that is attributable to Test-x not being perfectly reliable.

x_i is referred to as the "observed score" or the "obtained score," T_i is referred to as the "true score," and E_x is referred to as "reliability error." The subscript "i" attached to the shorthand

Student	Item Scores																				(Test Score)
i	4	3	5	2	1	11	8	10	9	13	12	7	6	18	15	20	19	16	17	14	u_i
11	1	1	1	1	1	1	1	1	1	1	1	1	1	1	1	1	1	1	1	1	20
6	1	1	1	1	1	1	1	1	1	1	1	1	1	1	1	1	1	1	1	1	20
10	1	0	1	1	1	1	1	0	1	1	1	1	1	1	1	1	1	1	1	1	18
3	1	1	1	1	1	1	1	1	1	1	1	1	1	1	1	0	0	1	1	0	17
13	1	1	1	1	1	1	1	1	1	1	1	1	1	1	1	0	1	1	0	0	17
19	1	1	1	1	1	1	1	1	1	1	1	1	1	1	1	0	1	0	1	0	17
14	1	1	1	1	1	1	1	1	1	1	1	1	0	1	1	1	1	0	0	0	16
25	1	1	0	0	1	1	1	1	1	1	1	1	1	1	1	1	1	1	0	0	16
15	1	1	1	1	1	1	1	1	1	1	1	1	1	1	1	0	0	0	0	0	16
4	1	1	1	1	1	1	1	1	1	0	1	0	1	0	1	1	1	1	1	0	16
21	1	1	1	1	1	1	1	1	1	1	1	1	1	1	1	0	0	0	0	0	15
20	1	1	1	1	1	1	1	1	1	0	0	0	1	1	0	1	1	0	0	1	15
18	1	1	1	1	1	1	1	1	1	1	1	1	0	1	1	0	0	0	1	0	15
7	1	1	1	1	1	1	1	1	1	1	1	0	1	0	0	1	1	1	0	0	15
5	1	1	1	1	1	0	1	1	1	1	0	1	0	1	1	1	0	0	0	0	13
12	1	1	1	1	0	1	1	1	0	0	1	0	1	0	0	0	0	1	1	1	12
22	1	1	1	0	1	1	0	1	0	1	0	1	0	1	1	0	1	0	0	1	12
1	1	1	1	1	1	0	0	1	0	0	1	1	1	1	0	1	1	0	0	0	12
24	1	1	1	1	1	1	1	1	0	0	0	1	1	0	0	1	0	0	0	0	11
17	1	1	1	1	1	0	0	0	0	0	1	0	1	0	1	0	1	1	0	0	10
9	1	1	0	1	0	0	1	0	1	1	1	1	1	0	0	0	0	0	0	0	9
23	1	1	1	1	0	1	1	1	1	1	0	0	0	0	0	0	0	0	0	0	9
16	1	1	0	0	1	0	0	0	0	0	0	1	0	0	0	0	0	1	0	0	5
8	1	1	0	0	0	1	0	0	0	0	0	0	0	0	0	1	0	0	1	0	5
2	1	0	0	0	0	0	0	0	0	0	0	0	0	0	0	0	0	1	0	1	3
Item Sums	25	23	20	20	20	19	19	19	17	17	17	17	17	15	15	13	13	12	9	7	

ILLUSTRATION 16.5

Item-by-Item Scores from a Test with Rows Arranged in Descending Order of Test Scores and Columns by Ascending Order of Item Difficulty

symbols for observed score and to the true score remind us that their values are associated with an individual student and, thus, vary depending on whether $i = 1$, $i = 2$, $i = 3, \ldots$, or $i = N$. On the other hand, E_x is a value that is associated with the cumulative results from Test-x.

Obviously, if you knew the true scores for your N students (i.e., $\{T_1, T_2, T_3, \ldots, T_N\}$), you would not need to administer Test-x. But true scores only exist in theory and are not directly accessible. To estimate the true-score sequence $\{T_i\}$, you administer Test-x and obtain an observed-score sequence $\{x_i\}$. Now, if you could estimate E_x, then you could get a better grip on $\{T_i\}$ by applying Spearman's equation as follows:

$$\text{Since } x_i = T_i + E_x, T_i = x_i - E_x.$$

To estimate E_x, you need to measure the reliability of Test-x. From your work with Chapter 4 and then again with the section "The Mini-Experiments' Outcomes Matrix" of this chapter, you conceptualize reliability as consistency. The concept of consistency is central to all aspects of measurement reliability:

- Internal consistency depends on the agreement among the results of individual test items (e.g., from Illustration 4.4 or Illustration 16.1).
- Intra-observer consistency depends on how well scores resulting from an observer employing the test items' rubrics to students' responses at one point in time agree with the scores resulting from that observer employing the rubrics to those same responses a second time.
- Inter-observer consistency depends on how well scores resulting from one observer employing the test items' rubrics to students' responses agree with the scores resulting from a second observer employing the rubrics to those same students' responses.

What we need is a usable way to quantify the degree of agreement among score sequences, whether the sequences are generated by different items from the same test or from two different observations of the same set of student responses. In the first quarter of the 20th century, that problem was addressed by Francis Galton, Karl Pearson, and other pioneers of psychometrics with the invention of correlational statistics (Ryans, 1938; Thorndike, 1988).

MEASURES OF CONSISTENCY

(+, +) AND (−, −) VERSUS (+, −) AND (−, +)

To begin our examination of correlational statistics, consider a problem of assessing the concurrent validity of a test rather than its reliability. To refresh your memory of concurrent validity, reread the explanation under "Concurrent Validity" from Chapter 14's section "Standardized Tests" on pages 532–533.

Suppose that you wanted to assess the concurrent validity of the results of Test-u with respect to Test-x. You begin by administering both tests to the same group of students. The results from both sequences of scores are displayed in Illustration 16.6.

Just how consistent is $\{u_i\}$ with $\{x_i\}$? Do you visualize a trend in which students with high scores from Test-u tend to have high scores from Test-x and students with low scores from Test-u have low scores from Test-x? How common is it for a student (e.g., Ira) to have obtained a low score on one test and a high score on the other?

Answers to these questions might be facilitated by getting a better feel for how high is a "high score" and how low is a "low score" on each test. As you understand from your work with Chapter 14, computing μ_x, σ_x, μ_u, and σ_u helps address that question. $\{x_i\}$ also appears in Illustration 14.15, and while working with Chapter 14, you computed μ_x to be 30.43 and σ_x to be 9.87. Therefore, you might think of scores that are at least 5 greater than 30 (i.e., about $\frac{1}{2}\sigma_x$ above μ_x) to be high scores from Test-x and scores that are less than 30 by 5 or more (i.e., about $\frac{1}{2}\sigma_x$ below μ_x) to be low scores from Test-x. Thus, x_i would be categorized as "high" if $x_i >$ 35, as "low" if $x_i < 25$, and as "about average" if $25 \leq x_i \leq 35$.

To use the same strategy to determine high and low scores from Test-u, you could compute μ_u, and σ_u and get $\mu_u \approx 28.65$ and $\sigma_u \approx 11.15$. So you might be inclined to think of scores greater than 33 to be high for Test-u and scores below 24 to be low. Now, you could categorize the scores as "high" with a "+," "low" with a "−," and "about average" with a "0." See Illustration 16.7.

i	Student	x_i	u_i	i	Student	x_i	u_i
1	A.J.	41	39	20	Jose	39	20
2	Arlene	10	13	21	Joy	31	33
3	Bill	42	14	22	Lucinta	43	41
4	Bonita	30	37	23	Luke	34	33
5	Buddy	17	20	24	Michael	18	18
6	Buhla	38	38	25	Melinda	12	0
7	Cameron	10	9	26	Nadine	37	39
8	Candice	34	21	27	Nettie	40	38
9	Celeste	16	40	28	Ory	23	31
10	Charles	37	37	29	Phyllis	28	33
11	Eloise	35	38	30	Quinn	33	23
12	Elvira	36	41	31	Raul	18	19
13	Evelyn	25	29	32	Ricardo	39	34
14	Garret	34	34	33	Rufus	39	40
15	Gilda	39	31	34	Sidney	14	10
16	Hans	32	36	35	Singh	21	16
17	Hilda	29	40	36	Tomaria	37	37
18	Ira	40	10	37	Zelda	40	31

ILLUSTRATION 16.6

Results from Administration of Test-x and Test-u to the Same Group of 37 Students

Pairs of +'s as well as pairs of −'s in Illustration 16.7 support the argument favoring Test-u's concurrent validity with respect to Test-x. On the other hand, mixed pairs with a + and − support the argument against Test-u's concurrent validity with respect to Test-x. The greater the ratio of pairs with the same signs to pairs with unlike signs, the stronger the consistency between the two sequences of test scores. Note that had we used the test means and standard deviations to convert the raw scores from the tests to z-scores, we may have come up with a more precise measure of consistency.

SCATTERPLOTS

Perhaps we could more readily read the trend between $\{u_i\}$ and $\{x_i\}$ if we expressed the 37 pairs of scores from Illustration 16.7 as a graph. Use Illustration 16.8's grid to plot the 37 co-ordinate points.

This type of graph is commonly referred to as a *scatterplot*. Your *scatterplot* for the 37 pairs of scores from Illustration 16.7 should appear similar to the one shown in Illustration 16.9.

Illustration 16.10 is identical to Illustration 16.9, except the points have been enclosed by a square that is subdivided into four quadrants labeled "I," "II," "III," and "IV." In which quadrant, I, II, III, or IV, do the points of students who scored high on both administrations of the test fall (e.g., Student–1's)?

Such points fall into quadrant I. In which quadrants do points of students who scored low on both tests fall (e.g., Student–7's)? They fall within quadrant III. Points that fall within either quadrant I or quadrant III are evidence that the two score sequences are consistent with each other.

i	x_i	-/0/+	u_i	-/0/+	i	x_i	-/0/+	u_i	-/0/+
1	41	+	39	+	20	39	+	20	−
2	10	−	13	−	21	31	0	33	0
3	42	+	14	−	22	43	+	41	+
4	30	0	37	+	23	34	0	33	0
5	17	0	20	−	24	18	−	18	−
6	38	+	38	+	25	12	−	0	−
7	10	−	9	−	26	37	+	39	+
8	34	0	21	−	27	40	+	38	+
9	16	−	40	+	28	23	−	31	0
10	37	+	37	+	29	28	0	33	0
11	35	0	38	+	30	33	0	23	−
12	36	+	41	+	31	18	−	19	−
13	25	0	29	0	32	39	+	34	+
14	34	0	34	+	33	39	+	40	+
15	39	+	31	0	34	14	−	10	−
16	32	0	36	+	35	21	−	16	−
17	29	0	40	+	36	37	+	37	+
18	40	+	10	−	37	40	+	31	0

ILLUSTRATION 16.7

Illustration 16.6's Results with Scores Categorized as "High," "Low," or "About Average"

In what quadrants do points of students who scored high on Test-x and low on Test-u fall (e.g., Student–18's)? Such points fall within quadrant IV. Finally, points of students who scored low on Test-x and high on Test-u fall into quadrant II (e.g., Student–9's). Points that fall within quadrants II or IV are evidence that the two score sequences are inconsistent with each other.

When the points of a scatterplot tend to cluster more in the odd quadrants than they do in the even quadrants, the two score sequences *correlate positively*. If, on the other hand, quadrants II and IV are more populated than quadrants I and III, the correlation is negative. Whenever the points are distributed about equally among all four quadrants, then no correlation or hardly any correlation exists between the two score sequences. Examine the six scatterplots of Illustration 14.14. Note how configurations of points reflect the degree and direction of a correlation.

CORRELATION COEFFICIENTS

Just prior to 1900, Karl Pearson devised a method for quantifying the consistency between two score sequences (Walker, 1929). A principal outcome of the work of Pearson and his colleagues is the *Pearson product-moment correlation coefficient*. The formula for this coefficient as well as the many alternate formulas for correlation coefficients are applied in the assessment of relationship between the results of two tests administered to the same group of students. By computing a correlation coefficient, you obtain a number between −1 and 1 inclusive that reflects how the points in a scatterplot are distributed. The Greek letter "ρ"

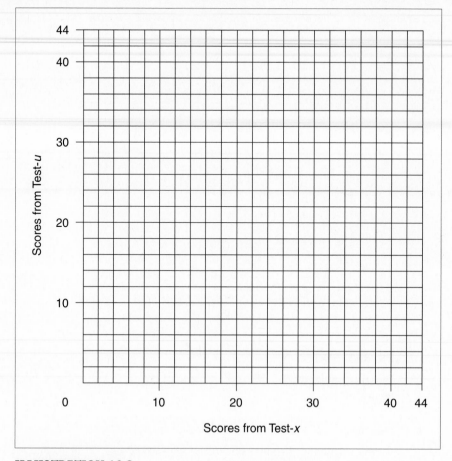

ILLUSTRATION 16.8

Grid for Plotting Coordinate Points from Illustration 16.7

(i.e., "rho") is commonly used to denote Pearson product-moment correlation coefficients. So the conventional symbol for the correlation coefficient relating two data sequences $\{a_i\}$ and $\{b_i\}$ is "$\rho_{a,b}$."

The Pearson product-moment correlation coefficient can be computed by the following formula:

$$\rho_{a,b} = \frac{1}{N} \sum_{i=1}^{N} z_{a_i} z_{b_i}$$

In the formula, $\rho_{a,b}$ is the correlation coefficient for $\{a_i\}$ and $\{b_i\}$; z_{a_i} is the z-score derived from a_i, μ_a, and σ_a; z_{b_i} is the z-score derived from b_i, μ_b, and σ_b; and N is the number of students.

To compute $\rho_{x,u}$ for $\{x_i\}$ and $\{u_i\}$ from Illustration 16.7, you would convert each score from $\{x_i\}$ to a z-score, z_{x_i}, and each score from $\{u_i\}$ to a z-score, z_{u_i}. Then the z-scores in

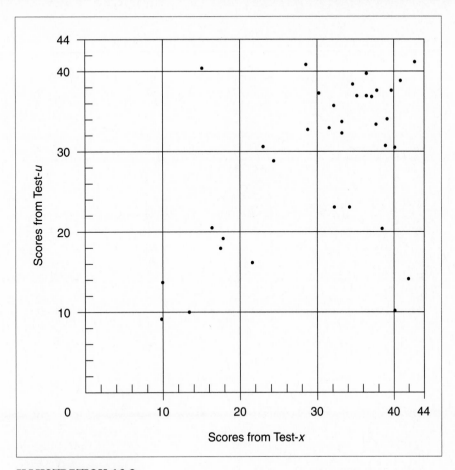

ILLUSTRATION 16.9

Scatterplot of 37 Pairs of Scores from Illustration 16.7

each corresponding pair of z-scores are multiplied to obtain N products (i.e., $z_{x_1} \cdot z_{u_1}$, $z_{x_2} \cdot z_{u_2}$, $z_{x_3} \cdot z_{u_3}$, $\ldots$ $z_{x_N} \cdot z_{u_N}$). The mean of those N products is then computed, resulting in the correlation coefficient $\rho_{x,u}$.

The computation resulting in $\rho_{x,u} \approx 0.58$ is displayed in Illustration 16.11. Note the following:

- For i such that $z_{x_i} > 0$ and $z_{u_i} > 0$, the coordinate point (x_i, u_i) is in quadrant I of the scatterplot and $z_{x_i} \cdot z_{u_i} > 0$, which increases the size of $\rho_{x,u}$.
- For i such that $z_{x_i} < 0$ and $z_{u_i} < 0$, the coordinate point (x_i, u_i) is in quadrant III of the scatterplot and $z_{x_i} \cdot z_{u_i} > 0$, which increases the size of $\rho_{x,u}$.
- For i such that $z_{x_i} > 0$ and $z_{u_i} < 0$, the coordinate point (x_i, u_i) is in quadrant IV of the scatterplot and $z_{x_i} \cdot z_{u_i} < 0$, which decreases the size of $\rho_{x,u}$.
- For i such that $z_{x_i} < 0$ and $z_{u_i} > 0$, the coordinate point (x_i, u_i) is in quadrant II of the scatterplot and $z_{x_i} \cdot z_{u_i} < 0$, which decreases the size of $\rho_{x,u}$.

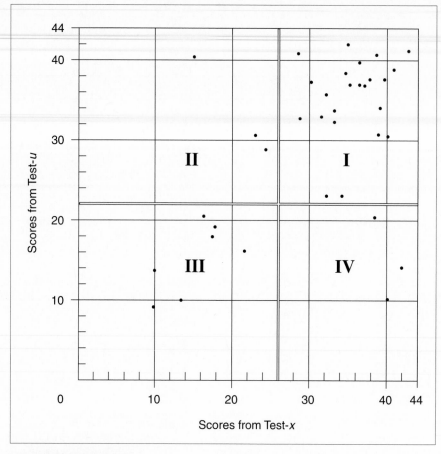

ILLUSTRATION 16.10

Illustration 16.9's Scatterplot Partitioned into Quadrants

The nearer the coefficient is to 1, the stronger the agreement between the two score sequences. The nearer the coefficient is to −1, the stronger the disagreement. The nearer the coefficient is to 0, the weaker the relationship. Turn back to Illustration 14.14. The correlation coefficient for the scatterplot in the top left of the illustration is about 0.40. For the middle scatterplot in the top row, it's about −1. For the top right scatterplot, it's about 0. For the bottom left scatterplot, it's about 1. For the bottom middle scatterplot, it's about −0.40. For the bottom right scatterplot, it's about 0.80.

You can use the computer software from the CD-ROM that accompanies this book to quickly compute correlation coefficients. Also, calculators with statistical functions are set up to compute correlation coefficients.

Now that you are cognizant of using correlation coefficients to measure consistency between two score sequences, you are ready to return your attention to assessing test reliability.

$\mu_x \approx 30.43, \ \sigma_x \approx 9.87$
$\mu_u \approx 28.65, \ \sigma_u \approx 11.15$

i	x_i	z_{xi}	u_i	z_{ui}	$z_{xi} \cdot z_{ui}$
1	41	1.071	39	0.928	0.99
2	10	-2.071	13	-1.403	2.91
3	42	1.172	14	-1.314	-1.54
4	30	-0.044	37	0.749	-0.03
5	17	-1.361	20	-0.776	1.06
6	38	0.767	38	0.839	0.64
7	10	-2.071	9	-1.762	3.65
8	34	0.362	21	-0.686	-0.25
9	16	-1.463	40	1.091	-1.49
10	37	0.666	37	0.749	0.50
11	35	0.463	38	0.839	0.39
12	36	0.564	41	1.108	0.62
13	25	-0.551	29	0.032	-0.02
14	34	0.362	34	0.480	0.17
15	39	0.868	31	0.211	0.18
16	32	0.159	36	0.659	0.10
17	29	-0.145	40	1.018	-0.15
18	40	0.970	10	-1.672	-1.62
19	35	0.463	37	0.749	0.35
20	39	0.869	20	-0.776	-0.67
21	31	0.056	33	0.390	0.02
22	43	1.274	41	1.108	1.41
23	34	0.362	33	0.390	0.14
24	18	-1.260	18	-0.955	1.20
25	12	-1.868	0	-2.569	4.80
26	37	0.666	39	0.928	0.62
27	40	0.970	38	0.839	0.81
28	23	-0.753	31	0.211	-0.16
29	28	-0.246	33	0.390	-1.10
30	33	0.260	23	-0.507	-0.13
31	18	-1.260	19	-0.865	1.09
32	39	0.868	34	0.480	0.42
33	39	0.868	40	1.018	0.88
34	14	-1.665	10	-1.672	2.78
35	21	-0.956	16	-1.134	1.08
36	37	0.666	37	0.749	0.50
37	40	0.970	31	0.211	0.20
					21.38

$\rho_{x,u} \approx 21.38 \div 37 \approx 0.58$

ILLUSTRATION 16.11

Computation of $\rho_{x,u}$ for $\{x_i\}$ and $\{u_i\}$ from Illustration 16.7

EVOLUTION OF RELIABILITY COEFFICIENTS

TEST-RETEST METHOD

Consider Case 16.1.

CASE 16.1

Ms. Vaughn, a physical education teacher, devised a test of basketball skills. Each of the test's 15 mini-experiments focused on a different subskill: (1) shooting layups, (2) medium-range shooting, (3) long-range shooting, (4) defensive positioning, (5) defensive movements, (6) rebounding, (7) setting screens, (8) making cuts, (9) dribbling, (10) moving up and down the floor, (11) foul shooting, (12) stationary passing, (13) stationary catching, (14) passing on the move, and (15) catching on the move.

The maximum possible score for each mini-experiment is 5 points, with the observer's rubric so specifically laid out that Ms. Vaughn does not believe that observer consistency presents a problem. However, she is concerned with the consistency among results from multiple administrations of the test. To assess reliability, she conducts an experiment with 32 students, 8 from each of her 4 physical education classes; each class period is 90 minutes long. In each class period, the experiment proceeds as follows:

> At the beginning of the period, she directs the 8 students to engage in a 5-minute warm-up exercise. Then she administers the test, with students working in pairs, rapidly and concurrently rotating through the 15 stations she has set up for the mini-experiments. The test is completed in 30 minutes. She then directs the students to take a drink of water and rest for 15 minutes. During the break she does not allow them to practice any of the skills nor to consume any food. They are only to rest and drink water. After the rest period, she has them engage in the warm-up exercise again and then administers the test a second time.

Illustration 16.12 lists the scores from the first administration of the test under "f_i" and the scores from the second administration under "s_i."

To measure the consistency of the results from the first administration with those from the retest administration, she computes a Pearson product-moment correlation coefficient using the computer software that accompanies this book. The result is $\rho_{f,s} \approx 0.83$. She judges that for this particular type of test, $\rho_{f,s} \approx 0.83$ reflects a satisfactory level of reliability.

In Case 16.1, Ms. Vaughn employed what is conventionally referred to in the psychometric literature as the *test-retest method* for measuring test reliability. As Ms. Vaughn was using this method, why do you suppose she directed her students to rest between the two administrations without practicing any of the basketball skills and to consume only water? For what variable do you think she was attempting to control by having students follow those directions before she administered the test a second time? Keep in mind that the purpose of her experiment was to assess the degree to which reliability error would cause $\{s_i\}$ to be inconsistent with $\{f_i\}$. Also keep in mind Spearman's equations:

$x_i = T_i + E_x$ where x_i is the score Student-i obtains on Test-x, T_i is the score Student-i would have obtained if Test-x had been perfectly reliable, and E_x is the error of measurement that is attributable to Test-x not being perfectly reliable.

A test is supposed to be sensitive to changes in true scores; that's what it is intended to measure. If T_i somehow manages to remain constant between the test and the retest, then any differences between f_i and s_i is a function of reliability error. Thus, Ms. Vaughn was attempting to prevent her students' basketball skills from fluctuating between administrations of the

i	f_i	s_i	i	f_i	s_i
1	48	50	17	59	55
2	33	41	18	12	20
3	33	33	19	64	54
4	20	13	20	34	35
5	51	39	21	49	47
6	40	42	22	35	33
7	29	31	23	62	58
8	39	41	24	40	46
9	22	45	25	31	29
10	47	44	26	36	39
11	42	47	27	35	37
12	34	30	28	21	17
13	32	34	29	54	40
14	49	53	30	30	35
15	22	21	31	39	42
16	17	35	32	55	57

ILLUSTRATION 16.12

Scores from the First and Second Administrations of Ms. Vaughn's Test

test. The test-retest method provides a correlation coefficient that measures the test's reliability only if $\{T_i\}$ is the same for both administrations.

The test-retest method is based on the following theoretical principle:

> If a measurement is administered at two different times to the same group of students, and if $\{T_i\}$ is the same for the second administration as it was for the first, then the greater the Pearson product-moment correlation coefficient computed from the results of the two administrations, the more reliable the measurement.

When a correlation coefficient is used for assessing the reliability of a measurement, it is called a *reliability coefficient*.

The test-retest method may be a realistic option for cases such as Case 16.1 in which $\{T_i\}$ can be held reasonably constant from one administration to the next. However, for most types of measurements that are relevant to cognitive or affective goals, test-retest is rarely a viable option. Cognitive and affective true scores can hardly be held constant over time; the very experience of taking most tests influences $\{T_i\}$. Building upon test-retest theory, more useful methods were developed throughout the first half of the 20th century.

EQUIVALENT FORM METHOD

Consider Case 16.2.

CASE 16.2

During the first week of the school year, Mr. Dunn plans to pre-assess his fourth-graders' reading comprehension skills to help him make some decisions about the year's language arts curriculum. With that purpose in mind, he develops a test with four mini-experiments. Mini-experiment #1's prompt consists of an intermediate third-grade-level reading passage followed by six comprehension-level questions for students to write one-sentence answers. The other three mini-experiments are similar, except that #2 uses an advanced third-grade-level passage with four questions, #3 uses a beginning fourth-grade-level passage with five questions, and #4 uses an intermediate fourth-grade-level passage with eight questions.

He thinks to himself as he decides how to assess the reliability of the test: "I could administer the test on Monday and then again on Wednesday and compute the reliability coefficient by running the two score sequences through the Pearson product-moment formula. Their true reading scores aren't likely to fluctuate much over that short period of time. Comprehension and communication skills aren't acquired or lost in just a day or two, like simple-knowledge and process-knowledge achievement. But if the time between the test and the retest is short enough so that their reading comprehension skills won't appreciably change, it'll also be short enough for them to remember their answers from the first administration during the second administration. In the retest, some won't even bother rereading the passages; they'll just recall their original answers. Some others will discuss their answers with one another before the retest. The test-retest method is not going to yield a meaningful reliability coefficient. What should I do?

"I'll have to make up an equivalent form of the test for the second administration—like the multiple forms standardized-test companies use. The form for the retest will have to be equivalent to the original test. So Item #1 on the retest form must also have six comprehension questions about an intermediate third-grade-level reading passage—but the passage must be different from Item #1's on the original test. I'm glad I have these resource materials for our reading program; the grade-level-specific reading selections will help me come up with the equivalent prompts. Let's see, for #2, I'll need another advanced-level third-grade passage."

Mr. Dunn develops the equivalent form of the test. Two days after administering the original test, he administers the equivalent form, thus obtaining two scores for each student. He uses the correlation coefficient based on the two score sequences as the reliability coefficient for the test.

In Case 16.2, Mr. Dunn employed what is conventionally referred to in the psychometric literature as the *equivalent form method* for measuring test reliability. Compared to the test-retest method, the equivalent form method has the advantage of obviating the effects of students' remembering responses from the first administration or sharing answers between administrations. Of course, the method depends on the two forms of the test actually being equivalent. Like the test-retest method, the equivalent form does not provide a meaningful coefficient for cases when true scores cannot or should not be kept stable between administrations.

SPLIT-HALVES METHOD

Consider Case 16.3.

CASE 16.3

Mr. Keldorf developed a history test consisting of 15 multiple-choice and 5 short-response dichotomously scored items. To assess its reliability, he develops an equivalent form of the test he considers administering a day or two after administering the original test. But then he thinks: "This isn't going to work. Some of my students will use the experience of taking the first test to guide their studying for the retest. I surely don't want to discourage that. After all, my job is to teach them more than it is to test them. Unfortunately, some of my other students will have crammed for the first test and have forgotten what they memorized by the time I retest with the equivalent form. I've got a problem to solve.

"I know! I'll minimize the time between the administrations of the original test and the equivalent form. I'll simply add the equivalent form of the test to the original version of the test and create what the kids will see as one long test. Brilliant! No wonder I'm a teacher! It'll take the full 90-minute period to administer both parts, but that's still more time efficient than two separate shorter administrations."

Mr. Keldorf then puts the two forms together so that Items #1–15 are multiple-choice, Items #16–20 are short-response, Items #21–35 are multiple-choice that are equivalent to Items #1–15, and Items #36–40 are short-response that are equivalent to Items #16–20.

From the single administrations of both halves to the test, he plans to extract two scores for each student: One based on Items #1–20 and a second based on Items #21–40. Those two score sequences can then be used with the Pearson product-moment correlation formula to obtain a reliability coefficient.

In Case 16.3, Mr. Keldorf employed what is conventionally referred to in the psychometric literature as the *split-halves method* for measuring test reliability. The advantage of the split-halves method is that both score sequences are obtained from a single administration of the test; thus, there is not time for the true scores to fluctuate.

ODD-EVEN METHOD

Case 16.4 is a continuation of Case 16.3.

CASE 16.4

Mr. Keldorf looks at the 40-point test with the 15 multiple-choice prompts, followed by 5 short-response prompts, followed by 15 more multiple-choice prompts, and finally 5 more short-response prompts. He thinks to himself: "This split-halves method makes sense theoretically, but I don't like the way this test is formatted. All the multiple-choice items ought to be together, and all the short-response prompts ought to be together. The students shouldn't have to make so many transitions from one format type to another. I have twice as many directions on this 'split-halves' test as I should. Furthermore, I really don't want to give a 90-minute, 40-point test; I want to give a 45-minute, 20-point test. I've got a problem to solve.

"I know! What if I just go back to my original 20-point test and administer it one time. Then for each student, I'll extract one score from the odd-numbered items—#1, #3, #5, . . . , #19—and then extract a second score from the even-numbered items—#2, #4, #6, . . . , #20. That's not exactly like equivalent-form split-halves, but by getting each score from every other item, there's a high probability that the test consisting of only the odd-number items is somewhat equivalent to the test consisting of only the even-numbered items. "

From the single administration of the one test, Mr. Keldorf plans to obtain a reliability coefficient by correlating the scores from the 10 odd-numbered items with the scores from the 10 even-numbered items.

In Case 16.4, Mr. Keldorf employed what is conventionally referred to in the psychometric literature as the *odd-even method* for measuring test reliability. Like the split-halves method, the odd-even method provides a reliability coefficient from only one administration of a test. In comparison to using split-halves, the odd-even method has the advantage of not requiring you to alter your test in order to assess its reliability. After all, are you really studying the validity of a test if you must change it in order to conduct the validation study?

ADJUSTED ODD-EVEN METHOD

Case 16.5 is a continuation of Case 16.4.

CASE 16.5

Mr. Keldorf is about to finalize his plans to apply the odd-even method for assessing the reliability of his history test when he thinks: "A test's reliability is greatly influenced by the number of items on the test. In most cases, you can increase reliability by increasing the number of test items (Cangelosi, 1982, pp. 229–231). The odd-even method treats my 20-item test as if it only had 10 items. That means I'll get a reliability coefficient based on a formula that assumes I have half as many points on my test as I actually have. I have a problem to solve."

Mr. Keldorf looks up several sources on educational measurement and psychometrics. He learns that several formulas have been developed that estimate how the reliability coefficient of a test would vary according to how many items the test has. He finds that the formula that is referred to most often is the Spearman-Brown Prophecy formula (Hopkins, 1998, pp. 121–122). The formula is displayed in Illustration 16.13, along with an explanation of how it is applied.

Mr. Keldorf reasons, "The reliability coefficient I would get via the odd-even method is going to underestimate the test's reliability because it treats my test as if it's half as long as it really is. I could go ahead and compute that odd-even reliability coefficient and then adjust it upward using the Spearman-Brown formula by plugging in 2 for t. That would estimate what the reliability would be for my 20-point test.

The Spearman-Brown Prophecy formula was designed to predict what the reliability coefficient of a test would be if the test were composed of more items than it actually contains. In other words, the formula estimates how much greater a reliability coefficient would be if additional items were added to the test (i.e., if k is increased) providing that the new items have the same statistical characteristics as the original items. The formula is as follows:

$$r_t = \frac{tr'}{(t-1)r' + 1}$$

where r_t is the estimate of what the reliability coefficient would be if the test were t times longer, and r' is the reliability coefficient computed for the actual test.

For example, suppose a reliability coefficient, r', was computed on a 15-item test and $r' = 0.50$. What would the Spearman-Brown estimate for the reliability coefficient be for that test if it had 45 more items added to it (i.e., if k were increased from 15 to 60)?

The new test would be 4 times longer, $t = 4$. Thus, r_4 would be computed as follows:

$$r_4 = \frac{(4)(.50)}{(4-1)(.50) + 1} = \frac{2}{2.5} = 0.80$$

ILLUSTRATION 16.13

The Spearman-Brown Prophecy Formula

In Case 16.5, Mr. Keldorf considered employing what is referred to as the *adjusted odd-even method* for measuring test reliability. The process for using the adjusted odd-even method is as follows:

1. Administer the test one time to a group of students.
2. Extract one score sequence, $\{o_i\}$, from the odd-numbered items and a second score sequence, $\{e_i\}$, from the even-numbered items.
3. Compute $\rho_{o,e}$.
4. Use the Spearman-Brown Prophecy formula shown in Illustration 16.13 to adjust $\rho_{o,e}$ by substituting 2 for t and $\rho_{o,e}$ for r'.

Note that for the special case of $t = 2$ for the adjusted odd-even method, the Spearman-Brown formula simplifies to the following form where r is the reliability coefficient:

$$r = \frac{2\rho_{o,e}}{\rho_{o,e} + 1}$$

KUDER-RICHARDSON METHODS
Discovery and Invention

Case 16.6 is a continuation of Case 16.5.

CASE 16.6

In Case 16.5, Mr. Keldorf decided that the adjusted odd-even method would provide a meaningful reliability coefficient for his history test. But before using the method, he read from a technical manual for a standardized test that the reliability coefficient for the standardized test was computed using the Kuder-Richardson formula 20. Curious as to what that meant, he located some sources on Kuder-Richardson formulas for assessing the internal consistency of tests. He learned that by using the appropriate Kuder-Richardson formula, he could obtain a reliability coefficient for his history test that would be at least as meaningful as the one he would get by the adjusted odd-even method. Furthermore, the Kuder-Richardson method would be much easier and less time-consuming than the adjusted odd-even method.

After determining that the Kuder-Richardson formula 21 would be appropriate for his history test, Mr. Keldorf obtained his reliability coefficient as follows:

1. He administered the 20-point history test to his 34 students, yielding $\{h_i\}$ with $\{h_i\}$ = (14, 19, 18, 9, 11, 20, 13, 19, 19, 10, 17, 12, 11, 15, 11, 19, 4, 11, 9, 20, 19, 10, 15, 13, 12, 17, 12, 13, 12, 10, 15, 17, 11, 16)
2. Knowing that the Kuder-Richardson formula 21 is a function of three variables (number of items, mean of the scores, and variance of the scores), he computes μ_h, and σ_h^2, resulting in the following: $\mu_h \approx 13.91$ and $\sigma_h^2 \approx 14.96$.
3. He computes the reliability coefficient, r_h, as shown in Illustration 16.14, resulting in $r_h \approx 0.75$.

You examined the item-by-item scores from tests while working with the section "Mini-Experiments' Outcomes Matrix" in this chapter. The characteristics of those matrices and the intercorrelations among item scores were a major focus of study in psychometrics throughout the 1930s and into the early 1940s. Brownell (1933), Mosier (1936), Kuder and Richardson (1937), Rulon (1939), and Hoyt (1941) were among those who worked with the matrices in an effort to develop meaningful and usable methods for assessing internal

The Kruder–Richardson formula 21 is as follows:

$$r = \frac{k\sigma^2 - \mu(k - \mu)}{\sigma^2(k - 1)}$$

where r is the reliability coefficient, k is the number of test items, μ is the mean of the test scores, and σ^2 is the variance of the test scores.

There are 20 items on Test-h, so $k_h = 20$. Also $\mu_h \approx 13.91$. And $\sigma_h^2 \approx 14.96$. Thus,

$$r_h = \frac{k_h\sigma_h^2 - \mu_h(k_h - \mu_h)}{\sigma_h^2(k_h - 1)} \approx \frac{20(14.96) - 13.91(20 - 13.91)}{14.96(19)} \approx 0.75$$

ILLUSTRATION 16.14

Mr. Keldorf Computes a Reliability Coefficient for His 20-Point History Test

consistency. A variety of formulas for reliability coefficients emerged, each with its own relative advantages and disadvantages, depending on the type of test to be assessed for reliability as well as characteristics of item-by-item test results. The second half of the 20th century brought additional formulas and refinements of previously published methods, as reflected in hundreds of reports appearing in journals such as *Psychometrika*, *Journal of Educational Measurement*, *Applied Psychological Measurement*, and *Journal of Educational Statistics* as well as papers presented at meetings of scholarly organizations such as the National Council on Measurement in Education, American Psychological Association, and American Educational Research Association. The development continues. However, the method that continues to be most often applied and recommended, especially for use by classroom teachers, is that based on the seminal work of G. Frederic Kuder and Marion W. Richardson (1937).

The Kuder-Richardson method is an improvement of the adjusted odd-even method because with the Kuder-Richardson formulas all possible split-halves, not only the odd-even split, are factored into the process. As suggested by Case 16.6, a Kuder-Richardson reliability coefficient is easier to compute than an adjusted odd-even reliability coefficient. Three Kuder-Richardson formulas are commonly applied in the assessment of measurement reliability: Coefficient alpha (α), Kuder-Richardson formula 20 (*KR20*), and Kuder-Richardson formula 21 (*KR21*).

Coefficient α

The general Kuder-Richardson formula which is applicable to more types of measurements than *KR20* or *KR21* but is not as easy to compute is coefficient α (Cronbach, 1951). The derivation of the formula for α is reported by Kuder and Richardson (1937) in their original article in *Psychometrika*, "The Theory of the Estimation of Test Reliability." However, for an easier to follow explanation of the derivation, you might want to read pages 311–326 of Robert Ebel's (1965) *Measuring Educational Achievement*. If you are so inclined, you might also see pages 326–328 of the same book for explanations of the derivations of the Spearman-Brown Prophecy formula as well as *KR20*.

The formula for α is as follows:

$$\alpha = \frac{k}{k-1}\left(1 - \frac{\displaystyle\sum_{j=1}^{k}\sigma_j^{\,2}}{\sigma^2}\right)$$

where α is the reliability coefficient, k is the number of test items, σ^2 is the variance of the test scores, and $\sigma_j^{\,2}$ is the variance of the scores from Item #j.

Thus,

$$\sum_{j=1}^{k}\sigma_j^{\,2} = \sigma_1^{\,2} + \sigma_2^{\,2} + \sigma_3^{\,2} + \cdots + \sigma_k^{\,2}$$

Consider Case 16.7.

CASE 16.7

Ms. Phares administers a 17-point test consisting of 1 short-response and 3 essay items to 18 students. Item #1, the short-response item, is dichotomously scored; the maximum possible points for the essay items are as follows: 6 for Item #2, 5 for Item #3, and 5 for Item #4.

Refer to the test as "Test-q." Test q's results, including item-by-item scores, are shown in Illustration 16.15.

Ms. Phares decides to use coefficient α in her assessment of Test-q's reliability. She computes α_q to be 0.81, which she considers indicative of a satisfactory level of internal consistency for this particular test. Her computations resulting in $\alpha_q \approx 0.81$ are explained in Illustration 16.16.

Note that the computer software on the CD-ROM that accompanies this book includes a routine for you to use to compute coefficient α. The CD-ROM also includes routines for *KR20*, *KR21*, and other statistical functions explained in this chapter.

Kuder-Richardson 20

Kuder and Richardson developed their formulas for a time when people did not have access to electronic calculators or high-speed computers. Their concern that coefficient α is too time-consuming to compute for tests with more than several items led them to devise *KR20*. However, *KR20* is restricted for use with tests that only include items that are dichotomously scored.

The formula for *KR20* is as follows:

$$KR20 = \frac{k}{k-1}\left(1 - \frac{\displaystyle\sum_{j=1}^{k}p_j(1 - p_j)}{\sigma^2}\right)$$

where *KR20* is the reliability coefficient, k is the number of test items, σ^2 is the variance of the test scores, and p_j is the proportion of students that scored 1 point for Item #j.

Thus,

$$\sum_{j=1}^{k}p_j(1 - p_j) = p_1(1 - p_1) + p_2(1 - p_2) + p_3(1 - p_3) + \cdots + p_k(1 - p_k)$$

| Students | Items (j) | | | | Test Scores |
(i)	1	2	3	4	q_i
1	1	4	3	2	10
2	1	4	2	3	10
3	1	6	5	5	17
4	1	6	5	5	17
5	0	0	0	0	0
6	0	5	5	1	11
7	1	3	2	1	7
8	1	4	5	4	14
9	1	6	5	5	17
10	1	2	4	3	10
11	0	1	2	0	3
12	0	0	1	2	3
13	1	5	3	5	14
14	1	5	5	4	15
15	1	6	5	3	15
16	0	6	3	3	12
17	0	2	4	5	11
18	0	3	3	1	7

ILLUSTRATION 16.15

Results of Ms. Phares's 17-Point Test (i.e., Test-q)

Consider Case 16.8.

CASE 16.8

Ms. Thompson administers a 15-point test consisting of 15 dichotomously scored items to 20 students. Refer to the test as "Test-c." Test c's results, including item-by-item scores, are shown in Illustration 16.17.

Ms. Thompson decides to use Kuder-Richardson formula 20 in her assessment of Test-c's reliability. She computes $KR20_c$ to be 0.48, which she believes indicates an unsatisfactory level of internal consistency for Test-c. Her computations resulting in $KR20_c \approx 0.48$ are explained in Illustration 16.18.

Keep in mind that $KR20$ is applicable only for tests consisting solely of dichotomously scored items. Also, statistical routines (e.g., computing μ, σ, ρ, α, and $KR20$) are helpful when we are attempting to extract meaning from a somewhat large data sequence. When you have more than just a few scores to analyze, statistical computations provide a mechanism for identifying aggregate characteristics of the score sequence (e.g., central tendency, variability, or internal consistency). But when your measurement results only contain a few scores (e.g., less than 10), statistical routines like the Kuder-Richardson formulas do not apply. How to assess the reliability of a measurement administered to only a few students is addressed in a subsequent section of this chapter.

$\sigma_1^2 \approx 0.24,\ \sigma_2^2 \approx 4.06,\ \sigma_3^2 \approx 2.36,\ \sigma_4^2 \approx 2.94$

$$\sum_{j=1}^{4} \sigma_j^2 \approx 0.24 + 4.06 + 2.36 + 2.94 = 9.60$$

$\sigma_q^2 \approx 24.53$

Therefore,

$$\alpha_q = \frac{k_q}{k_q - 1}\left(1 - \frac{\displaystyle\sum_{j=1}^{k_q} \sigma_j^2}{\sigma_q^2}\right) \approx \frac{4}{3}\left(1 - \frac{9.60}{24.53}\right) \approx 0.81$$

ILLUSTRATION 16.16

How Ms. Phares Computed α_q

Student (i)	\multicolumn{15}{c}{Items (j)}	(Test Score) c_i

Student (i)	1	2	3	4	5	6	7	8	9	10	11	12	13	14	15	c_i
1	1	1	1	1	1	0	1	0	0	1	1	1	0	1	0	10
2	0	1	1	1	1	1	1	0	0	0	1	1	1	1	0	10
3	0	0	1	1	1	1	1	1	0	1	1	1	1	1	0	11
4	1	0	1	1	1	1	1	1	0	1	1	0	1	1	1	12
5	0	0	0	1	1	0	0	0	0	1	1	1	1	1	1	8
6	1	1	1	1	1	1	1	1	1	1	1	1	1	1	0	14
7	1	0	1	1	1	1	1	0	0	1	1	1	0	1	0	10
8	1	0	1	1	0	1	1	0	1	1	1	1	1	1	0	11
9	0	1	0	0	1	1	0	0	0	1	1	1	1	1	0	8
10	1	0	0	1	1	1	1	1	1	1	1	1	0	1	0	11
11	1	1	1	1	1	1	1	1	1	1	0	1	1	1	1	14
12	0	1	0	1	1	1	1	0	1	1	1	1	0	1	0	10
13	0	1	1	1	1	1	1	1	1	1	1	1	0	0	0	11
14	1	1	0	1	1	1	1	1	1	1	1	1	1	1	0	13
15	1	0	0	0	1	0	0	1	0	0	1	1	0	0	0	5
16	1	0	1	1	1	1	1	1	1	1	1	1	0	1	0	12
17	1	1	0	1	0	1	1	0	1	1	1	1	0	0	0	9
18	1	1	1	1	1	1	1	1	1	1	1	1	0	1	0	13
19	1	1	1	1	1	1	1	1	1	1	1	0	0	0	0	11
20	1	0	1	1	1	1	1	1	1	1	1	0	0	0	0	10
21	1	1	1	1	1	1	1	1	1	1	1	1	0	1	0	13
22	1	1	1	1	0	0	1	1	1	1	1	1	0	0	1	11
23	1	1	1	1	1	1	1	1	1	1	1	1	1	1	1	15
24	1	1	1	1	1	1	1	1	1	1	1	1	0	1	0	13
25	0	0	0	1	1	1	1	1	1	1	1	1	0	1	0	10

ILLUSTRATION 16.17

Results of Ms. Thompson's 15-Point Test (i.e., Test-c)

Student (i)	Items (j) 1	2	3	4	5	6	7	8	9	10	11	12	13	14	15	(Test Score) c_i
1	1	1	1	1	1	0	1	0	0	1	1	1	0	1	0	10
2	0	1	1	1	1	1	1	0	0	0	1	1	1	1	0	10
3	0	0	1	1	1	1	1	1	0	1	1	1	1	1	0	11
4	1	0	1	1	1	1	1	1	0	1	1	0	1	1	1	12
5	0	0	0	1	1	0	0	0	0	1	1	1	1	1	1	8
6	1	1	1	1	1	1	1	1	1	1	1	1	1	1	0	14
7	1	0	1	1	1	1	1	0	0	1	1	1	0	1	0	10
8	1	0	1	1	0	1	1	0	1	1	1	1	1	1	0	11
9	0	1	0	0	1	1	0	0	0	1	1	1	1	1	0	8
10	1	0	0	1	1	1	1	1	1	1	1	1	0	1	0	11
11	1	1	1	1	1	1	1	1	1	1	0	1	1	1	1	14
12	0	1	0	1	1	1	1	0	1	1	1	1	0	1	0	10
13	0	1	1	1	1	1	1	1	1	1	1	1	0	0	0	11
14	1	1	0	1	1	1	1	1	1	1	1	1	1	1	0	13
15	1	0	0	0	1	0	0	1	0	0	1	1	0	0	0	5
16	1	0	1	1	1	1	1	1	1	1	1	1	0	1	0	12
17	1	1	0	1	0	1	1	0	1	1	1	1	0	0	0	9
18	1	1	1	1	1	1	1	1	1	1	1	1	0	1	0	13
19	1	1	1	1	1	1	1	1	1	1	1	0	0	0	0	11
20	1	0	1	1	1	1	1	1	1	1	1	0	0	0	0	10
21	1	1	1	1	1	1	1	1	1	1	1	1	0	1	0	13
22	1	1	1	1	0	0	1	1	1	1	1	1	0	0	1	11
23	1	1	1	1	1	1	1	1	1	1	1	1	1	1	1	15
24	1	1	1	1	1	1	1	1	1	1	1	1	0	1	0	13
25	0	0	0	1	1	1	1	1	1	1	1	1	0	1	0	10
Sum	18	15	17	23	22	21	22	17	17	23	24	22	10	19	5	

$\text{Sum}_j/25$
$= p_j$ .72 .60 .68 .92 .88 .84 .88 .68 .68 .92 .96 .88 .40 .76 .20

$1-p_j$ .28 .40 .32 .08 .12 .16 .12 .32 .32 .08 .04 .12 .60 .24 .80

$$\sum_{j=1}^{15} p_j(1-p_j) \approx (.72)(.28)+(.60)(.40)+(.68)(.32)+(.68)(.32)+(.92)(.08)+$$

$$(.88)(.12)+(.84)(.16)+(.88)(.12)+(.68)(.32)+(.92)(.08)+$$

$$(.96)(.04)+(.88)(.12)+(.40)(.60)+(.76)(.24)+(.20)(.80) \approx 2.53$$

$k_c = 15$ and $\sigma_c^2 \approx 2.53$. Thus,

$$KR20_c \approx \frac{15}{14}\left[1-\frac{2.53}{4.62}\right] \approx 0.48$$

ILLUSTRATION 16.18

How Ms. Thompson Computed $KR20_c$

Kuder-Richardson 21

In an attempt to devise an easy-to-compute estimate of *KR20*, Kuder and Richardson examined how the *KR20* formula could be simplified if the application is restricted to tests consisting only of dichotomously scored *items that are equally difficult*. How much simpler would the *KR20* formula be if $p_1 = p_2 = p_3 = \ldots = p_k$? They found that the formula simplifies considerably because one can compute it directly from the test scores with no need to input item-by-item scores. As shown in Illustration 16.19, the formula simplifies to the following form and is referred to as "Kuder-Richardson formula 21" or simply "*KR21*":

$$KR21 = \frac{k\sigma^2 - \mu(k - \mu)}{\sigma^2(k - 1)}$$

where k is the number of items, μ is the mean of the test scores, and σ^2 is the variance of the test scores.

Of course, no matter how easy *KR21* is to compute, it isn't very useful unless it provides a reasonably accurate estimate of *KR20*. It is rare for all the items on a test to be equally difficult. Of course, sometimes a test might be so easy that all students obtain the maximum score; for such a case, $p_1 = p_2 = p_3 = \ldots = p_k = 1.00$. Or a test might be so hard that all students score 0; in such a case, $p_1 = p_2 = p_3 = \ldots = p_k = 0.00$. But neither of these two cases is interesting because such perfectly homogeneous scores could not produce a reliability coefficient. Why not? What would σ equal? Note that formulas for ρ, α, *KR20* and *KR21* all require division by σ or by σ^2.

$$KR20 = \frac{k}{k-1}\left(1 - \frac{\sum_{j=1}^{k} p_j(1 - p_j)}{\sigma^2}\right)$$

Suppose $p_1 = p_2 = p_3 = \ldots = p_k = p$

Then $\sum_{j=1}^{k} p_j(1 - p_j) = \sum_{j=1}^{k} p(1 - p) = kp(1 - p)$

But because the test is dichotomously scored and $p_1 = p_2 = p_3 = \ldots = p_k = p$,

$p_1 + p_2 + p_3 + \ldots + p_k = \mu.$

But $p_j = P$ for $j = 1, 2, 3\ldots, k$. Thus, $kp = \mu$ which implies that $p = \dfrac{\mu}{k}$

which means that $kp(1 - p) = k\left(\dfrac{\mu}{k}\right)\left(1 - \dfrac{\mu}{k}\right) = \mu\left(1 - \dfrac{\mu}{k}\right)$

Therefore, $\dfrac{k}{k-1}\left(1 - \dfrac{\sum_{j}^{k} p_j(1 - p_j)}{\sigma^2}\right) = \dfrac{k}{k-1}\left(1 - \dfrac{\frac{\mu}{k}(k-\mu)}{\sigma^2}\right) = \dfrac{k}{k-1}\left(1 - \dfrac{\mu(k-\mu)}{k\sigma^2}\right) = \dfrac{k}{k-1} - \dfrac{k\mu(k-\mu)}{(k-1)k\sigma^2} =$

$\dfrac{k}{k-1} - \dfrac{k\mu(k-\mu)}{(k-1)k\sigma^2} = \dfrac{k\sigma^2 - \mu(k-\mu)}{\sigma^2(k-1)} = KR21$

ILLUSTRATION 16.19

Derivation of *KR21*

So the supposition under which the formula for *KR21* is deduced rarely holds. However, experiments in which both *KR20* and *KR21* are computed on a wide variety of score sequences from tests consisting of dichotomously scored items that are not all equally difficult demonstrate that *KR21* is an excellent estimate of *KR20* in many cases. *KR21* underestimates any positive *KR20* from a test consisting of dichotomously scored items that are not all equally difficult. Whenever σ^2 is sufficiently large (e.g., $\sigma^2 > 5$), the estimate is usually close enough to what *KR20* would be to produce a meaningful reliability coefficient.

In Case 16.6, Mr. Keldorf computed $KR21_h$ to be 0.75. Thus, he knows if he had taken the trouble to compute $KR20_h$, that $KR20_h$ would be at least 0.75. Noting that $\sigma_h^2 \approx 14.96$, I would guess that $KR20_h$ would have been less than 0.85, depending on the distribution of the item-by-item scores.

Just for practice, use your computer with the software from the CD-ROM that accompanies this book or your calculator to compute $KR21_d$ for Test-*d*, which consists of 45 dichotomously scored items administered to 22 students yielding $\{d_i\}$ such that $\{d_i\}$ = (39, 29, 40, 41, 33, 39, 35, 31, 40, 27, 30, 35, 34, 39, 31, 24, 34, 20, 37, 25, 35, 33). Illustration 16.20 displays the computation.

The following questions still need to be addressed in subsequent sections of this chapter: Once a reliability coefficient is computed (e.g., 0.74), what does it mean? How can reliability coefficients be used to estimate measurement error? How should reliability be assessed for measurements to which the Kuder-Richardson formulas do not apply? How should observer consistency be assessed?

INTERPRETING RELIABILITY COEFFICIENTS

RELIABILITY COEFFICIENTS YOU COMPUTE

A reliability coefficient, being a correlation coefficient, is never less than −1 or greater than 1. The closer the coefficient is to 1, the more reliable the measurement. How near 1 must a reliability coefficient be for the measurement in question to be judged reliable?

The question is simple, but the answer is complex. As you administer numerous measurements, compute reliability coefficients, and compare how students respond to different mini-experiments, you will develop a "feel" for how reliability coefficients vary for different types of measurements and circumstances. Usually it takes months for a person to develop this feel for when a reliability coefficient (e.g., 0.74) is indicative of a reliable test and when it is indicative of an unreliable test. Until you build your background of experiences, here is a rough guideline to help you interpret reliability coefficients that you compute yourself for measurements you administer to your own students:

> Usually, $r > 0.75$ is indicative of measurement results with a satisfactory degree of internal consistency; $r > 0.65$ is usually indicative of measurement results that are too internally inconsistent to be used for a formative judgment or summative evaluation.

What if $0.65 \leq r \leq 0.75$? Compare Case 16.9 to Case 16.10.

$k_d = 45$, $\mu_d \approx 33.23$, $\sigma_d \approx 5.57$, $\sigma_d^2 \approx 31.02$

$$KR21_d = \frac{k_d\sigma_d^2 - \mu_d(k_d - \mu_d)}{\sigma_d^2(k-1)} \approx \frac{45(31.02) - 33.23(45 - 33.23)}{31.02(44)} \approx 0.74$$

ILLUSTRATION 16.20

Computation of $KR21_d$

CASE 16.9

Ms. Fisher administers Illustration 2.28's test to help her make a summative evaluation regarding her 32 students' achievement of the goal stated in Illustration 2.9. Because the test includes mini-experiments with weighted scoring rubrics, she decides to use coefficient α in her assessment of the test's internal consistency. Using the software from the CD-ROM accompanying this book, she computes $\alpha \approx 0.71$.

She thinks to herself, "An alpha of 0.71 isn't all that high. But after all, this test is designed to be relevant to some really complex objectives—discover relationships, construct concepts, comprehension and communication skills, process knowledge, simple knowledge, and application. It's awfully tough to reliably measure such a complexly defined learning goal. Because of the complexity of what I was trying to measure, I used a variety of mini-experiment formats—not just all essay or all multiple-choice. Having such a variety of formats tends to introduce inconsistencies into students' responses. If I used fewer types of formats, the test would be less relevant. Also, these 32 students really went through this unit on civil rights together; they helped each other in a lot of cooperative learning activities. I shouldn't expect their theoretical true scores to vary widely. Thus, I shouldn't expect the standard deviation of the test scores to be great. A large standard deviation tends to jack up the reliability coefficient. Considering all the factors influencing the internal consistency of this test downward, $\alpha \approx 0.71$ is more than satisfactory."

CASE 16.10

For the purpose of evaluating how well her 32 students remember prominent facts, events, and personalities in U.S. history, Ms. Fisher administers a 42-point test consisting of 42 multiple-choice mini-experiments. Using the computer software from the CD-ROM accompanying this book, she plugs the results into the Kuder-Richardson formula 21, obtaining a reliability coefficient of 0.73.

She thinks to herself, "Even though *KR21* underestimates what *KR20* would have given me, 0.73 is very disappointing for a test like this. The test has only one type of item format and it's relevant to simple-knowledge achievement. Furthermore, with these historical facts and stuff coming from more than one unit, I bet the students' theoretical true scores vary quite a bit. All the factors favoring internally consistent results are in effect. For this situation, 0.73 is unacceptable. I'm going to disregard these results and analyze the test further to see how I can make it more reliable.

Frequently, interpretations of reliability coefficients between 0.65 and 0.75 are not as clear-cut as they are in Cases 16.9 and 16.10. Often it is necessary for you to weigh various factors—some which enhance and some which contaminate internal consistency—into your interpretations.

RELIABILITY COEFFICIENTS REPORTED BY COMMERCIAL TEST PUBLISHERS

As you understand from your work with Chapter 14, reliability coefficients for standardized tests are published in test manuals and advertisements for the test (e.g., on web sites and in publishers' catalogues). Such reliability coefficients are computed from the results of the tests being administered to norm groups. Typical norm-group samples include students from various grade levels who vary considerably regarding demographic characteristics. You can be sure that a standardized test norm group is considerably more heterogeneous with more highly variable true scores than any one class you teach. Consequently, you should expect the published reliability coefficient for a standardized test to be higher than it would be if it were computed on the results of the test from your class only. Furthermore, standardized tests are usually designed with greater attention to internal consistency than to relevance. Note, for example, that standardized tests do not use as wide a variety of item formats as Ms. Fisher used for her test in Case 16.9. Most group-administered standardized tests include only multiple-choice items. Therefore, you should set a much higher standard for acceptability of reliability coefficients reported for standardized tests than you set for reliability coefficients you compute yourself. Published reliability coefficients should be near or above 0.90 to be considered satisfactory.

STANDARD ERROR OF MEASUREMENT (SEM)

Instead of simply interpreting reliability coefficients as either satisfactory or unsatisfactory, consider using reliability coefficients to estimate reliability error (i.e., to solve for E_x in Spearman's equation $x_i = T_i + E_x$). This can be done with the *standard error of measurement* (*SEM*) function. *SEM* is a handy, easy-to-compute statistic that lends precision to the interpretation of reliability coefficients. After we manage to derive it, I believe you will appreciate its usefulness as a mechanism for assessing measurement error.

DERIVATION OF SEM

PIECES IN THE PUZZLE

Test-Retest Reliability Model

Suppose that Test-x is administered to a student, Marion. Now further suppose that Marion is readministered the test at a later date so that by some magical mechanism Marion's true score, T, is at exactly the same level for the retest as it was for the first administration. Also pretend that Marion's memory of having taken the test the first time does not influence how he responds to the test prompts the second time. In other words, the theoretical test-retest method is applied to only one student.

If Test-x is perfectly reliable and Marion's score from the first administration is 70, then what should his score be for the second administration? Keeping in mind that T remains constant, he should again obtain a score of 70. But if the test is not perfectly reliable, the score from the second administration will likely differ from the first even though T did not change. The results of a less than perfectly reliable test (i.e., if $r_x < 1$) would be expected to fluctuate from administration to administration even though T does not.

Now if under these theoretical circumstances specified by the test-retest model, Marion is retested time and time again, then a frequency distribution can be drawn from the results of these repeated administrations. Suppose the frequency distribution from this theoretical experiment looked like Illustration 16.21. What do you infer about r_x?

Illustration 16.21 suggests that $r_x = 1$. However, suppose the frequency distribution from these many, many retestings looked like Illustration 16.22 or Illustration 16.23. What would that imply about r_x? Does Illustration 16.22 suggest a different r_x than Illustration 16.23?

Unlike Illustration 16.21, the frequency distributions of Illustrations 16.22 and 16.23 show some variability. In other words, $\sigma_{16.22} > 1$ and $\sigma_{16.23} > 1$, whereas $\sigma_{16.21} = 0$. For what distribution does Test-x seem more reliable, Illustration 16.22's or Illustration 16.23's? The shorter, broader shape of Illustration 16.23's graph indicates that $\sigma_{16.22} > \sigma_{16.23}$. Thus, the results from Illustration 16.22 reflect a more reliable test than the results from Illustration 16.23.

ILLUSTRATION 16.21

Theoretical Results of a Perfectly Reliable Test Administered to Marion Many, Many Times Under Theoretical Test-Retest Conditions

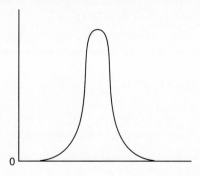

ILLUSTRATION 16.22

Theoretical Results of a Test with High, But Imperfect, Reliability Administered to Marion Many, Many Times Under Theoretical Test-Retest Conditions

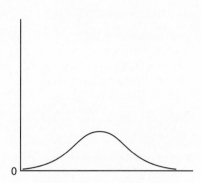

ILLUSTRATION 16.23

Theoretical Results of a Test with Relatively Low Reliability Administered to Marion Many, Many Times Under Theoretical Test-Retest Conditions

Thus, the standard deviation of the results from this theoretical test-retest, test-retest, . . . , test-retest experiment is a function of the reliability of the test. If we could find a practical way of estimating the standard deviation of this distribution due to reliability error, then we'd have a mechanism for estimating measurement error from a reliability coefficient. Of course, we don't actually readminister a test to a single student many times. In reality, we administer a test one time to many students. Fortunately, we can develop a practical means of estimating the standard deviation of the results from this theoretical test-retest experiment without actually conducting the experiment. But to do so, we need to collect a few more pieces for our puzzle.

A Normal Distribution of Reliability Error

From Chapter 14, reread the section "Normal Distributions" on pages 550–553.

The *central limit theorem* is a set of relationships upon which the study of inferential statistics is based. A phenomenon associated with the central limit theorem brings us a step closer to developing a formula for estimating the standard deviation of the theoretical test-retest experiment. The effect of that phenomenon on our theoretical repeated administrations of Test-*x* with Marion is as follows:

> As the number of retest scores increases from 100 to 200 to 1000 and on and on, the frequency distribution of the scores gets closer and closer to a normal frequency distribution.

By applying this effect to our theoretical test-retest experiment, we can assume that ultimately the error distributions from the continued retests will become normal. The advantage we gain is that we know how the standard deviation of a normal distribution behaves (e.g., about 68% of the scores fall within 1σ of μ and about 95% fall within 2σ of μ).

The Ratio Reliability Model and Theoretical True Scores

Besides the test-retest model, classical test theory also provides a way of defining reliability that is useful in our quest to derive a formula for the standard deviation of a normal distribution of reliability error; it is called the *ratio reliability model* (Ebel, 1965, pp. 330–331). With the ratio reliability model, a reliability coefficient for Test-*x*, r_x, is defined as follows:

$$r_x = \frac{\sigma_T^2}{\sigma_x^2}$$

where σ_T^2 is the variance of the theoretical true scores and σ_x^2 is the variance of the observed scores (i.e., the scores obtained from Test-*x*).

The rationale underlying the ratio model is based on the following:

Two sources of variability influence $\{x\}$: the variability of $\{T\}$ and variability due to imperfect reliability (i.e., the reason the standard deviations associated with Illustrations 16.22 and 16.23 are positive, whereas the standard deviation associated with the perfectly reliable test of Illustration 16.21 is 0). Thus, for a perfectly reliable test, $\sigma_x^2 = \sigma_T^2$, which means $\sigma_T^2/\sigma_x^2 = 1 = r_x$.

Since you cannot access $\{T_i\}$, you can hardly compute σ_T^2. However, because of Spearman's equation, $x_i = T_i + E_x$, you can deduce the following:

$\sigma_x^2 = \sigma_T^2 + \sigma_E^2$ where σ_E^2 is the error due to imperfect reliability. Thus, $\sigma_T^2 = \sigma_x^2 - \sigma_E^2$.

Now, we can rewrite the ratio reliability model definition of r_x as follows:

$$r_x = \frac{\sigma_x^2 - \sigma_E^2}{\sigma_x^2}$$

Think about what σ_E^2 in the above equation is. It's the variance of the error distribution due to imperfect reliability . If we solve for σ_E^2 and take its square root, we have σ_E. σ_E is the *SEM* we have been seeking.

SOLVING FOR THE STANDARD DEVIATION DUE TO RELIABILITY ERROR

To derive a formula for *SEM*, solve for σ_E in the above equation as follows:

$$r_x = \frac{\sigma_x^2 - \sigma_E^2}{\sigma_x^2} \qquad \text{which implies that}$$

$$\sigma_x^2 r_x = \sigma_x^2 - \sigma_E^2 \qquad \text{which implies that}$$

$$\sigma_E^2 = \sigma_x^2 - \sigma_x^2 r_x \qquad \text{which implies that}$$

$$\sigma_E^2 = \sigma_x^2(1 - r_x) \qquad \text{which implies that}$$

$$\sqrt{\sigma_E^2} = \sqrt{\sigma_x^2(1 - r_x)} \qquad \text{which implies that}$$

$$\sigma_E = \sigma_x\sqrt{1 - r_x}$$

σ_E is SEM_x, so our formula for the standard error of measurement for Test-*x* is as follows:

$$SEM_x = \sigma_x\sqrt{1 - r_x}$$

where σ_x is the standard deviation of $\{x_i\}$ and r_x is the reliability coefficient of Test-x.

Now we have a mechanism for estimating the reliability error of a test from simply administering the test one time to a group of students. After all, from one administration, you can compute r_x and σ_x and, thus, solve for SEM_x.

Compute SEM_h for Mr. Keldorf's Test-h from Case 16.6. Compute SEM_q for Ms. Phares' Test-q from Case 16.7. Compute SEM_c for Ms. Thompson's Test-c from Case 16.8. Compute SEM_d for Test-d from Illustration 16.20.

The computations are displayed in Illustration 16.24.

At first, it may seem odd that a test with a higher reliability coefficient (e.g., $r_q \approx 0.81$) would have lower SEM (e.g., $SEM_q \approx 2.18$) than a test with a lower reliability coefficient (e.g., $r_h \approx 0.75$ and $SEM_h \approx 1.94$). This can happen because SEM, like many other statistics, is expressed in standard deviation units. Whereas a lower reliability coefficient raises the SEM, a higher σ raises the SEM. It's a bit of a balancing act because, as you know, higher score variability is associated with greater reliability; thus, larger σ's tend to be associated with larger r's.

USING SEM TO INTERPRET SCORES

Using SEM to interpret measurement scores depends on the assumption that the distribution of reliability error (e.g., in Illustration 16.22) is normal. Keeping in mind that SEM is the standard deviation of that normal curve, SEM can be used to interpret scores as Mr. Keldorf does in Case 16.11.

Computation of SEM_h:

From Illustration 16.14, we get $\sigma_h^2 \approx 14.96$ which implies that $\sigma_h \approx \sqrt{14.96} \approx 3.87$. Also, $r_h \approx 0.75$.

Thus, $SEM_h = \sigma_h \sqrt{1 - r_h} \approx 3.87 \sqrt{1 - 0.75} = 3.87(.5) \approx 1.94$

Computation of SEM_q:

From Illustration 16.16, we get $\sigma_q^2 \approx 24.53$ which implies that $\sigma_q \approx 4.95$. Also, $r_q \approx 0.81$.

Thus, $SEM_q = \sigma_q \sqrt{1 - r_q} \approx 4.95 \sqrt{1 - 0.81} = 4.95 \sqrt{.19} \approx 4.95(.44) \approx 2.18$

Computation of SEM_c:

From Illustration 16.18, we get $\sigma_c^2 \approx 4.60$ which implies that $\sigma_c \approx 2.14$. Also, $r_c \approx 0.48$.

Thus, $SEM_c = \sigma_c \sqrt{1 - r_c} \approx 2.14 \sqrt{1 - 0.48} \approx 1.54$

Computation of SEM_d:

From Illustration 16.20, we get $\sigma_d \approx 5.57$ and $r_d \approx 0.74$.

Thus, $SEM_d = \sigma_d \sqrt{1 - r_d} \approx 5.57 \sqrt{1 - 0.74} \approx 2.84$

ILLUSTRATION 16.24

Computation of SEM_h, SEM_q, SEM_c, and SEM_d

CASE 16.11

In Case 16.6, Mr. Keldorf administered Test-*h* to his 34 history students. As displayed in Illustrations 16.14 and 16.24, he computed $r_h \approx 0.75$, and $SEM_h \approx 1.94$. He thinks, "1.94 is about 2. That means that in a theoretical test-retest experiment, I should expect retest scores to be within about 2 points of the obtained scores from Test-*h* about 68% of the time (i.e., $\pm SEM$) and within about 4 points of the obtained scores about 95% of the time (i.e., $\pm 2SEM$). Bart's score for example is 14" (i.e., $u_1 = 14$, as listed in Case 16.6). "So according to the SEM model, I'm about 68% sure that Bart's true score is between 12 and 16 (i.e., 14 ± 2) and 95% sure it's between 10 and 18 (i.e., 14 ± 4). I'll use a 95% confidence interval for everybody's scores; so I won't consider two scores significantly different unless they differ by at least 4 points."

Mr. Keldorf converts the 34 scores to grades via the compromise grading method explained in Chapter 3. He applies his 95% confidence interval rule to the grade conversion by requiring that scores be at least 4 points apart to justify being assigned different grades. As shown by his sketch in Illustration 16.25, he assigns grades as follows: F for $h_i < 5$, F or D for $5 \le h_i < 7$, D for $7 \le h_i < 9$, D or C for $9 \le h_i < 11$, C for $11 \le h_i < 13$, C or B for $13 \le h_i < 15$, B for $15 \le h_i < 17$, B or A for $17 \le h_i < 19$, and A for $19 \le h_i$.

Look at Illustration 14.3. Note the horizontal bars extending the percentile scores in the chart. Also next to the column listing the national percentile scores is a column referred to as "Range." The horizontal bars and range reflect the SEMs computed for the various subtest scores. Typically, standardized test reports include standard error of measurements. In Case 16.12, the teachers at one school take into account the reported SEM in their interpretation of standardized test results.

CASE 16.12

Students at Eugene Street Elementary School qualify for a special language-arts skills development program through a federally funded grant if they score below 30 on a particular standardized reading test. According to one of the test manuals, the standard error of measurement is 2.48. Most teachers believe that the decision as to whether or not a student should be placed in the special program should not hinge solely on a single test score. They would rather use more extensive assessment techniques. However, with

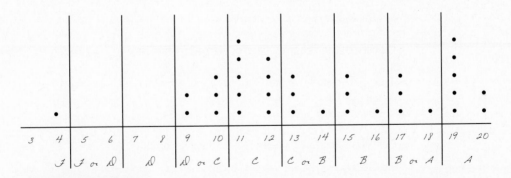

ILLUSTRATION 16.25

Sketch Mr. Keldorf Made as He Used the Compromise Grading Method in Conjunction with SEM_h

the reading skills of 633 students to be assessed at the beginning of the school year, extensive, in-depth measurements are ruled out by the school principal. Some of the teachers negotiate a compromise plan:

> The standardized test is administered to all 633 students. Those students with scores less than or equal to 25 (i.e., more than 2*SEM* below the cutoff score of 30) are automatically enrolled in the special program. Students with scores greater than or equal to 35 (i.e., more than 2*SEM* above the cutoff score of 30) are automatically excluded from the special program. Additional, more in-depth measurements are administered to students with scores between 25 and 35 (i.e., within 2*SEM* of the cutoff score of 30) to help determine whether or not they should be enrolled in the special program.

The plan was based on the teachers' understanding that scores need to be markedly different to justify using them to judge one student's true score to be different from another's. From the school principal's perspective, the compromise plan reduced the number of students with whom in-depth assessments would be used—in this case from 633 to 42. The principal believes 42 is a manageable number for whom interviews could be conducted and prior teachers consulted.

For example, Sam, a third-grader, scored 26 on the standardized test. However, a one-to-one interview mini-experiment and consultations with his second-grade teacher convince the teachers that Sam does not need to be in the program. On the other hand, the interview mini-experiment and consultations convince the teachers that Troy should be enrolled in the program although his score on the standardized test was 33.

ASSESSING RELIABILITY WHEN KUDER-RICHARDSON METHODS ARE INAPPROPRIATE

MEASUREMENTS USED FOR CRITERION-REFERENCED EVALUATIONS

The Problem

Of course, reliability is just as necessary for measurements used for making criterion-referenced evaluations as it is for making norm-referenced evaluations. However, the state of the art of assessing the reliabilities of tests used with criterion-referenced evaluations is not as advanced as it is for tests used with norm-referenced evaluations. The methods that use correlational statistics (e.g., Pearson product-moment correlation and Kuder-Richardson coefficients) are based on the assumption that greater score variability is more desirable than less score variability. Since measurements used for norm-referenced evaluations are designed for discriminating among various levels in a student population, this assumption is tenable for norm-referenced situations. However, measurements used for making criterion-referenced evaluations only need to discriminate around a criterion-level cutoff point; thus, high variability among students' scores is not necessarily desirable.

Consider strategies for assessing the reliabilities of measurements used for criterion-referenced evaluations in three types of situations: (1) when scores are used to assess the degree to which achievement levels exceed or fall below a criterion, (2) when scores are used only to discriminate between achievement levels that meet a criterion and levels that do not, and (3) when the true scores of the group tests are believed to be extremely homogeneous.

Variation from the Criterion

The levels of student achievement may vary widely around a criterion. In such cases, it may be desirable to have a measurement that finely discriminates how far above or below students' achievement levels are with respect to that criterion. In other words, test results (even for a criterion-referenced evaluation) may be used not only to help determine whether or not each student has achieved a criterion standard, but also exactly how far from the standard her or his achievement lies. For a test to make such fine discriminations among levels around the criterion point, it must necessarily produce scores that vary. For these types of tests, the traditional reliability coefficients designed for norm-referenced situations can appropriately be used.

If the criterion cutoff point is near the mean of scores, then reliability can be assessed using Kuder-Richardson methods. However, if the criterion point is quite deviant from the mean of the scores—either much higher or much lower—and the test effectively discriminates about the criterion point, then the Kuder-Richardson methods will yield inaccurately low coefficients. For such a case, you might consider computing a Kuder-Richardson reliability coefficient and then adjusting it by one of several formulas for "reliability of criterion-referenced measurements" that can be found in the literature published since 1972 (e.g., Brennan & Kane, 1977). One of the more popular and easy to compute of these formulas was proposed by S. A. Livingston (1972) and is as follows:

$$cr = \frac{(nr)(\sigma^2) + (\mu - C)^2}{\sigma^2 = (\mu - C)^2}$$

where cr is the adjusted reliability coefficient for the test to be used for a criterion-referenced evaluation, nr is the reliability coefficient computed as one would for a norm-referenced situation (e.g., $KR21$), and C is the criterion-level cutoff score.

The Livingston formula is applied in Case 16.13.

CASE 16.13

Ms. Bagshaw, a reading teacher, wants to evaluate her students' achievement of the following objective:

> Students accurately decode 80% of the words on the high-frequency word list (Cunningham, 1995) (simple knowledge).

In an interview, Ms. Bagshaw asks each student to read 20 words randomly selected from the high-frequency word list. She records each word correctly pronounced as "+1" and others as "+0." Thus, she has a measurement consisting of 20 dichotomously scored mini-experiments. The measurement yields the score sequence $\{v_i\}$ displayed in Illustration 16.26. She computes $KR21_v$, then adjusts the coefficient with the Livingston formula to obtain r_v. She also computes SEM_v, using it to help her judge which scores suggest student achievement of the objective is significantly above or below the 90% criterion. Illustration 16.26 displays her computations.

Either Meets or Fails to Meet the Criterion

Sometimes a measurement is used only as an indicator of whether or not the achievement level of each student is above or below a criterion level. In such cases, the evaluator is not concerned with how far from the criterion level the students' achievement levels lie. Test-retest or equivalent form methods for assessing reliabilities in this type of situation may be meaningful if, as in Case 16.1, students' true scores can be held reasonably constant and the first administration of the test does not influence the retest. The data from the two administrations might be handled as follows:

> A "+" is recorded for each score from the first administration that meets or exceeds the criterion cutoff and a "−" for each that does not. The scores from the second administration are recorded the same way.

Illustration 16.27 is an example.

$\{v_i\} = (17, 7, 16, 20, 11, 16, 13, 11, 8, 20, 17, 13, 13, 13, 12, 12, 11, 7, 11, 12, 11, 8, 20, 19, 18)$

$N_v = 25$

$\mu_v = 13.44$

$\sigma_v \approx 3.99$

$\sigma_v^2 \approx 15.92$

$k_v = 20$

$C_v = 16$ (since $(0.80)(20) = 16$)

$$KR21_v = \frac{k_v\sigma_v^2 - \mu_v(k_v - \mu_v)}{\sigma_v^2(k_v - 1)} \approx \frac{20(15.92) - 13.44(20 - 13.44)}{15.92(19)} \approx 0.76$$

$$r_v = \frac{(KR21_v)(\sigma_v^2) + (\mu_v - C_v)^2}{\sigma_v^2 + (\mu_v - C_v)^2} \approx \frac{.76(15.92) + (13.44 - 16)^2}{15.92 + (13.44 - 16)^2} \approx \frac{18.65}{22.47} \approx 0.83$$

$$SEM_v = \sigma_v\sqrt{1 - r_v} \approx 3.99\sqrt{1 - .83} \approx 1.65$$

ILLUSTRATION 16.26

Ms. Bagshaw's Computation of r_v and SEM_v

The consistency between the two results can be eye-balled or you may want to compute a percentage of test-retest pairs that are in agreement. In Illustration 16.27, the test and retest results are the same for 13 of 20 students (i.e., for $i = 1, 2, 3, 5, 8, 10, 11, 12, 13, 15, 17, 18$, and 19). Thus, 65% of the results are in agreement. The 65% is an indicator of the test's reliability, but it should not be interpreted as if it were a reliability coefficient computed by a traditional method.

An alternative method to computing the percentage of agreements is to compute a correlation coefficient and obtain an indicator that is more comparable to standard reliability coefficients. In cases where the results are expressed simply as +'s and −'s, the Pearson product-moment correlation formula is simplified considerably. The conventional symbol for the correlation coefficient computed with the simplified formula is "ϕ" (the Greek letter "phi") rather than "ρ." The formula for ϕ is as follows:

$$\phi = \frac{P_{1,2} - (P_1)(P_2)}{\sqrt{(P_1)(M_1)(P_2)(M_2)}}$$

where ϕ is the reliability coefficient, $P_{1,2}$ is the proportion of students who have +'s from both administrations, P_1 is the proportion of students with a + from the first administration, P_2 is the proportion of students with a + from the second administration, M_1 is the proportion of students with a − from the first administration, and M_2 is the proportion of students with a − from the second administration.

Illustration 16.28 displays the computation of ϕ for Illustration 16.27's results. $\phi \approx 0.30$ suggests that the test lacks a satisfactory degree of reliability.

Student	1st	2nd
i	Adm.	Adm.
1	+	+
2	+	+
3	−	−
4	−	+
5	−	−
6	+	−
7	+	−
8	−	−
9	−	+
10	+	+
11	−	−
12	+	+
13	+	+
14	−	+
15	+	+
16	−	+
17	−	−
18	−	−
19	+	+
20	+	−

ILLUSTRATION 16.27

Example of Scores from Two Administrations Recorded as Meeting or Not Meeting a Criterion Cutoff

$P_{1,2} = 7 \div 20 = 0.35$, $P_1 = 10 \div 20 = 0.50$, $P_2 = 11 \div 20 = 0.55$, $M_1 = 10 \div 20 = 0.50$, $M_2 = 9 \div 20 = 0.45$

Therefore,

$$\emptyset = \frac{.35 - (.50)(.45)}{\sqrt{(.50)(.50)(.55)(.45)}} = 0.30$$

ILLUSTRATION 16.28

Computation of ϕ for Illustration 16.27's Results

Homogeneous True Scores

Measurements that are used to make criterion-referenced evaluations regarding mastery level achievement do not ordinarily have high variances when used with students who almost all have achieved a mastery level. One possibility for assessing the reliability of such a measurement is to field test the measurement with a group of students before more than half of the students have "achieved mastery." Traditional methods for assessing reliability can produce meaningful coefficients with a group that hasn't been "homogenized" by instruction.

MEASUREMENTS WITH MANY WEIGHTED-SCORED ITEMS

Fortunately, there will be times when you find it necessary to assess the reliability of measurements that do not quite fit any of the known methods. I say "fortunately" because such situations give you practice developing your own strategies instead of only following technical rules. You will need to call upon concepts you've constructed and relationships you've discovered to develop methods to apply to new situations.

Recall Case 15.9 in which Mr. Doleac began conducting a validation study of Illustration 15.7's test. Case 16.14 is a continuation of Case 15.9.

CASE 16.14

In response to Mr. Doleac's memo shown in Illustration 15.11, Ms. Baker arranged for Illustration 15.7's 25-point test to be administered to 33 first-aid students. The resulting score sequence, $\{b_i\}$, is as follows: (20, 23, 13, 19, 20, 15, 10, 14, 25, 15, 14, 10, 7, 19, 10, 10, 2, 13, 13, 8, 13, 20, 8, 20, 23, 14, 13, 12, 5, 13, 24, 5, 12).

Mr. Doleac thinks as he decides how to assess reliability, "This test has 13 items. Section I of Part A has 9 dichotomously scored items. II and III of Part A and I and II of Part B use weighted scoring with A-II worth 2 points, A-III worth 5 points, B-I worth 5 points, and B-II worth 4 points. Too bad those last 4 items use weighted scoring, I really don't have the time to go into the item-by-item score matrix to compute coefficient α. But that's the right way to do it."

Mr. Doleac re-examines the scoring rubrics for the items, as shown in Illustration 15.7. Suddenly, he exclaims to himself, "Wait a minute, Kordel; maybe you don't need to compute α after all! The weighted scoring for each of these last four items is analytical, not global. That means that the 2 points for Item #A-II can be broken down into two separate parts—each part associated with a single student response. The same is true for the 5 points of Item #A-III, the 5 points of Item #B-I, and the 4 points of Item #B-II. It would be legitimate for me to treat Test-b as if it were a test consisting of 25 dichotomously scored items. Those last four items with analytical scoring are really 16 dichotomously scored items. So, if the variance is sufficiently large, I'll go ahead and estimate the reliability coefficient I would get with KR20 by computing KR21. I must remember to use 25 for K instead of 13."

Mr. Doleac's computations are shown in Illustration 16.29.

Of course, if the four weighted items on Illustration 15.7's test were globally scored, then Mr. Doleac's application of KR21 would not be tenable and he would need to compute coefficient α.

$$N_b = 33$$

$$k_b = 25$$

$$\mu_b = 14.00$$

$$\sigma_b \approx 5.73$$

$$\sigma_b^2 \approx 32.83$$

$$KR21_b = \frac{k_b \sigma_b^2 - \mu_b(k_b - \mu_b)}{\sigma_b^2(k_b - 1)} \approx \frac{25(32.83) - 14(25 - 14)}{32.83(24)} \approx 0.85$$

ILLUSTRATION 16.29

Mr. Doleac's Computation of a Reliability Coefficient for Illustration 15.7's Test

MEASUREMENTS ADMINISTERED TO ONLY A FEW STUDENTS

Whether a test is short or long or contains weighted or dichotomously scored items, reliability coefficients derived from Pearson product-moment correlations are not appropriate for only a small number of scores (e.g., $N \leq 10$). But a small N not only renders correlational statistics meaningless and unnecessary; a small N also renders *qualitative* assessments of measurement reliability usable. With only a few students, you can make multiple observations per student and compare consistency among the results of those observations. Using, for example, the idea of the equivalent-form method, you can discuss with a student why he or she responded differently to the prompts for two equivalent mini-experiments. When an inconsistency between two responses is detected, you can use qualitative strategies (e.g., think-aloud trials about which you learned from your work with Chapter 15) to determine if the inconsistency is a consequence of reliability error or a fluctuation in the student's true score.

ASSESSING OBSERVER CONSISTENCY

Reread Chapter 4's section "Observer Consistency" on pages 186–189.

Ms. Conine in Case 4.7 and Ms. Fisher in Case 4.8 employed sound methods for assessing intra-observer consistency of measurements. Consider routinely spot-checking the intra-observer and inter-observer consistency of a sample of measurements you make that include mini-experiments with rubrics that leave room for judgment. Such spot checks for mini-experiments with performance-observation, essay, product-examination, and oral-discourse formats will lead you to design better rubrics and to improve how consistently you follow rubrics.

For less frequent situations in which you need to conduct formal validation studies, statistical applications may be useful. Case 16.15 is a continuation of Case 16.14.

CASE 16.15

As shown in Illustration 16.29, Mr. Doleac used KR21 in his assessment of the internal consistency of Test-b (i.e., Illustration 15.7's test). But because of the Items #A-III, #B-I, and #B-II, he also decided to assess the inter-observer consistency of the test. To do this, he not only scored the 33 students' responses to Prompts #A-III, #B-I, and #B-II himself, but he had another first-aid teacher, Ms. Zhang, score them also. For Item #A-III, he made copies of the students' responses and gave the copies to Ms. Zhang. The two teachers read and scored the 33 descriptions and explanations independently of one another. For Item #B-I, he and Ms. Zhang observed each student execute the five-step process and, without seeing what was on the other's score sheet, recorded their scores for the performance. For Item #B-II, the two teachers examined each of the students' pressure bandages without comment, recording their scores out of 4 independently of one another.

A secretary scored students' responses to the 11 prompts for Parts A-I and A-II of the test because no judgment or teaching expertise was needed to follow the rubrics for those multiple-choice items. Illustration 16.30 displays the item-by-item results from Mr. Doleac's application of the rubrics for the 5 parts of #A-III, the 5 parts of #B-I, and the 4 parts of #B-II as well as students' total scores for the test. Illustration 16.31 displays the results from Ms. Zhang's application of the rubrics.

Using the most common method for checking inter-observer consistency, Mr. Doleac computes a Pearson product-moment correlation coefficient to measure the relationship between the test scores from his use of the rubrics, $\{b_i\}$, and the test scores from Ms. Zhang's use of the rubrics, $\{b_i'\}$. The resulting $\rho_{b,b'} \approx 0.92$ leads him to conclude that overall the test has satisfactory observer consistency.

Student i	A-III					B-I					B-II				(Test Score)* b_i
	1	2	3	4	5	1	2	3	4	5	1	2	3	4	
1	1	1	1	1	1	1	1	1	0	1	1	1	1	1	20
2	1	1	1	1	1	1	1	1	1	1	1	1	1	1	23
3	1	1	0	0	0	1	1	1	1	1	0	1	0	0	13
4	1	0	1	1	0	1	1	1	1	1	1	1	1	1	19
5	1	1	1	1	1	1	1	1	1	1	1	1	1	0	20
6	1	0	0	0	0	1	1	1	1	1	1	1	1	1	15
7	1	0	0	0	0	0	1	1	1	1	1	0	0	0	10
8	0	0	0	0	0	1	1	1	1	1	1	1	1	1	14
9	1	1	1	1	1	1	1	1	1	1	1	1	1	1	25
10	1	1	1	0	1	1	0	1	0	0	1	0	1	1	15
11	0	0	0	0	0	1	1	1	1	1	1	1	0	1	14
12	1	1	0	0	0	1	1	1	1	1	0	0	0	0	10
13	0	0	0	0	0	1	1	1	0	0	0	0	0	0	7
14	1	0	1	0	0	1	1	1	1	1	1	1	1	1	19
15	0	0	0	0	0	1	1	1	1	1	0	0	1	0	10
16	0	0	0	0	0	1	1	1	1	1	0	0	1	0	10
17	0	0	0	0	0	0	0	0	0	0	0	0	0	0	2
18	1	1	1	1	1	1	0	0	0	0	0	1	0	1	13
19	0	0	0	0	0	1	1	1	1	1	1	1	0	1	13
20	0	0	0	0	0	1	1	1	1	0	0	0	0	0	8
21	0	0	0	0	0	1	1	1	1	1	1	1	1	1	13
22	1	1	1	1	1	1	1	0	1	1	1	1	1	1	20
23	0	0	0	0	0	0	1	0	0	0	0	0	0	0	8
24	1	1	1	1	0	1	1	1	1	1	1	1	1	1	20
25	1	1	1	1	1	1	1	1	1	1	1	1	1	1	23
26	0	0	0	0	0	1	0	1	1	1	1	1	0	1	14
27	0	0	0	0	0	1	1	1	1	1	1	1	0	1	13
28	1	0	0	0	0	1	0	0	0	0	1	1	1	1	12
29	0	0	0	0	0	0	1	1	0	1	0	0	0	0	5
30	0	0	0	0	0	1	1	1	1	1	1	1	1	1	13
31	1	1	1	1	1	1	1	1	1	1	1	1	1	1	24
32	0	0	0	0	0	0	1	1	0	0	0	0	0	0	5
33	0	0	0	0	0	1	1	1	1	1	1	1	1	0	12

* Scores from Item #A-I and #A-II are included in these sums.

ILLUSTRATION 16.30

Results from Mr. Doleac's Scoring of Illustration 15.7's Test

He then does an item-by-item comparison of Illustration 16.30's matrix to Illustration 16.31's matrix by computing the percentage of observations in which he and Ms. Zhang agreed. To obtain this percentage, he notes that the matrix contains 462 item-score cells, since there are 33 students and 14 observation points to record a "0" or "1." He does not include the first 11 items that the secretary scored in this analysis.

Student	A-III					B-I					B-II				(Test Score)*
i	1	2	3	4	5	1	2	3	4	5	1	2	3	4	b'_i
1	1	1	1	1	1	0	1	1	0	1	1	1	0	1	18
2	1	0	1	1	1	1	1	1	1	1	1	1	1	1	22
3	1	0	1	0	0	0	1	1	1	1	1	1	0	0	13
4	1	0	1	1	1	1	1	1	1	1	1	1	1	1	20
5	1	0	1	1	0	1	1	1	1	1	1	1	1	0	18
6	0	0	0	0	0	1	1	1	1	1	1	1	1	0	13
7	0	0	0	0	0	0	1	1	1	1	1	1	0	0	10
8	0	0	0	0	0	1	1	1	1	1	1	1	1	1	14
9	1	1	1	1	1	1	1	1	1	1	1	1	1	1	25
10	1	1	1	0	1	1	1	0	1	0	1	1	1	1	17
11	1	0	0	0	0	1	1	1	1	1	1	1	1	1	16
12	1	0	0	0	0	1	1	1	1	1	0	0	0	0	9
13	0	0	0	0	0	1	1	0	0	0	0	0	0	0	6
14	1	1	1	0	0	1	1	1	1	1	1	1	1	1	20
15	0	0	0	0	0	1	1	1	1	1	0	0	1	0	10
16	0	0	0	0	0	1	1	1	1	1	0	0	1	0	10
17	0	0	0	0	0	0	0	0	0	0	0	0	0	0	2
18	1	1	1	1	1	1	0	0	0	0	0	1	0	0	12
19	0	0	0	0	0	1	1	1	1	1	1	1	1	0	13
20	0	0	0	0	0	1	1	1	0	0	0	0	0	0	7
21	1	0	1	0	0	1	1	1	1	1	1	1	1	1	15
22	1	1	1	1	1	1	1	0	1	1	1	1	1	1	20
23	0	0	0	0	0	0	1	0	0	0	0	0	0	0	8
24	1	1	1	1	0	1	1	1	1	1	1	1	1	1	20
25	1	1	1	1	1	0	0	0	0	0	0	1	1	0	16
26	0	0	0	0	0	1	1	1	1	1	1	1	0	1	15
27	0	0	0	0	0	1	1	1	1	1	1	1	0	1	13
28	1	0	0	0	0	1	0	0	0	1	1	0	1	1	12
29	0	0	0	0	0	0	0	1	0	1	0	0	0	0	4
30	0	0	0	0	0	1	1	1	1	1	1	1	0	1	12
31	1	1	1	1	1	1	1	1	1	1	1	1	1	1	24
32	0	0	0	0	0	0	1	1	0	0	0	0	0	0	5
33	0	0	0	0	0	1	1	1	1	1	1	1	1	1	13

* Scores from Item #A-I and #A-II are included in these sums.

ILLUSTRATION 16.31

Results from Ms. Zhang's Scoring of Illustration 15.7's Test

He counts the number of agreements (i.e., cells for which both he and Ms. Zhang recorded "0" or both recorded "1") to be 420. There are 42 discrepancies out of 462 opportunities. Thus, the two teachers agreed 420 out of a possible 462 times, which means that 91% of the cells are in agreement. The 91% is further evidence that the test has a satisfactory degree of observer consistency.

$$P_{1,2} = \frac{250}{462} \approx 0.54, \ P_1 = \frac{275}{462} \approx 0.60, \ M_1 = \frac{187}{462} \approx 0.40, \ P_2 = \frac{266}{462} \approx 0.58, \ M_1 = \frac{196}{462} \approx 0.42$$

$$\phi = \frac{P_{1,2} - P_1 P_2}{\sqrt{P_1 M_1 P_2 M_2}} \approx \frac{.54 - (.60)(.58)}{\sqrt{(.60)(.40)(.58)(.42)}} \approx \frac{.192}{.242} \approx 0.79$$

ILLUSTRATION 16.32

Mr. Doleac's Computations of ϕ

Although not necessary, Mr. Doleac decides to do one more computation relative to observer consistency. He uses the formula for a ϕ to correlate the cell-by-cell agreement between Illustration 30's matrix and Illustration 31's. With $P_{1,2}$ being the proportion of corresponding cells from the two matrices that both have 1's, P_1 as the proportion of Illustration 30's cells with 1's, P_2 as the proportion of Illustration 31's cells with 1's, M_1 as the proportion of Illustration 30's cells with 0's, and M_2 as the proportion of Illustration 31's cells with 0's, he computes $\phi \approx 0.79$. He considers that coefficient to be consistent with the two other indicators of observer consistency (i.e., $\rho_{b,b'} \approx 0.92$ and 91% of cell-by-cell agreement). Illustration 16.32 displays his computation of ϕ.

SYNTHESIS ACTIVITIES FOR CHAPTER 16

1. For each of the multiple-choice prompts, select the one best response that either answers the question or completes the statement:

   A. If KR20 is an accurate reliability coefficient for a particular test, then so is _____.
   a) KR21
   b) α

   B. Two achievement tests are administered to the same group of students. Which one of the following numbers would be an indication of whether or not the two tests were relevant to the same learning goal?
   a) The combined ratios of scores falling within one standard deviation of the mean on both tests.
   b) The difference between the two tests' standard deviations.
   c) The difference between the two test means.
   d) The correlation coefficient obtained on the two sequences of test scores.

   C. The Kuder-Richardson reliability coefficient a teacher computes on a test is 0.94. Such a test would probably yield results which are generally _____.
   a) valid
   b) dependable
   c) relevant at the 0.06 level
   d) 94% accurate

   D. A test has reliability coefficient of 0.28. Such a test would probably yield results _____.
   a) that are invalid
   b) with relatively low scores
   c) that include data with an unstable range
   d) that are not relevant at the 0.72 level

   E. A reliability coefficient is a(n) _____.
   a) evaluation of a test's reliability
   b) measurement of a test's reliability

   F. Which one of the following is probably the most useful method for assessing reliability of a mea-
      surement administered to only one student?
      a) computing α
      b) computing KR21
      c) comparing responses for consistency among various items
      d) computing the Pearson product-moment correlation coefficient with the measurement in ques-
         tion and that of a criterion measure
   G. Which one of the following is probably the most useful computation for assessing reliability of
      an 18-point test administered to 38 students if the test consists of 3 globally scored essay items?
      a) coefficient α
      b) Kuder-Richardson formula 20
      c) Kuder-Richardson formula 21
      d) Pearson product-moment correlation coefficient with the results from a test and a retest
   H. Maria's raw score on a test is 80. Statistical analysis of the test results obtained from Maria and
      her 27 classmates yielded a standard deviation of 6 and a Kuder-Richardson reliability coeffi-
      cient of 0.84. The SEM method of interpreting Maria's score in light of the reliability coefficient
      indicates which one of the following?
      a) Maria's actual level of achievement lies in the interval from 77.6 to 82.4.
      b) If Maria were retested many, many times under theoretical test-retest conditions, about 95%
         of the times her scores would be between 75 and 85.
   I. Relative to the relationship $x_i = T_i + E_x$ for Test-x, which one of the following variables repre-
      sents a measurement result?
      a) x_i
      b) T_i
      c) E_x
   J. Relative to the relationship $x_i = T_i + E_x$ for Test-x, which one of the following variables would
      a validation study be used to assess?
      a) x_i
      b) T_i
      c) E_x

2. With a colleague, compare and discuss your responses to the multiple-choice prompts from Synthesis Activity 1. Also, check your choices against the following key: A-b, B-d, C-b, D-a, E-b, F-c,
   G-a, H-b, I-a, and J-c.

3. When Mr. Doleac assessed the internal consistency of Test-b from Illustration 15.7, he used KR21
   rather than the more obviously appropriate coefficient α. Discuss with a colleague why coefficient
   α is appropriate. Then discuss Mr. Doleac's rationale for using KR21 instead (i.e., why he would
   want to and why what he did was tenable).

4. Use the statistics from Illustration 16.29 to compute SEM_b for Illustration 15.7's test. Then use SEM_b
   to partition the test scores from Illustration 16.30 into three groups: (1) Those that are significantly
   greater than the μ_b, (2) those that are not significantly different from μ_b, and (3) those that are significantly lower than μ_b. Compare your results to those of a colleague.

5. Suppose you were going to convert Test-b's scores from Illustration 16.30 to letter grades via the
   compromise method. Establish some cutoff scores for each letter grade (e.g., 15 for a C). In light of
   SEM_b you computed when you engaged in Synthesis Activity 4, convert the scores to grades similar to the way Mr. Keldorf did in Case 16.11.

6. With several colleagues, engage in a discussion addressing the following question: What can a reliability coefficient (e.g., coefficient α) tell you about the mini-experiments' outcomes matrix for a
   test without you having to actually lay out and examine the matrix?

7. Administer a measurement (preferably one which you designed yourself) to a group of students. Assess the internal consistency of the measurement as well as its observer consistency.

TRANSITIONAL ACTIVITY FROM CHAPTER 16 TO CHAPTER 17

In a discussion with two or more of your colleagues, address the following questions:

1. What is the difference between an effective mini-experiment and a mini-experiment that is either ineffective or defective?

2. From our work with Chapters 15 and 16, we can assess the validity of a measurement as a whole, but what strategies can we employ to find out how to make a measurement more valid? What can we do to distinguish between mini-experiments that contribute to a measurement's validity and those that contaminate validity?

Examining the Effectiveness of Mini-Experiments

⟻ GOAL OF CHAPTER 17

Chapter 17 is intended to lead you to develop strategies for assessing the effectiveness of individual mini-experiments. More specifically, the objectives are as follows:

A. You will explain how a measurement's mini-experiments' outcome matrix reflects the effectiveness of individual mini-experiments (discover a relationship) 15%.

B. You will explain how assessments of mini-experiments' effectiveness can be used to refine measurements and develop your own talents for designing mini-experiments (comprehension and communication skills) 10%.

C. You will explain how correlational statistics and item analysis data are used in the assessment of mini-experiment effectiveness (comprehension and communication skills) 20%.

D. You will develop and employ strategies for assessing the effectiveness of mini-experiments you use with your students (application) 45%.

E. You will incorporate the following technical phrases into your professional vocabulary: "effectiveness of mini-experiments," "classical item analysis," "index of discrimination," "index of difficulty," and "efficiency index" (comprehension and communication skills) 10%.

THE EFFECTIVENESS OF MINI-EXPERIMENTS

THE CONCEPT OF EFFECTIVENESS

Consider Case 17.1.

CASE 17.1

As indicated by Illustration 7.10, Ms. Ragusa defines the goal of her unit on magnetism with 10 objectives, including Objective A:

> A. Students discriminate between examples and non-examples of magnets and discover attributes of magnets (construct a concept).

During the unit, she conducts several mini-experiments intended to be relevant to Objective A. Illustration 17.1 displays three of them.

Mini-Experiment #1:

Interview Prompt:

Ms. Ragusa gives the student two identical-looking, bar-shaped pieces of metal. One is magnetized; the other is not. She then asks the student to determine which one of the two is a magnet and which one is not.

Observer's Rubric:

Ms. Ragusa observes what the student does with the two objects. The following is an example of a student's action that would be a positive indicator that the student has constructed the concept of a magnet:

> The student asks for or locates a piece of magnetic material (e.g., the steel leg of a table) and one at a time brings each object near the magnetic material to see if the object and the magnetic material pull together. Then the student identifies the object that attracted the magnetic material as the magnet.

Other actions may be negative indicators of objective achievement (e.g., checking to see which object is heavier, bringing the two objects together to see if they attract each other, or bringing the objects near non-magnetic material (e.g., a wooden desk top)). Ms. Ragusa scores the response +2 if the positive indicators clearly outweigh the negative indicators, +0 if the negative indicators clearly outweigh the positive indicators, or +1 if it is unclear as to whether or not the positive indicators outweigh the negative indicators.

Mini-Experiment #2:

Prompt:

Each student is seated at his/her desk with an answer sheet. Ms. Ragusa stands in front of the class holding a horseshoe- shaped piece of iron. On a table in front of her is an open container with iron filings. She directs the students, "Carefully watch what I do with this horseshoe. After I'm done, decide whether or not this horseshoe is a magnet. If you decide that it is, write 'yes' in blank number 2 of your answer sheet. If you decide it is not a magnet, then write 'no.' If you cannot tell from the demonstration whether or not it is a magnet, then write 'cannot tell'." She then brings the horseshoe [it is magnetized] over the container close enough for the filings to "jump up" and cling to the horseshoe.

ILLUSTRATION 17.1

Three Mini-Experiments Ms. Ragusa Intends to Be Relevant to Objective A

(Continued)

ILLUSTRATION 17.1 (Continued)

<u>Observer's Rubric</u>:

+1 for "yes;" +0 for "no" or "cannot tell."

<u>Mini-Experiment #3</u>:

<u>Prompt</u>:

Each student is seated at his/her desk with an answer sheet. Ms. Ragusa stands in front of the class holding a bar-shaped piece of iron. On a table in front of her is an open container with steel pins. She directs the students, "Carefully watch what I do with this bar. After I'm done, decide whether or not this bar is a magnet. If you decide that it is, write 'yes' in blank number 3 of your answer sheet. If you decide it is not a magnet, then write 'no.' If you cannot tell from the demonstration whether or not it is a magnet, then write 'cannot tell'." She then brings the bar [it is not magnetized] over to the pins, touching them. The pins do not cling to the bar; they remain in the container as she brings the bar away from them.

<u>Observer's Rubric</u>:

+1 for "no;" +0 for "yes" or "cannot tell."

When one student, Eicho, is confronted with Prompt #1, she thinks, "I need some iron or something that magnets attract. The leg of this chair is metal. I'll see which one of these bars will stick to it. Of course, it may not be the right kind of metal. If it's stainless steel or fake metal, then I'll have to find something else to test." She puts the two bars against the leg. One clings; the other doesn't. She tells, Ms. Ragusa, "This one is a magnet." Ms. Ragusa records "+1" by "#1" on Eicho's scoresheet.

When another student, Bryce, is confronted with Prompt #1, he thinks, "This is some kind of trick. A horseshoe is a magnet. These aren't horseshoes." He asks Ms. Ragusa, "Are you tricking me? These are not magnets." He brings them together; the two bars cling together. "They're not magnets," he says, as Ms. Ragusa records "+0."

When Eicho observes Ms. Ragusa's demonstration as part of Prompt #2 from Illustration 17.1, she thinks, "The filings jumped up on the magnet. The filings couldn't be magnets or they'd be sticking to one another and they'd lose their power anyway. The horseshoe has to be a magnet." She writes, "yes," in the blank for #2.

As soon as Bryce hears the directions for Prompt #2, he writes "yes" in the blank as he thinks, "It's a horseshoe, so it's got to be a magnet." He doesn't even bother to watch what happened with the filings.

When Eicho observes Ms. Ragusa's demonstration for Prompt #3, she thinks, "The bar didn't attract the pins, but maybe the pins aren't the right kind of metal. They may be stainless steel, and magnets don't attract stainless steel." She writes, "cannot tell" in the blank for #3.

As soon as Bryce hears the directions for Prompt #3, he writes "no" in the blank as he thinks, "It's not a magnet because it's not a horseshoe."

Eicho's score for Mini-Experiment #1 was +1; Bryce's was +0. Thus, Mini-Experiment #1 caused a difference in their two scores on the measurement. What caused Eicho to make a response that produced a score of +1 for Mini-Experiment #1? What caused Bryce to make a response that produced a score of +0 for Mini-Experiment #1?

From being able to read their thoughts in Case 17.1, it appears that Eicho's score of +1 reflected a rather sophisticated level of achievement of Objective A. Bryce's thoughts suggest that his response reflects a misconception about magnets. In other words, he does not seem to have achieved Objective A very well. Thus, Mini-Experiment #1 seems to have effectively discriminated in favor of Eicho's high level of achievement of Objective A and against Bryce's low level of achievement of Objective A. Is that not what a mini-experiment designed to be relevant to Objective A should do? Mini-experiments that discriminate in favor of high levels of achievement of the objective and against low levels of achievement are referred to as *"effective mini-experiments"* or *"effective items."*

Although Ms. Ragusa designed Mini-Experiment #2 to be relevant to Objective A just like Mini-Experiment #1, Mini-Experiment #2 did not discriminate between Eicho's achievement of Objective A and Bryce's lack of achievement of Objective A. Such mini-experiments that don't discriminate are referred to as *"ineffective mini-experiments"* or *"ineffective items."* Whereas, effective mini-experiments tend to raise the scores of students with higher levels of achievement over the scores of students with lower levels of achievement, ineffective mini-experiments do not contribute to the variability of measurement scores.

From reading Eicho's and Bryce's thoughts as they responded to Mini-Experiment #3 in Case 17.1, it appears that Mini-Experiment #3 discriminated against Eicho's high level of achievement and in favor of Bryce's low level of achievement. Mini-Experiment #3 tends to raise Bryce's score on the measurement above Eicho's. Mini-experiments that favor lower-levels of objective achievement over higher levels of achievement are referred to as *"defective mini-experiments"* or *"defective items."*

In general, a mini-experiment is *effective* to the degree to which it discriminates in favor of high levels of objective achievement and against low levels of objective achievement.

WHY ASSESS EFFECTIVENESS

The purpose of the first two stages of a validation study, assessment of relevance and reliability, is to provide information on the validity and overall results of a measurement. The purpose of the third stage, assessment of the effectiveness of mini-experiments, is to identify (1) mini-experiments that are contributing to the accuracy of the measurement (i.e., providing information), (2) mini-experiments that are not influencing the measurement's results (i.e., not providing information), and (3) mini-experiments that are detracting from the accuracy of the results (i.e., providing misinformation).

Assessments of relevance and reliability help determine measurement error. Assessments of mini-experiment effectiveness help determine how a measurement can be improved by replacing ineffective or defective mini-experiments with effective ones, thus reducing measurement error. A measurement can hardly be valid if it is dominated by faulty mini-experiments. But a valid measurement may have some faulty mini-experiments, and an invalid measurement may have some effective mini-experiments. Assessments of mini-experiment effectiveness are designed to identify strengths and weaknesses of measurements.

DEVELOPING A PROCESS FOR ASSESSING EFFECTIVENESS

Of course, if you could read your students' thoughts the way you were able to read Eicho's and Bryce's in Case 17.1, you could readily know about the effectiveness of mini-experiments. The closest you actually get to reading students' thoughts is whenever you conduct think-aloud trials, as Ms. Kromenhoek conducted in Case 15.8. But think-aloud trials are too time-consuming to be used routinely with more than a few students.

To assess how well a mini-experiment discriminates in favor of higher levels of objective achievement and against lower levels of objective achievement, you need to try out the mini-experiment with a group of students—some of whom you know have achieved the objective to a high degree and some of whom you know have not. If you had knowledge of your students' actual achievement levels, you wouldn't need to conduct any mini-experiments in the first place, but just for the purpose of getting us on track to develop a process for assessing effectiveness, suppose that you have access to 10 persons you know have achieved a particular objective to a relatively high degree. Refer to the objective as "Objective O" and the group with the high degree of achievement of Objective O as "Group H." Further suppose that you have access to a second group of 12 persons whose achievement of Objective O is relatively low; refer to this group as "Group L." Suggest a way for taking advantage of this hypothetical situation for assessing the effectiveness of a mini-experiment that is supposed to be relevant to Objective O. Refer to the mini-experiment as "Mini-Experiment #1." For simplicity, assume that Mini-Experiment #1 is dichotomously scored.

You could administer Mini-Experiment #1 to Group H as well as to Group L. Then you could compare the number of correct responses from the two groups. Because Group L has 12 people (i.e., $N_L = 12$), whereas Group H has only 10 (i.e., $N_H = 10$), you should compare the *proportion* of correct responses from Group H to the *proportion* of correct responses from Group L. Refer to Group H's proportion of correct responses to Mini-Experiment #1 as "PH_1" and Group L's proportion of correct responses to Mini-Experiment #1 as "PL_1." Suppose this hypothetical experiment yielded the results shown by Illustration 17.2.

From Group H, 7 out of 10 correctly responded to Mini-Experiment #1, so $PH_1 = 0.70$. From Group L, 4 out of 12 correctly responded to Mini-Experiment #1, so $PL_1 \approx 0.33$. $PH_1 > PL_1$ suggests that Mini-Experiment #1 is effective.

Group H		Group L	
Person i	Score for Mini-Exp. #1	Person i	Score for Mini-Exp. #1
1	1	11	1
2	0	12	1
3	1	13	0
4	1	14	0
5	1	15	1
6	0	16	0
7	1	17	0
8	1	18	0
9	0	19	0
10	1	20	0
		21	1

ILLUSTRATION 17.2

Results from Hypothetical Effectiveness Study of Mini-Experiment #1

Now, suppose that you took further advantage of your access to Groups H and L by trying out 11 more dichotomously scored mini-experiments designed to be relevant to Objective O. The results of those trials, as well as the one with Mini-Experiment #1, are shown by Illustration 17.3. Use Illustration 17.3's data to rank the 12 mini-experiments from most to least effective. In Case 17.2, Elwin and Kisha discuss their analysis of Illustration 17.3.

CASE 17.2

Elwin:	"First of all, I categorized the mini-experiments as either effective, ineffective, or defective."
Kisha:	"So whenever PH_j is greater than PL_j, you labeled the mini-experiment 'effective.'"
Elwin:	"Right. And for PH_j equal to PL_j, I said Mini-Experiment #j is 'ineffective.' And 'defective' for the cases where PH_j is less than PL_j."
Kisha:	"That makes sense. So you called Mini-Experiments #1, #2, #4, #6, #8, and #11 'effective'; #7, #9, and #10 'ineffective'; and #3, #5, and #12 'defective.'"
Elwin:	"Yeah, except there seems to be a lot of variation in the degree of effectiveness in each category. Like #2 is perfectly effective, whereas #11 is barely effective. Even though PH_{11} is greater than PL_{11}, it just seems like more of a chance difference."
Kisha:	"I see what you mean. $PH_{11} = 0.90$ means 9 out of 10 from H, and $PL_{11} = 0.83$ means—check with my calculator here—uhh, 10 out of 12 from L. That's hardly a resounding endorsement of Mini-Experiment #11's effectiveness."
Elwin:	"We were supposed to rank these mini-experiments according to effectiveness. What are your rankings?"
Kisha:	"#2 first, then #4, #6, #1, #11, and #8, then a tie for #7, #9, and #10, then in tenth place is #12, then #5 is second to worst, and finally #3 seems perfectly defective."
Elwin:	"That's exactly like my rankings."
Kisha:	"To rank them, we didn't only look to see if PH_j is greater than, equal to, or less than PL_j; we looked at how much greater than or less than they were."
Elwin:	"So a formula for measuring the degree of effectiveness is to subtract PL_j from PH_j."

ILLUSTRATION 17.3

$\{PH_j\}$ and $\{PL_j\}$ for $j = 1, 2, \ldots, 12$ from the Hypothetical Trials

Mini-Exp. j	PH_j	PL_j
1	0.70	0.33
2	1.00	0.00
3	0.00	1.00
4	0.90	0.25
5	0.30	0.50
6	0.80	0.33
7	0.50	0.50
8	0.70	0.67
9	1.00	1.00
10	0.00	0.00
11	0.90	0.83
12	0.08	0.20

The effectiveness of Mini-Experiment j can be measured by subtracting PL_j from PH_j. The greater that difference, the more effective the mini-experiment. Refer to the difference as the "*index of discrimination for Mini-Experiment #j*" and by the shorthand symbol "D_j." The formula Elwin suggested in Case 17.2 can be expressed as follows:

$$D_j = PH_j - PL_j$$

where D_j is the index of discrimination for Mini-Experiment #j, PH_j is the proportion of correct responses to Mini-Experiment #j from Group H, and PL_j is the proportion of correct responses to Mini-Experiment #j from Group L.

$\{D_j\}$ for Illustration 17.3's results is shown by Illustration 17.4.

What is the range of possible values for D_j? $-1 \le D_j \le 1$.

Our next task is to address the problem of finding a practical way of identifying a Group H and a Group L—a way that does not depend on reading students' thoughts.

CLASSICAL ITEM ANALYSIS

IDENTIFYING GROUPS OF VARYING ACHIEVEMENT LEVELS

Consider Case 17.3.

CASE 17.3

Ms. Youngberg designs three mini-experiments and inserts them into her computerized folder for Unit 4 of her health science course. The goal is defined by 9 objectives, A–I. One of the three mini-experiments is intended to be relevant to Objective B; the other two are for Objective F. All three are dichotomously scored. She would like to assess the effectiveness of the three mini-experiments before deciding whether or not to include them on an upcoming measurement of how well her 32 students achieved Unit 4's goal. However, as is usually the case, Ms. Youngberg is unable to conveniently locate

Mini-Exp. j	PH_j	PL_j	D_j
1	0.70	0.33	0.37
2	1.00	0.00	1.00
3	0.00	1.00	-1.00
4	0.90	0.25	0.65
5	0.30	0.50	-0.20
6	0.80	0.33	0.47
7	0.50	0.50	0.00
8	0.70	0.67	0.03
9	1.00	1.00	0.00
10	0.00	0.00	0.00
11	0.90	0.83	0.07
12	0.08	0.20	-0.12

ILLUSTRATION 17.4

$\{D_j\}$ for j = 1, 2, . . . , 12 from Illustration 17.3

a group of persons, comparable to her class, who she knows has achieved Objectives B and F. Not surprisingly, it is also too difficult to gain access to a comparable group with low levels of achievement of those objectives. She has ready access to her own health science students, and she could try the mini-experiments out on them, but if she already knew how well each of them had achieved the objectives, there would be no need to test them in the first place.

Unable to devise a reasonably convenient way to compute indices of discrimination before administering the measurement, Ms. Youngberg decides to go ahead and include these three untried mini-experiments in the measurement. In synthesizing the test, she applies strategies for designing relevant measurements as suggested in Chapter 6. On the test, the untried mini-experiment for Objective B is Prompt #3; the two for Objective F are Prompts #17 and #18. Convinced that the test is satisfactorily relevant, she administers it to her health science class and uses the results to compute a reliability coefficient of 0.89. Believing that the test is both relevant and reliable, she concludes that the scores are a valid indicator of her students' achievement of Unit 4's goal.

Although she has already used the test, she would still like to assess the effectiveness of those three mini-experiments in order to improve her own mini-experiment design skills and to refine the test for future use. She asks herself how she might use the results of the test to identify a Group H and a Group L for the purpose of computing D_3, D_{17}, and D_{18}. She thinks, "Because the test scores proved to be valid, they could serve as one mechanism for identifying H and L. Students with higher scores from the test would more likely have higher levels of achievement of Objectives B and F than those with lower test scores. So it's at least somewhat reasonable to compose Group H with the students who had the highest 10 or so test scores and Group L with the students who had the lowest 10 or so test scores. That'll be like correlating performance on each of the three mini-experiments with performance on the test as a whole.

"One weakness of this idea is that the three mini-experiments I want to assess influenced the test scores. That makes my logic a bit circular—comparing something to itself. But on the other hand, the maximum score for this test was 45. These three mini-experiments are only 1 point each. So each of them influenced the test results by only one–45th; that's only—here's my calculator—about 2% of the total possible score. So the circularity of the reasoning isn't all that great."

Ms. Youngberg ranks the students' scores as shown in Illustration 17.5.

Looking over the ranked scores, she thinks, "If I count down 10 from the top, I get to Student–21's 39. The next one's 38—no real difference between the 10th and 11th scores. But there's a 5-point break between the 11th and 12th scores. So I'll use the top 11 scores for Group H. Okay, now 10 up from the bottom gets me to Student–10's 26. But the break of 4 points occurs just before that. I think I'll go with bottom 9 scores for Group L."

She then checks Group H's and Group L's item scores for Mini-Experiments #3, #17, and #18, obtaining the results shown by Illustration 17.6. Also shown in Illustration 17.6 are the indices of discrimination she computed for those three mini-experiments.

$D_{17} \approx -0.20$ raises a red flag with Ms. Youngberg. She decides to re-examine Mini-Experiment #17 and to conduct a few think-aloud trials with two or three students to help her decide what is wrong with it and how she should change it in her computerized mini-experiment folders.

Note that Ms. Youngberg's method of computing indices of discrimination based on Groups H and L being determined by overall test scores provides a method for easily identifying mini-experiments that produce scores that are out of line with the ideal mini-experiments' outcomes matrix pictured by Illustration 16.2. Using her method, the smaller D_j, the more 1's in Item #j's column fall below the ideal diagonal and the more 0's will fall above that diagonal. Computing $\{D_j\}$ for $j = 1, 2, 3, \ldots, k$ is easier than laying out and analyzing the mini-experiments' outcomes matrix.

student i	t_i	i	t_i
11	44	23	31
9	43	15	29
2	43	5	29
4	40	6	28
20	40	17	28
24	40	25	28
29	40	10	26
7	40	30	22
1	39	13	22
21	39	14	21
31	38	27	20
3	33	8	20
28	33	32	20
12	32	26	15
19	32	18	15
22	32	16	15

ILLUSTRATION 17.5

Ms. Youngberg's Students' Test Scores Ranked from Highest to Lowest

	Group H				Group L		
Student i	Score for Mini-Exp. #3	#17	#18	Student i	Score for Mini-Exp. #3	#17	#18
11	1	1	1	30	0	0	1
9	1	0	1	13	1	1	0
2	1	1	1	14	0	1	0
4	1	0	1	27	0	0	0
20	1	0	1	8	0	1	0
24	1	0	1	32	0	0	1
29	1	1	1	26	0	1	1
7	1	1	1	18	0	0	0
1	0	0	1	16	0	1	1
21	1	0	1				
31	0	0	1				

$$D_3 = PH_3 - PL_3 = 9/11 - 1/9 \approx 0.81 - 0.11 = 0.70$$
$$D_{17} = PH_{17} - PL_{17} = 4/11 - 5/9 \approx 0.36 - 0.56 = -0.20$$
$$D_{18} = PH_{18} - PL_{18} = 11/11 - 4/9 \approx 1.00 - 0.44 = 0.56$$

ILLUSTRATION 17.6

D_3, D_{17}, and D_{18} That Ms. Youngberg Computed

Whenever overall test scores are used to determine Groups H and L as Ms. Youngberg did in Case 17.3, the procedure is referred to as "*classical item analysis*."

INDEX OF DISCRIMINATION (D_j)

Classical item analysis begins with a measurement being administered to students. If the measurement appears to be reasonably valid, the scores are partitioned into three groups: higher scores, in-between scores, and lower scores. The higher scores are used to identify Group H; the lower scores identify Group L. An index of discrimination is computed for each of the measurement's mini-experiments (i.e., $\{D_j\}$ for $j = 1, 2, 3, \ldots, k$).

How would you compute D_j if Mini-Experiment j uses weighted rather than dichotomous scoring? Suppose, for example, that in Case 17.3, Mini-Experiments #21, #22, and #23 on Ms. Youngberg's test had scoring rubrics indicating maximum possible points of 4, 5, and 10 respectively. Illustration 17.7 displays Group H's and Group L's scores for those three mini-experiments. Develop a formula for computing D_{21}, D_{22}, and D_{23}.

Students' responses to mini-experiments that are dichotomously scored are either correct or incorrect, whereas with weighted scores, students' responses have degrees of correctness. From Illustration 17.7, you can see that Student–11's response to Mini-Experiment #21 is completely correct, whereas Student–2's response to Mini-Experiment #21 is 3/4 or 75% correct. To compute PH_{21} and PL_{21}, it is reasonable to record each student's proportion as correct. In other words, Student–11's proportion is 4/4, Student–9's is 4/4, Student–2's is 3/4, . . . , Student–30's is 3/4, . . . , Student–32's is 2/4, . . . , and Student–16's is 4/4. Then PH_{21} and PL_{21}, as well as PH_{22}, PL_{22}, PH_{23}, and PL_{23} can be computed as shown by Illustration 17.8.

Note: Maximum possible points for the three mini-experiments
      are as follows:
           4 for #21, 5 for #22, and 10 for #23

	Group *H*				Group *L*		
Student	Score for Mini-Exp.			Student	Score for Mini-Exp.		
i	#21	#22	#23	*i*	#21	#22	#23
11	4	4	10	30	3	3	7
9	4	5	10	13	4	2	6
2	3	5	9	14	4	3	8
4	4	5	6	27	4	4	7
20	4	3	10	8	3	2	6
24	4	4	8	32	2	4	7
29	2	3	10	26	4	1	3
7	4	0	10	18	3	2	6
1	4	5	9	16	4	1	4
21	4	5	8				
31	4	5	8				

ILLUSTRATION 17.7

Group *H*'s and Group *L*'s Points for Three Mini-Experiments with Weighted Scoring

$$PH_{21} = \frac{1}{11}\left(\frac{4}{4}+\frac{4}{4}+\frac{3}{4}+\frac{4}{4}+\frac{4}{4}+\frac{4}{4}+\frac{2}{4}+\frac{4}{4}+\frac{4}{4}+\frac{4}{4}+\frac{4}{4}\right) = \frac{1}{11}\left(\frac{41}{4}\right) = \frac{41}{44} \approx 0.93$$

$$PL_{21} = \frac{1}{9}\left(\frac{3}{4}+\frac{4}{4}+\frac{4}{4}+\frac{4}{4}+\frac{3}{4}+\frac{2}{4}+\frac{4}{4}+\frac{3}{4}+\frac{4}{4}\right) = \frac{1}{9}\left(\frac{31}{4}\right) = \frac{31}{36} \approx 0.86$$

Thus, $D_{21} \approx 0.93 - 0.86 = 0.07$

$$PH_{22} = \frac{1}{11}\left(\frac{4}{5}+\frac{5}{5}+\frac{5}{5}+\frac{5}{5}+\frac{3}{5}+\frac{4}{5}+\frac{3}{5}+\frac{0}{5}+\frac{5}{5}+\frac{5}{5}+\frac{5}{5}\right) = \frac{1}{11}\left(\frac{44}{5}\right) = \frac{44}{55} \approx 0.80$$

$$PL_{22} = \frac{1}{9}\left(\frac{3}{5}+\frac{2}{5}+\frac{3}{5}+\frac{4}{5}+\frac{2}{5}+\frac{4}{5}+\frac{1}{5}+\frac{2}{5}+\frac{1}{5}\right) = \frac{1}{9}\left(\frac{22}{5}\right) = \frac{22}{45} \approx 0.49$$

Thus, $D_{22} \approx 0.80 - 0.49 = 0.31$

$$PH_{23} = \frac{1}{11}\left(\frac{10}{10}+\frac{10}{10}+\frac{9}{10}+\frac{6}{10}+\frac{10}{10}+\frac{8}{10}+\frac{10}{10}+\frac{10}{10}+\frac{9}{10}+\frac{8}{10}+\frac{8}{10}\right) = \frac{1}{11}\left(\frac{98}{10}\right) = \frac{98}{110} \approx 0.89$$

$$PL_{23} = \frac{1}{9}\left(\frac{7}{10}+\frac{6}{10}+\frac{8}{10}+\frac{7}{10}+\frac{6}{10}+\frac{7}{10}+\frac{3}{10}+\frac{6}{10}+\frac{4}{10}\right) = \frac{1}{9}\left(\frac{54}{10}\right) = \frac{54}{90} \approx 0.60$$

Thus, $D_{23} \approx 0.89 - 0.60 = 0.29$

ILLUSTRATION 17.8

One Possible Way to Compute PH_{21}, PL_{21}, PH_{22}, PL_{22}, PH_{23}, and PL_{23} from Illustration 17.7's Results

Illustration 17.8's computations display that formulas for computing PH_j and PL_j that do not require Mini-Experiment j to be dichotomously scored can be stated as follows:

$$PH_j = \frac{\sum_{i=1}^{N_H} j_i}{N_H w_j}$$

where N_H is the number of students in Group H, w_j is the maximum possible number of points for a student's response to Mini-Experiment j, and j_i is the score for Mini-Experiment j obtained by ith student from Group H.

$$PL_j = \frac{\sum_{i=1}^{N_L} j_i}{N_L w_j}$$

where N_L is the number of students in Group L, w_j is the maximum possible number of points for a student's response to Mini-Experiment j, and j_i is the score for Mini-Experiment j obtained by ith student from Group L.

Thus, the general formula for index of discrimination remains $D_j = PH_j - PL_j$. But we still have some questions to address:

• How large should Groups H and L be for classical item analysis?

- How well does D_j reflect the effectiveness of Mini-Experiment j when classical item analysis is used?
- How should D_j be interpreted?

SELECTING N_H AND N_L

Even a highly valid test only discriminates between achievement levels when the test scores are markedly different. In other words, the test scores from Group H need to be significantly higher than the scores from Group L. Group H's test scores are more likely to be significantly higher than Group L's when a reasonably large number of students with in-between scores are excluded from the classical item analysis process. In other words, if you administer Test-x to N_x students, the larger $N_x - (N_H + N_L)$, the greater the gap between the lowest test score from Group H and the highest test score from Group L. Of course, the larger the number of students with in-between scores you exclude from both Groups H and L, the fewer students you will have in Groups H and L. Thus, there is an advantage to minimizing N_H and N_L. But minimizing N_H and N_L has its drawbacks.

Chance factors, such as guessing and momentary distractions, can be very influential on one student's response to a prompt. But for a large number of students, the occurrence of such fortuitous factors is predictable and occurs with about equal frequency in two large groups. One student in either Group H or Group L may have better fortune guessing responses to a prompt than a student in the other group. But if both N_H and N_L are reasonably large, the influence of chance factors on responses to a prompt should be about equal for the two groups. Thus, there is an advantage to maximizing N_H and N_L.

So you have reasons to both minimize and maximize N_H and N_L. You can't do both. The trick is to make both N_H and N_L large enough to mitigate the influence of chance factors, but small enough to have a reasonably large number of students with in-between scores excluded from both Groups H and L. This is easily done if you've administered Test-x to nearly 30 or more students. With $N_x \approx 30$, you can let $N_H \approx 10$, $N_L \approx 10$, and $N_x \approx 10$. For most classroom situations, about 10 in each group is a nice compromise between minimizing and maximizing N_H and N_L. Obviously, the larger N_x, the easier it is to deal with these two conflicting factors. In any case, use Ms. Youngberg's strategy from Case 17.3 and look for gaps in the ranked test scores when choosing values for N_H and N_L.

D_J AS A MEASURE OF EFFECTIVENESS

How well does D_j reflect the effectiveness of Mini-Experiment j when classical item analysis is used? The answer, of course, varies from case to case. We have already seen that classical item analysis requires that the test be administered to a sufficiently large number of students. Furthermore, the test needs to be a reasonably valid measure of the goal, which is partially defined by the objective to which Mini-Experiment j is supposed to be relevant. The test is supposed to be relevant to the overall goal, whereas Mini-Experiment j is supposed to be relevant to only one of the objectives that defines that goal. So one might argue that a student's achievement of the objective might differ from her or his achievement of the goal. However, if the objective is truly a logical component of the goal, then for a *group* of students, there should be a high enough correlation between objective achievement and goal achievement for the test scores to serve as a means for identifying Groups H and L.

You might also recall that in Case 17.3, Ms. Youngberg was concerned that classical item analysis is based on circular reasoning. That is, each mini-experiment that the process compares for consistency with the overall test scores is a contributing factor to those scores. This weakness is diminished for tests with many mini-experiments. The more mini-experiments, the less the contribution of any one mini-experiment to the overall test results. Thus, the indices of discrimination produced by classical item analysis better indicate effectiveness when the test has more rather than fewer mini-experiments.

INTERPRETING D_j

If D_j is positive, then you have some evidence that Mini-Experiment j is effective rather than ineffective or defective. But how close to 1 does D_j need to be for it to be considered satisfactorily effective? That's another question with an answer that depends on other variables—primarily on how difficult Mini-Experiment j was for the students. You need to understand the relationship between D_j and the proportion of students correctly responding to Mini-Experiment j before you are in a position to interpret D_j. You'll gain that understanding from your work with the next four subsections of this chapter. You will also develop a feel for what a relatively high D_j is from your experiences employing item analysis with your own tests. But for the moment, take a look at the following very rough guides from Robert Ebel (1965, p. 364): (1) $0.40 \leq D_j \leq 1.00$ suggests that Mini-Experiment j is very effective, (2) $0.30 \leq D_j < 0.40$ suggests that it is reasonably effective but possibly subject to improvement, (3) $0.20 \leq D_j < 0.30$ suggests that it is only marginally effective and probably subject to being refined, and (4) $-1.00 \leq D_j < 0.20$ suggests it is inadequately effective and should be modified or rejected.

Ebel's guides are presented here only as a start as you develop your talents for interpreting $\{D_j\}$. Do not take Ebel's guides to heart, especially when $0 \leq D_j < 0.20$. As you will learn, classical item analysis often produces near zero indices of discrimination for mini-experiments, not because they are ineffective, but because they are either very easy or very hard. This is why we must examine another statistic related to Mini-Experiment j before interpreting D_j; that statistic is P_j (the *index of difficulty*).

INDEX OF DIFFICULTY (P_j)

The *index of difficulty* of Mini-Experiment j is the mean of PH_j and PL_j and is expressed as "P_j." Thus,

$$P_j = \frac{PH_j + PL_j}{2}$$

Use Illustrations 17.6 and 17.8 to compute P_3, P_{17}, P_{18}, P_{21}, P_{22}, and P_{23}. Check your figures with those in Illustration 17.9. Rank Mini-Experiments #3, #17, #18, #21, #22, and #23 from easiest to hardest for Ms. Youngberg's students. What is the range of possible values for P_j?

The range of possible values of P_j is $0 \leq P_j \leq 1$. The closer P_j is to 0, the harder Mini-Experiment j; the closer P_j is to 1, the easier Mini-Experiment j.

Do you detect a relationship between P_j and D_j?

A REFINEMENT OF CLASSICAL ITEM ANALYSIS

DEPENDENCE OF D_j ON P_j

The dependence of D_j on P_j is not obvious from Illustration 17.9. The relationship comes into clearer focus if we compute $\{P_j\}$ for several more mini-experiments from Ms. Youngberg's Test-t. The item-analysis data from Illustration 17.9 are extended in Illustration 17.10.

Mini-Exp.				
j	PH_j	PL_j	D_j	P_j
3	0.81	0.11	0.70	0.46
17	0.36	0.56	-0.20	0.46
18	1.00	0.44	0.56	0.72
21	0.93	0.86	0.07	0.90
22	0.80	0.49	0.31	0.65
23	0.89	0.60	0.29	0.75

ILLUSTRATION 17.9

How Does D_j Depend on P_j?

Mini-Exp.				
j	PH_j	PL_j	D_j	P_j
3	0.81	0.11	0.70	0.46
17	0.36	0.56	-0.20	0.46
18	1.00	0.44	0.56	0.72
21	0.93	0.86	0.07	0.90
22	0.80	0.49	0.31	0.65
23	0.89	0.60	0.29	0.75
24	1.00	1.00	0.00	1.00
25	0.18	0.00	0.18	0.09
26	0.64	0.44	0.20	0.54
27	1.00	0.89	0.11	0.95

ILLUSTRATION 17.10

An Extension of Illustration 17.9's (D_j, P_j)

The difference between PH_j and PL_j determines how much D_j deviates from 0. But if Mini-Experiment j is very easy and, thus, P_j is near 1, then $1 \approx PH_j \approx PL_j$ and, consequently, $D_j \approx 0$. In fact, if $P_j = 1$, then $PH_j - PL_j = 1 - 1 = 0$. In other words, very easy mini-experiments necessarily have indices of discrimination near 0.

Similarly, very difficult mini-experiments will also have indices of discrimination near 0. If P_j is near 0, then $0 \approx PH_j \approx PL_j$ and, consequently, $D_j \approx 0$. In fact, if $P_j = 0$, then $PH_j - PL_j = 0 - 0 = 0$.

In order for D_j to approach either 1 or -1, P_j must deviate from both 0 and 1 and approach 0.50. In other words, $|D_j|$ will be relatively large only for moderately difficult mini-experiments. Just because Mini-Experiment j is moderately difficult (i.e., P_j approaches 0.50) does not imply that D_j will deviate from 0, but if Mini-Experiment j is either very easy (i.e., P_j approaches 1) or very difficult (i.e., P_j approaches 0), then D_j will be near 0.

Does the combination of $D_j \approx 0$ and $P_j \approx 1$ suggest that Mini-Experiment j is ineffective and should be modified or eliminated? The answer depends on whether you want to include easy mini-experiments on your measurements. For most classroom measurements, I believe a few easy mini-experiments should be included. Why? For two reasons: (1) As suggested in Chapter 6, easy mini-experiments are needed to measure rudimentary achievement levels. (2) Easy mini-experiments provide opportunities for all students to experience a degree of success on tests and may encourage some students to attempt other mini-experiments.

Similarly, does the combination of $D_j \approx 0$ and $P_j \approx 0$ suggest that Mini-Experiment j is ineffective and should be modified or eliminated? The answer depends on whether you want to include hard mini-experiments on your measurements. For most classroom measurements, I believe a few hard mini-experiments should be included. Why? For two reasons: (1) As suggested in Chapter 6, hard mini-experiments are needed to measure advanced achievement levels. (2) Hard mini-experiments provide challenges for students with sophisticated achievement levels to extend what they have learned.

When classical item analysis is applied to moderately difficult mini-experiments, Ebel's guides for interpreting indices of discrimination are meaningful. But for mini-experiments you intend to be very easy or very hard, indices of discrimination should be interpreted in light of the fact that D_j is limited by P_j being near either 1 or 0. Re-examine $\{(D_j, P_j)\}$ in Illustration 17.10. Which mini-experiments appear to behave in line with the mini-experiments' outcomes matrix of a perfectly reliable test? Which ones appear to deviate from that ideal?

P_3 is near 0.50; thus, if Mini-Experiment #3 is effective, you would expect D_3 to be high, and it is. The negative D_{17} suggests that Mini-Experiment #17 is probably faulty. No red flags are raised by the combination $(D_{18}, P_{18}) = (0.56, 0.72)$. D_{21} is nearly 0, but P_{21} is near 1. The item analysis data for Mini-Experiment #21 simply indicate that it was very easy. If Ms. Youngberg intended for Mini-Experiment #21 to be easy, then the data are consistent with her wishes. $(D_{22}, P_{22}) = (0.31, 0.65)$ is not alarming, but I wonder why such a moderately difficult mini-experiment doesn't have a higher index of discrimination. Ms. Youngberg might consider checking to see if something went awry with Mini-Experiment #22. Although $D_{23} < D_{22}$, I think the data look better for Mini-Experiment #23 than for #22. Why? Because D_{23} and D_{22} are near in value, but P_{22} is nearer to 0.50 than P_{23}. Mini-Experiment #24 is too easy to discriminate, and #25 is too difficult for D_{25} to deviate very much from 0. $D_{26} > D_{25}$ and $D_{26} > D_{27}$. But Ms. Youngberg should be much more concerned about Mini-Experiment #26 being faulty than either #25 or #27. Why? We can see why D_{25} is so near 0; it is because P_{25} is so near 0. We can also see why D_{27} is so near 0; it is because P_{27} is so near 1. But considering that $P_{26} = 0.54$, we should wonder what is wrong with Mini-Experiment #26 for D_{26} not to be any higher.

Fortunately, Richard Hofmann (1975) developed a process by which indices of discrimination could be used to compare the effectiveness of mini-experiments even when the indices of difficulty (i.e., $\{P_j\}$) varied widely from 0.50. He discovered the following relationships:

- If $P_j \leq 0.50$, then the maximum possible value for D_j is $2P_j$. For example, if $P_j = 0.35$, then D_j can be no greater than 0.70 no matter how effective Mini-Experiment j is.
- If $P_j > 0.50$, then the maximum possible value for D_j is $2(1 - P_j)$. For example, if $P_j = 0.85$, then D_j can be no greater than 0.30 no matter how effective Mini-Experiment j is.
- If $P_j \leq 0.50$, then the minimum possible value for D_j is $-2P_j$. For example, if $P_j = 0.35$, then D_j can be no less than -0.70 no matter how defective Mini-Experiment j is.
- If $P_j > 0.50$, then the minimum possible value for D_j is $-2(1 - P_j)$. For example, if $P_j = 0.85$, then D_j can be no less than -0.30 no matter how defective Mini-Experiment j is.

P_j	$\text{Max}\lvert D_j \rvert$	Range of Possible Values for D_j
0.00	0.00	$D_j = 0$
0.05	0.10	$-.10 \leq D_j \leq .10$
0.10	0.20	$-.20 \leq D_j \leq .20$
0.15	0.30	$-.30 \leq D_j \leq .30$
0.20	0.40	$-.40 \leq D_j \leq .40$
0.25	0.50	$-.50 \leq D_j \leq .50$
0.30	0.60	$-.60 \leq D_j \leq .60$
0.35	0.70	$-.70 \leq D_j \leq .70$
0.40	0.80	$-.80 \leq D_j \leq .80$
0.45	0.90	$-.90 \leq D_j \leq .90$
0.50	1.00	$-1.00 \leq D_j \leq 1.00$
0.55	0.90	$-.90 \leq D_j \leq .90$
0.60	0.80	$-.80 \leq D_j \leq .80$
0.65	0.70	$-.70 \leq D_j \leq .70$
0.70	0.60	$-.60 \leq D_j \leq .60$
0.75	0.50	$-.50 \leq D_j \leq .50$
0.80	0.40	$-.40 \leq D_j \leq .40$
0.85	0.30	$-.30 \leq D_j \leq .30$
0.90	0.20	$-.20 \leq D_j \leq .20$
0.95	0.10	$-.10 \leq D_j \leq .10$
1.00	0.00	$D_j = 0$

ILLUSTRATION 17.11

Max$\lvert D_j \rvert$ for Selected Values of P_j

Let the maximum possible value of D_j as determined by Hofmann's relationships be designated by "Max$\lvert D_j \rvert$." Illustration 17.11 is a table relating selected values of P_j with Max$\lvert D_j \rvert$. Compute $\{\lvert \text{Max}\lvert D_j \rvert \rvert\}$ for $\{P_j\}$ from Illustration 17.10.

Did you obtain $\{\lvert \text{Max}\lvert D_j \rvert \rvert\} = (0.92, 0.92, 0.56, 0.20, 0.70, 0.50, 0.00, 0.18, 0.92, 0.10)$ for $j = 3, 17, \ldots, 27$ respectively? Note that Max$\lvert D_{27} \rvert = 0.10$ but that D_{27} was computed to be 0.11. Isn't it impossible for $D_j \leq \text{Max}\lvert D_j \rvert$? Yes, it is impossible. The discrepancy is caused by rounding error in the computation of PL_j. Of the 9 students in Group L, 8 correctly responded to Mini-Experiment #27. $8 \div 9 = 0.888 \ldots$, which was rounded to 0.89. When 0.89 was used to compute P_{27} instead of $0.888 \ldots$, we obtained $(1 + 0.89) \div 2 = 0.945$, which we rounded up to 0.95. Had we used $0.888 \ldots$ to compute P_{27}, we would have obtained $(1 + 0.888 \ldots) \div 2 = 0.9444 \ldots$, which we would have rounded down to 0.94. Then we would have computed Max$\lvert D_{27} \rvert$ as $2(1 - 0.9444 \ldots) = 2(0.0555 \ldots) = 0.111 \ldots$, which D_{27} does not exceed.

The point to keep in mind is that with item analysis statistics as well as statistics computed for assessing reliability and establishing norms, more than 2-decimal accuracy is unnecessary. The numbers are just not that exact. However, I do not want you to think that Hofmann's relationships between P_j and Max$\lvert D_j \rvert$ are in error.

INDEX OF ITEM EFFICIENCY (E_j)

Hofmann (1975) reasoned that a mini-experiment's effectiveness should be judged in light of how closely its index of discrimination approaches the maximum possible value. Thus, he formulated what is referred to as an *index of item efficiency*. It is computed as follows:

$$E_j = \frac{D_j}{Max|D_j|}$$

where E_j is the index of item efficiency for Mini-Experiment j.

Compute $\{E_j\}$ for $\{D_j, P_j, Max|D_j|\}$ from Illustration 17.10. Check your results against Illustration 17.12. Note how the values for E_j relate to our previous analysis of Illustration 17.10 when we assessed mini-experiment effectiveness in light of both D_j and P_j.

INTERPRETING ITEM ANALYSIS DATA

Generally speaking, the greater E_j, the more effective Mini-Experiment j. Illustration 17.12 suggests that, statistically speaking, Mini-Experiments #3, #18, #25, and #27 performed very well on Ms. Youngberg's test. Clearly, Mini-Experiment #17 should be examined to find out why students' scores for it correlated negatively with their scores on the test as a whole. E_{26} seems low compared to the other efficiency indices; thus, Ms. Youngberg should consider examining it for possible weaknesses. Mini-Experiment #24 was simply very easy. The data don't raise any red flags about Mini-Experiments #21, #22, or #23. Statistically, they seemed to have performed satisfactorily.

Of course, item analysis data are not capable of indicating what is wrong or what is right about mini-experiments or how faulty ones should be modified. Item analysis data can call your attention to mini-experiments from your measurements that should be scrutinized and

Mini-Exp. j	PH_j	PL_j	D_j	P_j	$Max|D_j|$	E_j
3	0.81	0.11	0.70	0.46	0.92	0.76
17	0.36	0.56	-0.20	0.46	0.92	-0.22
18	1.00	0.44	0.56	0.72	0.56	1.00
21	0.93	0.86	0.07	0.90	0.20	0.35
22	0.80	0.49	0.31	0.65	0.70	0.44
23	0.89	0.60	0.29	0.75	0.50	0.58
24	1.00	1.00	0.00	1.00	0.00	none*
25	0.18	0.00	0.18	0.09	0.18	1.00
26	0.64	0.44	0.20	0.54	0.92	0.22
27	1.00	0.89	0.11	0.95	0.10	1.00**

* E_{24} cannot be computed since division by 0 is meaningless.

** Computed D_{27} exceeds $Max|D_{27}|$ because of rounding error.

ILLUSTRATION 17.12

$\{Max|D_j|\}$ and $\{E_j\}$ Added to Illustration 17.10

discussed with your students for the purpose of detecting possible flaws. The data also call your attention to the types of mini-experiments that seem to work well.

ASSESSING EFFECTIVENESS OF MINI-EXPERIMENTS WHEN CLASSICAL ITEM ANALYSIS IS INAPPROPRIATE

WHEN THE MEASUREMENT LACKS VALIDITY

When the relevance or reliability of a measurement is unsatisfactory, refinement of that measurement is obviously in order. However, to use classical item analysis in such a case would be correlating outcomes from the measurement's mini-experiments to the measurement's invalid scores. The resulting indices of discrimination would not be indicators of effectiveness. A measurement whose scores do not satisfactorily pertain to students' achievement of the goal should be redesigned. Think-aloud trials with some of the mini-experiments may be helpful; little can be gained from computing item analysis data.

Unsatisfactory measurement reliability is often a consequence of low score variability. A relevant test may have low score variability because either (1) nearly all of its mini-experiments are very easy, (2) nearly all of its mini-experiments are very difficult, or (3) a significant share of its mini-experiments produce conflicting results (i.e., scores from one mini-experiment correlate negatively with scores from another).

If the unreliable measurement is relevant but the mini-experiments are mostly very easy, then the test should be refined by replacing a portion of the very easy mini-experiments with moderately difficult ones. Similarly, if the lack of score variability is caused by too many very hard mini-experiments, a portion of the hard mini-experiments should be replaced by moderate ones. In either case, computing $\{P_j\}$ will guide which mini-experiments should be replaced.

Computation of $\{D_j, P_j, E_j\}$ using classical item analysis can be helpful to determine if a relevant test is unreliable because a significant share of its mini-experiments produced conflicting results. For measurements with unsatisfactorily low reliability coefficients, E_j should not be considered an indicator of Mini-Experiment j's effectiveness, but only as how consistent its results are with those of the test as a whole. Replacing or modifying mini-experiments with low efficiency indices often increases score variability, which in turn improves reliability.

WHEN THE NUMBER OF MINI-EXPERIMENTS IS SMALL

Classical item analysis is designed to call attention to mini-experiments that should be modified. For a test with many items (e.g., $k > 20$), this process reduces the amount of time you need to spend refining your measurement. $\{D_j, P_j, E_j\}$ provides you with a screening device for guiding which mini-experiments should be scrutinized for possible modification or rejection. Thus, instead of spending time examining all k mini-experiments, you may choose to only examine those few with lower efficiency indices. Computing $\{D_j, P_j, E_j\}$, especially with the aid of the computer software on the CD-ROM that accompanies this book, is not nearly as time-consuming as examining the way prompts are presented and rubrics applied, conducting think-aloud trials with students, and pinpointing design flaws in mini-experiments. For a lengthy test, classical item analysis reduces to a manageable size the number of mini-experiments to be scrutinized.

But when a measurement includes only a small number of mini-experiments (e.g., $k < 7$), the number of mini-experiments to be scrutinized is already manageable. Thus, for measurements with only a few mini-experiments, classical item analysis doesn't serve a useful purpose.

WHEN THE NUMBER OF STUDENTS IS SMALL

Conventional statistical techniques (e.g., classical item analysis and computation of reliability coefficients) are generally applicable to measurements administered to a reasonably large group of students (e.g., $N > 20$). With smaller groups of students, you can employ more qualitative methods such as think-aloud trials. Having fewer students also allows for more in-depth measurement formats (e.g., using interviews) by which measurement error is qualitatively detected.

USING ITEM ANALYSIS DATA

Consider Case 17.4.

CASE 17.4

Ferriday Elementary School's primary-grade teachers decide to develop a diagnostic mathematics achievement test to be administered to all second-graders near the beginning of each school year. They agree on a set of weighted objectives to which they want the test to be relevant. During July, they use methods described in Chapter 6 to develop the test. In September, they administer it to about 100 second-graders for the purpose of assessing its reliability as well as the effectiveness of its mini-experiments.

On the basis of a reliability coefficient of 0.87, they conclude that the test is satisfactorily reliable. They then conduct classical item analysis with $N_H = N_L = 20$, obtaining $\{D_j, P_j, E_j\}$ for $j = 1, 2, 3, \ldots ,$ 37. Mini-Experiment #14, which is shown by Illustration 17.13, is intended to be relevant to the following objective:

Students read the time on a circular clock to the nearest quarter hour (process knowledge).

Prompt:

(The question is to be read aloud to the students in a group; students are directed to write their answers in the blank.)

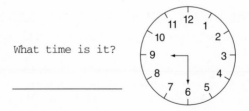

What time is it?

_____

Scoring Rubric:

+1 for "9:30" or the equivalent, +0 otherwise.

ILLUSTRATION 17.13

Mini-Experiment #14 on Ferriday Elementary School's Diagnostic Mathematics Achievement Test for Second-Graders

The teachers are initially surprised to find out $E_{14} = -0.15$. Then they take a closer look at the picture of the clock in the prompt and note that the hour hand is not in the correct position for 9:30. One teacher, Ms. Toone, suggests that students with sophisticated time-telling skills recognize the impossible combination of hand positions and were less likely to write "9:30" in the blank than students with less sophisticated time-telling skills. Ms. Toone's conjecture is supported by a review of the responses from Groups H and L. One student from Group H wrote "broken." Two put "?" and three left the blank empty. Because the teachers had not scored the responses themselves, they would not have noticed these particulars had the $E_{14} = -0.15$ not called their attention to the item. They revise the prompt by repositioning the hour hand in the sketch.

Illustration 17.14 displays the prompts for Mini-Experiments #1 through #8. The 8 items are intended to be relevant to the following objective:

Students discriminate between examples and non-examples of ½ (construct a concept).

According to the scoring rubrics, students respond correctly by circling the sketches for Prompts #3, #4, #5, and #8 and by leaving the other four sketches alone.

The item analysis data for Mini-Experiments #1 through #8 are shown by Illustration 17.15.

What do Illustration 17.15's data suggest to you regarding Mini-Experiments #1 through #8? Do you think any of the mini-experiments need to be scrutinized? Do you think any of the prompts need to be modified? If so, how?

Case 17.5 is a continuation of Case 17.4.

CASE 17.5

Ms. Toone finds nothing alarming about Illustration 17.5's data. However, she's perplexed by the fact that E_8 is so much lower than efficiency indices for the other seven. She thinks, "I thought these 8 items should be equivalent to one another. But apparently something is different about the way the children responded to #8 as compared to the others. It could be just a chance thing. But I'd better check it out."

Ms. Toone sits down with Vanica, who had one of the higher scores on the test but did not circle Prompt #8's figure, and engages her in the following interview.

Ms. Toone: "Look at this picture."

Ms. Toone shows Vanica Prompt #5's shaded circular region.

Ms. Toone: "Does it show one-half?"
Vanica: "Yes."
Ms. Toone: "Tell me why."
Vanica: "Because the same amount is black that is white."
Ms. Toone: "Thank you. What about this one? Does it show one-half?"

Ms. Toone displays Prompt #7's shaded rectangular region.

Vanica: "No, because there's more white part than there's black part."
Ms. Toone: "Thank you. What about this one? Does it show one-half?"

Ms. Toone displays Prompt #8's shaded triangular region.

Vanica: "No it doesn't."
Ms. Toone: "Why not?"

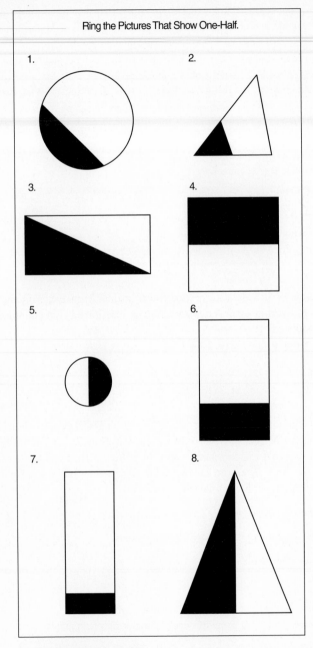

Ring the Pictures That Show One-Half.

ILLUSTRATION 17.14

Prompts for Mini-Experiments #1–8 on Ferriday Elementary School's Diagnostic Mathematics Achievement Test for Second-Graders

Mini-Exp. j	PH_j	PL_j	D_j	P_j	$\text{Max}\,\lvert D_j\rvert$	E_j
1	0.95	0.25	0.70	0.60	0.80	0.88
2	1.00	0.30	0.70	0.65	0.70	1.00
3	0.95	0.20	0.75	0.58	0.84	0.89
4	1.00	0.40	0.60	0.70	0.60	1.00
5	1.00	0.60	0.40	0.80	0.40	1.00
6	1.00	0.30	0.70	0.65	0.70	1.00
7	0.95	0.55	0.40	0.75	0.50	0.80
8	0.60	0.30	0.30	0.45	0.90	0.33

ILLUSTRATION 17.15

Item Analysis Data for Mini-Experiments #1–8 on Ferriday Elementary
School's Diagnostic Mathematics Achievement Test for Second-Graders

Vanica:	"Well, you can't tell for sure because you can't see the whole thing. But I don't think it is—'cause even if the other side is black, the bottom isn't the same size."
Ms. Toone:	"Vanica, show me with your hands what this figure is like."
Vanica:	"Well, it's one of those pyra-things like in Egypt—you know."

Vanica's gestures indicate to Ms. Toone that Vanica perceives Prompt #8's figure to be a three-dimensional tetrahedron—solid with four surfaces. Ms. Toone looks at the figure. Suddenly, she also sees it as a three-dimensional solid. She thinks, "The way the triangular region is shaded makes it look like an Egyptian pyramid with the surface on the right facing the sun. Of course! Primary grade children would perceive the characteristics of what is being pictured rather than characteristics of the picture itself."

Ms. Toone's interview with another student from Group H supports her belief that because of the shape and shading of Prompt #8's figure, some students perceived a four-sided tetrahedron. She discusses her findings with the other teachers. They decide to modify Prompt #8 by shortening and rotating the triangle. They conduct a few think-aloud trials with students and decide that the revised figure should be included on the test.

SYNTHESIS ACTIVITIES FOR CHAPTER 17

1. Call to mind Cases 15.9, 16.14, and 16.15, in which Mr. Doleac assessed the relevance and reliability of the test displayed by Illustration 15.7. Illustration 17.16 presents the item-by-item results he obtained from the test. In collaboration with a colleague, use classical item analysis procedures to compute $\{D_j, P_j, E_j\}$ for the 14 mini-experiments. Use your results to decide which mini-experiments should be scrutinized.

2. Mr. Doleac also used Illustration 17.16 to compute $\{D_j, P_j, E_j\}$. He decided to use the 10 highest and the 10 lowest scores to determine Groups H and L. Compare you and your colleague's item analysis data from having engaged in Synthesis Activity 1 to those Mr. Doleac obtained as displayed by

Student	Item A-I									Item A-II		Item A III	Item B I	Item B II	(Test Score)
i	1	2	3	4	5	6	7	8	9	1	2	III	I	II	b_i
9	1	1	1	1	1	1	1	1	1	1	1	5	5	4	25
31	1	1	1	1	0	1	1	1	1	1	1	5	5	4	24
2	1	1	1	0	0	1	1	1	1	1	1	5	5	4	23
25	1	1	1	0	0	1	1	1	1	1	1	5	5	4	23
1	1	0	1	1	1	0	1	1	0	1	0	5	4	4	20
5	1	1	0	0	0	1	1	1	0	1	1	5	5	3	20
22	1	0	1	0	0	1	1	0	1	1	1	5	4	4	20
24	1	1	1	1	0	0	1	0	1	0	1	4	5	4	20
4	1	1	1	0	0	1	0	1	1	0	1	3	5	4	19
14	1	1	1	1	0	1	1	1	1	0	0	2	5	4	19
6	1	0	1	0	0	1	0	1	0	1	0	1	5	4	15
10	1	0	1	0	1	0	1	1	0	0	1	4	2	3	15
8	1	1	0	0	0	1	1	0	1	0	0	0	5	4	14
11	1	0	1	1	0	0	1	0	0	1	1	0	5	3	14
26	1	0	1	1	1	1	0	1	0	0	0	0	4	3	14
3	1	1	0	0	0	1	1	1	0	0	0	2	5	1	13
18	0	0	0	1	0	1	1	0	1	1	0	5	1	2	13
19	1	0	1	0	0	1	1	1	0	0	0	0	5	3	13
21	1	1	0	1	1	0	0	0	0	0	0	0	5	4	13
27	0	1	0	0	0	1	0	0	1	1	1	0	5	3	13
30	1	1	1	0	0	1	0	0	0	0	0	0	5	4	13
28	1	1	0	0	1	0	0	1	0	1	1	1	1	4	12
33	1	1	0	0	0	0	1	0	1	0	0	0	5	3	12
7	1	0	0	0	1	0	0	1	1	0	0	1	4	1	10
12	1	0	0	1	1	0	0	0	0	0	0	2	5	0	10
15	1	0	0	1	0	1	0	0	0	0	1	0	5	1	10
16	0	1	0	0	1	0	1	0	1	0	0	0	5	1	10
20	1	0	1	0	1	0	0	0	0	0	1	0	4	0	8
23	0	1	1	1	1	1	1	0	0	1	0	0	1	0	8
13	1	0	1	1	1	0	0	0	0	0	0	0	3	0	7
29	0	0	0	0	1	0	0	0	1	0	0	0	3	0	5
32	1	0	0	0	1	0	0	1	0	0	0	0	2	0	5
17	0	0	0	0	0	0	0	1	0	0	1	0	0	0	2

ILLUSTRATION 17.16

Item-by-Item Results Mr. Doleac Obtained from Illustration 15.17's Test (Test Scores Rank Ordered)

Illustration 17.17. Keep in mind that your data and his data may differ if you did not choose $N_H = N_L = 10$ as he did.

3. Read Case 17.6.

CASE 17.6

A standardized reading-readiness test is administered in December to first-grade students in a Florida school district. The prompts for Mini-Experiments #4 and #5 from that test are shown in Illustration 17.18. For each prompt, students are directed to cut the three pictures and arrange them in order from what happened first, to what happened next, to what happened last. Both mini-experiments are intended to be relevant to the following objective:

> Students arrange events in a story in a time sequence (comprehension and communication skills).

According to the scoring rubrics, the correct response to Prompt #4 is (1) left-side picture first, (2) right-side picture second, and (3) middle picture third. For Prompt #5, it is (1) middle picture first, (2) right-side picture second, and (3) left-side picture third.

Classical item analysis yields the following data on the two items: $D_4 = 0.40$, $P_4 = 0.73$, $E_4 = 0.75$, $D_5 = -0.20$, $P_5 = 0.50$, $E_5 = -0.20$.

In light of its poor performance under item analysis, discuss with a colleague what might be wrong with Mini-Experiment #5.

Mini-Exp. j	PH_j	PL_j	D_j	P_j	Max$|D_j|$	E_j
A-I-1	1.00	0.60	0.40	0.80	0.40	1.00
A-I-2	0.80	0.20	0.60	0.50	1.00	0.60
A-I-3	0.90	0.30	0.60	0.60	0.80	0.75
A-I-4	0.50	0.40	0.10	0.45	0.90	0.11
A-I-5	0.20	0.80	-0.60	0.50	1.00	-0.60
A-I-6	0.80	0.20	0.60	0.50	1.00	0.60
A-I-7	0.90	0.10	0.80	0.50	1.00	0.80
A-I-8	0.80	0.30	0.50	0.55	0.90	0.56
A-I-9	0.80	0.30	0.50	0.55	0.90	0.56
A-II-1	0.70	0.10	0.60	0.40	0.80	0.75
A-II-2	0.80	0.20	0.60	0.50	1.00	0.60
A-III	0.88	0.06	0.82	0.47	0.94	0.94
B-I	0.96	0.64	0.32	0.80	0.40	0.80
B-II	0.98	0.08	0.90	0.53	0.94	0.96

ILLUSTRATION 17.17

Item Analysis Data Mr. Doleac Computed from Illustration 17.16's Matrix

Directions: Paste the pictures in the order so that they tell a story.

ILLUSTRATION 17.18

Prompts #4 and #5 from a Reading Readiness Test Administered to Students in Florida

TRANSITIONAL ACTIVITY FROM THEORY TO PRACTICE

After completing your work with each of the first 16 chapters of this book, you and your colleagues addressed questions for the transitional activity from that chapter to the next. Now that you have nearly completed your work with all 17 chapters, get together with your colleagues one more time to revisit those 16 sets of questions. You may find yourself speaking to those questions much differently than you did the first time. This time, pay particular attention to how you will incorporate assessment strategies for monitoring students' learning into your own unique teaching situation.

GLOSSARY

Achievement test: An *achievement test* is a measurement that is used in the evaluation of what students have learned or how well they have achieved certain goals.

Affective domain: A learning objective falls within the *affective domain* if its intent is for students to develop a particular attitude or feeling (e.g., a desire to read or willingness to attempt a task).

Agility: *Agility* is the ability of a person to make controlled changes in body position both rapidly and accurately while moving through space.

Alternative assessment: *Alternative assessment* refers to an *authentic assessment* based on non-traditional measurement results (e.g., results from measurements with performance-observation mini-experiments rather than multiple-choice items).

Analytical scoring: A mini-experiment with *weighted scoring* is *analytically scored* if its rubric specifies exactly how each single point should be distributed.

Application: An objective requiring students to use deductive reasoning to decide how, if at all, to utilize the *subject-content* specified by the objective is at the *application learning level*.

Appreciation: Students achieve an objective at the *appreciation learning level* by believing that the *subject-content* specified by the objective has value.

Aptitude test: An *aptitude test* is a measurement whose scores are used to evaluate students' potential for achieving certain goals if the students engage in reasonably appropriate learning activities.

Authentic assessment: *Authentic assessment* is the practice of basing formative judgments and summative evaluations of student achievement on measurement results that are *relevant* to stated learning objectives, especially learning objectives that specify reasoning-level cognition (i.e., construct a concept, discover a relationship, comprehension and communication skills, application, and creative thinking), affective, and psychomotor achievement.

Blueprint, Measurement: A *measurement blueprint* is an outline specifying the features a teacher wants to build into a measurement he or she plans to develop from the prompts stored in mini-experiment files. Typically, the *blueprint* indicates (1) the goal to be measured or the name of the measurement, (2) anticipated

administration dates and times, (3) provisions for accommodating students with special needs, (4) types of mini-experiment formats to be used, (5) approximate number of mini-experiments to be included, (6) the targeted mix of difficulty levels for mini-experiments, (7) an approximation of the maximum possible score for the measurement, (8) how points should be distributed among the objectives that define the goal (based on the weights of the objectives), (9) the overall structure of the measurement, and (10) for summative evaluations, the method for converting scores to grades.

Body composition: *Body composition* is the ratio of fat mass to lean body mass (Heyward & Stolarczyk, 1996). Lean body mass is composed of bone, muscle, and other body tissues exclusive of fat, except for the essential fat stored in bone marrow, the brain, spinal cord, and internal organs.

Cardiovascular endurance: *Cardiovascular endurance* is how well a person's circulatory and respiratory systems efficiently deliver oxygen and fuel for muscles so that the person is able to sustain an activity for an extended period of time.

Central tendency of a sequence of scores: The *central tendency* of a sequence of scores is a reflection of the magnitude of the scores. Many statisticians consider "average" to be synonymous with *central tendency*. However, it is also very common for people to use the word "average" as a synonym for the best known measure of central tendency—arithmetic mean. Herein, "average" is used in the broader sense (i.e., as a synonym for "central tendency.")

Checking-off objectives: With the *checking-off objectives* method for reporting summative evaluations, either (1) the objectives judged to be achieved by the student are listed or (2) the percentage of objectives judged to be achieved by the student is reported.

Cognitive domain: A learning objective falls within the *cognitive domain* if its intent is for students to be able to do something mentally (e.g., to construct a concept or remember a statement of a relationship).

Commercially produced test: *Commercially produced tests* are tests that can be purchased from publishers of educational and psychological materials.

Comprehension and communication skills: An objective focusing on students being able to use language to communicate as well as to extract and interpret meaning from expressions is at the *comprehension-and-communication-skills learning level.*

Compromise grading method: With the *compromise grading method* for converting measurement scores to grades, cutoff points for each letter grade are established prior to the administration of the measurement. All scores that are only insignificantly below or insignificantly above a grade cutoff point according to some criterion (e.g., within one *standard error of measurement*) are assigned the grade associated with that cutoff point. A significant difference between two scores is required in order for the two scores to be assigned different grades.

Concept: A *concept* is a category people mentally construct from a set of two or more *specifics* that have some common attributes. "Concept" is one of the subject-content categories in the advanced organizer for formulating learning objectives that is introduced in Chapter 5.

Concept attribute: An *attribute of a concept* is any characteristic that is common to all examples of that concept.

Concurrent validity: A test has *concurrent validity* with respect to another test to the same degree that results from the two tests positively correlate. In other words, results from administrations of both tests to the same group of students displayed a group trend in which (1) students with higher ranking scores on one test tended to have higher ranking scores on the second test, and (2) students with lower ranking scores on one test tended to have lower ranking scores on the second test.

Construct a concept: An objective requiring students to use inductive reasoning to distinguish between examples and non-examples of a concept is at the *construct-a-concept learning level.*

Convergent reasoning: *Convergent reasoning* is reasoning that is typical and usual for the majority of the people of a specific population.

Coordination: *Coordination* is the ability of the body to concurrently execute multiple motor tasks. Typically, coordination involves the integration of eye, hand, limb, and trunk movements.

Correction-for-guessing technique: A *correction-for-guessing* technique is sometimes employed with multiple-choice items. When such a technique is employed, students are directed to select only alternatives to multiple-choice prompts that they are reasonably certain to be correct. If they are unsure about which alternative to select, they are directed either not to select any of the alternatives or to select an alternative with wording equivalent to "I don't know." Measurement scores are then computed using one of several correction-for-guessing formulas. (Note that you are advised against using correction-for-guessing techniques.)

Creative thinking: An objective requiring students to use *divergent reasoning* to originate ideas, hypotheses, procedures, or problem solutions is at the *creative-thinking learning level.*

Criterion-referenced evaluation: A summative evaluation of a student's achievement is *criterion-referenced* if the evaluation is influenced by how the measurement results relevant to that student's achievement compare to a standard that is not dependent on results obtained from others.

Curriculum: A *school curriculum* is a system of planned experiences (e.g., coursework, school-sponsored social functions, and contacts with school-supported services, such as the library) designed to educate students. A *course or classroom curriculum* is a sequence of teaching units designed to provide students with experiences that help them achieve specified learning goals.

Curve grading method, Classical: With the *classical curve grading method* for converting measurement scores to grades, each score from a measurement is ranked from highest to lowest so that A's are assigned to the highest 7% of the scores, B's are assigned to the next 24% of the scores, C's are assigned to the middle 38% of the scores, D's are assigned to the next 24% of the scores, and F's are assigned to the lowest 7% of the scores.

Deductive reasoning: *Deductive reasoning* is deciding whether or not a specific problem is subsumed by a generality. The use of *syllogisms* is inherent in deductive reasoning.

Defective mini-experiments: (See "Effectiveness of mini-experiments.")

Derived score: A *derived score* is a test score that is the result of an arithmetic computation involving a raw score and other data (e.g., test norms). Standardized test results are commonly reported in terms of derived scores (e.g., percentiles, stanines, grade equivalents, deviation IQs, NCEs, and scaled scores) that automatically rank each student's raw score with those from the norm group.

Dichotomous scoring: A mini-experiment is *dichotomously scored* if its rubric is such that there are only two possible categories for students' responses; the observer classifies a response as either meeting a criterion or not.

Difficulty, Index of (P_j): P_j is an estimate of the proportion of the maximum possible points from Mini-Experiment j obtained by a group of students. P_j is calculated from the results of a group of students with relatively high test scores and a group with relatively low test scores.

Difficulty of a mini-experiment: The *difficulty of a mini-experiment* depends on the proportion of students whose responses to the prompt receive high scores. The difficulty level is *easy* if the vast majority of students' responses receive high scores; it is *hard* if only a relative few responses receive high scores. *Moderately difficult* mini-experiments are neither particularly easy or hard. The *index of difficulty* of Mini-Experiment j (P_j) is a measure of whether the mini-experiment is easy, moderate, or hard.

Discover a relationship: An objective requiring students to use inductive reasoning to discover that a particular relationship exists or why the relationship exists is at the *discover-a-relationship learning level.*

Discrimination, Index of (D_j): D_j is a measure of the degree to which students' scores from Mini-Experiment j correlate with another indicator of achievement. In classical item analysis, D_j is an indicator of the consistency between performance on Mini-Experiment j and scores from the test that included Mini-Experiment j.

Display-process format: A mini-experiment that prompts students to complete a task and exhibit evidence of the steps used to attempt the task has a *display-process format.*

Distractor, Multiple-choice: (See "Multiple-choice format.")

Divergent reasoning: *Divergent reasoning* is atypical reasoning that deviates from the norm of a specific population; thoughts that reflect unanticipated and unusual, but reasonable, responses are divergent.

Dynamic balance: *Dynamic balance* is the ability to maintain equilibrium while in motion.

Easy mini-experiment: (See "Difficulty of a mini-experiment.")

Edition of a standardized test: The *edition of a standardized test* is the number of times it has been revised and normed. Each edition is associated with a copyright date.

Effectiveness of mini-experiments: A mini-experiment is *effective* to the degree to which it discriminates in favor of high levels of objective achievement and against low levels of objective achievement. Mini-experiments that favor lower-levels of objective achievement over higher levels of achievement are referred to as *defective mini-experiments* or *defective items*. Mini-experiments that favor neither lower or higher levels of achievement are referred to as *ineffective*.

Efficiency, Index of item (E_j): The *index of item efficiency* is a refinement of the *index of discrimination* in that the calculation of E_j adjusts for the influence of the difficulty of Mini-Experiment j on D_j.

Empirical observation: An *empirical observation* is the use of hearing, sight, smell, taste, or touch to detect stimuli or information from one's surrounding.

Equivalent forms of a test: Two different forms or versions of a test are *equivalent* if they have almost exactly the same number and types of items, are relevant to the same goals, and are equally difficult.

Error-pattern analysis: An *error-pattern analysis* is a strategy teachers employ to obtain formative feedback on exactly what steps students are executing in a process.

Essay format: A mini-experiment that prompts students to write a composition of at least one paragraph, but normally not more than several pages, has an *essay format*.

Example noise: *Example noise* is a characteristic of a particular concept that is not an *attribute* of that concept.

Example of a concept: An *example of a concept* is a *specific* possessing all of the defining attributes of that concept.

Flexibility, Psychomotor: *Flexibility* is the range of motion for various joints and combination of joints.

Foil, Multiple-choice: (See "Multiple-choice format.")

Folder of mini-experiment files, Computerized: A *computerized folder of mini-experiment files* is space in a computer's memory containing files for mini-experiments that are all intended to be relevant to students' achievement of the same unit's learning goal.

Form, Standardized test: Most popular standardized tests are published in multiple *forms*. Two different forms of the same level of a test are designed to be *equivalent*. (See "Equivalent forms of a test.")

Formative judgment: A *formative judgment* is a decision made by a teacher that influences how she or he teaches.

Frequency distribution of a sequence of scores: A *frequency distribution* is an association of each possible score value in a sequence with the number of scores having that value.

Global scoring: A mini-experiment with *weighted scoring* is *globally scored* if its rubric allows the observer leeway to rate the degree to which a student's response meets the criterion.

Goal, Learning: A *learning goal* is a statement specifying what students will do or be able to if a teaching unit is successful. The learning goal is the purpose of a teaching unit.

Government-mandated test: A *government-mandated test* is a *systemwide test* that is required by a government agency (e.g., a state office of education), usually for evaluating achievement of some broad curriculum standards.

Grade equivalent score, Standardized test: A *grade equivalent score* of g.m is associated with a raw score x_i if x_i is approximately equal to the mean of the raw scores of those students in the norm group who were in the *g.m grade level* when they took the test.

Grade level, Student's standardized test: For purposes of standardized testing, a *student's grade level* is expressed in the form "*g.m*," where g is what grade the student is in when she or he takes the test and m is the month of the school year in which the test was administered. Thus, a student who takes a standardized test in October while in fifth grade is assigned a grade level of 5.2 for that test (assuming September was the first month of that school year). A student's grade level determines (1) which level of the test she or he will be administered, and (2) the grade-level norms to which her or his scores will be compared.

Grading: *Grading* the measurement is the process of assigning a qualitative value to the score.

Hard mini-experiment: (See "Difficulty of a mini-experiment.")

High-stakes testing: A test is considered *high stakes* if it is administered for the purpose of (1) accountability for student achievement, or (2) evaluations affecting promotion, retention, or graduation (U.S. General Accounting Office, 1993).

Inductive reasoning: *Inductive reasoning* is generalizing from encounters with *specifics*. Moreover, inductive reasoning is the cognitive process by which a person groups specifics into categories to either *construct a concept* or *discover a relationship*.

Ineffective mini-experiments: (See "Effectiveness of mini-experiments.")

Internal consistency of a measurement: A measurement is *internally consistent* to the degree results from its mini-experiments agree (i.e., correlate positively).

Inter-observer consistency: A mini-experiment has *inter-observer consistency* to the degree that different trained observers faithfully follow the rubric so that the results are not influenced by who makes the observation. A measurement's *inter-observer consistency* depends on the inter-observer consistencies of its mini-experiments.

Interpretive understanding: Students understand a message at the *interpretive level* if they can infer implicit meaning and explain how aspects of the communication are used to convey the message.

Interview format: A mini-experiment has an *interview format* if a teacher (or other interviewer) engages a student one-to-one in a process that includes the following features:

1. A sequence of questions or directives are orally presented to the student (sometimes complemented by visual prompts).
2. The student orally responds to each question or directive as it is presented, usually with the opportunity to elaborate.
3. Subsequent questions or directives may be influenced by responses the student makes to prior questions or directives.
4. The rubric is such that the interviewer takes notes or marks a scorer's form as the student completes each response either during the interview itself or while the interviewer listens to or views a taped recording of the interview.

Intra-observer consistency: A mini-experiment has *intra-observer consistency* to the degree that the observer (e.g., the teacher) faithfully follows the rubric so that the results are not influenced by fluctuations in the mood of the observer or in the way the observation is conducted. A measurement's *intra-observer consistency* depends on the intra-observer consistencies of its mini-experiments.

Item analysis: *Item analysis* is a process for measuring the effectiveness of mini-experiments.

Item analysis, Classical: *Classical item analysis* is an item analysis strategy by which students' scores from a mini-experiment are correlated with their overall scores on the measurement of which the mini-experiment is a part.

Learning level: The *learning level of an objective* is the way the objective specifies for students to think about, behave with, or interact with *subject-content*. Chapter 5 presents an advanced organizer for categorizing learning levels.

Learning-level relevance, Measurement: A measurement has *learning-level relevance* to the degree that its mini-experiments require students to operate at the learning levels specified by the learning objectives.

Literal understanding: Students *literally understand* a message if they can accurately translate its explicit meaning.

Local norm group: (See "Norm group.")

Manual, Standardized test: The test manuals for a particular standardized test are booklets with information about the test. Typically, these manuals include (1) detailed directions for how the test should be administered uniformly, (2) reliability coefficients (i.e., measures of reliability), (3) demographic information on the norm group, (4) information on how the test was normed, (5) explanations on how scores should be interpreted, and (6) information on appropriate uses of the test. Depending on test publishers, manuals have various titles, including Administrator's Guide, User's Manual, and Technical Manual.

Matching multiple-choice format: Matching prompts are a common variation of the multiple-choice format. A *matching prompt* presents students with two lists and the task of associating each entry of one list with an entry from the second.

Mean deviation of a sequence of scores (*MD*): One measure of variability is the *mean deviation*. The mean deviation of a sequence of scores is the arithmetic mean of the absolute values of the differences between each score and the arithmetic mean of scores. If $\{x_i\}$ is the sequence of scores from Test X, the arithmetic mean of $\{x_i\}$ is symbolized by μ_x, and $\{x_i\}$ has N_x scores, then MD_x is given by the following formula:

$$MD_x = \frac{\sum_{i=1}^{N_x} |x_i - \mu_x|}{N_x}$$

Mean of a sequence of scores, Arithmetic (μ): The *arithmetic mean* of a sequence of scores is a measure of central tendency that is the sum of scores divided by the number of scores. If $\{x_i\}$ is the sequence of scores from Test X, the arithmetic mean of $\{x_i\}$ is symbolized by μ_x, and $\{x_i\}$ has N_x scores, then μ_x is given by the following formula:

$$\mu_x = \frac{\sum_{i=1}^{N_x} x_i}{N_x}$$

Meaningful learning: Learning is *meaningful* to a student if she or he is able to apply what is learned in situations she or he considers important.

Measurement: A *measurement* is the process by which (1) information is collected through empirical observations, and (2) that information is remembered or recorded.

Measurement, Planned: A *planned measurement* is a sequence of mini-experiments a teacher deliberately conducts for the purpose of collecting information to be used to make a formative judgment or summative evaluation.

Measurement, Unplanned: *Unplanned measurements* are the continual flow of information from ongoing empirical observations that occur in the course of daily activities. Unplanned measurement results influence decision-making although they are not deliberately designed for that purpose.

Measurement error: *Measurement error* is the difference between the results of a measurement and what the results would be if the measurement had been perfectly valid.

Measurement results: The memory or record of the information yielded by a measurement is the *measurement result*.

Median of a sequence of scores: One measure of central tendency of a sequence of scores is its *median*. If the sequence has an odd number of scores, its median is the middle score. If the sequence has an even number of scores, its median is half the sum of the two middle scores.

Memory-level objective: Achievement of a *memory-level objective* requires students to remember a specified *subject-content*.

Message, Particular: A *particular message* is a specific communication transmitted from one person or group to another that is intended to convey information, ideas, directions, meanings, arguments, or other types of thoughts. Examples of particular messages include (1) Martin Luther King Jr.'s "I Have a Dream" speech, (2) the definition of "rational number" as stated in a particular mathematics textbook, (3) a particular science teacher's explanation of how solar cells convert sunlight into electricity, and (4) the directions that appear on your computer screen when you insert the CD-ROM that accompanies this textbook into your CD-ROM drive.

Mini-experiment: A *mini-experiment* is a component of a measurement used to monitor student learning that consists of a prompt for students' responses and an observer's rubric for recording or quantifying those responses. Traditional test items are examples of such mini-experiments. Herein, "mini-experiment" is used instead of the more conventional "test item," "measurement item," or "test question" for the following reasons: (a) The author's experiences working with teachers and teacher-educators suggest that the conventional terms connote only traditional item formats (e.g., multiple-choice and essay). (b) "Mini-experiments" reminds teachers that in order to gather evidence of student learning they need to create situations in which students behave in observable ways that are either consistent or inconsistent with achievement of a learning objective (i.e., the teachers are performing an experiment). (c) "Mini-experiment" reminds teachers that they are free to design an information-gathering device that may look much different from anything they've ever before seen.

Mini-experiment file: A computer file containing a set of prompts and rubrics for mini-experiments intended to be relevant to the same objective is a *mini-experiment file*.

Mini-experiment format: "*Mini-experiment format*" refers to the mode by which a mini-experiment's prompt is presented and students are expected to respond. Commonly used mini-experiment formats include, but are not limited to, multiple-choice, performance observation, essay, oral discourse, matching, interview, product examination, and short-response.

Mnemonic: A *mnemonic* is any device used to help one remember information.

Mode of communication: A *mode of communication* is a vehicle by which people send and receive messages. Examples of modes of communication are spoken words, books, maps, graphs, drawing, body language, music, American Sign Language, and writing.

Mode of a sequence of scores: One measure of central tendency of a sequence of scores is its *mode* or *modes*. The *mode* is the most frequently occurring *score value* in a sequence. Some sequences of scores have more than one mode.

Moderately difficult mini-experiment: (See "Difficulty of a mini-experiment.")

Monitoring students' learning: *Monitoring students' learning* is the ongoing process by which a teacher gauges students' progress and activities throughout their learning experiences.

Multiple-choice format: A mini-experiment that prompts students to select a response from a given list of alternatives has a *multiple-choice format*. A multiple-choice prompt is presented in two parts: (1) A *stem* that asks a question, gives a direction, or pro-

vides an incomplete statement, and (2) a number of *alternatives* from which students are to select the one that answers the question, follows the directions, or correctly completes the statement presented in the stem. The alternatives, except for the correct one, are referred to as "*distractors*" or "*foils*."

Muscular endurance: *Muscular endurance* is the ability of various muscle groups to repeatedly exert force. A muscle group's endurance depends on the frequency with which that group can exert a force before resting.

Muscular strength: *Muscular strength* is the capacity of various muscle groups to exert force. The strength of a muscle group is dependent on the amount of force that group is able to exert.

National norm group: (See "Norm group.")

Non-example of a concept: Relative to a particular concept, a *non-example* is a *specific* that does not possess all the *attributes* of that concept.

Norm group: A *norm group* for a standardized test is the sample of students with whom the test is field-tested and whose scores provide the standards for interpreting scores from subsequent administrations of the test. The more popular standardized tests that appeal to a nationwide market are *nationally normed*. In other words, the norm groups for these tests are samples drawn from geographic regions widely spread across the United States. Often, students' scores on standardized tests are also compared to the scores from *local norm groups*. A local norm group is a sample of test-takers within a particular geographic region.

Normal curve equivalent score (*NCE*): An NCE score is a type of standard score and can be computed for a raw score x_i as follows:

$NCEx_i = 21.06z_{x_i} + 50$ where z_{x_i} is the z-score associated with a raw score value of xi.

Like percentiles, NCE score values are positive numbers less than 100. But unlike percentiles, NCE values are equally spaced. (See Illustration 14.39.)

Normal frequency distribution: A frequency distribution is *normal* if its graph has a bell-shaped appearance similar to the curve shown by Illustration 14.33 and it includes the characteristics shown by Illustration 14.34. More specifically, a normal frequency function is generated by the following function where e is Euler's constant (i.e., $e \approx 2.71828$) and μ and σ are, respectively, the mean and standard deviation of the domain:

$$f(x) = \frac{1}{\sigma\sqrt{2\pi}} e^{-(x-\mu)^2/2\sigma^2}$$

Norm-referenced evaluation: A summative evaluation of a student's achievement is *norm-referenced* if the evaluation is influenced by how the measurement results relevant to that student's achievement compare to results obtained from others.

Norms, Test: *Test norms* are statistics computed from the norm group's scores that provide the (1) standard to which subsequent scores are compared (i.e., an average of scores from the norm group) and (2) unit of measure for making those comparisons (i.e., a measure of the variability of the scores from the norm group).

Objective, Learning: A *learning objective* is a statement specifying what students will do or be able to do if a lesson is successful. The learning objective is the purpose of a lesson.

Observer consistency: A measurement has *observer consistency* to the degree it has both *intra-observer consistency* and *inter-observer consistency*.

Observer's rubric: A mini-experiment's *observer's rubric* is the set of rules, key, or procedures a teacher or other observer follows to record an analysis of a student's response to the mini-experiment's prompt.

Oral-discourse format: A mini-experiment that prompts students to give a talk or speech that is more complex than a simple recitation has an *oral-discourse format*.

Overlapping alternatives: Two *multiple-choice alternatives* overlap if one cannot be correct unless the other is also correct.

Overlearning: Students *overlearn* by continuing to practice recalling subject-content even after they have memorized it. Overlearning increases resistance to forgetting and facilitates long-term retention of information.

Parallel alternatives, Multiple-choice: Two alternatives in a multiple-choice prompt are *parallel* if they pose the same question to students—a question about a specific subject-content.

Parallel concepts: Two concepts are *parallel* if neither is *subordinate* to the other.

Percentage-averaging method: With the *percentage-averaging method* for converting grades from different measurements to a single grade, the percentage scores from individual measurements are averaged to determine the overall percentage. The overall percentage is converted to an overall grade. (See Case 3.12 for an example. Note that you are advised not to use this method.)

Percentage grading method, Traditional: With the *traditional percentage grading method* for converting measurement scores to grades, each score from a measurement is converted to a percentage of the maximum possible score and translated to a letter grade by some predetermined scale (e.g., 94% to 100% for an A, 86% to 93% for a B, 78% to 85% for a C, 70% to 77% for a D, and 00% to 69% for an F).

Percentile: A raw score x_i converts to a *percentile* of p if x_i is greater than $p\%$ of the norm-group's raw scores and x_i is less than $(100 - p)\%$ of the norm-group's raw scores.

Performance assessment: (See "Authentic assessment.")

Performance observation format: A mini-experiment has a *performance-observation format* if it is designed for the teacher (or other designated observer) to use the rubric as students are responding to the prompt so that what the students do is the focus of the observation rather than the end product of the response.

Physical fitness: Objectives at the *physical-fitness learning level* are concerned with students improving their physical states of well-being that allow them to "perform daily activities with vigor, reduce the risk of health problems related to lack of exercise, and establish a fitness base for participation in a variety of physical activities" (McSwegin, Pemberton, Petray, & Going, 1989, p. 1).

Portfolio, Individualized student: An *individualized student portfolio* is a collection of products, artifacts, and demonstrations of the student's schoolwork assembled for the purpose of providing a representative sample of the student's achievement. Three types of portfolios are commonly identified in the teacher-education literature (Alleman & Brophy, 1997, p. 341): The (1) *working portfolio*, (2) *showcase portfolio*, and (3) *record-keeping portfolio*. The *working portfolio* is a mechanism for documenting the student's ongoing progress. The *showcase portfolio* is a mechanism for reflecting the student's significant and prominent accomplishments. The *record-keeping portfolio* is a mechanism for maintaining a comprehensive record of the student's schoolwork.

Portfolio assessment: *Portfolio assessment* is the use of individualized student portfolios as devices for communicating summative evaluations of student achievement.

Power, Psychomotor: *Psychomotor power* is the ability to generate maximum force in an explosive, nearly instantaneous way.

Predictive validity: An *aptitude test* has *predictive validity* to the degree that (1) students with high scores from the test of their potential for success with targeted goals actually do achieve those goals, and (2) students with low scores fail to achieve those goals.

Process: A *process* is a systematic, step-by-step method by which a task is accomplished. "Process" is one of the subject-content categories in the advanced organizer for formulating learning objectives that is introduced in Chapter 5.

Process knowledge: An objective requiring students to remember the sequence of steps in a procedure is at the *process-knowledge learning level*.

Product-examination format: A *product-examination* mini-experiment prompts students to complete a production task; the rubric is a scheme for either judging the quality of what the students produce or detecting features of the product.

Prompt of a mini-experiment: A *prompt of a mini-experiment* is the aspect of the mini-experiment that stimulates students to behave or respond in a manner that is indicative of what the mini-experiment is designed to measure.

Psychomotor domain: A learning objective falls within the *psychomotor domain* if its intent is for students to develop some physical attribute (e.g., muscle flexibility) or physical skill (e.g., manipulate a pencil well enough to form legible manuscript letters).

Psychomotor skill: *Psychomotor-skill* objectives focus on students' abilities to execute physical tasks as they cognitively know the task should be executed.

Range of a sequence of scores: The *range* of a score sequence is the difference between the greatest and least score values. The range is one measure of score variability.

Raw score: The *raw score* a student obtains from a test is simply the sum of the points from the individual mini-experiments composing the test.

Reaction time: *Reaction time* is how quickly the body initiates a controlled movement in response to a stimulus signaling the need to make that movement.

Real-life problem: A real-life problem is a perplexing or puzzling question, issue, or task an individual is motivated to address.

Reasoning-level objective: Achievement of a *reasoning-level objective* requires students to use reasoning to make judgments relative to a specified *subject-content*.

Relationship: A *relationship* is a particular association between either (1) *concepts*, (2) a concept and a *specific*, or (3) specifics. "Relationship" is one of the subject-content categories in the advanced organizer for formulating learning objectives that is introduced in Chapter 5.

Relationship, Discoverable: A relationship is *discoverable* if one can use reasoning or experimentation to find out that the relationship exists.

Relationship of Convention: A *relationship of convention* is a relationship that exists because it has been established through tradition or agreement.

Relevance, Measurement: A measurement is *relevant* to the degree that it provides information that is pertinent to the decision influenced by the measurement results. To be relevant to students' achievement of a learning goal, the measurement must have both *subject-content relevance* as well as *learning-level relevance*.

Reliability, Measurement: A measurement is *reliable* to the degree to which it can be depended upon to provide non-contradictory information. To be reliable, a measurement must produce *internally consistent* results and have *observer consistency*.

Scaled scores: *Scaled scores* are derived scores from a standardized test that allow results from different levels of the test to be compared. Scaled score values are positive numbers less than 1,000, with raw scores from lower grade levels (e.g., 1.2) associated with lower scaled scores (e.g., 109) and raw scores from higher grade levels (e.g., 11.7) associated with higher ones (e.g., 722). The particular correspondences between scaled scores and other types of scores as well as grade levels differ, depending on the test and the edition of the test.

Scorer consistency: (See "Observer consistency.")

Scoring: *Scoring* a student's measurement responses is the process of adhering to the observer's rubric for each of the measurement's mini-experiments and compiling the results into a single measurement score.

Short-response format: A mini-experiment that prompts students to respond with a brief verbal expression (either orally or in writing) has a *short-response format*.

Simple knowledge: An objective requiring students to remember a specified response (but not a step-by-step process) to a specified stimulus is at the *simple-knowledge learning level*.

Specific: A *specific* is any unique entity. "Specific" is one of the subject-content categories in the advanced organizer for formulating learning objectives that is introduced in Chapter 5.

Speed, Psychomotor: *Speed* is the ability of the body to rapidly move between two points—especially when running a relatively short distance (e.g., 50 m).

Standard deviation of a sequence of scores (σ). One measure of variability is the *standard deviation*, symbolized by "σ" (sigma). The standard deviation of a sequence of scores is the square root of the *variance* of scores. If $\{x_i\}$ is the sequence of scores from Test X, the arithmetic mean of $\{x_i\}$ is symbolized by μ_x, and $\{x_i\}$ has N_x scores, then σ_x^2 is given by the following formula:

$$\sigma_x = \sqrt{\frac{\sum_{i=1}^{N_x} (x_i - \mu_x)^2}{N_x}}$$

Standard error of measurement (SEM): A standard error of measurement is a statistical estimate or the reliability error of a measurement. SEM_x is the standard error of measurement of a sequence of measurement scores, $\{x_i\}$, if

$$SEM = \sigma_x \sqrt{1 - r_x}$$

where σ_x is the standard deviation of $\{x_i\}$ and r_x is the reliability coefficient of the measurement.

Standard score: A *standard score*, Sx_i, is any derived score that is computed by the following formula:

$Sx_i = D(z_{x_i}) + M$ where z_{x_i} is the z-score associated with a raw score value of x_i, D is a constant (whatever the inventor of the standard score wants the standard deviation of the standard-score scale to be) and M is a constant (whatever the inventor of the standard score wants the mean of the standard score scale to be).

Standardized test: A *standardized test* is a planned measurement that has been field-tested to assess its reliability and to establish normative standards to be used in interpreting scores from subsequent administrations of the test.

Stanine score: To convert raw scores to *stanine scores*, the raw scores are collapsed into 9 categories or intervals so that each raw score is reported simply as either a "1," "2," . . . , or "9." Raw scores very near the norm-group mean (i.e., μ) are assigned to the middle interval, which is stanine 5. The length of each of the 9 stanine intervals (except for the two most extreme ones) is one-half a norm-group standard deviation (i.e., $^1/_2\sigma$). The 9 *stanines* are defined as follows:

1. If x_i is a raw score such that $z_{x_i} < -1.75$, then x_i is assigned to stanine 1.
2. If x_i is a raw score such that $-1.75 \leq z_{x_i} < -1.25$, then x_i is assigned to stanine 2.
3. If x_i is a raw score such that $-1.25 \leq z_{x_i} < -0.75$, then x_i is assigned to stanine 3.
4. If x_i is a raw score such that $-0.75 \leq z_{x_i} < -0.25$, then x_i is assigned to stanine 4.

5. If x_i is a raw score such that $-0.25 \leq z_{x_i} < 0.25$, then x_i is assigned to stanine 5.
6. If x_i is a raw score such that $0.25 \leq z_{x_i} < 0.75$, then x_i is assigned to stanine 6.
7. If x_i is a raw score such that $0.75 \leq z_{x_i} < 1.25$, then x_i is assigned to stanine 7.
8. If x_i is a raw score such that $1.25 \leq z_{x_i} < 1.75$, then x_i is assigned to stanine 8.
9. If x_i is a raw score such that $1.75 < z_{x_i}$, then x_i is assigned to stanine 9.

Static balance: *Static balance* is the ability to maintain equilibrium in a stationary position.

Stem, Multiple-choice: (See "Multiple-choice format.")

Subject-content: *Subject-content* refers to the academic material or aspects of a discipline (e.g., art, physical education, mathematics, or history) upon which learning objectives are focused. Chapter 5 presents an advanced organizer for categorizing subject-content.

Subject-content relevance, Measurement: A measurement has *subject-content relevance* to the degree that its mini-experiments involve students in the subject-content specified by the learning objectives.

Subordinate concept: One concept is *subordinate* to a second concept if the first is subsumed by the second. For example, the concept "cat" is subordinate to the concept "mammal."

Summative evaluation: A *summative evaluation* is a decision about the success of a teaching cycle.

Superordinate concept: One concept is *superordinate* to a second concept if the first subsumes the second. For example, the concept "mammal" is superordinate to the concept "cat."

Syllogism: A *syllogism* is a scheme for making a conclusion from a *major premise* and a *minor premise*. Illustration 10.1 displays examples of syllogisms.

Synectics: *Synectics* is an instructional strategy for fostering creative thinking by which *metaphors* and *analogies* are used to lead students into an illogic state for situations where rational logic fails. The intent is for students to free themselves of convergent thinking and to develop empathy with ideas that conflict with their own.

Systemwide test: A test is *systemwide* if it is administered to nearly all or a representative sample of all students in at least one grade level (e.g., third grade) or in one subject-content area (e.g., U.S. history) in a school district or state (Phelps, 1996).

Teaching cycle: A *teaching cycle* is any sequence of events in which a teacher (1) recognizes a need one or more students have, (2) decides to address that need by determining an objective or a set of learning objectives, (3) decides how to lead students to achieve the objectives, (4) implements the plan, and (5) determines how well students achieved the objectives.

Test: A formal *planned measurement*.

Test battery: A *test battery* is a sequence of individual tests that are administered under a single title (e.g., "State Core-Curriculum Tests" or "*Stanford Achievement Test 9*") within a single time interval (e.g., three consecutive days with three or four *subtests* per day). An individual test in a battery is referred to as a *subtest*.

Test item: A *test item* is a *mini-experiment*.

Test level, Standardized: *Test level* for a standardized test refers to the particular part of the standardized test that is designed for administration to students within a particular grade-level range. Different test levels are associated with different ranges of grade levels. (See Illustrations 14.12 and 14.13 for examples.)

Think-aloud trial: A *think-aloud trial* is used to provide an indication of the cognitive activity a mini-experiment's prompt triggers in a student's mind. To conduct a think-aloud trial for a mini-experiment, a teacher directs a student to speak her or his thoughts aloud as she or he responds to the prompt.

Unit, Teaching: A *teaching unit* is a part of a course focusing on a particular topic or content area; a teaching unit includes four components: (1) A learning goal defined by a set of specific objectives, (2) a planned sequence of lessons, each designed to lead students to achieve one of the specific objectives, (3) mechanisms for monitoring student progress and using formative feedback to guide lessons, and (4) summative evaluations of student achievement of the learning goal.

Usability, Measurement: A measurement is *usable* to the degree that it is inexpensive, does not consume time, is easy to administer and score, is safe for students and other personnel, and does not interfere with other activities.

Usefulness, Measurement: A measurement is *useful* to the degree that it is both *valid* and *usable*.

Validity, Measurement: A measurement is *valid* to the degree that it is both *relevant* and *reliable*.

Variability of a sequence of scores: The *variability* of a sequence of scores is a reflection of how dispersed the scores tend to be; the greater the differences among scores, the greater the variability of the sequence.

Variance of a sequence of scores (σ^2): One measure of variability is the *variance*, symbolized by "σ^2." The variance of a sequence of scores is the arithmetic mean of the squares of differences between each score and the arithmetic mean of scores. If $\{x_i\}$ is the sequence of scores from Test X, the arithmetic mean of $\{x_i\}$ is symbolized by μ_x, and $\{x_i\}$ has N_x scores, then σ^2_x is given by the following formula:

$$\sigma_x^{\,2} = \frac{\sum_{i=1}^{N_x} (x_i - \mu_x)^2}{N_x}$$

Visual inspection grading method: With the *visual inspection grading method* for converting measurement scores to grades, the frequency distribution of the scores from a measurement are graphed so that grades are assigned according to gaps in the distribution. Every score within a single cluster of scores is assigned the same grade, with clusters of higher scores assigned higher grades, and clusters of lower scores assigned lower grades.

Weighted-averaging method: With the weighted-averaging method for converting grades from different measurements to a single grade, the teacher weights each individual measurement grade according to the degree to which she or he decides that measurement grade should influence the overall grade. Then the overall grade is determined by an algorithm that factors in the weights assigned by the teacher. (See Case 3.11 for an example.)

Weighted scoring: A mini-experiment has *weighted scoring* if there are more than two possible categories for students' responses; the observer classifies a response in terms of the degree to which it meets a criterion.

Weighting objectives: *Weighting objectives* is the process by which a teacher assigns a percentage value to each objective in a set of objectives for the purpose of indicating the relative impor-

tance of that objective with respect to goal achievement. More important objectives are assigned higher percentages than less important objectives.

Willingness to try: Students achieve an objective at the *willingness-to-try learning level* by choosing to attempt a task specified by the objective.

z-score: The *z-score* associated with a particular raw score is the number of standard deviations that the raw score falls above the mean. If x_i is a raw score from Test x, the *z*-score associated with x_i (z_{x_i}) is given by the following:

$$z_{x_i} = \frac{x_i - \mu_x}{\sigma_x}$$

REFERENCES

Alleman, J., & Brophy, J. (1997). Elementary social studies: Instruments, activities, and standards. In G.D. Phye (Ed.), *Handbook of classroom assessment: Learning, adjustment, and achievement* (pp. 321–356). San Diego: Academic Press.

American Psychological Association, American Educational Research Association, & National Council on Measurement in Education. (1985). *Standards for educational and psychological testing* (5th ed.). Washington: Author.

Ashburn, R. R. (1938). An experiment in the essay type question. *Journal of Experimental Education, 7,* 1–3.

Barber, B. L., Paris, S. G., Evans, M., & Gadsen, V. L. (1992). Policies for reporting test results to parents. *Educational Issues and Practices, 11,* 15–20.

Bass, R. I. (1939). An analysis of the components of semi-circular canal function and of static and dynamic balance. *Research Quarterly, 10,* 33–42.

Bauman, M. (1997). What grades do for us, and how to do without them. In S. Tschudi (Ed.), *Alternatives to grading student writing* (pp. 162–178). Urbana, IL: National Council of Teachers of English.

Beyer, B. K. (1987). *Practical strategies for teaching of thinking.* Boston: Allyn and Bacon.

Bloom, B. S. (Ed.). (1984). *Taxonomy of educational objectives: The classification of educational goals book I: Cognitive domain.* New York: Longman.

Bourne, L. E., Dominowski, R. L., Loftus, E. F., & Healy, A. F. (1986). *Cognitive processes* (2nd ed.). Englewood Cliffs, NJ: Prenctice Hall.

Brandes, B. (1986). *Academic honesty: A special study of California students.* Sacramento: Bureau of Publications, California State Department of Education.

Brennan, R. L., & Kane, M. T. (1977). An index of dependability for mastery tests. *Journal of Educational Measurement, 14,* 277–289.

Brophy, J. (1998). *Motivating students to learn.* Boston: McGraw- Hill.

Brophy, J., & Good, T. L. (1986). Teacher behavior and student achievement. In M.C. Wittrock (Ed.), *Handbook of research on teaching* (3rd ed.) (pp. 328–375). New York: Macmillan.

Brownell, W. A. (1933). On the accuracy with which reliability may be measured by correlating test halves. *Journal of Experimental Education, 1,* 204–215.

Bushway, A., & Nash, W. (1977). School cheating behavior. *Review of Educational Research, 47,* 623–632.

Cangelosi, J.S. (1982). *Measurement and evaluation: An inductive approach for teachers.* Dubuque, IA: W. C. Brown.

Cangelosi, J. S. (1990). *Designing tests for evaluating student achievement.* New York: Longman.

Cangelosi, J. S. (1991). *Evaluating classroom instruction.* New York: Longman.

Cangelosi, J. S. (1992). *Systematic teaching strategies.* New York: Longman.

Cangelosi, J. S. (1993, April). *Cheating on tests: Issues in elementary and secondary school classrooms.* Paper presented at a joint session of the American Educational Research Association and the National Council for Measurement in Education, Atlanta.

Cangelosi, J. S. (1996). *Teaching mathematics in secondary and middle school: An interactive approach* (2nd ed.). Englewood Cliffs, NJ: Prentice-Hall.

Cangelosi, J. S. (1997). *Classroom management strategies: Gaining and maintaining students' cooperation* (3rd ed.). New York: Longman.

Cangelosi, J. S. (1998). *Measurement-development practices of classroom teachers.* Unpublished survey. Logan: Utah State University.

Chance, P. (1988). *Learning and behavior* (2nd ed.). Belmont, CA: Wadsworth.

Conoley, J. C., & Impara, J. C. (Eds.). (1995). *The twelfth mental measurement yearbook.* Lincoln, NE: Buros Institute of Mental Measurements.

Cronbach, L. J. (1951). Coefficient alpha and the internal structure of tests. *Psychometrika, 16,* 297–335.

Cunningham, P. M. (1995). *Phonics they use: Words for reading and writing* (2nd ed.). New York: HarperCollins.

Davey, L. (1992). The case for a national test. *Clearinghouse on Tests, Measurement, and Evaluation* EDO-TM–91–1 [online]. Available: http://ericae.net/ft/nattest/natfor.htm.

Davey, L. & Neill, M. (1991). The case against a national test. *ERIC/TM Digest* ED338703 [on-line]. Available: http://eri-cae.net/db/digs/ed338703.htm

Davis, R. B., Maher, C. A., & Noddings, N. (Ed.). (1990). *Constructivist views on the teaching and learning of mathematics.* Reston, VA: National Council of Teachers of Mathematics.

Douglas, G. (1988). Latent trait measurement models. In J. P. Keeves (Ed.), *Educational research, methodology, and measurement: An international handbook* (pp. 282–286). Oxford, UK: Pergamon Press.

Driver, R. (1995). Constructivist approaches to science teaching. In L. P. Steffe & J. Gale (Eds.), *Constructivism in education* (pp. 385–400). Hillsdale, NJ: Lawrence Erlbaum.

Duell, O. K. (1986). Metacognitive skills. In G. D. Phye & T. Andre (Eds.), *Cognitive classroom learning: Understanding thinking, and problem solving* (pp. 205–242). San Diego: Academic Press.

Ebel, R. L. (1965). *Measuring educational achievement.* Englewood Cliffs, NJ: Prentice-Hall.

Ellis, H. C., & Hunt, R. R. (1983). *Fundamentals of human memory and cognition* (3rd ed.). Dubuque: IA: W. C. Brown.

Ertmer, P. A., Newby, T. J., & MacDougall, M. (1996). Students' responses and approaches to case-based instruction: The role of reflective self-regulation. *American Educational Research Journal, 33,* 719–752.

Evans, E. D., & Craig, D. (1990). Teacher and student perceptions of academic cheating in middle and senior high schools. *Journal of Educational Research, 84,* 44–52.

Fischer, C., & King, R. (1995). *Authentic assessment: A guide to implementation.* Thousand Oaks, CA: Corwin Press.

Gaffney, R. F., & Maguire, T. O. (1971). Use of optically scored test answer sheets with young children. *Journal of Educational Measurement, 8,* 103–106.

Gagné, N. L. (1985). Hard gains in the soft sciences: The case of pedagogy. *Phi Delta Kappan, 67,* 4–11.

Gagné, E. D., Yekovich, C. W., & Yekovich, F. R. (1993). *Cognitive psychology of school learning* (2nd ed.). New York: HarperCollins College Publishers.

Gallager, J. D. (1998). *Classroom assessment for teachers.* Upper Saddle River, NJ: Prentice-Hall.

Ginott, H. G. (1972). *Teacher and child.* New York: Avon.

Gordon, W. J. J. (1961). *Synectics.* New York: Harper & Row.

Gowan, J. C., Demos, G. D., & Torrance, E. P. (1967). *Creativity: Its educational implications.* New York: John Wiley.

Greene, S., & Ackerman, J.M. (1995). Expanding the constructivist metaphor: A rhetorical perspective on literacy research and practice. *Review of Educational Research, 65,* 383–420.

Gronlund, N. E. (1982). *Constructing achievement tests* (3rd ed.). Englewood Cliffs, NJ: Prentice-Hall

Guilford, J. P. (1959). *Personality.* New York: McGraw-Hill.

Guskey, T. R., & Kifer, E. W. (1990). Ranking school districts on the basis of statewide tests results: Is it meaningful or misleading? *Educational Issues and Practices, 9,* 11–16.

Hallahan, D. P., & Kauffman, J. M. (1997). *Exceptional learners: Introduction to special education* (7th ed.). Boston: Allyn and Bacon.

Hambleton, R. K., & Swaminathan, H. (1985). *Item response theory.* Boston: Kluwer-Nijhoff Publishing.

Harrow, A. J. (1974). *A taxonomy of the psychomotor domain: A guide for developing behavioral objectives.* New York: McKay.

Herman, J. L., & Golan, S. (1995). The effects of standardized testing on teaching and schools. *Educational Issues and Practices, 12,* 20–25+.

Heyward, W. H., & Stolarczyk, L. M. (1996). *Applied body composition assessment* (4th ed.). Champaign, IL: Human Kinetics.

Hofmann, R. J. (1975). The concept of efficiency in item analysis. *Educational and Psychological Measurement, 35,* 621–640.

Hopkins, K. E. (1998). *Educational and psychological measurement and evaluation* (8th ed.). Boston: Allyn and Bacon.

Hoyt, C. J. (1941). Test reliability estimated by analysis of variance. *Psychometrika, 6,* 153–160.

Hurd, J. (1998). The effect of the estimate of resting metabolic rate on the correlation between energy expenditure as estimated using self-reports of physical activity and food intake records in older adults. Dissertation. Utah State University.

Institute for Aerobics Research. (1992). *The Prudential FIT-NESSGRAM test administration manual.* Dallas: Author.

Jones, K. (1997). Portfolio assessment as an alternative to grading student writing. In S. Tchudi (Ed.), *Alternatives to grading student writing* (pp. 255–263). Urbana, IL: National Council of Teachers of English.

Joyce, B., Weil, M., & Showers, B. (1992). *Models of teaching* (4th ed.). Boston: Allyn and Bacon.

Kelley, D. (1988). *The art of reasoning.* New York: W. W. Norton.

Keeves, J. P. (1988a). Scaling achievement test scores. In J. P. Keeves (Ed.), *Educational research, methodology, and measurement: An international handbook* (pp. 403–419). Oxford, UK: Pergamon Press.

Keeves, J. P. (1988b). Social theory and educational research. In J. P. Keeves (Ed.), *Educational research, methodology, and measurement: An international handbook* (pp. 20–27). Oxford, UK: Pergamon Press.

Kleinbaum, D. G., Kupper, L. L., & Muller, K. E. (1988). *Applied regression analysis and other multivariable methods* (2nd ed.). Boston: PWS-KENT Publishing.

Krathwohl, D., Bloom, B. S., & Masia, B. (1964). *Taxonomy of educational objectives, the classification of educational goals, handbook 2: Affective domain.* New York: Longman.

Kuder, G.F., & Richardson, M.W. (1937). The theory of the estimation of test reliability. *Psychometrika, 2,* 151–160.

Lassiter, K. (1987, April). An examination of performance differences using two types of answer media. Paper presentation at the annual meeting of the National Council on Measurement in Education. Washington.

Lavoie, R. D. (1989). *Understanding learning disabilities: How difficult can this be? The F.A.T city workshop.* [videotape]. Greenwhich, CT: Eagle Hill Outreach. A Peter Rose Production distributed by PBS Video.

Livingston, S. A. (1972). Criterion-referenced applications of classical test theory. *Journal of Education Measurement, 9,* 12–36.

Mager, R. (1961). *Preparing instructional objectives*. Belmont, CA: Fearon Publishers.

McCombs, B. L. (1988). Motivational skill training: Combining metacognitive, cognitive, and affective learning strategies. In C.E. Weinstein, E.T. Goetz, & P.A. Alexander (Eds.), *Learning and study strategies: Issues in assessment, instruction, and evaluation* (pp. 141–169). San Diego: Academic Press.

McMillan, J. H. (1997). *Classroom assessment: Principles and practice for effective instruction*. Boston: Allyn and Bacon.

McSwegin, P., Pemberton, C., Petray, C., & Going, S. (1989). *Physical best: The AAH-PERD guide to physical fitness education and assessment*. Reston, VA: American Alliance for Health, Physical Education, Recreation, and Dance

Metz, K. E. (1995). Reassessment of developmental constraints on children's science instruction. *Review of Educational Research, 65*, 193–127.

Moore, K. D. (1992). *Classroom teaching skills* (2nd ed.). New York: McGraw-Hill.

Mosier, C. I. (1936). A note on item analysis and the criterion of internal consistency. *Psychometrika, 1*, 275–282.

Murphy, L. L., Conoley, J. C., & Impara, J. C. (1994). *Tests in print* (4th ed.). Lincoln, NE: Buros Institute of Mental Measurements.

National Center for History in the Schools. (1997). *National standards for history grades K–4: Expanding children's world in time and space*. Los Angeles: Author.

National Council of Teachers of English & International Reading Association. (1996). *Standards for the English Language Arts*. Urbana, IL: Author.

National Council of Teachers of Mathematics. (1989). *Curriculum and evaluation standards for school mathematics*. Reston, VA: Author.

National Council of Teachers of Mathematics. (1995). *Assessment standards for school mathematics*. Reston, VA: Author.

National Research Council. (1996). *National science education standards*. Washington, DC: National Academy Press.

Neill, D. M. (1997). Transforming student assessment. *Phi Delta Kappan, 79*, 34–40+.

New Jersey Department of Education. (1997). *New Jersey Core Curriculum Content Standards*. Trenton, NJ: Author.

Nolen, S. B., Haladyna, T. M., & Haas, N. S. (1992). Uses and abuses of achievement tests scores. *Educational Measurement: Issues and Practices, 11*, 9–15.

Nunnally, J. C. (1978). *Psychometric theory* (2nd ed.). New York: McGraw-Hill.

O'Hagan, L. K. (1997). It's broken—fix it! In S. Tschudi (Ed.), *Alternatives to grading student writing* (pp. 3–13). Urbana, IL: National Council of Teachers of English.

O'Malley, M., Russo, R. P., Chamot, A. U., & Stewner-Manzanares, G. (1988). Applications of learning strategies by students learning English as a second language. In C. E. Weinstein, E. T. Goetz, & P. A. Alexander (Eds.), *Learning and study strategies: Issues in assessment, instruction, and evaluation* (pp. 215–231). San Diego: Academic Press.

Pangrazi, R. P. (1998). *Dynamic physical education for elementary school children* (2nd ed.). Boston: Allyn and Bacon.

Plake, B. S., & Impara, J. C. (1997). Teacher assessment literacy: What do teachers know about assessment? In G. D. Phye (Ed.), *Handbook of classroom assessment: Learning, adjustment, and achievement* (pp. 53–68). San Diego: Academic Press.

Phelps, R. P. (1996). Are U.S. students the most heavily tested on earth? *Educational Measurement: Issues and Practices, 15*, 19–27.

President's Council on Physical Fitness and Sports. (1991). *The President's challenge physical fitness program packet*. Washington, DC: Author.

Prince, G. (1968). The operational mechanism of synectics. *Journal of Creative Behavior, 2*, 1–13.

Pulaski, M.A.S. (1980). *Understanding Piaget: An introduction to children's cognitive development* (2nd ed.). New York: Harper & Row.

Rogoff, B. (1990). *Apprenticeship in thinking*. New York: Oxford University Press.

Romesburg, H. C. (1984). *Cluster analysis for researchers*. Belmont, CA: Lifetime Learning Publications.

Roscoe, J. T. (1969). *Fundamental research statistics for the behavioral sciences*. New York: Holt, Rinehart, and Winston.

Rowley, E. R. (1996). Alternative assessments of meaningful learning of calculus content: A development and validation of item pools. Dissertation. Utah State University.

Rulon, P. J. (1939). A simplified procedure for determining the reliability of a test by split-halves. *Harvard Educational Review, 9*, 99–103.

Ryans, D. G. (1938). Francis Galton's statistical contributions. *School and Society, 48*, 312–316.

Safrit, M. J. (1995). *Complete guide to youth fitness testing*. Champaign, IL: Human Kinectics.

Safrit, M. J., & Wood, T. M. (1995) *Introduction to measurement in physical education and exercise science* (3rd ed.). St. Louis: Mosby.

Santa, C. M., & Havens, L. T. (1991). Learning through writing. In C. M. Santa & D. E. Alverman (Eds.),. *Science learning: Process and applications* (pp. 122–133). Newark, DE: International Reading Association.

Schab, F. (1991). Schooling without learning: Thirty years of cheating in high school. *Adolescence, 26*, 839–847.

Schoenfeld, A. H. (1985). *Mathematical problem solving*. San Diego, CA: Academic Press.

Schoenfeld, A. H. (1992). Learning to think mathematically: Problem solving, metacognition, and sense making in mathematics. In D. A. Grouws (Ed.), *Handbook of research on mathematics teaching and learning* (pp. 334–370). New York: Macmillan.

Schunk, D. H. (1996). Goal and self-evaluative influences during children's cognitive skill learning. *American Educational Research Journal, 33*, 359–382.

Sheppard, L. A., Flexer, R. J., Hiebert, E. H., Marion, S. F., Mayfield, V., & Weston, T. J. (1996). Effects of introducing classroom performance assessments on student learning. *Educational Measurement: Issues and Practices, 15*, 7–18.

Shuell, T. J. (1990). Phases of meaningful learning. *Review of Educational Research, 60*, 531–547.

Smith, F., & Adams, S. (1972). *Educational measurement for the classroom teacher* (2nd ed.). New York: Harper & Row.

Smith, M. U., & Sims, O. S. (1992). Cognitive development, problem solving, and genetics instruction: A critical review. *Journal of Research in Science Teaching, 29,* 701–713.

Soar, R. S., Medley, D. M., & Coker, H. (1983). Teacher evaluation: A critique of currently used methods. *Phi Delta Kappan, 65,* 239–246.

Spandel, V., & Culham, R. (1995). *Putting portfolio stories to work.* Portland, OR: Northwest Regional Educational Laboratory.

Spearman, C. (1904). The proof and measurement of association between two things. *American Journal of Psychology, 15,* 201–293.

Stalnaker, J. M. (1936). The problem of the English examination. *Educational Record, 17,* 41.

Stanley, J. C., & Hopkins, K. D. (1972). *Educational and psychological measurement and evaluation.* Englewood Cliffs, NJ: Prentice-Hall.

Starko, A. J. (1995). *Creativity in the classroom: Schools of curious delight.* New York: Longman.

Steffe, L. P., & Gale, J. (Eds.) (1995). *Constructivism in education.* Hillsdale, NJ: Lawrence Erlbaum.

Stiggins, R. J. (1988). Revitalizing classroom assessment: The highest priority. *Phi Delta Kappan, 69,* 363–368.

Stiggins, R. J., & Conklin, N. F. (1992). *In teachers' hands: Investigating the practices of classroom assessment.* Albany, NY: State University of New York Press.

Strom, R. D. (1969). *Psychology for the classroom.* Englewood Cliffs, NJ: Prentice Hall.

Tallmadge, G. K. (1985). Normalizing the NCE. *Educational Measurement: Issues and Practices, 4,* 30.

Tallmadge, G. K., & Wood, C. T. (1976). *User's guide ESEA Title I evaluation and reporting system.* Mountain View, CA: RMC Research Corporation and the U.S. Department of Health, Education, and Welfare.

Taylor, K., & Walton, S. (1997). Co-opting standardized tests in the service of learning. *Phi Delta Kappan, 79,* 66–70.

Thorndike, R. M. (1988). Correlational procedures. In J. P. Keeves (Ed.), *Educational research, methodology, and measurement: An international handbook* (pp. 613–621). Oxford, UK: Pergamon Press.

Thurstone, L. L. (1928). Attitudes can be measured. *American Journal of Sociology, 33,* 529–554.

Tobin, K., Tippins, D. J., & Gallard, A. J. (1994). Research on instructional strategies for teaching science. In D. L. Gabel (Ed.), *Handbook of research on science teaching and learning* (pp. 45–93). New York: Macmillan.

Torrance, E. P. (1962). *Guiding creative talent.* Englewood Cliffs, NJ: Prentice-Hall.

Torrance, E. P. (1988). The nature of creativity as manifest in its testing. In R. J. Sternberg (Ed.), *The nature of creativity.* New York: Cambridge University Press.

Turnbull, H. R., & Turnbull, A. P. (1998). *Free appropriate public education* (5th ed.). Denver: Love Publishing Co.

U.S. General Accounting Office. (1993). *Student testing: Current extent and expenditure, with cost estimates for a national examination* (GAO/PEDM–93–8). Washington: Author.

Utah State Office of Education. (1995). *Mathematics Core Curriculum: Grade 6.* Salt Lake City, UT: Author.

von Glasersfeld, E. (1995) A constructivist approach to teaching. In L. P. Steffe & J. Gale (Eds.), *Constructivism in education* (pp. 3–15). Hillsdale, NJ: Lawrence Erlbaum.

Walker, H. M. (1929). *Studies in the history of statistical methods.* Baltimore: Williams and Wilkins Company.

Williams, C. S., Harageones, E. G., Johnson, D. J., & Smith, C. D. (1995). *Personal fitness: Looking good, feeling good* (3rd ed.). Dubuque, IA: Kendall/Hunt Publishing.

Wolff, L. (1995). An English department's fusion: Portfolios as a place to begin department talk. *Iowa English Bulletin, 45,* 53–59.

Woolfolk, A. E. (1993). *Educational psychology* (5th ed.). Boston: Allyn and Bacon.

NAME INDEX

Ackerman, J. M., 57, R2
Adams, S., 163, R4
Alexander, P. A., R3
Alleman, J., 289, G6, R1
Alverman, D. E., R3
Andre, T., R2
Ashburn, R.R., 335, R1

Barber, B.L., 514, R1
Bass, R.I., 439, R1
Bauman, M., 148, R1
Beyer, B. K., 452, R1
Bloom, B. S., 230, R1, R2
Bourne, L. E., 372, 451, 452, R1
Brandes, B., 286, R1
Brennan, R.L., 628, R1
Brophy, J., 91, 122, 289, G7, R1
Brownell, W.A., 613, R1
Bushway, A., 286, R1
Cangelosi, J.S., 2, 57, 66, 71, 82, 86, 115, 122, 124, 148, 200, 225, 230, 238, 256, 257, 283, 284, 286, 288, 297, 335, 344, 467, 514, 515, 525, 562, R1

Chamot, A.U., 91, R3
Chance, P., 374, R1
Coker, H., 514, 515, 562, R4
Conklin, N.F., 256, R4
Conoley, J. C., 527, R1, R3
Craig, D., 286, R1
Cronbach, L. J., 614, R1
Culham, R., 114, R4
Cunningham, P.M., 628, R1

Davey, L., 525, R1
Davis, R.B., 57, R2
Demos, G. D., R2
Dominowski, R. L., 372, 451, 452, R1
Douglas, G., 558, R2
Driver, R., 347, R2
Duell, O.K., 91, R2

Ebel, R. L., 614, 624, 650, R2
Ellis, H. C., 347, R2

Ertmer, P.A., 91, R2
Evans, E.D., 286, R2
Evans, M., 514, R1

Fischer, C., 289, R2
Flexer, R.J., 525, R3

Gabel, D. L., R4
Gadsen, V.L., 514, R1
Gaffney, R.F., 523, R2
Gagné, E. D., 91, R2
Gagné, N. L., 347, R2
Gale, J., 57, R2, R4
Gallager, J.D., 152, R2
Gallard, A.J., 57, R4
Galton, F., 601
Ginott, H.G., 122, R2
Goetz, E. T., R3
Going, S., 243, G7, R3
Golan, S., 514, R2
Good, T.L., 91, R1
Gordon, W. J. J., 450, 451, 452, R2
Gowan, J. C., 451, R2
Greene, S., 57, R2
Gronlund, N.E., 334, R2
Grouws, D. A., R4
Guilford, J. P., 230, R2
Guskey, T.R., 513, 516, R2

Haas, N.S., 519, R3
Haladyna, T. M., 519, R3
Hallahan, D. P., 279, R2
Hambleton, R. K., 559, R3
Harageones, E.G., 485, R4
Harrow, A.J., 230, R2
Havens, L.T., 39, R4
Healy, A. F., 372, 451, 452, R1
Herman, J.L., 514, R2
Heyward, W.H., 486, G1, R2
Hiebert, E.H., 525, R4
Hofmann, R.J., 652, 654, R2
Hopkins, K.D., 335, R4
Hopkins, K.E., 612, R2
Hoyt, C.J., 613, R2

Hunt, R. R., 347, R2
Hurd, J., 486, R2

Impara, J. C., 256, 527, R3, R4

Johnson, D.J., 485, R4
Jones, K. S., 152, R2
Joyce, B., 372, 450, R2

Kane, M.T., 628, R1
Kauffman, J.M., 279, R2
Keeves, J.P., 513, 558, R2, R3, R4
Kelley, D., 225, 297, R2
Kifer, E.W., 513, 516, R2
King, R., 289, R2
Kleinbaum, D.G., 592, R2
Krathwohl, D., 230, R2
Kuder, G.F., 613, 614, 619, R2
Kupper, L.L., 592, R2

Lassiter, K., 523, R2
Lavoie, R.D., 280, R2
Livingston, S.A., 628, R2
Loftus, E. F., 372, 451, 452, R1

MacDougall, M., 91, R2
Mager, R., 217, 218, 219, R3
Maguire, T.O., 523, R2
Maher, C.A., 57, R2
Marion, S.F., 525, R4
Masia, B., 230, R3
Mayfield, V., 525, R5
McCombs, B. L., 91, R3
McMillan, J.H., 114, R3
McSwegin, P., 243, G6, R3
Medley, D.M., 514, 515, 562, R4
Metz, K. E., 225, 297, R3
Moore, K. D., 218, 219, R3
Mosier, C.I., 613, R3
Muller, K.E., 592, R3
Murphy, L.L., 527, R3
Nash, W., 286, R1
Neill, D. M., 200, R3
Neill, M., 525, R2

Newby, T.J., 91, R2
New Jersey Department of Education, 452, R3
Noddings, N. 57, R2
Nolen, S.B., 519, R3
Nunnally, J.C., 344, 559, R3

O'Hagan, L.K., 148, 257, R3
O'Malley, M., 91, R3

Pangrazi, R.P., 244, 485, R3
Paris, S.G., 514, R1
Pearson, K., 601, 603
Pemberton, C., 243, G7, R2
Petray, C., 243, G6, R2
Phelps, R.P., 517, 525, G8, R3
Phye, G. D., R2, R3
Plake, B.S., 256, R3
Prince, G., 452, R3
Pulaski, M.A.S., 287, R3

Richardson, M.W., 613, 614, 619, R2
Rogoff, B., 287, R3
Romesburg, H.C., 592, R3
Roscoe, J.T., 524, R3
Rowley, E.R., 257, R3
Rulon, P.J., 613, R3
Russo, R.P., 91, R3

Ryans, D.G., 601, R3

Safrit, M.J., 230, 244, 491, R3
Santa, C.M., 39, R4
Schab, F., 286, R4
Schoenfeld, A. H. 91, R4
Schunk, D.H., 91, R4
Sheppard, L.A., 525, R4
Showers, B., 372, 450, R2
Shuell, T. J., 57, R4
Sims, O. S., 347, R4
Smith, C.D., 485, R4
Smith, F., 163, R4
Smith, M. U., 347, R4
Soar, R.S., 514, 515, 562, R4
Spandel, V., 114, R4
Spearman, C., 599, 600, 608, 624, R4
Stalnaker, J.M., 335, R4
Stanley, J.C., 335, R5
Starko, A.J., 450, 452, 455, 457, R4
Steffe, L.P., 57, R2, R4
Sternberg, R. J., R4
Stewner-Manzanares, G., 91, R4
Stiggins, R.J., 157, 256, R4
Stolarczyk, L. M., 486, G1, R4
Strom, R. D., 450, 451, 452, R4
Swaminathan, H., 559, R2

Tallmadge, G.K., 558, R4
Taylor, K., 201, R4
Thorndike, R. M., 601, R4
Thurstone, L.L., 559, R4
Tippins, D.J., 57, R4
Tobin, K., 57, R4
Torrance, E. P., 450, 451, R2, R4
Tschudi, S., R1, R2, R4
Turnbull, A.P., 279, R4
Turnbull, H.R., 279, R4

von Glasersfeld, E., 217, R4

Walker, H.M., 603, R4
Walton, S., 201, R4
Weil, M., 372, 450, R2
Weinstein, C. E., R2, R4
Weston, T.J., 525, R4
Williams, C.S., 485, R4
Wittrock, M. C., R1
Wolff, L., 152, R4
Wood, C.T., 558, R4
Wood, T.M., 230, 491, R3
Woolfolk, A. E., 217, 372, 450, R4

Yekovich, C. W., 91, R2
Yekovich, F. R., 91, R2

SUBJECT INDEX

Accommodations for students with special
needs, 276, 278–280
Achievement test, 200–201, 510–571, G1. *See
also* Measurement, Planned
Affective domain, 231, 242–243, 246–247,
463–483, G1
Agility, 486, 492, G1
Alternative assessment, xvii–xx, G1. *See also*
Mini-experiment; Relevance, Measurement
American Educational Research Association,
148, 614, R1
American Psychological Association, 148,
515, R1
Application learning level, 57–59, 238–240,
246–247, 433–447, G1
Appreciation learning level, 242–243,
246–247, 463–477, G1
Aptitude test, 526, 529–530, G1
Attitudes, Students'. *See* Affective domain
Authentic assessment, xvii–xx, G1. *See also*
Mini-experiment; Relevance, Measurement

Battery, Test, 514, 517, 519, 527–528, G9
Behavioral objectives, 217–219
Blueprint, Measurement, 275–282,
577–578, G1
Body composition, 486, G1

California Achievement Tests, 527
Cardiovascular endurance, 485, G1
Central tendency, 537–540, G1
Cheating on tests, 192–193, 284–289, 521,
523–525
Classroom arrangement, 81–85
Classroom and behavior management, 2–8, 33,
61–70, 86–91, 138–141, 284–289,
463–469
Cognitive Abilities Test, 529
Cognitive domain, 230–242, 246–247, G1
Commercially-produced test, 199–201, 344, 577,
621–622, G2. *See also* Standardized test
Comprehension and communication skills,
57–59, 237–238, 246–247, 408–431, G1–G2
Comprehensive Test of Basic Skills, 527

Computer technology, Application of, 46, 81,
257–275. *See also* Measurement and
Analysis Tool
Concept, 222–225, 246–247, 293–345, G2
Concept attribute, 222, 293–345, G2
Example noise, 293–345, G3
Example of a concept, 293–345, G3
Parallel concepts, 225, G6
Subordinate concept, 225, G8
Superordinate concept, 225, G8
Concurrent validity, 532–533, 601–607, G2
Conferences, Student-parent-teacher, 117–118,
122–124, 145, 148, 562–571
Construct a concept, 2–5, 57–59, 236–237,
293–345, G2
Convergent reasoning, 241–242, 454, G2
Cooperative learning, 6–7, 137–138, 295–297
Coordination, 489, 495, G2
Core-curriculum tests, 200–201, 510–522
Correction-for-guessing technique, 344, G2
Correlation coefficient, 532–534, 601–613,
627–630, 632–635
Creative thinking, 57–59, 240–242,
450–461, G2
Criterion-referenced evaluation, 131–138,
154–166, 519, 627–630, G2
Culture Fair Intelligence Tests, 529
Curriculum, 44–61, G2
Curriculum standards, xx, 44, 148, 152,
216–217, 452, 525

Deductive reasoning 240, 433–437, G2
Derived score, 531, 549–550, 553–570, G2
Difficulty, Index of (P_j), 650–654, G2
Direct instruction, 57, 59, 211–217, 368–376,
388–397, 491, 494–505
Discover a relationship, 57–59, 237, 246–247,
345–362, G2
Discovery learning. *See* Inquiry instruction
Discrimination, Index of (D_j), 647–659, G2
Display-process format, 398, G2–G3
Divergent reasoning, 240–242, 450–461, G3
Dynamic balance, 489, 494, G3

Educational Testing Service (ETS), 527, 529
Efficiency, Index of Item (E_j), 650–659, G3
Empirical observation, 19, 30, G3
Engagement, Student. *See* Classroom and
behavior management
Equivalent forms of a test, 531–532,
609–610, G3
Error of measurement. *See also* Measurement,
Measurement error;
Standard error of measurement
Error-pattern analysis, 108–109, 395,
398–406, G3
Essay format, 191–192, 328–336, G3
Expert judges of measurement relevance,
578–579, 592

Feedback, Formative. *See* Formative judgment
Flexibility, Psychomotor, 486, 490, G3
Folder of mini-experiment files, Computer-
ized, 257–275, G3
Formative judgment, 43–118, 473, G3
Frequency distribution of a sequence of scores,
541–553, G3

Goal, Learning, 51–60, 248–250, G3
Goodenough-Harris Drawing Test, 529
Government-mandated test, 199–201,
510–525, G3
Grade equivalent score, Standardized test, 514,
560–563, G3
Grade level, Student's standardized test,
550, G3
Grade reports, 125–154
Grading, 125–173, 473, G3
Checking-off objectives method, 157,
159, G1
Compromise method, 164–166,
626–627, G2
Curve grading method, Classical, 163, G2
Percentage-averaging method,
171–172, G6
Percentage grading method, Traditional,
154–157, G6

Visual inspection grading method, 163–164, G8

Weighted-averaging method, 171–172, G8–G9

Graduate Record Examination (GRE), 533–534

Hennon-Nelson Tests of Mental Ability, 529

High-stakes testing, 199, 286–287, 510–525, G3

Homework, 10–29, 141, 143

Individualized education program (IEP), 279

Individuals with Disabilities Education Act (IDEA), 278–280

Inductive reasoning, 297, G3

Inquiry instruction, 57–61, 211–217, 293–325, 345–352, 408–428, 433–440, 452–455

Institute for Aerobics Research, 490, R2

Internal consistency of a measurement, 183–186, 595–620, G3

International Reading Association, xx, 148, 217, 452, R4

Inter-observer consistency, 189, 601, 632–635, G4

Interpretive understanding, 409–416, 422–423, G3–G4

Interview format, 190, 344–345, G4

Intra-observer consistency, 186–188, 601, 632–635, G4

Iowa Test of Basic Skills, 528

Iowa Test of Educational Development, 528

Item analysis, 638–662, G4

Kaufman Assessment Battery for Children, 529

Kuhlmann-Anderson Intelligence Test, 529

Learning level, 217–250, G4

Lesson planning, 2–5, 57–64, 217

Literal understanding, 409–422, G4

Mastery learning. *See* Direct instruction

Matching multiple-choice format, 384–388, G4

Matrix, Mini-experiment outcome, 595–601, 613, 616–618, 633–635

Mean deviation of a sequence of scores (*MD*), 546–548, G4

Mean of a sequence of scores, Arithmetic (μ), 539, 601–602, G4

Meaningful learning, 211–217, 238, G4

Measurement, 10–39, 177–203, 255–289, G4

    Measurement error, 37–39, 177–180, 599–601, 622–627, G4

    Measurement results, 30, G4

    Planned measurement, 33–37, G5. *See also* Mini-experiment; Achievement test

    Unplanned measurement, 31–33, 201–202, G4

Measurement and Analysis Tool, xxi, 268–269, 273–275, 290, 549, 558, 606, 615, 620, 621

Median of a sequence of scores, 538–539, G4

Memory-level objective, 231–236, 246–247, 368–406, G4

Mental Measurement Yearbooks, 527–530, R2

Message, Particular, 237–238, 408–423, G4

Metropolitan Achievement Tests, 528

Mini-experiment, 34–37, 257–275, 325–345, 352–362, 376–388, 397–406, 428–431, 440–447, 455–457, 471–483, 505–507, 638–659, G5

    Defective mini-experiments, 641, G2

    Difficulty of a mini-experiment, 259, 267–268, 339, 380–382, 596, 650–654, G2

    Easy mini-experiment, 267, G3

    Effectiveness of mini-experiments, 638–662, G3

    File, Mini-experiment, 257–275, G5

    Format, Mini-experiment, G5

    Hard mini-experiment, 267, G4

    Ineffective mini-experiments, 641, G4

    Moderately difficult mini-experiment, 267, G5

Mnemonic, 372–373, G5

Mode of communication, 237–238, 416, 423, G5

Mode of a sequence of scores, 539, G5

Monitoring students' learning, 31, 70–114, 292–508, G5

Multiple-choice format, 336–344, 380–388, 405–406, G5

    Distractor, Multiple-choice, 337, G2

    Foil, Multiple-choice, 337, G2

    Overlapping alternatives, 382–383, G6

    Parallel alternatives, Multiple-choice, 339–341, G6

    Stem, Multiple-choice, 336–337, G8

Muscular endurance, 486, 492, G5

Muscular strength, 486, 491, G5

National Center for History in the Schools, xx, 217, 452, R3

National Council of Teachers of English, xxx, 148, 217, 452, R3

National Council of Teachers of Mathematics, xx, 44, 148, 152, 217, 452, R3

National Council on Measurement in Education, 148, 614, R1

National Education Association, 521

National Research Council, xviii, xx, 44, 148, 217, 452, R3

Noise, Example. *See* Concept, Example noise.

Non-example of a concept, 225, 297–309, G5

Norm group, 526–531, 535, 621–622, G5

    Local norm group, 526, 528, G3

    National norm group, 526, 528, G5

Normal curve equivalent score (*NCE*), 557–560, G5

Normal frequency distribution, 550–558, 623–625, G5

Norm-referenced evaluation, 131–138, 163–166, 519, 526, 535–571, G5

Norms, Test, 528, 535–571, G5–G6

Objective, Learning, 51–57, 211–250, G6

Observer consistency, 189, 198–199, 334–335, 601, 632–635, G6

Observer's rubric, 35–37, 186–189, G7. *See also* Mini-experiment

On-task behavior. *See* Classroom and behavior management

Oral-discourse format, 336, G6

Otis-Lennon School Ability Test, 529

Overlearning, 374, 395, 505, G6

Parents, Communicating with, 117–118, 122–154, 562–571

Pearson's equation, 599–601, 608, 622–624

Percentile, 553–559, 564–571, G6

Performance assessment, xvii–xx, G6. *See also* Mini-experiment.

Performance observation format, 328, 400–405, 505–507, G6

Physical fitness, 243–244, 246–247, 484–491, G6

Portfolios, Student, 50, 111–114, 128, 148–154, 173, 289–290, G6

Power, Psychomotor, 489, 496, G6

Predictive validity, 533–534, G6

President's Council on Physical Fitness and Sports, 491–492, R3

Problem solving, 239–240, 433–447

Process, 230, 236, 244, 246–247, 388–398, 491–505, G6

Process knowledge, 57–59, 230, 236, 246–247, 388–406, 491, 493, G6

Product-examination format, 144–145, 345, 440, 443, G6

Professional trust, 122–125

Prompt of a mini-experiment, 35, G7. *See also* Mini-experiment

Psychomotor domain, 230–231, 243–247, 485–507, G6

Psychomotor skill, 244–247, 484, 491–507, G6

Questionnaire, 11–17, 64–67, 71–73

Range of a sequence of scores, 546, G6

Raw score, 528, G6

Reaction time, 489, 497, G7

Real-life problem, 239–240, G7

Reasoning-level objective, 231–242, 246–247, 293–362, 408–462, G7

Relationship, 226–230, 237, 345–362, G7

    Discoverable relationship, 226–228, 345–362, G7

    Relationship of convention, 228–230, G7

Relevance, Measurement, 181–183, 189–190, 203, 248–250, 292–483, 576–592, G7

    Learning-level relevance, Measurement, 182–183, G3

    Subject-content relevance, Measurement, 181–182, G8

Reliability, Measurement, 183–199, 523, 595–635, G7

Reliability coefficient, 532, 599–635

Adjusted odd-even method, 611–614
Coefficient α, 614–615
Equivalent form method, 609–610, 628
Kuder-Richardson 20, 615–618, 621
Kuder-Richardson 21, 619–621, 629, 631
Kuder-Richardson methods, 613–621
Odd-even method, 611
Ratio-reliability model, 624
Split-halves method, 610–611
Test-retest method, 608–609, 622–625, 628
Reporting grades, 125–154
Rubric. *See* Observer's rubric
Scaled scores, 558–560, G7
Scatterplot, 533, 602–606
Scorer consistency, 189, 198–199, 334–335, 632–635, G7
Scoring, G8. *See also* Observer's rubric
Analytical scoring, 198–199, 335, G1
Dichotomous scoring, 198–199, 595–596, G2
Global scoring, 198–199, 335, G3
Weighted scoring, 198–199, 596–597, G9
Short-response format, 379–380, G7
Simple knowledge, 57–59, 231–235, 246–247, 368–388, G7
Slosson Intelligence Test, 529
Spearman-Brown prophecy formula, 612–614
Special needs, Accommodating students with, 276, 278–280

Specific, 219–222, 246–247, G7
Speed, Psychomotor, 489, G7
Standard deviation (σ), 549–570, 601–602, G7
Standard error of measurement (SEM), 523, 622–629, G8
Standard score, 553, G7
Standardized test, 50, 200–201, 286–287, 509–571, 621–622, G7
Edition of a standardized test, 532, 559, G2
Form, Standardized test, 531–532, G2
Manual, Standardized test, 530, 532, 621–622, G4
Test battery, 514, 517, 519, 527–528, G8
Test level, Standardized, 531–532, G8
User's manual, 526, 530, 559
Stanford Achievement Tests, 526, 528
Stanine score, 563–571, G7
Static balance, 489, 493, G8
Subject-content, 181–182, 217–230, 246–247, 445–446, 465–468, G8
Summative evaluation, 43–44, 121–173, 473, G8
Syllogism, 433–434, G8. *See also* Deductive reasoning
Synectics, 452–455, G8
Systemwide test, 509–571, 577, G8

Teaching cycle, 2–10, G8
Test, G8. *See also* Measurement, Planned
Test item, 526, G8. *See also* Mini-experiment
Tests in Print, 527, 529, R3
Think-aloud trial, 584–586, 656–659, G8
True score, 599–601, 608, 622–624, 630

Unit, Teaching, 51–57, G8
Usability, Measurement, 180, 181, G8
Usefulness, Measurement, 177–203, G8
U.S. General Accounting Office, 519, G3, R4
Utah State Office of Education, 519, 520, R4

Validation study, Measurement, 577–659
Validity, Measurement, 177–203, G8. *See also* Relevance, Measurement; Reliability, Measurement
Variability of a sequence of scores, 543–549, G8
Variance of a sequence of scores (σ²), 548, G8

Wechsler Intelligence Scale of Children, 530
Weighting objectives, 248–250, 257, 280–281, G9
Willingness to try, 34, 243, 246–247, 463–470, 477–482, G9

z-score, 549–571, 603–607, G9